Sophie Tison (Ed.)

Trees in Algebra and Programming – CAAP '94

19th International Colloquium
Edinburgh, U.K., April 11-13, 1994
Proceedings

Springer-Verlag
Berlin Heidelberg New York
London Paris Tokyo
Hong Kong Barcelona
Budapest

Series Editors

Gerhard Goos
Universität Karlsruhe
Postfach 69 80
Vincenz-Priessnitz-Straße 1
D-76131 Karlsruhe, Germany

Juris Hartmanis
Cornell University
Department of Computer Science
4130 Upson Hall
Ithaca, NY 14853, USA

Volume Editor

Sophie Tison
LIFL, University of Lille 1
Bât. M3, F-59655 Villeneuve d'Ascq Cedex, France

CR Subject Classification (1991): F, D.1, E.1, G.2.2

ISBN 3-540-57879-X Springer-Verlag Berlin Heidelberg New York
ISBN 0-387-57879-X Springer-Verlag New York Berlin Heidelberg

CIP data applied for

Printed in Germany

Typesetting: Camera-ready by author
SPIN: 10132003 45/3140-543210 - Printed on acid-free paper

Lecture Notes in Computer Science 787

Edited by G. Goos and J. Hartmanis

Dedicated to the memory of Ahmed Saoudi

Preface

This volume contains the papers selected for presentation at the 19th Colloquium on Trees in Algebra and Programming (CAAP'94), which was held jointly with the 5th European Symposium on Programming (ESOP'94) during 11–13 April in Edinburgh. CAAP is held annually in conjunction either with TAPSOFT or ESOP. Its predecessors were held in France, Italy, Spain, Germany and the UK.

Originally this colloquium series was devoted to the algebraic and combinatorial properties of trees, and their role in various fields of computer science. In keeping with CAAP's tradition and taking into account the evolution of computer science, CAAP'94 focuses on logical, algebraic and combinatorial properties of discrete structures (strings, trees, graphs, etc.); the topics include also applications to computer science provided that algebraic or syntactic methods are involved.

The programme committee received 51 submissions, from which 21 were accepted; invited papers were presented by Hubert Comon and Joost Engelfriet.

Programme Committee

J. Almeida, Porto
A. Arnold, Bordeaux
V. Bruyère, Mons
H. Comon, Orsay
B. Courcelle, Bordeaux
A. De Luca, Naples
V. Diekert, Stuttgart
J. Karhumaki, Turku
G. Mauri, Milan
M. Nivat, Paris
D. Niwinski, Warsaw
A. Restivo, Palermo
H. Seidl, Passau
C. Stirling, Edinburgh
W. Thomas, Kiel
S. Tison, Lille (chairperson)

CAAP/ESOP was organized by the Laboratory for Foundations of Computer Science of the University of Edinburgh. It was held in cooperation with ACM SIGPLAN and was sponsored by Hewlett Packard, LFCS, and the University of Edinburgh.

Local Arrangements Committee

G. Cleland (chairman)
S. Gilmore
M. Lekuse
D. Sannella

I would like to express my sincere gratitude to the members of the programme committee and their referees (see below) for their care in reviewing and selecting the submitted papers. I am also grateful to the members of the local arrangements committee and especially to Donald Sanella for their hard work.

Lille, January 1994 Sophie Tison

Referees for CAAP'94:

J. Almeida
A. Arnold
P. Audebaud
M. Benke
M. Bertol
F. Bossut
L. Bougé
M. Bousquet-Mélou
J.C. Bradfield
V. Bruyère
F. Cardone
A.C. Caron
A. Carpi
H. Comon
J.L. Coquidé
B. Courcelle
M. Dauchet
A. De Luca
J.P. Delahaye
N. Dershowitz
G. Di Battista
V. Diekert
V. Di Jesu
M. Droste
W. Ebinger
R. Echahed
J. Engelfriet
J. Esparza
C. Ferdinand
M. Fernández
P.A. Gardner
L. Gąsieniec
R. Gilleron
P. Goralcik
D. Gouyou-Beauchamps
G. Grudziński
R. Hoogen
S.B. Jones
R. Kaivola
J. Karhumaki
A. Kuhn
D. Le Métayer
S. Limet
J. Longley
C. Marché
A. Mateescu
A. Matos
G. Mauri
M. Mériaux
A. Middledorp
A. Mifsud
F. Mignosi
A. Mignotte
M. Nivat
D. Niwiński
J.C. Penaud
D. Perrin
W. Plandowski
A. Potthoff
J.C. Raoult
A. Rauzy
P. Ressmanith
A. Restivo
N. Sabadini
N. Saheb
A. Salooma
G. Sanniti di Baja
P.H. Schmitt
P. Seebold
D. Seese
H. Seidl
K. Sieber
P.V. Silva
J.M. Steyaert
C. Stirling
D. Teodosiu
S. Tison
W. Thomas
U. Trier
M. Torelli
P. Urzyczyn
F. van Raamsdonk
S. Varrichio
M. Venturini Zilli
W. Vogler
I. Walukiewicz
R. Werchner
T. Wilke
P. Wolper
H. Zantema
V. Zissimopoulos

Contents

Invited papers

Contributed papers

Ordering Constraints on Trees

Hubert Comon[1*] and Ralf Treinen[2**]

[1] CNRS and LRI, Bat. 490, Université de Paris Sud, F-91405 ORSAY cedex, France, E-mail: comon@lri.lri.fr

[2] German Research Center for Artificial Intelligence (DFKI), Stuhlsatzenhausweg 3, D-66123 Saarbrücken, Germany, E-mail: treinen@dfki.uni-sb.de

Abstract. We survey recent results about ordering constraints on trees and discuss their applications. Our main interest lies in the family of *recursive path orderings* which enjoy the properties of being total, well-founded and compatible with the tree constructors. The paper includes some new results, in particular the undecidability of the theory of lexicographic path orderings in case of a non-unary signature.

1 Symbolic Constraints

Constraints on trees are becoming popular in automated theorem proving, logic programming and in other fields thanks to their potential to represent large or even infinite sets of formulae in a nice and compact way. More precisely, a *symbolic constraint system*, also called a *constraint system on trees*, consists of a fragment of first-order logic over a set of predicate symbols $\mathcal{P}$ and a set of function symbols $\mathcal{F}$, together with a fixed interpretation of the predicate symbols in the algebra of finite trees $T(\mathcal{F})$ (or sometimes the algebra of infinite trees $I(\mathcal{F})$) over $\mathcal{F}$. The *satisfiability problem* associated with a constraint system is to decide whether a formula has a solution. There are plenty of symbolic constraint systems, some important examples are:

- *unification problems* in which the formulae are conjunctions of equations and where the equality symbol is interpreted as a congruence relation generated by a finite set E of equational axioms. (See [12] for a survey).
- *disunification problems* in which the formulae are conjunctions of equations and negated equations (called *disequations*), or more generally, arbitrary formulae involving no other predicate symbol than equality. Such formulae are interpreted in the free or quotient algebras of $T(\mathcal{F})$. (See [6] for a survey).
- *membership constraints* in which the formulae involve membership constraints of the form $t \in \zeta$ where ζ belongs to an infinite set of *sort expressions*, generally built from a finite set of sort symbols, logical connectives and applications of function symbols. The membership predicate symbols are interpreted using (some kind of) tree automata. (See for example [4]).

* Supported by the Esprit working group CCL, contract EP 6028.

** Supported by the Bundesminister für Forschung und Technology, contract ITW 9105, and by the Esprit working group CCL, contract EP 6028. The result Theorem 8 was obtained while the second author visited LRI.

- *ordering constraints* which are the subject of this survey paper. The set $\mathcal{P}$ now involves, besides equality, a binary predicate symbol $\geq$. This symbol is interpreted as an ordering on trees; we will discuss later which kind of interpretations are relevant.
- many other systems, like *set constraints*, *feature constraints* etc. We refer to [7] for a short survey.

Symbolic constraints, besides their own interest, can be used together with a logical language, hence leading to *constrained formulae*. A constrained formula is a pair (ϕ, c) (actually written $\phi|c$) where ϕ is a formula in some first-order logic built upon a set $\mathcal{Q}$ of predicate symbols and a set $\mathcal{F}'$of function symbols, and c is a formula (called *constraint*) in some constraint system over $\mathcal{P} \subseteq \mathcal{Q}, \mathcal{F} \subseteq \mathcal{F}'$ As sketched above, any constraint system comes with a satisfaction relation $\models$ such that, for any assignment σ of the free variables of c, $\sigma \models c$ iff $c\sigma$ holds in the given interpretation. Then, $\phi|c$ can be simply interpreted as the (possibly infinite) set of formulae

$$[\![\phi \mid c]\!] = \{\phi\sigma \mid \sigma \models c\}$$

It should be clear from the above interpretation that constraints may help in expressing large or infinite sets of formulae. For example, unification problems can be used for compacting the information, allowing for sharing, as in the example:

$$\phi[f(x, x, x)] \quad | \quad x = \text{Bigterm} \quad \text{standing for} \quad \phi[f(\text{Bigterm,Bigterm,Bigterm})]$$

The reader is referred to e.g. [15] for more details.

Constraint systems can also be used in expressing *deduction strategies*. For example, the *basic strategy* for paramodulation and completion can be nicely expressed using the constraint system of unification problems [1, 19]. Let us go further in this direction since this is indeed where ordering constraints come into the picture. First, let us make an excursion into rewrite system theory.

2 Ordered Strategies

Let E be a finite set of equations, for example the classical three equations defining group theory:

$$\begin{cases} (x \times y) \times z = x \times (y \times z) \\ x \times 1 = x \\ x \times x^{-1} = 1 \end{cases}$$

A classical problem is to decide whether a given equation, for example $(x \times y)^{-1} = y^{-1} \times x^{-1}$ in group theory, is a logical consequence of E. This problem, also known as the *word problem*, has been subject to intensive research. The brute force search for a proof using the replacement of equals by equals, although complete, rarely leads to an actual solution. One of the most successful approaches is to use *ordered strategies*. Knuth and Bendix in their famous paper [16] proposed to use the equations in one way only, i.e. as *rewrite rules*. Of course, such a strategy is incomplete in general, but completeness can be restored using a completion mechanism based on the computation of some particular equational consequences called *critical pairs*. One requirement of the original method was the *termination* of the rewrite system: the replacement of equals by equals using the ordered strategies should always end up after a finite number of replacement steps.

In the above example of group theory, it is quite easy to fulfill this termination requirement by choosing carefully the way in which to orient the equations. The situation changes if we consider the *commutative groups*, adding the equation $x \times y = y \times x$ to the above system. Now the completion procedure fails because commutativity cannot be oriented in either way without loosing termination. Several solutions have been studied to overcome this problem. It is beyond the scope of this paper to investigate all of them (see [10]). They can be mainly divided into two families: rewriting modulo and ordered rewriting. Rewriting modulo seems interesting when the non-orientable axioms are fixed and known, since it is then possible to tailor the computation of critical pairs and any other operation required during the completion process. In general, however, it may also fail. In contrast, ordered completion never fails but may run forever. The idea is very simple: use every equation in one way or the other, depending on the ordering on *the instances on which it is applied.* For example consider the commutativity axiom and assume a total ordering on terms, e.g compare lexicographically the arguments of $\times$, from left to right. Then if $a > b$, $a \times b$ rewrites to $b \times a$ using $x \times y = y \times x$, but not the other way around, since $a \times b > b \times a$, but $b \times a \not> a \times b$. This idea is developed in e.g. [11]. To be more precise, let us introduce some notations.

We use notations consistent with [10]; missing definitions can be found there. A set of *positions* is a (finite) set of strings of positive integers which is closed by prefix and by the lexicographic ordering. Λ is the empty string. For example $\{\Lambda, 1, 2, 21\}$ is a set of position whereas $\{\Lambda, 1, 21\}$ and $\{\Lambda, 2, 21\}$ are not. Given a set of function symbols $\mathcal{F}'$ together with their arity, a *term* t is a mapping from a set of positions P to $\mathcal{F}'$ such that, if $p \in P$ and $t(p)$ has arity n, then $p \cdot n \in P$ and $p \cdot (n+1) \notin P$. $t|_p$ is the subterm of t at position p and $t[u]_p$ is the term obtained by replacing $t|_p$ with u in t (see [10] for the definitions). In $\mathcal{F}'$, we distinguish a particular set of nullary symbols called *variables*. This subset is denoted by $\mathcal{X}$. The set of all positions of a term t is written $Pos(t)$ and the set of its non-variable positions is $\mathcal{F}Pos(t)$.

Now, the deduction rule for the standard completion procedure can be stated as follows:

$$\frac{l \rightarrow r \qquad g \rightarrow d}{l[d]_p\sigma = r\sigma} \quad \text{If } p \in \mathcal{F}Pos(l) \text{ and } \sigma = \text{mgu}(l|_p, g)$$

This rule is classically associated with an *orientation rule* w.r.t. a given ordering on terms:

$$\frac{l = r}{l \rightarrow r} \quad \text{If } l > r$$

Now the ordered completion consists of a single rule (besides simplification rules which we do not consider so far):

$$\frac{l = r \quad g = d}{l[d]_p\sigma = r\sigma} \quad \text{If } p \in \mathcal{F}Pos(l),\ \sigma = mgu(l|_p, g),\ l\sigma \not\leq r\sigma \text{ and } g\sigma \not\leq d\sigma$$

which deduces a new equation only for equations which actually can form a critical pair.

In the light of constrained logics, this rule can be reformulated as the (classical) critical pair computation between $l = r \mid l \not\leq r$ and $g = d \mid g \not\leq d$. Going further in this direction it is possible to improve the above deduction rule, expressing the conditions at the object level, thus keeping track of which instances of the equations can lead to a critical pair. We get then the following constrained deduction rule:

$$\frac{l = r \mid c \qquad g = d \mid c'}{l[d]_p = r \ \mid \ l|_p = g \wedge c \wedge c' \wedge l > r \wedge g > d} \quad \text{If } p \in \mathcal{F}Pos(l)$$

(Note that we replaced here $\not\leq$ by $>$, assuming that the ordering is total on ground terms). This strategy is strictly more restrictive than the ordered deduction rule because we keep track of the reason why some former equations have been generated: the constraint contains in some sense the "history" of the deduction. This point of view has been extended to arbitrary clauses and shown to be complete (see e.g. [20]).

This new rewriting point of view has however a drawback: at some point it is necessary to decide whether the constraint is indeed satisfiable: all these systems are quite useless if we are computing with empty sets $[\![\phi \mid c]\!]$. This is the motivation for the study of *ordering constraint solving* which is the subject of the next sections. First we will precise which interpretations of the ordering are relevant.

3 Orderings on Trees

With respect to ordered strategies in first-order logic with equality, the ordering we consider must have the following properties:

- To be well founded
- To be *monotonic* i.e. $f(\ldots, s, \ldots) > f(\ldots, t, \ldots)$ whenever $s > t$.
- To be total on ground terms. (i.e. terms without variables).

Totality is mandatory only for completeness of the strategy, whereas the two first properties are already necessary for the completeness of the rules themselves. Monotonicity is required because, along the proofs, equality steps can take place at any positions in the terms.

Typical orderings which fulfill the above three properties are the *recursive path orderings* introduced by N. Dershowitz [9]. We consider these orderings as well as some extensions in sections 4, 5.

Originating from quite different problems, other interpretations of the orderings have been studied in the literature. For example, $\geq$ can be interpreted as the ***subterm ordering***. To be more precise, let us introduce some terminology. The *existential fragment* of a the theory of $\mathcal{P}, \mathcal{F}$ (in a given interpretation) is the set of formulae $\exists \mathbf{x}.\phi$ which hold in the interpretation, where ϕ is any quantifier-free formula built over $\mathcal{P}, \mathcal{F}$ and $\mathbf{x}$ is the set of variables occurring in ϕ. More generally, the Σ_n fragment of the theory is the set of (closed, i.e. without free variables) formulae $\exists^* \mathbf{x_1} \forall^* \mathbf{x_2} \exists^* \ldots \mathbf{x_n}.\phi$ which hold true in the interpretation, where ϕ is quantifier free. It is shown in [26] that existential fragment of the theory of subterm ordering is decidable. On the other side, it is also shown in [26] that the Σ_2 fragment of the theory of subterm ordering is undecidable, which sets up a quite precise boundary between decidability and undecidability in this case. Subterm ordering is also studied in the case of infinite trees: again the existential fragment of the theory is decidable [25] and the Σ_2 fragment is undecidable [24].

Let us finally consider yet another ordering on trees: the ***encompassment ordering***. We say that s encompasses t (noted $s \trianglerighteq t$) if some instance of t is a subterm of s. For example, $s = g(f(f(a,b), f(a,b)))$ encompasses $t = f(x,x)$ since instantiating x with $f(a,b)$, we get a term $t\sigma$ which is a subterm of s. The encompassment ordering plays a central role in the so-called ***ground reducibility problem*** in rewriting theory. Given a rewrite system $\mathcal{R}$, a term t is ground reducible w.r.t. $\mathcal{R}$ if all the ground instances of t (i.e. instances without variables) are reducible by $\mathcal{R}$. A reducible term is always ground reducible, but the converse is false. For example, consider $\mathcal{R} = \{s(s(0)) \rightarrow 0\}$ and $t = s(s(x))$ and assume that the set of function symbols only consists of $0, s$. Then t is ground reducible because the tail of any of its ground instances will be $s(s(0))$. However, it is not reducible. Ground reducibility has been shown decidable by D. Plaisted [22]. However, as noticed in [3], this property can be nicely expressed using the encompassment ordering: t is ground reducible by a rewrite system whose left members are $l_1, \ldots, l_n$ iff

$$\forall x, \mathbf{z}.\ x \trianglerighteq t \rightarrow (x \trianglerighteq l_1 \vee \ldots \vee x \trianglerighteq l_n)$$

where $\mathbf{z}$ is the set of variables of t.

Theorem 1 [3]. *The first-order theory of finitely many (unary) predicate symbols* $\trianglerighteq l_1, \ldots, \trianglerighteq l_n$ *is decidable.*

This shows in particular that ground reducibility is decidable.

4 Recursive Path Ordering Constraints

4.1 The lexicographic path ordering

Given a *precedence* $\geq_{\mathcal{F}}$ (which we assume so far to be an ordering) on $\mathcal{F}$, the *lexicographic path ordering* on $T(\mathcal{F})$ is defined as follows: $s = f(s_1, \ldots, s_n) >_{lpo} g(t_1, \ldots, t_m) = t$ iff one of the following holds:

- $f >_{\mathcal{F}} g$ and, for all i, $s >_{lpo} t_i$
- for some i, $s_i \geq_{lpo} t$
- $f = g$ (and $n = m$) and there is a $j < n$ such that
  - $s_1 = t_1, \ldots, s_j = t_j$ and $s_{j+1} >_{lpo} t_{j+1}$
  - and, for all i, $s >_{lpo} t_i$

Proposition 2 [9, 14]. *$\geq_{lpo}$ is a well-founded ordering. It is monotonic and, if $\geq_{\mathcal{F}}$ is total on $\mathcal{F}$, then $\geq_{lpo}$ is total on $T(\mathcal{F})$.*

This shows, according to the previous section, that the lexicographic path ordering is a good candidate for ordered strategies. Fortunately, there is a positive result on constraint solving in this interpretation:

Theorem 3 [5]. *The existential fragment of the theory of a total lexicographic path ordering is decidable.*

The original proof has been actually simplified in [18] where two other problems are considered: the satisfiability *over an extended signature* and complexity issues. A conjunction of inequations, built over an initial set of function symbols $\mathcal{F}$ is satisfiable over an extended signature if there is an (finite) extension $\mathcal{F} \cup \mathcal{F}'$ of the set of function symbols and an extension of the precedence to this new set of function symbols in which the formula is satisfiable. This kind of interpretation is actually useful for the applications in automated theorem proving (see [20]).

Theorem 4 [18]. *The satisfiability problems for quantifier-free total LPO ordering constraints over a given signature and over an extended signature are both NP-complete.*

Actually, the NP-hardness result can be strengthened:

Proposition 5. *Let $\geq$ be interpreted as a total $\geq_{lpo}$. Deciding satisfiability of a single inequation $s > t$ is NP-complete.*

Sketch of the proof. According to the above theorem, we only have to prove NP-hardness. We encode 3SAT. $\mathcal{F} = \{f, g, h, 0\}$ with the precedence $g > h > f > 0$ and we assume g unary, h, f binary and 0 constant. We will use also the abbreviations: $1 = f(0,0)$ and $2 = f(0, f(0,0))$. Then, we use the following translations:

- each positive literal P is translated into $h(2, x_P) > f(h(x_P, x_P), h(2,0))$ which holds iff x_P is assigned to 1.
- each negative literal $\neg P$ is translated into $1 > x_P$ which holds iff x_P is assigned to 0.
- each clause $s_1 > t_1 \;\vee\; s_2 > t_2 \;\vee\; s_3 > t_3$ is equivalent (w.r.t. the $\geq_{lpo}$ interpretation) to

$$f(g(C_1(C(0))), f(g(C_2(C(0))), g(C_3(C(0))))) > h(0, g(C(C(0))))$$

  where $C(x) \stackrel{\text{def}}{=} f(t_1, f(t_2, f(t_3, x)))$, $C_1(x) \stackrel{\text{def}}{=} f(s_1, f(t_2, f(t_3, x)))$, $C_2(x) \stackrel{\text{def}}{=} f(t_1, f(s_2, f(t_3, x)))$ and $C_3(x) \stackrel{\text{def}}{=} f(t_1, f(t_2, f(s_3, x)))$.

– the conjunction $s_1 > t_1 \wedge \ldots \wedge s_n > t_n$ is equivalent to the single inequation

$$C_h(s_1, \ldots, s_n, t_1, \ldots, t_n)$$
$$> C_f(C_h(t_1, s_2, \ldots, s_n, t_1, \ldots, t_n), \ldots, C_h(s_1, \ldots, s_{n-1}, t_n, t_1, \ldots, t_n))$$

where C_h and C_f are the right "combs" recursively defined by: $C_\alpha(t, L) \stackrel{\text{def}}{=} \alpha(t, C_\alpha(L))$ and $C_\alpha(\emptyset) \stackrel{\text{def}}{=} 0$.

The coding is in $O(n^2)$. It is a routine verification that the resulting inequation is satisfiable iff the set of clauses is satisfiable. □

The proposition also holds for satisfiability over an extended signature, with a minor modification: $\neg P$ has to be translated in a slightly more complicated way: $f(0, f(1, x_P)) > f(1, 0) \wedge f(0, f(1, 0)) > f(1, x_P)$ which is in turn expressed using a single inequation as we did above.

4.2 The recursive path ordering with status

The recursive path ordering with status is slightly more general than the lexicographic path ordering. In addition to the precedence, we assume, for each function symbol, given a *status* which can be either "multiset" or "lexicographic" (other status are also available, but w.r.t. constraint solving only these two are relevant).

The definition of the ordering is exactly the same as in section 4.1 except when $f = g$. In that case, we get the status of f and compare the terms as before if the status is lexicographic, whereas, if the status is multiset, $s >_{rpo} t$ iff $\{s_1, \ldots, s_n\} \gg \{t_1, \ldots, t_n\}$ where $\gg$ is the multiset extension of $>_{rpo}$ (see [9, 10] for more details). This ordering is not total on ground terms as permuting the direct subterms of a function symbol whose status is multiset leads to incomparable terms. However, modulo such permutations, the (quasi-)ordering is total. With such an extension to a total quasi-ordering, constraint solving is still possible:

Theorem 6 [13]. *The existential fragment of the theory of a total recursive path (quasi-)ordering with status is decidable.*

Actually, as above, the fragment is NP-complete. Satisfiability over an extended signature is NP-complete as well [18].

4.3 Partial recursive path orderings

Although less interesting from the applications point of view, the question arises of whether the above results can be extended to arbitrary (non-total) recursive path orderings. This turns out to be a difficult question, which is not answered so far.

The only progress in this direction is the study of *tree embedding constraints*. This is yet another interpretation of the ordering on trees. Tree embedding is the least recursive path ordering: it extends the precedence where any two symbols are uncomparable. It can also be defined as the least monotonic ordering which contains the subterm relation. Up to our knowledge, there is only one result about tree embedding and, more generally, partial recursive path orderings:

Theorem 7 [2]. *The positive existential fragment of the theory of tree embedding is decidable.*

In the *positive* existential fragment, negation is not allowed in the quantifier-free part of the formula.

4.4 The first-order theory of recursive path orderings

Now, extending the language allowing for some more quantifiers may be useful for deciding some other properties (such as for *simplification rules* as described in [15]). Unfortunately, we fall into the undecidability side as soon as we try to enlarge the class of formulae. R. Treinen first shows that the Σ_4 fragment of the theory of a partial lexicographic path ordering is undecidable [24]. But this leaves still some room and most properties for which a decision procedure would be welcome can be expressed in the Σ_2 fragment. Moreover the result did not apply to total orderings, which are the most interesting ones. Extending the technique of [24], it is possible to show the following:

Theorem 8. *The Σ_2 fragment of the theory of any (partial or total) lexicographic path ordering is undecidable, as soon as there is at least a binary function symbol.*

We give a sketch of the proof, the full (quite technical) proof of this result can be found in [8].

We reduce the Post Correspondence Problem (PCP) to the theory of a lexicographic path ordering following the line of [24]. Let F be a finite set of function symbols, such that 0 is a minimal constant, f is a binary function symbol which is minimal in $F - \{0\}$ and g is a minimal unary symbol larger than f. Let $P = (p_i, q_i)_{i=1\dots n}$ be an instance of the PCP over the alphabet $\{a, b\}$. We can device an injective coding function $\mathsf{cw}\colon \{a,b\}^* \to T(\{f,0\})$ and formulae $\underline{\mathsf{empty}}(x)$ and $\underline{\mathsf{prefix}}_v(x,y)$ for every $v \in \{a,b\}^*$, such that $\models \underline{\mathsf{empty}}(x)$ iff $x = \mathsf{cw}(\epsilon)$, and that $\models \underline{\mathsf{prefix}}_v(x, \mathsf{cw}(w))$ iff $x = cw(v \circ w)$. Now it is not hard to device an injective pairing function $\mathsf{pair}\colon T(\{f,0\}) \times T(\{f,0\}) \to T(\{f,0\})$ and a formula $x \sqsupset y$,such that

$$\mathsf{pair}(x,y) \sqsupset \mathsf{pair}(x',y') \leftrightarrow \bigvee_{(p,q)\in P} \underline{\mathsf{prefix}}_p(x,x') \wedge \underline{\mathsf{prefix}}_q(y,y')$$

and such that $\sqsupset$ is well-founded but nevertheless $t \sqsupset t'$ implies $t <_{lpo} t'$. Intuitively, $t \sqsupset t'$ reads "the pair represented by t' is obtained form the pair represented by t by one construction step of P. It is important that $\sqsupset$ is a well-founded relation, this can be achieved by counting in $\sqsupset$ (not in pair) the maximal number of construction steps to go.

The idea is now to design a sentence $\underline{\text{solv}}$ which holds iff there is a sequence $t_0, \ldots, t_n$ such that $t_0 = \mathsf{pair}(\mathsf{cw}(\epsilon), \mathsf{cw}(\epsilon))$, $t_n = \mathsf{pair}(\mathsf{cw}(w), \mathsf{cw}(w))$ for some $w \neq \epsilon \in \{a,b\}^*$ and $\models t_i \sqsupset t_{i+1}$ for every $0 \leq i < n$. Let $\mathcal{I}(x)$ be a formula which holds iff $x = \mathsf{pair}(\mathsf{cw}(\epsilon), \mathsf{cw}(\epsilon))$, and let $\mathcal{F}(x)$ be a formula which holds iff $x = \mathsf{pair}(\mathsf{cw}(w), \mathsf{cw}(w))$ for some $w \neq \epsilon \in \{a,b\}^*$. In the following formula $\underline{\text{solv}}$, some parts are not yet defined. The intended meaning of $x\,\underline{\text{head}}\,y$ is that x is the head of the sequence y, $\underline{\text{nonempty}}(y)$ expresses that y has a head and $(x,y')\,\underline{\text{sub}}\,y$ should express that the sequence $cons(x,y')$ is a subsequence of y.

$$\begin{aligned}&\exists y(\ \exists x, y'(\mathcal{I}(x) \wedge (x,y')\,\underline{\text{sub}}\,y) \wedge \\ &\quad \forall x, y'((x,y')\,\underline{\text{sub}}\,y \rightarrow [\mathcal{F}(x) \vee (\underline{\text{nonempty}}(y') \wedge \forall x'(x'\,\underline{\text{head}}\,y' \rightarrow x \sqsupset x'))]\end{aligned}$$

Now, we have to show that the above formula $\underline{\text{solv}}$ holds iff P has a solution. We give first some characterizations of the "if" and "only if" parts respectively in terms of properties of the formulas $\underline{\text{nonempty}}$(x), x $\underline{\text{head}}$ y and (x,y) $\underline{\text{sub}}$ z. Then, we will sketch how (x,y) $\underline{\text{sub}}$ z is constructed. This is the most complicated part; the constructions of x $\underline{\text{head}}$ y and $\underline{\text{nonempty}}$(x) are skipped here. We will also sketch why (x,y) $\underline{\text{sub}}$ z follows the requirements.

In order to show that $\underline{\text{solv}}$ holds if P has a solution, we have to design a coding cs of sequences of elements from $T(\{f,0\})$. $\mathsf{cs}: T(\{f,0\})^* \rightarrow T(F)$. This is given by $\mathsf{cs}(\epsilon) \stackrel{\text{def}}{=} 0$, and $\mathsf{cs}(cons(t,\bar{t})) \stackrel{\text{def}}{=} f(g(t), \mathsf{cs}(\bar{t}))$. Now, $\underline{\text{solv}}$ holds if P has a solution, provided that the following relations are satisfied:

$$\begin{array}{ll}\models \underline{\text{nonempty}}(\mathsf{cs}(s)) & \Leftrightarrow s \neq \epsilon \\ \models t\,\underline{\text{head}}\,\mathsf{cs}(t_0, \ldots, t_n) & \Leftrightarrow t_0 = t \\ \models (t,u')\,\underline{\text{sub}}\,\mathsf{cs}(t_0,\ldots,t_n) & \Leftrightarrow \text{exists } i \leq n,\ t = t_i,\ u' = \mathsf{cs}(t_{i+1}, \ldots, t_n)\end{array} \quad (1)$$

Once we have the definition of $\underline{\text{sub}}$ with property (1), it follows immediately that $\underline{\text{solv}}$ holds if P has a solution: We take y to be the coding of the solution to P.

Conversely, P has a solution if $\underline{\text{solv}}$ holds, provided that the following relations are satisfied:

$$\underline{\text{nonempty}}(y) \rightarrow \exists x\ x\,\underline{\text{head}}\,y \quad (2)$$

$$(x,y')\,\underline{\text{sub}}\,y \wedge x'\,\underline{\text{head}}\,y' \wedge x \sqsupset x' \rightarrow \exists y''\ (x',y'')\,\underline{\text{sub}}\,y \quad (3)$$

This claim is easily proven by well-founded induction on $\sqsupset$. The lemmata (2) and (3) give exactly the argument needed in the induction step. Using well-founded induction at this place is a central idea in [24].

Appropriate definitions of $\underline{\text{nonempty}}(y)$ and $x\,\underline{\text{head}}\,y$ are given easily. Now, let us sketch the construction of $(x,y)\,\underline{\text{sub}}\,z$. The first step is the definition

$$\phi_1(x,y) \stackrel{\text{def}}{=} f(g(x), g(x)) \geq y > g(x)$$

It is easily proven by structural induction on u, that $\models \phi_1(t,u)$ implies that $g(t)$ is the maximal subterm of u which is headed by a symbol not smaller than g. For instance, if g is the greatest symbol in F, this means that $g(t)$ is the maximal g-headed subterm of u. In this proof, we exploit the fact that $f < g$. It is not always true, that for any y containing a g there is an x such that $\phi_1(x,y)$. On the other hand, the definition of <u>nonempty</u>(y) will have to ensure this fact, as can be seen from the definition of <u>sub</u> given below. The formula $\exists x\, \phi_1(x,y)$ does the job but introduces an existential quantifier at the wrong place, which would throw <u>solv</u> out of the Σ_2 fragment. A working formula $\psi(y)$ using only universal quantifiers can be found in the full paper [8]. Now it can be shown that always

$$\models \phi_1(x, \mathsf{cs}(t_0,\ldots,t_n)) \leftrightarrow x = t_n \tag{4}$$

which gives us access to the greatest pair of a list. Note that in our representation of lists, the greatest term stands at an *innermost* position; it is by no means obvious that we can access this term when the ordering might be total. This was a main difficulty which was not solved in the result on partial precedences in [24]. The complete definition of $(x,y')\,\underline{\mathrm{sub}}\,y$ is

$$\begin{array}{l}(\phi_1(x,y) \wedge y' = 0)\\ \vee \exists w\, (f(g(x), f(g(x),y')) > y \geq f(g(x),y') > g(w) > g(x) \wedge \phi_1(w,y))\end{array}$$

Let us sketch now the main part of the proof, namely that the definition of $(x,y')\,\underline{\mathrm{sub}}\,y$ satisfies (1). The "$\Leftarrow$" direction of (1) is easy, let us prove the "$\Rightarrow$" direction. If the first case of <u>sub</u> applies, then the claim holds by (4). Otherwise,

$$\begin{array}{l}\models f(g(t), f(g(t),u')) > \mathsf{cs}(t_0,\ldots,t_n) \geq f(g(t),u') > g(r) > g(t)\\ \quad \wedge \phi_1(r, \mathsf{cs}(t_0,\ldots,t_n))\end{array}$$

holds for some $r \in T(F)$. In fact, $r = t_n$ by (4). Now, $\models g(r) > g(t)$, hence $t_n >_{lpo} t$. Let i be the smallest index such that $t_i \geq_{lpo} t$. Such an i exists since $t_n >_{lpo} t$. Hence, $t_{i'} \not\geq_{lpo} t$ for all $i' < i$. Using the lpo rules, $\mathsf{cs}(t_0,\ldots,t_n) \geq_{lpo} f(g(t),u')$ is simplified into $\mathsf{cs}(t_i,\ldots,t_n) \geq_{lpo} f(g(t),u')$, hence $\mathsf{cs}(t_i,\ldots,t_n) >_{lpo} u'$.

Now let j be the smallest index such that $t \not\geq_{lpo} t_j$. Note that j is well defined since $t \not\geq_{lpo} t_n$. Since $f(g(t), f(g(t),u')) >_{lpo} \mathsf{cs}(t_0,\ldots,t_n)$, it follows that $f(g(t), f(g(t),u')) >_{lpo} \mathsf{cs}(t_j,\ldots,t_n)$. Since by construction $t \not\geq_{lpo} t_j$, this inequality is equivalent to $u' \geq_{lpo} \mathsf{cs}(t_j,\ldots,t_n)$. Together we have

$$\mathsf{cs}(t_i,\ldots,t_n) >_{lpo} u' \geq_{lpo} \mathsf{cs}(t_j,\ldots,t_n)$$

and hence $i < j$. By our construction of j this means $t \geq_{lpo} t_i$. On the other hand we have $t_i \geq_{lpo} t$, hence $t = t_i$. Using the definition of an lpo, we can now simplify

$$\begin{array}{rl}f(g(t_i), f(g(t_i),u')) >_{lpo} \mathsf{cs}(t_0,\ldots,t_n) \Rightarrow^* & f(g(t_i), f(g(t_i),u')) >_{lpo} \mathsf{cs}(t_i,\ldots,t_n)\\ \Rightarrow & f(g(t_i),u') >_{lpo} \mathsf{cs}(t_{i+1},\ldots,t_n)\\ \Rightarrow & u' \geq_{lpo} \mathsf{cs}(t_{i+1},\ldots,t_n)\end{array}$$

On the other hand, we have

$$\begin{array}{rl}\mathsf{cs}(t_0,\ldots,t_n) \geq_{lpo} f(g(t_i),u') \Rightarrow^* & \mathsf{cs}(t_i,\ldots,t_n) \geq_{lpo} f(g(t_i),u')\\ \Rightarrow & \mathsf{cs}(t_{i+1},\ldots,t_n) \geq_{lpo} u'\end{array}$$

Hence, $u' = \mathsf{cs}(t_{i+1}, \ldots, t_n)$. □

In case there are only unary symbols we can use another reduction technique and show:

Proposition 9. *The first-order theory of strings embedding is undecidable.*

The theory of strings involves a binary concatenation function, but the undecidability result in fact holds if we restrict ourselves to unary functions which prefix a string with a fixed symbol. With the representation of strings as terms, this kind of left concatenation corresponds to the application of a unary function symbol.

Sketch of the proof: We encode the concatenation of words, whose first-order theory is known to be undecidable (see e.g. [23]). We use an additional symbol # and successively express the following properties:

$x\# \leq z$, where x contains no #:

$$\phi_1(x, z) \stackrel{\text{def}}{=} x \leq z \wedge \forall y(\# y \leq z \leftrightarrow y = \Lambda)$$

$z = x\# y$ (and x, y are #-free):

$$\begin{aligned}\phi_2(x, y, z) \stackrel{\text{def}}{=} \; & \# \not\leq x \wedge \# \not\leq y \wedge \#\# \not\leq z \wedge \\ & \forall u[\#\# \not\leq u \rightarrow (z \leq u \leftrightarrow (\phi_1(x, u) \wedge \# y \leq u))]\end{aligned}$$

This reads: "z is minimal with the property that z contains at most one #, $x\# \leq z$ and $\# y \leq z$."

x, y, u are #-free and $z = xy$:

$$\phi_3(x, y, u) \stackrel{\text{def}}{=} \exists z.(\phi_2(x, y, z) \wedge \# \not\leq u \wedge \forall v(u \leq v \leq z \leftrightarrow (v = u \vee v = z)))$$

Since u doesn't contain #, it must be the immediate predecessor of z obtained by deleting the # of z. □

The decidability of the theory of a total lexicographic path ordering on strings remains open.

5 Extensions

We list below a number of extensions which have still to be investigated.

- As we have seen in section 2, using ordering constraints avoids failure even in presence of associative-commutative (AC) function symbols. This particular case of unorientable equations occurs very often. On the other hand, however, although the use of ordering constraints prevents failure, completion procedures often run forever in such situations. Hence, from the practical point of view, it is important to design dedicated techniques for this particular situation. In general, AC equations are not treated like the other relations;

this theory is built-in, which implies the use of AC-unification (or AC equality constraints). Using ordering constraints in this context requires first an AC-compatible ordering which is total on ground terms. For a long time no such ordering was known. P. Narendran and M. Rusinowitch [17] were the first to give such an ordering, which is based on polynomial interpretations. An rpo-style AC-compatible ordering, total on ground terms was then given in [21]. Is it possible to design a constraint solving algorithm for such an ordering? This is an open question which is currently under investigation.

- Another important question is the *combination* of constraint systems on terms. Indeed, we may consider the problem of using ordered strategies on constrained equations (or clauses). The combination of ordering constraints and equations and disunification constraints is quite obvious (equational constraints are already considered within the ordering constrains and $s \neq t$ is equivalent to $s > t \vee t > s$ when the ordering is total). More relevant is the combination with membership constraints. This is another open question currently under investigation: is the existential fragment of the theory of $\geq, \in \zeta$, for a family of unary predicate symbols $\in \zeta$, as explained in introduction, decidable?
- Finally, we already mentioned some open questions about the theory of recursive path orderings. In case of partial orderings, we don't know whether the existential fragment is decidable. Similarly, the problem of the first-order theory of a total lexicographic path ordering on unary function symbols is open.

References

1. L. Bachmair, H. Ganzinger, C. Lynch, and W. Snyder. Basic paramodulation and superposition. In D. Kapur, editor, *Proc. 11th Int. Conf. on Automated Deduction, Saratoga Springs, NY*, Lecture Notes in Computer Science, vol. 607, pages 462–476. Springer-Verlag, June 1992.
2. A. Boudet and H. Comon. About the theory of tree embedding. In M. C. Gaudel and J.-P. Jouannaud, editors, *Proc. Int. Joint Conf. on Theory and Practice of Software Development*, Lecture Notes in Computer Science, vol. 668, pages 376–390, Orsay, France, Apr. 1993. Springer-Verlag.
3. A.-C. Caron, J.-L. Coquidé, and M. Dauchet. Encompassment properties and automata with constraints. In C. Kirchner, editor, *Proc. 5th. Int. Conf. on Rewriting Techniques and Applications*, Lecture Notes in Computer Science, vol. 690, pages 328–342, Montreal, Canada, 1993. Springer-Verlag.
4. H. Comon. Equational formulas in order-sorted algebras. In *Proc. 17th Int. Coll. on Automata, Languages and Programming, Warwick*, Lecture Notes in Computer Science, vol. 443, pages 674–688, Warwick, July 1990. Springer-Verlag.
5. H. Comon. Solving symbolic ordering constraints. *International Journal of Foundations of Computer Science*, 1(4):387–411, 1990.
6. H. Comon. Disunification: a survey. In J.-L. Lassez and G. Plotkin, editors, *Computational Logic: Essays in Honor of Alan Robinson*, pages 322–359. MIT Press, 1991.

7. H. Comon. Constraints in term algebras (short survey). In T. R. M. Nivat, C. Rattray and G. Scollo, editors, *Proc. Conf. on Algebraic Methodology and Software Technology*, Univ. of Twente, 1993. Springer Verlag, series Workshop in Computing. Invited talk.
8. H. Comon and R. Treinen. The first-order theory of lexicographic path orderings is undecidable. Research Report RR-93-42, Deutsches Forschungszentrum für Künstliche Intelligenz, Stuhlsatzenhausweg 3, D-66123 Saarbrücken, Germany, Sept. 1993. Anonymous ftp from `duck.dfki.uni-sb.de:/pub/ccl/dfki-saarbruecken`.
9. N. Dershowitz. Orderings for term rewriting systems. *Theoretical Computer Science*, 17(3):279–301, Mar. 1982.
10. N. Dershowitz and J.-P. Jouannaud. Rewrite systems. In J. van Leeuwen, editor, *Handbook of Theoretical Computer Science*, volume B, pages 243–309. North-Holland, 1990.
11. J. Hsiang and M. Rusinowitch. On word problems in equational theories. In *Proc. in 14th ICALP Karlsruhe*, July 1987.
12. J.-P. Jouannaud and C. Kirchner. Solving equations in abstract algebras: A rule-based survey of unification. In J.-L. Lassez and G. Plotkin, editors, *Computational Logic: Essays in Honor of Alan Robinson*, pages 257–321. MIT-Press, 1991.
13. J.-P. Jouannaud and M. Okada. Satisfiability of systems of ordinal notations with the subterm property is decidable. In *Proc. 18th Int. Coll. on Automata, Languages and Programming, Madrid*, Lecture Notes in Computer Science, vol. 510, pages 455–468, 1991. Springer-Verlag.
14. S. Kamin and J.-J. Lévy. Two generalizations of the recursive path ordering. Available as a report of the department of computer science, University of Illinois at Urbana-Champaign, 1980.
15. C. Kirchner, H. Kirchner, and M. Rusinowitch. Deduction with symbolic constraints. *Revue Française d'Intelligence Artificielle*, 4(3):9–52, 1990. Special issue on automatic deduction.
16. D. E. Knuth and P. B. Bendix. Simple word problems in universal algebras. In J. Leech, editor, *Computational Problems in Abstract Algebra*, pages 263–297. Pergamon Press, 1970.
17. P. Narendran and M. Rusinowitch. Any ground associative-commutative theory has a finite canonical system. In R. V. Book, editor, *Proc. 4th Rewriting Techniques and Applications, Como*, Lecture Notes in Computer Science, vol. 488, pages 423–434. Springer-Verlag, Apr. 1991.
18. R. Nieuwenhuis. Simple LPO constraint solving methods. *Inf. Process. Lett.*, 47:65–69, Aug. 1993.
19. R. Nieuwenhuis and A. Rubio. Basic superposition is complete. In B. Krieg-Bruckner, editor, *Proc. European Symp. on Programming*, Lecture Notes in ComputerScience, vol. 582, pages 371–389, Rennes, 1992. Springer-Verlag.
20. R. Nieuwenhuis and A. Rubio. Theorem proving with ordering constrained clauses. In D. Kapur, editor, *Proc. 11th Int. Conf. on Automated Deduction, Saratoga Springs*, NY, Lecture Notes in Computer Science, vol. 607, pages 477–491. Springer-Verlag, June 1992.
21. R. Nieuwenhuis and A. Rubio. A precedence-based total AC-compatible ordering. In C. Kirchner, editor, *Proc. 5th Rewriting Techniques and Applications, Montréal*, Lecture Notes in Computer Science, vol. 690, pages 374–388. Springer-Verlag, June 1993.
22. D. Plaisted. Semantic confluence tests and completion methods. *Information and Control*, 65:182–215, 1985.

23. W. V. Quine. Concatenation as a basis for arithmetic. *Journal of Symbolic Logic*, 11(4), 1946.
24. R. Treinen. A new method for undecidability proofs of first order theories. *Journal of Symbolic Computation*, 14(5):437–458, Nov. 1992.
25. S. Tulipani. Decidability of the existential theory of infinite terms with subterm relation. To appear in *Information and Computation*, 1994.
26. K. N. Venkataraman. Decidability of the purely existential fragment of the theory of term algebras. *J. ACM*, 34(2):492–510, 1987.

Graph Grammars and Tree Transducers

Joost Engelfriet*

Department of Computer Science, Leiden University
P.O.Box 9512, 2300 RA Leiden, The Netherlands

Abstract. Regular tree grammars can be used to generate graphs, by generating expressions that denote graphs. Top-down and bottom-up tree transducers are a tool for proving properties of such graph generating tree grammars.

1 Introduction

The most well-known way of generating graphs is to replace a subgraph by another subgraph, analogous to string rewriting systems. The resulting theory of graph grammars has been developed since the seventies (see, e.g., [41, 20, 19, 32, 7]). Of particular interest are the context-free graph grammars, in which the replaced subgraph is a single edge or node. Such grammars model graph properties that can be defined in a recursive way.

A conceptually completely different way of generating graphs is to use symbolic computation, as follows. First a set of operations on graphs is selected (such as disjoint union of graphs, addition of edges, identification of nodes, graph substitution, etc.). Then one uses a tree grammar to generate expressions over these operations. Expressions are viewed as trees in the usual way. Finally, interpreting the expressions as graphs, one obtains a graph generating device. This method of symbolic generation was first considered in general by Mezei and Wright [40], using regular tree grammars to generate objects of an arbitrary semantic domain. For graphs it was introduced and investigated by Courcelle (see, e.g., [1, 7, 9, 15]); it turned out that, with a suitable choice of graph operations, both ways of generating graphs are equivalent (for several types of context-free graph grammar).

Just as tree grammars can be used to generate graphs (or any other objects), tree transducers can be used to symbolically compute transductions of objects of arbitrary semantic domains (as pointed out in [23, 17]) and hence, in particular, to compute graph transductions. This last possibility has turned up recently in the work of Courcelle, as a tool in proofs of properties of graph generating tree grammars (see, e.g. [8, 14, 12]). Of particular interest are the (usual) top-down and bottom-up tree transducers (see, e.g., [31]) because they are syntax-directed, i.e., compute recursively on the structure of the input tree. Moreover, implicitly in [6, 5, 35, 36, 16, 45] and explicitly by Drewes in [17], the top-down tree transducer was formulated as a model for the computation of boolean

* Supported by the ESPRIT BRWG No.7183 COMPUGRAPH II

and numerical functions on graphs, i.e., the translation of graphs into booleans or natural numbers, using boolean operations or numerical operations such as addition and multiplication. Numerical functions on graphs (such as the number of nodes of the graph, or the number of its connected components) are of interest for the decidability of boundedness properties of graph grammars, as shown by Habel, Kreowski, and Vogler in [36].

The graph generation power of a tree grammar critically depends on the chosen set of graph operations. Thus, we consider several different sets of operations in Section 3 and compare their power in Section 4. Tree transducers are used to transform an expression over one set of operations into an equivalent one over another set of operations, where 'equivalent' means that they denote the same graph. Numerical functions on graphs, computed by tree transducers, are considered in Section 5.

The main aim of this paper is to give the reader some insight in the use of top-down and bottom-up tree transducers for proving properties of graph generating regular tree grammars. No knowledge of the usual kinds of graph grammars is required, and none will be obtained from reading this paper. The reader is assumed to be familiar with elementary tree language theory (see [31]).

2 Tree Terminology

N denotes the set of natural numbers 0,1,2,.... A partial function $f : A \to B$ is, as usual, also viewed as the set of pairs $\{(a,b) \mid f(a) = b\}$. The domain and range of f are denoted by dom(f) and ran(f), respectively. The composition of relations $R_1 \subseteq A \times B$ and $R_2 \subseteq B \times C$ is denoted $R_2 \circ R_1$.

We assume the reader to be familiar with elementary tree language theory (see, e.g., [31, 21, 42]), but we recall some concepts and notations.

A set Σ with a mapping rank: $\Sigma \to \mathbf{N}$ is called a *ranked set* (or signature, or set of operators); if Σ is finite, it is called a ranked alphabet. The set of all trees (or terms, or expressions) over Σ is denoted T_Σ. Formally, expressions are written in parenthesis-free prefix notation, but we also use the more convenient notation with parentheses and comma's, possibly also with infix notation. Thus, if $+$ is a binary operator, f is unary, and c is a constant, then we write also $+(+(c, f(c)), c)$ or $(c + f(c)) + c$ or even $c + f(c) + c$ (assuming left-association) instead of the formal $+ + cfcc$. A tree language over a ranked alphabet Σ is a subset of T_Σ.

A *regular tree grammar* G is a context-free grammar such that the terminal and nonterminal alphabets Σ and N are ranked, all nonterminals have rank 0, and the right-hand side of every production is a tree over $\Sigma \cup N$. The language $L(G)$ generated by G is a tree language over Σ, and is called a regular tree language.

A *top-down tree transducer* τ has a ranked input alphabet Σ, a ranked output alphabet Δ, a finite ranked set Q of states such that every state has rank 1, an initial state $q_0 \in Q$, and a finite set of rules. Let $X = \{x_1, x_2, \ldots\}$ be the set of variables, of rank 0, and let $X_n = \{x_1, \ldots, x_n\}$ for every $n \in \mathbf{N}$. Each rule of τ is of the form $q(\sigma(x_1,\ldots,x_n)) \to t$ with $q \in Q$, $\sigma \in \Sigma$, $n = \text{rank}(\sigma)$, and t is a tree over $\Delta \cup Q \cup X_n$ such that the child of each state in t is a variable. The rules of τ are used as term rewriting rules in the usual way, and the relation computed by τ, also denoted by τ, is $\{(t,s) \in T_\Sigma \times T_\Delta \mid q_0(t) \Rightarrow^* s\}$. A top-down tree transducer τ is *total deterministic* if for every $q \in Q$ and $\sigma \in \Sigma$ there is exactly one rule with left-hand side $q(\sigma(x_1,\ldots,x_n))$. In that case τ computes a function $T_\Sigma \to T_\Delta$ and we denote by $\tau(t)$ the unique tree s such that $q_0(t) \Rightarrow^* s$; similarly, we denote by $\tau_q(t)$ the unique tree s such that $q(t) \Rightarrow^* s$. A *tree homomorphism* is a total deterministic top-down tree transducer with one state only.

A *bottom-up tree transducer* τ is similar to a top-down tree transducer, but its rules have the form $\sigma(q_1(x_1),\ldots,q_n(x_n)) \to q(t)$ with $q_1,\ldots,q_n,q \in Q$, $\sigma \in \Sigma$, $n = \text{rank}(\sigma)$, and t is a tree over $\Delta \cup X_n$. It does not have an initial state but a set of final states $F \subseteq Q$, and it computes the relation $\{(t,s) \in T_\Sigma \times T_\Delta \mid t \Rightarrow^* q(s)$ for some $q \in F\}$. A bottom-up tree transducer τ is *total deterministic* if for every $\sigma \in \Sigma$ of rank n and all states $q_1,\ldots,q_n$ there is exactly one rule with left-hand side $\sigma(q_1(x_1),\ldots,q_n(x_n))$, and, moreover, all its states are final. In that case τ computes a function $T_\Sigma \to T_\Delta$; if $t \Rightarrow^* q(s)$, we write $\tau(t) = s$, and we say that τ arrives in state q after processing input t. A *bottom-up tree automaton* is a bottom-up tree transducer of which all rules are of the form $\sigma(q_1(x_1),\ldots,q_n(x_n)) \to q(\sigma(x_1,\ldots,x_n))$. It recognizes the tree language $\{t \in T_\Sigma \mid t \Rightarrow^* q(t)$ for some $q \in F\}$. It is *total deterministic* if there is exactly one rule with left-hand side $\sigma(q_1(x_1),\ldots,q_n(x_n))$ for all σ and $q_1,\ldots,q_n$ (but not all its states need be final). A tree language is regular iff it is recognized by a total deterministic bottom-up tree automaton.

A top-down or bottom-up tree transducer is *linear* if each variable x_i occurs at most once in the right-hand side of each rule.

The following basic results will be used in this paper. For a tree language L and a tree transducer τ, we write $\tau(L) = \{s \mid (t,s) \in \tau$ for some $t \in L\}$, as usual. By TB* we denote the class of all tree relations $\tau_n \circ \cdots \circ \tau_2 \circ \tau_1$, $n \geq 1$, where each τ_i is a bottom-up or top-down tree transducer.

Proposition A. *If L is a regular tree language and τ is a linear top-down or bottom-up tree transducer, then $\tau(L)$ is a regular tree language.*

Proposition B. *It is decidable for a regular tree language L and a tree relation τ in* TB* *whether or not $\tau(L)$ is finite.*

Proposition A is proved in Lemma 6.5 (and Corollary 6.6) of [31] (see also Corollary 4.55 of [21]). Proposition B is proved for top-down tree transducers τ in a Corollary of Theorem 4 of [43]; the proof technique is extended to the general case in Theorem 4.90 of [21] (the basic idea is that the set of paths through the trees of $\tau(L)$ is a regular language).

3 Graph Languages Generated by Tree Grammars

For a given set of operations on graphs, a regular tree grammar can be used to generate a set of expressions over these operations. Interpreting the expressions as graphs, a set of graphs is obtained that will be called a context-free graph language. Clearly, this notion of context-free graph language depends on the given operations: different sets of operations may determine different classes of context-free graph languages. In this section we first define the general notion of a context-free graph language, and then consider several sets of graph operations. In the next section we compare the power of the resulting classes of context-free graph languages.

This approach to the generation of graphs was introduced in [1] (see also [7]); it is a special case of the general method of generating elements of an algebra as described in [40]. The presentation in this section is closely related to the one of Courcelle in [9].

For simplicity we consider directed graphs of which only the edges are labeled by symbols; moreover we do not allow loops or multiple edges with the same label. Let A be an infinite set of *edge labels*. A *graph* is a pair $g = (V, E)$ where V is a finite set of nodes, and $E \subseteq \{(v, a, w) \mid a \in A, v, w \in V, v \neq w\}$ is a finite set of edges. By GR we denote the set of all graphs. A *graph language* is a subset of GR.

In order to define some elementary operations on graphs such as the identification of two nodes or the addition of an edge, we need a means to specify which nodes have to be identified or to which nodes the edge has to be attached, respectively. Since we do not distinguish between isomorphic graphs, the concrete nodes themselves cannot be used. Instead, we label them with so-called port labels (and we call them ports).

Let P be an infinite set of *port labels*. A *graph with ports* is a triple $g = (V, E, \mathrm{port})$ where (V, E) is a graph and $\mathrm{port} : V \to P$ is a partial function from V to P. For given g, its components V, E, and port are also denoted by V_g, E_g, and port_g. The nodes in $\mathrm{dom}(\mathrm{port}_g)$ are the *ports* of g, and a port v with label $\mathrm{port}_g(v) = p \in P$ is called a *p-port*. The *type* of g, denoted $\mathrm{type}(g)$, is the finite set $\mathrm{ran}(\mathrm{port}_g)$ of port labels that occur in g. By $\mathrm{GR_p}$ we denote the set of all graphs with ports. We identify a graph (V, E) with $(V, E, \emptyset)$, the corresponding graph with ports that has no ports (where $\emptyset$ is the partial function $V \to P$ with empty domain). Thus, $\mathrm{GR} \subseteq \mathrm{GR_p}$. From now on we will also say graph instead of graph with ports. As observed above, we do not distinguish between isomorphic graphs (where an isomorphism is a bijection between nodes that preserves edges and port labels). Thus, we consider abstract rather than concrete graphs.

We now define the notion of a context-free graph language. By a *graph operation* of rank n we mean a mapping $\mathrm{GR_p^n} \to \mathrm{GR_p}$, for some $n \geq 0$. Let F be a (possibly infinite) set of graph operations. We will also use F to denote the set of operators that denote these operations. Thus, T_F is the set of expressions over the operators in F. For an expression (or term, or tree) $t \in T_F$ we write $\mathrm{val}(t)$ for the graph it denotes. Thus, val is a mapping from T_F to $\mathrm{GR_p}$. For a tree language $R \subseteq T_F$, $\mathrm{val}(R) = \{\mathrm{val}(t) \mid t \in R\}$, as usual.

Definition 1. A graph language $L \subseteq \mathrm{GR}$ is *F-context-free* if there is a finite subset Σ of F and a regular tree language $R \subseteq T_\Sigma$ such that $L = \mathrm{val}(R)$.

In this way we can use regular tree grammars to generate context-free graph languages. According to the main result of [40], the F-context-free graph languages are exactly the F-equational sets of graphs, i.e., the sets of graphs that can be obtained as the least solution of a regular tree grammar viewed as a set of equations for sets of graphs. In fact, the result of [40] does not only hold for graphs, but for the elements of any algebra.

Since Σ is finite, the regular tree grammar that generates $R \subseteq T_\Sigma$ uses a finite number of constants (i.e., graph operations of rank 0, i.e., graphs), and uses a finite number of graph operations of rank ≥ 1 to build larger graphs from smaller graphs, starting from the constants. To this aim, F will usually contain all constants in $\mathrm{GR_P}$ (another choice is to allow only a number of elementary constant graphs, such as all one- or two-node graphs).

A basic graph building operation is *disjoint union*, a binary operation. For graphs g and h, their disjoint union $g+h$ is $(V_g \cup V_h, E_g \cup E_h, \mathrm{port}_g \cup \mathrm{port}_h)$ where we assume that V_g and V_h are disjoint (otherwise disjoint isomorphic copies of g and h should be taken).

In general, we also need operations to change or remove port labels. For every partial function $z : P \to P$ with finite domain, the *port relabeling* π_z is the unary graph operation that transforms $g \in \mathrm{GR_P}$ into the graph $\pi_z(g) = (V_g, E_g, z\circ\mathrm{port}_g) \in \mathrm{GR_P}$. Thus, every port label $p \in \mathrm{dom}(z)$ is changed into $z(p)$, and every port label not in $\mathrm{dom}(z)$ is removed. It is easy to see that $\pi_z(g+h) = \pi_z(g) + \pi_z(h)$, and that $\pi_z(\pi_{z'}(g)) = \pi_{z\circ z'}(g)$.

Disjoint union can only be used to build very disconnected graphs. In order to put the pieces together, we choose between two methods: identification of nodes or addition of edges. This turns out to be a basic choice. The resulting classes of context-free graph languages correspond to two distinct well-known types of graph grammar in the literature, one of which is based on edge replacement and the other on node replacement.

Node identification is the unary graph operation δ that, for a given graph $g \in \mathrm{GR_P}$, identifies all ports of g with the same label. Loops and multiple edges that are, intuitively, formed by this identification, are removed. Formally, let $\equiv$ be the equivalence relation on V_g such that $v \equiv w$ iff either $v = w$ or $v, w \in \mathrm{dom}(\mathrm{port}_g)$ and $\mathrm{port}_g(v) = \mathrm{port}_g(w)$. Let $[v]$ denote the equivalence class of v, and let $[V_g]$ denote the set of all equivalence classes. Then $\delta(g) = ([V_g], E, \mathrm{port})$, where $E = \{([v], a, [w]) \mid (v, a, w) \in E, [v] \neq [w]\}$ and $\mathrm{port} = \{([v], p) \mid (v, p) \in \mathrm{port}_g\}$.

For every finite set $C \subseteq P \times A \times P$, the *edge addition* η_C is the unary graph operation that transforms the graph g into the graph $\eta_C(g) = (V_g, E_g \cup E, \mathrm{port}_g)$ where $E = \{(v, a, w) \mid v \neq w, (\mathrm{port}_g(v), a, \mathrm{port}_g(w)) \in C\}$. Thus, for every (p, a, q) in C, all a-labeled edges from p-ports to q-ports are added to g (as far as they did not exist already). Note that, if $C = \{c_1, \ldots, c_n\}$, then $\eta_C = \eta_{\{c_n\}} \circ \cdots \circ \eta_{\{c_1\}}$.

Two important sets of operations are now defined: HR and VR. Both HR and VR contain disjoint union $+$, all port relabelings π_z, and all constants in $\mathrm{GR_P}$. Moreover, HR contains node identification δ, and VR contains all edge additions η_C. Using Definition 1, we obtain two different types of context-free graph languages: the *HR-context-free* and the *VR-context-free* graph languages. We give some simple examples.

Examples 2. For $p \in P$ we denote the one-node graph $(\{x\}, \emptyset, \{(x,p)\})$ by c_p, and for $p, q \in P$ and $a \in A$ we denote the one-arc graph $(\{x,y\}, \{(x,a,y)\}, \{(x,p),(y,q)\})$ by c_{paq}. Similarly we use ϵ to indicate that a node has no port label; thus, c_ϵ denotes the one-node graph $(\{x\}, \emptyset, \emptyset)$ and $c_{pa\epsilon}$ the graph $(\{x,y\}, \{(x,a,y)\}, \{(x,p)\})$. These graphs will be used as constants in the example grammars.

(1) The set of all stars S_n is an HR-context-free graph language, where $S_n = (\{0,1,\ldots,n\}, \{(0,a,i) \mid 1 \leq i \leq n\}), n \geq 0$. It is generated by the regular tree grammar G with nonterminals S and B (of which S is the initial nonterminal), and productions $S \rightarrow \pi_\emptyset \delta B$, $B \rightarrow +Bc_{pa\epsilon}$, and $B \rightarrow c_p$. More informally, the productions can be written $S \rightarrow \pi_\emptyset(\delta(B))$, $B \rightarrow B + c_{pa\epsilon}$, and $B \rightarrow c_p$. As an example, G generates the tree $t = \pi_\emptyset(\delta(((c_p + c_{pa\epsilon}) + c_{pa\epsilon}) + c_{pa\epsilon})) = \pi_\emptyset(\delta(c_p + c_{pa\epsilon} + c_{pa\epsilon} + c_{pa\epsilon}))$. The value of the subtree $c_p + c_{pa\epsilon} + c_{pa\epsilon} + c_{pa\epsilon}$, generated by B, is the graph consisting of one copy of c_p and three copies of $c_{pa\epsilon}$, all disjoint. The value of t is obtained from this graph by identifying its four p-ports, and then removing the port label p. Hence, val(t) is the graph S_3. Thus, obviously, $\text{val}(L(G)) = \{S_n \mid n \geq 0\}$.

(2) Another simple example of an HR-context-free graph language is the set L of all cycles that are labeled with strings from the language $\{a^k b^k \mid k \geq 1\}$, where we use the symbol s to indicate the start of the string (with $a, b, s \in A$). Formally, L is the set of all graphs $(\{0,1,\ldots,n\}, \{(i-1, a_i, i) \mid 1 \leq i \leq n\} \cup \{(n,s,0)\})$ such that $a_1 a_2 \cdots a_n \in \{a^k b^k \mid k \geq 1\}$. It is generated by a regular tree grammar G that uses four port labels: p, q, p', and q'. G has nonterminals S and B, where S is the initial nonterminal and B generates all chains $(\{0,1,\ldots,n\}, \{(i-1, a_i, i) \mid 1 \leq i \leq n\}, \{(0,p),(n,q)\})$ with $a_1 a_2 \cdots a_n \in \{a^k b^k \mid k \geq 1\}$. G has productions $S \rightarrow \pi_\emptyset(\delta(B + c_{qsp}))$, $B \rightarrow \pi_z(\delta(c_{p'ap} + B + c_{qbq'}))$, $B \rightarrow \pi_z(\delta(c_{p'ap} + c_{pbq'}))$, where z is the partial function $\{(p',p),(q',q)\}$, i.e., $\text{dom}(z) = \{p',q'\}$ and $z(p') = p$, $z(q') = q$. By the third production, B generates a chain corresponding to the string ab. Production $B \rightarrow \pi_z(\delta(c_{p'ap} + B + c_{qbq'}))$ explains how to obtain the chain g_{k+1} corresponding to $a^{k+1}b^{k+1}$ from the chain g_k corresponding to $a^k b^k$: add copies of $c_{p'ap}$ and $c_{qbq'}$ to g_k, identify node 0 of g_k with the p-port of $c_{p'ap}$ and node $2k$ of g_k with the q-port of $c_{qbq'}$, remove port labels p and q, and remove the primes from port labels p' and q'. Thus, g_{k+1} is obtained from g_k by gluing an a-edge at its "left" and a b-edge at its "right". The production $S \rightarrow \pi_\emptyset(\delta(B + c_{qsp}))$ turns the chain into a cycle, and removes port labels p and q.

(3) The set of all complete graphs K_n is not an HR-context-free graph language (see the discussion after Proposition 10), but it is a VR-context-free graph language, with $K_n = (\{1,\ldots,n\}, \{(i,a,j) \mid 1 \leq i,j \leq n, i \neq j\})$. It is generated by the regular tree grammar with productions $S \rightarrow \pi_\emptyset(B)$, $B \rightarrow \pi_z(\eta_C(B + c_q))$, $B \rightarrow c_p$, where $C = \{(p,a,q),(q,a,p)\}$ and $z = \{(p,p),(q,p)\}$. Nonterminal B generates all graphs K'_n, i.e., all K_n with port label p on each node. K'_{n+1} is obtained from K'_n by adding a node x with label q, adding all possible edges

between x and the nodes of K'_n, and changing q into p. Another grammar that generates all K_n has productions $S \to \pi_\emptyset(\eta_{\{(p,a,p)\}}(B))$, $B \to B + c_p$, $B \to c_p$.

(4) The set of all complete bipartite graphs $K_{m,n}$ is also VR-context-free, where $K_{m,n}$ has nodes $v_1, \ldots, v_m, w_1, \ldots, w_n$ (with $m, n \geq 1$) and edges (v_i, a, w_j) and (w_j, a, v_i) for all $1 \leq i \leq m, 1 \leq j \leq n$. It is generated by the regular tree grammar with productions $S \to \pi_\emptyset(\eta_C(B))$, $B \to B + c_p$, $B \to B + c_q$, $B \to c_p$, $B \to c_q$, where $C = \{(p, a, q), (q, a, p)\}$. TheVR-context-free graph language $\{K_{n,n} \mid n \geq 1\}$ is generated by the regular tree grammar with productions $S \to \pi_\emptyset(\eta_C(B))$, $B \to B + c_p + c_q$, $B \to c_p + c_q$. □

The set of operations HR is a variant of the sets of operations defined in [1, 9, 8, 13], which are all equivalent, in the sense that they give the same class of context-free graph languages (see [9, 12, 14]). The equivalence of HR with these sets of operations will be shown in Proposition 8. Thus, they all define the HR-context-free graph languages. It was proved in [1] that these are exactly the graph languages generated by the Hyperedge Replacement graph grammars of [33, 32, 18, 1].

The set of operations VR was defined in [15]. To be precise, it was defined for a more general type of graphs (in which one node can have several port labels); the equivalence of the two sets of operations was shown in Lemma 1.1 of [8] (using a tree transducer and applying Proposition A, as in the next section). It was shown in [15] that the VR-context-free graph languages are exactly the graph languages generated by the C-edNCE graph grammars of [37, 2, 44, 24, 25]; this is the largest class of context-free NLC-like node replacement graph grammars, and was re-baptized Vertex Replacement graph grammars in [9, 11]. In this paper we will not consider these graph grammars. Let us just have a short look at the possibly counter-intuitive idea that (HR) node identification is related to edge replacement, whereas (VR) edge addition is related to node replacement.

First edge replacement. Consider a graph g with an edge $e = (v, a, w)$, and let v and w be the only ports of g, with labels p and q, respectively. Then g can naturally be written as $g = \delta(h + c_{paq})$, where h is obtained from g by removing (v, a, w) from E_g. Now let d be another graph, with exactly two ports, labeled p and q. Then the result of replacing edge e by graph d in g is the graph $\delta(h + d)$. This means that, after removing e, the ports of d are glued to the corresponding ports of g. It is, roughly speaking, the way in which (hyper)edge replacement graph grammars work.

Next node replacement. Consider now a graph g that has exactly one p-port v and several other ports. Assume moreover that g can be written as $g = \eta_C(h + c_p)$ where h is obtained from g by removing node v and all its incident edges, and for each triple (q, a, r) in C either $q = p$ or $r = p$. Let d be another graph, and assume that d has p-ports only. Then the result of replacing node v by graph d in g is the graph $\eta_C(h + d)$. This means that, after removing v, each p-port of d is connected (by edges) to h in the same way as v was. It is a (simple) example of how node replacement graph grammars work.

4 Comparison of Graph Operations

One aspect of the unary operations δ and η_C that is intuitively not very nice, is that they are able to identify nodes or add edges throughout the argument graph g. One could ask whether it is not possible for the grammar to identify these nodes or add these edges during the generation of the graph g. This suggests that nodes should only be identified, or edges added, when two graphs g_1 and g_2 are put together by the operation of disjoint union, and, to be more precise, only nodes of g_1 should be identified with nodes of g_2, or edges added between nodes of g_1 and g_2. We will show that this is indeed possible. We start with the VR case.

For every finite set $C \subseteq P \times A \times P$, the *edge connection* $\wedge_C$ is the binary graph operation that transforms (disjoint) graphs g and h into the graph $g \wedge_C h = (V_g \cup V_h, E_g \cup E_h \cup E, \text{port}_g \cup \text{port}_h)$ where $E = \{(v, a, w) \mid (\text{port}_g(v), a, \text{port}_h(w)) \in C$ or $(\text{port}_h(v), a, \text{port}_g(w)) \in C\}$. Thus, for every (p, a, q) in C, all a-labeled edges from p-ports of g to q-ports of h and from p-ports of h to q-ports of g, are added to $g + h$. Note that $g \wedge_\emptyset h = g + h$.

As an example, the set of cographs [4] is generated by the regular tree grammar with productions $S \to \pi_\emptyset(B)$, $B \to B \wedge_C B$, $B \to B + B$, $B \to c_p$, where $C = \{(p, a, p)\}$.

The set VR$\wedge$ of graph operations is defined to contain all edge connections $\wedge_C$, all port relabelings π_z, and all constants in GR_p. This gives the notion of a *VR$\wedge$-context-free* graph language. We will now show that a graph language is VR$\wedge$-context-free iff it is VR-context-free, using linear tree transducers to transform expressions over VR$\wedge$ into equivalent expressions over VR, and vice versa. The basic underlying result from tree language theory is that the class of regular tree languages is closed under linear tree transductions (Proposition A).

We need the following technical concept. Let Σ be a finite set of graph operations of the types discussed until now. Since Σ is finite, it uses only finitely many port labels. By $P(\Sigma)$ we denote the finite subset of P that is the union of all type(g) with g a constant graph in Σ, all dom(z) and ran(z) for π_z in Σ, and all sets $\{p \in P \mid (p, a, q) \in C$ or $(q, a, p) \in C$ for some $a \in A$ and $q \in P\}$ for all η_C and all $\wedge_C$ in Σ. Obviously, type(val(t)) $\subseteq P(\Sigma)$ for every $t \in T_\Sigma$.

In one direction the proof is quite easy because $\wedge_C$ is in fact a (linear) derived operation of VR.

Proposition 3. *For every finite $\Sigma \subseteq$ VR$\wedge$ there are a finite $\Delta \subseteq$ VR and a linear tree homomorphism $\tau : T_\Sigma \to T_\Delta$ such that* $\text{val}(\tau(t)) = \text{val}(t)$ *for every $t \in T_\Sigma$.*

Proof. Let $P'(\Sigma) = \{p' \mid p \in P(\Sigma)\}$ be a "new" set of port labels, disjoint with $P(\Sigma)$. It is easy to check that, for graphs g and h with type(g), type(h) $\subseteq P(\Sigma)$, and for $\wedge_C$ in Σ, $g \wedge_C h = \pi_z(\eta_{C'}(g + \pi_{z'}(h)))$ where $z'(p) = p'$ for all $p \in P(\Sigma)$, $C' = \{(p, a, q') \mid (p, a, q) \in C\} \cup \{(p', a, q) \mid (p, a, q) \in C\}$, and $z(p') = z(p) = p$ for all $p \in P(\Sigma)$. The required tree homomorphism τ has one state q and the following rules: $q(x_1 \wedge_C x_2) \to \pi_z(\eta_{C'}(q(x_1) + \pi_{z'}(q(x_2))))$ for every $\wedge_C$ in Σ

(where z, C', z' are as defined above), $q(\pi_z(x_1)) \to \pi_z(q(x_1))$ for every π_z in Σ, and $q(g) \to g$ for every constant graph g in Σ. The output alphabet $\Delta \subseteq \mathrm{VR}$ of τ is just the finite set of all operations that appear in the right-hand sides of these rules. By the above equation, $\mathrm{val}(\tau(t)) = \mathrm{val}(t)$ for every $t \in T_\Sigma$. □

In the other direction we need a more complicated tree transducer.

Proposition 4. *For every finite $\Sigma \subseteq \mathrm{VR}$ there are a finite $\Delta \subseteq \mathrm{VR}\wedge$ and a linear total deterministic top-down tree transducer $\tau : T_\Sigma \to T_\Delta$ such that $\mathrm{val}(\tau(t)) = \mathrm{val}(t)$ for every $t \in T_\Sigma$.*

Proof. As observed before, we have to show that edges need only be added just after a disjoint union, and only between the two argument graphs. The possibility to do this is based on the following equations. For graphs g and h, and for $C, C' \subseteq P \times A \times P$ and $z : P \to P$,

$$\eta_C(g + h) = \eta_C(g) \wedge_C \eta_C(h),$$
$$\eta_C(\eta_{C'}(g)) = \eta_{C \cup C'}(g), \text{ and}$$
$$\eta_C(\pi_z(g)) = \pi_z(\eta_D(g)), \text{ where } D = \{(p, a, q) \mid (z(p), a, z(q)) \in C\}.$$

The required top-down tree transducer τ has a state q_C for every $C \subseteq P(\Sigma) \times A \times P(\Sigma)$, initial state $q_\emptyset$, and the following rules (for the operations in Σ):

$$q_C(x_1 + x_2) \to q_C(x_1) \wedge_C q_C(x_2),$$
$$q_C(\eta_{C'}(x_1)) \to q_{C \cup C'}(x_1),$$
$$q_C(\pi_z(x_1)) \to \pi_z(q_D(x_1)), \text{ where } D \text{ is as defined above, and}$$
$$q_C(g) \to \eta_C(g) \text{ for every constant } g.$$

Note that the right-hand side of the last rule is a constant that denotes the graph $\eta_C(g)$. Hence, the output alphabet of τ is in $\mathrm{VR}\wedge$. It is now straightforward to prove that for every $t \in T_\Sigma$, $\mathrm{val}(\tau_{q_C}(t)) = \eta_C(\mathrm{val}(t))$; the proof is by induction on t, using the above equations. Hence, $\mathrm{val}(\tau(t)) = \eta_\emptyset(\mathrm{val}(t)) = \mathrm{val}(t)$. □

Proposition 5. *A graph language is $\mathrm{VR}\wedge$-context-free iff it is VR-context-free.*

Proof. (If) Let L be VR-context-free, i.e., $L = \mathrm{val}(R)$ where R is a regular tree language over a finite subset Σ of VR. By Proposition 4 there exist a finite subset Δ of $\mathrm{VR}\wedge$ and a linear total deterministic top-down tree transduction τ such that $\mathrm{val}(\tau(t)) = \mathrm{val}(t)$ for every $t \in T_\Sigma$, and so $\mathrm{val}(\tau(R)) = \mathrm{val}(R)$ where $\tau(R) = \{\tau(t) \mid t \in R\}$. Since the regular tree languages are closed under linear tree transductions (Proposition A), $\tau(R)$ is a regular tree language over Δ. Since $L = \mathrm{val}(\tau(R))$, L is $\mathrm{VR}\wedge$-context-free.

The only-if direction is analogous, using Proposition 3. □

We now turn to an analogous result for HR. For HR we will show moreover that it suffices to consider graphs g for which port_g is injective (i.e., g contains at most one p-port for every $p \in P$). The *node connection* $//$ is the binary graph operation that transforms (disjoint) graphs g and h into the graph $g//h = \delta(g + h)$. Thus, if port_g and port_h are injective, the p-port of g is identified with the

p-port of h for every $p \in \mathrm{type}(g) \cap \mathrm{type}(h)$. Note that for arbitrary g and h, $\delta(g+h) = \delta(g)//\delta(h)$. For a finite subset Q of P, the *port restriction* res_Q is the unary graph operation that equals π_z where z is the identity on Q, i.e., $z = \{(q,q) \mid q \in Q\}$. Thus, res_Q throws away all port labels not in Q, and does not change those in Q. Note that $\mathrm{res}_\emptyset = \pi_\emptyset$.

The set HR// of graph operations is defined to contain the node connection //, all port restrictions res_Q, and all constants g in $\mathrm{GR_P}$ such that port_g is injective. Note that port_g is injective for every graph $g \in \mathrm{val}(T_{HR//})$. The set HR// was introduced in [9] (with arbitrary port relabelings). The operation of node connection was introduced in [12], where it is called gluing; in [9, 8, 13] it is called parallel composition. The set HR// is very close to the set of all graph substitution operations (see, e.g., [10]), and hence very close to the Hyperedge Replacement graph grammars of [32].

As usual, we obtain the notion of an *HR//-context-free* graph language. As in the VR case, we will show that this coincides with the notion of an HR-context-free graph language, using linear tree transducers.

As an example we show that the graph language L of Example 2(2) is HR//-context-free. A regular tree grammar generating L and using the operations of H// has the following productions: $S \to \mathrm{res}_\emptyset(B//c_{qsp})$,
$B \to \mathrm{res}_{\{p,q\}}(c_{pap'}//C//c_{q'bq})$, $B \to \mathrm{res}_{\{p,q\}}(c_{pap'}//c_{p'bq})$,
$C \to \mathrm{res}_{\{p',q'\}}(c_{p'ap}//B//c_{qbq'})$, $C \to \mathrm{res}_{\{p',q'\}}(c_{p'ap}//c_{pbq'})$.
Nonterminal B generates the same graphs as in Example 2(2), with port labels p and q, whereas C generates the same graphs as B, but with port labels p' and q', respectively.

Proposition 6. *For every finite $\Sigma \subseteq$ HR// there are a finite $\Delta \subseteq$ HR and a linear tree homomorphism $\tau : T_\Sigma \to T_\Delta$ such that* $\mathrm{val}(\tau(t)) = \mathrm{val}(t)$ *for every $t \in T_\Sigma$.*

Proof. The proof is even easier than the one of Proposition 3, because $g//h = \delta(g+h)$ by definition and thus // is a derived operation of HR (and hence a tree homomorphism can again be used). □

Proposition 7. *For every finite $\Sigma \subseteq$ HR there are a finite $\Delta \subseteq$ HR// and a linear total deterministic top-down tree transducer $\tau : T_\Sigma \to T_\Delta$ such that* $\mathrm{val}(\tau(t)) = \mathrm{val}(t)$ *for every $t \in T_\Sigma$ with* $\mathrm{type}(\mathrm{val}(t)) = \emptyset$.

Proof. Note that we may restrict attention to trees with $\mathrm{type}(\mathrm{val}(t)) = \emptyset$, because we are only interested in graph languages $\subseteq$ GR.

For every $z : P(\Sigma) \to P(\Sigma)$ we fix some $z' : P(\Sigma) \to P(\Sigma)$ such that $\mathrm{dom}(z') = P(\Sigma) - \mathrm{dom}(z)$, $\mathrm{ran}(z') \subseteq P(\Sigma) - \mathrm{ran}(z)$, and z' is injective.

We will define a tree transducer that has states to compute the operations $\delta \circ \pi_z$ for every $z : P(\Sigma) \to P(\Sigma)$ (which are similar to the fuse′ operations of [13]). The correctness of this transducer is based on the following equations. For graphs g and h, and $z, u : P \to P$,

$$\delta(\pi_z(g+h)) = \delta(\pi_z(g))//\delta(\pi_z(h)),$$

$\delta(\pi_z(\pi_u(g))) = \delta(\pi_{z \circ u}(g))$, and
$\delta(\pi_z(\delta(g))) = \mathrm{res}_{\mathrm{ran}(z)}(\delta(\pi_{z \cup z'}(g)))$, where z' is defined above.

The linear total deterministic top-down tree transducer τ based on these equations has a state q_z for every $z : P(\Sigma) \to P(\Sigma)$, with initial state $q_\emptyset$. It has the following rules (for the operations in Σ):

$q_z(x_1 + x_2) \to q_z(x_1)//q_z(x_2)$,
$q_z(\pi_u(x_1)) \to q_{z \circ u}(x_1)$,
$q_z(\delta(x_1)) \to \mathrm{res}_{\mathrm{ran}(z)}(q_{z \cup z'}(x_1))$, and
$q_z(g) \to \delta(\pi_z(g))$ for every constant g

where (again) the right-hand side of the last rule is a constant (and clearly it is a constant of HR//).

It follows from the above equations that for every $t \in T_\Sigma$, $\mathrm{val}(\tau_{q_z}(t)) = \delta(\pi_z(\mathrm{val}(t)))$. Hence, if $\mathrm{type}(\mathrm{val}(t)) = \emptyset$, then $\mathrm{val}(\tau(t)) = \delta(\pi_\emptyset(\mathrm{val}(t))) = \mathrm{val}(t)$. □

The next proposition now follows from Propositions 6 and 7, in the same way as Proposition 5 followed from Propositions 3 and 4.

Proposition 8. *A graph language is HR//-context-free iff it is HR-context-free.*

We now show that every HR-context-free graph language is VR-context-free. This result is well known, through proofs based on graph grammars [30, 46] or based on logic [14, 25]. Here we give a proof based on graph operations and linear tree transducers (this time bottom-up).

Proposition 9. *For every finite $\Sigma \subseteq$ HR// there are a finite $\Delta \subseteq$ VR and a linear total deterministic bottom-up tree transducer $\tau : T_\Sigma \to T_\Delta$ such that $\mathrm{val}(\tau(t)) = \mathrm{val}(t)$ for every $t \in T_\Sigma$ with $\mathrm{type}(\mathrm{val}(t)) = \emptyset$.*

Proof. Consider an arbitrary $t \in T_\Sigma$ with $\mathrm{val}(t) = g$. The idea is to define a bottom-up tree transducer τ that transforms t into a tree s with $\mathrm{val}(s) = h$, where h is the graph obtained from g by removing all its ports with their incident edges. However, to keep track of the missing information, τ labels the nodes of h with finite information that codes the edges with which they were connected to the ports (note that this is possible because port_g is injective). Moreover, in its finite state τ stores the information which ports are missing (i.e., $\mathrm{type}(g)$) and what were the edges between the ports.

Let $P'(\Sigma)$ be the set of all nonempty subsets of $(A \times P(\Sigma)) \cup (P(\Sigma) \times A)$. We may assume that $P'(\Sigma) \subseteq P$ (disjoint with $P(\Sigma)$), i.e., we will use the elements of $P'(\Sigma)$ as new port labels. For every graph g with $\mathrm{type}(g) \subseteq P(\Sigma)$, we now define the graph $\mathrm{nop}(g)$ with $\mathrm{type}(\mathrm{nop}(g)) \subseteq P'(\Sigma)$; $\mathrm{nop}(g)$ is the graph h discussed above. Intuitively, if a node v of $\mathrm{nop}(g)$ has port label $I \in P'(\Sigma)$, a pair $(a, p) \in I$ means that in g there is an a-labeled edge from v to the p-port of g, and similarly for $(p, a) \in I$ an edge in the other direction. Formally, $\mathrm{nop}(g) = (V_g - \mathrm{dom}(\mathrm{port}_g), E, \mathrm{port})$, where E is the restriction of E_g to the nodes of $\text{nop}(g)$, and port is defined as follows: for $v \in V_g - \text{dom}(\text{port}_g)$, let $\text{conn}(v) = \{(a,p) \mid (v,a,x) \in E_g$ for an x with $\text{port}_g(x) = p\} \cup \{(p,a) \mid (x,a,v) \in E_g$ for an x with $\text{port}_g(x) = p\}$; then $\text{dom}(\text{port}) = \{v \mid \text{conn}(v) \neq \emptyset\}$ and $\text{port}(v) = \text{conn}(v)$.

The states of τ are all graphs $k \in \text{GR}_\text{p}$ with $\text{type}(k) \subseteq P(\Sigma)$ and $\text{port}_k : V_k \to P(\Sigma)$ is a total injective function. Note that (modulo isomorphism) there are only finitely many such graphs. In what follows it will often be convenient to use the port labels as nodes of k, i.e., to assume that port_k is the identity on $\text{type}(k)$. All states of τ are final. For a graph g with port_g injective and $\text{type}(g) \subseteq P(\Sigma)$, we define $\text{ind}(g)$ to be $g[\text{dom}(\text{port}_g)]$, i.e., the subgraph of g induced by its ports (for a set $V \subseteq V_g$, $g[V]$ denotes the subgraph of g induced by V); clearly, $\text{ind}(g)$ is a state of τ. Note that $\text{type}(\text{ind}(g)) = \text{type}(g)$.

We will define τ in such a way that, for every $t \in T_\Sigma$, $\text{val}(\tau(t)) = \text{nop}(\text{val}(t))$, and if τ arrives in state q after processing t, then $q = \text{ind}(\text{val}(t))$. In the case that $\text{type}(\text{val}(t)) = \emptyset$ this means that $\text{val}(\tau(t)) = \text{val}(t)$ (and q is the empty graph). The rules of τ are based on the following equations. For graphs g and h with port_g and port_h injective and $\text{type}(g), \text{type}(h) \subseteq P(\Sigma)$,

$$\text{ind}(g//h) = \text{ind}(g)//\text{ind}(h),$$
$$\text{nop}(g//h) = \text{nop}(g) + \text{nop}(h),$$
$$\text{ind}(\text{res}_Q(g)) = \text{ind}(g)[Q], \text{ and}$$
$$\text{nop}(\text{res}_Q(g)) = \pi_z(\eta_C(\text{nop}(g) + c)), \text{ where}$$

$c = \text{ind}(g)[V_{\text{ind}(g)} - Q]$, $C = \{(I,a,p) \mid I \in P'(\Sigma), (a,p) \in I, p \notin Q\} \cup \{(p,a,I) \mid I \in P'(\Sigma), (p,a) \in I, p \notin Q\}$, for $p \in P(\Sigma) - Q$, $z(p) = \{(a,r) \mid (p,a,r) \in E_{\text{ind}(g)}, r \in Q\} \cup \{(r,a) \mid (r,a,p) \in E_{\text{ind}(g)}, r \in Q\}$ and for $I \in P'(\Sigma)$, $z(I) = I \cap ((A \times Q) \cup (Q \times A))$, where $z(p) = \emptyset$ or $z(I) = \emptyset$ means that $z(p)$ or $z(I)$ is undefined. Note that we have assumed that the port labels of $\text{ind}(g)$ are also its nodes.

From all considerations above it should now be clear that the rules of τ can be taken as follows (for the operations in Σ):

$q_1(x_1)//q_2(x_2) \to q(x_1 + x_2)$, where $q = q_1//q_2$,
$\text{res}_Q(q_1(x_1)) \to q(\pi_z(\eta_C(x_1 + c)))$, where $q = q_1[Q]$ and c, C, and z are defined as above, except that q_1 should be used for $\text{ind}(g)$,
$g \to q(g')$ for every constant g, where $q = \text{ind}(g)$ and $g' = \text{nop}(g)$.

This ends the proof of the proposition. □

Proposition 10. *Every HR-context-free graph language is VR-context-free.*

Proof. Let L be an HR-context-free graph language. By Proposition 8, L is HR//-context-free. Using the same argument as in the proof of Proposition 5, Proposition 9 implies that L is VR-context-free. □

The other direction of Proposition 10 is not true. It has recently been shown in [8] that it is decidable whether a VR-context-free graph language is HR-context-free. This result is based on an elegant structural characterization of the HR-context-free graph languages within the class of VR-context-free graph languages: a VR-context-free graph language L is HR-context-free if and only if there exists an n such that $K_{n,n}$ (cf. Example 2(4)) is not an induced subgraph of any graph in L (when disregarding the direction of the edges). Thus, the VR-context-free graph languages of Example 2(3,4) are not HR-context-free.

The characterization of [8] implies the, previously known [27, 3], fact that a graph language of bounded degree is VR-context-free iff it is HR-context-free (where L is of bounded degree if there is a uniform bound on the degree of all nodes of all graphs of L). In fact, the class of HR-context-free (or VR-context-free) graph languages of bounded degree is a class of context-free graph languages in its own right, as will be shown next. We need a new graph operation that is a variant of $//$. The *node attachment* Π is the binary graph operation such that, for graphs g and h, $g \Pi h = \mathrm{res}_Q(g//h)$, where $Q = (\mathrm{type}(g) \cup \mathrm{type}(h)) - (\mathrm{type}(g) \cap \mathrm{type}(h))$, i.e., the symmetric difference of type(g) and type(h). This means that the port labels that are used for the node identification in $g//h$ (the port labels in $\mathrm{type}(g) \cap \mathrm{type}(h)$) are thrown away immediately. Let HRΠ be the set of graph operations containing node attachment Π and all constants g in $\mathrm{GR_P}$ such that port_g is injective. Note that restrictions are not needed in HRΠ; they can be simulated by an appropriate node attachment with a discrete graph.

As an example we show that the language L of Example 2(2) is HRΠ-context-free. Note that L is of bounded degree 2. L is generated by the regular tree grammar over HRΠ with the following productions (see also the grammar for L just before Proposition 6): $S \to B \Pi c_{qsp}$, $B \to c_{pap'} \Pi C \Pi c_{q'bq}$, $B \to c_{pap'} \Pi c_{p'bq}$, $C \to c_{p'ap} \Pi B \Pi c_{qbq'}$, $C \to c_{p'ap} \Pi c_{pbq'}$.

Proposition 11. *A graph language is HRΠ-context-free iff it is HR-context-free and of bounded degree.*

Proof. (Sketch) The only-if direction is not difficult. It follows from the above definition of node attachment that one can use linear total deterministic bottom-up tree transducers to transform trees over HRΠ into trees over HR$//$ with the same value. For an input tree t, the transducer should compute type(val(t)) in its state (in order to determine the appropriate restrictions res_Q). This implies that every HRΠ-context-free graph language is HR$//$-context-free, in the usual way. It is also quite obvious that every HRΠ-context-free graph language is of bounded degree: port labels can be used at most once for node identification; thus, for a given regular tree grammar over HRΠ, the nodes of the generated graphs have a degree that is at most two times the degree of the nodes of the graphs that are used as constants by the grammar.

In the other direction we need the result of [28] (see also [26]): every HR-context-free graph language of bounded degree can be generated by a so-called Apex HR graph grammar. Using a result similar to the one on Apex VR graph grammars in [29], it is then not difficult to show (analogous to the method in [1]) that the language is HRΠ-context-free. It is not clear whether, in this direction, there is a direct proof without the use of HR graph grammars. □

Finally, the reader may have wondered what happens if one takes all discussed operations together, i.e., what are the (HR $\cup$ VR)-context-free graph languages.

It can be shown by methods similar to those used in this section that a graph language is (HR$\cup$VR)-context-free iff it is VR-context-free. This can also be seen from logical arguments, using the result of [25]. Of course the question remains which natural operations can still be added to VR, giving a new natural notion of context-free graph language. It is shown in [12] that the addition to VR (or HR) of all unary operations that can be defined by quantifier-free first-order logical formulas (in a certain way) does not increase the power of VR (or HR, respectively).

5 Numerical Functions on Graphs

For many types of context-free graph grammars (in particular HR and VR graph grammars) it is quite straightforward to decide the emptiness or finiteness of the generated graph language. In our case, it is also straightforward to decide whether or not a given regular tree grammar G (over any set of graph operations F) generates an empty graph language: $\mathrm{val}(L(G)) = \emptyset$ iff $L(G) = \emptyset$ (and emptiness of regular tree languages is decidable). However, for the finiteness problem (which is decidable for regular tree languages) it is not so straightforward: even if $L(G)$ is infinite $\mathrm{val}(L(G))$ may be finite, because for a given graph g there are infinitely many expressions t such that $\mathrm{val}(t) = g$ (for instance, $\pi_z(g) = g$ where z is the identity on $\mathrm{type}(g)$). We will show in this section how the finiteness problem for HR- and VR-context-free graph languages can be reduced to the tree language theoretic problem in Proposition B, i.e., by the use of tree transducers.

Let $\#\mathrm{nod} : \mathrm{GR} \to \mathbf{N}$ be the function such that, for every graph $g \in \mathrm{GR}$, $\#\mathrm{nod}(g)$ is the number of nodes of g. Obviously, for a graph language L, L is finite iff $\#\mathrm{nod}(L)$ is finite (where, for a function $f : \mathrm{GR} \to \mathbf{N}$, $f(L)$ is the set of natural numbers $\{f(g) \mid g \in L\}$). In what follows we will consider arbitrary numerical functions on graphs (rather than just #nod), and for each such function f : $\mathrm{GR} \to \mathbf{N}$ we will consider the f-finiteness problem, i.e., the problem to decide for a given context-free graph language L whether or not $f(L)$ is finite. Thus, $f(g)$ may be the number of connected components of g, or the maximal degree of the nodes of g, etc. The f-finiteness problem is also called the *f-boundedness problem*, because $f(L)$ is finite iff there exists $k \in \mathbf{N}$ such that $f(g) \leq k$ for all $g \in L$. Thus, if $f(g)$ is the maximal degree of the nodes of g, $f(L)$ is finite iff L is of bounded degree.

General conditions on f that guarantee the decidability of the f-boundedness problem were first investigated by Habel, Kreowski, and Vogler in [36], for HR-context-free languages (see also Chapter VII of [32]). Later work is in [25, 45, 47, 17, 38]. It was realized by Drewes in [17] that the conditions of [36] could be expressed in terms of top-down tree transducers that transform a graph expression for a graph g into a numerical expression for the number $f(g)$. In this section we follow the approach and terminology of [17] (though not in detail).

Let DTB* denote the class of all tree functions $\tau_n \circ \cdots \circ \tau_2 \circ \tau_1$, $n \geq 1$, where each τ_i is a total deterministic top-down or bottom-up tree transducer (not necessarily linear).

Let F be a set of graph operations, and let F' be a set of numerical operations, i.e., mappings $\mathbf{N}^k \to \mathbf{N}$, $k \geq 0$. As for F, we will use F' also to denote the set of corresponding operators, and, for a tree $t \in T_{F'}$ we write val(t) for the number denoted by t.

Definition 12. A function $f : \mathrm{GR} \to \mathbf{N}$ is *F-F'-transducible* if for every finite subset Σ of F there are a finite subset Δ of F' and a tree function $\tau : T_\Sigma \to T_\Delta$ in DTB* such that $\mathrm{val}(\tau(t)) = f(\mathrm{val}(t))$ for every $t \in T_\Sigma$ with $\mathrm{type}(\mathrm{val}(t)) = \emptyset$.

This means that τ computes f on the expression level, i.e., symbolically (see [23, 17]): for every graph expression t with value g, τ computes a numerical expression $\tau(t)$ with value $f(g)$. We say that f is *effectively F-F'-transducible* if there is an algorithm that produces Δ and τ from Σ. We note here (once and for all) that all the results in this paper are effective.

Following [36], we will mostly take $F' =$ PTM, where PTM consists of the usual binary numerical operations + (plus), $\cdot$ (times), max (maximum), and all constants in $\mathbf{N}$. For this reason we will say that f is *F-transducible* if it is F-PTM-transducible (for a set of graph operations F).

Taking F' to be the set of all boolean operations, transducible boolean functions were introduced in [6, 5], where they are called inductive predicates. In [35] they are called compatible predicates (for a different, but equivalent, F). Transducible numerical functions (called compatible functions) were introduced in [36] and also studied in [16] (where they are called inductively computable). Definition 12 is more general than these concepts, in the spirit of [17]. In fact, in all the above papers only top-down tree transducers are allowed (rather than compositions of top-down and bottom-up tree transducers), and the top-down tree transducer τ should depend on Σ in a certain uniform way. Moreover, the rules of τ should be "valid" for graphs; this amounts to the following requirement: for every state q of τ and all input trees t_1 and t_2, if $\mathrm{val}(t_1) = \mathrm{val}(t_2)$ then $\mathrm{val}(\tau_q(t_1)) = \mathrm{val}(\tau_q(t_2))$. All these restrictions seem unnecessary (though they will usually be satisfied in concrete cases).

Note that Definition 12 is very similar to the statements in Propositions 3, 4, 6, 7, and 9. In fact, for an even more general notion of transducibility (see [17]), they express that the identity on GR is F-F'-transducible, for the appropriate sets F and F' of graph operations. This similarity gives the following easy result.

Proposition 13. *Let F' be a set of numerical operations, and let f be a numerical function* GR $\to$ **N**. *Then*
f is VR-F'-transducible iff it is VR$\wedge$-F'-transducible,
f is HR-F'-transducible iff it is HR//-F'-transducible, and
if f is VR-F'-transducible, then f is HR-F'-transducible.

Proof. As an example we show that if f is VR-F'-transducible, then f is HR//-F'-transducible. The other statements can be shown in the same way. Let f be VR-F'-transducible, and let Σ be a finite subset of HR//. By Proposition 9 there are a finite subset Ω of VR and a total deterministic tree transducer

$\tau_1 : T_\Sigma \to T_\Omega$ such that $\mathrm{val}(\tau_1(t)) = \mathrm{val}(t)$ for every $t \in T_\Sigma$ with $\mathrm{type}(\mathrm{val}(t)) = \emptyset$. Since f is VR-F'-transducible, there are a finite subset Δ of F' and a tree function $\tau_2 : T_\Omega \to T_\Delta$ in DTB* such that $\mathrm{val}(\tau_2(s)) = f(\mathrm{val}(s))$ for every $s \in T_\Omega$ with $\mathrm{type}(\mathrm{val}(s)) = \emptyset$. Take $\tau = \tau_2 \circ \tau_1$. Then τ is in DTB*, and for every $t \in T_\Sigma$ with $\mathrm{type}(\mathrm{val}(t)) = \emptyset$: $\mathrm{val}(\tau(t)) = \mathrm{val}(\tau_2(\tau_1(t))) = f(\mathrm{val}(\tau_1(t))) = f(\mathrm{val}(t))$. This shows that f is HR//-F'-transducible. □

At the end of the secton we will give an example of an HR-transducible function that is not VR-transducible. We now give two very simple examples of transducible functions; more complicated examples can be found in [32, 36, 16].

Examples 14. (1) As a first example we show that the numerical function #nod is (effectively) VR-transducible. Let Σ be a finite subset of VR. We define the tree homomorphism τ with the following rules (for the operations in Σ):

$$q(x_1 + x_2) \to q(x_1) + q(x_2),$$
$$q(\pi_z(x_1)) \to q(x_1),$$
$$q(\eta_C(x_1)) \to q(x_1), \text{ and}$$
$$q(g) \to n, \text{ where } n = \#\mathrm{nod}(g).$$

Note that in the first rule, the first + is from VR and the second + from PTM.

Clearly, $\mathrm{val}(\tau(t)) = \#\mathrm{nod}(\mathrm{val}(t))$ for every $t \in T_\Sigma$. Hence #nod is VR-transducible. From Proposition 13 it follows that #nod is also (effectively) HR-transducible. A direct proof of this would be (slightly) more complicated.

(2) As a second example we show that the maximal degree function md is (effectively) HR//-transducible, and hence HR-transducible. For a graph g, we define $\mathrm{md}(g)$ to be the maximal degree of the non-ports of g. Thus, for $g \in \mathrm{GR}$, $\mathrm{md}(g)$ is the maximal degree of its nodes. For a graph g with port_g injective, and $p \in P$, we denote by $\mathrm{d}_p(g)$ the degree of the p-port of g (and $\mathrm{d}_p(g) = 0$ if g has no p-port). We now have the following equations for graphs g and h with port_g, port_h injective (and the operations of a finite $\Sigma \subseteq \mathrm{HR}//$):

$$\mathrm{md}(g//h) = \max(\mathrm{md}(g), \mathrm{md}(h)),$$
$$\mathrm{d}_p(g//h) = \mathrm{d}_p(g) + \mathrm{d}_p(h),$$
$$\mathrm{md}(\mathrm{res}_Q(g)) = \max(\mathrm{md}(g), \mathrm{d}_{p_1}(g), \ldots, \mathrm{d}_{p_n}(g)) \quad \text{where } \{p_1, \ldots, p_n\} = P(\Sigma) - Q,$$
$$\mathrm{d}_p(\mathrm{res}_Q(g)) = 0 \quad \text{for } p \in P(\Sigma) - Q, \text{ and}$$
$$\mathrm{d}_p(\mathrm{res}_Q(g)) = \mathrm{d}_p(g) \text{ for } p \in Q.$$

It is straightforward to turn these equations into the rules of a total deterministic top-down tree transducer $\tau : T_\Sigma \to T_{\mathrm{PTM}}$ with initial state q_0 and states q_p for every $p \in P(\Sigma)$, such that for every tree $t \in T_\Sigma$, $\mathrm{val}(\tau_{q_0}(t)) = \mathrm{md}(\mathrm{val}(t))$ and $\mathrm{val}(\tau_{q_p}(t)) = \mathrm{d}_p(\mathrm{val}(t))$. As an example, the third equation is turned into the rule $q_0(\mathrm{res}_Q(x_1)) \to \max(q_0(x_1), \max(q_{p_1}(x_1), \ldots, \max(q_{p_{n-1}}(x_1), q_{p_n}(x_1)) \ldots))$. That shows that md is HR//-transducible. A slightly more complicated transducer can be constructed to show that md is even VR$\wedge$-transducible, and hence VR-transducible. □

The main aim of this section is to give a tree-oriented proof of the main result of [36]: the decidability of the f-boundedness problem for effectively HR-transducible functions f. The proof works for arbitrary F instead of HR.

Proposition 15. *Let F be a set of graph operations and let f : GR $\to$ **N** be an effectively F-transducible function. It is decidable for an F-context-free graph language L whether or not $f(L)$ is finite.*

Thus, as an example, it follows from Example 14(2) and this proposition, that it is decidable for an HR-context-free graph language L whether or not it is of bounded degree (i.e., by Proposition 11, whether or not L is HRΠ-context-free).

The proof of Proposition 15 is based on Proposition B and the following easy lemma's. For $F' \subseteq$ PTM, let $T_{F'}(\geq 2)$ be the set of all $t \in T_{F'}$ that do not contain any subtree of the form $s + 0$, $0 + s$, $s \cdot 1$, or $1 \cdot s$, with $s \in T_{\mathrm{PTM}}$ (in other words, if 0 occurs in t then $t = 0$, and if 1 occurs in t then $t = 1$). Let PT $=$ PTM $-$ {max}.

Lemma 16. *For any tree language $L \subseteq T_{\mathrm{PT}}(\geq 2)$,* val$(L)$ *is finite iff L is finite.*

Proof. For arbitrary natural numbers $m, n \geq 2$, we have that $m + n > m$, $m + n > n$, $m \cdot n > m$, and $m \cdot n > n$. This implies that for every tree $t \in T_{\mathrm{PT}}(\geq 2)$, val$(t) \geq$ height(t). If L is infinite, then there are trees t in L of arbitrary height, and hence of arbitrary large value. □

Lemma 17. *For every finite $\Delta \subseteq$ PTM there is a total deterministic bottom-up tree transducer $\tau : T_\Delta \to T_\Delta$ such that $\tau(t) \in T_\Delta(\geq 2)$ and* val$(\tau(t)) =$ val(t) *for every $t \in T_\Delta$.*

Proof. This is an easy exercise in writing tree transducers. The tree transducer τ has state set $Q = \{q_0, q_1, q_2\}$, where states q_0, q_1, and q_2 indicate that the value of the processed tree is 0, 1, and ≥ 2, respectively. It has the following rules (in which we use x and y instead of x_1 and x_2):
$0 \to q_0(0)$, $1 \to q_1(1)$, and $n \to q_2(n)$ for every $n \geq 2$, $n \in \Delta$,
$q_0(x) + q(y) \to q(y)$ and $q(x) + q_0(y) \to q(x)$ for every $q \in Q$,
$q(x) + q'(y) \to q_2(x + y)$ for all $q, q' \in \{q_1, q_2\}$,
$q_0(x) \cdot q(y) \to q_0(0)$ and $q(x) \cdot q_0(y) \to q_0(0)$ for every $q \in Q$,
$q_1(x) \cdot q(y) \to q(y)$ and $q(x) \cdot q_1(y) \to q(x)$ for every $q \in \{q_1, q_2\}$,
$q_2(x) \cdot q_2(y) \to q_2(x \cdot y)$,
$\max(q_0(x), q(y)) \to q(y)$ and $\max(q(x), q_0(y)) \to q(x)$ for every $q \in Q$,
$\max(q_1(x), q(y)) \to q(y)$ and $\max(q(x), q_1(y)) \to q(x)$ for every $q \in \{q_1, q_2)$,
$\max(q_2(x), q_2(y)) \to q_2(\max(x, y))$. □

Lemma 18. *For every finite $\Delta \subseteq$ PTM there is a top-down tree transducer $\tau \subseteq T_\Delta \times T_\Delta$ such that $\tau(T_\Delta(\geq 2)) \subseteq T_{\mathrm{PT}}(\geq 2)$ and, for every $L \subseteq T_\Delta$,* val(L) *is finite iff* val$(\tau(L))$ *is finite.*

Proof. The (nondeterministic) tree transducer τ has one state q, and the rules $q(\max(x_1,x_2)) \to q(x_1)$ and $q(\max(x_1,x_2)) \to q(x_2)$, $q(x_1+x_2) \to q(x_1)+q(x_2)$, $q(x_1 \cdot x_2) \to q(x_1) \cdot q(x_2)$, and $q(n) \to n$ for every n in Δ. Thus, τ replaces each expression $\max(t_1,t_2)$ by one of its arguments t_1 or t_2. Consider $t \in T_\Delta$, and let $\tau(t) = \{s \in T_\Delta \mid q(t) \Rightarrow^* s\}$. Clearly $\mathrm{val}(s) = \mathrm{val}(t)$ for some $s \in \tau(t)$. Moreover, since $+$ and $\cdot$ are monotonic in each argument, $\mathrm{val}(s) \leq \mathrm{val}(t)$ for every $s \in \tau(t)$. This implies that $\mathrm{val}(\tau(L))$ is finite iff $\mathrm{val}(L)$ is finite, for every $L \subseteq T_\Delta$. □

We are now ready for the proof of Proposition 15.

Proof of Proposition 15. Let L be an F-context-free graph language, i.e., $L = \mathrm{val}(R)$ for some regular tree language $R \subseteq T_\Sigma$ with $\Sigma \subseteq F$ finite. Since f is F-transducible, there are a finite subset Δ of PTM and a tree function $\tau_1 : T_\Sigma \to T_\Delta$ in DTB* such that $\mathrm{val}(\tau_1(t)) = f(\mathrm{val}(t))$ for every $t \in T_\Sigma$ with $\mathrm{type}(\mathrm{val}(t)) = \emptyset$. Hence $\mathrm{val}(\tau_1(R)) = f(\mathrm{val}(R))$, i.e., $f(L) = \mathrm{val}(\tau_1(R))$. By Lemma 17 there is a tree transducer $\tau_2 : T_\Delta \to T_\Delta$ such that $\tau_2(s) \in T_\Delta(\geq 2)$ and $\mathrm{val}(\tau_2(s)) = \mathrm{val}(s)$ for every $s \in T_\Delta$. Hence $\tau_2(\tau_1(R)) \subseteq T_\Delta(\geq 2)$ and $\mathrm{val}(\tau_2(\tau_1(R))) = \mathrm{val}(\tau_1(R)) = f(L)$. Finally, by Lemma 18, there is a tree transducer $\tau_3 \subseteq T_\Delta \times T_\Delta$ such that for every $L \subseteq T_\Delta(\geq 2)$ $\tau_3(L) \subseteq T_{\mathrm{PT}}(\geq 2)$, and $\mathrm{val}(L)$ is finite iff $\mathrm{val}(\tau_3(L))$ is finite. Hence $\tau_3(\tau_2(\tau_1(R))) \subseteq T_{\mathrm{PT}}(\geq 2)$, and $f(L)$ is finite iff $\mathrm{val}(\tau_3(\tau_2(\tau_1(R))))$ is finite. Thus, by Lemma 16, $f(L)$ is finite iff $\tau_3(\tau_2(\tau_1(R)))$ is finite. Now, since $\tau_3 \circ \tau_2 \circ \tau_1$ is in TB*, finiteness of $\tau_3(\tau_2(\tau_1(R)))$ can be decided by Proposition B. □

The proof of Proposition 15 only uses a few easy properties of the plus (+) and times ($\cdot$) operations. Thus, the result remains true if one adds binary numerical operations ϕ to PTM that are monotonic in both arguments, are growing (i.e., $\phi(x,y) > x$ and $\phi(x,y) > y$ for $x, y \geq 2$), and satisfy some easy laws for the arguments 0 and 1 (easy in the sense that they can be implemented on a bottom-up tree transducer, as in the proof of Lemma 17). For instance, the function x^y can be added to PTM.

It is shown in [45] that there is in fact a polynomial time algorithm to decide the f-boundedness of an effectively F-transducible function f, for the case of top-down tree transducers with at most d states, for some fixed d (and provided τ can be obtained from Σ in polynomial time).

An important special case of F-transducible functions are the boolean ones: they determine graph properties that can be computed symbolically by tree transducers. The f-boundedness problem for such functions is of course trivial. The main result about boolean F-transducible functions f is that the class of F-context-free graph languages is closed under f, i.e., under intersection with the graph language $\{g \in \mathrm{GR} \mid f(g) = 1\}$ (see Proposition 1.10 of [6]). This closure result follows easily from the following proposition (see Propositions 1.5 and 1.7 of [6]).

Proposition 19. *Let F be a set of graph operations with the property that $\{t \in T_\Sigma \mid \mathrm{type}(\mathrm{val}(t)) = \emptyset\}$ is regular for every finite $\Sigma \subseteq F$.*
For $f : \mathrm{GR} \to \{0,1\}$, f is F-transducible iff for every finite subset Σ of F the tree language $\{t \in T_\Sigma \mid \mathrm{type}(\mathrm{val}(t)) = \emptyset, f(\mathrm{val}(t)) = 1\}$ is regular.

Proof. For $\Sigma \subseteq F$, let $R_\Sigma = \{t \in T_\Sigma \mid \text{type}(\text{val}(t)) = \emptyset, f(\text{val}(t)) = 1\}$.
(Only if). Let f be F-transducible, and let $\Sigma \subseteq F$ be finite. There are a finite $\Delta \subseteq$ PTM and a tree function τ in DTB* such that $\text{val}(\tau(t)) = f(\text{val}(t))$ for every $t \in T_\Sigma$ with $\text{type}(\text{val}(t)) = \emptyset$. Clearly, the tree language $S_\Delta = \{s \in T_\Delta \mid \text{val}(s) = 1\}$ is regular (a bottom-up tree automaton recognizing S_Δ can easily be obtained from the tree transducer in the proof of Lemma 17). Obviously $R_\Sigma = \tau^{-1}(S_\Delta) \cap \{t \in T_\Sigma \mid \text{type}(\text{val}(t)) = \emptyset\}$. Since the class of regular tree languages is closed under inverse bottom-up and top-down tree transductions (see Lemma 1.2 of [22]) and under intersection, R_Σ is regular.

(If). To show that f is F-transducible, let Σ be a finite subset of F. Consider a total deterministic bottom-up tree automaton $\mathcal{A}$ that recognizes R_Σ, and let Q_{fin} be its set of final states. Construct the total deterministic bottom-up tree transducer τ with the same states as $\mathcal{A}$ and the following rules: if $\sigma(q_1(x_1), \ldots, q_n(x_n)) \to q(\sigma(x_1, \ldots, x_n))$ is a rule of $\mathcal{A}$, then τ has the rule $\sigma(q_1(x_1), \ldots, q_n(x_n)) \to q(1)$ if $q \in Q_{\text{fin}}$ and the rule $\sigma(q_1(x_1), \ldots, q_n(x_n)) \to q(0)$ if $q \notin Q_{\text{fin}}$. Obviously, for every $t \in T_\Sigma$ with $\text{type}(\text{val}(t)) = \emptyset$, $\text{val}(\tau(t)) = 1$ if $t \in R_\Sigma$ (i.e., $f(\text{val}(t)) = 1$) and $\text{val}(\tau(t)) = 0$ if $t \notin R_\Sigma$. Thus $\text{val}(\tau(t)) = f(\text{val}(t))$. This shows that f is F-transducible. We note that an alternative proof can be given with a top-down tree transducer. □

Note that the assumption of this proposition is satisfied for the F's that we have discussed sofar. A bottom-up tree automaton recognizing the tree language $\{t \in T_\Sigma \mid \text{type}(\text{val}(t)) = \emptyset\}$ can easily be based on equations like $\text{type}(g + h) = \text{type}(g) \cup \text{type}(h)$ and $\text{type}(\pi_z(g)) = z(\text{type}(g))$.

From Proposition 19 it easily follows that the class of F-context-free graph languages is closed under intersection with $\{g \in \text{GR} \mid f(g) = 1\}$, i.e., if L is an F-context-free graph language then $L_f = \{g \in L \mid f(g) = 1\}$ is F-context-free. In fact, let $L = \text{val}(R)$ for some regular tree language $R \subseteq T_\Sigma$. Then $L_f = \text{val}(R')$ with $R' = R \cap \{t \in T_\Sigma \mid f(\text{val}(t)) = 1\}$. R' is regular by Proposition 19 and the closure of the regular tree languages under intersection. Hence L_f is F-context-free. Note that this implies that it is decidable whether or not $L_f = \emptyset$, and, because the regular tree languages are closed under complement, also whether or not $L_f = L$ (see Corollary 1.11 of [6]; see also [35, 39]).

By Proposition 19, the notion of a boolean F-transducible function $f : \text{GR} \to \{0, 1\}$ is closely related to that of an F-recognizable graph language, in the sense of [40] (and first considered for graphs in [6]). Let us here define a graph language $L \subseteq \text{GR}$ to be F-recognizable if the tree language $\{t \in T_\Sigma \mid \text{val}(t) \in L\}$ is regular for every finite $\Sigma \subseteq F$. This definition is slightly more general than the one in [6] (cf. Proposition 1.7 of [6]) where the bottom-up tree automaton recognizing $\{t \in T_\Sigma \mid \text{val}(t) \in L\}$ should depend on Σ in a uniform way (note that the definition of recognizability of [40] is not applicable directly because F contains infinitely many operations). With this notion of F-recognizability, Proposition 19 says that the boolean function f is F-transducible iff $\{g \in \text{GR} \mid f(g) = 1\}$ is F-recognizable. Equivalences similar to those in Proposition 13 (for boolean functions) are given in [34, 13].

We note here that Propositions 15 and 19 are independent of the properties of graphs; they also hold for an arbitrary semantic domain with a set F of operations on its elements.

Finally, we consider an HR-transducible function that is not VR-transducible, using an idea from [7]. Let hc be the boolean function GR $\rightarrow \{0,1\}$ such that hc$(g) = 1$ iff g is Hamiltonian (i.e., has a Hamiltonian circuit). By the results of [6], hc is HR-transducible (see also Section 5.3 of [35]). Assume now that hc is VR-transducible, and consider $\Sigma = \{+, \eta_C, \pi_\emptyset, c_p, c_q\} \subseteq$ VR, with $C = \{(p,a,q),(q,a,p)\}$. Then, by Proposition 19, the tree language $H = \{t \in T_\Sigma \mid \text{type}(\text{val}(t)) = \emptyset, \text{hc}(\text{val}(t)) = 1\}$ is regular. From this it easily follows that the tree language $H' = \{t \in T_{\Sigma'} \mid \text{val}(\pi_\emptyset(\eta_C(t)))$ is Hamiltonian$\}$, with $\Sigma' = \{+, c_p, c_q\}$, is also regular (because $H' = \{t \in T_{\Sigma'} \mid \pi_\emptyset(\eta_C(t)) \in H\}$). Clearly, for $t \in T_{\Sigma'}$, val$(\pi_\emptyset(\eta_C(t)))$ is the complete bipartite graph $K_{m,n}$ (see Example 2(4)) where m (n) is the number of constants c_p (c_q) occurring in t. Since $K_{m,n}$ is Hamiltonian iff $m = n$, $H' = \{t \in T_{\Sigma'} \mid t$ contains the same number of occurrences of c_p and $c_q\}$. But this tree language is not regular, contradicting our assumption that hc is VR-transducible.

For many concrete functions f : GR $\rightarrow$ **N** the results of this section (such as the decidability of the f-boundedness problem) can also be obtained (and usually much quicker) by means of general results that employ monadic second order logic (see, e.g., [7, 6, 25, 14, 16]). The precise relationships between transducibility and monadic seccond-order definability are not yet completely clear.

References

1. M.Bauderon, B.Courcelle; Graph expressions and graph rewritings, Math. Syst. Theory 20 (1987), 83-127
2. F.J.Brandenburg; On polynomial time graph grammars, Proc. STACS 88, Lecture Notes in Computer Science 294, Springer-Verlag, Berlin, pp.227-236
3. F.J.Brandenburg; The equivalence of boundary and confluent graph grammars on graph languages of bounded degree, in *Rewriting Techniques and Applications* (R.V.Book, ed.), Lecture Notes in Computer Science 488, Springer-Verlag, Berlin, 1991, pp.312-322
4. D.G.Corneil, H.Lerchs, L.Stewart Burlingham; Complement reducible graphs, Discr. Appl. Math. 3 (1981), 163-174
5. B.Courcelle; An axiomatic definition of context-free rewriting and its application to NLC graph grammars, Theor. Comput. Sci. 55 (1987), 141-181
6. B.Courcelle; The monadic second-order logic of graphs I: Recognizable sets of finite graphs, Inform. and Comput. 85 (1990), 12-75
7. B.Courcelle; Graph rewriting: an algebraic and logic approach, in *Formal Models and Semantics*, Handbook of Theoretical Computer Science Volume B (J.van Leeuwen, ed.), Elsevier, Amsterdam, 1990, pp.193-242
8. B.Courcelle; On the structure of context-free sets of graphs generated by vertex replacement, Report 91-44, Bordeaux-1 University (A short version is Context-free graph grammars: separating vertex replacement from hyperedge replacement, Proc. FCT'93 (Z.Ésik, ed.), Lecture Notes in Computer Science 710, Springer-Verlag, Berlin, pp.181-193)

9. B.Courcelle; Graph grammars, monadic second-order logic and the theory of graph minors, in Proc. of the A.M.S. Conference on Graph Minors, Seattle, 1993 (preliminary version in Bulletin of the EATCS 46 (1992), 193-226)
10. B.Courcelle; The monadic second-order logic of graphs V: on closing the gap between definability and recognizability, Theor. Comput. Sci. 80 (1991), 153-202
11. B.Courcelle; Monadic second-order definable graph transductions, invited lecture, Proc.CAAP '92 (J.-C.Raoult, ed.), Lecture Notes in Computer Science 581, Springer-Verlag, Berlin, 1992
12. B.Courcelle; The monadic second-order logic of graphs VII: Graphs as relational structures, Theor. Comput. Sci. 101 (1992), 3-33
13. B.Courcelle; Recognizable sets of graphs: equivalent definitions and closure properties, Research Report 92-06, Bordeaux-1 University
14. B.Courcelle, J.Engelfriet; A logical characterization of the sets of hypergraphs generated by hyperedge replacement grammars, Research Report 91-41, Bordeaux-1 University, to appear in Math. Syst. Theory.
15. B.Courcelle, J.Engelfriet, G.Rozenberg; Handle-rewriting hypergraph grammars, J. Comp. Syst. Sci. 46 (1993), 218-270
16. B.Courcelle, M.Mosbah; Monadic second-order evaluations on tree-decomposable graphs, Theor. Comput. Sci. 109 (1993), 49-82
17. F.Drewes; Transducibility - symbolic computation by tree-transductions, Universität Bremen, Bericht Nr: 2/93, 1993
18. F.Drewes, H.-J.Kreowski; A note on hyperedge replacement, in [19], pp. 1-11
19. H.Ehrig, H.-J.Kreowski, G.Rozenberg (eds.); *Graph-Grammars and their Application to Computer Science*, Lecture Notes in Computer Science 532, Springer-Verlag, Berllin, 1991
20. H.Ehrig, M.Nagl, G.Rozenberg, A.Rosenfeld (eds.); *Graph-Grammars and their Application to Computer Science*, Lecture Notes in Computer Science 291, Springer-Verlag, Berlin, 1987
21. J.Engelfriet; *Tree automata and tree grammars*, Lecture Notes, DAIMI FN-10, Aarhus, 1975
22. J.Engelfriet; Top-down tree transducers with regular look-ahead, Math. Syst. Theory 10 (1977), 289-303
23. J.Engelfriet; Some open questions and recent results on tree transducers and tree languages, in *Formal language theory; perspectives and open problems* (R.V.Book, ed.), Academic Press, New York, 1980
24. J.Engelfriet; Context-free NCE graph grammars, Proc. FCT '89, Lecture Notes in Computer Science 380, Springer-Verlag, Berlin, pp.148-161
25. J.Engelfriet; A characterization of context-free NCE graph languages by monadic second-order logic on trees, in [19], pp.311-327
26. J.Engelfriet; A Greibach normal form for context-free graph grammars, Proc. ICALP '92 (W.Kuich, ed.), Lecture Notes in Computer Science 623, Springer-Verlag, Berlin, pp.138-149
27. J.Engelfriet, L.M.Heyker; Hypergraph languages of bounded degree, Report 91-01, Leiden University, to appear in J. Comp. Syst. Sci.
28. J.Engelfriet, L.M.Heyker, G.Leih; Context-free graph languages of bounded degree are generated by apex graph grammars, Report 91-16, Leiden University, to appear in Acta Informatica
29. J.Engelfriet, G.Leih, G.Rozenberg; Nonterminal separation in graph grammars, Theor. Comput: Sci. 82 (1991), 95-111

30. J.Engelfriet, G.Rozenberg; A comparison of boundary graph grammars and context-free hypergraph grammars, Inform. and Comput. 84 (1990), 163-206
31. F.Gécseg, M.Steinby; *Tree automata*, Akadémiai Kiadó, Budapest, 1984
32. A.Habel; *Hyperedge replacement: grammars and languages*, Lecture Notes in Computer Science 643, Springer-Verlag, Berlin, 1992
33. A.Habel, H.-J.Kreowski; May we introduce to you: hyperedge replacement, in [20], pp. 15-26
34. A.Habel, H.-J.Kreowski, C.Lautemann; A comparison of compatible, finite, and inductive graph properties, Theor. Comput. Sci. 110 (1993), 145-168
35. A.Habel, H.-J.Kreowski, W.Vogler; Metatheorems for decision problems on hyperedge replacement graph languages, Acta Informatica 26 (1989), 657-677
36. A.Habel, H.-J.Kreowski, W.Vogler; Decidable boundedness problems for sets of graphs generated by hyperedge-replacement, Theor. Comput. Sci. 89 (1991), 33-62
37. M.Kaul; Syntaxanalyse von Graphen bei Präzedenz-Graph-Grammatiken, Ph. D. Thesis, Osnabrück, 1985
38. S.Kuske; A maximum path length pumping lemma for edge-replacement languages, Proc. FCT'93 (Z.Ésik, ed.), Lecture Notes in Computer Science 710, Springer-Verlag, Berlin, pp.342-351
39. T.Lengauer, E.Wanke; Efficient decision procedures for graph properties on context-free graph languages, J. of the ACM 40 (1993), 368-393
40. J.Mezei, J.B.Wright; Algebraic automata and context-free sets, Inform. and Control 11 (1967), 3-29
41. M.Nagl; *Graph-Grammatiken*, Vieweg, Braunschweig, 1979
42. M.Nivat, A.Podelski (eds.); *Tree automata and languages*, North-Holland, Amsterdam, 1992
43. W.C.Rounds; Mappings and grammars on trees, Math. Syst. Theory 4 (1970), 257-287
44. R.Schuster; Graphgrammatiken und Grapheinbettungen: Algorithmen und Komplexität, Ph.D.Thesis, Report MIP-8711, Passau, 1987
45. H.Seidl; Finite tree automata with cost functions, Proc. CAAP'92 (J.-C.Raoult, ed.), Lecture Notes in Computer Science 581, Springer-Verlag, Berlin, pp.279-299
46. W.Vogler; On hyperedge replacement and BNLC graph grammars, Discr. Appl. Math. 46 (1993), 253-273
47. E.Wanke; On the decidability of integer subgraph problems on context-free graph languages, Proc. FCT '91 (L.Budach, ed.), Lecture Notes in Computer Science 529, Springer-Verlag, Berlin, pp.415-426

Type Preorders *

Fabio Alessi

Dipartimento di Matematica e Informatica,
via Zanon 6, 33100, Udine (Italy)
e-mail: alessi@udmi5400.cineca.it

Abstract. Various type structures, called Intersection Type Structures, have been introduced in the literature in order to define models of λ-calculus and simultaneously to reason in a finitary way about λ-terms. All these systems are only employed as meet-semilattices generated by preorders built on *prime* types. For this reason these structures are linguistically redundant. Starting from this observation we introduce the category of *Type Preorders*, which arises naturally when we eliminate redundant types from Intersection Type Structures. We give a Stone-duality type result for Type Preorders, showing that they are equivalent to the category of prime-algebraic complete lattices and Scott continuous functions. Thus we clarify the domain-theoretic description of Intersection Type Structures, which often appears opaque. As an application we give the domain-theoretic reading of the Intersection Union Type Structure.

1 Introduction

The present paper deals with structures employed to provide semantics to various kinds of λ-calculi, namely Intersection Type Structures (ITS's).
The first example of ITS was given in [BCD] in order to define a model for untyped λ-calculus. Since then many more have been introduced (see [Abr2], [BD], [CDHL], [CDZ], [DdLP], [EHR], [HL], [HR]).
An ITS can be viewed as a particular Information System [Sco]: it consists of a countable set of types, to be thought as observable properties of computations, related by a preorder relation and closed w.r.t. a meet operation '$\wedge$'. ITS's fall within the Stone-duality scenario, as generalized by Abramsky [Abr1] where finitary structures (Information Systems, ITS's, Domain Prelocales etc.) are interpreted as endogenous logics associated to the domain topologies. In this framework type theories describe suitable bases (or subbases) of domain topology: a logical judgment $\sigma \leq \tau$ between types corresponds to set-theoretic inclusion $O_\sigma \subseteq O_\tau$, where O_t denotes the open set associated to the type t. The points of the domains are recovered by taking suitable subsets of types (*upper sets, filters, prime filters, completely prime filters* according to the cases).

* Work partially supported by Science Project MASK Sci#-CT92-0776, 60%-40% MURST

Here is a list of important algebraic subcategories of **CPO** together with the corresponding categories of finitary structures which are Stone-dual to them:

2/3-SFP Domains $\leftrightarrow$ Coherent Algebraic Locales;
SFP Domains $\leftrightarrow$ Domain Prelocales;
Scott Domains $\leftrightarrow$ Information Systems;
ω-algebraic Lattices $\leftrightarrow$ Intersection Type Structures.

Working in the categories on the right in the table, one can build domains for semantics in a concrete and effective way (see e.g. [Abr1], [BCD], [CDHL], [LW], [Sco]) and reason about programs by finitary techniques (Type Assignment Systems and similar formal systems: see e.g. [Abr1], [Abr2], [BCD], [CDZ], [DdLP]). In order to take advantage of these properties, a finitary structure should be defined as concisely and clearly as possible. ITS's meet these requirements better than Information Systems or Domain Prelocales. However, as regards ITS's introduced in the literature, (see e.g. [Abr2], [BCD], [CDHL], [CDZ], [DM], [DdLP]) one can immediately observe that

the meet operator '$\wedge$' always plays a 'decorative' rôle. In fact ITS's are always defined as meet-semilattices generated by preorders over 'prime' types.

The domain-theoretic consequence of this fact is that ITS's are actually employed to describe only *prime-algebraic* complete lattices (p-ALG's, see [NPW]), i.e. those ω-algebraic complete lattices (ω-ALG's) whose elements are l.u.b's of the prime elements they dominate.
This fact suggests to simplify further the syntax of ITS's by eliminating the meet operator, in order to get even more concise and clear structures.
In such a way we get *Type Preorders* (TP's).
Quite similar structures have already been introduced in [NPW] and referred to as *Elementary Event Structures.* The difference between Elementary Event Structures and Type Preorders consists in considering opposite preorder relations when relating types to open sets of the lattice topology.
TP's are Stone-duals to p-ALG's. In particular they describe the *coprime-and-prime* open sets subbasis of the p-ALG's topologies.
TP's provide a reasonably expressive framework for denotational semantics: in fact p-ALG's are closed under the same constructions (namely $\times$, $(\cdot)_\perp$, $\rightarrow$, $\rightarrow_\perp$, $\mathcal{P}_H$, $\mathcal{P}_S$) just as ω-ALG's. Various important models for λ-calculus can actually be described by TP's, e.g. classical Scott models for untyped λ-calculus or models defined e.g. in [Abr2], [BCD], [Bou], [CDZ], [DdLP] are p-ALG's. Therefore it is possible to provide simple and concise descriptions of them via TP's.
The aim of the paper is to investigate in detail TP's and their relations with ITS's and p-ALG's.
As a by-product we can clarify the domain-theoretic reading of ITS's.
The paper is organized as follows.
First we give the necessary preliminaries and introduce p-ALG's.
Secondly we introduce ITS's and show how they admit a more concise description via TP's. Then we prove a Stone-duality result between **p-ALG** and **TP** and discuss constructions over TP's. In order to provide a machinery for translating p-ALG's in TP's we introduce the auxiliary notions of *association* and

bi-embedding. These notions are useful if one wants to understand compositionally domain constructions and relate solutions of domain equations in **p-ALG** to solutions of the corresponding equations in **TP**.
Finally, as an application addressed to clarify semantics of ITS's via TP's, we study the *Intersection Union Type Structure* of [BD] and give a domain-theoretic reading of it.

2 Notation and Preliminaries

In this section we recall some classical definitions and fix notations. Moreover we introduce the category **p-ALG** and discuss some of its properties.

Notations:
I, J, K, H etc. are used to denote finite sets of indexes (possibly empty). Given a set X, $\mathcal{P}(X)$ denotes the powerset of X; $Y \subseteq_f X$ [$Y \subseteq_{fne} X$] means Y is a finite [finite not empty] subset of X. $\mathcal{P}_f(X)$ [$\mathcal{P}_{fne}(X)$] denotes the set of finite [finite not empty] subsets of X.
If $P = (P, \sqsubseteq)$ is a preorder, $X, Y \subseteq P$ and $z \in P$ then:
- $\downarrow X = \{y \in P \mid \exists x \in X. y \sqsubseteq x\}$ ($\downarrow z$ stands for $\downarrow \{z\}$);
- $\uparrow X = \{y \in P \mid \exists x \in X. x \sqsubseteq y\}$ ($\uparrow z$ stands for $\uparrow \{z\}$);
- $U(P) = \{X \subseteq P \mid X = \uparrow X\}$ (set of *upper subsets* of P);
- $L(P) = \{X \subseteq P \mid X = \downarrow X\}$ (set of *lower subsets* of P);
- $X \sqsubseteq_H Y \iff \forall x \in X. \exists y \in Y. x \sqsubseteq y$ (Hoare preorder over $\mathcal{P}(P)$);
- $X \sqsubseteq_S Y \iff \forall y \in Y. \exists x \in X. x \sqsubseteq y$ (Smyth preorder over $\mathcal{P}(P)$).

If P is a meet-semilattice, a *filter* in P is a not empty set $\xi \subseteq P$ such that:

$\xi = \uparrow \xi; \quad x, y \in \xi \Longrightarrow x \wedge y \in \xi.$

We denote $Fil(P)$ the set of the filters in P.
Let D be an ω-algebraic cpo.
The *Hoare [Smyth] powerdomain* of D, $\mathcal{P}_H(D)$ [$\mathcal{P}_S(D)$], is the ideal completion of $\mathcal{P}_{fne}(K(D))$ ordered by Hoare [Smyth] preorder:

$\mathcal{P}_{\mathrm{W}}(D) = (Idl(\mathcal{P}_{fne}(K(D)), \sqsubseteq_{\mathrm{W}}), \subseteq) \quad (\mathrm{W{=}H,S}).$

Let $D = (D, \sqsubseteq)$ be an ω-algebraic lattice. An open set $A \in \Omega(D)$ is *completely coprime* (*coprime* for short), iff

$\forall X \subseteq \Omega(D). (A \subseteq \bigcup X \implies \exists B \in X. A \subseteq B).$

Dually A is *completely prime* (*prime*) iff

$\forall X \subseteq \Omega(D). (A \supseteq \bigcap X \implies \exists B \in X. A \supseteq B).$

$Cpr(\Omega(D))$ [$Pr(\Omega(D))$] denotes the set of coprime open sets [prime open sets] in D. Recall that $(Cpr(\Omega(D)), \subseteq) \simeq (K(D), \sqsubseteq^{op})$ as partial orders.
The previous definitions have to be dualized when applied to the points. Thus $p \in D$ is *completely prime* (*prime*) iff $\forall X \subseteq D. p \sqsubseteq \bigvee X \Longrightarrow \exists x \in X. p \sqsubseteq x$.
$Pr(D)$ denotes the set of the prime elements in D.
D is *prime-algebraic* iff $Pr(D)$ is a basis for D: $\forall x \in D. x = \bigvee Pr(x)$.
We now focus on prime-algebraic complete lattices as they are the domain-theoretic counterpart of Type Preorders.
A function $i : D \to D'$ between p-ALG's is a *prime embedding* if it preserves

prime elements, is injective and commutes with joins. If i is a prime embedding, then it admits a right adjoint $j : D' \to D$ such that:

$$j \circ i = Id_D; \quad i \circ j \sqsubseteq Id_{D'}.$$

j is the projection associated to i and commutes with arbitrary meets and joins. Denote **p-ALG** [**p-ALG**^{E}] the category whose objects are prime-algebraic complete lattices and morphisms Scott continuous functions [prime embeddings].

The next lemma is useful for placing p-ALG's in the Stone-duality framework of [Abr1]. It determines the canonical open sets subbasis by which it is possible to recover the whole topology of p-ALG's. The lemma is the topological counterpart of the equivalence of the categories **p-ALG** and **TP** stated below.

Lemma 1.

i) Let D be a p-ALG. Then the set $\{\uparrow p \mid p \in Pr(D)\}$ is the smallest subbasis generating $\Omega(D)$.

ii) If D is an ω-algebraic lattice, then D is prime-algebraic iff $\forall A \in Cpr(\Omega(D)).\exists B_i \in Cpr(\Omega(D)) \cap Pr(\Omega(D)).A = \cap_I B_i \quad (i \in I)$. $\diamond$

By the previous lemma, given a p-ALG D we obtain a canonical and simple presentation for its topology. Consider in fact $\mathrm{Fr}\langle G_D, R\rangle$ (for this notation see [Vic]) where the set of generators is $G_D = \{\gamma_p \mid p \in Pr(D)\}$ and the set of relations consists of $R = \{\gamma_p \leq \gamma_{p'} \mid \uparrow p \subseteq \uparrow p'\}$. Then $\mathrm{Fr}\langle G_D, R\rangle$ is (isomorphic to) the frame $\Omega(D)$.

The next theorem shows that **p-ALG** is closed with respect to the same constructors just as ω-**ALG**. Moreover we can derive the existence of colimits of towers in **p-ALG**^{E}. Hence we can restrict ourselves to considering just p-ALG's instead of ω-ALG's, without weakening the power of the semantics.

Theorem 2.

i) $\times$, $\to$, $\to_\perp$, $(\cdot)_\perp$, $\mathcal{P}_H$ and $\mathcal{P}_S$ are continuous functors over **p-ALG**.

ii) **p-ALG** is a CCC.

iii) A tower $\langle D_n, i_n : D_n \to D_{n+1}\rangle_n$ in **p-ALG**^{E} admits colimits. $\diamond$

For each of the constructions above, here is the description of prime elements:

$$Pr(D_\perp) = \{0\} \times Pr(D) \ \cup \ \{(0, \perp_D)\};$$
$$Pr(D \times E) = Pr(D) \times \{\perp_E\} \ \cup \ \{\perp_D\} \times Pr(E);$$
$$Pr([D \to E]) = \{\mathrm{step}_{d,q} \mid d \in K(D), q \in Pr(E)\};$$
$$Pr([D \to_\perp E]) = \{\mathrm{step}_{d,q} \mid d \in K(D) \setminus \{\perp_D\}, q \in Pr(E)\};$$
$$Pr(\mathcal{P}_H(D)) = \{\downarrow d \mid d \in K(D) \setminus \{\perp_D\}\};$$
$$Pr(\mathcal{P}_S(D)) = \{\uparrow A \mid A \subseteq_{fne} Pr(D)\}.$$

Remark: Notice that our choice of considering just prime-algebraic *lattices* makes it possible to obtain a category closed for Smyth powerdomain constructor. This would fail if we consider prime-algebraic domains which are not necessarily lattices (e.g. dI-domains). For example $\mathbb{N}_\perp$ is a dI-domain but its Smyth powerdomain is not prime-algebraic.

3 Type Preorders

In this section we recall the main properties of the category of Intersection Type Structures, and show how it is possible to give concise and clear descriptions of ITS's. Then we are led to introduce Type Preorders. These structures are quite similar to Elementary Event Structures introduced in [NPW]. We define an appropriate notion of *approximable mapping* for TP's and check the equivalence between the categories **p-ALG** and **TP**.

We start from the definition of ITS. Our definition is different from the classical one in that we do not introduce the arrow type constructor '$\rightarrow$'. The explicit introduction of '$\rightarrow$' allows immediately to get functional types. These yield powerful *Type Assignment Systems* (see e.g. [Abr2], [CDHL], [CDZ], [DdLP], [DM], [HR]) which induce domain logics (in the sense of [Abr1]) for reasoning about *solutions of domain equations which involve the function space constructor.* Thus if one wants to capture the domain-theoretic aspect of ITS's in general, then only intersection type constructor '$\wedge$' is taken as primitive. Intersection Type Structures that we define coincide, a part from the different notation, with the Information Systems introduced in [Bou], and are particular cases of Scott's Information Systems [Sco].

Notation: From now on each set of types is intended to be countable.

Definition 3.

i) An *Intersection Type Structure* is a quadruple $A = (|A|, \leq_A, \omega_A, \wedge)$ such that:
  - $|A|$ is a countable set of types;
  - $\omega_A \in |A|$;
  - $\wedge : |A| \times |A| \rightarrow |A|$ is a binary operation;
  - $\leq_A$ ($\leq$ for short) is a preorder relation over $|A|$ such that ($\sigma, \sigma', \tau, \tau'$ range over $|A|$):
    a) $\sigma \leq \omega_A$;
    b) $\sigma \leq \sigma \wedge \sigma$;
    c) $\sigma \wedge \tau \leq \sigma, \quad \sigma \wedge \tau \leq \tau$;
    d) $\sigma \leq \sigma' \ \& \ \tau \leq \tau' \implies \sigma \wedge \tau \leq \sigma' \wedge \tau'$.

    We write $\sigma \sim \tau$ when $\sigma \leq \tau$ and $\tau \leq \sigma$.

ii) Let A and B two ITS's. An *approximable mapping* $R : A \rightarrow B$ is a subset $R \subseteq |A| \times |B|$ such that the following properties are satisfied:
  a) $\sigma R \tau \ \& \ \sigma R \tau' \implies \sigma R(\tau \wedge \tau')$;
  b) $(\sigma \leq_A \sigma', \sigma' R \tau', \tau' \leq_B \tau) \implies \sigma R \tau$. $\diamond$

Regarded as a category an ITS A is a countable preorder which has terminal object ω_A and finite products.

We now give the theorem relating ITS's with ω-ALG's. ITS's provide a description of the coprime open sets basis of ω-ALG's topologies. This fact guarantees that the information given by an ITS is enough to recover the whole domain.

Theorem 4.
The category **ITS** whose objects are Intersection Type Structures and morphisms are approximable mappings is equivalent to the category of ω-ALG's and Scott continuous functions (see [Bou]). $\diamond$

More precisely, the equivalence is obtained as follows.
Given a ω-ALG D define $\mathcal{G}(D)$ as the partial order $(Cpr(\Omega(D)), \subseteq)$.
Viceversa, given an ITS A define $\mathcal{F}(A)$ as the lattice $(Fil(A), \subseteq)$.
$\mathcal{F}$ and $\mathcal{G}$ provide the equivalence between **ITS** and **ω-ALG** (the action of $\mathcal{F}, \mathcal{G}$ on morphisms is omitted).

We now turn our attention to the rôle of '$\wedge$' in ITS's.
In order to give a complete description of lattice topology, we need to use the connective '$\wedge$' between types. However ITS's considered in the literature describe prime-algebraic lattices and hence admit simpler descriptions. Actually ITS's are defined (see e.g. [Abr2], [BCD], [BDdL], [Bou], [CDHL], [CDZ], [DdLP], [HR]) by giving:

i) a syntax which generates all types in by means of suitable type constructors (e.g. constants, $\rightarrow, \vee$).
ii) an appropriate preorder relation which enforces the right behaviour of the considered type constructors.

From a domain-theoretic point of view this corresponds to solving a domain equation $D = F(D)$ by building the colimit of a suitable tower. The functor F is related to the type constructions employed in the definition of the ITS.
As an example consider the ITS T introduced in [BCD].
Type syntax for $|T|$ is the following:
$\sigma ::= t \mid \omega \mid \sigma \wedge \sigma \mid \sigma \rightarrow \sigma.$
Preorder relation over $|T|$ satisfies conditions of Definition 3 and moreover:

- $\omega \leq \omega \rightarrow \omega$;
- $\sigma \leq \sigma' \;\&\; \tau' \leq \tau \Longrightarrow \sigma' \rightarrow \tau' \leq \sigma \rightarrow \tau$;
- $(\sigma \rightarrow \rho) \wedge (\sigma \rightarrow \tau) \leq \sigma \rightarrow (\rho \wedge \tau)$.

Notice that these additional conditions serve to give the intended functional character to the type constructor '$\rightarrow$'.
We would like to stress the following remark about ITS's introduced in the literature:

definitions of ITS's involve constructors preserving prime-algebricity.

As a consequence all ITS's studied in the literature are actually defined as meet-semilattices built on underlying preorders of *prime* types, and their domain-theoretic counterparts are p-ALG's. Therefore ITS's are linguistically redundant structures. In the following we try to simplify ITS's by eliminating redundant types (due to the presence of '$\wedge$').

Definition 5.
Let A an ITS. A is *prime* if and only if there exists a subset $|P(A)| \subseteq |A|$ of *prime types* such that:

a) $\forall \sigma \in |P(A)|.(\wedge_I \tau_i \leq \sigma \Longrightarrow \exists i \in I. \tau_i \leq \sigma)$;
b) $\forall \tau \in A. \exists \sigma_i \in |P(A)|.\ \tau \sim \wedge_I \sigma_i \quad (i \in I)$. $\diamond$

If A is prime then it is the free ITS generated by the preorder $P(A)$ defined as $(|P(A)|, \leq_A)$.
The next lemma characterizes prime ITS's from the domain-theoretic point of view. Moreover it shows how filters over prime ITS's correspond to upper-sets over TP's.

Lemma 6.
i) Let A be a prime ITS. Then $(Fil(A), \subseteq)$ is a p-ALG.
ii) $(Fil(A), \subseteq) \simeq (U(P(A)), \subseteq)$. $\diamond$

$P(A)$ is more concise and clear than A.
Thus it is natural to replace **ITS** with a suitable category of *Type Preorders*. In particular one wants to get simpler descriptions of lattice models employed in denotational semantics.
We will therefore introduce the category **TP** of Type Preorders. However, before doing this, we need to introduce the notion of *lifted Hoare powerdomain*.
In fact, we want to capture the notion of Scott continuous function between p-ALG's by that of *prime approximable mapping* between TP's. A Scott continuous function $f : D \to D'$ is completely determined by its action on $K(D)$, but the information about the images of prime elements does not suffice to recover it. For this reason we need to consider $K(D)$ as the *prime elements basis* of a new p-ALG. This turns out to be the lifted Hoare powerdomain of D, $\mathcal{P}_{H,\perp}(D)$ (more formally $(K(D), \sqsubseteq_D) \simeq (Pr(\mathcal{P}_{H,\perp}(D)), \sqsubseteq_{\mathcal{P}_{H,\perp}(D)})$).
Notation: From now on, in order to avoid confusion, when we write $\wedge^e_I \sigma_i$ the set I is intended to be finite (possibly empty). If we write $\wedge_I \sigma_i$, I is intended to be finite not empty.

Definition 7.
i) Let $A = (|A|, \leq_A)$ be a TP. Define $\mathcal{P}_{H,\perp}(A)$ as the TP such that
$$|\mathcal{P}_{H,\perp}(A)| = \{(\wedge^e_I \sigma_i) \mid \forall i \in I. \sigma_i \in A\}$$
and $\leq_{\mathcal{P}_{H,\perp}(A)}$ is the preorder relation over $|\mathcal{P}_{H,\perp}(A)|$ such that
$$(\wedge^e_I \sigma_i) \leq_{\mathcal{P}_{H,\perp}(A)} (\wedge^e_J \sigma'_j) \iff (\forall j \in J. \exists i \in I.\ \sigma_i \leq_A \sigma'_j).^2$$
Given an upper set $x \subseteq A$ we write $x \models (\wedge^e_I \sigma_i) \iff \forall i \in I. \sigma_i \in x$.
ii) A *prime approximable mapping* (*p.a.m.* for short) $R : A \to B$ is a relation $R \subseteq \mathcal{P}_{H,\perp}(A) \times B$ such that:
$$(\wedge^e_I \sigma_i) \leq_{\mathcal{P}_{H,\perp}(A)} (\wedge^e_J \sigma'_j) \,\&\, (\wedge^e_J \sigma'_j)\, R\, \tau' \,\&\, \tau' \leq_B \tau \implies (\wedge^e_I \sigma_i)\, R\, \tau.$$
Composition between p.a.m.'s is defined as follows.
Let $R : A \to B$ and $S : B \to C$. Then
$$\wedge^e_I \sigma_i\ S \circ R\ \rho \iff \exists \tau_j \in |B|\ (j \in J)\,.\forall j\ \wedge^e_I \sigma_i\ R\ \tau_j \,\&\, \wedge^e_J \tau_j\ S\ \rho.$$

---

[2] Notice that $\wedge_I \sigma_i$ is a 'formal' meet, i.e. it stands for the finite set $\{\sigma_i \mid i \in I\}$. The order introduced above is essentially the Smyth preorder ($\leq_{\mathcal{P}_{H,\perp}(A)} \equiv (\leq_A)_S$). Since TP's reverse the ordering of finite elements in the lattices, Smyth preorder corresponds to Hoare powerdomain construction. From a categorical point of view $\mathcal{P}_{H,\perp}(A)$ is the finite-product completion of A, i.e. it corresponds to the free ITS generated by A.

iii) A *prime embedding* (*p.e.* for short) is a mapping $\phi : |A| \to |B|$ preserving and reflecting preorder relations:
$\forall \sigma, \sigma' \in |A|.\ \sigma \leq_A \sigma' \iff \phi(\sigma) \leq_B \phi(\sigma')$.

iv) A is *substructure* of B ($A \trianglelefteq B$) if $A \subseteq B$ and the inclusion map is a prime embedding.

v) Denote **TP** [**TP**^{E}] the category whose objects are TP's and morphisms p.a.m.'s [p.e.'s]. ◇

Notice that each p.e. ϕ determines a p.a.m. R_ϕ defined by $(\wedge_I^e \sigma_i) R_\phi \tau \iff \exists i \in I. \phi(\sigma_i) \leq \tau$. Viceversa, let $R : A \to B$ be a p.a.m. with the following properties:
- $(\wedge_I^e \sigma_i)\, R\, \tau \iff \exists i \in I.\ \sigma_i R \tau$;
- $\forall \sigma \in |A|. \exists \tau_\sigma \in |B|.\ \sigma R \tau_\sigma\ \&\ \forall \tau \in B.(\sigma R \tau \implies \tau_\sigma \leq \tau)$.

Then ϕ_R defined by: $\phi_R(\sigma) = \tau_\sigma$ is a prime embedding.

Theorem 8.
p-ALG and **TP** are equivalent categories. ◇

This can be verified by considering the functors $\mathcal{U}$ and $\mathcal{P}r$ defined below.
$\mathcal{U} : \mathbf{TP} \to \mathbf{p\text{-}ALG}$ is defined as follows.
$\mathcal{U}(A) = (U(A), \subseteq)$. For each $R : A \to B$ p.a.m. and $x \in U(A)$,
$\mathcal{U}(R)(x) = \{\tau \mid \exists (\wedge_I^e \sigma_i) \in \mathcal{P}_{H,\perp}(A).\ (\wedge_I^e \sigma_i)\, R\, \tau\ \&\ x \models (\wedge_I^e \sigma_i)\}$.
$\mathcal{P}r : \mathbf{p\text{-}ALG} \to \mathbf{TP}$ is defined as follows.
$\mathcal{P}r(D) = (G_D, \leq)$, where $G_D = \{\gamma_p \mid p \in Pr(D)\}$ and $\leq$ is the (pre)order relation over G_D such that $\uparrow p \subseteq \uparrow p' \iff \gamma_p \leq \gamma_{p'}$.
If $f : D \to E$ is a continuous function then
$(\wedge_I^e \gamma_{p_i})\, \mathcal{P}r(f)\, \gamma_q \iff \bigcap_I \uparrow p_i \subseteq f^{-1}(\uparrow q)$.
We can now define natural transformations:
$\eta : I_{\mathbf{p\text{-}ALG}} \to \mathcal{U} \circ \mathcal{P}r,\ \ \varepsilon : I_{\mathbf{TP}} \to \mathcal{P}r \circ \mathcal{U}$;
$\eta_D(x) = \{\sigma \in \mathcal{U} \circ \mathcal{P}r(D) \mid \exists p \in Pr(x).\ \gamma_p \leq \sigma\}$;
$(\wedge_I^e \sigma_i)\, \varepsilon_A\, \gamma_{\uparrow\tau} \iff \exists i \in I.\ \sigma_i \leq \tau$.
Then $(\mathcal{P}r, \mathcal{U}, \eta, \varepsilon) : \mathbf{p\text{-}ALG} \simeq \mathbf{TP}$ is an equivalence of categories. Similarly **p-ALG**^{E} is equivalent to **TP**^{E}.

4 Associations and Bi-embeddings

In this section we introduce the notions of *association* and *bi-embedding*, in order to provide a methodology which allows to relate explicitly TP's to the colimits which solve domain equations in **p-ALG**^{E}. Moreover we extend to *non-initial* cases the technique introduced in [LW] in order to get initial solutions of domain equations in the category of Information Systems. Finally we combine these, and by Theorem 14 we provide TP's which describe colimit solutions of domain equations in **p-ALG**.

Definition 9.
i) Let D be a p-ALG. A TP A is *associated* to D if there exists a surjection $h : |A| \to Pr(D)$ such that for each $\sigma, \tau \in |A|$ we have
$\sigma \leq \tau \iff h(\tau) \sqsubseteq h(\sigma)$.

When A is associated to D via h we write $[A, h, D]$. h is said a *finitary description* of D. The triple $[A, h, D]$ is said an *association*.[3]
ii) Let $[A, h, D]$, $[A', h', D']$ and $\phi : A \to A'$, $i : D \to D'$ be p.e.'s. (ϕ, i) is said a *bi-embedding* from $[A, h, D]$ to $[A', h', D']$ (denoted by $[h, (\phi, i), h']$) iff $i \circ h = h' \circ \phi$. $\diamond$

As an immediate consequence of the previous definition, if A is associated to D then $\mathcal{U}(A) \simeq D$.

We give now the important notion of *associated functors*, by which we achieve a translation of colimits of TP's into colimits of p-ALG's and viceversa. For this aim we first need to introduce the *category of associations* **AS**.

Definition 10.
AS is the category whose objects are associations and morphisms bi-embeddings, with composition:

$$(\phi, i) \circ (\psi, j) = (\phi \circ \psi, i \circ j). \diamond$$

Definition 11.
Let $F : (\mathbf{p\text{-}ALG}^E)^n \to \mathbf{p\text{-}ALG}^E, \bar{F} : (\mathbf{TP}^E)^n \to \mathbf{TP}^E$ two continuous functors. Suppose that for each n-tupla of associations $[A_m, h_m, D_m]$ $(1 \leq m \leq n)$ there exists an association $[\bar{F}(A_1, \ldots, A_n), F^\star(h_1, \ldots, h_n), (F(D_1, \ldots, D_n)]$.
Define $\mathbb{F} : \mathbf{AS}^n \to \mathbf{AS}$ as follows:

- $\mathbb{F}([A_1, h_1, D_1], \ldots, [A_n, h_n, D_n]) =$
  $= [\bar{F}(A_1, \ldots, A_n), F^\star(h_1, \ldots, h_n), F(D_1, \ldots, D_n)]$.
- If $[B_m, k_m, E_m]$ and $[h_m, (\phi_m, i_m), k_m]$ $(1 \leq m \leq n)$, then:
  $\mathbb{F}((\phi_1, i_1), \ldots, (\phi_n, i_n)) = (\bar{F}(\phi_1, \ldots, \phi_n), F(i_1, \ldots, i_n))$.

$\bar{F}$ and F are *associated* if $\mathbb{F}$ is a functor over **AS**, i.e.

$$[F^\star(h_1, \ldots, h_n), (\bar{F}(\phi_1, \ldots, \phi_n), F(i_1, \ldots, i_n)), F^\star(k_1, \ldots, k_n)]. \diamond$$

In order to describe solutions of domain equations in $\mathbf{p\text{-}ALG}^E$ by TP's we define colimits in $\mathbf{TP}^E$ as *set-theoretic unions* of TP's in the spirit of [LW]. This is done by the next two lemmata. Then, by exploiting the notion of associated functors, we can relate constructions of colimits in the two categories.

Lemma 12.
Let $\phi : B \to A$ be a p.e. Define B_ϕ and $\hat{\phi} : |B_\phi| \to |A|$ in the following way:

- $|B_\phi| = |A| \cup |B|$;
- $\hat{\phi}(\sigma) = \begin{cases} \sigma & \text{if } \sigma \in |A| \setminus |B| \\ \phi(\sigma) & \text{if } \sigma \in |B| \end{cases}$;
- $\sigma \leq_{B_\phi} \sigma' \iff \hat{\phi}(\sigma) \leq_A \hat{\phi}(\sigma')$.

Then $B \trianglelefteq B_\phi$, $A \trianglelefteq B_\phi$, and $\hat{\phi} : B_\phi \to A$ is an isomorphism. $\diamond$

---

[3] Regarded as categories, A is associated to D if and only if A is equivalent to $(Pr(D), \sqsubseteq^{op})$.

Lemma 13.
Let $\langle A_n, \phi_n : A_n \rightarrow A_{n+1}\rangle_n$ be a tower of TP's.
Define, for each $n \in \omega$, B_n and $\hat{\phi}_n : B_{n+1} \rightarrow A_{n+1}$ in the following way:
- $B_0 = A_0$;
- $B_{n+1} = \widehat{(B_n)}_{\phi_n \circ \hat{\phi}_{n-1}}$;
- $\hat{\phi}_n = \phi_n \circ \hat{\phi}_{n-1}$ ($\hat{\phi}_{-1}$ is the identity on A_0).

Let $A_\infty = (\bigcup_{n\in\omega} |B|_n, \bigcup_{n\in\omega} \leq_{B_n})$ and $\iota_n : A_n \rightarrow A_\infty$ be the inclusion maps.
Then $\langle A_\infty, \iota_n\rangle_n$ is a colimits of the tower $\langle A_n, \phi_n\rangle_n$. ◇

We now recall some standard facts and notations.
Let $F : \textbf{p-ALG}^E \rightarrow \textbf{p-ALG}^E$ be a continuous functor. In order to solve the domain equation $D = F(D)$ one starts from an initial domain D_0 and a prime embedding $i_0 : D_0 \rightarrow F(D_0)$.
Denote $D_\infty(F, i_0)$ the colimit in $\textbf{p-ALG}^E$ of the tower $\langle F^n(D_0), F^n(i_0)\rangle_n$, with cocone $\alpha_n : F^n(D_0) \rightarrow D_\infty(F, i_0)$. Define $A_\infty(\bar{F}, \phi_0)$, the colimit of a tower $\langle \bar{F}^n(A_0), \bar{F}^n(\phi_0)\rangle_n$, as A_∞ of Lemma 13.
Since the definitions of ITS's mostly determine colimits $A_\infty(\bar{F}, \phi_0)$, the next theorem is the key to give the domain-theoretic reading of ITS's.

Theorem 14.
Let $\bar{F}$ and F be associated, $[A_0, h_0, D_0]$ and $[h_0, (\phi_0, i_0), F^\star(h_0)]$.
Then $[A_\infty(\bar{F}, \phi_0), h_\infty, D_\infty(F, i_0)]$ where h_∞ is the surjection defined as follows:
$\forall \sigma \in A_n \subseteq A_\infty.\ h_\infty(\sigma) = \alpha_n \circ \bar{F}^n(h_0)(\sigma)$. ◇

5 Constructions

In this section we give the main constructions over the category **TP**.
In the following A, B, A', B' are TP's, $R : A \rightarrow A', R' : A' \rightarrow A, S : B \rightarrow B'$ are prime approximable mappings, and $[A, h, D]$, $[B, k, E]$ are associations.
For each of the next definitions 'i)' describes the action of the functor on objects, 'ii)' the action on morphisms. 'iii)' gives the appropriate transformations of finitary descriptions (provided by '$F^\star$' in the previous section).
Notice how definitions of constructions are immediate and involve few axioms and rules, with respect to Scott's Information Systems or Abramsky's Domain Prelocales.
We conclude the section by stating the theorem which provides the connection between solutions of domain equations in $\textbf{p-ALG}^E$ and $\textbf{TP}^E$. It is the key for giving domain-theoretic readings of TP's and ITS's.

Definition 15.
i) The *lift* of A,$A_\perp$, is defined in the following way:
- $|A_\perp| = (\{0\} \times |A|) \cup \omega_{A_\perp}$;
- $\sigma \leq_{A_\perp} \sigma' \iff (\sigma' \equiv \omega_{A_\perp}$ or $(\sigma \equiv (0, \tau)\ \&\ \tau \equiv (0, \tau')\ \&\ \tau \leq_A \tau'))$.

ii) $R_\perp : A_\perp \rightarrow A'_\perp$ is the p.a.m. defined as follows:
$\sigma R_\perp \sigma' \iff \sigma' \equiv \omega_{B_\perp}$ or $(\sigma \equiv (0, \tau)\ \&\ \tau \equiv (0, \tau')\ \&\ \tau R \tau')$.

iii) $h_\perp : |A_\perp| \to Pr(D_\perp)$ is defined as follows:
$h_\perp(0,\sigma) = (0, h(\sigma))$;
$h_\perp(\omega_{A_\perp}) = \perp_{D_\perp}$. $\diamond$

Definition 16.

i) The *product* of A and B, $A \times B$, is defined in the following way:
- $|A \times B| = (\{0\} \times |A|) \cup (\{1\} \times |B|)$;
- $\sigma \leq_{A\times B} \tau \iff$
$\sigma \equiv (0,\sigma_0) \,\&\, \tau \equiv (0,\tau_0) \,\&\, \sigma_0 \leq_A \tau_0$ or
$\sigma \equiv (1,\sigma_1) \,\&\, \tau \equiv (1,\tau_1) \,\&\, \sigma_1 \leq_B \tau_1$.

ii) $R \times S : A \times B \to A' \times B'$ is the p.a.m. defined as follows:
$\sigma\, R \times S\, \sigma' \iff$
$\sigma \equiv (0,\sigma_0) \,\&\, \sigma' \equiv (0,\sigma'_0) \,\&\, \sigma_0 R \sigma'_0$ or
$\sigma \equiv (1,\sigma_1) \,\&\, \sigma' \equiv (1,\sigma'_1) \,\&\, \sigma_1 S \sigma'_1$.

iii) $(h \times k) : |A \times B| \to Pr(D \times E)$ is defined as follows:
$(h \times k)(0,\sigma_0) = (h(\sigma_0), \perp_E)$;
$(h \times k)(1,\sigma_1) = (\perp_D, k(\sigma_1))$. $\diamond$

The next definition is slightly different from the one given for $\mathcal{P}_{H,\perp}$ in that we do not admit empty meets. Notice that the interpretation we give to intersection types is quite different to the standard one in ITS's. This difference depends upon the fact that we recover domains by taking upper sets (not filters).

Definition 17.

i) The *Hoare powerdomain* of A, $\mathcal{P}_H(A)$, is defined in the following way:
- $|\mathcal{P}_H(A)| = \{(\wedge_I \sigma_i) \mid \forall i \in I.\, \sigma_i \in A\}$;
- $(\wedge_I \sigma_i) \leq_{\mathcal{P}_H(A)} (\wedge_J \tau_j) \iff \forall j \in J. \exists i \in I.\, \sigma_i \leq_A \tau_j$.

ii) $\mathcal{P}_H(R) : \mathcal{P}_H(A) \to \mathcal{P}_H(B)$ is the p.a.m. defined as follows:
$(\wedge_I \sigma_i)\, \mathcal{P}_H(R)\, (\wedge_J \sigma'_j) \iff \forall j \in J.\, \exists i \in I.\, \sigma_i R \sigma'_j$.

iii) $\mathcal{P}_H(h) : |\mathcal{P}_H(A)| \to Pr(\mathcal{P}_H(D))$ is defined as follows:
$\mathcal{P}_H(h)(\wedge_I \sigma_i) = \downarrow \bigvee_I h(\sigma_i)$. $\diamond$

$\mathcal{P}_{H,\perp}$, $\mathcal{P}_H \circ (\cdot)_\perp$ and $(\cdot)_\perp \circ \mathcal{P}_H$ lead to isomorphic TP's. $\mathcal{P}_{H,\perp}$ is introduced to keep type notation more compact. In particular notice that $\wedge_\emptyset \sigma_i$ is the type of $\mathcal{P}_{H,\perp}$ corresponding to $\omega_{\mathcal{P}_H(A)}$ in $(\mathcal{P}_H(A))_\perp$.

Definition 18.

i) The *Smyth powerdomain* of A, $\mathcal{P}_S(A)$, is defined in the following way:
- $|\mathcal{P}_S(A)| = \{(\vee_I \sigma_i) \mid \forall i \in I.\, \sigma_i \in A\}$;
- $(\vee_I \sigma_i) \leq_{\mathcal{P}_S(A)} (\vee_J \tau_j) \iff \forall i \in I. \exists j \in J.\, \sigma_i \leq_A \tau_j$.[4]

ii) $\mathcal{P}_S(R) : \mathcal{P}_S(A) \to \mathcal{P}_S(B)$ is the p.a.m. defined as follows:
$(\vee_I \sigma_i) \mathcal{P}_S(R) (\vee_J \sigma'_j) \iff \forall i \in I. \exists j \in J.\, \sigma_i R \sigma'_j$.

iii) $\mathcal{P}_S(h) : |\mathcal{P}_S(A)| \to Pr(\mathcal{P}_S(D))$ is defined as follows:
$\mathcal{P}_S(h)(\vee_I \sigma_i) = \uparrow \{h(\sigma_i) \mid i \in I\}$. $\diamond$

[4] From a categorical point of wiew $\mathcal{P}_S(A)$ corresponds to the finite (non-empty) coproduct completion of A.

Definition 19.

i) The *function space* from A to B, $(A \to B)$ is defined in the following way:
- $A \to B = \{(\wedge_I^e \sigma_i) \to \tau \mid (\wedge_I \sigma_i) \in \mathcal{P}_{H,\perp}(A),\ \tau \in B\}$;
- $(\wedge_I^e \sigma_i) \to \tau \leq_{A \to B} (\wedge_J^e \rho_j) \to \chi \iff$
  $(\wedge_J^e \rho_j) \leq_{\mathcal{P}_{H,\perp}(A)} (\wedge_I^e \sigma_i)\ \&\ \tau \leq_B \chi$.

ii) $R' \to S : (A \to B) \to (A' \to B')$ is the p.a.m. defined as follows:
$((\wedge_I^e \sigma_i) \to \tau)(R' \to S)((\wedge_J^e \sigma'_j) \to \tau') \iff$
$(\wedge_J^e \sigma'_j)\mathcal{P}_{H,\perp}(R')(\wedge_I^e \sigma_i)\ \&\ \tau S \tau'$.

iii) $(h \to k) : |(A \to B)| \to Pr([D \to E])$ is defined as follows:
$(h \to k)((\wedge_I^e \sigma_i) \to \tau) = \text{step}_{(\bigvee_I h(\sigma_i)),k(\tau)}$. ◇

Definition 20.

i) The *strict function space* from A to B, $(A \to_\perp B)$ is defined in the following way:
- $|A \to_\perp B| = \{(\wedge_I \sigma_i) \to \tau \mid (\wedge_I \sigma_i) \in \mathcal{P}_H(A),\ \tau \in B\}$;
- $(\wedge_I \sigma_i) \to \tau \leq_{A \to_\perp B} (\wedge_J \rho_j) \to \chi \iff$
  $(\wedge_J \rho_j) \leq_{\mathcal{P}_H(A)} (\wedge_I \sigma_i) \& \tau \leq_B \chi$.

ii) $R' \to_\perp S : (A \to_\perp B) \to (A' \to_\perp B')$ is the p.a.m. defined as follows:
$((\wedge_I \sigma_i) \to \tau)(R' \to_\perp S)((\wedge_J \sigma'_j) \to \tau') \iff$
$(\wedge_J \sigma'_j)\mathcal{P}_H(R')(\wedge_I \sigma_i) \& \tau S \tau'$.

iii) $(h \to_\perp k) : |(A \to_\perp B)| \to Pr([D \to_\perp E])$ is defined as follows:
$(h \to_\perp k)((\wedge_I \sigma_i) \to \tau) = \text{step}_{\bigvee_I h(\sigma_i),k(\tau)}$. ◇

We conclude the section by giving the theorem stating the expected connection between functors over **p-ALG** and functors over **TP**. In order to study domain equations we consider also the *diagonal* functor $\Delta : \mathbf{TP} \to \mathbf{TP} \times \mathbf{TP}$ and the *constant* functors $Const_A : \mathbf{TP} \to \mathbf{TP}$ (A is a Type Preorder):

$\Delta(B) = \langle B, B \rangle, \quad \Delta(R) = \langle R, R \rangle;$
$Const_A(B) = A, \quad Const_A(R) = Id_A.$

Theorem 21.
The functors $(\cdot)_\perp$, $\times$, $\mathcal{P}_H$, $\mathcal{P}_S$, $\to$, $\to_\perp$, Δ, $Const_A$ are associated to their analogues over **p-ALG**. ◇

By combining Theorem 14 with the previous one, we get the final theorem enabling us to relate colimit solutions in the two categories $\mathbf{p\text{-}ALG}^E$ and $\mathbf{TP}^E$.

Theorem 22.
Let $F : \mathbf{p\text{-}ALG}^E \to \mathbf{p\text{-}ALG}^E$ be a functor defined by composition using the domain constructors above and $\bar{F} : \mathrm{TP}^E \to \mathrm{TP}^E$ be the functor defined in the same way by using the corresponding constructors over TP^E.
Suppose that $[A_0, h_0, D_0]$ are associations and $[h_0, (\phi_0, i_0), F^\star(h_0)]$.
Then $A_\infty(\bar{F}, \phi_0)$ and $D_\infty(F, i_0)$ are associated. ◇

6 A Domain Equation for Intersection Union Types

In this section we give an application of the previous results by giving the domain-theoretic reading of the Intersection Union Type Structure *Type*, (see [BD], [BDdL], [DdLP]).
Type provides an appropriate framework for the semantics of various λ-calculi extended with non-deterministic operators. Due to the introduction of *union* types, *Type* seems to be similar to Domain Prelocales of [Abr1]. Nevertheless this is not the case. In Domain Prelocales points are recovered by taking *prime* filters of types, while points of *Type* are recovered by taking (simple) filters. As a consequence of this, in the first case union types describe compact open sets of the domain topology; in the second case they are related to coprime open sets of the Smyth powerdomain topology. The investigation about *Type* is developed by using TP's. In such a way we get a definition of *Type* by few axioms and rules, enabling us to understand easily its domain-theoretic reading.

The definition of *Type* makes use of two type constructors, '$\rightarrow$' and '$\vee$', and introduces a countable set of type variables in order to make the structure non-trivial and to have a different atomic type for each term variable.

Definition 23. The Intersection Union Type Structure, *Type*, is the ITS defined as follows. $|Type|$ consists of a set of types generated by the syntax:

$\tau \ ::= \ t \mid \omega \mid \tau \rightarrow \tau \mid \tau \wedge \tau \mid \tau \vee \tau$

(t ranges over a countable set *Var* of type variables).

$\leq$ is the minimal preorder relation over $|Type|$ such that conditions of Definition 3 are satisfied and moreover:

- $\omega \leq \omega \rightarrow \omega$;
- $\tau \vee \tau \leq \tau$;
- $\sigma \leq \sigma \vee \tau, \quad \tau \leq \sigma \vee \tau$;
- $\sigma \leq \sigma' \ \& \ \tau \leq \tau' \implies \sigma \vee \tau \leq \sigma' \vee \tau'$;
- $(\sigma \vee \tau) \wedge \rho \leq (\sigma \wedge \rho) \vee (\tau \wedge \rho)$;
- $(\sigma \rightarrow \tau) \wedge (\sigma \rightarrow \rho) \leq \sigma \rightarrow (\tau \wedge \rho)$;
- $\sigma' \leq \sigma \ \& \ \tau \leq \tau' \implies \sigma \rightarrow \tau \leq \sigma' \rightarrow \tau'$. ◇

We now proceed to clarify the domain-theoretic aspect of *Type*. First notice that *Type* is a prime ITS's. $P(Type) = (|P(Type)|, \leq)$ consists of types generated by the following syntax:

$\sigma \ ::= \ t \mid (\wedge_I^e \sigma_i) \rightarrow \sigma \mid \sigma \vee \sigma$ (t ranges over a countable set *Var*).

We can equivalently define another (more compact) grammar for $|P(Type)|$ in the following way:

$\sigma \ ::= \ \vee_I((\wedge_H^e \sigma_{ih}) \rightarrow \sigma_i) \vee (\vee_L t_l) \quad (I \cup L \neq \emptyset)$.

$\leq$ is the minimal preorder relation such that:

a) $\sigma \vee \sigma \leq \sigma$;

b) $\sigma \leq \sigma \vee \tau, \quad \tau \leq \sigma \vee \tau$;

c) $\sigma \leq \sigma' \ \& \ \tau \leq \tau' \implies \sigma \vee \tau \leq \sigma' \vee \tau'$;

d) $(\forall i \in I. \exists j \in J. \sigma'_j \leq \sigma_i) \ \& \ \tau \leq \tau' \implies (\wedge_I^e \sigma_i) \rightarrow \tau \leq (\wedge_J^e \sigma'_j) \rightarrow \tau'$.

We now show how *Type* corresponds to a colimit construction in $\mathbf{TP}^E$.
First consider the functor $\bar{F} = \mathcal{P}_S \circ (((\rightarrow \circ \Delta) \times Const_V) \circ \Delta)$ where V is the TP's consisting of a countable set of atomic types with the empty preorder relation (actually V is associated to the powerset of ω, $\mathcal{P}\omega$).
For sake of completeness here is the action of $\bar{F}$ on objects and morphisms:

i) $\bar{F}(A) = \mathcal{P}_S((A \rightarrow A) \times V)$.
By the way notice that:
- types in $|\bar{F}(A)|$ can be defined by the syntax:
$\tau ::= (\vee_I((\wedge_H \sigma_{ih})) \rightarrow \rho_i) \vee (\vee_L t_l) \ \ (\sigma_{ih}, \rho_i \in |A|, t_l \in |V|, I \cup L \neq \emptyset)$;
- preorder relation in $\bar{F}(A)$ satisfies conditions a),..,d) above.

ii) Let $R : A \rightarrow B$ be a p.a.m. Then $\bar{F}(R) : \bar{F}(A) \rightarrow \bar{F}(B)$ is defined as follows:
$(\vee_I((\wedge_H \sigma_{ih}) \rightarrow \rho_i) \vee (\vee_L t_l))\bar{F}(R)(\vee_J((\wedge_K \sigma'_{jk}) \rightarrow \rho'_j) \vee (\vee_M t'_m)) \Longleftrightarrow$
$(\forall i \in I.\exists j \in J.(\forall h \in H.\exists k \in K.\sigma'_{jk} R \sigma_{ih})\ \&\ \rho_i R \rho'_j)\ \&$
$\forall l \in L.\exists m \in M.t_l = t'_m$.

As shown in the discussion above, $P(Type)$ is strictly related to $\bar{F}$. In fact the following result holds.

Theorem 24.
Let A_0 be the empty Type Preorder $(\emptyset, \emptyset)$ and $\phi_0 : A_0 \rightarrow \bar{F}(A_0)$ the trivial p.e. Then $P(Type) = A_\infty(\bar{F}, \phi_0)$. ◇

We can now exploit Theorem 22 in order to get the domain-theoretic reading of *Type*. First consider the one-element lattice $D_0 = \{\bot\}$ associated to the TP $(\emptyset, \emptyset)$. Then take the functor F associated to $\bar{F}$:

$F = \mathcal{P}_S \circ (((\rightarrow \circ \Delta) \times Const_{\mathcal{P}\omega}) \circ \Delta)$.

Consider the trivial prime embedding $i_0 : D_0 \rightarrow F(D_0)$.
By Theorem 22 we get immediately:

$P(Type) = A_\infty(\bar{F}, \phi_0)$ *is associated to* $D_\infty(F, i_0)$.

Finally notice that $\mathcal{U}(P(Type)) \simeq Fil(Type)$.
It is now possible to give the domain-theoretic reading of *Type*.

Theorem 25.
Fil(*Type*) is the initial solution of the domain equation $D = \mathcal{P}_S([D \rightarrow D] \times \mathcal{P}\omega)$ computed in the category of prime algebraic complete lattices. ◇

Acknowledgments
The author is greatly indebted to Furio Honsell for illuminating discussions. I wish to thank Mariangiola Dezani-Ciancaglini, Ugo de' Liguoro, Pietro Di Gianantonio for comments and two anonymous referees for their remarks.

References

[Abr1] S. Abramsky: *Domain Theory in Logical Form.* Annals of Pure and Applied Logic, 51 (1991) 1-77.

[Abr2] S. Abramsky: *A The lazy λ-calculus.* In D. Turner ed. *Research Topics in Functional Programming.* Addison-Wesley, Reading, MA.

[BCD] H.P. Barendregt, M. Coppo, M. Dezani-Ciancaglini: *A Filter λ-models and Completeness of Type Assignment.* Journal of Symbolic Logic, 48 (1983) 931-940.

[BD] F. Barbanera, M. Dezani-Ciancaglini: *Intersection and Union Types* TACS'91, LNCS, 526 (1991), 651-674.

[BDdL] F. Barbanera, M. Dezani-Ciancaglini, U. de' Liguoro: *Intersection and Union Types: Syntax and Semantics.* Information and Computation, to appear.

[Bou] G. Boudol: *Lambda-Calculi for (strict) Parallel Functions.* INRIA / Sophia-Antipolis Technical Report 1387, (1991) To appear on Information and Computation.

[CDHL] M. Coppo, M. Dezani-Ciancaglini, F. Honsell, G. Longo: *Extended Type Structures and Filter λ-models.* In G. Lolli, G. Longo, A. Morcja editors, Logic Colloquium '82 , North Holland, Amsterdam (1984) 241-262.

[CDZ] M. Coppo, M. Dezani-Ciancaglini, M. Zacchi: *Type Theories, Normal Forms and* $D_\infty - \lambda$*-models.* Information and Computation, 72 (1987) 85-116.

[DdLP] M. Dezani-Ciancaglini, U. de' Liguoro, A. Piperno: *Filter λ-models for a Parallel and Non-Deterministic λ-calculus.* In A.M. Borzyszkowsky, S. Sokolowsky editors, *18th International Symposium on Mathematical Foundation of Computer Science*, Gdansk (Poland) (1993) 403-412. Springer-Verlag LNCS Vol 711.

[DM] M. Dezani-Ciancaglini, I. Margaria: *A Characterization of F-complete Type Assignments.* Theoretical Computer Science, 45 (1986) 121-157.

[Comp] G.K. Gierz, K.H. Hoffmann, K. Keimel, J.D. Lawson, M. Mislove, D.S. Scott: *A Compendium of Continuous Lattices.* Springer-Verlag, Berlin, 1980.

[EHR] L. Egidi, F. Honsell, S. Ronchi della Rocca: *Operational, Denotational and Logical Descriptions: a case study.* Fundamenta Informaticae 16 (2) (1992) 149-169.

[HL] F. Honsell, M. Lenisa: *Some Results on the Full Abstraction Problem for Restricted Lambda Calculi.* In A.M. Borzyszkowsky, S. Sokolowsky editors, *18th International Symposium on Mathematical Foundation of Computer Science*, Gdansk (Poland) (1993) 84-104. Springer-Verlag LNCS Vol 711.

[HR] F. Honsell, S. Ronchi della Rocca: *An Approximation Theorem for Scott Topological Lambda Models and the Topological Incompleteness of Lambda Calculus.* To appear on Journal of Computer and System Science.

[Joh] P.T. Johnstone: *Stone Spaces.* Volume 3 of *Cambridge Studies in Advanced Mathematics.* Cambridge University Press, Cambridge, 1982.

[LW] K.G. Larsen, G. Winskel: *Using Information Systems to Solve Recursive Domain Equation Effectively.* In D.B MacQueen, G. Khan and G. Plotkin editors, *Semantics of Data Types*, 109-130, Berlin (1984) Springer-Verlag LNCS Vol. 173.

[NPW] M. Nielsen, G. Plotkin, G. Winskel: *Petri Nets, Event Structures and Domains. part I.* Theoretical Computer Science, 13 (1981) 85-108.

[Sco] D.S. Scott: *Domain for Denotational Semantics.* In M. Nielson, E.M. Schmidt editors, Automata, Languages and Programming: Proceedings 1982. Berlin (1982) Springer-Verlag LNCS 140.

[SP] M. Smyth, G. Plotkin: *The Category Theoretic Solution of Recursive Domain Equations.* SIAM Journal Computing 11 (1982) 761.

[Vic] S. Vickers: *Topology via Logic.* Cambridge Tracts in Theoretical Computer Science. Cambridge University Press, 1988.

Compilative Constructive Negation in Constraint Logic Programs

Paola Bruscoli, Francesca Levi, Giorgio Levi, Maria Chiara Meo

Dipartimento di Informatica, Università di Pisa,
C.so Italia, 40 - 56125 Pisa, Italy
e-mail: paola@csr.unibo.it {levifran, levi, meo}@di.unipi.it

Abstract. In this paper we define a new compilative version of constructive negation (intensional negation) in CLP and we prove its (non-ground) correctness and completeness wrt the 3-valued completion. We show that intensional negation is essentially equivalent to constructive negation and that it is indeed more efficient, as one would expect from the fact that it is a compilative technique, with the transformation and the associated normalization process being performed once and for all on the source program. We define several formal non-ground semantics, based either on the derivation rule or on the least fixpoint of an immediate consequence operator. All these semantics are proved to correctly model the observable behavior, from the viewpoint of answer constraints. We give some equivalence theorems and we show that all our denotations are the non-ground representation of a single partial interpretation, which is $\Phi_P \uparrow \omega$, where Φ_P is the Fitting's operator [12].

1 Introduction

The most popular semantics for normal logic programs is based on $SLDNF$-resolution (SLD-resolution with Negation As Failure) as operational semantics and on the program completion as declarative semantics [9, 20]. The reference fixpoint semantics is usually based on Fitting's operator [12]. Unfortunately, the nice equivalence and completeness results proved for the semantics of positive logic programs [30, 2, 20, 1] are not valid in the case of normal programs. In particular, we need to impose strong conditions on programs and goals, in order to deal with various incompleteness problems (e.g. floundering, inconsistency of the completion, the combination of tertium non datur and non-termination). The completeness of $SLDNF$-resolution holds for a larger class of programs, if we consider the logical consequences of the completion $Comp(P)$ in a 3-valued logic. Let P be a normal program, $G = L_1, \ldots, L_n$ be a normal goal, such that $P \bigcup \{G\}$ is *allowed*, if $(L_1 \wedge \ldots \wedge L_n)\theta$ is a 3-valued logical consequence of $Comp(P)$, then there exists an $SLDNF$-refutation of $P \bigcup \{G\}$ which computes an answer τ more general than θ.

The 3-valued completion is also strongly related to the Fitting's operator Φ_P [12], which acts upon 3-valued interpretations. The minimal 3-valued model M_P

of $Comp(P)$ is its least fixpoint $\Phi_P \uparrow \alpha$. Kunen's semantics [17] is also defined in terms of Φ_P, namely $\{L \mid \Phi_P \uparrow n \models_3 L \text{ for a finite } n\} = \{L \mid Comp(P) \models_3 L\}$.

If we choose the 3-valued completion, the only source of incompleteness has to do with the floundering problem, i.e. with non-ground negative literals. Another serious drawback of $SLDNF$ is also related to the non-ground literal problem, namely the fact that Negation As Failure can only be used as a test and never computes answers.

The problem of handling "non-ground" literals was tackled by various extensions of Negation As Failure, called *constructive negation*. Examples are *intensional negation* [3, 4], Chan's *constructive negation* [7, 8], *fail substitutions* [21] and *fail answers* [11, 10]. The idea of intensional negation, originally sketched in [26] and then formalized for positive logic programs in [3, 4], is the following. Given a normal program P, we derive a new program P', which contains clauses which allow us to compute the answers to negative queries.

Example 1. Let P be the program $\{even(0) \quad , \quad even(s(s(X))) \leftarrow even(X)\}$. The new clauses in P' generated by intensional negation are the following: $\{even^{\neg}(s(0)) \quad , \quad even^{\neg}(s(s(X))) \leftarrow even^{\neg}(X)\}$.
A (possibly non-ground) literal of the form $\neg even(t)$ (in a goal or in the body of a normal clause) is transformed to $even^{\neg}(t)$ and evaluated in P'.

The new clauses are built in such a way that the answers to negative queries are "the complement" of the set of answers to the corresponding positive query. The complement is computed by assuming the Domain Closure Axiom (DCA). The negative literals (not only in the goal, but also in clause bodies) can be replaced by (positive) calls to the new predicates. Note that if the result of intensional negation were really a positive program, we could simply apply SLD-resolution. Moreover, the standard least Herbrand model and least fixpoint of T_P semantics would be applicable. Finally, the resulting denotation could be viewed as a 3-valued interpretation. Unfortunately, there exist logic programs for which the intensional negation transformation introduces universal quantification in clause bodies, coming from local variables in the original program. The standard semantics of positive logic programs is then applicable to the result of the intensional negation transformation for restricted classes of normal programs only [23]. The range of applicability of intensional negation was increased by defining an extended derivation rule for positive logic programs with universal quantification parametric w.r.t. the DCA [19].

Chan's constructive negation, in its original formulation [7] can be described as follows. Let $\neg A$ be a (possibly non-ground) literal in the normal program P. Let $\mathcal{T}$ be the complete SLD-tree rooted at A and let $e_1, \ldots, e_n$ be the sets of equations in solved form corresponding to the answer substitutions computed by the success paths in $\mathcal{T}$. The answer to $\neg A$ is the (normalization of the) constraint $\neg(e_1 \vee \ldots \vee e_n)$.

The normalization is a disjunction of constraints, i.e. equalities and inequalities. Note that Chan's constructive negation does not require the DCA. The application of the above inference rule is undefined when the SLD-tree is infinite. The mechanism of negative literals evaluation, inherited from Negation

As Failure, is not "incremental", since it requires the construction of a full SLD-tree. This problem was solved in [8], by considering a *finite* part of the SLD-tree, defined by a *frontier*, instead of the complete $SLD-$tree. Using the Constraint Logic Programming (CLP) notation [16, 15], each node of the frontier is a goal $e_i \Box B_i$ containing both constraints (equalities) and literals. The literal $\neg A$ is now rewritten as the result of the normalization of the formula $\neg(e_1 \Box B_1 \vee \ldots \vee e_n \Box B_n)$. The result of the computation is independent from the choice of the frontier. The above technique was then extended to CLP [28, 29] and a completeness result was proved.

The problem of handling negation constructively has an alternative solution in the idea of using explicitely the formulas in the completion (first order program) as rewrite rules, with a suitable constraint extraction procedure. [25] has shown a top-down interpreter which is sound and complete w.r.t. three-valued logical consequences semantics. A similar method with a different proof of completeness is given in [5]. Stuckey's constructive negation can be shown to be an implementation of the above operational semantics. The distinctive feature of constructive negation, however, is that it handles general clauses rather than more complex first order programs and that it is defined as an extension of standard SLD-resolution (to which it gracefully reduces in the case of positive clauses). The idea is therefore that of using as much as possible the standard logic programming technology. We push forward this idea by defining a compilative version of constructive negation in the line of intensional negation. As was the case of Stuckey's constructive negation we prove the (correctness and) completeness w.r.t. three-valued logic, without going through first order programs.

Intensional negation is clearly a "compile-time" technique. The transformation and the associated normalization process are performed once and for all on the source program. All the versions of constructive negation are instead interpretative. Intensional negation is therefore much more efficient. We show that both intensional and constructive negation can simply be viewed as mechanisms to efficiently implement "computing in the completion". The optimization is concerned with the management of disjunctions, which are handled by using essentially the $SLD-$tree structure of positive Horn clauses. The resulting theory allows us to identify commonalities and differences between the various constructive negation techniques. It is worth noting that there exists one example [11, 10] of constructive negation technique, which is not based on the program completion and is not therefore easily comparable to our technique.

The second contribution of the paper is related to the formal semantics. None of the existing semantics for constructive negation correctly models answer constraints. We propose several formal (non-ground) denotations which are based either on the top-down derivation rules or on the bottom-up application of immediate consequences operators. All these semantics are proved to be correct (and fully abstract) with respect to the answer constraints observable. We give some equivalence theorems and we show that all our denotations are the non-ground representation of a single partial interpretation, which is $\Phi_P \uparrow \omega$.

There are several motivations for choosing the CLP setting instead of the logic programming one. First, even if we start from normal logic programs, constructive negation forces the introduction of (universally quantified) inequalities. One can stay within the logic programming setting based on substitutions only by assuming the DCA. This is, for example, the solution chosen in [21]. The most natural solution is then choosing the instance of CLP, where constraints are equalities and inequalities on the Herbrand domain. Moving to CLP allows us to get more generality and to use the only existing formalization of constructive negation [28] for which there exists a completeness theorem. All the proofs of the results reported in the paper can be found in [6].

2 The language and its semantic domains

We will first recall the basic CLP concepts as defined in [16]. A first order language is defined on a function symbol set denoted by Σ, a predicate symbol set denoted by Π and a collection of variables denoted by V. $\tau(\Sigma \cup V)$ and $\tau(\Sigma)$ denote the set of terms and ground terms (i.e. terms without variables) built on Σ and V. A (Π, Σ)-atom is an element $p(t_1, \dots, t_n)$ where $p \in \Pi$ is n-ary and $t_i \in \tau(\Sigma \cup V)$, $i = 1, \dots, n$. A (Π, Σ)-literal is a (Π, Σ)-atom or its negation. A (Π, Σ)- constraint is a well formed formula over the alphabets Π and Σ. The empty constraint is denoted by *true*. In the following the symbol $\bar{}$ will denote a finite sequence of objects (variables, terms, atoms etc.). If t is a syntactic object, $FV(t)$ is the set of variables which are not explicitly quantified in t. A sentence is a well formed formula with no free variables.

Definition 1. *(CLP normal programs)* [16] Let $\Pi = \Pi_C \cup \Pi_B$ and $\Pi_C \cap \Pi_B = \emptyset$. A (Π, Σ)-normal program is a finite set of clauses of the form

$$H \leftarrow c\Box \qquad or \qquad H \leftarrow c\Box B_1, \dots, B_n$$

where c is a finite (Π_C, Σ)-constraint, H (the head) is a (Π_B, Σ)-atom of the form $p(\bar{X})$, where $\bar{X}$ is a sequence of distinct variables and $B_1, \dots, B_n$ (the body) are (Π_B, Σ)-literals. A *normal goal* is a program clause with no head and with a non-empty body.

Definition 2. Let $\Pi = \Pi_C \cup \Pi_B$ and $\Pi_C \cap \Pi_B = \emptyset$. A (Π_B, Σ)-constrained atom is an object of the form $c\Box p(\bar{X})$, where c is a (Π_C, Σ)-constraint and $p(\bar{X})$ is a (Π_B, Σ)-atom.

A *structure* $\Re(\Pi_C, \Sigma)$ over the alphabets Π_C and Σ, where Π_C contains the equality symbol consists of a non empty set $(D\Re)$ and any interpretation of each function and predicate symbol according to its arity. We do not make any assumption on Σ. Rather we require that the structure $\Re(\Pi_C, \Sigma)$ be a model of the standard theory CET, given in [9] to axiomatize unification. Moreover if the set of function symbols Σ is finite we assume the (weak) DCA be added to CET, thus achieving the completeness of the theory CET in the case of a language with finite set of function symbols. Informally the DCA [22] ensures that in the interpretation domain of any model of the theory every object is a value of a non-variable term (under some variable valuation). By $th(\Re)$ we denote the set of all the (Π_C, Σ)- constraints *true* in $\Re$. A $\Re(\Pi, \Sigma)$-valuation for a (Π, Σ)-expression is a mapping $\theta : V \to D\Re$. The notion of $\Re$-valuation is extended in the obvious way to terms and constraints. A negation of an equation $s = t$ (a *disequation* or *inequality*) will be written as $s \neq t$. If $\bar{t} = (t_1, \ldots, t_n)$ and $\bar{s} = (s_1, \ldots, s_n)$ are two sequences of terms, $\bar{t} = \bar{s}$ will be denote the set of equations $\{t_1 = s_1, \ldots, t_n = s_n\}$. A constraint c is $\Re$-satisfiable iff there exists a $\Re$-valuation θ such that $th(\Re) \models c\theta$. θ is called an $\Re$-solution of c. A constrained atom $c\Box p(\bar{X})$ is $\Re$-satisfiable iff c is $\Re$-satisfiable. The structures considered in *CLP* are the "solution compact" ones as defined in [16, 15]. In the following we will denote by P^* the completed definitions of the predicates in P.

3 Partial π-interpretations

We extend the notion of π-interpretation as introduced in [14] in order to provide three-valued models of the completion of a *CLP* program. First of all, a *partial* interpretation, as defined in [17] is any total function F from the set of all ground atoms into $\{\mathbf{t}, \mathbf{f}, \mathbf{u}\}$, where $\{\mathbf{t}, \mathbf{f}, \mathbf{u}\}$ are interpreted as *true*, *false* and *undefined.* According to our notation, we will represent such a function F as a pair $\langle F^+, F^- \rangle$, where $F^+ = \{p(\bar{t}) \mid F(p(\bar{t})) = \mathbf{t}\}$ and $F^- = \{p(\bar{t}) \mid F(p(\bar{t})) = \mathbf{f}\}$. The extension of a partial interpretation to ground constraints and to ground formulas is defined in [28], by the following rules.

- Let c be a ground constraint. c is true in F iff $th(\Re) \models c$ and c is false in F iff $th(\Re) \models \neg c$.
- We assume the usual strong three-valued interpretation of the symbols $\wedge, \vee, \neg$, $\forall, \exists, \rightarrow$, and following Kunen, we use Lukasiewicz's truth table for the connective $\leftrightarrow$. Moreover the symbols $\Box$ and "," will be interpreted as $\wedge$.

All the following definitions are related to a given $\Re$ (and thus to a given (Π, Σ)).

Definition 3. [16] The set of "domain instances" $[c\Box p(\bar{X})]$ of a constrained atom $c\Box p(\bar{X})$ is defined as $[c\Box p(\bar{X})] = \{p(\bar{X})\theta \mid \theta \textit{ is an } \Re\text{-solution of } c\}$. Let S be a set of constrained atoms. Then $[S] = \bigcup_{A \in S}[A]$.

Definition 4. Let $\mathcal{A}$ be the set of the constrained atoms for program P. We define a preorder $\sqsubseteq$ on $\mathcal{A}$ as $c_1\Box p(\bar{X}) \sqsubseteq c_2\Box p(\bar{X})$ iff $[c_1\Box p(\bar{X})] \subseteq [c_2\Box p(\bar{X})]$. The equivalence induced by $\sqsubseteq$ on the set of atoms is denoted by $\equiv$.
The relation on constraints $c_1 \equiv_{|\bar{X}} c_2$ is a notation for $c_1\Box p(\bar{X}) \equiv c_2\Box p(\bar{X})$, for any predicate symbol p.

Definition 5. *(π-base)* Let P be a (Π, Σ)-program and $\mathcal{A}$ be the set of all the $\Re(\Pi, \Sigma)$-satisfiable constrained atoms for P. The π-base of interpretations $\mathcal{B}$ is the quotient set of $\mathcal{A}$ w.r.t. the equivalence relation $\equiv$.

The ordering induced by $\sqsubseteq$ on $\mathcal{B}$ will still be denoted by $\sqsubseteq$. For the sake of simplicity A will represent the equivalence class of the constrained atom A.

Definition 6. *(partial π-interpretation)* A partial π-interpretation is a pair $I_p = \langle I_p^+, I_p^- \rangle$ such that

i) I_p^+ and I_p^- are subsets of $\mathcal{B}$ and

ii) $\forall c_1 \Box p(\bar{X}) \in I_p^+$ and $\forall c_2 \Box p(\bar{X}) \in I_p^-$ $[c_1 \Box p(\bar{X})] \cap [c_2 \Box p(\bar{X})] = \emptyset$.

The set of all the partial π-interpretations is denoted by $\mathcal{I}$.

Given a partial π-interpretation I_p we denote by I_p^+ (I_p^-) its first (second) component. Informally I_p^+ and I_p^- are sets of satisfiable constrained atoms, which are true or false in I_p, respectively. Condition **ii)** ensures the consistency of I_p. Given a partial π-interpretation I_p, we will denote by $[I_p]$ the *partial* interpretation $\langle [I_p^+], [I_p^-] \rangle$. Note that, given $S = \langle S_1, S_2 \rangle$, where S_i is a set of constrained atoms, $[S]$ is not a partial interpretation. In fact, if there exists a ground atom $p(\bar{t})$ such that $p(\bar{t}) \in [S_1] \cap [S_2]$, then $[S]$ cannot be viewed as a function from the set of all ground atoms into $\{\mathbf{t}, \mathbf{f}, \mathbf{u}\}$ (i.e. as a *partial* interpretation). Such a problem does not arise if we consider a partial π-interpretation. In fact the *consistency* condition of a partial π-interpretation ensures that, given a π-intepretation I_p, $[I_p^+] \cap [I_p^-] = \emptyset$.

Definition 7. *(π-truth)* Let P be a normal CLP program, I_p be a partial π-interpretation and S be a formula of P^*. S has π-truth value $\mathbf{v}$ in I_p iff S has truth value $\mathbf{v}$ in $[I_p]$.

4 Intensional negation in *CLP*

In this section we show how intensional negation is syntactically related to a specific decomposition of the program completion. This feature was originally proposed for normal programs parametric with respect to the assumption of the DCA. By abstracting the DCA, equality and inequality constraints are explicitely introduced in the clause bodies. These constraints are more adequately treated by considering CLP, which allows us to handle more general constraint systems. Moreover CLP provides a common framework in which to compare the intensional negation and constructive negation as defined by Stuckey. The generation of a positive program able to compute the logical consequence of P^* is achieved also in [24]. However, even in this case, the resulting program is a first order program (without negation) whereas our aim is to stick as much as possible to positive clauses.

Let P be a normal program, p be a predicate symbol and

$\{C_1 = p(\bar{X}) \leftarrow c_1 \Box \bar{B}_{1,1}, \bar{B}_{1,2} \quad \ldots\ldots \quad C_n = p(\bar{X}) \leftarrow c_n \Box \bar{B}_{n,1}, \bar{B}_{n,2}\}$

be the clauses defining p in P, where $\forall i = 1, \ldots, n$, $\bar{Y}_i = FV(C_i) \setminus \{\bar{X}\}$ (local variables of C_i), $\bar{B}_{i,1} = L_{i,1}, \ldots, L_{i,k_i}$, $\bar{B}_{i,2} = L'_{i,1}, \ldots, L'_{i,h_i}$, such that the $L_{i,j}$'s and the $L'_{i,j}$'s are literals and $FV(\bar{B}_{i,1}) \cap \bar{Y}_i = \emptyset$ (there are no local variable occurrences in the $\bar{B}_{i,1}$'s). Intensional negation can be understood in terms of P^*. The formula defining p in P^* is $p(\bar{X}) \leftrightarrow (\exists \bar{Y}_1.(c_1 \wedge \bar{B}_{1,1} \wedge \bar{B}_{1,2})) \vee \ldots \vee (\exists \bar{Y}_n.(c_n \wedge \bar{B}_{n,1} \wedge \bar{B}_{n,2}))$. Then we can derive $\neg p(\bar{X}) \leftrightarrow (\forall \bar{Y}_1.(\neg c_1 \vee \neg \bar{B}_{1,1} \vee \neg \bar{B}_{1,2})) \wedge \ldots \wedge (\forall \bar{Y}_n.(\neg c_n \vee \neg \bar{B}_{n,1} \vee \neg \bar{B}_{n,2}))$.

In order to obtain a set of clauses defining $\neg p$ we perform the following steps.

- Transformation of the right hand side of the equivalence in a disjunction ($F_1 \vee \ldots \vee F_k$). We have the following sequence of logically equivalent formulas: $\forall i = 1, \ldots, n,$
$\forall \bar{Y}_i.(\neg c_i \vee \neg \bar{B}_{i,1} \vee \neg \bar{B}_{i,2})$ $\equiv$ since $FV(\bar{B}_{i,1}) \cap \bar{Y}_i = \emptyset$
$\forall \bar{Y}_i.(\neg c_i \vee \neg \bar{B}_{i,2}) \vee \neg \bar{B}_{i,1}$ $\equiv$ since $\forall \bar{Y}_i.(\neg c_i \vee \neg \bar{B}_{i,2}) \equiv \forall \bar{Y}_i.(\neg c_i) \vee \forall \bar{Y}_i.(\neg c_i \vee \neg \bar{B}_{i,2})$
$\forall \bar{Y}_i.(\neg c_i) \vee \forall \bar{Y}_i.(\neg c_i \vee \neg \bar{B}_{i,2}) \vee \neg \bar{B}_{i,1}$ $\equiv$ by definition of $\bar{B}_{i,1}$
$\forall \bar{Y}_i.(\neg c_i) \vee \forall \bar{Y}_i.(\neg c_i \vee \neg L'_{i,1} \vee \ldots \vee \neg L'_{i,h_i}) \vee \neg L_{i,1} \vee \ldots \vee \neg L_{i,k_i}.$
Finally, if $L_{i,j}$ or $L'_{i,j}$ has the form $\neg A$, where A is an atom, then $\neg\neg A$ is simplified to A. The disjunction ($F_1 \vee \ldots \vee F_k$) is the disjunctive normal form of the conjunction of the simplification of those of the above formulas whose constraints are satisfiable.
- Renaming of the negative literals. For each predicate symbol q we introduce a new predicate symbol $q^\neg$. ($F'_1 \vee \ldots \vee F'_k$) is obtained by replacing each occurrence of a literal $\neg q(\bar{t})$ by $q^\neg(\bar{t})$ in ($F_1 \vee \ldots \vee F_k$). The symbol $\Box$ is a syntactic variant of conjunction, used to separate constraints out.
- Generation of the "positive clauses" for the new predicate symbols $p^\neg$.
$\{p^\neg(\bar{X}) \leftarrow F'_1, \ldots\ldots, p^\neg(\bar{X}) \leftarrow F'_k.\}$

Given a program P, we obtain a *transformed* program $P' = P^+ \cup P^-$, corresponding to P, where P^+ is obtained from P by replacing each occurrence of a literal $\neg q(\bar{t})$ by $q^\neg(\bar{t})$ and P^- is obtained from the completed definitions as described above. For each predicate symbol q not defined in P, $q^\neg$ is defined in P^- by the unique clause $q^\neg(\bar{X}) \leftarrow$. Note that we do not use the DCA.

Example 2. Let P be the following normal program

$$\left\{\begin{array}{l} p(X) \leftarrow true\Box\neg q(X,Y) \\ q(X,Y) \leftarrow X = a\Box\neg r(X,Y,Y) \\ q(X,Y) \leftarrow X \neq a\Box r(X,Y,Z) \\ r(X,Y,Z) \leftarrow Y = b\Box \end{array}\right\}$$

Then, the transformed program P' is

$$\left\{\begin{array}{ll} p(X) \leftarrow true\Box q^\neg(X,Y) & q^\neg(X,Y) \leftarrow X \neq a\Box\forall Z.(X = a \vee r^\neg(X,Y,Z)) \\ q(X,Y) \leftarrow X = a\Box r^\neg(X,Y,Y) & q^\neg(X,Y) \leftarrow X = a\Box r(X,Y,Y) \\ q(X,Y) \leftarrow X \neq a\Box r(X,Y,Z) & q^\neg(X,Y) \leftarrow true\Box\forall Z.(X = a \vee r^\neg(X,Y,Z)), \\ r(X,Y,Z) \leftarrow Y = b\Box & \qquad\qquad r(X,Y,Y) \\ p^\neg(X) \leftarrow true\Box\forall Y.q(X,Y) & r^\neg(X,Y,Z) \leftarrow Y \neq b\Box \end{array}\right\}$$

The clauses of P' can contain universally quantified disjunctions of literals in the body. Therefore we need a notion of complex goal, similar to the one introduced for constructive negation [28], and the derivation rule must be defined for complex goals. In addition to universally quantified disjunctions, since all the quantifiers need to be made explicit, complex goals contain also existentially quantified conjunctions.

Definition 8. A complex goal is:
- $p(\bar{t})$, for every predicate symbol p occurring in the transformed program.

- $\exists \bar{Z}.(c\Box B_1,\ldots,B_n)$ where $\bar{Z}$ is a (possibly empty) set of variables, c is a constraint and the B_i's are complex goals.
- $\forall \bar{Z}.(c \vee B_1 \vee \ldots \vee B_n)$, where $\bar{Z}$ is a (possibly empty) set of variables, c is a constraint and the B_i's are complex goals.

A goal G can be viewed as the (operationally equivalent) goal $(true\Box G)$. The following definitions give the syntax of ***transformed programs***, generated by intensional negation, and the corresponding sequential $SLD^{\forall}$-derivation. $G \overset{\forall}{\rightarrow}_{P'} G'$ denotes an $SLD^{\forall}$-derivation of the goal G' from G in the transformed program P', corresponding to P.

Definition 9. A transformed program clause has the form $H \leftarrow c\Box B_1,\ldots,B_n$, where H is an atom of the form $p(\bar{X})$ or $p^{\neg}(\bar{X})$, c is a constraint and each B_i is a complex goal, for $i = 1,\ldots,n$. A transformed program P' is a set of transformed program clauses.

Definition 10. *($SLD^{\forall}$-resolution step)* Let P' be a transformed program, G_k be a complex goal and R be a selection rule. G_{k+1} is derived from G_k in P' by R iff the following conditions hold.

1. if $G_k = p(\bar{t})$ then if there exists a renamed apart clause $C = p(\bar{X}) \leftarrow c\Box\bar{B} \in P'$, such that $\bar{Y} = FV(C)$ and $c' = \exists\bar{Y}.(c \wedge \bar{X} = \bar{t})$ is satisfiable then
   $G_{k+1} = (c'\Box)$ if $\bar{B}$ is empty, (i)
   $G_{k+1} = (c'\Box\exists\bar{Y}.(c \wedge \bar{X} = \bar{t}\Box\bar{B}))$ otherwise. (ii)
2. if $G_k = \exists\bar{Z}.(c_q\Box B_1,\ldots,B_j,\ldots,B_n)$ then let B_j be the goal selected by R in G_k and $(c'\Box\bar{B})$ be the goal derived in one $SLD^{\forall}$-resolution step from B_j. If $c_q \wedge c'$ is satisfiable then
   $G_{k+1} = \exists\bar{Z}.(c_q \wedge c'\Box B_1,\ldots,B_{j-1},\bar{B},B_{j+1},\ldots,B_n)$.
3. if $G_k = \forall\bar{Z}.(c_q \vee B_1 \vee \ldots \vee B_j \vee \ldots \vee B_n)$ then let B_j be the goal selected by R in G_k and $F = \{(c_1\Box\bar{B}_1),\ldots,(c_m\Box\bar{B}_m)\}$ be the set of all the subgoals obtained from B_j in one $SLD^{\forall}$-resolution step. If F is empty then
   $G_{k+1} = \forall\bar{Z}.(c_q \vee B_1 \vee \ldots \vee B_{j-1} \vee B_{j+1} \vee \ldots \vee B_n)$. (i)
   Otherwise let $I \subseteq \{1,\ldots,m\}$ such that $\forall r = 1,\ldots,m$, $r \in I$ iff $\bar{B}_r$ is not empty, $J = \{1,\ldots,m\} \setminus I$ and let $c' = \forall\bar{Z}.(c_q \vee \bigvee_{j\in J} c_j)$. Then, if c' is satisfiable,
   $G_{k+1} = (c'\Box)$, (ii)
   and if $\neg c'$ is satisfiable,
   $G_{k+1} = \forall\bar{Z}.((c_q \vee \bigvee_{j\in J} c_j) \vee B_1 \vee \ldots \vee B_{j-1} \vee \bigvee_{i\in I}(c_i\Box\bar{B}_i) \vee B_{j+1} \vee \ldots \vee B_n)$.

Some remarks about the above definition are in order. The G_{k+1} computed in 1.*ii* contains the constraint $c' = \exists\bar{Y}.(c \wedge \bar{X} = \bar{t})$. Such a choice is motivated by the fact that the final constraint computed by G_k is more specified than c'. Therefore c' allows us to prune those branches that would fail in conjunction with other goals. Note that the correctness of definition 1 derives from the equivalence $\exists\bar{X}.(c \wedge \bar{B}) \leftrightarrow \exists\bar{X}.(c) \wedge \exists\bar{X}.(c \wedge \bar{B})$. In case 3, in order to ensure the completeness we must extract as much constraint information as possible from the set of all the subgoals obtained from B_j. This is reflected in case 3.*ii*. In order to achieve this result we separate the constraints out by using the equivalence $\forall\bar{X}.(c \vee \bar{B}) \leftrightarrow \forall\bar{X}.(c) \vee \forall\bar{X}.(c \vee \bar{B})$.

Example 3. Let P be the normal program defining the function plus

$$P = \left\{ \begin{array}{l} plus(X,U,Z) \leftarrow U = 0 \wedge Z = X\Box \\ plus(X,U,Z) \leftarrow U = s(Y) \wedge Z = s(W)\Box plus(X,Y,W) \end{array} \right\}$$

P' is the union of P with the set of clauses defining $plus^{\neg}$.
$plus^{\neg}(X,U,Z) \leftarrow (U \neq 0 \vee Z \neq X) \wedge \forall Y,W.(U \neq s(Y) \vee Z \neq s(W))\Box$
$plus^{\neg}(X,U,Z) \leftarrow (U \neq 0 \vee Z \neq X)\Box\forall Y,W.((U \neq s(Y) \vee Z \neq s(W)) \vee plus^{\neg}(X,Y,W))$.
Given the goal $G = plus^{\neg}(s(0), s(0), Z)$, the $SLD^{\forall}$-derived goal is
$G_1 = c_0\Box\forall Y,W.(c_1 \vee \underline{plus^{\neg}(s(0),Y,W)})$,
where $c_1 = (s(0) \neq s(Y) \vee Z \neq s(W))$ and $c_0 = (s(0) \neq 0 \vee Z \neq s(0)) \equiv_{|Z} true$, and thus, it can be omitted.
By selecting the underlined goal we obtain two derived goals

- $G_2' = \forall Y,W.c'\Box$ where
  $c' = c_1 \vee ((Y \neq 0 \vee W \neq s(0)) \wedge \forall Y_1,W_1.(Y \neq s(Y_1) \vee W \neq s(W_1)))$ and
  $\forall Y,W.c' \equiv_{|Z}$
  $\forall Y,W,Y_1,W_1.((s(0) \neq s(Y) \vee Z \neq s(W)) \vee$
  $((Y \neq 0 \vee W \neq s(0)) \wedge (Y \neq s(Y_1) \vee W \neq s(W_1)))) \equiv_{|Z}$
  $\forall Y,W,Y_1,W_1.((Y \neq 0 \vee Z \neq s(W) \vee W \neq s(0) \vee Y \neq s(Y_1)) \wedge$
  $(Y \neq 0 \vee Z \neq s(W) \vee W \neq s(0) \vee W \neq s(W_1))) \equiv_{|Z}$
  $\forall Y,W,W_1.(true \wedge (Z \neq s(W) \vee W \neq s(0) \vee W \neq s(W_1))) \equiv_{|Z}$
  $Z \neq s(s(0))$.
- $G_2'' = \forall Y,W.(c' \vee Y \neq 0 \vee W \neq s(0)\Box$
  $\forall Y_1,W_1.((Y \neq s(Y_1) \vee W \neq s(W_1)) \vee plus^{\neg}(s(0),Y_1,W_1)))$.

Note that from G_2' we obtain the expected solution.

4.1 Top-down semantics

Given a normal program P and the corresponding transformed one P', we define the top-down semantics of P in such a way that it fully characterizes the computed answer constraints. We first introduce an intermediate semantics $\mathcal{O}'(P')$ for a transformed program P'. Since in P' we have atoms of the form $p^{\neg}(\bar{t})$ where $p^{\neg}$ is a new predicate symbol, we need to consider an extension of $\mathcal{B}$ (denoted by $\mathcal{B}^{\neg}$), by introducing the constrained atoms over such new predicates.

Definition 11. Let P' be a transformed program.

$$\mathcal{O}'(P') = \{c\Box p(\bar{X}) \in \mathcal{B}^{\neg} \mid true\Box p(\bar{X}) \overset{\forall}{\rightarrow}_{P'} c\Box \text{ and } \bar{X} \text{ are distinct variables}\}.$$

Definition 12. Let P be a normal program and P' be the corresponding transformed program. The top-down semantics of P is $\mathcal{O}^{\forall}(P) = \langle \mathcal{O}^{\forall}_{+}(P), \mathcal{O}^{\forall}_{-}(P)\rangle$, where $\mathcal{O}^{\forall}_{+}(P) = \{c\Box p(\bar{X}) \in \mathcal{B} \mid c\Box p(\bar{X}) \in \mathcal{O}'(P')\}$ and
$\mathcal{O}^{\forall}_{-}(P) = \{c\Box p(\bar{X}) \in \mathcal{B} \mid c\Box p^{\neg}(\bar{X}) \in \mathcal{O}'(P')\}$.

As shown in the following, this top-down semantics fully characterizes the computed answer constraints for normal goals.

Example 4. Let P be the normal program in example 2.
$\mathcal{O}^{\forall}_{+}(P)=\{X \neq a\Box p(X),\ \ X=a\Box p(X),\ \ Y=b\Box r(X,Y,Z),$
$X=a \wedge Y \neq b\Box q(X,Y),\ \ X \neq a \wedge Y = b\Box q(X,Y)\}$
$\mathcal{O}^{\forall}_{-}(P)=\{X \neq a \wedge Y \neq b\Box q(X,Y),\ X=a\wedge Y=b\Box q(X,Y),\ Y\neq b\Box r(X,Y,Z)\}.$

We can now define the equivalence $\simeq_{\forall}$ on programs induced by computed answers and we show that $\mathcal{O}^{\forall}(P)$ correctly captures answer constraints.

Definition 13. Let P_1, P_2 be normal programs, P_1', P_2' be the corresponding transformed programs, G be a normal goal and $\tilde{G}$ be the complex goal obtained by replacing each literal $\neg p(\bar{t})$ in G with $p^{\neg}(\bar{t})$. $P_1 \simeq_{\forall} P_2$ if for each normal goal G, $\tilde{G} \overset{\forall}{\rightarrow}_{P_1'} c_1\Box$ iff $\tilde{G} \overset{\forall}{\rightarrow}_{P_2'} c_2\Box$ and $c_1 \equiv_{|\bar{X}} c_2$ where $\bar{X} = FV(G)$.

Theorem 14. *Let P' be a transformed program and $G = (c_0\Box r_1(\bar{t}_1), \ldots, r_k(\bar{t}_k))$ be a complex goal. Then $G \overset{\forall}{\rightarrow}_{P'} c$ iff $\forall i = 1, \ldots, k$, there exists $c_i'\Box r_i(\bar{X}_i) \in \mathcal{O}'(P')$, renamed apart, such that $c' = (c_0 \wedge \bigwedge_{i=1,\ldots,k} c_i' \wedge \bigwedge_{i=1,\ldots,k} \bar{X}_i = \bar{t}_i)$ is satisfiable and $c \equiv_{|FV(G)} c'$.*

Corollary 15. *Let P_1 and P_2 be normal programs. $P_1 \simeq_{\forall} P_2$ iff $\mathcal{O}^{\forall}(P_1)=\mathcal{O}^{\forall}(P_2)$.*

We give a formal top-down semantics also for constructive negation. $G \overset{CN}{\rightarrow}_P G'$ denotes an $SLDCN$-derivation of the goal G' from G in the normal program P, as defined in [28, 29].

Definition 16. Let P be a normal program. The top-down semantics of P is denoted by $\mathcal{O}^{CN}(P) = \langle \mathcal{O}^{CN}_{+}(P), \mathcal{O}^{CN}_{-}(P)\rangle$, where

$$\mathcal{O}^{CN}_{+}(P) = \{c\Box p(\bar{X}) \mid true\Box p(\bar{X}) \overset{CN}{\rightarrow}_P c\Box \text{ and } \bar{X} \text{ are distinct variables}\},$$
$$\mathcal{O}^{CN}_{-}(P) = \{c\Box p(\bar{X}) \mid true\Box\neg p(\bar{X}) \overset{CN}{\rightarrow}_P c\Box \text{ and } \bar{X} \text{ are distinct variables}\}.$$

Results similar to those proved for intensional negation on the observational equivalence and on the correctness wrt answer constraints are valid for constructive negation as well [6].

Example 5. Let P be the normal program defined in example 2
$\mathcal{O}^{CN}_{+}(P) = \{X \neq a\Box p(X),\ \ \ X = a\Box p(X),\ \ \ Y = b\Box r(X,Y,Z),$
$X = a \wedge Y \neq b\Box q(X,Y),\ \ \ X \neq a \wedge Y = b\Box q(X,Y)\}$
$\mathcal{O}^{CN}_{-}(P) = \{X \neq a \wedge Y \neq b\Box q(X,Y),\ \ \ X = a \wedge Y = b\Box q(X,Y),$
$(X \neq a \wedge Y \neq b) \vee (X = a \wedge Y = b)\Box q(X,Y),\ \ \ Y \neq b\Box r(X,Y,Z)\}$

Note that the denotations $\mathcal{O}^{\forall}(P)$ and $\mathcal{O}^{CN}(P)$ for the program in example 2 are quite similar, even if not identical. This issue will be discussed later.

4.2 Bottom-up semantics

We define the bottom-up semantics of P by introducing an immediate consequence operator $T_{P'}$ for the corresponding transformed program P'.

The definition of $T_{P'}$ is based on an *unfolding* operator $Unf_C(I)$, where C is a clause and $I \subseteq \mathcal{B}^{\neg}$. In turn such an operator is based on $\Gamma_G(I)$, which denotes the unfolding of a goal G wrt $I \subseteq \mathcal{B}^{\neg}$.

Definition 17. Let G be a complex goal and let $I \subseteq \mathcal{B}^{\neg}$. The unfolding of G wrt I, $\Gamma_G(I)$, is defined as follows.

- $G = p(\bar{t})$ (or $G = p^{\neg}(\bar{t})$).
  $\Gamma_G(I) = \{c \mid$ there exists $c'\Box p(\bar{X}) \in I$, renamed apart, $\bar{Z} = FV(c'\Box p(\bar{X}))$, $c = \exists\bar{Z}.(c' \wedge (\bar{X} = \bar{t}))$, c is satisfiable$\}$.
- $G = \exists\bar{Z}.(c_q \Box B_1, \ldots, B_n)$.
  $\Gamma_G(I) = \{c \mid \forall i = 1, \ldots, n,$ there exists $c_i \in \Gamma_{B_i}(I), c = \exists\bar{Z}.(c_q \wedge \bigwedge_{i=1,\ldots,n} c_i)$, c is satisfiable$\}$.
- $G = \forall\bar{Z}.(c_q \vee B_1 \vee \ldots \vee B_n)$.
  $\Gamma_G(I) = \{c \mid \forall i = 1, \ldots, n, J_i$ finite subset of $\Gamma_{B_i}(I)$, $c_i = \bigvee_{d \in J_i} d$, $c = \forall\bar{Z}.(c_q \vee \bigvee_{i=1,\ldots,n} c_i)$, c is satisfiable$\}$.

Definition 18. Let $C = p(\bar{X}) \leftarrow c_0 \Box L_1, \ldots, L_k$ be a transformed clause and let $I \subseteq \mathcal{B}^{\neg}$. The unfolding of C wrt I, $Unf_C(I)$ is defined as follows
$$Unf_C(I) = \{\exists\bar{Z}.c\Box p(\bar{X}) \mid c \in \Gamma_{(c_0 \Box L_1, \ldots, L_k)}(I),\ \bar{Z} = FV(C) \setminus \bar{X}\}$$
The unfolding of a set of transformed clauses Q wrt I is $Unf_Q(I) = \bigcup_{C \in Q} Unf_C(I)$.

Definition 19. Let P' be a transformed program and $I \subseteq \mathcal{B}^{\neg}$. $T_{P'}(I) = Unf_{P'}(I)$.

In the following, given a partial π-interpretation I_p, we denote by
$$\widehat{I_p} = I_p^+ \cup \{c\Box p^{\neg}(\bar{X}) \mid c\Box p(\bar{X}) \in I_p^-\} \in \wp(\mathcal{B}^{\neg}).$$
We define the immediate consequence transformation associated to a normal program P as follows.

Definition 20. Let P be a normal program, P' be the associated transformed one and I_p be a partial π-interpretation. Then
$$T_P^{\forall}(I_p) = \langle\{c\Box p(\bar{X}) \mid c\Box p(\bar{X}) \in T_{P'}(\widehat{I_p})\}, \{c\Box p(\bar{X}) \mid c\Box p^{\neg}(\bar{X}) \in T_{P'}(\widehat{I_p})\}\rangle.$$

The following proposition shows that $T_P^{\forall}$ is well defined, i.e. given a partial π-interpretation I_p, $T_P^{\forall}(I_p)$ is a partial π-interpretation too. In other words the result of the application of the operator $T_P^{\forall}$ to a partial π-interpretation is a pair $\langle J_p^+, J_p^-\rangle$ which satisfies the consistency condition of a partial π-interpretation (i.e. $[J_p^+] \cap [J_p^-] = \emptyset$).

Proposition 21. *Let P be a normal program and let I_p be a partial π-interpretation. Then $T_P^{\forall}(I_p)$ is a partial π-interpretation.*

Corollary 22. *Let P be a normal program. Then $T_P^{\forall} \uparrow \omega$ is a partial π-interpretation.*

In what follows, we show that $T_P^{\forall}$ is continuous wrt $\mathcal{I}$ ordered by set inclusion on the components of the pairs. First we introduce the partial order relation $\subseteq_3$ on the set of partial π-interpretations $\mathcal{I}$.

Definition 23. Let I_p, $J_p \in \mathcal{I}$. $I_p \subseteq_3 J_p$ iff $\widehat{I_p} \subseteq \widehat{J_p}$.

The relation $\subseteq_3$ is an ordering on $\mathcal{I}$. Given $S \subseteq_3 \mathcal{I}$ there exists $glb(S) = \langle \bigcap_{I_p \in S} I_p^+, \bigcap_{I_p \in S} I_p^- \rangle \in \mathcal{I}$. The bottom element of $(\mathcal{I}, \subseteq_3)$ is the partial π-interpretation $\langle \emptyset, \emptyset \rangle$. Note that, given two partial π-interpretations I and J, $lub\{I, J\}$ does not necessarily exist. This holds for the consistency condition of partial π-interpretations. For example let us consider $I = \langle \{X = a\Box p(X)\}, \emptyset \rangle$ and $J = \langle \emptyset, \{X = a\Box p(X)\} \rangle$. An upper bound $U = \langle U^+, U^- \rangle$ of $\{I, J\}$ must be such that $\langle \{X = a\Box p(X)\}, \{X = a\Box p(X)\} \rangle \subseteq_3 U$. Therefore $[U^+] \cap [U^-] \neq \emptyset$. However every chain in $(\mathcal{I}, \subseteq_3)$ has a least upper bound in $\mathcal{I}$ obtained by componentwise union of the elements in the chain. Therefore $(\mathcal{I}, \subseteq_3)$ is a complete semi-lattice.

Proposition 24. *Let P be a normal program. $T_P^{\forall}$ is continuous in $(\mathcal{I}, \subseteq_3)$.*

The fixpoint semantics of normal programs is the following.

Definition 25. Let P be a normal program. $\mathcal{F}^{\forall}(P) = lfp(T_P^{\forall}) = T_P^{\forall} \uparrow \omega$.

By corollary 22 it follows that $\mathcal{F}^{\forall}(P)$ is a partial π-interpretation.

4.3 Relations between the top-down and the bottom-up semantics

We give some results which relate top-down and bottom-up semantics. In particular we prove that, given a normal program P, $\mathcal{O}^{\forall}(P) \subseteq_3 \mathcal{F}^{\forall}(P)$ and $\mathcal{F}^{\forall}(P) \leq_3 \mathcal{O}^{\forall}(P)$, where the ordering $\leq_3$ is defined below. The equality $\mathcal{O}^{\forall}(P) = \mathcal{F}^{\forall}(P)$ does not hold. Therefore the functional semantics does not characterize the operational behavior of the program wrt answer constraints. However the equality $[\mathcal{O}^{\forall}(P)] = [\mathcal{F}^{\forall}(P)]$ holds.

Proposition 26. *Let P be a normal program. $\mathcal{O}^{\forall}(P) \subseteq_3 \mathcal{F}^{\forall}(P)$.*

A corollary of proposition 26 is that $\mathcal{O}^{\forall}(P)$ is a partial π-interpretation. In order to better reflect the properties of partial π-interpretations, we introduce a new preorder $\leq$ on sets in $\wp(\mathcal{B}^{\neg})$, and we generalize it to partial π-interpretations providing the new preorder $\leq_3$.

Definition 27. Let $I_1, I_2 \in \wp(\mathcal{B}^{\neg})$, $I_p, J_p \in \mathcal{I}$.
$I_1 \leq I_2$ iff $\forall A_1 \in I_1\ \exists A_2 \in I_2$ such that $A_1 \sqsubseteq A_2$ and $I_p \leq_3 J_p$ iff $\widehat{I}_p \leq \widehat{J}_p$.

Corollary 28. *Let P be a normal program. $\mathcal{F}^{\forall}(P) \leq_3 \mathcal{O}^{\forall}(P)$.*

From corollary 28 and proposition 26, the ground instances of the operationally derived constrained atoms are exactly the ones obtained by using the bottom-up technique. Note that in the case of a goal $G = \forall \bar{Z}.(c_q \vee B_1 \vee \ldots \vee B_k)$, the behavior of the top-down rule differs from the one of $T_{P'}$, since in the first one choice only of the computed constraints for $(B_1 \vee \ldots \vee B_k)$ is allowed while in the latter the possible choices are all the subsets of computed constraints for those subgoals. A different definition for $T_{P'}$, reflecting exactly the operational behavior, would lead to an operator non-monotonic wrt $(\mathcal{I}, \subseteq_3)$.

Theorem 29. *Let P be a normal program. $[\mathcal{F}^{\forall}(P)] = [\mathcal{O}^{\forall}(P)]$.*

5 Correctness and completeness

In this section we show that $[\mathcal{O}^{\forall}(P)] = [\mathcal{F}^{\forall}(P)] = \Phi_P \uparrow \omega$, where Φ_P is Fitting's operator described in [12] and extended to constraint logic programs in [13]. The proof is based on the analysis of the relation between $[\mathcal{F}^{\forall}(P)]$ and Φ_P. In such a way a completeness and correctness result is inherited by intensional negation. Given a complex goal G, we denote by $\breve{G}$ the formula obtained from G by replacing each occurrence of an atom of the form $p^{\neg}(\bar{t})$ by $\neg p(\bar{t})$. Moreover, given a normal goal G, we denote by $\tilde{G}$ the complex goal obtained from G by replacing each occurrence of a literal of the form $\neg p(\bar{t})$ by $p^{\neg}(\bar{t})$.

Proposition 30. *Let P be a normal program and I_p be a finite partial π-interpretation. Then $[T_P^{\forall}(I_p)] = \Phi_P([I_p])$.*

We now show that $T_P^{\forall} \uparrow n$ has the same ground information as $\Phi_P \uparrow n$, for finite n. The equivalence holds since for each finite n, $T_P^{\forall} \uparrow n$ is a finite partial π-interpretation.

Proposition 31. *Let P be a normal program. $\forall n \geq 0$, $[T_P^{\forall} \uparrow n] = \Phi_P \uparrow n$ and $[\mathcal{O}^{\forall}(P)] = [\mathcal{F}^{\forall}(P)] = \Phi_P \uparrow \omega$.*

Using our terminology, theorem 6 of [27] (which is a generalization of theorem 6.3 in [17] for languages other than those with infinitely many function symbols of all arities) can be stated for CLP as follows. The notation $th(\Re) \wedge P^* \models_3 S$ shows that the sentence S is a *three-valued* logical consequence of the theory $th(\Re) \wedge P^*$.

Theorem 32. (correctness and completeness of Φ_P)*[27] Let P be a normal program over the structure $\Re$ and let S be a sentence. Then the following are equivalent:* 1) $th(\Re) \wedge P^* \models_3 S$; 2) *$S$ has truth value* $\mathbf{t}$ *in $\Phi_P \uparrow n$, for a finite n.*

Corollary 33. (correctness and completeness of $T_P^{\forall}$) *Let P be a normal program over the structure $\Re$ and let S be a sentence. $th(\Re) \wedge P^* \models_3 S$ iff S has π-truth value* $\mathbf{t}$ *in $T_P^{\forall} \uparrow n$ for a finite n.*

The following theorems show the correctness and the completeness of $SLD^{\forall}$-resolution with respect to the 3-valued logical consequences of $th(\Re) \wedge P^*$. Similar theorems were proved for constructive negation in [29]. Our proofs are strongly based on properties of $\mathcal{F}^{\forall}(P)$. $\forall F$ denotes the universal closure of F.

Theorem 34. (correctness) *Let P be a normal program over the structure $\Re$, P' be the corresponding transformed program and $G = (c_0 \square B_1, \ldots, B_k)$ be a normal goal. If $\tilde{G} \overset{\forall}{\rightarrow}_{P'} c\square$ then $th(\Re) \wedge P^* \models_3 \forall(c \rightarrow B_1 \wedge \ldots \wedge B_k)$.*

Proposition 35. *Let P be a normal program over $\Re$ and F be a formula such that $th(\Re) \wedge P^* \models_3 \forall F$. Then there exists a finite partial π-interpretation $J \subseteq_3 \mathcal{F}^{\forall}(P)$ such that $\forall F$ has truth value* $\mathbf{t}$ *in $[J]$.*

Theorem 36. (completeness) *Let P be a normal program over the structure $\Re$, P' be the corresponding transformed program and $G = (c_0 \Box B_1, \ldots, B_k)$ be a normal goal, such that c_0 is satisfiable.*
If $th(\Re) \wedge P^* \models_3 \forall(c_0 \rightarrow B_1 \wedge \ldots \wedge B_k)$ then there exists a finite number of derivations $\tilde{G} \overset{\forall}{\rightarrow}_{P'} c_i\Box$, $i = 1, \ldots, r$, such that $th(\Re) \models \forall(c_0 \leftrightarrow c_1 \vee \ldots \vee c_r)$.

6 Comparisons

In general there is not an injective correspondence between the $SLD^{\forall}$-tree and the $SLDCN$-tree of a given goal G. In fact, one $SLDCN$-derivation might compute an answer which is equivalent to the answer computed by a subtree of the corresponding $SLD^{\forall}$-tree.

Example 6. Let P be the normal program $P = \{q(X) \leftarrow \neg p(X),\ p(X) \leftarrow X = a\Box,$ $p(X) \leftarrow X = b\Box\}$. The associated program is $P' = \{q(X) \leftarrow p^{\neg}(X),\ q^{\neg}(X) \leftarrow p(X),$ $p(X) \leftarrow X = a\Box,\ p(X) \leftarrow X = b\Box,\ p^{\neg}(X) \leftarrow X \neq a \wedge X \neq b\Box\}$.
Intensional negation computes for the goal $q^{\neg}(X)$ two distinct answer constraints $c_1 = \{X = a\}$ and $c_2 = \{X = b\}$. On the other hand constructive negation for the goal $\neg q(X)$ computes the only answer constraint $c = \{X = a \vee X = b\}$ s.t. $th(\Re) \models c \rightarrow c_1 \vee c_2$.

Obviously in intensional negation $\neg(\neg(p(X))$ is operationally equivalent to $p(X)$, differently from constructive negation. As a consequence, in presence of nested negation, constructive negation might compute an answer more general than the one computed by intensional negation.

This means that we can only state the logical equivalence between complete answers (i.e. disjunctions of leaves) in the $SLDCN$ and $SLD^{\forall}$ trees, as shown by the following theorem. Informally the correspondence between $\mathcal{O}^{CN}(P)$ and $\mathcal{O}^{\forall}(P)$ holds since the set of all derived goals computed from $p(\bar{X})$ (and $\neg p(\bar{X})$), in the $SLDCN$ and in the $SLD^{\forall}$ derivations is logically equivalent to (the negation of) the right hand side of the completed definition of p in P^*.

Theorem 37. *Let P be a normal program over the structure $\Re$. For any constrained atom $c\Box p(\bar{X}) \in \mathcal{O}^{CN}_{+}(P)$ ($c\Box p(\bar{X}) \in \mathcal{O}^{CN}_{-}(P)$) there exists a finite number of constrained atoms $c_i\Box p(\bar{X}) \in \mathcal{O}^{\forall}_{+}(P)$, $i = 1, \ldots, n$, ($c_i\Box p(\bar{X}) \in \mathcal{O}^{\forall}_{-}(P)$, $i = 1, \ldots, n$), s.t. $th(\Re) \models \forall(c \rightarrow \bigvee_{i=1,\ldots,n} c_i)$ and vice versa.*

The differences between $\mathcal{F}^{\forall}(P)$ and $\mathcal{O}^{\forall}(P)$ and between $\mathcal{O}^{\forall}(P)$ and $\mathcal{O}^{CN}(P)$ (examples 4 and 5, theorem 37) are related to the fact that $SLD^{\forall}$-resolution, $SLDCN$-resolution and the computation rule embedded in $T^{\forall}_{P}$ do arbitrarily partition into separate paths, by using different strategies, what would be the computation of one disjunctive answer constraint. We can easily realize that, if we choose the frontier at depth one, also constructive negation is simply an implementation of computing with the completion.

A few more remarks on the relation between constructive and intensional negation are in order. The two techniques can easily be compared from the performance viewpoint, if we choose the frontier at depth one in constructive negation. Intensional negation has a much better performance in handling the nesting of negation, which occurs whenever we consider a negative call to a procedure which has a negation in the body. In fact, constructive negation delivers a partial answer to the initial goal only after the evaluation of its complex normal subgoals, while intensional negation is able to incrementally provide an answer after one derivation step. Constructive negation can lead to more efficient derivations by choosing a deeper frontier. However the same result can be obtained in intensional negation by a preliminary unfolding on the clauses of P. Note also that, if p is defined in P by clauses that do not contain local variables, $p^{\neg}$ in P' is defined by standard definite clauses only. In such a case, negation can therefore be fully processed at compile time.

References

1. K. R. Apt. Introduction to Logic Programming. In J. van Leeuwen, editor, *Handbook of Theoretical Computer Science*, volume B: Formal Models and Semantics, pages 495–574. Elsevier, Amsterdam and The MIT Press, Cambridge, 1990.
2. K. R. Apt and M.H. van Emden. Contributions to the theory of logic programming. *Journal of the ACM*, 29(3):841–862, 1982.
3. R. Barbuti, P. Mancarella, D. Pedreschi, and F. Turini. Intensional Negation of Logic Programs: Examples and Implementation Techniques. In H. Ehrig, R. Kowalski, G. Levi, and U. Montanari, editors, *TAPSOFT '87*, volume 250 of *Lecture Notes in Computer Science*, pages 96–110. Springer-Verlag, Berlin, 1987.
4. R. Barbuti, P.Mancarella, D. Pedreschi, and F. Turini. A transformational approach to negation in logic programming. *Journal of Logic Programming*, 8:201–228, 1990.
5. A. Bottoni and G. Levi. The inverse of Fitting's functional. In *Proc. of the 3rd Kurt Goedel Colloquium on Computational Logic and Proof Theory*, Lecture Notes in Computer Science. Springer-Verlag, Berlin, 1993. To appear.
6. P. Bruscoli, F. Levi, G. Levi, and M. C. Meo. Intensional negation in Constraint Logic Programs. Technical Report 11/93, Dipartimento di Informatica, Università di Pisa, 1993.
7. D. Chan. Constructive Negation Based on the Completed Database. In R. A. Kowalski and K. A. Bowen, editors, *Proc. Fifth Int'l Conf. on Logic Programming*, pages 111–125. The MIT Press, Cambridge, Mass., 1988.
8. D. Chan. An Extension of Constructive Negation and its Application in Coroutining. In E. Lusk and R. Overbeek, editors, *Proc. North American Conf. on Logic Programming'89*, pages 477–493. The MIT Press, Cambridge, Mass., 1989.
9. K. L. Clark. Negation as Failure. In H. Gallaire and J. Minker, editors, *Logic and Data Bases*, pages 293–322. Plenum Press, New York, 1978.
10. W. Drabent. SLS-resolution without floundering. In L. M. Pereira and A. Nerode, editors, *Logic Programming and Non-monotonic Reasoning, Proceedings of the Second International Workshop*, pages 82–98. The MIT Press, Cambridge, Mass., 1993.
11. W. Drabent. What is Failure? An Approach to Constructive Negation. *Acta Informatica*, 1993. To appear.

12. M. Fitting. A Kripke-Kleene semantics for logic programs. *Journal of Logic Programming*, 2:295–312, 1985.
13. M. Fitting and M. Ben-Jacob. Stratified and Three-valued Logic Programming Semantics. In R. A. Kowalski and K. A. Bowen, editors, *Proc. Fifth Int'l Conf. on Logic Programming*, pages 1054–1069. The MIT Press, Cambridge, Mass., 1988.
14. M. Gabbrielli and G. Levi. Modeling Answer Constraints in Constraint Logic Programs. In K. Furukawa, editor, *Proc. Eighth Int'l Conf. on Logic Programming*, pages 238- 252. The MIT Press, Cambridge, Mass., 1991.
15. J. Jaffar and J.-L. Lassez. Constraint Logic Programming. In *Proc. Fourteenth Annual ACM Symp. on Principles of Programming Languages*, pages 111–119. ACM, 1987.
16. J. Jaffar and J.-L. Lassez. Constraint Logic Programming. Technical report, Department of Computer Science, Monash University, June 1986.
17. K. Kunen. Negation in logic programming. *Journal of Logic Programming*, 4:289–308, 1987.
18. F. Levi. Negazione e quantificazione universale in programmazione logica. Master's thesis, Dipartimento di Informatica, Università di Pisa, 1991. in italian.
19. F. Levi, P. Mancarella, and D. Pedreschi. Negazione Costruttiva e Quantificazione Universale in Programmazione Logica con Vincoli. In S. Costantini, editor, *Proc. Seventh Italian Conference on Logic Programming*, pages 273–287, 1992.
20. J. W. Lloyd. *Foundations of Logic Programming*. Springer-Verlag, Berlin, 1987. Second edition.
21. J. Maluszyński and T. Näslund. Fail Substitutions for Negation as Failure. In E. Lusk and R. Overbeek, editors, *Proc. North American Conf. on Logic Programming'89*, pages 461–476. The MIT Press, Cambridge, Mass., 1989.
22. P. Mancarella, S. Martini, and D. Pedreschi. Complete Logic Programs with Domain Closure Axiom. *Journal of Logic Programming*, 5(3):263–276, 1988.
23. P. Mancarella, D. Pedreschi, M. Rondinelli, and M. Tagliatti. Algebraic Properties of a Class of Logic Programs. In S. K. Debray and M. Hermenegildo, editors, *Proc. North American Conf. on Logic Programming'90*, pages 23–39. The MIT Press, Cambridge, Mass., 1990.
24. T. Sato. Equivalence-preserving first-order unfold/fold transformation systems. *Theoretical Computer Science*, 105:57–84, 1992.
25. T. Sato and F. Motoyoshi. A Complete Top-down Interpreter for First Order Programs. In V. Saraswat and K.Ueda, editors, *Proc. 1991 Int'l Symposium on Logic Programming*, pages 35–53, 1991.
26. T. Sato and H. Tamaki. Transformational Logic Programs Synthesis. In *Proceedings of the International Conference of Fifth Generation Computer Systems, 1984*, pages 195–201, 1984.
27. J. C. Shepherdson. Language and equality theory in logic programming. Technical Report PM-91-02, School of Mathematics, University of Bristol, 1991.
28. P. J. Stuckey. Constructive Negation for Constraint Logic Programming. In *Proc. Sixth IEEE Symp. on Logic In Computer Science*, pages 328–339. IEEE Computer Society Press, 1991.
29. P. J. Stuckey. Constructive Negation for Constraint Logic Programming. Technical report, Department of Computer Science, University of Melbourne, 1991.
30. M. H. van Emden and R. A. Kowalski. The semantics of predicate logic as a programming language. *Journal of the ACM*, 23(4):733–742, 1976.

A New Linear Algorithm for Modular Decomposition

Alain Cournier and Michel Habib

LIRMM, 161, Rue Ada, 34392 Montpellier cedex 5 France
email: {cournier, habib}@lirmm.fr

Abstract. We present here a new algorithm linear in time and space complexity for Modular Decomposition. This algorithm relies on structural properties of prime graphs (see theorems 7, and 8), on properties of modules (see property 1 and corollary 1) but also on the cograph recognition algorithm [CPS85]. Our algorithm builds and explores the decomposition tree of any undirected graph in a depth-first search way. As a by-product we show that a vertex-splitting operation is really a central tool for modular decomposition algorithms.

Keywords : Graphs, autonomous subsets, modules, clans, substitution, graph decomposition trees, prime graphs, cographs, vertex-splitting. cotrees.

1 Introduction

Modular decomposition definition is quite natural for discrete structures and has been discovered and studied in many areas (graphs, 2-structures, hypergraphs, categories, boolean functions, matroids, ...) under various names such as substitution [MR84], ordinal sum [Sab59] and X-join [Sum71]. It has both theoretical and practical applications. Möhring and Radermacher [MR84] give an excellent survey of the various aplications of this decomposition. Modules that subsets of vertices which allow when contracted to a single vertex modular graph decompositions have also been called autonomus sets [MR84], clans [ER90b], closed sets [Gal67], committees [Sha68], externally related subsets [HM79], intervals [Ill91], partitive sets [Gol80], and even "parties homogènes" by some french authors [MC78]. We present here a general linear decomposition framework for various notions of modular (or substitution) decomposition. Since the first published algorithms by Cowan, James and Stanton [CJS72], Habib and Maurer [HM79], Möhring [Möh85, Möh89] an impressive amount of research has been done in the last few years about algorithmic aspects of substitution decomposition. In particular Muller and Spinrad [MS89] and McConnell [McC92] proposed $O(n^2)$ algorithms, Spinrad $O(n+m\alpha(m,n))$ [Spi92], Cournier and Habib $O(n+m\log n)$ [CH93a] and finally McConnell and Spinrad can get rid of the α function and propose a linear algorithm [MS93]. Efficient decomposition algorithms can be shared into two classes. The first one is made up with the so called "incremental" algorithms. They process by updating an already constructed decomposition tree, when a new vertex x is added. Roughly speaking this insertion operation can be described as follows: while the neighbourhood of x is visited, its neighbours are marked in the decomposition tree, and using syntactic rules the new tree is constructed. The famous linear cograph recognition algorithm from Corneil, Perl and Stewart [CPS85] (denoted by *CPS-algorithm* in the following), but also Muller and Spinrad's incremental algorithm [MS89], are in this class. For the algorithms of the second class, the main idea is to increase in a stepwise manner the size of a prime subgraph found in the original graph. This approach relies on the structure of prime graphs, and uses some vertex-splitting operation. Cournier and Habib's [CH93a] algorithm belongs to this class. Spinrad's algorithm [Spi92] with its P_4-tree structure originated this class of algorithms. In this paper we present a new linear algorithm which uses both paradigms. It maintains both a collection of prime subgraphs and a collection of local cotrees decomposition. When a vertex x is considered, first a vertex-spliting with x is achieved, and then x is introduced in its local cotree. Theoretically, modular decomposition has been used to obtain fastest known algorithms ($O(n^2)$) for transitive orientation, recognition of permutation graphs or comparability graphs [Spi85]. Furthermore, we believe that linear decomposition algorithms would help to further improve some of these algorithms up to optimality (i.e. linear time). Similarly such a linear substitution decomposition algorithm with reasonable overhead allows now substitution decomposition to be used practically in real life applications as a preprocessing for many optimization problems. For example substitution decomposition has been recently used for drawing nicely acyclic graphs on a screen [MCGW93], or to decompose inheritance graphs in Object Oriented Programming [HHS90]. Moreover the algorithm presented here can easily be generalized to some other decompositions, namely: substitution of directed graphs, 2-structures, and some other slight variations on the graph substitution decomposition.

All graphs considered here are finite, simple (without multiple edges), loopless and undirected. We use the notation $G = (X, E)$ to represent such a graph, X being its vertices set and $E \subseteq X^2$ its edges set, with $n = \mid X \mid$ and $m = \mid E \mid$. For each $x \in X$, we denote the *neighbourhood* of x by $N(x) = \{y \in X/(x,y) \in E\}$. For any $Y \subseteq X$ we denote by G_Y the subgraph induced by Y. For each set $Y \subseteq X$, Y is a *module* (or *autonomous set* or *clan*) if and only if $\forall(x,z) \in Y^2, N(x) - Y = N(z) - Y$ (i.e. x and z have identical neighbourhoods out of Y). $Y \subseteq X$ is a *trivial module* if and only if $\mid Y \mid = 0$, $\mid Y \mid = 1$ or $\mid Y \mid = \mid X \mid$. G is a *prime graph* if it only contains trivial modules. A subset Y of X induces a *maximal prime subgraph* if and only if, G_Y is a prime subgraph, and $\forall Z, Y \subseteq Z \subseteq X$, G_Z is a prime subgraph, yields $Z = Y$. Graphs with 1 or 2 vertices are trivially prime, but one can notice that ANY graphs with 3 vertices are decomposable.

Definition 1 *A module M is a strong module or a strongly autonomous set [Kel85] if and only if for any module M', one of the following statements holds:* $M \cap M' = \emptyset, \quad M \subseteq M', \quad M' \subseteq M$

Definition 2 *Let W and A be two subsets of X, A is a W-module if and only if A is a module of the subgraph $G_{W \cup A}$.*

It is well known (Chein, Habib and Maurer [CHM81], Möhring and Radermacher

[MR84], or Ille [Ill91]) that modules have some algebraic properties:

Property 1 *Let A and B be two modules of $G = (X, E)$ then:*
1. $A \cap B$ is a module. 2. If $B \not\subseteq A$ then $A - B$ is a module.
3. If $A \cap B \neq \emptyset$ then $A \cup B$ is a module.
4. If $Y \subseteq X$ then $A \cap Y$ is a module of G_Y.

Corollary 1 *Let X_1, X_2 and M be subsets of X. If M is a module of the two subgraphs $G_{X_1 \cup M}$ and $G_{X_2 \cup M}$, then M is a module of the subgraph $G_{X_1 \cup X_2 \cup M}$.*

There are two particular cases of substitution decomposition. Unless G is connected, the *parallel decomposition* divides G into its connected components. Unless $\overline{G}$ is connected, the *serial decomposition* divides G into the connected components of $\overline{G}$. Therefore if G is a prime with more than 2 vertices, it admits neither parallel decomposition nor serial decomposition.

Theorem 1 (Decomposition theorem, [Hab81, HM79, Sum71]) *Let G be an undirected graph with at least two vertices then one and only one of the three following statements holds:*

1. *G is disconnected, and it can be decomposed into its connected components (Parallel decomposition).*
2. *$\overline{G}$ is disconnected, and G can be decomposed into the connected components of $\overline{G}$ (Serial decomposition).*
3. *There exists $Y \subseteq X$, and a unique partition P such that:*
   (a) $|Y| > 3$.
   (b) G_Y is a maximal prime subgraph of G.
   (c) $\forall S \in P$, S is a module and $|S \cap Y| = 1$.

Using recursively Theorem 1, one can associate to any undirected graph its decomposition tree. Only three kinds of nodes are needed, namely: *Parallel* nodes, also called 0 nodes, associated with *Parallel decomposition. Serial* nodes, also called 1 nodes, associated with *Serial decomposition.* And, *Prime* nodes, associated with the last case of theorem 1. Prime nodes correspond to maximal prime subgraphs of the graph G. Each leaf of the tree correspond to a unique vertex of the graph. Therefore to each vertex x of the tree, corresponds a module M(x) made up with the vertices associated to the leaves of the subtree rooted in x. It should be noticed that those modules M(x) are exactly the strong modules of G. In the following we only consider prime graphs with strictly more than 2 vertices. $P4$ (graph described by Fig. 1) is the smallest non-trivial prime graph.

Property 2 ([Sum71]) *Let G be a prime undirected graph, there exists four vertices a, b, c, d such that $G_{\{a,b,c,d\}}$ is a P_4 (see Fig. 1).*

A *cotree* is a substitution decomposition tree which only contains *Parallel* and *Serial* nodes. A graph is called a *cograph* if and only if its decomposition tree is a cotree. Using property 2 and theorem 1 G is a cograph if and only if it has no induced $P4$ (i.e. a subgraph isomorphic to a $P4$). The *Parallel* and *Serial* nodes are easy to find, since they correspond to connected components of some subgraph of G or $\overline{G}$. So one would expect an $O(n^2)$ algorithm to recognize cographs, but Corneil *et al* [CPS85] found a linear (thus optimal) algorithm that recognizes cographs and produces a decomposition tree.

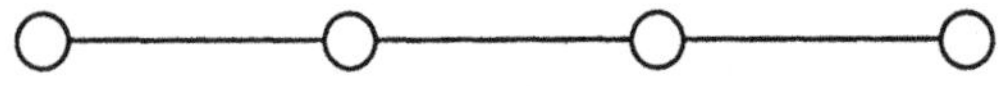

Fig. 1. The first non-trivial prime graph: P_4.

So, here is a first informal version of a recursive decomposition algorithm:
Algorithm DecomposeDraft

data : G : a graph; **result:** T : a decomposition tree;
processing:
if *G is a cograph* **then** $T \leftarrow$ *the cotree obtained via CPS-algorithm*;
else
Let $abcd$ be any P_4 in G.
Find a maximal prime subgraph G_Y containing $abcd$.
Find its associated partition P.
for each $S \in P$ **do** *DecomposeDraft* (G_S); **endfor**;
create the final tree T.
endif
End algorithm.

MAIN INVARIANT: each node of the constructed tree corresponds to a strong module of G.

Such an algorithm would be nice, but as far as we know, the search in linear time of a maximal prime subgraph and its associated partition is far from obvious. Therefore in the following sections incremental algorithms that begin with a P_4 and end up with a maximal prime subgraph will be presented.

2 Prime graphs and partitions of vertices

Using definition 2, and a prime graph G_Y we will try to amalgamate vertices of G into *Y-modules* as big as possible. To achieve this objective, we put together vertices of X sharing the same neighbourhood in Y. But we can also put together a vertex y in Y and a vertex x in X if x and y share the same neighbourhood in $Y - \{y\}$ ($\{x, y\}$ is an Y-module). This is the aim of the following definition.

Definition 3 ([CH93a]) *Let $Y \subseteq X$ such that G_Y is a prime subgraph. $\forall (x, z) \in X$, xR_Yz if and only if one of the two following statements holds:*

1. $N(x) \cap Y = N(z) \cap Y$
2. $(N(x) \Delta N(z)) \cap Y = \{y\}$ *and*
$N(x) \cap (Y - \{y\}) = N(z) \cap (Y - \{y\}) = N(y) \cap Y$.

R_Y is an equivalence relation. It yields a partition of the vertices of G. We will denote by $EC(R_Y)$ this partition. The classes of $EC(R_Y)$ can be divided into the four following sets: $YEquivalent = \{C \in EC(R_Y) / \mid C \cap Y \mid = 1\}$;
$YSerial = \{C \in EC(R_Y)/\forall c \in C,\ N(c) \cap Y = Y\} = \{C_s\}$;
$YParallel = \{C \in EC(R_Y)/\forall c \in C,\ N(c) \cap Y = \emptyset\} = \{C_p\}$;
$YExtension = EC(R_Y) - (YEquivalent \cup YSerial \cup YParallel)$.

In the following, each time a partition $EC(R_Y)$ is used, the induced subgraph G_Y of G is supposed to be prime.

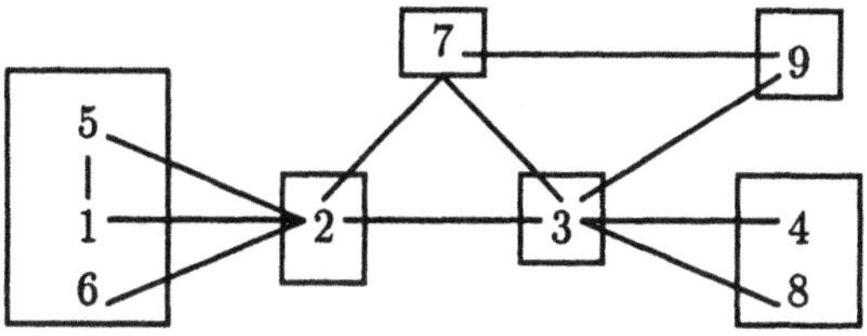

Fig. 2. A graph and the partition induced by the prime subgraph $G_{\{1,2,3,4,7\}}$.

Theorem 2 (**[CH93a]**) *Let G be an undirected graph, G_Y be a prime subgraph of G, $EC(R_Y)$ be its associated partition and M be a module of G then one of the two following statements holds: 1. $\exists C \in EC(R_Y)$ such that $M \subseteq C$.*
2. Each class C of $YExtension$ and $YEquivalent$ is a subset of M.

Therefore such a partition can be understood as an approximation of the module decomposition, with respect to the prime subgraph G_Y.

Property 3 *Each class of $EC(R_Y)$ is a strong Y-module.*

Definition 4 (**[CH93a]**) *Let C be an equivalence class of $EC(R_Y)$. We associate to C a vertex $r(C)$, in the following way: If $C \in YEquivalent$ then $r(C)$ is the vertex in $C \cap Y$; If $C \in YExtension$ then $r(C)$ is any vertex of C.*

Property 4 (**[CH93a]**) *Let G be a graph, G_Y be a prime subgraph of G, and $EC(R_Y)$ be the associated partition. If C is a class of YExtension then $G_{Y\cup\{r(C)\}}$ is also a prime subgraph of G. If C is a class of YEquivalent then either C is a module of G or there exists $x \in C$ and $z \in X - C$ such that $G_{Y\cup\{x,z\}}$ is also a prime subgraph of G.*

3 Vertex-splitting as a central tool

Most of the algorithms for modular decomposition and related decompositions deal with a partition of the vertices into subsets and process by updating it while traversing the graph. The basic operation called *splitting* or *vertex-splitting* , is made with a simple scan of the neighbourhood of a given vertex. This search may

split some sets of vertices into pieces, if some violation of the module definition is found. We will use this split operation to refine partitions (which are associated to some prime subgraph G_Y and are approximations of the decomposition), until we reach a maximal decomposition into modules. The decomposition tree being obtained recursively. More precisely, we define in the following section a split operation, which associates to each vertex x (called the *splitter*) and each set of vertices C, a partition of C denoted by *split*(x, C).
Let C be a subset of X and x be a vertex of $X - C$. If $M \subset C$ is a module of G, it necessarily must be included in one of the two following sets: $C_1 = C \cap N(x)$ or $C_2 = C - N(x)$. Suppose now that C is a class of *YEquivalent*, it contains a distinguishable vertex called $r(C)$. Only one of these two new sets C_1 and C_2 can contain $r(C)$. Let K be the other set, if M is a module included in K, it must necessarily be included in one of the two following sets: $K_1 = K \cap N(r(C))$ or $K_2 = K - N(r(C))$. All these facts are used in the following definition:

Definition 5 ([CH93a, Cou93]) *Let C be a class of $EC(R_Y)$ and x be a vertex of G. We will associate to this couple (x, C), a partition of C (denoted $Split(x, C)$) containing at most three subsets of C, in the following way:*

If $x \in C$ then $Split(x, C) = \{C\}$.
If $x \in C_p \cup C_s$ then $Split(x, C_p) = \{C_p\}$, $Split(x, C_s) = \{C_s\}$.
If $x \notin C_p \cup C_s$ then
- $Split(x, C_p) = \{C_p \cap N(x),\ C_p - N(x)\}$
- $Split(x, C_s) = \{C_s \cap N(x),\ C_s - N(x)\}$.

If $x \notin C$ and $C \in YExtension$ then $Split(x, C) = \{C \cap N(x),\ C - N(x)\}$.
If $x \notin C$ and $C \in YEquivalent$ then
- *If $r(C) \in N(x)$ then*
  $Split(x, C) = \{C \cap N(x), (C - N(x)) \cap N(r(C)), (C - N(x)) - N(r(C))\}$.
- *If $r(C) \notin N(x)$ then*
  $Split(x, C) = \{C - N(x), (C \cap N(x)) \cap N(r(C)), (C \cap N(x)) - N(r(C))\}$.

Property 5 *Let C be a class of $EC(R_Y)$ and x be vertex of $X - C$. If $Split(x, C) = \{C_1, C_2, C_3\}$ (some of these sets may be empty), then for any subset S of C_1 (respectively of C_2 or C_3), $Split(x, S) = \{S\}$.*

Proof: Every C_i is an $\{x\}$-module of G, and the split operation just consider the behavior C_i of with respect to $N(x)$, which insures the desired property.□
The previous definition can be enlarged to the whole partition $EC(R_Y)$:

Definition 6 ([CH93a]) $SPLIT(x, EC(R_Y)) = \bigcup_{C \in EC(R_Y)} Split(x, C)$

From this definition we immediately have the consequence:

Property 6 *Let M be a module of G, included in some class C of $EC(R_Y)$, then for every x in X, M is included in some element of $SPLIT(x, EC(R_Y))$.*

Therefore with respect to the decomposition into modules, for every x in X, $P = SPLIT(x, EC(R_Y))$ is a better approximation than $EC(R_Y))$. In fact

every element of P is an $\{x\}$-module of G, and thus $SPLIT(x, P) = P$. Furthermore if G_Y and $G_{Y\cup\{z\}}$ are prime subgraphs of G then $EC(R_{Y\cup\{z\}}) = SPLIT(z, EC(R_Y))$. Although it may be possible that :
$SPLIT(x, SPLIT(y, P)) \neq SPLIT(y, SPLIT(x, P))$ it is always true that for every x and y,
$SPLIT(x, SPLIT(y, SPLIT(x, P))) = SPLIT(y, SPLIT(x, SPLIT(y, P)))$.
Therefore such a sequence of three SPLITS will be denoted by: $SPLIT(\{x, y\}, P)$, and x, y a pair of splitters.
Let us state more formally these properties of the SPLIT operation, which show that updating the partition $EC(R_Y)$ can be done via this operation.

Theorem 3 ([CH93a, Cou93]) *Let G_Y be a prime subgraph of G and $EC(R_Y)$ be its associated partition. Then one of the three following mutually exclusive statements holds:*

1. *There exists $\{z\}$ such that $G_{Y\cup\{z\}}$ is also a prime graph of G then: $EC(R_{Y\cup\{z\}}) = SPLIT(z, EC(R_Y))$.*
2. *YExtension is empty and there exists $\{z, t\}$ such that $G_{Y\cup\{z,t\}}$ is a prime graph of G then: $EC(R_{Y\cup\{z,t\}}) = SPLIT(\{z, t\}, EC(R_Y))$*
3. *G_Y is a maximal prime subgraph of G.*

Theorem 4 ([CH93a, Cou93]) *Let G_Y be a prime subgraph of G and $EC(R_Y)$ be its associated partition. If YExtension is empty and C is a class of YEquivalent the three following statements are equivalent:*
1. C is a module of G.
2. For each vertex $c \in C$, $SPLIT(c, EC(R_Y)) = EC(R_Y)$.
3. For each vertex $x \in X - C$, $Split(x, C) = \{C\}$.

Corollary 2 ([CH93a, Cou93]) *Let G_Y be a prime subgraph of G and $EC(R_Y)$ be its associated partition. The two following statements are equivalent:*
1. G_Y is a maximal prime subgraph of G.
2. YExtension is empty and each class C of YEquivalent is a module.

Corollary 3 *Let G_Y be a maximal prime subgraph and $EC(R_Y)$ be its associated partition, the union of all YEquivalent classes is a strong module of G.*

Theorems 3 and 4 also yield some known structural results on prime graphs, which are nice generalisations of property 2.

Corollary 4 ([Ill90, ST91, CH93a, ER90a]) *Let G be a prime undirected graph, and $Y \subset X$ such that G_Y is a prime subgraph of G then at least one of the two following statements holds:*
1. $\exists x \in (X - Y)/G_{Y\cup\{x\}}$ is prime.
2. $\exists x, y \in (X - Y)/G_{Y\cup\{x,y\}}$ is prime.

So, we can extend a prime subgraph G_Y fo G in a stepwise manner by adding vertices, one by one until *Y-Extension* is empty and then by choosing a class C in *YEquivalent* and testing if C is a module of G. In the cases where C is not a module of G, we know that there exists two vertices that can be added to Y, keeping its primality. This is the basis of the following algorithm.

Algorithm Decompose1

data : G : a graph; cot : a cotree; **result:** T : a tree;
variable : P : a partition of the vertices;
processing:
if G *is a cograph* **then** $T \leftarrow$ *The cotree of* G
else
  Let *abcd* be a P_4; $P \leftarrow PrimeMax(abcd, G)$
  create a prime node PN labeled with this prime graph.
  for each $C \in YModule$ **do**
    compute cot_C and G_C; $T' \leftarrow Decompose1(cot_C, G_C)$
    put T' as a child of PN
  endfor
  $T \leftarrow Decompose1(cot_{C_p \cup C_s \cup \{y\}}, G_{C_p \cup C_s \cup \{y\}})$
  replace in T the leave y by the tree PN.
endif
End algorithm.

Procedure PrimeMax

{This procedure looks for a maximal prime subgraph of G containing the given $P4$}
data : P4 : a set of 4 vertices inducing a P_4 in G; G : graph;
result : P : a partition of the vertices;
processing:
let a, b, c, d be a P_4; *initpartition*(P_4, P);
while $YExtension \neq \emptyset$ **do** *IncreaseY*(P); **endwhile**
while $\neg Stop(P)$ **do** *FindModule*(P); **endwhile**
End procedure.

Procedure FindModule

{This procedure computes if a class C is a module. If C is not a module it computes the maximal modules included in C.}
data/result : P : a partition of the vertices ;
variable : Continue : boolean; copy : list of vertices;
processing:
Continue $\leftarrow$ *false*; "Choose a class C"; *copy* $\leftarrow$ *a copy of* C;
for each $x \in copy$ **do**
  $P \leftarrow SPLIT(x, P)$; {**label : A**}
  while $YExtension \neq \emptyset$ **do** *Continue* $\leftarrow$ *true*; IncreaseY(P); **Endwhile**
endfor
if *Continue* **then**
  let P' be the new partition of *copy*
  $P \leftarrow P - P'$; FindModule (P'); $P \leftarrow P \cup P'$
else
  if $C \in YEquivalent$ **then** Put C in $YModule$; **endif**
endif
End procedure.

Procedure IncreaseY

{This procedure introduces a new vertex in Y and computes the new associated partition}
data/result : P : a partition;
processing:
Remove C from *YExtension*; Take x in C;
$SPLIT(x, P)$; Insert C in *YEquivalent*
End procedure.

The above algorithm also uses a function Stop, not detailed here, but which simply returns true if *YExtension* is empty and if for every class C in *YEquivalent*, C is a module.

Before proving the algorithm we need an extra technical lemma to handle the particular cases of *YParallel* and *YSeries* classes, respectively denoted by S and P in the following lemma. Let G_Y be a maximal prime subgraph and A be the union of all classes in *YEquivalent.*

Lemma 1 *If M is a module of $G_{S \cup P \cup \{y\}}$ with $y \in Y$ then either $y \notin M$ and M is a module of G or $y \in M$ and $M \cup A$ is a module of G.*

So the decomposition tree of G, can be obtained from that of $G_{S \cup P \cup \{y\}}$, by replacing the leaf y, by a tree having a prime node labeled with Y as a root, the sons of which are the decomposition trees of the G_C's where C is a class of YEquivalent.

Theorem 5 *The algorithm Decompose1 computes the decomposition tree of any undirected graph.*

Proof: If G is a cograph, the result comes from CPS-algorithm. Else the algorithm manages a partition of the vertices P. At each step i of the algorithm, let us denote by P_i the partition, and by Y_i the set $\{y | y$ is a distinguished vertex in some class of $P_i\}$. Therefore we can state the basic property of the algorithm.
MAIN INVARIANT: each class C of P_i is a strong Y_i-module of G.
A class C is introduced during the algorithm as a module in the tree decomposition of G, only if it satisfies the property $\forall x \in C$, $SPLIT(x, P_i) = P_i$, and therefore is a module of G. Since any module of G is a Y-module of G for any $Y \subseteq X$, our main invariant shows us that we have not missed any intermediate module and so the modules inserted in the decomposition tree are strong modules of G. Furthermore the special treatment done during the algorithm to YParallel and YSeries classes can be easily justified by the above lemma 1.□

4 Complexity issues

As a consequence one can notice that the SPLIT operation play a crucial role, since we can build a decomposition algorithm based on it. Therefore we will need an efficient way to implement it, see proposition 7.

4.1 Split implementation

Property 7 *For every x in X, $SPLIT(x, EC(R_Y))$ can be computed in $O(|N(x)|)$ elementary operations from G and $EC(R_Y)$.*

Proof: (See [CH93a, Cou93, CH93b])□

4.2 Initial Partition

Property 8 *From any P_4 on four vertices a, b, c, d in G the initial partition, denoted by $EC(P_4)$, can be computed in $O(|N(a)| + |N(b)| + |N(c)| + |N(d)|)$ elementary operations.*

Proof: (See [CH93a, Cou93, CH93b])□
Therefore we can assume that the cost of the function initpartition is linear in the size of the neighbourhood of the considered P_4.

4.3 CPS-algorithm revisited

In fact we precisely need a variation of the CPS-algorithm, i.e. an incremental algorithm which processes by inserting a new vertex x in an already existing cotree T associated to a subgraph G_V. Either $G_{V \cup \{x\}}$ is a cograph, then the vertex x is inserted in the cotree or the algorithm produces a P_4. In both cases, the treatment of this new vertex x has be done in $O(|N(x)|)$ elementary operations. Such a modification of CPS-Algorithm is possible and is left to the reader, but also can be found in [Cou93].

4.4 Complexity of Decompose1

Theorem 6 *The algorithm Decompose1 requires $O(n + m \log n)$ elementary operations to build the modular decomposition tree of any undirected graph.*

Proof: (See [CH93a, Cou93, CH93b])□
But for such an algorithm, in some examples the neighbourhood of a given vertex can be visited $\Omega(\log n)$ times, in order to avoid this, we propose the following method in which neighbourhoods of vertices are visited at most three times.

Corollary 5 ([CH93a]) *Let G be a prime graph. From any prime subgraph G_Y there exists an algorithm which produces in $O(n + m \log n)$ time complexity a finite series of subgraphs G_{Y_i} such that:*
1. $G_{Y_0} = G_Y$.
2. $\forall i$ G_{Y_i} is a subgraph of $G_{Y_{i+1}}$ (i.e. $Y_i \subset Y_{i+1}$) and $|Y_{i+1}| \leq |Y_i| + 2$.

Corollary 6 *For any prime graph G, there exists an ordering of the vertices x_1, ..., x_n such that, x_1, x_2, x_3, x_4 is a P_4, and there exists a sequence of partitions of the vertices: $Q_4 = EC(P_4)$, for every $i \geq 4$: $Q_i = SPLIT(x_i, Q_{i-1})$ or $Q_i = SPLIT(\{x_{i-1}, x_i\}, Q_{i-1})$. Furthermore, the final partition of the sequence Q_f is the partition made up with singletons.*

Hence, if one could *guess* this ordering on the vertices, using proposition 7 this would imply a linear time algorithm to recognize prime graphs.

5 Towards a linear algorithm

In order to avoid an unbounded number of splits for a given vertex, our second algorithm when managing a partition of the vertices yielded by a prime graph, will also search recursively for P_4 included in some class. In this approach each class is associated to some cotree, and during the test if a class C is a module of G, a vertex $x \in C$ is first splitted and then inserted in some cotree. Therefore some P_4 may be found inside a class, and a the partition is now a tree (called *partition-tree*) in which a new level is created. Therefore the next presented algorithm has the two following simple invariants:

Invariant 1 *The sets corresponding to the leaves of the partition-tree partition the vertices of G. To each leaf of the partition-tree is associated a cotree.*

Let us suppose that we find a prime subgraph G_Z such that $Z \subset C$ and for all z in Z $SPLIT(z, EC(R_Y)) = EC(R_Y)$. We can compute a new partition $EC(R_Z)$ and one can notice that each class $K \neq C$ in $EC(R_Y)$ is included in a class of *ZParallel* or *ZSerial*. So we just need to remember the partition of C induced by the vertices of Z and therefore in the following $EC(R_Z)$ will denote the partition of C induced by the prime subgraph G_Z. These two partitions must satisfy theorem 2, since G_Y and G_Z are two prime subgraphs of G.

Let us suppose that there exists a vertex x in a class of *ZEquivalent* or *ZExtension* and a class W in $EC(R_Y)$ such that $Split(x, W) \neq W$, it yields that there exists w in W such that:
1. $G_{Y \cup \{x,w\}}$ is a prime subgraph of G.
2. $G_{Z \cup \{x,w\}}$ is a prime subgraph of G.
But we can also claim that the graph $G_{(Y-\{r(C)\}) \cup Z \cup \{x,w\}}$ is also a prime subgraph of G. This is the result introduced in theorem 7 (proof in [CH93b]).

Theorem 7 *Let G be a graph, G_Y be a prime subgraph of G, $EC(R_Y)$ be its associated partition such that YExtension is empty and C be a class of YEquivalent. Let $Z \subset C$ such that:*
1. G_Z is a prime subgraph of G.
2 $\forall z \in Z$, $SPLIT(z, EC(R_Y)) = EC(R_Y)$.
We will denote $EC(R_Z)$ its associated partition. Let x be a vertex of a class of ZEquivalent or ZExtension and W a class of $EC(R_Y)$ such that $Split(x, W) \neq W$. Then there exists w in W such that $G_{(Y-\{r(C)\}) \cup Z \cup \{x,w\}}$ is a prime subgraph.

Considering the associated partitions we have (proof in [CH93b]):

Theorem 8 *Let G be a graph, G_Y a prime subgraph of G, $EC(R_Y)$ the associated partition such that YExtension is empty and C be a class of YEquivalent. Let $Z \subset C$ such that:*

- *G_Z is a prime subgraph of G.*
- *$\forall z \in Z$, $SPLIT(z, EC(R_Y)) = EC(R_Y)$.*
- *$EC(R_Z)$ is the partition of C induced by G_Z.*

Let x be a vertex of a class of ZEquivalent or ZExtension and W a class of $EC(R_Y)$ such that $Split(x, W) \neq W$. Then there exists $w \in W$ such that $Q = Z \cup (Y - \{r(C)\}) \cup \{x, w\}$ induce a prime subgraph of G_Y and we can compute $EC(R_Q)$ in the following way first we compute a partition D.
DSerial = YSerial; DParallel = YParallel;
DEquivalent = (YEquivalent - $\{C\}$) $\cup$ ZEquivalent
DExtension = ZExtension $\cup$ ZParallel $\cup$ ZSerial then
$EC(R_Q) = SPLIT(\{x, w\}, D))$.

When in the algorithm some case described in the above theorems will be found, we have a *collapsing rule* to apply in the partition-tree between the levels of Z and Y. Such a collapsing will be very easy to handle since the algorithm will examine the classes in a depth-first way, and then a collapse can be done in $O(1)$ between two consecutive levels of the partition-tree. Moreover, when a collapse is executed, a vertex of Y is replaced by at least four vertices of Z (at least a P_4), with their corresponding edges. Therefore the total number of collapses in the algorithm will be bounded by m.

6 Managing the Cotrees

The algorithm uses cotrees to find P_4's in the graph G. But it seems too costly to maintain a bijection between classes and cotrees, since each time a class is splitted we would have to split its cotree. Therefore when a P_4 is found and the associated partition is calculated, some of the classes of this partition do not contain any element of the cotree. So a cotree is created for each such a class. The algorithm manages all these cotrees and keeps a link from a class to its cotree. So, it uses these cotrees to generate P_4, and to verify modules properties.

6.1 Insert a vertex in a cotree

As we take a class C in $YExtension$, either there exists a vertex v of C previously introduced in the associated cotree, and then we can use this vertex for the $SPLIT$ operation or there is no such a vertices and we can create a cotree for the class C. But if we take a class C in $YEquivalent$ ($YExtension = \emptyset$), we will try to choose in this class a vertex v and we insert it in the associated cotree. If we cannot introduce v in the cotree, we obtain a P_4.
1. $P4 \subseteq C$: we can compute a new partition of C using this P_4.
2. The $P4$ meets two classes: Let K be the other class, then v Splits K into at least 2 classes and there exists v' in K which splits C into at least 2 classes.
3. The $P4$ meets three classes. Since $r(C)$ does not create a $P4$ with the other vertices of the $P4$, v splits one of these classes.
4. The $P4$ meets four classes. Since $r(C)$ does not create a $P4$ with the other vertices of the $P4$, v splits one of these classes.
Therefore in all cases, when a P_4 is found it allows to refine some class in the current partition. This is the option we have taken in the algorithm, let us

describe it. When a vextex $v \in C$ is chosen, first we compute $SPLIT(v, P)$, where P represent the current partition, and if no split is detected, *then* we try to insert v in the cotree of C. So the cases 3 and 4 described above are not possible. In the case 1, we just create a new level in the partition-tree and study this level (following the depth first idea). It only remains to consider the case 2. In this case we just execute $SPLIT(v', P)$, and we know that v can be choosen as the distinguished vertex of his new class. Therefore the only P_4's considered explicitely by the algorithm are those totally included in the current class.

6.2 Finding a Module in a cotree

Since the algorithm process by splitting a class while it contains a P_4, necessarily a step is reached where classes yield subgraphs of G which are cographs. Let us consider how these modules can be spread a cotree. Let G be a cograph and T the associated cotree. M is a module of G yields:

- $\exists N \in T$ such that N is the lowest ancestor of M in the cotree.
- For each son f of N, either the subtree rooted by f does not contain any element of M or f contains only elements of M.

Let C be a class of *YEquivalent* such that each vertices of C are in a cotree *cot*. Therefore, the subgraph G_C is a cograph. So one can notice that if $I \subseteq C$ is a module of G then it must be a module of the subgraph G_C. Now it remains to find those modules of G included in a cograph. In this section we will denote by L_{cot} the set of vertices described by the cotree *cot*, if N is a node of a cotree, then L_N will denote the set of vertices described by the subcotree rooted by N. We assume that C is a class of *YEquivalent* associated with a cotree *cot* such that $C \subseteq L_{cot}$. Using corollary 1 one can notice that if $M \subseteq C$ is a module of the subgraphs G_C and $G_{(X-C)\cup M}$, then M is a module of the whole graph G. But if $M \subseteq C$ is a module of the subgraph G_C and M is not a module of G then necessarily there is no module of G between M and C (see property 1). Modules of G ina cograph described by its cotree can be found using syntactic rules as in the CPS-algorithm based on SPLIT (explanation can be found in [CH93b]).

7 Description of the Algorithm

7.1 The Main Algorithm

1. Initialize data structures:
   - Cotrees are empty
   - Create a level 0 partition, containing a single set X.
   - Create an empty Stack Aliases.
2. Call the BuildTree Operation.
3. Create the final tree.

7.2 The BuildTree operation

This operation called for each level i of the partition creates the decomposition tree of each class in YEquivalent at this level. Any time the partition of level i disapears its associated BuildTree operation also disappears. To achieve this object, we take any class C of YEquivalent (at level i). So we take any vertex c of C-cot and compute SPLIT(x, P) and insert x in the appropriate cotree, until SPLIT(x, P) $\neq$ P or we find a P4 in C or C-cot is empty. In the first case (SPLIT(x, P) $\neq$ P) either we apply theorems 7 and 8 and the partition of level i and there is no more partition of level i, or we clean out YExtension, then we choose a new class in YEquivalent. In the third case G_C is a cograph, then we verify module property on C, and choose another class. In the second cases, we can build a new partition at a level i+1, then we clean out YExtension at the level i+1 and then if the partition of C still exists at level i+1 we call recursively BuildTree. At the end of this recursive operation, either the answer in tree associated with a subset of C, and we can compress all this subset to a single vertex x (since this subset is a module of G) or the partition of C go out from the level i+1. In the first subcase we just introduce in the partition at level i a new class (x, YSerial$_{i+1}$, YParallel$_{i+1}$). In the second subcase we choose a new class C and follows the depth first search. At the end of this loops if the partition at level i still exists, we can build the modular decomposition tree rooted by the prime node labeled with the prime subgraph Y_i.

8 A draft version of the algorithm

Algorithm Decompose2

processing:
init data structures; $T \leftarrow$ *BuildTree*; GraftTree
End algorithm.

Algorithm BuildTree

processing:
BeginLevel $\leftarrow$ The deepest level of the partition;
while *YEquivalent at BeginLevel not empty* **do**
  Choose such a class C; $P4 \leftarrow LookForP4(C)$
  if *a partition at level BeginLevel+1 occurs* **then**
    {*i.e.* We find a P4 in C and it creates a new partition}
    ClearOutYExtension
    if *partition at level BeginLevel+1 still exists* **then**
      $T' \leftarrow$ *BuildTree*; **endif**
    if *partition at level BeginLevel+1 still exists* **then**
      {We found a maximal prime subgraph and its partition}
      Create a new vertex x
      x will replace in G all the vertices in T'
      Introduce in YEquivalent at level BeginLevel new class: (x, C_s^{i+1}, C_p^{i+1});
        Delete partition at level BeginLevel+1; **endif**
  else

{either partition at BeginLevel goes out or YExtension at BeginLevel is not empty or each vertex of C is in a cotree}
if *partition at BeginLevel still exists* **then**
if *YExtension not empty* **then** ClearOutYExtension
else
if *BeginLevel* = 0 **then** return the cotree of C
else VerifyModule (C)
endif
endif; ClearOutYExtension
endwhile
End algorithm.

The function ClearOutYExtension not detailed here simply ...

Theorem 9 *The algorithm Decompose2 produces the decomposition tree of any undirected graph.*

Proof: We build and explore the tree in a depth-first search way. This algorithm is a variation of decompose1, and the differences has been explained and proved in previous properties. *INVARIANT*: Each leaf of the partition-tree is a strong Y-module of G, where Y is the set of the distinguished vertices of the classes of the current partition (made up with the leaves of the partition-tree).□

9 Complexity of the algorithm

Theorem 10 *The algorithm decompose2 builds in linear time the decomposition tree of any undirected graphs.*

Proof: First we notice that using our CPS-revisited algorithm, the overall complexity needed by inserted a vertex in a cotree of finding a P_4 and its associated partition is linear in the neighbourhood of the considered vertices. Secondly as we have seen previoulsy there are at most $O(m)$ time required for collapsing the levels during the algorithm. When a vertex-splitting operation effectively splits the current partition, then this splitter enters in some prime graphs, and its neighbourhood will never be considered again. The overall complexity of these operations is bounded by $O(n+m)$. Let us now consider the bad case, some vertex $x \in C$ for which $SPLIT(x, P) = P$ splitter. The first case to consider is when C is a cograph, then x will be splitted again once the find the modules in C. Now suppose that C is not a cograph, therefore G_C contains a P_4 which yields a new partition Q of C . Either x is a distinguished element in some class of Q and then another split operation could be done for x, or x just belongs to some class and then x will not be used as a splitter again (**because it already is inserted in a cotree**) until its class is a cograph. Therefore in the worst case, a vertex is used as a bad splitter, (those that do not refine the the current partition), at most three times. This gives the linearity of the algorithm. □

10 Conclusions

This algorithm can be generalized to directed graphs, we only need a linear algorithm for directed cographs recognition (which can be achieved see Cournier [Cou93]), and the list of the samllest prime graphs (in the directed case, there exist prime graphs having 3 vertices). Then all the techniques developped above may be adapted, taking into account the direction of the edges (for example in the SPLIT operation), and the linearity of the algorithm is preserved. Similar work can be done for 2-structures, which can be seen as a genreralization of substitution decomposition for labeled graphs. Furthermore, an implementation in C++ programmed by C. Capelle is now available, and some details of the data structures involved can be found in [CH93b].

The authors wish to thank Bruno Courcelle, Hervé Dicky, Dieter Kratsch, Rolf Möhring, Stephan Olariu, Jerry Spinrad, Ross McConnel, and many others for stimulating and fruitful discussions on graph decompositions.

References

[CH93a] A. Cournier and M. Habib. An efficient algorithm to recognize prime undirected graphs. In E. W. Mayr, editor, *Lectures notes in Computer Science, 657.Graph-Theoretic Concepts in Computer Science. 18th International Workshop, WG'92. Wiesbaden-Naurod, Germany, June 1992. Proceding*, pages 212–224. Springer-Verlag, 1993.

[CH93b] A. Cournier and M. Habib. A new linear algorithm for modular decomposition. Raport de recherche, LIRMM, 161, Rue Ada, 34392 Montpellier Cedex 5, 1993.

[CHM81] M. Chein, M. Habib, and M. C. Maurer. Partitive hypergraphs. *Discrete Mathematics*, (37):35–50, 1981.

[CJS72] D. D. Cowan, L. O. James, and R. G. Stanton. Graph decomposition for undirected graphs. In R. B. Levow eds. F. Hoffman, editor, *3rd S-E Conf. Combinatorics, Graph Theory and computing, Utilitas Math*, pages 281–290, Winnipeg, 1972.

[Cou93] A. Cournier. *Sur Quelques Algorithmes de Décomposition de Graphes.* PhD thesis, Université Montpellier II, 161 rue Ada, 34392 Montpellier Cedex 5, France, février 1993.

[CPS85] D. G. Corneil, Y. Perl, and L. K. Stewart. A linear recognition algorithm for cographs. *SIAM journal of computing*, (14):926–934, november 1985.

[ER90a] A. Ehrenfeucht and G. Rozenberg. Primitivity is hereditary for 2-structures (fundamental study). *Theoretical Comp. Sci.*, 3(70):343–358, 1990.

[ER90b] A. Ehrenfeucht and G. Rozenberg. Theory of 2-structures, part i: clans, basic subclasses and morphisms (fundamental study). *Theoretical Comp. Sci.*, 3(70):277–303, 1990.

[Gal67] T. Gallai. Transitiv orienterbare graphen. *Acta Math. Acad. Sci. Hungar.*, (18):25–66, 1967. MR 36 #5026.

[Gol80] M. C. Golumbic. *Algorithmic graph theory and perfect graphs.* Academic Press, New-York, 1980.

[Hab81] M. Habib. *Substitution des structures combinatoires, théorie et algorithmes.* PhD thesis, Université Pierre et Marie Curie (Paris VI), 1981.

[HHS90] M. Habib, M. Huchard, and J. Spinrad. A linear algorithm to decompose inheritance graphs into modules. Rapport de Recherche CRIM-81, to appear in Algorithmica, 1990.

[HM79] M. Habib and M. C. Maurer. On the x-join decomposition for undirected graphs. *Discrete Applied Math*, (3):198–207, 1979.

[Ill90] P. Ille. Indecomposable relations. preprint Université de Marseille, 1990.

[Ill91] P. Ille. L'ensemble des intervalles d'une multirelation binaire et réflexive. *Zeitschr. f. math. Logik und Grundlagen d. Math. Bd.*, (37):227–256, 1991.

[Kel85] D. Kelly. Comparability graphs. In I. Rival, editor, *Graphs and Orders*, pages 3–40. D. Reidel Publishing Company, 1985.

[MC78] M.C. Vilarem M. Chein, M. Habib. Hypergraphes homogènes et ensembles de parties homogènes d'un graphe ou d'un hypergraphe. *C.R. Acad Sciences Paris*, (287):285–287, 1978.

[McC92] R. M. McConnell. A practical $o(n^2)$ algorithm for substitution decomposition. Dept. of computer science, University of colorado at Boulder, Boulder, CO 80309 USA, 1992.

[MCGW93] C.L. McCreary, C.L. Combs, D.H. Gill, and J.V. Warren. An automated graph drawing system using graph decomposition. In *Graph Drawing'93*, 1993.

[Möh85] R. H. Möhring. Algorithmic aspects of the substitution decomposition in optimization over relations, set systems and boolean functions. *Annals of Operations Research*, 6:195–225, 1985.

[Möh89] R. H. Möhring. Computationaly tractable classes of ordered sets. In I. Rival, editor, *Algorithms and Orders*, pages 105–193. Kluwer Academic Publishers, 1989. volume : 255, series C: Mathematical and Physical Sciences.

[MR84] R. H. Möhring and F. J. Radermacher. Substitution decomposition for discrete structures and connections with combinatorial optimization. *Ann. Discrete math*, (19):257–356, 1984.

[MS89] J. H. Muller and J. Spinrad. Incremental modular decomposition. *Journal of the association for Computing Machinery*, (1):1–19, January 1989.

[MS93] R. M. McConnell and J. Spinrad. Linear-time modular decomposition and efficient transitive orientation of undirected graphs. Dept. of computer science, University of colorado at Boulder, Boulder, CO 80309 USA, 1993.

[Sab59] J. Sabidussi. The composition of graphs. *Duke Math.Journal*, (26):693–696, 1959.

[Sha68] L. S. Shapley. In F. Zwycky and A. Wilson, editors, *New Methods of Thought and Procedure*, number 26, pages 693–696. New-York, 1968.

[Spi85] J. Spinrad. On comparability and permutation graphs. *SIAM J. COMPUT.*, 14(3):658–670, August 1985.

[Spi92] J. Spinrad. P4-trees and substitution decomposition. *Discrete Applied Mathematics*, (39):263–291, 1992.

[ST91] J. H. Schmerl and W. T. Trotter. Critically indecomposable partially ordered sets, graphs, tournaments and other binary relational structures. preprint, 1991.

[Sum71] D. P. Sumner. *Indecomposable graphs.* PhD thesis, University of Massachussets, Amherts, 1971.

A CPS-Translation of the $\lambda\mu$-Calculus

Philippe de Groote

INRIA-Lorraine - CRIN - CNRS
Campus Scientifique - B.P. 239
54506 Vandœuvre-lès-Nancy Cedex - FRANCE
e-mail: degroote@loria.fr

Abstract. We present a translation of Parigot's $\lambda\mu$-calculus [10] into the usual λ-calculus. This translation, which is based on the so-called *continuation passing style*, is correct with respect to equality and with respect to evaluation. At the type level, it induces a logical interpretation of classical logic into intuitionistic one, akin to Kolmogorov's negative translation. As a by-product, we get the normalization of second order typed $\lambda\mu$-calculus.

1 Introduction

During the last three years, several authors have introduced various systems that clarify the computational content of classical proofs [2, 3, 5, 6, 8, 9, 10]. In this paper, we investigate one of these systems, namely Parigot's $\lambda\mu$-calculus [10].

Our investigation tool is merely syntactic: we propose a translation of the $\lambda\mu$-calculus into the well known λ-calculus. This interpretation, which obey a continuation passing style, works for any $\lambda\mu$-term. It is therefore more general than the one introduced by M. Parigot in [11], which works only for bounded $\lambda\mu$-terms.

The notion of continuation has been developed in the framework of programming language semantics in order to model control. Since Griffin's work [6], one knows that there is a connection between classical proofs and control. With this respect, our interpretation enlighten the relation between the $\lambda\mu$-calculus and the notion of control: a μ-abstraction is interpreted as a λ-abstraction whose bound variable stands for some possible continuation.

The main properties of our translation are that it is correct with respect to equality and evaluation: two $\lambda\mu$-terms are equal if and only if their translations are (*translation property*); the evaluation of a $\lambda\mu$-term may be simulated faithfully by the evaluation of its translation (*simulation property*).

Up to a slight modification, the interpretation of the typed $\lambda\mu$-calculus that results from our translation does also make sense from a proof-theoretic point of view. It amounts to a negative translation of classical logic into intuitionistic one, akin to Kolmogorov's. This allow us to establish the normalization of second-order classical natural deduction, which is a property that has been recently proven in [12].[1]

[1] Actually, M. Parigot proves more, namely strong normalization.

The remainder of this paper is organized as follows. The next section is a short introduction to Parigot's $\lambda\mu$-calculus. In Section 3, we define our translation of the $\lambda\mu$-calculus into the λ-calculus, and we prove its correctness with respect to equality. In Section 4, we address the problem of the correctness of the translation with respect to evaluation. The proof-theoretic interpretation of the translation is investigated in Section 5. Finally we present our conclusions in Section 6.

2 The $\lambda\mu$-Calculus

This section is a short introduction to the $\lambda\mu$-calculus. The reader may refer to [10, 11, 12] for further details.

The $\lambda\mu$-calculus, introduced by M. Parigot in [10], extends the λ-calculus in order to give an algorithmic interpretation to classical proofs. This interpretation is based on cut-elimination as it is in the case of intuitionistic logic. Nevertheless, in addition to the so-called *logical reductions* of intuitionistic logic, some other kind of reduction is needed in order to handle the double-negation rule of classical logic. This gives rise to an extension of the syntax of the λ-calculus (addition of *μ-abstractions* and *named terms*), and to a new notion of reduction (the one of *structural reduction*).

The terms of the $\lambda\mu$-calculus ($\lambda\mu$-terms, for short) are built from two distinct alphabets of variables: the set of λ-variables, and the set μ-variables. The raw syntax of the language is given by the following grammar:

$$T \ ::= \ x \mid (\lambda x.\, T) \mid (T\,T) \mid (\mu\delta.\, T) \mid [\delta]T,$$

where x ranges over λ-variables, and δ ranges over μ-variables. A $\lambda\mu$-term of the form $\mu\delta.\, T$ is called a *μ-abstraction*, and a $\lambda\mu$-term of the form $[\delta]T$ is called a *named term*. The operator μ is a binding operator as is λ. Therefore, the free occurrences of a μ-variable δ in T become bound in $\mu\delta.\, T$. In order to be protected from clashes between free and bound variables, we adopt Barendregt's variable convention [4] for μ-variables as well as for λ-variables.

The reduction relation of the $\lambda\mu$-calculus is induced by three different notions of reduction. The first one is the usual notion of reduction β:

$$(\lambda x.\, M)\, N \to M[x := N]$$

where $M[x := N]$ denotes the usual capture-avoiding substitution.

The second notion of reduction is the one of *structural reduction*. This notion may be intuitively explained as follows: in a $\lambda\mu$-term $\mu\alpha.\, M$ of type $A \to B$, only the subterms named by α are *really* of type $A \to B$ (see the typing rules hereafter); hence, when such a μ-abstraction is applied to an argument, this argument must be passed over to the subterms named by α. This intuition is formalized as follows:

$$(\mu\delta.\, M)\, N \to M[\delta \Leftarrow N],$$

where the structural substitution is inductively defined as follows:

(i) $x[\delta \Leftarrow N] = x$;
(ii) $(\lambda x.\, M)[\delta \Leftarrow N] = \lambda x.\, M[\delta \Leftarrow N]$;
(iii) $(M\, O)[\delta \Leftarrow N] = M[\delta \Leftarrow N]\, O[\delta \Leftarrow N]$;
(iv) $(\mu\gamma.\, M)[\delta \Leftarrow N] = \mu\gamma.\, M[\delta \Leftarrow N]$;
(v) $([\delta]\, M)[\delta \Leftarrow N] = [\delta]\, (M[\delta \Leftarrow N]\, N)$;
(vi) $([\gamma]\, M)[\delta \Leftarrow N] = [\gamma]\, M[\delta \Leftarrow N]$ *if* $\delta \neq \gamma$.

The third notion of reduction, which is called *renaming*, is the following:

$$[\delta]\,(\mu\gamma.\, M) \rightarrow M[\gamma := \delta]$$

We will write $\rightarrow_\mu$ for the one-step reduction relation induced by the three notions of reduction as above. Similarly, we will respectively write $\twoheadrightarrow_\mu$ and $=_\mu$ for the reflexive, transitive closure, and the reflexive, transitive, symmetric closure of the one-step reduction relation.

The type system of the $\lambda\mu$-calculus is defined by means of a classical sequent calculus. The sequents are either of the form $M \;:\; \Gamma \vdash \Delta$ or of the form $M \;:\; \Gamma \vdash A,\, \Delta$. In such sequents, M is a $\lambda\mu$-term; the antecedent Γ is a set of second-order formulas indexed by λ-variables; the succedent Δ is a set of second-order formulas indexed by μ-variables; A is a non-indexed second-order formula. The typing rules are the following:

Logical rules

$$x \;:\; A^x \vdash A$$

$$\frac{M \;:\; \Gamma,\, A^x \vdash B,\, \Delta}{\lambda x.\, M \;:\; \Gamma \vdash A \rightarrow B,\, \Delta} \qquad \frac{M \;:\; \Gamma \vdash A \rightarrow B,\, \Delta \qquad N \;:\; \Pi \vdash A,\, \Sigma}{M\, N \;:\; \Gamma,\, \Pi \vdash B,\, \Delta,\, \Sigma}$$

$$\frac{M \;:\; \Gamma \vdash A[x := y],\, \Delta}{M \;:\; \Gamma \vdash \forall x.A,\, \Delta} \qquad \frac{M \;:\; \Gamma \vdash \forall x.A,\, \Delta}{M \;:\; \Gamma \vdash A[x := t],\, \Delta}$$

$$\frac{M \;:\; \Gamma \vdash A[X := Y],\, \Delta}{M \;:\; \Gamma \vdash \forall X.A,\, \Delta} \qquad \frac{M \;:\; \Gamma \vdash \forall X.A,\, \Delta}{M \;:\; \Gamma \vdash A[X := B],\, \Delta}$$

where the *eigenvariablen* y and Y must obey the usual proviso.

Naming rules

$$\frac{M \;:\; \Gamma \vdash A,\, \Delta}{[\alpha]\, M \;:\; \Gamma \vdash A^\alpha,\, \Delta} \qquad \frac{M \;:\; \Gamma \vdash A^\alpha,\, \Delta}{\mu\alpha.\, M \;:\; \Gamma \vdash A,\, \Delta}$$

When a judgement of the form $M \;: \vdash A$ is derivable according to these typing rules, we will write $\vdash_\mu\; M : A$.

If one forgets about the naming rules (and therefore, about μ-abstractions and named terms), the above type system amounts to Krivine's AF_2 [7]. When dealing with pure λ-calculus or with AF_2, we will allow only for the notion of reduction β. Then, we will respectively write $\rightarrow_\lambda$, $\twoheadrightarrow_\lambda$, and $=_\lambda$ for the relations of one-step reduction, reduction, and conversion induced by β. When dealing with the intuitionistic sequents of AF_2, we will use the standard notation, that is $\Gamma \vdash M : A$ instead of $M : \Gamma \vdash A$. Finally, when a judgement of the form $\vdash M : A$ is derivable according to the typing rules of AF_2, we will write $\vdash_{AF_2} M : A$.

3 The CPS-translation

There is a strong connection between classical proofs and control operators like scheme's `call/cc` [6]. Control operators act on the evaluation ordering of programs. Similarly, a feature such as the μ-abstraction may be seen as a construct allowing the evaluation context of a term to be changed by passing over a stack of arguments to some subterms.

Control and evaluation ordering may be modeled in pure λ-calculus by using a technique known as the continuation passing style (CPS, for short) [13]. It is therefore not too surprising that the same technique may be used to give a translation of the $\lambda\mu$-calculus into the λ-calculus.

For the purpose of this CPS-translation, we consider that pure λ-terms are built upon an alphabet of variables made of the sets of λ- and μ-variables of the $\lambda\mu$-calculus plus two distinguished variables, k and m.[2]

Definition 3.1 (CPS-Translation) *The CPS-translation $\underline{M}$ of a $\lambda\mu$-term M is inductively defined as follows:*

(i) $\underline{x} = \lambda k.\, x\, k;$

(ii) $\underline{\lambda x.\, M} = \lambda k.\, k\, (\lambda x.\, \underline{M});$

(iii) $\underline{M\, N} = \lambda k.\, \underline{M}\, (\lambda m.\, m\, \underline{N}\, k);$

(iv) $\underline{\mu\delta.\, M} = \lambda\delta.\, \underline{M};$

(v) $\underline{[\delta]\, M} = \lambda k.\, \underline{M}\, \delta\, k.$

This translation, which is based on Plotkin's call-by-name CPS-simulation [13], gives an interesting interpretation of the operations of μ-abstraction and naming. A μ-abstraction $\mu\delta.\, M$ corresponds to a λ-abstraction waiting for some continuation represented by the formal parameter δ. Then, the naming of a subterm corresponds simply to the application of the given subterm to the continuation δ.

It remains to show that our translation is correct with respect to equality. More precisely, we intend to prove the following proposition:

Proposition 3.2 (Translation) *$\underline{M} =_\lambda \underline{N}$ if and only if $M =_\mu N$, for any $\lambda\mu$-terms M and N.* □

[2] Actually, the variables k and m will always occur bound. Nevertheless, for a technical reason that will appear in the sequel, we consider their names as relevant.

We first establish the if part of this proposition. To this end, a couple of lemmas are needed.

Lemma 3.3 $\lambda k.\, \underline{M}\, k =_\lambda \underline{M}$, *for any* $\lambda\mu$*-term* M.

Proof. The CPS-translation $\underline{M}$ of any $\lambda\mu$-term M is a λ-abstraction. □

Lemma 3.4 $\underline{M}[x := \underline{N}] =_\lambda \underline{M[x := N]}$, *for any* $\lambda\mu$*-terms* M *and* N.

Proof. A straightforward induction on the structure of M, using Lemma 3.3 when M is x. □

Lemma 3.5 $\underline{M}[\delta := \lambda m.\, m\, \underline{N}\, \delta] =_\lambda \underline{M[\delta \Leftarrow N]}$, *for any* $\lambda\mu$*-terms* M *and* N.

Proof. By induction on the structure of M. We consider only the case $M = [\delta] M'$, the other cases being straightforward.

$$\begin{aligned}
\underline{[\delta] M'}[\delta := \lambda m.\, m\, \underline{N}\, \delta] &= (\lambda k.\, \underline{M'}\, \delta\, k)[\delta := \lambda m.\, m\, \underline{N}\, \delta] \\
&= \lambda k.\, \underline{M'}[\delta := (\lambda m.\, m\, \underline{N}\, \delta)]\, (\lambda m.\, m\, \underline{N}\, \delta)\, k \\
&=_\lambda \lambda k.\, \underline{M'[\delta \Leftarrow N]}\, (\lambda m.\, m\, \underline{N}\, \delta)\, k \text{ by induction hypothesis} \\
&=_\lambda \lambda k.\, (\lambda k.\, \underline{M'[\delta \Leftarrow N]}\, (\lambda m.\, m\, \underline{N}\, k))\, \delta\, k \\
&= \lambda k.\, \underline{M'[\delta \Leftarrow N]\, N}\, \delta\, k \\
&= \underline{[\delta](M'[\delta \Leftarrow N]\, N)} \\
&= \underline{([\delta] M)[\delta \Leftarrow N]}
\end{aligned}$$

□

Thanks to the above lemmas, the proof of the if part of Proposition 3.2 becomes rather easy:

Proof of Proposition 3.2 (if part). The proof is by induction on the derivation of $M =_\mu N$. The inductive steps being straightforward, we will only focus on the base cases. We consider the case of structural reduction step below, and we leave the two other cases to the reader.

$$\begin{aligned}
\underline{(\mu\delta.\, M)\, N} &= \lambda k.\, (\lambda\delta.\, \underline{M})\, (\lambda m.\, m\, \underline{N}\, k) \\
&=_\alpha \lambda\delta.\, (\lambda\delta.\, \underline{M})\, (\lambda m.\, m\, \underline{N}\, \delta) \\
&=_\lambda \lambda\delta.\, \underline{M}[\delta := \lambda m.\, m\, \underline{N}\, \delta] \\
&=_\lambda \lambda\delta.\, \underline{M[\delta \Leftarrow N]} && \text{by Lemma 3.5} \\
&= \underline{\mu\delta.\, M[\delta \Leftarrow N]}
\end{aligned}$$

□

To establish the only-if part of Proposition 3.2 is more intricate. The proof that we will give is adapted from a proof by G. Plotkin in [13]. Let us first explain where the difficulties are.

The proof of the if part of Proposition 3.2 demonstrates that the contraction of a β-redex in a $\lambda\mu$-term is simulated by a sequence of contractions in the

CPS-transform. Among these contractions, only one corresponds to the original contraction in the $\lambda\mu$-term. The other ones, which are related to the management of the continuations, are what G. Plotkin calls *administrative* reduction-steps.

Because of these administrative reductions, we do not have that, when $\underline{M} \twoheadrightarrow_\lambda N$, there is a N' such that $\underline{N'} = N$. To circumvent this problem, we will define a binary relation $M \sim N$ between $\lambda\mu$-terms and λ-terms, with the meaning that N may be obtained from $\underline{M}$ by administrative reductions.

In order to define the relation $\sim$, we must be able to distinguish proper reductions from administrative ones. For this reason, the names of the bound variables k and m introduced in Definition 3.1 will be considered as relevant. For the same reason, the α-conversion step that appears in the simulation of a structural reduction step (see the proof of the if part of Proposition 3.2) will be considered as mandatory.

The relation $\sim$ is defined by the following formal system, where x ranges over λ-variables, δ ranges over μ-variables, and k, m stand for themselves:

$$\text{I.} \quad x \sim \lambda k.\, x\, k$$

$$\text{II.} \quad \frac{M_1 \sim M_2}{\lambda x.\, M_1 \sim \lambda k.\, k\,(\lambda x.\, M_2)}$$

$$\text{III.a.} \quad \frac{M_1 \sim M_2 \quad N_1 \sim N_2}{M_1\, N_1 \sim \lambda k.\, M_2\,(\lambda m.\, m\, N_2\, k)} \qquad \text{III.b.} \quad \frac{M_1 \sim \lambda k.\, M_2 \quad N_1 \sim N_2}{M_1\, N_1 \sim \lambda k.\, M_2[k := \lambda m.\, m\, N_2\, k]}$$

$$\text{IV.} \quad \frac{M_1 \sim M_2 \quad N_1 \sim N_2}{(\lambda x.\, M_1)\, N_1 \sim \lambda k.\, (\lambda x.\, M_2)\, N_2\, k}$$

$$\text{V.} \quad \frac{M_1 \sim M_2}{M_1 \sim \lambda k.\, M_2\, k}$$

$$\text{VI.} \quad \frac{M_1 \sim M_2}{\mu\delta.\, M_1 \sim \lambda\delta.\, M_2}$$

$$\text{VII.a.} \quad \frac{M_1 \sim M_2}{[\delta]\, M_1 \sim \lambda k.\, M_2\, \delta\, k} \qquad \text{VII.b.} \quad \frac{M_1 \sim \lambda k.\, M_2}{[\delta]\, M_1 \sim \lambda k.\, M_2[k := \delta]\, k}$$

The advantage of the above definition is that we may now establish the two following key properties:

$$\textit{If } M_1 \sim N_1 \textit{ and } N_1 \rightarrow_\lambda N_2 \textit{ then } M_1 \twoheadrightarrow_\mu M_2 \textit{ and } M_2 \sim N_2\textit{, for some } M_2. \quad (1)$$

$$\textit{If } M_1 \sim N \textit{ and } M_2 \sim N \textit{ then } M_1 = M_2. \quad (2)$$

The three next lemmas concern Property 1.

Lemma 3.6 *Let M_1, N_1 be $\lambda\mu$-terms and M_2, N_2 be λ-terms. If $M_1 \sim M_2$ and $N_1 \sim N_2$, then $M_1[x := N_1] \sim M_2[x := N_2]$.*

Proof. A straightforward induction on the derivation of $M_1 \sim M_2$. □

Lemma 3.7 *Let M_1, N_1 be $\lambda\mu$-terms and M_2, N_2 be λ-terms. If $M_1 \sim M_2$ and $N_1 \sim N_2$, then $M_1[\delta \Leftarrow N_1] \sim M_2[\delta := \lambda m.\, m\, N_2\, \delta]$.*

Proof. By induction on the derivation of $M_1 \sim M_2$. The only cases that are not straightforward are those for which $M_1 \sim M_2$ is the conclusion of Rule VII.a or Rule VII.b. These cases are similar to the case $M = [\delta]\, M'$ in the proof of Lemma 3.5. □

Lemma 3.8 (Property 1) *Let M_1 be a $\lambda\mu$-term and N_1, N_2 be λ-terms. If $M_1 \sim N_1$ and $N_1 \rightarrow_\lambda N_2$, then there exists a $\lambda\mu$-term M_2 such that $M_1 \twoheadrightarrow_\mu M_2$ and $M_2 \sim N_2$.*

Proof. By induction on the derivation of $M_1 \sim N_1$, using Lemmas 3.6 and 3.7. When $M_1 \sim N_1$ is the conclusion of Rule III.b, a secondary induction is needed. □

Property 2 will be established by induction on the definition of the relation $\sim$. In order to distinguish between different subcases when performing this induction, we must first characterize the form of the λ-terms that belong to the codomain of the relation $\sim$. Consider the following grammar, where x ranges over λ-variables, δ ranges over μ-variables, and k, m stand for themselves:

$$
\begin{array}{lcl}
\mathcal{A} & ::= & \lambda k.\, x\, k \\
\mathcal{B} & ::= & \lambda k.\, k\, (\lambda x.\, \mathcal{H}) \\
\mathcal{C} & ::= & \lambda k.\, x\, \mathcal{K} \mid \lambda k.\, \mathcal{K}\, (\lambda x.\, \mathcal{H}) \mid \lambda k.\, \mathcal{H}\, \mathcal{K} \mid \lambda k.\, (\lambda x.\, \mathcal{H})\, \mathcal{H}\, \mathcal{K} \mid \lambda k.\, \mathcal{G}'\, \mathcal{K} \\
\mathcal{K} & ::= & \lambda m.\, m\, \mathcal{H}\, k \mid \lambda m.\, m\, \mathcal{H}\, \mathcal{K} \\
\mathcal{D} & ::= & \lambda k.\, (\lambda x.\, \mathcal{H})\, \mathcal{H}\, k \\
\mathcal{E} & ::= & \lambda k.\, \mathcal{H}\, k \\
\mathcal{F} & ::= & \lambda \delta.\, \mathcal{H} \\
\mathcal{G} & ::= & \lambda k.\, \mathcal{G}'\, k \\
\mathcal{G}' & ::= & x\, \Delta \mid \Delta\, (\lambda x.\, \mathcal{H}) \mid \mathcal{H}\, \Delta \mid (\lambda x.\, \mathcal{H})\, \mathcal{H}\, \Delta \mid \mathcal{G}'\, \Delta \\
\Delta & ::= & \delta \mid \lambda m.\, m\, \mathcal{H}\, \Delta \\
\mathcal{H} & ::= & \mathcal{A} \mid \mathcal{B} \mid \mathcal{C} \mid \mathcal{D} \mid \mathcal{E} \mid \mathcal{F} \mid \mathcal{G}
\end{array}
$$

This grammar characterizes the codomain of the relation $\sim$ as follows:

Lemma 3.9 *Let M be a $\lambda\mu$-term and N be a λ-term. If $M \sim N$ then $N \in \mathcal{H}$. Moreover, $N \in \mathcal{A}$ iff the last rule used in the derivation of $M \sim N$ is I; $N \in \mathcal{B}$ iff the last rule is II; $N \in \mathcal{C}$ iff the last rule is III.a or III.b; $N \in \mathcal{D}$ iff the last rule is IV; $N \in \mathcal{E}$ iff the last rule is V; $N \in \mathcal{F}$ iff the last rule is VI; and $N \in \mathcal{G}$ iff the last rule is VII.a or VII.b.*

Proof. The proof is by induction on the derivation of $M \sim N$, the different cases and subcases are numerous but not difficult. □

Thanks to the above lemma, Property 2 may be now established:

Lemma 3.10 (Property 2) *Let M_1, M_2 be a $\lambda\mu$-terms, and N be a λ-term. If $M_1 \sim N$ and $M_2 \sim N$ then $M_1 = M_2$ (where "=" stands for syntactic equivalence modulo α-conversion).*

Proof. By induction on the derivation of $M_1 \sim N$.

By Lemma 3.9, when the last rule of the derivation of $M_1 \sim N$ is respectively I, II, IV, V, or VI, so is the last rule of the derivation of $M_2 \sim N$. Moreover, the form of N determines univocally the forms of the premises. Therefore, in these cases, the induction is straightforward.

If the last rule of the derivation of $M_1 \sim N$ is III.a or III.b, the same reasoning applies except when $N = \lambda k.\, N_1\,(\lambda m.\, m\, N_2\, k)$ because there is a possibility of overlapping. Nevertheless, in this last case, the two possible derivations are the following:

$$\text{III.a.}\ \frac{\dfrac{\vdots}{M_{11} \sim N_1} \quad \dfrac{\vdots}{M_{12} \sim N_2}}{M_{11}\, M_{12} \sim \lambda k.\, N_1\,(\lambda m.\, m\, N_2\, k)} \qquad \text{III.b.}\ \frac{\text{V.}\ \dfrac{\dfrac{\vdots}{M_{21} \sim N_1}}{M_{21} \sim \lambda k.\, N_1\, k} \quad \dfrac{\vdots}{M_{22} \sim N_2}}{M_{21}\, M_{22} \sim \lambda k.\, N_1\,(\lambda m.\, m\, N_2\, k)}$$

Therefore, for this case, the induction is also straightforward.

Finally, when the last rule of the derivation is VII.a or VII.b, the only possibility of overlapping is similar to the previous one, and the induction is also straightforward. □

We are now in the position of proving the only-if part of Proposition 3.2:

Proof of Proposition 3.2 (only-if part). Let $\underline{M} =_\lambda \underline{N}$. By the theorem of Church-Rosser, there exists a λ-term O such that $\underline{M} \twoheadrightarrow_\lambda O$ and $\underline{N} \twoheadrightarrow_\lambda O$. As $M \sim \underline{M}$, by Lemma 3.8, there is a $\lambda\mu$-term M' such that $M \twoheadrightarrow_\mu M'$ and $M' \sim O$. Similarly, there is a $\lambda\mu$-term N' such that $N \twoheadrightarrow_\mu N'$ and $N' \sim O$. Then, by Lemma 3.10, $M' = N'$. Therefore, $M =_\mu N$. □

4 Simulation

The proposition established in the previous section is concerned with the correction of the CPS-translation with respect to equality. If one considers the $\lambda\mu$-calculus as a programming language, this criterion of correction is not sufficient any more because it does not say anything about evaluation.

In this section, we intend to answer the following natural question: does the CPS-transform simulate faithfully the evaluation of the $\lambda\mu$-terms. More precisely, is there a mapping Φ such that:

$$\mathrm{eval}_\lambda(\underline{M}) = \Phi(\mathrm{eval}_\mu(M)) \tag{1}$$

In order to give a meaning to this equation, we must first define the functions of evaluation. Traditionally, this is done by giving some abstract machines. In order to be machine independent, we simply define $\mathrm{eval}_\mu(M)$ as the normal form of M, if any. We define $\mathrm{eval}_\lambda(N)$ similarly. These definitions are not ambiguous because both calculi satisfy the Church-Rosser property. They also make sense from an operational point of view, the evaluation functions corresponding to a call-by-name strategy [13].

The two evaluation functions are partial. For this reason, we must also precise the meaning of the equality in (1). We adopt Kleene's complete equality, that is: if one member of the equation is defined, so is the other one and their values are the same. Therefore, in proving an equation similar to (1), we must first establish that the left-hand side is defined if and only if the right-hand side is defined. If Φ is a total function, this amounts to show that a $\lambda\mu$-term is normalizable if and only if its CPS-translation is normalizable. Half of this property may be proven with the tools that we have introduced in the previous section.

Lemma 4.1 *Let M be a $\lambda\mu$-term and N be a λ-term such that $M \sim N$. If N is in λ-normal form then M is in μ-normal form.*

Proof. By induction on the derivation of $M \sim N$, using Lemma 3.9 to distinguish between the different subcases. □

Lemma 4.2 *Let M be a $\lambda\mu$-term. If $\underline{M}$ is λ-normalizable then M is μ-normalizable.*

Proof. Let Z be the λ-normal form of $\underline{M}$. As $M \sim \underline{M}$, by Lemma 3.8, there is a $\lambda\mu$-term Y such that $M \twoheadrightarrow_\mu Y$ and $Y \sim Z$. Then, by Lemma 4.1, Y is the μ-normal form of M. □

To establish that $\underline{M}$ is normalizable whenever M is, we must face two problems. The first one is related to the administrative reductions: in general, when M is in μ-normal form, we do not have that $\underline{M}$ is in λ-normal form. The second one is related to the simulation of the structural reduction: if $M_1 \rightarrow_\mu M_2$ by structural reduction, we do not have that $\underline{M_1} \twoheadrightarrow_\lambda \underline{M_2}$; this is due to the β-expansion step that appears in the proof of Lemma 3.5.

The solution to these problems is to modify the definition of the CPS-transform in such a way that some of the administrative redexes disappear:

Definition 4.3 (Modified CPS-Translation) *The modified CPS-translation $\underline{\underline{M}}$ of a $\lambda\mu$-term M is inductively defined as follows:*

(i) $\underline{\underline{x}} = \lambda k.\, x\, k$;

(ii) $\underline{\underline{\lambda x.\, M}} = \lambda k.\, k\, (\lambda x.\, \underline{\underline{M}})$;

(iii) $\underline{\underline{M\, N}} = \lambda k.\, (\underline{\underline{M}} : \lambda m.\, m\, \underline{\underline{N}}\, k)$;

(iv) $\underline{\underline{\mu\delta.\, M}} = \lambda\delta.\, \underline{\underline{M}}$;

(v) $\underline{\underline{[\delta]M}} = \lambda k.\overline{[\delta]M}\,k;$

where:

(vi) $x : K = x\,K;$

(vii) $(\lambda x.\,M) : K = K\,(\lambda x.\,\underline{\underline{M}});$

(viii) $(M\,N) : K = M : \lambda m.\,m\,\underline{\underline{N}}\,K;$

(ix) $(\mu\delta.\,M) : K = (\lambda\delta.\,\underline{\underline{M}})\,K;$

(x) $([\delta]M) : K = \overline{[\delta]M} : K;$

(xi) $\overline{[\delta]x} = x\,\delta;$

(xii) $\overline{[\delta](\lambda x.\,M)} = \delta\,(\lambda x.\,\underline{\underline{M}});$

(xiii) $\overline{[\delta](M\,N)} = M : (\lambda m.\,m\,\underline{\underline{N}}\,\delta);$

(xiv) $\overline{[\delta](\mu\gamma.\,M)} = (\lambda\gamma.\,\underline{\underline{M}})\,\delta;$

(xv) $\overline{[\delta]([\gamma]M)} = \overline{[\gamma]M}\,\delta.$

This new definition is compatible with the previous one in the following sense:

Lemma 4.4 *$\underline{M} \twoheadrightarrow_\lambda \underline{\underline{M}}$, for any $\lambda\mu$-term M.*

Proof. By induction on the structure of M, using auxiliary inductions when M is an application or a named term. □

As expected, the modified CPS-transform maps normal forms to normal forms:

Lemma 4.5 *Let M be a $\lambda\mu$-term in μ-normal form. Then $\underline{\underline{M}}$ is in λ-normal form.*

Proof. By induction on the structure of M. □

These two lemmas allow us to show that if M is normalizable, so is $\underline{M}$:

Lemma 4.6 *Let M be a $\lambda\mu$-term. If M is μ-normalizable then $\underline{M}$ is λ-normalizable.*

Proof. Let Z be the μ-normal form of M. By Proposition 3.2, $\underline{M} =_\lambda \underline{Z}$. On the other hand, by Lemma 4.4, $\underline{Z} \twoheadrightarrow_\lambda \underline{\underline{Z}}$, and this last term is in β-normal form by Lemma 4.5. Finally, by Church-Rosser, $\underline{M} \twoheadrightarrow_\lambda \underline{\underline{Z}}$. □

Lemmas 4.2, 4.4, 4.5, and 4.6, allow us to prove Equation (1) where the mapping Φ is nothing but the modified CPS-transform. Therefore, we have the following:

Proposition 4.7 (Simulation) $\mathrm{eval}_\lambda(\underline{M}) = \underline{\underline{\mathrm{eval}_\mu(M)}}$, *for any $\lambda\mu$-term M.* □

We end this section by a remark. Traditionally, the evaluation of a program is simulated by the evaluation of its CPS-translation applied to the empty continuation $\lambda x.\,x$. This make sense because a program is defined to be a closed term of atomic type. Now, the only closed normal form of atomic types are basic constants and the CPS-transform of a basic constant a is defined to be $\lambda k.\, k\, a$. Therefore, for any program P, we have that $\mathrm{eval}(P) = \mathrm{eval}(\underline{P}(\lambda x.\, x))$.

We did not follow this traditional approach for two reasons. The first one is that in the $\lambda\mu$-calculus, as in AF_2, the basic data-structures are not of atomic type. For instance, the type of natural numbers is represented by the following second order formula that asserts that n is a natural number:

$$\forall X.(X(0) \to \forall y.(X(y) \to X(sy)) \to X(n)).$$

The second reason, as we will see in the next section, is that $\underline{M}(\lambda x.\, x)$ is not always well-typed.

5 Logical Interpretation

Up to now, we have worked in the framework of the untyped $\lambda\mu$-calculus. In this section, we intend to answer questions such as the following ones: does the CPS-translation make sense in a typed framework? is it typable? if yes, does it induce some interesting translation at the type level? These different questions are summarized by the following one: is there a translation acting on the types such that this translation and the CPS-translation would commute with the typing relations of $\lambda\mu$ and AF_2?

The answer is positive. The translation at the type level corresponds to a logical interpretation of classical logic into intuitionistic one akin to Kolmogorov's negative translation.

Definition 5.1 (Negative Translation) *The negative translation A^{k} of a first-order formula A is inductively defined as follows:*

(i) $A^{\mathrm{k}} = \neg\neg A,$ *(for A an atomic formula);*
(ii) $(A \to B)^{\mathrm{k}} = \neg\neg(A^{\mathrm{k}} \to B^{\mathrm{k}});$
(iii) $(\forall x.A)^{\mathrm{k}} = \neg\neg\forall x.A^{\mathrm{k}};$
(iv) $(\forall X.A)^{\mathrm{k}} = \neg\neg\forall X.A^{\mathrm{k}};$

where $\neg A = A \to \mathbf{f}$, and $\mathbf{f} = (\bot \to \bot) \to \bot$.

The proposition that we are going to establish in this section is the following:

Proposition 5.2 (Logical Interpretation) *If $\vdash_\mu M : A$ then $\vdash_{\mathrm{AF}_2} \underline{M} : A^{\mathrm{k}}$, for any $\lambda\mu$-term M and any second-order formula A.* □

In trying to prove the above proposition, we will encounter a problem related to the introduction of the quantifiers. Indeed, whenever $\vdash_{\mathrm{AF}_2} \underline{M} : A^{\mathrm{k}}$, we may conclude that $\vdash_{\mathrm{AF}_2} \underline{M} : \forall x.A^{\mathrm{k}}$. But this is not sufficient because one does not have that $(\forall x.A)^{\mathrm{k}} = \forall x.A^{\mathrm{k}}$.

A solution to this problem is to extend Definition 3.1 by defining the CPS-translation of the typed $\lambda\mu$-terms by induction on the derivations of the typing judgments. The only typing rules that are not reflected by the syntax of the $\lambda\mu$-terms are the ones related to the quantifiers. Therefore, we extend Definition 3.1 by adding the two following clauses:

(vi) $\underline{M} = \lambda k.\, k\,\underline{M}$, *if M is obtained by first- or second-order $\forall$-introduction;*

(vii) $\underline{M} = \lambda k.\, \underline{M}\,(\lambda m.\, m\, k)$, *if M is obtained by first- or second-order $\forall$-elimination.*

Then Propositions 3.2 and 4.7 must be restated in terms of proof reduction. This gives rise to the following additional reduction steps (we give them for the first-order case, the second-order case being completely similar):

$$\dfrac{\dfrac{\begin{matrix}\mathbf{\Pi}\\ \vdots\\ M \,:\, \Gamma \vdash A,\, \Delta\end{matrix}}{M \,:\, \Gamma \vdash \forall x.A,\, \Delta}}{M \,:\, \Gamma \vdash A[x:=t],\, \Delta} \quad \text{reduces to} \quad \dfrac{\begin{matrix}\mathbf{\Pi}[x:=t]\\ \vdots\end{matrix}}{M \,:\, \Gamma \vdash A[x:=t],\, \Delta}$$

This logical reduction step is simulated by the reduction of the following λ-term:

$$\lambda k.\, (\lambda k.\, k\,\underline{M})\,(\lambda m.\, m\, k).$$

$$\dfrac{\dfrac{\begin{matrix}\dfrac{\begin{matrix}\vdots\\ M_i \,:\, \Gamma_i \vdash \forall x.A,\, \Delta_i\end{matrix}}{[\alpha]M_i \,:\, \Gamma_i \vdash \forall x.A^{\alpha},\, \Delta_i}\\ \vdots\\ M \,:\, \Gamma \vdash \forall x.A^{\alpha},\, \Delta\end{matrix}}{\mu\alpha.M \,:\, \Gamma \vdash \forall x.A,\, \Delta}}{\mu\alpha.M \,:\, \Gamma \vdash A[x:=t],\, \Delta} \quad \text{reduces to} \quad \dfrac{\begin{matrix}\dfrac{\dfrac{\begin{matrix}\vdots\\ M_i \,:\, \Gamma_i \vdash \forall x.A,\, \Delta_i\end{matrix}}{M_i \,:\, \Gamma_i \vdash A[x:=t],\, \Delta_i}}{[\alpha]M_i \,:\, \Gamma_i \vdash A[x:=t]^{\alpha},\, \Delta_i}\\ \vdots\\ M \,:\, \Gamma \vdash A[x:=t]^{\alpha},\, \Delta\end{matrix}}{\mu\alpha.M \,:\, \Gamma \vdash A[x:=t],\, \Delta}$$

This structural reduction step is simulated by the reduction of the following λ-term:

$$\lambda k.\, (\lambda\alpha.\, \underline{M})\,(\lambda m.\, m\, k).$$

In order to prove Proposition 5.2, we must be able to represent classical sequents by intuitionistic ones. A possible solution to this problem is to negate each formula of the succedent and to add this sequence of negated formulas to the antecedent. In our case, we may not apply this idea roughly because we do not want to deal with triple negations. Therefore, given a second-order formula A, we define $A^{\mathsf{k}-}$ to be the unique formula such that $A^{\mathsf{k}} = \neg A^{\mathsf{k}-}$.

Proof of Proposition 5.2 We interpret any sequent

$$M \,:\, \Gamma \vdash A,\, \Delta \tag{1}$$

of the $\lambda\mu$-calculus by the following intuitionistic sequent of AF_2:

$$\Gamma^{\mathrm{k}}, \Delta^{\mathrm{k}-} \vdash \underline{M} : A^{\mathrm{k}}, \tag{2}$$

and we show that if (1) is derivable so is (2).

Given a second-order formula A, we define A^* to be the formula such that $A^{\mathrm{k}} = \neg\neg A^*$. Then, we have that $A^{\mathrm{k}-} = \neg A^*$. We will use these notations in the sequel of the proof, which is done by induction on the derivation of (1). We only handle some interesting cases, leaving the other ones to the reader.

Elimination of second-order quantification:

$$\mathbf{\Pi}\left\{\frac{\dfrac{\dfrac{m : \forall X.A^{\mathrm{k}} \vdash m : \forall X.A^{\mathrm{k}}}{m : \forall X.A^{\mathrm{k}} \vdash m : \neg\neg A^*[X := B^*]} \qquad k : \neg A^*[X := B^*] \vdash k : \neg A^*[X := B^*]}{m : \forall X.A^{\mathrm{k}}, k : \neg A^*[X := B^*] \vdash m\,k : \mathbf{f}}}{k : \neg A^*[X := B^*] \vdash \lambda m.\, m\,k : \neg\forall X.A^{\mathrm{k}}}\right.$$

$$\frac{\dfrac{\begin{array}{c}\textit{induction hypothesis}\\ \vdots \\ \Gamma^{\mathrm{k}}, \Delta^{\mathrm{k}-} \vdash \underline{M} : \neg\neg\forall X.A^{\mathrm{k}}\end{array} \qquad \begin{array}{c}\mathbf{\Pi}\\ \vdots \\ k : \neg A^*[X := B^*] \vdash \lambda m.\, m\,k : \neg\forall X.A^{\mathrm{k}}\end{array}}{\Gamma^{\mathrm{k}}, \Delta^{\mathrm{k}-}, k : \neg A^*[X := B^*] \vdash \underline{M}\,(\lambda m.\, m\,k) : \mathbf{f}}}{\Gamma^{\mathrm{k}}, \Delta^{\mathrm{k}-} \vdash \lambda k.\, \underline{M}\,(\lambda m.\, m\,k) : (A[X := B])^{\mathrm{k}}}$$

μ-Abstraction:

$$\frac{\begin{array}{c}\textit{induction hypothesis}\\ \vdots \\ \Gamma^{\mathrm{k}}, \Delta^{\mathrm{k}-}, \delta : \neg A^* \vdash \underline{M} : \mathbf{f}\end{array}}{\Gamma^{\mathrm{k}}, \Delta^{\mathrm{k}-} \vdash \lambda\delta.\, \underline{M} : \neg\neg A^*}$$

Naming:

$$\frac{\dfrac{\dfrac{\begin{array}{c}\textit{induction hypothesis}\\ \vdots \\ \Gamma^{\mathrm{k}}, \Delta^{\mathrm{k}-} \vdash \underline{M} : \neg\neg A^*\end{array} \qquad \delta : \neg A^* \vdash \delta : \neg A^*}{\Gamma^{\mathrm{k}}, \Delta^{\mathrm{k}-}, \delta : \neg A^* \vdash \underline{M}\,\delta : \mathbf{f}} \qquad k : \bot \to \bot \vdash k : \bot \to \bot}{\Gamma^{\mathrm{k}}, \Delta^{\mathrm{k}-}, \delta : \neg A^*, k : \bot \to \bot \vdash \underline{M}\,\delta\,k : \bot}}{\Gamma^{\mathrm{k}}, \Delta^{\mathrm{k}-}, \delta : \neg A^* \vdash \lambda k.\, \underline{M}\,\delta\,k : \mathbf{f}}$$

□

The reason why we did define $\neg A$ as $A \to \mathbf{f}$ appears in the last case of the above proof. We could get a simpler negative translation by simplifying, in the definition of the CPS-translation, Clauses (i) and (v) as follows:

(i) $\underline{x} = x$;

(v) $\underline{[\delta]M} = \underline{M}\,\delta$.

With this definition, however, Lemma 3.3 does not hold any more and therefore some sort of η-reduction would be needed.[3]

The well-typed terms of AF_2 are normalizable [7]. Therefore, we get the following proposition as a corollary.

Corollary 5.3 (Normalization) *Any well-typed $\lambda\mu$-term is normalizable.* □

6 Conclusions

We have presented a CPS-translation of the $\lambda\mu$-calculus into the λ-calculus that satisfies *translation* and *simulation* properties similar to the ones introduced in [13]. As we pointed out in the introduction, this CPS-translation is general in the sense that it works for any (untyped) $\lambda\mu$-term. Moreover, it maps typed $\lambda\mu$-terms to typed λ-terms and this allows us to get the normalization of the typed $\lambda\mu$-calculus for free.

In [13], G. Plotkin also establishes indifference results with respect to call-by-name and call-by-value strategies. We did not make such an analysis in this paper. Nevertheless, the reader familiar with [13], may check that all the β-redexes that are contracted during the simulation of the evaluation of a $\lambda\mu$-term are in fact β_V-redexes. Therefore our work gives also an interpreter-independent operational semantics to the $\lambda\mu$-calculus. The interest of this result is not only theoretic. Indeed, the continuation passing style is a technique that is actually used in compiling [1].

Finally, we want to stress that the notion of continuation is not only syntactic and that it has been widely used for semantic purposes. While the work that we have presented in this paper remains merely syntactic, it can be the starting point of some semantic investigations of classical proofs. Indeed, our translation allows $\lambda\mu$-terms to be interpreted in λ-algebras.

References

[1] A. W. Appel. *Compiling with continuations.* Cambridge University Press, 1992.

[2] F. Barbanera and S. Berardi. Continuations and simple types: a strong normalization result. In *Proceedings of the ACM SIGPLAN Workshop on Continuations.* Report STAN-CS-92-1426, Stanford University, 1992.

[3] F. Barbanera and S. Berardi. Extracting constructive content from classical logic via control-like reductions. In M. Bezem and J.F. Groote, editors, *Proceedings of the International Conference on on Typed Lambda Calculi and Applications*, pages 45–59. Lecture Notes in Computer Science, 664, Springer Verlag, 1993.

[3] This problem seems to have been overlooked in [13] where Theorem 6, as it is stated, fails

[4] H.P. Barendregt. *The lambda calculus, its syntax and semantics.* North-Holland, revised edition, 1984.

[5] J.-Y. Girard. A new constructive logic: Classical logic. *Mathematical Structures in Computer Science*, 1:255–296, 1991.

[6] T. G. Griffin. A formulae-as-types notion of control. In *Conference record of the seventeenth annual ACM symposium on Principles of Programming Languages*, pages 47–58, 1990.

[7] J.-L. Krivine. *Lambda-calcul, types et modèles.* Masson, 1990.

[8] C. R. Murthy. An evaluation semantics for classical proofs. In *Proceedings of the sixth annual IEEE symposium on logic in computer science*, pages 96–107, 1991.

[9] C. R. Murthy. A computational analysis of Girard's translation and LC. In *Proceedings of the seventh annual IEEE symposium on logic in computer science*, pages 90–101, 1992.

[10] M. Parigot. $\lambda\mu$-Calculus: an algorithmic interpretation of classical natural deduction. In A. Voronkov, editor, *Proceedings of the International Conference on Logic Programming and Automated Reasoning*, pages 190–201. Lecture Notes in Artificial Intelligence, 624, Springer Verlag, 1992.

[11] M. Parigot. Classical proofs as programs. In G. Gottlod, A. Leitsch, and D. Mundici, editors, *Proceedings of the third Kurt Gödel colloquium – KGC'93*, pages 263–276. Lecture Notes in Computer Science, 713, Springer Verlag, 1993.

[12] M. Parigot. Strong normalization for second order classical natural deduction. In *Proceedings of the eighth annual IEEE symposium on logic in computer science*, pages 39–46, 1993.

[13] G. D. Plotkin. Call-by-name, call-by-value and the λ-calculus. *Theretical Computer Science*, 1:125–159, 1975.

A lower bound on the growth of functions computed by tree transductions

Frank Drewes

Universität Bremen, Fachbereich 3, D–28334 Bremen (Germany)

E-mail: drewes@informatik.uni-bremen.de

Abstract. Tree transducers may be used to perform symbolic computations. A function f from one algebra into another is computed by a transduction that yields for any term t representing an element a a term t' representing $f(a)$. We consider the case where the input algebra is a term algebra, the target algebra is given by the natural numbers with operations $\sqcup$, $+$, $\cdot$, and f is injective. In this case f may be seen as a coding of terms as natural numbers. It is shown that functions computed by deterministic top-down tree transducers cannot compress totally balanced trees: The binary representation of $f(t)$ is at least as long as t up to a constant factor.

1 Introduction

In theory as well as in practice symbolic computation is a field that has received great interest. Many models for symbolic computation, among which attribute grammars are probably the most famous one, have been developed and studied, and certainly this research will continue for quite a while. Basically, the idea of symbolic computation can be described quite generally as follows. Suppose there are two algebras A and B with their respective term algebras $\mathrm{T}(A)$ and $\mathrm{T}(B)$ and we want to compute some function f from A to B. Then a term $t \in \mathrm{T}(A)$ provides a structured representation of its value a in A that may be exploited by a suitable device in order to figure out $f(a)$. In particular, this device may be a tree transducer out of some predefined class, that is, an automaton that on input t yields some tree $t' \in \mathrm{T}(B)$ whose value in B is $f(a)$. This view was developed by the author in an earlier paper [Dre93b], where the name *transducibility* was introduced to describe that situation. The diagram looks as depicted in Figure 1.

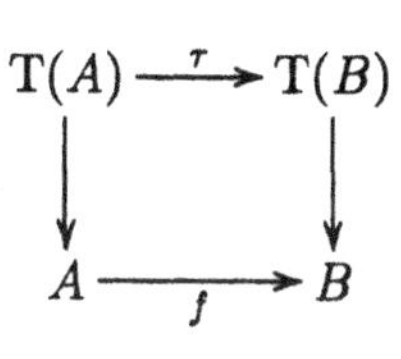

Figure 1: The basic situation of transducibility (see [Dre93b]).

Here, τ is a transducer out of the given class, so that the diagram commutes, in which case we say that f is *transducible*. (Actually, the notion is a bit more complex (see [Dre93b]), but for the purpose of this paper it is not necessary to introduce transducibility formally, anyway.)

Obviously, the question of whether a function f is transducible depends highly on three parameters: the operations available in A and B, and the class of admissable transducers. One class of tree transductions might be suitable for computing a particular type of functions from A to B, another one may be especially suited for the target algebra B', or two classes of tree transducers might serve equally well for some purpose although in general they are different in power.

This is the overall motivation for the study of various aspects of transducibility — to find out the strong and the weak points of different classes of tree transducers if applied in different situations and to get some insight into the relations between the components of the diagram. The present paper contributes to this area by studying the power of deterministic top-down tree transducers to compute a particular class of functions. In the following A will be the term algebra with one binary and one nullary symbol, B will be the algebra $\mathcal{N}$ consisting of the natural numbers with the operations maximum, addition, and multiplication, and, as already mentioned, the class of tree transducers considered is the set of all deterministic top-down tree transducers (for references see, e.g., [GS84, Eng75, Eng80]).

The interest in the target algebra $\mathcal{N}$ came from the work by Habel, Kreowski, and Vogler [HKV91], who studied *compatibile* functions and found out nice decidability results (for this, see also [Sei92, CM93, Wan91]) that carry over to transducible functions into $\mathcal{N}$ (see [Dre93b]), because the notion of transducibility is a generalization of compatibility.

The main result proved in this paper is a lower bound on the growth of transducible codings. If f is injective it provides a coding of the argument term as a natural number. It is shown that, if f can be computed by a deterministc top-down tree transducer tr with k states, this implies a constant $c \leq 2^{2^{2k}}$ such that $\|f(t)\| > |t|/c$ for all totally balanced trees t.[1] Observe that this is a statement about particular terms. It does not only say that there are terms whose value exceeds the mentioned bound, but rather that for every fixed, totally balanced tree t we have $\|f(t)\| > |t|/c$. It can be shown that the result is optimal in the sense that there are transducers that compress *all* totally balanced input trees by a constant factor c' doubly exponential in the number of states.

The lower bound is proved for deterministic top-down tree transducers, but it carries over to the whole class of (possibly nondeterministic) top-down tree transducers *with regular look-ahead* (with different c, however), because these devices have the same power for what concerns the computation of functions into $\mathcal{N}$. (The proof of the latter result, which might be of independent interest, can be found in [Dre93a]; unfortunately, there is not enough room to include it here, but the result itself is quoted in Section 3.)

[1] For a natural number n we denote by $\|n\|$ the length of the binary representation of n.

The paper is partitioned into sections as follows. The next section provides the basic definitions and notations, whereas Section 3 concentrates on the definitions around tree transducers. Section 4 provides examples of transducible codings. Section 5 contains an upper bound used to prove the main result, which is shown in Section 6. In Section 7 optimality is shown and the final section contains a short discussion of the results. Because of the limited space some of the proofs had to remain a bit sketchy, but I hope they are all comprehensible.

2 Basic definitions and notations

Let us agree on some basic definitions and notations. We denote by $\mathbb{N}$ the set of all natural numbers (including 0) and by $\mathbb{N}_+$ the set of all positive natural numbers, that is, $\mathbb{N}_+ = \mathbb{N} - \{0\}$. The length of the binary representation of $n \in \mathbb{N}$ (without leading zeroes) is denoted by $||n||$. If x is a tuple we denote by x_i its i-th component, the first one being x_1.

The composition of functions f, f', first f then f', is denoted by $f' \circ f$. As usual, f^0 is the identity and $f^{n+1} = f \circ f^n$. A relation $r \subseteq A \times B$ will also be looked at as a function from A into the powerset of B, that is, $r(a) = \{b \in B \mid (a, b) \in r\}$ for $a \in A$. We do not distinguish between $\{a\}$ and a.

A *signature* (usually denoted by Σ, Σ', etc.) is a finite set of operation symbols each of which has an arity $n \in \mathbb{N}$. If $f \in \Sigma$ is of arity n this is indicated (if necessary) by writing $f^{(n)}$. The symbols $x_1, x_2, \ldots$ denote variables, where $x_i \neq x_j$ for $i, j \in \mathbb{N}$, $i \neq j$. By $\mathrm{T}(\Sigma, k)$, k a natural number, we denote the set of terms over Σ with variables in $\{x_1, \ldots, x_k\}$. We set $\mathrm{T}(\Sigma) = \mathrm{T}(\Sigma, 0)$. If t is a term in $\mathrm{T}(\Sigma, k)$ we let $t[t_1, \ldots, t_k]$ denote the term t with x_i being replaced by t_i, for $i = 1, \ldots, k$. The *size* of a term $t \in \mathrm{T}(\Sigma)$ is the number $|t|$ of operation symbols in it, that is, $|f(t_1, \ldots, t_n)| = 1 + \sum_{i=1}^{n} |t_i|$. The *height* of $t = f(t_1, \ldots, t_n)$ is given by

$$height(t) = \begin{cases} 0 & \text{if } n = 0 \\ 1 + \max_{1 \leq i \leq n} height(t_i) & \text{if } n > 0. \end{cases}$$

If Σ is a signature, a Σ-algebra A is defined as usual: It consists of a domain $dom(A)$ and a function $f_A \colon dom(A)^n \to dom(A)$ for every $f^{(n)} \in \Sigma$, called the *interpretation* of f in A. In the following the index A will be omitted, thus writing f instead of f_A, since no confusion is likely to arise. If $t \in \mathrm{T}(\Sigma, k)$ its value in A is denoted by $\langle t \rangle_A$. It is defined in the obvious way, yielding a function in k variables. In particular, $\langle t \rangle_A \in dom(A)$ for all $t \in \mathrm{T}(\Sigma)$.

If a Σ-algebra A is given we frequently use the notation $\mathrm{T}(A)$ to mean $\mathrm{T}(\Sigma)$. Two algebras will be of special interest in the following. The first one, denoted by $\mathcal{N}$, is given by the natural numbers, that is, $dom(\mathcal{N}) = \mathbb{N}$, and the operations $\sqcup^{(2)}$, $+^{(2)}$, $\cdot^{(2)}$, $0^{(0)}$, $1^{(0)}$ together with their standard interpretation of maximum, addition, multiplication, zero, and one. The second algebra is the boolean algebra $\mathcal{B}$ whose domain is the set $\{\mathbf{true}, \mathbf{false}\}$ of truth values and whose operations are $\neg^{(1)}$, $\wedge^{(2)}$, $\vee^{(2)}$, $\mathbf{true}^{(0)}$, and $\mathbf{false}^{(0)}$ with their usual meaning.

3 Tree transducers and their computed functions

We now introduce the class of tree transducers considered in the paper. Let us start by defining tree transductions and the relations specified by them.

3.1 Definition (*tree transduction*)

Let Σ, Σ' be signatures. A tree transduction is a relation $\tau \subseteq \mathrm{T}(\Sigma) \times \mathrm{T}(\Sigma')$. If A is a Σ'-algebra we denote by $\langle\tau\rangle_A \subseteq \mathrm{T}(\Sigma) \times A$ the relation defined by

$$\langle\tau\rangle_A(t) = \{\langle t'\rangle_A \mid t' \in \tau(t)\}$$

for all $t \in \mathrm{T}(\Sigma)$. ◇

In the following sections we will only consider functional tree transductions. For these, $\langle\tau\rangle_A(t) = \langle\tau(t)\rangle_A$, by definition. If the algebra A referred to is clear from the context we write $\langle\tau\rangle$ instead of $\langle\tau\rangle_A$.

Next, we define the class of tree transducers — finite state automata that compute tree transductions — considered in this paper: the so-called *top-down tree transducers* (also called root-to-frontier tree transducers in the literature). These are tree transducers that process their input trees from the root towards the leaves.

3.2 Definition (*top-down tree transducer*, cf. [GS84])

Let Σ, Σ' be signatures and let Q be a set of *states* disjoint with $\Sigma \cup \Sigma'$, considered as a signature of unary symbols.

Let $q \in Q$ and $f^{(n)} \in \Sigma$. A *qf-rule* is a (left-linear) term rewrite rule

$$q(f(x_1, \ldots, x_n)) \rightarrow t[q_1(x_{i_1}), \ldots, q_m(x_{i_m})]$$

such that $t \in \mathrm{T}(\Sigma', m)$ and $q_j(x_{i_j}) \in \mathrm{T}(Q, n)$ for $j = 1, \ldots, m$.

A *top-down tree transducer* $tr\colon \mathrm{T}(\Sigma) \rightarrow \mathrm{T}(\Sigma')$ from $\mathrm{T}(\Sigma)$ into $\mathrm{T}(\Sigma')$ is a pair $tr = (q_0, R)$ such that

- q_0, called the *initial state*, is an element of Q, and
- R is a finite set of qf-rules, with $q \in Q$, $f \in \Sigma$.

The rewrite relation $\rightarrow_{tr}$ and its reflexive, transitive closure $\rightarrow^*_{tr}$ are defined as usual for term rewrite systems. For every $q \in Q$ we let

$$tr[q](t) = \{t' \in \mathrm{T}(\Sigma') \mid q(t) \xrightarrow[tr]{*} t'\}.$$

The transduction $tr[q_0]$, usually denoted by tr, is the transduction tr computes. ◇

In the following we omit the attribute *top-down* since no other sorts of transducers will be dealt with. If tr is a tree transducer into $\mathrm{T}(A)$, A an algebra, we denote by $\langle tr\rangle$ the relation $\langle tr\rangle_A$.

A tree transducer tr is *total* if $tr(t) \neq \emptyset$ for all $t \in \mathrm{T}(\Sigma)$ and is *deterministic* if there is at most one qf-rule for every $(q, f) \in Q \times \Sigma$. Clearly, the transductions defined by deterministic tree transducers are functional; hence total deterministic tree transducers define total functions. Observe also that total deterministic tree transducers can be assumed to be *reduced* in the sense that $tr[q]$ is total for all states q of tr. This is because states without this property must be unreachable (to keep tr total), so removing them does not affect the transduction.

To end this section let us quote the equivalence result for deterministic tree transducers and tree transducers with regular look-ahead mentioned in the introduction. (A tree transducer with regular look-ahead is a tree transducer in which every qf-rule (f of arity n) is equipped with n regular sets $T_1, \ldots, T_n$ of trees. The application of such a rule is then restricted to terms $f(t_1, \ldots, t_n)$ with $t_i \in T_i$ for $i = 1, \ldots, n$.)

3.3 Proposition (cf. [Dre93a])

Let Σ be a signature and let $\mathcal{N}'$ be an algebra over $\mathbb{N}$ containing as operations at least addition and multiplication. For every tree transducer $tr^R\colon \mathrm{T}(\Sigma) \rightarrow \mathrm{T}(\mathcal{N}')$ with regular look-ahead, if $\langle tr^R\rangle$ is functional, there is a deterministic tree transducer $tr\colon \mathrm{T}(\Sigma) \rightarrow \mathrm{T}(\mathcal{N}')$ such that

$$\langle tr\rangle(t) = \begin{cases} \langle tr^R\rangle(t) & \text{if } \langle tr^R\rangle(t) \neq \emptyset \\ 0 & \text{otherwise} \end{cases}$$

for all terms $t \in \mathrm{T}(\Sigma)$. ◇

In [Dre93a] Proposition 3.3 is formulated (and proved) for $\mathcal{N}' = \mathcal{N}$ but the proof uses only the fact that $\mathcal{N}$ contains $+$ and $\cdot$. Using Proposition 3.3 the linear bound proved in Section 6 carries over to the whole class of (possibly nondeterministic) tree transducers with regular look-ahead, which are, on the level of trees, strictly more powerful than deterministic tree transducers without.

4 Codings defined by tree transducers

For the rest of the paper we want to consider as input terms the set $\mathbf{T} = \mathrm{T}(\Sigma)$, the set of all binary trees with $\Sigma = \{bin^{(2)}, \bot^{(0)}\}$, and $\mathcal{N}$, the algebra with domain $\mathbb{N}$ and operations $\sqcup$, $+$, $\cdot$, 0, 1, as defined already in Section 2. We study the power of deterministic tree transducers that compute codings of terms, that is, injective functions from $\mathbf{T}$ into the natural numbers. In this section two such codings are given.

The terms of $\mathbf{T}$ may easily be coded as words over $\{0,1\}$ by defining $\overline{code}(\bot) = 0$ and $\overline{code}(bin(t,t')) = 1\overline{code}(t)\overline{code}(t')$. This function is well-known to be injective, and the leftmost digit of $\overline{code}(t)$ is 1 unless $t = \bot$. Therefore, $\overline{code}$ gives rise to the injective function $code: \mathbf{T} \to \mathbb{N}$ such that $\overline{code}(t)$ is the binary representation of $code(t)$. We may compute $code$ by a deterministic tree transducer using two states val and len. Let $cod = (val, R)$ where

$$\begin{aligned} R = \{\ & val(\bot) \to 0, \\ & len(\bot) \to 2, \\ & val(bin(x_1,x_2)) \to (len(x_1) + val(x_1)) \cdot len(x_2) + val(x_2), \\ & len(bin(x_1,x_2)) \to 2 \cdot len(x_1) \cdot len(x_2) \quad \}. \end{aligned}$$

(We use 2 as a shorthand for the term $1+1$.) By induction on $|t|$ it follows that $\langle cod[len]\rangle(t) = 2^{|t|}$ and thus $\langle cod\rangle = code$.

Using $code$ the representation of a term t as a natural number $n = code(t)$ satisfies $|t| = \|n\|$. In other words: the representation of a term is always as long as the term itself; no term gets compressed. Can we do better? Is there a deterministic tree transducer computing a coding that compresses suitable terms? The answer is *yes*.

Consider the set $\mathbf{T}' \subseteq \mathbf{T}$ of terms that have the form $bin(bin(\cdots bin(\bot,\bot)\cdots))$. If $t \in \mathbf{T}'$ we can represent t as $|t|$, thus obtaining a coding of logarithmic length for these chain terms. Define for $t \in \mathbf{T}$

$$code'(t) = \begin{cases} |t| & \text{if } t \in \mathbf{T}' \\ code(t) & \text{otherwise.} \end{cases}$$

This new function is injective, too, since $code(t)$ is always even whereas $|t|$ is always odd. Let us notice that $\mathbf{T}'$ is recognizable. Therefore, using Proposition 3.3 it follows that there is a deterministic tree transducer from $\mathbf{T}$ to $\mathrm{T}(\mathcal{N})$ computing $code'$. (A direct construction could be based on Theorem 7.1, which is in fact also the key to the proof of Proposition 3.3.)

The example of $code'$ shows that deterministic tree transducers can compute codings that compress input terms of a suitable type. However, from an intuitive point of view it is clear that this ability is quite limited. In the following we want to consider the subset $\mathbf{T}_b$ of $\mathbf{T}$ that consists of all totally balanced binary trees in $\mathbf{T}$. For a tree in $\mathbf{T}_b$ the only thing we must know in order to reconstruct it is its height. So, one can easily define an injective function $code'': \mathbf{T} \to \mathbb{N}$ such that $\|code''(t)\| \in O(\log\log|t|)$ for all $t \in \mathbf{T}_b$. Can a function like $code''$ ever be computed by a deterministic tree transducer? In the following two sections it is shown that this is not the case. For every deterministic tree transducer there is a constant $c \leq 2^{2^k}$ (where k is the number of states of the transducer used) such that every $t \in \mathbf{T}_b$ gets compressed by at most the factor c. Hence even $O(\log|t|)$ is impossible to achieve, not to mention $O(\log\log|t|)$.

5 Intermezzo: An upper bound

In this section an upper bound is proved that is used in the next section to show the main result. The upper bound concerns the maximum length of anti-chains in $\mathbb{N}^k$ — sequences of pairwise incomparable elements of $\mathbb{N}^k$ — obtained using $\sqcup$, $+$, and $\cdot$. We show that the length of these chains cannot exceed a certain (exponential) upper bound. Later on, this will be used in order to show that there must be two terms of at most exponential height, so that every entry in the k-tuple of values the transducer computes for the first is smaller than or equal to the corresponding entry in the tuple obtained for the second.

General assumption. Within this section, let k be an arbitrary, but fixed natural number.

As explained in Section 2, for every Σ-algebra A a term $t \in \mathrm{T}(\Sigma, l)$ defines a function $\langle t \rangle_A \colon dom(A)^l \to dom(A)$. Let us denote the class of these functions by $P_{A,l}$, where we omit l in case $l = k$. Every k-tuple $p \in P_A^k$ can be looked at as a function from $dom(A)^k$ into $dom(A)^k$, where $p(a) = (p_1(a), \ldots, p_k(a))$ for all $a \in dom(A)^k$.

In all what follows we omit the index A whenever $A = \mathcal{N}$. We are going to show the following theorem.

5.1 Theorem

For all $p \in P^k$ and $x \in \mathbb{N}^k$ there exist $c < c' < 2^{2k}$ such that $p^c(x) \leq p^{c'}(x)$.[2] $\diamond$

In order to prove Theorem 5.1 consider some fixed $p \in P$ and define a graph G that has as its nodes the numbers $1, \ldots, k$, where there is an edge directed from v to v' if $p_{v'}$ depends on its v-th argument.[3] Let us call a node in G a c-node if it lies on a cycle in G. Clearly, the proof of Theorem 5.1 must especially consider the cycles and it must exploit the monotonicity of the operations in $\mathcal{N}$ to show that these components of the tuple must eventually grow (or at least stay constant). However, we cannot conclude that a component within a cycle of length l grows after at most l steps because its old value may get "deleted" by multiplication with 0 somewhere on the course of the computation. Therefore, three lemmas are proved before the proof of the theorem. The first one deals with the indices not on a cycle. In the second we look at c-nodes, but in the easier situation where there is neither a 0 in x nor in p (that is, no component of p is the constant function 0). The third lemma synthesizes these two.

Remark. The reader might wonder whether it is perhaps easier to find a way to detect and remove multiplications with 0 in advance. However, this would have

[2] For k-tuples $x, y \in \mathbb{N}^k$ we define $x \leq y$ if $x_i \leq y_i$ for $i = 1, \ldots, k$.

[3] A function $f \colon A^k \to B$ depends on its i-th argument ($1 \leq i \leq k$) if there are $a_1, \ldots, a_k, a_i' \in A$ such that $f(a_1, \ldots, {}_{-k}) \neq f(a_1, \ldots, a_{i-1}, a_i', a_{i+1}, \ldots, a_k)$.

to happen on the level of transducers and since we work with top-down devices it does not seem to be possible to achieve this without using nondeterminism — which would complicate the situation instead of simplifying it. ◇

In the lemma given below it is stated that, if the values of c-nodes always grow after c steps, the others will also grow, with only a small delay. The reason should be clear: The value of a component not on any cycle depends only on the values of c-nodes. It is determined by the value these components had a number of steps before, that number resulting from the distances to cyclic nodes from which it can be reached.

5.2 Lemma

Suppose there are l c-nodes among $1, \ldots, k$ and let $c \in \mathbb{N}$ and $x \in \mathbb{N}^k$ be such that $p^i(x)_j \leq p^{c+i}(x)_j$ for $j = 1, \ldots, l$ and $i \in \mathbb{N}$. Then $p^{k-l}(x) \leq p^{c+k-l}(x)$.

Proof. Assume without loss of generality that $1, \ldots, l$ are the c-nodes and let $x^i = p^i(x)$ with $x^0 = x$. By assumption $x^i_j \leq x^{c+i}_j$ for $j = 1, \ldots, l$ and all $i \geq 0$. Consider some index j, $l < j \leq k$, and let $w_1, \ldots, w_m$ be the (directed) paths from c-nodes $start(w_i)$ to j that do not pass a c-node. It is easy to show by induction on the maximum length of the w_i that there is some $q \in P_{\mathcal{N},m}$ such that for all $n \geq \max_{1 \leq i \leq m} |w_i|$ we have $x^n_j = q\left(x^{n-|w_1|}_{start(w_1)}, \ldots, x^{n-|w_m|}_{start(w_m)}\right)$, that is, x^n_j depends only on the values the entries $start(w_1), \ldots, start(w_m)$ assumed $|w_1|, \ldots, |w_m|$ steps before. But since these entries are c-nodes whose values increase after at most c steps we get $x^{k-l} \leq x^{c+k-l}$ because $n \leq k - l$. □

Let us now concentrate on the c-nodes, assuming $p_i \neq 0 \neq x_i$ for $i = 1, \ldots, k$.

5.3 Lemma

Suppose that $p_i \neq 0$ for $i = 1, \ldots, k$ and let there be l c-nodes among $1, \ldots, k$. There is a constant c, $1 \leq c < 2^l$ such that $x_i \leq p^c(x)_i$ for all i, $1 \leq i \leq l$, and all $x \in \mathbb{N}^k_+$.

Proof. Again, let $1, \ldots, l$ be the c-nodes and let $x^i = p^i(x)$ with $x^0 = x$. Since for all $n_1, n_2 \in \mathbb{N}_+$ and each $\odot \in \{\sqcup, +, \cdot\}$ we have $n_i \leq n_1 \odot n_2$ $(i = 1, 2)$ it holds that $x^i \in \mathbb{N}^k_+$ for all i. Hence, if there is a path of length i from j_1 to j_2 in G we get $x_{j_1} \leq x^i_{j_2}$. Suppose c_i is the length of the shortest cycle the node i is contained in, for $i = 1, \ldots, l$, and let $c = \mathrm{lcm}(c_1, \ldots, c_l)$[4]. We have $x_i \leq x^{nc_i}_i$ and hence $x_i \leq x^c_i$ for $i = 1, \ldots, l$. In fact, it even suffices to define $c = g(l) = \max\{\mathrm{lcm}(a_1, \ldots, a_j) \mid \sum_{i=1}^{j} a_i = l\}$ since $c_i \leq l$ and if some node

[4]By $\mathrm{lcm}(c_1, \ldots, c_l)$ we denote the least common multiple of $c_1, \ldots, c_l$.

i lies on a cycle of length c_i the other $c_i - 1$ nodes also on that cycle do not contribute to the lcm. Induction on l shows $g(l) < 2^l$:[5] For $l = 1$ this is trivial and otherwise we obtain

$$g(l) \leq \max_{l_1+l_2=l} g(l_1) \cdot g(l_2) < \max_{l_1+l_2=l} 2^{l_1} 2^{l_2} = 2^l. \qquad \square$$

Together, the two previous lemmas yield the following.

5.4 Lemma

Suppose that $p_i \neq 0$ for $i = 1, \ldots, k$. There are constants $c < c' < 2^k$ such that $p^c(x) \leq p^{c'}(x)$ for all $x \in \mathbb{N}_+^k$.

Proof. Let l be the number of c-nodes, $c = k - l$ and $c' = c_0 + k - l$, where $c_0 < 2^l$ is obtained from Lemma 5.3. Together, Lemmas 5.2 and 5.3 yield $p^c(x) \leq p^{c'}(x)$ for all $x \in \mathbb{N}_+^k$. But $k - l \leq 2^{k-l}$ and hence $c' < 2^l + k - l \leq 2^k$. $\square$

We are now able to prove Theorem 5.1. In the proof we will make use of the homomorphism $^-$ from $\mathcal{N}$ to $\mathcal{B}$ given by $\bar{\cdot} = \wedge$ and $\overline{+} = \overline{\sqcup} = \vee$, that is,

$$\overline{x} = \begin{cases} \textbf{false} & \text{if } x = 0 \\ \textbf{true} & \text{otherwise.} \end{cases}$$

The natural extensions of $^-$ to $\mathcal{N}^k$, P, and P^k also get denoted by $^-$.

Proof of Theorem 5.1. Since $^-$ is a homomorphism, for all $n \in \mathbb{N}$ and all i ($1 \leq i \leq k$) we have $\overline{p}^n(\overline{x})_i = \textbf{false}$ if and only if $p^n(x)_i = 0$. Due to the fact that the cardinality of $\mathcal{B}^k$ is 2^k we can find $c_0 < c_1 \leq 2^k$ such that $\overline{p}^{c_0}(\overline{x}) = \overline{p}^{c_1}(\overline{x})$. With $\Delta = c_1 - c_0$ we therefore get $\overline{p}^{c_0}(\overline{x}) = \overline{p}^{i\Delta + c_0}(\overline{x})$ for all $i \in \mathbb{N}$. Defining $\tilde{p} = p^{\Delta}$ and $\tilde{x} = p^{c_0}(x)$ we now get $\tilde{p}^n(\tilde{x})_i = 0$ if and only if $\tilde{x}_i = 0$. Thus we may assume that p_i depends on its j-th argument only if $x_j \neq 0$. Say $\tilde{x}_1, \ldots, \tilde{x}_l \neq 0$ and $\tilde{x}_{l+1}, \ldots, \tilde{x}_k = 0$. Then Lemma 5.4 applies to $q = (\tilde{p}_1, \ldots, \tilde{p}_l)$ and $y = (\tilde{x}_1, \ldots, \tilde{x}_l)$ saying that there are constants $m < m' \leq 2^l \leq 2^k$ such that $q^m(y) \leq q^{m'}(y)$. This reveals $\tilde{p}^m(\tilde{x}) = (q^m(y), 0, \ldots, 0) \leq (q^{m'}(y), 0, \ldots, 0) = \tilde{p}^{m'}(\tilde{x})$, so that for $c = m\Delta + c_0$ and $c' = m'\Delta + c_0$

$$p^c(x) = p^{m\Delta}(p^{c_0}(x)) = \tilde{p}^m(\tilde{x}) \leq \tilde{p}^{m'}(\tilde{x}) = p^{m'\Delta}(p^{c_0}(x)) = p^{c'}(x).$$

So, we are ready since $c < c' = m'\Delta + c_0 \leq 2^k(c_1 - c_0) + c_0 \leq 2^k c_1 \leq 2^{2k}$. $\square$

[5] In the literature, $g(l)$ is known as *Landau's function* with $g(l) \approx e^{\sqrt{n \cdot \log_e n}}$ (as I was kindly told by a referee), named after a prominent German number theorist from the first half of the century.

6 Consequence: A lower bound

We now prove the main result of the paper. In the following we assume that all total deterministic tree transducers we deal with are reduced (see Section 3), that is, if tr is a total deterministic tree transducer, then $tr[q]$ is total for all states q of tr. This simplifies the formulation of the next lemma, but it means no loss of generality, as argued in Section 3. The lemma draws the connection between the results of the previous section and the context we are interested in.

6.1 Lemma

Let $tr\colon \mathbf{T} \to \mathrm{T}(\mathcal{N})$ be a reduced, total deterministic tree transducer with k states such that $\langle tr \rangle$ is injective. There are totally balanced trees $t, t' \in \mathbf{T}$ of height less than 2^{2k} such that $t \neq t'$ and $\langle tr[q] \rangle(t) \leq \langle tr[q] \rangle(t')$ for all states q of tr.

Proof. Since tr is reduced, there is exactly one qf-rule in tr for every state q and every $f \in \{bin, \perp\}$. Let $q_1, \ldots, q_k$ be the states of tr and define $p = (p_1, \ldots, p_k)$ as follows. If t_i is obtained from the right-hand side of the $q_i bin$-rule by replacing all subterms of the form $q_j(x_l)$ ($j = 1, \ldots, k$ and $l = 1, 2$) by x_j then $p_i = \langle t_i \rangle_{\mathcal{N}}$. With $x = (\langle tr[q_1] \rangle(\perp), \ldots, \langle tr[q_k] \rangle(\perp))$ this definition yields

$$(\langle tr[q_1] \rangle(t), \ldots, \langle tr[q_k] \rangle(t)) = p^{height(t)}(x)$$

for all totally balanced trees $t \in \mathbf{T}$, as is easy to show by induction on $height(t)$. Now the assertion follows directly from Theorem 5.1. □

Using the previous lemma we are able to prove the promissed theorem. Notice that the proof idea is *not* to iterate the reasoning that led to Lemma 6.1, because this would only yield $\langle tr \rangle(t) \in \Omega(height(t))$, that is, $\|\langle tr \rangle(t)\| \in \Omega(\log\log|t|)$. Instead, the idea is to consider a totally balanced term t with n subtrees of the form t_1 (observe that n is of order $|t|$) and to replace some of the t_1 by t_0 (with t_0, t_1 as in Lemma 6.1). Then the values of the resulting terms must be different (by injectivity) and they all must be smaller than the one of t (by monotonicity and choice of t_0, t_1), hence $\langle tr \rangle(t) \geq 2^n - 1$.

6.2 Theorem

Let $tr\colon \mathbf{T} \to \mathrm{T}(\mathcal{N})$ be a total deterministic tree transducer with k states such that $\langle tr \rangle$ is injective. There is some $c \leq 2^{2^{2k}}$ such that for all totally balanced trees $t \in \mathbf{T}$

$$\|\langle tr \rangle(t)\| > |t|/c. \qquad \diamond$$

Proof. Assume without loss of generality that tr is reduced and let $t_0, t_1 \in \mathbf{T}$ be minimal, totally balanced trees such that $t_0 \neq t_1$ and $\langle tr[q] \rangle(t_0) \leq \langle tr[q] \rangle(t_1)$ for all states q of tr. By Lemma 6.1 t_0 and t_1 exist and $height(t_0), height(t_1) < 2^{2k}$.

Assume without loss of generality that $height(t_0) < height(t_1)$ and consider some totally balanced term $t \in \mathbf{T}$ at least as large as t_1. Then $n = 2^{height(t)-height(t_1)}$ is the number of subterms of t of the form t_1. Denote for every $w \in \{0,1\}^n$ by t_w the term obtained from t by replacing the i-th occurrence of t_1 by t_0 if $w_i = 0$. By monotonicity of the operations in $\mathcal{N}$ we get $\langle tr\rangle(t) \geq \langle tr\rangle(t_w)$ for all $w \in \{0,1\}^n$. Furthermore, since $\langle tr\rangle$ is injective, $\langle tr\rangle(t_w) \neq \langle tr\rangle(t_{w'})$ whenever $w \neq w'$, and therefore $\langle tr\rangle(t) \geq 2^n - 1$, that is, $\|\langle tr\rangle(t)\| \geq n$ and the following inequality completes the proof:

$$|t| = n - 1 + n\,|t_1| \leq n - 1 + 2^{2^{2k}-1}n < 2^{2^{2k}}n = cn. \qquad \square$$

Although the emphasis of this paper lies on the study of ⊔, +, and · as operations of the target algebra, it is worthwhile to notice that the proof of Theorem 6.2 itself does not rely on any other property than the monotonicity of operations. Hence if we are not interested in a bound for the constant c the result holds for all sets of monotone operations, as stated in the corollary below.

6.3 Corollary

Let $\mathcal{N}'$ be an algebra over $\mathbb{N}$ that contains monotone operations only and let $tr\colon \mathbf{T} \to \mathrm{T}(\mathcal{N}')$ be a total deterministic tree transducer such that $\langle tr\rangle$ is injective. There is some $c \in \mathbb{N}$ such that for all totally balanced trees $t \in \mathbf{T}$

$$\|\langle tr\rangle(t)\| \geq |t|/c. \qquad \diamond$$

Proof. This is clear as soon as we can show that there are c, c' satisfying Theorem 5.1 if the additional requirement $c < c' < 2^{2k}$ is omitted. But this follows from the fact that $\leq$ is a well-quasi-order on $\mathbb{N}^k$, which implies that there are no infinite anti-chains, that is, for all infinite sequences $(x_i)_{i\in\mathbb{N}}$ $(x_i \in \mathbb{N}^k)$ there are $i, j \in \mathbb{N}$, $i < j$, such that $x_i \leq x_j$ (see [NW63]). □

Together with Proposition 3.3 we obtain one further generalization:

6.4 Corollary

Let $\mathcal{N}'$ be an algebra over $\mathbb{N}$ that contains monotone operations only and let $tr^R\colon \mathbf{T} \to \mathrm{T}(\mathcal{N}')$ be a tree transducer with regular look-ahead such that $\langle tr^R\rangle$ is injective. There is some $c \in \mathbb{N}$ such that for all totally balanced trees $t \in \mathbf{T}$

$$\|\langle tr^R\rangle(t)\| \geq |t|/c. \qquad \diamond$$

Proof. This is a direct consequence of Corollary 6.3 and Proposition 3.3. □

However, observe that the corollaries lack the bound on c known from Theorem 6.2.

7 Optimality

At first sight, the doubly exponential constant c provided by Theorem 6.2 seems unreasonably large and one could hope to be able to reduce it by a more sophisticated proof. But we can show that it must indeed be doubly exponential. This can be seen by exploiting an idea that allows to code truth values as pairs of natural numbers, as made precise in the following.

7.1 Theorem

Let Σ be a signature and let $tr\colon \mathrm{T}(\Sigma) \to \mathrm{T}(\mathcal{B})$ be a deterministc tree transducer. Then there is a deterministc tree transducer $tr'\colon \mathrm{T}(\Sigma) \to \mathrm{T}(\mathcal{N})$ such that tr' contains states $q, \hat{q}$ for every state q of tr (and no further states) such that

$$\langle tr'[q]\rangle(t) = 1 - \langle tr'[\hat{q}]\rangle(t) = \begin{cases} 1 & \text{if } \langle tr[q]\rangle(t) = \mathbf{true} \\ 0 & \text{otherwise} \end{cases}$$

for all $t \in \mathrm{T}(\Sigma)$.

Proof. A *nondeleting* transducer is one in which every variable that occurs in the left-hand side of a rule occurs also in the right-hand side of that rule. It is known from a result by Baker [Bak79] that for every deterministc tree transducer tr and every nondeleting deterministc tree transducer tr' there is a deterministc tree transducer tr'' whose states set is the cartesian product of the states sets of tr and tr', such that for all its states (q', q) we have $tr''[(q', q)] = tr'[q'] \circ tr[q]$.

Define a nondeleting transducer $tr' = (h, R_0)$ using states h, $\hat{h}$ by

$$\begin{aligned} R_0 = \{\ & h(\mathbf{true}) && \to && 1, \\ & h(\mathbf{false}) && \to && 0, \\ & h(\neg x_1) && \to && \hat{h}(x_1), \\ & h(x_1 \wedge x_2) && \to && h(x_1) \cdot h(x_2), \\ & h(x_1 \vee x_2) && \to && h(x_1) \cdot h(x_2) + h(x_1) \cdot \hat{h}(x_2) + \hat{h}(x_1) \cdot h(x_2), \\ \\ & \hat{h}(\mathbf{true}) && \to && 0, \\ & \hat{h}(\mathbf{false}) && \to && 1, \\ & \hat{h}(\neg x_1) && \to && h(x_1), \\ & \hat{h}(x_1 \wedge x_2) && \to && h(x_1) \cdot \hat{h}(x_2) + \hat{h}(x_1) \cdot \hat{h}(x_2) + \hat{h}(x_1) \cdot h(x_2), \\ & \hat{h}(x_1 \vee x_2) && \to && \hat{h}(x_1) \cdot \hat{h}(x_2)\ \ \} \end{aligned}$$

By induction on $|t|$ the following can be verified for all $t \in \mathrm{T}(\mathcal{B})$:

$$\langle tr'\rangle(t) = 1 - \langle tr'\rangle(t) = \begin{cases} 1 & \text{if } \langle t\rangle_{\mathcal{B}} = \mathbf{true} \\ 0 & \text{if } \langle t\rangle_{\mathcal{B}} = \mathbf{false} \end{cases}$$

Now for $tr = (q_0, R)$ the composition result by Baker proves the theorem if we identify q with (h, q) and $\hat{q}$ with $(\hat{h}, q)$ for all states q of tr. □

(It is worth noticing the following closure property that results from the closure of deterministic tree transductions under nondeleting deterministic tree transductions: For each two deterministic tree transducers $tr\colon \mathrm{T}(\Sigma) \to \mathrm{T}(\Sigma')$ and $tr'\colon \mathrm{T}(\Sigma') \to \mathrm{T}(\mathcal{N})$ we can find a deterministic tree transducer $tr''\colon \mathrm{T}(\Sigma) \to \mathrm{T}(\mathcal{N})$ such that $\langle tr'' \rangle = \langle tr' \rangle \circ tr$. This holds true because every transducer into $\mathcal{N}$ can be made nondeleting by replacing a right-hand side t in which the variable x_i does not occur by $t + 0 \cdot q(x_i)$ (where q is a new state with $tr[q](t) \neq \emptyset$ for all $t \in \mathrm{T}(\Sigma)$).)

Using the previous theorem we can mimic the behaviour of a deterministic tree transducer $tr\colon \mathrm{T}(\Sigma) \to \mathrm{T}(\mathcal{B})$ by a transducer $tr'\colon \mathrm{T}(\Sigma) \to \mathrm{T}(\mathcal{N})$, and the latter needs at most twice as many states as the former. This enables us to exploit the next lemma for the proof of the optimality result directly following it.

7.2 Lemma

For all $c \in \mathbb{N}$ there is some $c' \in \mathbb{N}$ such that for all $k \in \mathbb{N}$ there is a deterministic tree transducer $tr\colon \mathbf{T} \to \mathrm{T}(\mathcal{B})$ using $k + c'$ states such that for all $t \in \mathbf{T}$ we have $\langle tr \rangle(t) = \mathbf{true}$ if and only if $height(t) = 2^k + c$.

Proof. It suffices to prove the statement for a particular pair c, c' because for $c + d$ we may then choose $c' + d$, simply counting the first d levels of a tree using the d additional states. Therefore, consider $c = -2$ and $c' = 1$.

Let us interpret a sequence $x_1 \cdots x_k$ of truth values as the binary representation of a natural number. Then we can define a deterministic tree transducer $tr = (q_0, R)$ with states $q_0, \ldots, q_k$, such that $\langle tr[q_1] \rangle(t) \cdots \langle tr[q_k] \rangle(t)$ represents the number

$$\#(t) = \begin{cases} 0 & \text{if } t = \bot \\ \#(t_1) + 1 & \text{if } t = bin(t_1, t_2) \text{ and } \#(t_1) = \#(t_2) < 2^k - 1 \\ 2^k - 1 & \text{otherwise.} \end{cases}$$

For the i-th bit $(1 \leq i \leq k)$ the necessary rules are $q_i(\bot) \to 0$ and, with $x \oplus y = x \wedge \neg y \vee \neg x \wedge y$ denoting the *xor* operation,

$$\begin{aligned} q_i(bin(x_1, x_2)) \to\ & q_1(x_1) \wedge \cdots \wedge q_k(x_1) \vee q_1(x_2) \wedge \cdots \wedge q_k(x_2) \\ & \vee\ (q_1(x_1) \oplus q_1(x_2)) \vee \cdots \vee (q_k(x_1) \oplus q_k(x_2)) \\ & \vee\ (q_i(x_1) \oplus (q_{i+1}(x_1) \wedge \cdots \wedge q_k(x_1))) . \end{aligned}$$

Here, the first row sets bit i to 1 (that is, **true**) if the values for one of the subterms represent the number $2^k - 1$. The same happens if the values for the subterms differ at some place (second row), and otherwise the bit is set or not, according to the result of adding 1 to the number assigned to the subterms.

Now, it suffices to include two further rules for q_0 so that

$$\langle tr[q_0]\rangle(t) = \langle tr[q_1]\rangle(t) \wedge \cdots \wedge \langle tr[q_{k-1}]\rangle(t) \wedge \neg\langle tr[q_k]\rangle(t),$$

that is, $\langle tr[q_0]\rangle(t) = \mathbf{true}$ if $\langle tr[q_1]\rangle(t) \cdots \langle tr[q_k]\rangle(t)$ represents the number $2^k - 2$. This finishes the proof. □

7.3 Theorem

There is a constant c, so that for all $k \in \mathbb{N}$ a deterministic tree transducer $tr\colon \mathbf{T} \to \mathrm{T}(\mathcal{N})$ with $2k + c$ states exists, such that $\langle tr\rangle$ is injective and

$$\|\langle tr\rangle(t)\| < |t| / 2^{2^k}$$

for all sufficiently large, totally balanced terms $t \in \mathbf{T}$.

Proof. Denote by $t_{(i)}$ the totally balanced term of height i and let, for $t \in \mathbf{T}$, $\tilde{t}$ be the term in which every subterm $t_{(2^k+2)}$ is replaced by $t_{(2)}$ and every $\perp$ not part of a subterm $t_{(2^k+2)}$ is replaced by $bin(bin(\perp, \perp), \perp)$. Then $\tilde{\ }$ is injective.

Theorem 7.1 and Lemma 7.2 provide a deterministic tree transducer tr' with $2k + c$ states such that

$$\langle tr'[q_0]\rangle(t) = 1 - \langle tr'[\hat{q}_0]\rangle(t) = \begin{cases} 1 & \text{if } height(t) = 2^k + 2 \\ 0 & \text{otherwise} \end{cases}$$

for all $t \in \mathrm{T}(\Sigma)$.

Now, it is not hard to combine tr' with the tree transducer *cod* used to compute *code* in Section 4 in such a way that $\langle tr\rangle(t) = code(\tilde{t})$. Then for $i \geq 2^k + 2$ we get $\|\langle tr\rangle(t_{(i)})\| = \|code(t_{(i-2^k)})\| = |t_{(i-2^k)}|$, so

$$2^{2^k} \|\langle tr\rangle(t_{(i)})\| = 2^{2^k} |t_{(i-2^k)}| = 2^{2^k}(2^{i-2^k+1} - 1) = |t_{(i)}| + 1 - 2^{2^k} < |t_{(i)}|. \ \square$$

8 Discussion

Tree transducers can be used to perform symbolic computations from one algebra into another. In particular, they may yield codings of trees by computing for every input tree a unique natural number. We have seen that, if this work is performed by a top-down tree transducer (with or without regular look-ahead) and the operations in the target algebra are monotone the obtained coding cannot compress any totally balanced tree by more than a constant factor.

The main interest, however, was devoted to the case where $\sqcup$, $+$, and $\cdot$ are the operations available and deterministic top-down tree transducers perform the computations. In this case, there is a constant $c \leq 2^{2^{2k}}$ (where k is the transducer's number of states) such that the length (in binary digits) of the number computed for any totally balanced tree t is at least $|t| / c$.

It was shown that this result is optimal in two respects. At first, it is really necessary to use a constant doubly exponential in the number of states of the considered automaton. Secondly, there exist coding functions that compress *every* totally balanced input term by this amount. Hence it is impossible to obtain a smaller constant even if we allow for a finite number of exceptions.

The results indicate that top-down tree transducers have quite a limited power for what concerns the computation of functions into $\mathbb{N}$ — at least if the operations that may be used are monotone. Although this might be considered a negative result it is not just disappointing because, as mentioned in the introduction, the main aim was not to actually use tree transducers for the computation of codings, but to gain some first insight into the properties of transducible functions. Of course, one of the next steps must be to try and find some more general statements about the power of top-down tree transducers (and other ways to define tree transductions) in the framework of transducibility.

Acknowledgement. I thank the referees for a number of valuable hints which — as I hope — led to some improvements. (If not, it's not their fault, of course.)

References

[Bak79] B.S. Baker. Composition of top-down and bottom-up tree transductions. *Information and Control* 41, 186–213, 1979.

[CM93] B. Courcelle, M. Mosbah. Monadic second order evaluations on tree-decomposable graphs. *Theoretical Computer Science* 109, 49–82, 1993.

[Dre93a] F. Drewes. A lower bound on the growth of functions computed by tree transducers. Report 4/93, Univ. Bremen, 1993.

[Dre93b] F. Drewes. Transducibility — symbolic computation by tree-transductions. Report 2/93, Univ. Bremen, 1993.

[Eng75] J. Engelfriet. Bottom-up and top-down tree transformations — a comparison. *Mathematical Systems Theory* 9(3), 198–231, 1975.

[Eng80] J. Engelfriet. Some open questions and recent results on tree transducers and tree languages. In R.V. Book, editor, *Formal Language Theory: Perspectives and Open Problems*, 241–286. Academic Press, New York, 1980.

[GS84] F. Gécseg, M. Steinby. *Tree Automata*. Akadémiai Kiadó, Budapest, 1984.

[HKV91] A. Habel, H.-J. Kreowski, W. Vogler. Decidable boundedness problems for sets of graphs generated by hyperedge-replacement. *Theoretical Computer Science* 89, 33–62, 1991.

[NW63] C.St.J.A. Nash-Williams. On well-quasi-ordering trees. In *Proc. Cambridge Phil. Soc. 59*, 833–835, 1963.

[Sei92] H. Seidl. Finite tree automata with cost functions. In J.-C. Raoult, editor, Proc. CAAP 92, *Lecture Notes in Computer Science* 581, 279–299, 1992.

[Wan91] E. Wanke. On the decidability of integer subgraph problems on context-free graph languages. In L. Budach, editor, Proc. Fundamentals of Computation Theory, *Lecture Notes in Computer Science* 529, 415–426, 1991.

On the Decidability of Model Checking for Several μ-calculi and Petri Nets

Javier Esparza

Laboratory for Foundations of Computer Science
University of Edinburgh
King's Buildings
Edinburgh EH9 3JZ
e-mail: je@dcs.ed.ac.uk

Abstract. The decidability of the model checking problem for several μ-calculi and Petri nets is analysed. The linear time μ-calculus without atomic sentences is decidable; if simple atomic sentences are added, it becomes undecidable. A very simple subset of the modal μ-calculus is undecidable.

1 Introduction

Research on decidability issues for Petri nets (or vector addition systems, a closely related model) has a long tradition. Two milestones are the introduction by Karp and Miller of coverability graphs [9] – which can be used to prove, among other properties, the decidability of boundedness – and the proof by Mayr and Kosaraju of the decidability of the reachability problem [12, 10]. A natural next step is to examine the decidability of the model checking problem for temporal logics able to express a large class of properties. This problem was first studied by Howell and Rosier in [6]; they observed that a simple linear time temporal logic is undecidable even for conflict-free Petri nets, a fairly small class. This logic is interpreted on the infinite occurrence sequences of the net, and consists of atomic sentences, the usual boolean connectives, and the operator **F** (eventually). The atomic sentences are of type $ge(s, c)$ (with intended meaning 'at the current marking, the number of tokens on place s is greater than or equal to c') or of type $fi(t)$ (with intended meaning 'transition t is the next one in the sequence'). In a subsequent paper [7], Howell, Rosier and Yen showed that the model checking problem for the positive fragment of this logic (in which negations are only applied to atomic sentences) can be reduced to the reachability problem, and is thus decidable. Jančar showed in [8] that the positive fragment with **GF** (always eventually) as operator, instead of **F**, is decidable as well.

We analyse in this paper the decidability of several μ-calculi, logics with fixpoint operators [15]. Our three results are:

- The linear time μ-calculus without atomic sentences is decidable.
- The linear time μ-calculus with atomic sentences of the form $s = 0$ – meaning 'at the current marking, the place s contains 0 tokens' – is undecidable,

even for formulas with one single fixpoint, and for Petri nets in which every transition has at most one input place and at most one output place.
- The modal μ-calculus is undecidable, even for formulas with one single fixpoint and for the same class of Petri nets.

The third result (which is a small modification of Theorem 5.4 in [1]) is not very surprising, because the modal μ-calculus is known to be a extremely powerful logic, which properly contains many branching time logics such as PDL, CTL or CTL*. Since the decidability of branching time logics seems not to have been explored so far, we complement the paper with a fourth result, unfortunately negative:

- a weak branching time subset of the modal μ-calculus, which extends propositional logic with possibility operators, is undecidable.

The note is organised as follows: sections 2 and 3 contain basic definitions about Petri nets and the linear time μ-calculus, respectively. Sections 4 and 5 prove the first and second results above. Section 6 proves the other two.

2 Petri Nets

A *labelled net* N is a fourtuple (S, T, F, l), where

- S and T are two disjoint, finite sets,
- F is a relation on $S \cup T$ such that $F \cap (S \times S) = F \cap (T \times T) = \emptyset$, and
- l is a surjective mapping $T \longrightarrow Act$, where Act is a set of actions (surjectivity is assumed for convenience).

The elements of S and T are called *places* and *transitions*, respectively. Places and transitions are genericaly called *nodes*.

Given a node x of N, ${}^\bullet x = \{y \mid (y, x) \in F\}$ is the *preset* of x and $x^\bullet = \{y \mid (x, y) \in F\}$ is the *postset* of x.

Given a set of nodes X of N, we define ${}^\bullet X = \bigcup_{x \in X} {}^\bullet x$ and $X^\bullet = \bigcup_{x \in X} x^\bullet$.

A *marking* of N is a mapping $M\colon S \longrightarrow \mathbb{N}$. A marking M *enables* a transition t if it marks every place in ${}^\bullet t$. If t is enabled at M, then it can *occur*, and its occurrence leads to the successor marking M' which is defined for every place s by

$$M'(s) = \begin{cases} M(s) & \text{if } s \notin {}^\bullet t \text{ and } s \notin t^\bullet \text{ or } s \in {}^\bullet t \text{ and } s \in t^\bullet \\ M(s) - 1 & \text{if } s \in {}^\bullet t \text{ and } s \notin t^\bullet \\ M(s) + 1 & \text{if } s \notin {}^\bullet t \text{ and } s \in t^\bullet \end{cases}$$

(a token is removed from each place in the preset of t and a token is added to each place in the postset of t).

A marking M is called *dead* if it enables no transition of N.

A *labelled Petri net* is a pair $\Sigma = (N, M_0)$ where N is a labelled net and M_0 is a marking of N. The expression $M_1 \xrightarrow{a} M_2$, where M_1, M_2 are markings of N, denotes that M_1 enables some transition t labelled by a, and that the marking reached by the occurrence of t is M_2. A sequence $M_0 \xrightarrow{a_1} M_1 \xrightarrow{a_2} \cdots \xrightarrow{a_n} M_n$ is a *finite occurrence sequence* leading from M to M_n and we write $M_0 \xrightarrow{a_1 \ldots a_n} M_n$. The empty sequence ϵ is an occurrence sequence: we have $M \xrightarrow{\epsilon} M$ for every marking M. A sequence $M_0 \xrightarrow{a_1} M_1 \xrightarrow{a_2} \cdots$ is an infinite occurrence sequence. We write $M \xrightarrow{a_1 a_2 \ldots}$.

We assume that if two transitions have the same label, then they do not have the same preset and postset. Under this assumption, every label of an occurrence sequence can be uniquely mapped to its underlying transition. Making implicit use of this property, we sometimes speak about the transitions that occur in an occurrence sequence.

A sequence of actions σ is *enabled* at a marking M if $M \xrightarrow{\sigma} M'$ for some marking M' (if σ is finite) or $M \xrightarrow{\sigma}$ (if σ is infinite).

An occurrence sequence is *maximal* if either it is infinite or it leads to a dead marking. The *language* of Σ, denoted by $L(\Sigma)$, is the set of words obtained by dropping the intermediate markings in the maximal occurrence sequences of Σ.

Unlabelled Petri nets are obtained from labelled ones by dropping the labelling function. Equivalently, one can think of unlabelled Petri nets as labelled Petri nets in which the labelling function assigns to a transition its own name. With this convention, the definition of language carries over to unlabelled Petri nets.

3 The Linear Time μ-calculus

The linear time μ-calculus without atomic sentences has the following syntax:

$$\phi ::= Z \mid \neg\phi \mid \phi \wedge \phi \mid O_a\phi \mid \nu Z.\phi$$

where a ranges over a set *Act* of *actions*, and Z over propositional variables. *Free* and *bound* occurrences of variables are defined as usual. A formula is *closed* if no variable occurs free in it.

Formulas are built out of this grammar, subject to the monotonicity condition that all free occurrences of X lie in the scope of an even number of negations.

Let $Act^\star$, Act^ω be the set of finite and infinite words on Act, and let $Act^\infty = Act^\star \cup Act^\omega$. A valuation $\mathcal{V}$ of the logic assigns to each variable X a set of words $\mathcal{V}(X)$ in Act^∞. We denote by $\mathcal{V}[W/Z]$ the valuation $\mathcal{V}'$ which agrees with $\mathcal{V}$ except on Z, where $\mathcal{V}'(Z) = W$. Given a word $\sigma = a_1\, a_2 \ldots$ on Act^∞, $\sigma(1)$ denotes the first action of σ, i.e., a_1, and σ^1 denotes the word $a_2\, a_3 \ldots$. With these notations, the denotation $||\phi||_\mathcal{V}$ of a formula ϕ is the set of words of Act^∞ inductively defined by the following rules:

$$\begin{aligned}
||Z||_\mathcal{V} &= \mathcal{V}(Z)\\
||\neg\phi||_\mathcal{V} &= Act^\infty - ||\phi||_\mathcal{V}\\
||\phi \wedge \psi||_\mathcal{V} &= ||\phi||_\mathcal{V} \cap ||\psi||_\mathcal{V}\\
||O_a\phi||_\mathcal{V} &= \{\sigma \in Act^\infty \mid \sigma(1) = a \wedge \sigma^1 \in ||\phi||_\mathcal{V}\}\\
||\nu Z.\phi||_\mathcal{V} &= \cup\{W \subseteq Act^\infty \mid W \subseteq ||\phi||_{\mathcal{V}[W/Z]}\}
\end{aligned}$$

Therefore, $||\nu Z.\phi||_{\mathcal{V}}$ is the greatest fixpoint of the function which assigns to a set W of words the set $||\phi||_{\mathcal{V}[W/Z]}$.

The denotation of a closed formula ϕ is independent of the valuation; we then use the symbol $||\phi||$. We also use the following abbreviations: $tt = \nu Z.Z$ and $\mu Z.\phi = \neg\nu Z.\phi[\neg Z/Z]$. Observe that $||tt|| = Act^{\infty}$.

Let Σ be a labelled Petri net and ϕ a closed formula of the linear time μ-calculus. We say that Σ satisfies ϕ if $L(\Sigma) \subseteq ||\phi||$. Notice that, with this definition of satisfaction, it can be the case that Σ satisfies neither a formula nor its negation.

4 Decidability of the Linear Time μ-calculus

We define the model checking problem for the linear time μ-calculus as follows: given a Petri net Σ and a closed formula ϕ, determine if Σ satisfies ϕ or not. We prove in this section that this problem is decidable. The decision procedure is based on an automata-theoretic characterisation of the logic [16]. We show that there exist two automata $A_{\neg\phi}$, $B_{\neg\phi}$ that accept the finite and infinite words of $||\neg\phi||$, respectively. It follows that Σ satisfies ϕ if and only if $L(\Sigma) \cap L(A_{\neg\phi}) = \emptyset$ and $L(\Sigma) \cap L(B_{\neg\phi}) = \emptyset$. To decide these two properties, we construct Petri net representations of $A_{\neg\phi}$ and $B_{\neg\phi}$, and combine them with Σ in a way similar to the product of automata; it is then easy to show that the two properties are equivalent to two decidable properties of Petri nets.

An automaton over an alphabet Act is a fourtuple $(Q, q_0, \delta, \mathcal{F})$, where Q is the set of states, q_0 the initial state, $\delta: Q \times Act \rightarrow Q$ the transition function and $\mathcal{F}$ the set of final states. Finite and Büchi automata are automata with different acceptance conditions: a finite automaton A accepts a word w in $Act^{\star}$ if the computation of A on w ends in some final state; a Büchi automaton B accepts a word w in Act^{ω} if the computation of B on w passes infinitely often through some final state.

Dam provides in [3] a procedure to construct, given a formula ϕ of a different version of the linear time μ-calculus, a Büchi automaton whose language is the denotation of the formula. Dam's version has one single next operator O, instead of an operator O_a for every action a. Given a finite set V of propositional variables, the denotation of a formula with free variables in V is a set of words over the alphabet 2^V. The rules defining the denotation of a formula are like the ones given above for $\neg$, $\wedge$ and greatest fixpoints, plus the following rule for the new next operator:

$$||O\phi||_{\mathcal{V}} = \{\sigma \in Act^{\infty} \mid \sigma^1 \in ||\phi||_{\mathcal{V}}\}$$

We briefly discuss how to adapt Dam's construction to our case. Dam's automaton has $\mathcal{P}(V) \times \mathcal{P}(V)$ as alphabet, where $\mathcal{P}(V)$ is the powerset of V. The automaton is constructed in a compositional way. A word w is accepted by the automaton if and only if there is an accepting run

$$q_0 \xrightarrow{(\alpha_1^+, \alpha_1^-)} q_1 \xrightarrow{(\alpha_2^+, \alpha_2^-)} \cdots$$

such that at the ith point of w all variables in α_i^+ hold and no variable in α_i^- holds.

For our version of the linear time μ-calculus, we enrich the alphabet of the automaton to $\mathcal{P}(V) \times \mathcal{P}(V) \times (Act \cup \{\tau\})$, where $\tau \notin Act$. Dam's construction can now be easily modified to take this third component of the alphabet into account. A word w is accepted by the new automaton if and only if there is an accepting run

$$q_0 \xrightarrow{(\alpha_1^+, \alpha_1^-, a_1)} q_1 \xrightarrow{(\alpha_2^+, \alpha_2^-, a_2)} \cdots$$

such that at the ith point of w all variables in α_i^+ hold, no variable in α_i^- holds, and the third component of w at this point is a_i.

If ϕ is a closed formula, we choose $V = \emptyset$; then, the automaton we obtain has just $Act \cup \{\tau\}$ as alphabet. The rôle of the action τ is the following: in our case, the Büchi automaton does not accept exactly $||\phi||$, because $||\phi||$ may contain finite words (for instance, $a \in ||O_a tt||$), while a Büchi automaton only accepts infinite ones. If $||\phi||$ contains a finite word w, then the automaton accepts $w\,\tau^\omega$. The action τ only appears in transitions of the form (q, τ, q).

Proposition 1.

Let ϕ be a closed formula of the linear time μ-calculus over a a set of actions Act. There exist a Büchi automaton B with alphabet $Act \cup \{\tau\}$ which accepts a word w iff $w \in ||\phi|| \cap Act^\omega$ or $w = w'\tau^\omega$ and $w' \in ||\phi|| \cap Act^\star$.

Proof:

Use Dam's construction with the modifications discussed above. ■

It is convenient for our analysis to split the automaton B of Proposition 1 into a finite automaton which accepts the finite words of $||\phi||$ and a Büchi automaton which accepts the infinite ones.

Proposition 2.

Let ϕ be a closed formula of the linear time μ-calculus over a set of actions Act. There exist a finite automaton A_ϕ and a Büchi automaton B_ϕ, both with alphabet Act, such that $L(A_\phi) = ||\phi|| \cap Act^\star$, and $L(B_\phi) = ||\phi|| \cap Act^\omega$.

Proof:

A_ϕ and B_ϕ are the same automaton (i.e., they differ only in the acceptance condition), obtained by just removing the transitions of the form (q, τ, q) from δ. ■

We now assign to a given automaton a Petri net. Let $A = (Q, q_0, \delta, \mathcal{F})$ be an automaton over an alphabet Act. The labeled Petri net $\Sigma^A = (S, T, F, M_0, l)$ – with labels on Act – is defined as follows:

$$S = Q$$
$$T = \delta$$

$$F = \{(q,(q,a,q')),((q,a,q'),q') \mid (q,a,q') \in \delta\}$$
$$M_0(q) = \begin{cases} 1 & \text{if } q = q_0 \\ 0 & \text{otherwise} \end{cases}$$
$$l((q,a,q')) = a$$

It follows immediately from this construction that the finite automaton A_ϕ accepts a word σ if and only if σ is an occurrence sequence of the Petri net Σ^{A_ϕ} leading to a marking in which some final state is marked (recall that the places of Σ^{A_ϕ} are the states of A). Similarly, B_ϕ accepts a word σ if and only if σ is an infinite occurrence sequence such that infinitely many intermediate markings along the sequence put one token in some of the final states of B_ϕ. If $T_\mathcal{F}$ is the set of input transitions of these states, then an equivalent condition is that σ contains infinitely many occurrences of some transition of $T_\mathcal{F}$.

Let $\Sigma_1 = (S_1, T_1, F_1, l_1, M_{01})$, $\Sigma_2 = (S_2, T_2, F_2, l_2, M_{02})$ be two labelled Petri nets with disjoint sets of nodes. The labelled Petri net $\Sigma_1 \times \Sigma_2 = (S, T, F, l, M_0)$ is defined as follows:

$$S = S_1 \cup S_2$$
$$T = \{\{t_1, t_2\} \mid t_1 \in T_1 \wedge t_2 \in T_2 \wedge l_1(t_1) = l_2(t_2)\}$$
$$F = (S \times T) \cap \{(s, \{t_1, t_2\}) \mid (s, t_1) \in F_1 \vee (s, t_2) \in F_2\}$$
$$\cup\, (S \times T) \cap \{(\{t_1, t_2\}, s) \mid (t_1, s) \in F_1 \vee (t_2, s) \in F_2\}$$
$$M_0(s) = \begin{cases} M_{01}(s) & \text{if } s \in S_1 \\ M_{02}(s) & \text{if } s \in S_2 \end{cases}$$
$$l(\{t_1, t_2\}) = l_1(t_1)$$

Observe that this product operation is very similar to the usual product of automata.

Every marking M of $\Sigma_1 \times \Sigma_2$ projects onto a marking M_1 of Σ_1 and a marking M_2 of Σ_2; moreover, these two projections determine M. Making use of this property, we denote $M = (M_1, M_2)$. So, in particular, $M_0 = (M_{01}, M_{02})$.

The following lemma is an immediate consequence of the definitions and the occurrence rule for Petri nets.

Lemma 3.
$(M_1, M_2) \xrightarrow{\sigma} (M_1', M_2')$ iff $M_1 \xrightarrow{\sigma} M_1'$ and $M_2 \xrightarrow{\sigma} M_2'$. (where M_1, M_1' are markings of Σ_1 and M_2, M_2' markings of σ_2)

Proof:
($\Rightarrow$): Let $\{t_1, u_1\}\, \{t_2, u_2\} \ldots$ be the sequence of transitions of $\Sigma_1 \times \Sigma_2$ underlying σ. Then, $t_1\, t_2 \ldots$ and $u_1\, u_2 \ldots$ are sequences of transitions underlying the occurrence sequence σ in Σ_1 and Σ_2, respectively.
($\Leftarrow$): Similar to ($\Rightarrow$). ■

We can now reduce $L(\Sigma) \cap L(B_\phi) \neq \emptyset$ to a property of the Petri net $\Sigma \times \Sigma^{B_\phi}$.

Lemma 4.
$L(\Sigma) \cap L(B_\phi) \neq \emptyset$ iff $\Sigma \times \Sigma^{B_\phi}$ has an occurrence sequence which contains infinitely many occurrences of some transition $\{t, u\}$, where $u \in T_{\mathcal{F}}$.

Proof:
($\Rightarrow$): Let σ be a word of $L(\Sigma) \cap L(B_\phi)$. Then σ is the sequence of labels of two occurrence sequences in Σ and Σ^{B_ϕ}; moreover, σ contains infinitely many occurrences of some transition u of $T_{\mathcal{F}}$. By Lemma 3, σ is the sequence of labels of an occurrence sequence in $\Sigma \times \Sigma^{B_\phi}$, in which transitions of the form $\{t, u\}$ occur infinitely often.
($\Leftarrow$): Let $(M_{01}, M_{02}) \xrightarrow{\sigma}$ be an infinite occurrence sequence of $\Sigma \times \Sigma^{B_\phi}$ which contains infinitely many occurrences of of some transition $\{t, u\}$, where $u \in T_{\mathcal{F}}$. By Lemma 3, $M_{02} \xrightarrow{\sigma}$ is an occurrence sequence of Σ^{B_ϕ}. Let $M_{02} \xrightarrow{a_1} M_1 \xrightarrow{a_2} M_2 \xrightarrow{a_3} \ldots$ be the full representation of $M_{02} \xrightarrow{\sigma}$. By the definition of Σ^{B_ϕ}, each marking M_i puts one token in exactly one place of Σ^{B_ϕ}, and no tokens in the rest. So each marking M_i is univoquely associated to a state of B_ϕ, and the whole sequence to a computation. The state associated to the markings succeeding an occurrence of $\{t, u\}$ is a final state of B_ϕ; so B_ϕ accepts σ. ■

The condition on $\Sigma \times \Sigma^{B_\phi}$ of Lemma 4 was shown to be decidable by Jantzen and Valk [4]. Yen shows in [17] that it is decidable within exponential space.

Lemma 5. *[17]*
Let Σ be a Petri net with n nodes, and let T_0 be a subset of transitions of Σ.. It can be decided in $O(2^{c \cdot n \cdot logn})$ space, for some constant c, if some infinite occurrence sequence of Σ contains infinitely many occurrences of some transition of T_0. ■

Proof:
There exists such an infinite occurrence sequence iff there exists a finite occurrence sequence $M_0 \xrightarrow{\sigma_1} M_1 \xrightarrow{\sigma_2} M_2$ such that $M_1 \leq M_2$ and σ_2 contains some occurrence of a transition of T_0 (then M_1 enables the sequence σ_2^ω). This can be expressed as a formula on paths of Petri nets which belongs to the class of formulas defined by Yen in [17]. Yen shows that any of these formulas can be decided using the space indicated in the lemma. ■

$L(\Sigma) \cap L(A_\phi) \neq \emptyset$ can also be reduced to a suitable property of $\Sigma \times \Sigma^{A_\phi}$.

Lemma 6.
$L(\Sigma) \cap L(A_\phi) \neq \emptyset$ iff there exists a reachable dead marking of $\Sigma \times \Sigma^{A_\phi}$ which puts one token in some final state of A_ϕ.

Proof:
($\Rightarrow$): Let σ be a word of $L(\Sigma) \cap L(A_\phi)$. Then, $M_{01} \xrightarrow{\sigma} M_1$ in Σ and $M_{02} \xrightarrow{\sigma} M_2$ in Σ^{A_ϕ}; moreover, M_1 is a dead marking of Σ, and M_2 puts a token in some final state of A_ϕ. By Lemma 3, $(M_{01}, M_{02}) \xrightarrow{\sigma} (M_1, M_2)$ is an occurrence sequence of $\Sigma \times \Sigma^{A_\phi}$. Since M_1 is a dead marking of Σ, (M_1, M_2) is a dead marking of $\Sigma \times \Sigma^{A_\phi}$.

($\Leftarrow$): Let $(M_{01}, M_{02}) \xrightarrow{\sigma} (M_1, M_2)$ be an occurrence sequence of Σ such that (M_1, M_2) is a dead marking, and M_2 puts a token in some final state of A_ϕ. By Lemma 3, $M_{02} \xrightarrow{\sigma} M_2$ is an occurrence sequence of Σ^{A_ϕ}, and therefore $\sigma \in L(A_\phi)$.

It remains to prove that σ belongs to the language of Σ, i.e., that $M_{01} \xrightarrow{\sigma} M_1$ is a maximal occurrence sequence of Σ.

Assume this is not the case. Then there exists an occurrence sequence $M_{01} \xrightarrow{\sigma} M_1 \xrightarrow{a} M_1'$. Let t be the transition underlying the occurrence of a. By the definition of A_ϕ, a belongs to the alphabet of A_ϕ, and therefore to the alphabet of Σ^{A_ϕ} as well. So Σ^{A_ϕ} contains a transition (q, a, q'), where q is the final state marked at M_2. This transition is enabled at M_2. By Lemma 3, $\{t, (q, a, q')\}$ is enabled at (M_1, M_2), which contradicts that (M_1, M_2) is a dead marking. ∎

The existence of the dead marking of lemma 6 can be decided by solving an exponential number of instances of the *submarking reachability problem* [5]. Given a net with a set of places S, a *submarking* of the net is a *partial* mapping from S onto $\mathbb{N}$. The submarking reachability problem is the problem of deciding, given a Petri net $\Sigma = (N, M_0)$ and a submarking P of N, if some reachable marking coincides with P on all the places where P is defined. The submarking reachability problem is reducible (in polynomial time) to the reachability problem [5].

Lemma 7.

Let Σ be a Petri net, and let S_0 be a subset of places of Σ. It is decidable if some dead marking of Σ puts a token on some place of S_0.

Proof:

If M is a dead marking, then for every transition t some input place of t is unmarked at M. The set of submarkings which specify that, for every transition t, some input place of t is unmarked, and moreover that some place of S contains one token, is finite: it contains at most $|S|^{|T|} \cdot |S_0|$ elements, where S, T are the sets of places and transitions of the net. The property of the lemma can then be decided by solving the submarking reachability problem for these sets. ∎

The complexity of the reachability problem is still open. The most efficient algorithm is not primitive recursive, while the best known lower bound is exponential space [11]. If exponential space suffices, then the complexities of deciding $L(\Sigma) \cap L(B_\phi) = \emptyset$ and $L(\Sigma) \cap L(A_\phi) = \emptyset$ are similar. Otherwise, deciding the second property is more involved.

Theorem 8.

Let Σ be a labelled Petri net, and let ϕ be a closed formula of the linear time μ-calculus. It is decidable if Σ satisfies ϕ.

Proof:

Σ satisfies ϕ iff $L(\Sigma) \subseteq ||\phi||$, or, by the semantics of negation, iff $L(\Sigma) \cap ||\neg\phi|| = \emptyset$.

By Proposition 2, $L(\Sigma)\cap||\neg\phi|| = \emptyset$ iff $L(\Sigma)\cap L(A_{\neg\phi}) = \emptyset$ and $L(\Sigma)\cap L(B_{\neg\phi}) = \emptyset$. Use then Lemmas 4, 5, 6 and 7. ■

5 Adding Atomic Sentences

It is well known that Petri nets have less computing power than Turing machines. In particular, it is impossible to construct a Petri net model of a counter. Crudely speaking, the reason is that Petri nets cannot 'test for zero'. This means that it is not possible in general to add new places and transitions to a given Petri net having a distinguished place s, in such a way that (1) the behaviour of the old net is not disturbed, and (2) one of the new transitions is enabled exactly when s is *not* marked. If Petri nets are enriched with inhibitor arcs, which allow to 'test for zero', they become Turing powerful [14].

Instead of enriching Petri nets, we can enrich the linear time μ-calculus, and allow it to 'test for zero': it suffices to supplement the logic with atomic sentences of the form $s = 0$, meaning 'the place s contains no tokens at the current marking'. We show that this addition makes the model checking problem undecidable, even for formulas with one single fixpoint and for a small class of unlabelled Petri nets. The proof is by reduction from the halting problem for register machines; it is a modification of Bradfield's construction in [1].

Let us start by giving the semantics of the extended logic. We interpret the sentence $s = 0$ on Petri nets $\Sigma = (N, M_0)$ having a place s. We then extend valuations in the following way:

$$\mathcal{V}(s = 0) = \{\sigma \in L((N, M)) \mid M(s) = 0\}$$

A register machine $\mathcal{R}$ is a tuple

$$(\{q_0, \ldots, q_{n+1}\}, \{R_1, \ldots, R_m\}, \{\delta_0, \ldots, \delta_n\})$$

where R_i are the registers, q_i are the states with q_0 being the initial state and q_{n+1} the unique halting state, and δ_i is the transition rule for state q_i ($0 \leq i \leq n$): δ_i is either (1) '$R_j := R_j + 1$; goto q_k' for some j, k, or (2) 'if $R_j = 0$' then goto q_k else ($R_j := R_j - 1$; goto $q_{k'}$)' for some j, k, k'. We denote the set of transition rules of the first and second kind by Δ_1 and Δ_2, respectively. The register R_j used by δ_i is denoted by $reg(\delta_i)$.

The halting problem for register machines is defined thus: given a register machine $\mathcal{R}$ and a set $v_1, \ldots, v_m$ of nonnegative integers, to decide if the computation of $\mathcal{R}$ with the registers initialised to $v_1, \ldots, v_m$ ever reaches the halting state. This problem is known to be undecidable [13], even for machines with only two registers.

We define an unlabelled net $N_{\mathcal{R}}$ as follows: the places of $N_{\mathcal{R}}$ are

$$q_0, \ldots, q_n, R_1, \ldots, R_m.$$

For every register R_i the net contains two transitions $inc(R_i)$, $dec(R_i)$, such that ${}^\bullet inc(R_i) = dec(R_i) = \emptyset$ and $inc(R_i)^\bullet = {}^\bullet dec(R_i) = \{R_i\}$. The rest of the transitions and the flow relation are determined by the δ_i: if $\delta_i \in \Delta_1$, then there is a transition δ_i^+ with ${}^\bullet\delta_i^+ = \{q_i\}$ and $\delta_i^{+\bullet} = \{q_k\}$; and if $\delta_i \in \Delta_2$, then there are transitions δ_i^0 and δ_i^- such that ${}^\bullet\delta_i^0 = {}^\bullet\delta_i^- = \{q_i\}$, $\delta_i^{0\bullet} = \{q_k\}$ and $\delta_i^{-\bullet} = \{q_{k'}\}$. Finally, there is a transition *halt*, such that ${}^\bullet halt = \{q_{n+1}\}$ and $halt^\bullet = \emptyset$.

Observe that every transition of $N_\mathcal{R}$ has at most one input place and at most one output place.

If we put $v_1, \ldots, v_m$ tokens in the places $R_1, \ldots, R_m$ of $N_\mathcal{R}$, and one token in the place q_0, then an occurrence sequence of the Petri net so obtained simulates the computation of $\mathcal{R}$ on the initial values $v_1, \ldots, v_m$. It is namely the sequence in which an occurrence of δ_i^+ (δ_i^-) is always followed by the occurrence of the transition $inc(reg(\delta_i))$ ($dec(reg(\delta_i))$), and in which a transition δ_i^0 occurs only at markings in which the place $reg(\delta_i)$ contains no tokens. There exist, however, many other occurrence sequences which do not correspond to any computation.

Define the formula $halt(\mathcal{R})$ as:

$$\mu Z.\ O_{halt}\, tt$$
$$\bigvee_{\delta_i \in \Delta_1} O_{\delta_i^+} O_{inc(reg(i))} Z$$
$$\bigvee_{\delta_i \in \Delta_2} (reg(\delta_i) = 0 \ \wedge \ O_{\delta_i^0} Z) \ \vee \ O_{\delta_i^-} O_{dec(reg(i))} Z$$

Theorem 9.

Let $\mathcal{R}$ be a register machine, and let $v_1, \ldots, v_m$ be initial values for the registers of $\mathcal{R}$. Let $\Sigma_\mathcal{R} = (N_\mathcal{R}, M)$ be a Petri net, where M is the marking that puts v_i tokens on the place R_i and one token on the place q_0. $\mathcal{R}$ halts for these initial values iff $\Sigma_\mathcal{R}$ does not satisfy $\neg halt(\mathcal{R})$.

Proof:

Σ_R satisfies $\neg halt(\mathcal{R})$ iff $L(\Sigma_\mathcal{R}) \subseteq ||\neg halt(\mathcal{R})||$ iff $L(\Sigma_\mathcal{R}) \cap ||halt(\mathcal{R})|| = \emptyset$. Let σ be a sequence of $||halt(\mathcal{R})||$. It follows from the semantics of the linear time μ-calculus that $\sigma = \sigma_1 \ldots \sigma_k\, halt$, where every σ_i is of the form $\delta_i^+\ inc(reg(\delta_i))$, $\delta_i^-\ dec(reg(\delta_i))$ or δ_i^0. Moreover, whenever we have $M_1 \xrightarrow{\delta_i^0} M_2$ along the occurrence sequence corresponding to σ, $M_1(reg(\delta_i)) = 0$. Such an ocurrence sequence simulates a halting computation of the register machine. Conversely, from a halting computation of the register machine we can easily obtain a sequence of $halt(\mathcal{R})$. So $L(\Sigma_\mathcal{R}) \cap ||halt(\mathcal{R})|| \neq \emptyset$ iff $\mathcal{R}$ halts with input $v_1, \ldots, v_m$. ∎

As mentioned above, the transitions of the Petri nets derived from register machines have at most one input place and at most one output place. In particular, they are Petri net representations of Basic Parallel Processes, a subset of CCS [2].

It seems difficult to find an interesting class of Petri nets with infinite state spaces, and properly included in the class derived from register machines. Since the formula $halt(\mathcal{R})$ is also rather simple, this undecidability result seems to determine the decidability border rather neatly.

6 Branching Time Logics

The modal μ-calculus, has the same syntax as the linear time μ-calculus (although $O_a\phi$ is usually replaced by $\langle a\rangle\phi$), but is interpreted on labelled transition systems. Let $\mathcal{T} = (\mathcal{S}, \xrightarrow{a}_{a\in Act})$ be a labelled transition system. Given a valuation $\mathcal{V}$ that assigns to each variable a subset of $\mathcal{S}$, the denotation of a formula is defined by the following rules:

$$\begin{aligned}
||Z||_{\mathcal{V}} &= \mathcal{V}(Z)\\
||\neg\phi||_{\mathcal{V}} &= \mathcal{S} - ||\phi||_{\mathcal{V}}\\
||\phi_1 \wedge \phi_2||_{\mathcal{V}} &= ||\phi_1||_{\mathcal{V}} \cap ||\phi_2||_{\mathcal{V}}\\
||\langle a\rangle\phi||_{\mathcal{V}} &= \{s \in \mathcal{S} \mid \exists s' \in \mathcal{S}. s \xrightarrow{a} s' \wedge s' \in ||\phi||_{\mathcal{V}}\}\\
||\nu Z.\phi||_{\mathcal{V}} &= \bigcup\{A \subseteq \mathcal{S} \mid A \subseteq ||\phi||_{\mathcal{V}[A/Z]}\}
\end{aligned}$$

As in the case of the linear time μ-calculus, the denotation of a closed formula is independent of the valuation.

Given a labelled Petri net $\Sigma = (N, M_0)$, the transition system associated to Σ, denoted by $\mathcal{T}(\Sigma)$, has the set of reachable markings as states; there is a transition labelled by a between two markings M_1, M_2 if and only if $M_1 \xrightarrow{a} M_2$. We say that Σ satisfies a formula ϕ if $M_0 \in ||\phi||_{\mathcal{V}}$.

It is undecidable if a Petri net satisfies a formula. In order to prove it, it suffices to proceed as for the linear time μ-calculus, but change in the formula $halt(\mathcal{R})$ the atomic sentence $reg(\delta_i) = 0$ into the formula $\neg\langle dec(reg(\delta_i))\rangle tt$. Observe that $||\langle dec(reg(\delta_i))\rangle tt||$ are the markings which enable the transition $dec(reg(\delta_i))$, which are exactly the markings that put no tokens on $reg(\delta_i)$. So, in fact, in the modal μ-calculus we can 'test for zero' without having to add atomic sentences.

In spite of its simplicity, this undecidability result has a consequence which may be a little bit surprising. For the class of Basic Parallel Processes (BPPs), bisimulation equivalence has been shown to be decidable [2]; moreover, since BPPs are image-finite, two Basic Parallel Processes are bisimilar if and only if they satisfy the same properties of the modal μ-calculus. So it is decidable if two BPPs satisfy the same properties. However, the model checking problem is undecidable.

Since the μ-calculus is known to be an extremely powerful logic, it could be expected to find some weaker but interesting, decidable logic. Unfortunately, there is little hope of obtaining such a result: we now show that one of the weakest non-trivial branching time logics is still undecidable. It extends propositional logic with an operator $\Diamond_a$ for each action a of the set Act. The syntax is:

$$\phi ::= tt \mid \neg\phi \mid \phi_1 \wedge \phi_2 \mid \Diamond_a\phi$$

Formulas are interpreted on a transition system $\mathcal{T} = (\mathcal{S}, \xrightarrow{a}_{a\in Act})$. Define $\overset{a}{\Longrightarrow}$ as the relation $(\bigcup_{b\in Act} \xrightarrow{b})^{\star} \xrightarrow{a}$. The denotation of a formula ϕ is a set of states $||\phi||$ defined according to the following rules:

$$\begin{aligned} ||tt|| &= \mathcal{S} \\ ||\neg\phi|| &= \mathcal{S} - ||\phi|| \\ ||\phi_1 \wedge \phi_2|| &= ||\phi_1|| \cap ||\phi_2|| \\ ||\Diamond_a \phi|| &= \{s \in \mathcal{S} \mid \exists s' \in \mathcal{S}. s \stackrel{a}{\Longrightarrow} s' \wedge s' \in ||\phi||\} \end{aligned}$$

(see [1] for an embedding of this logic in the modal μ-calculus)

When interpreted on Petri nets, a marking satisfies $\Diamond_a \phi$ if it enables some sequence σ a, whose occurrence leads to a marking which satisfies ϕ. We use the abbreviation $\Box_a = \neg\Diamond_a\neg$. A marking M satisfies $\Box_a \phi$ if every sequence σ a enabled at M leads to a marking satisfying ϕ.

We prove undecidability by a reduction from the *containment problem.* An instance of the problem consists of two Petri nets Σ_1, Σ_2 with the same number of places, and a bijection f between the sets of places of Σ_1 and Σ_2. f can be extended to a bijection between markings in the obvious way. The question to decide is whether for every reachable marking M of Σ_1, $f(M)$ is a reachable marking of Σ_2. Rabin showed that this problem is undecidable; the proof can be found in [5].

Let Σ_1, Σ_2 and f be an instance of the containment problem, and let S_1, S_2 be the sets of places of Σ_1, Σ_2. Assume also, without loss of generality, that the sets of nodes of Σ_1 and Σ_2 are disjoint. We construct an unlabelled Petri net $\Sigma = (N, M_0)$ in several stages. At each stage we add some places and transitions. For transitions we use the notation $X \rightarrow Y$, meaning that the transition t has the sets X and Y of places as preset and postset, respectively (the flow relation is thus specified at the same time as the set of transitions). To give a transition $X \rightarrow Y$ the name t, we write $t: X \rightarrow Y$.

- Add $\Sigma_1 \cup \Sigma_2$.
- Add three places A, B, C, and two transitions $t_{AB}: \{A\} \cup S_1 \rightarrow \{B\} \cup S_1$ and $t_{BC}: \{B\} \cup S_2 \rightarrow \{C\} \cup S_2$. Put one token on A, and no tokens on B and C.
- For every place s of Σ_1, add a transition $\{s, f(s), C\} \rightarrow \{C\}$.
- For every place s added so far, with the exception of C, add a transition $\{s\} \rightarrow \{s\}$.

Every marking M of Σ projects onto a marking M_1 of Σ_1, a marking M_2 of Σ_2, and a marking M_3 of the three places A, B and C; moreover, these three projections determine M. Making use of this property, we write $M = (M_1, M_2, M_3)$; also, we write M_3 as a string of three numbers representing the number of tokens in A, B, and C. Finally, the null marking, i.e., the marking that puts no token in any place, is denoted by $\mathbf{0}$.

The following lemma follows easily from the definition of Σ.

Lemma 10.
If $(M_{01}, M_{02}, 100) \xrightarrow{\sigma} (M_1, M_2, 001)$ *is an occurrence sequence of* Σ, *then there exist sequences* $\sigma_1, \sigma_2, \sigma_3$ *such that* $\sigma = \sigma_1\, t_{AB} \sigma_2\, t_{BC}\, \sigma_3$. ∎

We can now characterise the 'yes' instances of the containment problem in terms of occurrence sequences of Σ.

Lemma 11.
Σ_1, Σ_2, f *is a 'yes' instance of the containment problem iff every occurrence sequence* $(M_{01}, M_{02}, 100) \xrightarrow{\sigma\, t_{AB}} (M_1, M_{02}, 010)$ *of* Σ *can be extended to a maximal occurrence sequence* $(M_{01}, M_{02}, 100) \xrightarrow{\sigma\, t_{AB}\, \tau} (\mathbf{0}, \mathbf{0}, 001)$.

Proof:
($\Rightarrow$): M_1 is a reachable marking of Σ_1. Since M_1 is reachable in Σ_2 as well, there exists a sequence $\sigma_2\, t_{BC}$ such that

$$(M_1, M_{02}, 010) \xrightarrow{\sigma_2\, t_{BC}} (M_1, M_1, 001)$$

Let σ_3 be a sequence which contains each transition of the form $\{s, f(s), C\} \to \{C\}$ $M(s)$ times, and no occurrence of any other transition. We then have $(M_1, M_1, 001) \xrightarrow{\sigma_3} (\mathbf{0}, \mathbf{0}, 001)$. By the definition of Σ, no transition is enabled at the marking $(\mathbf{0}, \mathbf{0}, 001)$, and therefore

$$(M_0, M_0, 100) \xrightarrow{\sigma\, t_{AB}\, \sigma_2\, t_{BC}\, \sigma_3} (\mathbf{0}, \mathbf{0}, 001)$$

is maximal.
($\Leftarrow$): Let M_1 be a reachable marking of Σ_1. Then, we have

$$(M_{01}, M_{02}, 100) \xrightarrow{\sigma_1} (M_1, M_{02}, 100) \xrightarrow{t_{AB}} (M_1, M_{02}, 010)$$

for some sequence σ_1. So there exists a sequence τ such that

$$(M_{01}, M_{02}, 010) \xrightarrow{\sigma\, t_{AB}\, \tau} (\mathbf{0}, \mathbf{0}, 001)$$

is a maximal occurrence sequence. By Lemma 10, $\tau = \sigma_2\, t_{BC}\, \sigma_3$ for some sequences σ_2 and σ_3. Let

$$(M_1, M_{02}, 010) \xrightarrow{\sigma_2\, t_{BC}} (M_1', M_2, 010) \xrightarrow{\sigma_3} (\mathbf{0}, \mathbf{0}, 100)$$

We show $M_1' = M_1 = M_2$, which proves that M_1 is reachable in Σ_2.
Since σ_2 occurs after t_{AB} has occurred, no transition of Σ_1 occurs in σ_2. So $M_1' = M_1$.
Since σ_3 occurs after t_{BC}, only transitions of the form $\{s\} \to \{s\}$ for some place s can occur in σ_3. Since these transitions remove one token from s and one from $f(s)$, we have $M_1' - \mathbf{0} = M_2 - \mathbf{0}$. So $M_1' = M_2$. ∎

To finish the undecidability proof, it suffices to encode the characterisation of Lemma 11 into the temporal logic defined above. Define the operator $\diamond$ as $\bigvee_{a \in Act} \diamond_a$. It follows from the semantics of the logic that $\diamond\phi$ holds at a marking M if and only if some succesor marking M', $M' \neq M$ satisfies ϕ. In particular, $\diamond\, tt$ holds at a marking M if and only if M has some successor, i.e., it is not dead.

Theorem 12.
Σ_1, Σ_2, f is a 'yes' instance of the containment problem iff Σ satisfies the formula

$$\Box_{t_{AB}} \Diamond \neg \Diamond tt.$$

Proof:
$\neg\Diamond\, tt$ holds at a marking M iff M enables no transition. Therefore, the formula of the theorem states that every occurrence sequence $\sigma_1\, t_{AB}$ of Σ can be extended to an occurrence sequence $\sigma_1\, t_{AB}\, \tau$ leading to a marking at which no transition of Σ is enabled. By the definition of Σ, this marking can only be $(\mathbf{0}, \mathbf{0}, 001)$. Apply then Lemma 11. ■

7 Conclusions

We have examined the decidability of the model checking problem for several μ-calculi and Petri nets. The decidability border turns out to be rather neat: if we consider μ-calculi without atomic sentences, the whole linear time μ-calculus is decidable, while a very weak branching time subset of the modal μ-calculus is undecidable. The addition of very simple atomic sentences makes the linear time μ-calculus undecidable, even for formulas with one fixpoint and Petri nets in which every transition has at most one input and at most one output place.

Acknowledgements

I thank Julian Bradfield, Søren Christensen, Mads Dam and Colin Stirling for very helpful discussions.

References

1. J. C. Bradfield: Verifying Temporal Properties of Systems. Birkhäuser, Boston, Massachussets ISBN 0-8176-3625-0 (1991).
2. S. Christensen, Y. Hirshfeld and F. Moller: Bisimulation Equivalence is Decidable for Basic Parallel Processes. Proceedings of CONCUR'93, LNCS 715, 143–157 (1993).
3. M. Dam: Fixpoints of Büchi automata. LFCS Report ECS-LFCS-92-224, University of Edinburgh (1992).
4. M. Jantzen and R. Valk: The Residue of Vector Sets with Applications to Decidability Problems in Petri Nets. Acta Informatica 21, 643–674 (1985)
5. M.H.T. Hack: Decidability questions for Petri nets. Ph. D. Thesis, MIT (1976).
6. R.R. Howell and L.E. Rosier: Problems concerning fairness and temporal logic for conflict-free Petri nets. Theoretical Computer Science 64, 305–329 (1989).
7. R.R. Howell, L.E. Rosier and H. Yen: A taxonomy of fairness and temporal logic problems for Petri nets. Theoretical Computer Science 82, 341–372 (1991).
8. P. Jančar: Decidability of a temporal logic problem for Petri nets. Theoretical Computer Science 74, 71–93 (1990).

9. R.M. Karp and R.E. Miller: Parallel Program Schemata. Journal of Computer and System Sciences 3, 147–195 (1969).
10. S.R. Kosaraju: Decidability of reachability in vector addition systems. Proceedings of the 6th Annual ACM Symposium on the Theory of Computing, 267–281 (1982).
11. R. Lipton: The Reachability Problem Requires Exponential Space. Technical Report 62, Yale University (1976).
12. E.W. Mayr: An algorithm for the general Petri net reachability problem. SIAM Journal of Computing 13, 441-460 (1984).
13. M. Minsky: Computation: Finite and Infinite Machines. Prentice-Hall (1967).
14. J.L. Peterson: Petri Net Theory and the Modelling of Systems. Prentice-Hall (1981).
15. C. Stirling: Modal and Temporal Logics. In S. Abramsky, D. Gabbay and T. Maibaum (eds.) Handbook of Logic in Computer Science. Oxford University Press (1991)
16. M.Y. Vardi and P. Wolper: Automata Theoretic Techniques for Modal Logics of Programs. Journal of Computer and System Sciences 32, 183–221 (1986).
17. H. Yen: A Unified Approach for Deciding the Existence of Certain Petri Net Paths. Information and Computation 96(1), 119–137 (1992).

Generalizations of the Periodicity Theorem of Fine and Wilf

R. Giancarlo[1] and F. Mignosi[2]

[1] AT&T Bell Laboratories, Murray Hill NJ, USA. On leave from Dipartimento di Matematica ed Applicazioni, Universitá di Palermo, Italia
[2] Dipartimento di Matematica ed Applicazioni, Universitá di Palermo, Italia

Abstract. We provide three generalizations to the two-dimensional case of the well known *periodicity theorem* by Fine and Wilf [4] for strings (the one-dimensional case). The first and the second generalizations can be further extended to hold in the more general setting of Cayley graphs of groups. Weak forms of two of our results have been developed for the design of efficient algorithms for two-dimensional pattern matching [2, 3, 6].

1 Introduction

Periodicity, overlap, power, repetition. All these words could be considered as synonym of the same notion. For instance, for algebraic structures such notion is the iterated product of the same element, i.e., *a power.* For combinatorics on words and algorithmic applications derived from it, the notion is the "periodic appearence" of the same sequence of letters, i.e, *periodicity.*

M. P. Shutzenberger in [9, ch. 8] says that: " Periodicity is an important property of words, that is often used in applications of combinatorics on words. Main results characterizing it are the Theorem of Fine and Wilf and the Theorem of the Critical Factorization..."

Indeed, apart from its intrinsic mathematical interest, periodicity of words is a very important tool for the design and analysis of algorithms on words. For instance, to the best of our knowledge, there is no optimal (sequential or parallel) string matching algorithm that does not use one of the two main theorems of periodicity either for the design or for the analysis of the algorithm. The reader is referred to [1] for a survey of such algorithms.

Despite the rich body of knowledge available for perodicity of words [9], very little was known about such notion in higher dimensions, e.g., coverings of two-dimensional space by means of a repeated pattern. Motivated by applications in low level image processing [12], namely the design of efficient two-dimensional run length compressed matching algorithms, Amir and Benson [2] started a formal characterization of the intuitive idea of what two-dimensional periodicity should be. Indeed, in their seminal paper [2], they came up with a definition of periodicity for two-dimensional patterns, provided a classification of such patterns in four periodicity classes and devised efficient algorithms that decide in which class a given input pattern falls into. Such combinatorial study has been successfully applied by Amir and Benson to the design of efficient two-dimensional pattern matching algorithms on compressed data [2] and by Amir, Benson and Farach [3] to make progress towards a two-dimensional pattern matching algorithm that runs in linear time, independent of the alphabet size. Motivated by this second problem, Galil and Park have brought to light additional properties of two-dimensional periodicity and have applied them to obtain the first truly alphabet independent two-dimensional pattern matching algorithm. We point out that the two-dimensional periodicity studied in [2, 6, 7] is a natural extension of periodicity for words and that the results they prove about it can be regarded as the two-dimensional analog of the *Periodicity Lemma* for words [10]. It is well known that the Peridicity Lemma is a weak form of the Fine and Wilf Theorem [4].

Recently, Regnier and Rostami [13] have provided a framework for the study of d-dimensional periodicities. Based on it, they identify $2^{d-1}+1$ classes of periodicities for a d-dimensional pattern. For $d = 2$, their classification is a refinement of the one in [2, 6]. They also proved results that can be considered d-dimensional generalizations of the Periodicity Lemma. Algorithmic applications of such theory are claimed in [11].

In this paper we introduce the notion of periodicity on Cayley graphs of groups. Roughly speaking, that corresponds to placing the notion of higher dimensional periodicity discussed in [2, 6, 13] into a very general setting. Moreover, in that setting, we prove three generalizations of the theorem of Fine and Wilf for words. The first and the second generalizations hold in Cayley graphs of groups while the third holds only in the case in which we restrint the group to be Z^2. The relationship between the results previosly known for d-dimensional periodicity [2, 6, 13] and ours is the same as the one between the Periodicity Lemma and the Theorem of Fine and Wilf for words. Indeed, the Peridicity Lemma provides conditions for a word to be periodic while the Theorem of Fine and Wilf provides the *tightest possible* conditions for a word to be periodic. Indeed, weak forms of the second and the third of our generalizations have been obtained by Amir and Benson [2] and Galil and Park [7] and used in the design and analysis of their algorithms [2, 7].

The remainder of this abstract is organized as follows. In the second section we give some basic notations and discuss some preliminaries. In the third section we states three theorems and we show that each of them is a generalization of the Theorem of Fine and Wilf; proofs of these results are given in the fourth section. The last section presents conclusions and some open problems.

2 Preliminaries

For any notation not explicitely defined in this paper we refer to [9] and to [10].

We present now few group-theoretic preliminaries.

Let G be an additive group. Given any subgroup L of G, for every $g \in G$, $g + L = \{g + l \mid l \in L\}$ is the right *coset* of L containing g.

The set of right cosets of L is a partition of G, *i. e.* each element of G belongs to exactly one right coset. The cardinality of the set of right cosets is denoted by $i(L)$; we remark that $i(L)$ is not necessarly a finite number. A transversal T_L is a subset of G containing exactly one element from every right coset. It is clear that $Card(T_L) = i(L)$.

Let G be a group and let S be a set of generators for G. The associated *Cayley graph* Γ is a directed graph defined as follows. The node-set is the group G and for each $g \in G, s \in S$, there is an arc labeled s from g to $g+s$. For any fixed group G there are infinitely many sets S that generate G, and, consequently, infinitely many Caley graphs. Our main results concerning Cayley graphs do not depend on the choice of a set of generators for G.

In what follows, whenever we write "unidimensional case" or "bidimensional case" we refer to the Cayley graph of $\mathbb{Z}$ and of $\mathbb{Z}^2$ generated respectively by 1 and by $(1,0)$ and $(0,1)$.

We give now some classical notations of words and periodicity on words.

Let A be a set called *alphabet*; the elements of A are called *letters*.

Let A^* be the free monoid generated by A; the elements of A^* are called *words*. If w is a word, usually we write

$$w = a_1 a_2 .... a_n \ , \ a_i \in A.$$

The length n of the word w is denoted by $\mid w \mid$. Any word of the form $v = a_i....a_j \ , \ 0 < i \leq j \leq n$ is called a *factor* of the word w. The empty word is a factor of any word.

If $v = a_1....a_j \ , \ 0 < j \leq n$ then v is called a *prefix* of w; if $v = a_i....a_n \ ; \ 0 < i \leq n$ then v is called a *suffix* of w.

Let $w = a_1 a_2 ....a_n$; if for every i, $0 < i \leq n-p$, $a_i = a_{i+p}$ then we say that w is *p-periodic*. A word w is p-periodic iff the prefix of w of length $n-p$ is equal to the suffix of w of length $n-p$.

We now present the definitions of words and periodicity in Cayley graphs of groups; these definitions coincide in the unidimensional case with the classic ones. Examples will be given in the unidimensional and in the bidimensional case.

Let G be a group, let S be a set of generators for G and let Γ be the associated Cayley graph. Let X be a finite subset of G and let A be a set called alphabet.

Definition 1. Any function f from X to the alphabet A is called pointed word; X is called the support of f (supp(f) in short). If X is connected in the Cayley graph Γ then f is called connected pointed word.

Remark. The connection is a property of Γ and, consequently, depends on the set of generators S of G.

Let us now define an equivalence relation $\mathbf{R}$ in the set of pointed words: we say that $f_1 \mathbf{R} f_2$ if and only if there exist $g \in G$ such that $g + supp(f_1) = supp(f_2)$ and for any $x \in supp(f_1)$, $f_1(x) = f_2(g+x)$.

It is easy to see that if $f_1 \mathbf{R} f_2$ then f_1 is connected if and only if f_2 is connected.

Definition 2. Any equivalence classe $w = [f]$ of the previous equivalence relation $\mathbf{R}$ is called word; if f is a connected pointed word then w is called connected word.

In the unidimensional case the notion of connected word defined as above coincides with the classical notion; indeed we can define the associative product between two connected words as the "concatenation" of them (the formal definition of "concatenation" by using the previous definitions is left to the reader). Moreover if $w = [f]$ the length $| w |$ of w can be easly defined as $Card(supp(f))$.

The next two examples show one connected pointed word in the unidimensional case and one in the bidimensional case.

Example 1. Let $X = \{1,2,3,4,5,6,7,8\}$ and let $A = \{a,b\}$. Let us define the connected pointed word f

$$f(1) = a,\ f(2) = b,\ f(3) = a,\ f(4) = a,\ f(5) = b,\ f(6) = a,\ f(7) = b,\ f(8) = a.$$

Thus

$$w = [f] = abaababa.$$

Example 2. Let f be a pointed word in the bidimensional case. In this and in the following examples we associate to any element (x,y) of $\mathbb{Z}^2$ the unit square that has (x,y) as top-left corner; in order to describe f we write the letter $f((x,y))$ inside this square. If we want to describe the word $w = [f]$ we do not write in the figure the point $(0,0)$.

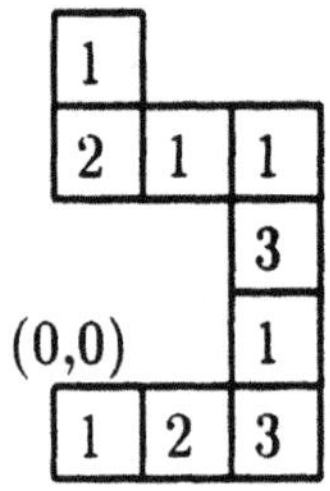

Let L be a subgroup of G.

Definition 3. A (connected) pointed word f is L-periodic if and only if for any $s_1,\ s_2 \in supp(f)$ one has

$$s_1 - s_2 \in L \Rightarrow f(s_1) = f(s_2).$$

In other words all elements in the same right coset have the same image.

Definition 4. A (connected) word w is L-periodic if and only if there exists a representative f of w that is L-periodic.

Remark. If a pointed word f_1 is L-periodic then any pointed word f_2 such that $f_1 \mathbf{R} f_2$ and $g + supp(f_1) = supp(f_2)$, with $g \in L$, is also L-periodic. If L is a normal subgroup of G then any pointed word f_2 such that $f_1 \mathbf{R} f_2$ is also L-periodic. Recall that any subgroup L of $\mathbb{Z}^n$ is normal.

Often we write $s_1 = s_2\,(mod\,L)$ to indicate that s_1 and s_2 are in the same right coset (i.e. $s_1 - s_2 \in L$).

In the unidimensional case the notion of periodic connected word defined as above coincides with the classical one, up to identifying any subgroup of $\mathbb{Z}$ (that one can think always generated by one element) with its generator.

Example 3. Let f be defined as in the Example 1. We want to check that f is $< 5 >$-periodic, where $< 5 >$ is the subgroup of $\mathbb{Z}$ generated by 5. Since $< 5 > = \{..., -5, 0, 5, 10, ...\}$ then

$$1, 6 \in < 5 > +1; 2, 7 \in < 5 > +2; 3, 8 \in < 5 > +3; 4 \in < 5 > +4; 5 \in < 5 > +0.$$

One has also that

$$f(1) = f(6),\ f(2) = f(7),\ f(3) = f(8).$$

Hence $w = [f]$ is $< 5 >$-periodic.

Note that $w = [f]$ is also $< 7 >$-periodic and that, in general, by this definition a word w is $< m >$-periodic for any $m \geq |w|$.

Example 4. In this example it is shown as to construct, given a subgrup L of $\mathbb{Z}^2$, an L-periodic word. We take $L = < (2, 1), (-1, 2) >$; then we start to give the same letter (number 1 in this case) to the elements of L. We continue giving the same letter to elements in the same right coset.

				1					1
		1					1		
1					1				
			1					1	
	1					1			
				1					1
		1					1		
1					1				
			1					1	
	1					1			

2		3		1	2		3		1
3		1	2		3		1	2	
1	2		3		1	2		3	
	3		1	2		3		1	2
	1	2		3		1	2		3
2		3		1	2		3		1
3		1	2		3		1	2	
1	2		3		1	2		3	
	3		1	2		3		1	2
	1	2		3		1	2		3

2	4	3		1	2	4	3		1
3		1	2	4	3		1	2	4
1	2	4	3		1	2	4	3	
4	3		1	2	4	3		1	2
	1	2	4	3		1	2	4	3
2	4	3		1	2	4	3		1
3		1	2	4	3		1	2	4
1	2	4	3		1	2	4	3	
4	3		1	2	4	3		1	2
	1	2	4	3		1	2	4	3

2	4	3	5	1	2	4	3	5	1
3	5	1	2	4	3	5	1	2	4
1	2	4	3	5	1	2	4	3	5
4	3	5	1	2	4	3	5	1	2
5	1	2	4	3	5	1	2	4	3
2	4	3	5	1	2	4	3	5	1
3	5	1	2	4	3	5	1	2	4
1	2	4	3	5	1	2	4	3	5
4	3	5	1	2	4	3	5	1	2
5	1	2	4	3	5	1	2	4	3

Example 5. In this example we show a word that is L_1-periodic, where L_1 is the subgroup of $\mathbb{Z}^2$ generated by $(2,1)$.

z	*v*	*t*	*s*	*r*	*q*	*p*	*n*	*l*	*k*
t	*s*	*r*	*q*	*p*	*n*	*l*	*k*	*j*	*h*
r	*q*	*p*	*n*	*l*	*k*	*j*	*h*	*g*	*f*
p	*n*	*l*	*k*	*j*	*h*	*g*	*f*	1	2
l	*k*	*j*	*h*	*g*	*f*	1	2	4	3
j	*h*	*g*	*f*	1	2	4	3	5	6
g	*f*	1	2	4	3	5	6	7	9
1	2	4	3	5	6	7	9	8	*a*
4	3	5	6	7	9	8	*a*	*b*	*c*
5	6	7	9	8	*a*	*b*	*c*	*e*	*d*

In the above examples we have shown the "most general" periodic words, in the sense that all the other L-periodic (L_1-periodic) words having same support can be obtained by these words with a *letteral projection* (for instance we can replace all the letter 1 by the letter 2 or by the letter a). Indeed the word in Example 4 is also L_1 periodic, and this is not surprising because L_1 is a subgroup of L. Notice that all subgroups of $\mathbb{Z}$ either are ciclic, as L_1, and have infinite index or are generated by two elements, as L, and have finite index.

We now state the Periodicity Lemma and the Theorem of Fine and Wilf with the classical notations (see [10] and [4]).

Periodicity Lemma (Lyndon and Shutzenberger 1962) *Let w be a p-periodic and q-periodic word.*

If $|w| \geq p+q$ then w is $gcd(p,q)$-periodic.

Theorem 5. (Fine and Wilf 1965) *Let w be a p-periodic and q-periodic word.*

1) *If $|w| \geq p+q-gcd(p,q)$ then w is $gcd(p,q)$-periodic .*
2) (tightness) *For any p,q there exists a word w, $|w| \geq p+q-gcd(p,q)-1$ that is p-periodic and q-periodic but it is not $gcd(p,q)$-periodic.*

The Theorem of Fine and Wilf improves the Periodicity Lemma because the property required for w to be $gcd(p,q)$-periodic is weaker and because of the tightness of this property.

We end this section by stating the Theorem of Fine and Wilf using the notations given above. We just recall that in the unidimensional case, given two positive integer p and q, the subgroup of $\mathbb{Z}$ generated by $gcd(p,q)$ is the smaller subgroup containing the subgroup generated by $<p>$ and the subgroup generated by $<q>$; with the group theoretic notation

$$<gcd(p,q)> = << p >, < q >> .$$

Theorem 6 (Fine and Wilf revisited). *Let w be a connected word in the unidimensional case and let L_1 and L_2 be two subgroups of $\mathbb{Z}$; let us suppose that w is L_1-periodic and L_2-periodic.*

1) *If $| w | \geq i(L_1) + i(L_2) - i(< L_1, L_2 >)$ then w is $< L_1, L_2 >$-periodic.*
2) (tightness) *There exists a word w, $| w | = i(L_1) + i(L_2) - i(< L_1, L_2 >) - 1$ that is L_1-periodic and L_2-periodic but it is not $< L_1, L_2 >$-periodic.*

3 Main Results

In this section we present three generalizations of the Theorem of Fine and Wilf; each generalization has a statement that is similar to the statement of Theorem 2. But no one of such generalizations implies or is implied by the others.

We state our results for pointed words; the extension to words is left to the reader, that must consider the remark to Definition 4.

Proposition 7. *Let f be a pointed word and let L_1 and L_2 be two subgroups of finite index. Let us suppose that f is L_1-periodic and L_2-periodic and that supp$(f) = G$. then f is $< L_1, L_2 >$-periodic.*

The above proposition states in the unidimensional case that if a biinfinite word has two periodicity p, q, then it is also $gcd(p, q)$-periodic. In order to get an extension of the Theorem of Fine and Wilf, further conditions on the support of the word are required.

Theorem 8. *Let f be a pointed word and let L_1 and L_2 be two subgroups of finite index; let us suppose that f is L_1-periodic and L_2-periodic. There exist a connected subset X of the Cayley graph Γ of G with $Card(X) \leq i(L_1) + i(L_2) - i(< L_1, L_2 >)$ such that*

1) *If supp(f) contains a set of the form $g + X$ for some element $g \in L_1 \cap L_2$ then f is $< L_1, L_2 >$-periodic.*
2) (tightness) *For any subset Y of the Cayley graph Γ of G with $Card(Y) = i(L_1) + i(L_2) - i(< L_1, L_2 >) - 1$, containing transversals T_{L_1} and T_{L_2} of L_1 and L_2, there exists a pointed word f, such that supp$(f) = Y$ that is L_1-periodic and L_2-periodic but it is not $< L_1, L_2 >$-periodic.*

Remark 1. If L_1 and L_2 are normal subgroups of G then condition 1 can be weakened by the following: *If supp(f) contains a set of the form $g + X$ for some element $g \in G$ then f is $< L_1, L_2 >$-periodic.* This leads to an easy extension of the previous theorem to words in the case of $G = \mathbb{Z}^n$ that has only normal subgroups.

Remark 2. Previous theorem holds for any set of generators S of G; this is why we did not mention the set S talking about the fact that X is a connected set.

The set X in the above theorem can have cardinality strictly smaller than $i(L_1)+i(L_2)-i(<L_1,L_2>)$, but not in the unidimensional case, unless we do not make the request of connettivity. For instance let $L_1 =< 2 >$, $L_2 =< 3 >$ and $X = \{1,4\}$. All pointed word f, 2-periodic and 3-periodic such that *supp*(f) contains a translated of X is also 1-periodic (i.e. in f it appears just one letter).

Of course, by Theorem 3.2, if $Card(X) < i(L_1)+i(L_2)-i(<L_1,L_2>)$ then X cannot contain a transversal T_{L_1} *and* a transversal T_{L_2} but it is possible to prove that in any case X must contain a transversal T_{L_1} *or* a transversal T_{L_2}.

In the unidimensional case, since all the sets of the form $g+X$ for some element $g \in Z$ are connected and $Card(g+X) = Card(X) \leq i(L_1)+i(L_2)-i(<L_1,L_2>)$, and since any connected subset Y of cardinality $i(L_1)+I(L_2)-i(<L_1,L_2>)-1$ contains transversals of L_1 and of L_2 then *supp*(f) contains a set of the form $g+X$ if and only if

$$Card(supp(f)) \geq i(L_1)+i(L_2)-i(<L_1,L_2>).$$

Since in the unidimensional case, if we suppose that $w = [f]$, the length $| w |$ of w is $Card(supp(f))$, then it is not difficult to prove that the extension of previous theorem to words is a generalization of the theorem of Fine and Wilf.

Definition 9. An element $q \in G$ is called periodicity vector for a pointed word f if and only if for any $x \in supp(f)$ such that $q+x \in supp(f)$ one has that $f(x) = f(q+x)$.

The following proposition is an immediate consequence of the definitions.

Proposition 10. *A pointed word f is L-periodic if and only if all $q \in L$ are periodicity vectors for f.*

Remark. It is not true that if q is a periodicity vector for f then f is $L =< q >$-periodic. This fact is true only in very particular cases as, for instance, in the unidimensional case for connected pointed words and in the bidimensional case for "rectangles". Obviously, from previous proposition, if f is $L =< q >$-periodic then q is a periodicity vector for f.

It is possible to represent in the unidimensional case non connected words with the aid of a letter ϕ that is not in the alphabet. For instance, the word $w = a\phi b\phi c\phi d$ has as representative the pointed word f where *supp*(f) $= \{1,3,5,7\}$ and $f(1) = a$, $f(3) = b$, $f(5) = c$, $f(7) = d$. This pointed word f is not 1-periodic but 1 is a periodicity vector for f. The letter ϕ is usually called "do not care symbol".

Before stating next theorem we give a definition.

Definition 11. Let L be a subgroup of a group G and let $q \in G$. We say that a set X is of the form $T_L \setminus T_{<L,q>}$ if and only if there exist a transversal $T_{<L,q>}$ of $<L,q>$ such that $X \cap T_{<L,q>} = \emptyset$, and $X \cup T_{<L,q>}$ is a transversal of L. Therefore

$$Card(X) = Card(T_L) - Card(T_{<L,q>}) = i(L) - i(<L,q>).$$

Theorem 12. *Let L be a subgroup of finite index of a group G. Let f be a pointed word that is L-periodic and let q be a periodicity vector for f.*

1) If $(q + supp(f)) \cap supp(f)$ *contains a set of the form*

$$T_L \setminus T_{<L,q>}$$

then f *is* $< L, q >$*-periodic.*

2) (tightness) *Let* Y *be a set of the form* $T_L \setminus T_{<L,q>}$. *There exists an element* $y \in Y$ *and a pointed word* f *such that* $(q + supp(f)) \cap supp(f)$ *contains the set*

$$\{T_L \setminus T_{<L,q>}\} \setminus \{y\}.$$

This pointed word f *is L-periodic,* q *is a periodicity vector for* f *but it is not* $< L, q >$*-periodic.*

In the unidimensional case we can suppose that $L =< p >$. If f is a connected pointed word then

$$Card((q + supp(f)) \cap supp(f)) = Card(supp(f)) - q.$$

If $(q + supp(f)) \cap supp(f)$ contains a set of the form

$$T_L \setminus T_{<L,q>}$$

then

$$Card((q + supp(f)) \cap supp(f)) \geq i(L) - i(< L, q >) = p - gcd(p, q).$$

Thus

$$Card(supp(f)) \geq p + q - gcd(p, q).$$

Conversely it is not difficult to see that if $Card(supp(f)) \geq p + q - gcd(p, q)$ then $(q + supp(f)) \cap supp(f)$ contains a set of the form $T_L \setminus T_{<L,q>}$.

Hence it is easy to prove that the extension of previous theorem to words is a generalization of the Theorem of Fine and Wilf.

A weak form of previous theorem in the bidimensional case and for "rectangles" was proved in [7].

Notice that it is possible to apply previous theorem to non connected pointed words. Thus this theorem leads to a generalization of the Theorem of Fine and Wilf to words with "do not care" symbols.

The next theorem holds only in the bidimensional case.

Theorem 13. *Let* $L_1 =< (c_1, r_1) >$ *and* $L_2 =< (c_2, r_2) >$ *be two ciclic subgroups of* $\mathbb{Z}$. *Let us suppose that* f *is a pointed word* L_1*-periodic and* L_2*-periodic; moreover let us suppose that* $c_1 \geq 0$, $r_1 \geq 0$, $c_2 > 0$, $r_2 \leq 0$, $(c_1, r_1) \neq (0, 0)$, *and that* $supp(f)$ *is a rectangle, i.e. a set of the form* $\{1, 2, ..., m\} \times \{1, 2, ..., n\}$.

1) If $Card(((c_1, r_1) + supp(f)) \cap supp(f)) + Card(((c_2, r_2) + supp(f)) \cap supp(f)) + i(< L_1, L_2 >) \geq Card(supp(f))$ *then* f *is* $< L_1, L_2 >$*-periodic.*

2) (tightness) *For any rectangle* Y *such that*

$$Card(((c_1, r_1) + Y) \cap Y) + Card(((c_2, r_2) + Y) \cap Y) + i(< L_1, L_2 >) < Card(Y)$$

there exists a word f, *such that* $supp(f) = Y$ *that is* L_1*-periodic and* L_2*-periodic but it is not* $< L_1, L_2 >$*-periodic.*

In previous theorem we use the notation that, in the case $i(< L_1, L_2 >)$ is not a finite number (i.e. if and only if $r_1 = 0$ and $r_2 = 0$), then $i(< L_1, L_2 >) = gcd(c_1, c_2) \times n$.

We can identify a connected pointed word in the unidimensional case with a pointed word in the bidimensional case having as support a rectangle of the form $\{1, 2, ..., m\} \times \{1\}$, and we can identify the subgroups L_1 and L_2 generated by p and q with the subgroups generated by $(p, 0)$ and by $(q, 0)$.

Since, in this case, $Card(((p, 0) + supp(f)) \cap supp(f)) = Card(supp(f)) - p$, $Card(((q, 0) + supp(f)) \cap supp(f)) = Card(supp(f)) - q$ and $i(< L_1, L_2 >) = gcd(p, q)$ then the property that f must verify in the point 1) is equivalent to

$$Card(supp(f)) - p + Card(supp(f)) - q + gcd(p, q) \geq Card(supp(f)),$$

that is

$$Card(supp(f)) \geq p + q - gcd(p, q).$$

Therefore it is easy to prove that the extension of previous theorem to words is a generalization of the Theorem of Fine and Wilf.

The following consequence of the previous theorem was firstly proved in [2].

Corollary 14. *Let f be a pointed word with $supp(f) = \{1, 2, ..., m\} \times \{1, 2, ..., n\}$. Let $(c_1, r_1)$and(c_2, r_2) be two periodicity vectors for f with $c_1 \geq 0$, $r_1 > 0$, $c_2 > 0$, $r_2 \leq 0$. If $c_1 + c_2 \leq m$ and $r_1 + r_2 \leq n$, then any element in $L =< (c_1, r_1), (c_2, r_2) >$ is a periodicity vector.*

4 Proofs

In this section give short sketch of some proofs of the results in Section 3.

Proof of Proposition 7. We want to prove that if $p, q \in G$ and $p - q \in < L_1, L_2 >$ then $f(p) = f(q)$. Since $< L_1, L_2 >$ is generated by L_1 and L_2, we can write:

$$p - q = l_1 + l_2 + \ldots + l_{2n}$$

where $l_{2i} \in L_2$ and $l_{2i-1} \in L_1$. Since f is L_1 periodic, it make sense to write (with abuse of notation) $f(L_1 + q) = f(q)$. But f is also L_2 periodic and, consequently, $f(L_2 + q) = f(q) = f(L_1 + q)$. We know that $L_2 + l_{2n} + q = L_2 + q$; consequently $f(L_1 + q) = f(L_2 + l_{2n} + q) = f(L_1 + l_{2n} + q)$. It is not difficult to iterate above argument and prove that

$$f(q) = f(L_1 + q) = f(L_1 + l_1 + l_2 + \ldots + l_{2n} + q) = f(L_1 + p) = f(p). \Box$$

Proof of Theorem 8. We give the sketch of the proof only in the case $< L_1, L_2 >= G$, i.e. when the two subgroups are coprime: the general case is proved in an analogous way.

We want to show now that there exists a set X with $Card(X) \le i(L_1)+i(L_2)-1$ such that, if f is L_1 and L_2-periodic and $supp(f)$ contains X then f is $< L_1, L_2 >$-periodic. It is sufficient to show that there exists a set X with $Card(X) \le i(L_1) + i(L_2) - 1$ such that, if f is L_1 and L_2-periodic and $supp(f)$ contains X then $f(q) = f(p)$ for all p, q in a transversal of L_1 or in a transversal of L_2.

Let us define a bipartite graph, where the set of vertices is $V_1 \cup V_2$. V_1 is the set of right cosets of L_1 and V_2 is the set of right cosets of L_2. There are only arcs between V_1 and V_2, and one arc connects $H \in V_1$ with $K \in V_2$ if and only if there exists one element $g \in G$ that is a representative of H and of K.

This graph has $Card(G)$ arcs and $i(L_1) + i(L_2)$ vertices.

The argument developed in the previous proposition shows that this graph is connected. Let us take one spanning tree of this graph, that is represented by a set of $i(L_1)+i(L_2)-1$ elements of G. It is not difficult to prove that this set X contains a transversal of L_1 *and* a transversal of L_2 and that for all $p, q \in X$, $f(q) = f(p)$.

It remains to prove that it is possible, for any (finite) set of generator S of G to choose this set X in order that it would be connected in the Cayley graph Γ; we do not report here the scheme of this step. □

The formal proof of Theorem 12 is rather technical, purely algebraic and it is not reported here. We now just describe the idea on which this proof is based. Let us suppose for semplicity that $< L, q >= G$, since the general case can be proved in an analogous way. Since q is a periodicity vector then if $s = q + t$, $z = q + q + t$ and t, s, z are still in $supp(f)$ then $f(L+s) = f(L+z) = f(L+t)$. If $q+q+q+t$ does not belong to $supp(f)$ we look for an element t' in the same right coset of $z = q + q + t$ that allows us to "add the vector q" at least another time. If $g + Supp(f) \cap Supp(f)$ is "large" enough then the sequence of equalities $f(L+t) = f(L+s) = \cdot = f(L+t')$ create a cicle where all right cosets of L appear as arguments of f; consequently the pointed word f is a constant function. Even if we cut this cicle in one position (this happens when the cardinality of $g + Supp(f) \cap Supp(f)$ is tight) we obtain the same result, but if we cut this cicle in two position then the word f can be a non-costant function.

Our proof of Theorem 13 is not algebraic and it uses the weaker Corollary 14. The most elegant and very easy part of this proof is the prooof of the tightness.

Proof of Theorem 13, tightness. We can think to any $f((x, y))$ as a variable; hence we have $supp(f)$ variables. To any element $(p, q) \in (c_i, r_i) + supp(f) \cap supp(f)$, $i = 1, 2$ it corresponds one equality between "variables" :

$$f((p, q)) = f((p - c_i, q - r_i)), i = 1, 2.$$

Even in the worst case where no equality is implied by the others, we can construct a word f that is $< (c_1, r_1) >$ and $< (c_2, r_2) >$-periodic and where we have

$$Card(supp(f)) - Card(((c_1, r_1) + supp(f)) \cap supp(f)) - \\ - Card(((c_2, r_2) + supp(f)) \cap supp(f)) > i(< (c_1, r_1), (c_2, r_2) >)$$

degrees of freedom (i.e. different letters). Thus f cannot be $< (c_1, r_1), (c_2, r_2) >$-periodic because any L-periodic (pointed) word contains less than or equal to $i(L)$ letters. □

5 Conclusions

Since in the bidimensional case the subgroup L of $\mathbb{Z}^2$ are such that either $i(L)$ is a finite number or they are generated by only one element. Thus our three theorems are "exaustive" in some sense in the case of $\mathbb{Z}^2$. We are trying to extend Theorem 13 to $\mathbb{Z}^n$ and more in general to Cayley graphs of groups. Just remark that the tightness of the condition in Theorem 13 does not depend on the shape of the support of the word f. Does this condition hold also for "parallelograms" (or other shapes)?

We verified sperimentally for "small" subgroups that in the bidimensional case it is possible to choose the set X in Theorem 8 not only connex but also convex. We do not believe that this is true for subgroup of very large index but we have not, up to now, counterexamples.

Weak versions of Theorem 12 and of Theorem 13 were used in [3], [2], [6] were used in optimal, alphabet independent, bidimensional pattern mathching algorithms. No algorithms with these properties are known at the moment for dimension greater than two.

We hope that Theorem 12 could be a tool for creating optimal, alphabet independent, n-dimensional pattern mathching algorithms.

One even more difficult task would be to create optimal pattern matching algorithms on Cayley graphs of groups.

References

1. Aho A. V.: Algorithms for Finding Pattern in Strings. In *Handbook of Theoretical Computer Science*, J. van Leeuwen editor, Elsevier Science Publishers B.V. 1990, 257–295
2. Amir, A., Benson, G. E.: Two-Dimensional Periodicity and its Applications. Proc. 3rd ACM-SIAM Symp. on Discr. Algorithms (1992) 440–452
3. Amir, A., Benson, G. E.: Alphabet Independent Two-Dimensional Pattern Matching. Proc. 24th ACM Symp. Theory on Comp. (1992) 59–68
4. Fine, N. J., Wilf, H. S.: Uniqueness Theorem for Periodic Functions. Proc. Am. Math. Soc. **16** (1965) 109–114
5. Galil, Z., Giancarlo, R.: On the Exact Complexity of String Matching: Upper Bounds. SIAM J. Comp. **20** number 6 1008–1020
6. Galil, Z., Park, K.: Truly Alphabet Independent Two-Dimensional Pattern Matching Proc. 33th IEEE Symp. on Foundations of Computer Science (1992) 247–256
7. Galil, Z., Park, K.: Truly Alphabet Independent Two-Dimensional Pattern Matching preprint (1993)
8. Lyndon, R.C., Schupp, P.E.: Combinatorial Group Theory, Springer Verlag 1977
9. Lothaire: Combinatorics on Words. Encyclopedia of Mathemathics and its Applications, **17** Addison-Wesley 1983
10. Lyndon,R. C., Schutzemberger M. P.: The Equation $a^m = b^n c^p$ in a Free Group. Michigan Math. J. **9** number 4 (1962) 289–298
11. Nicodeme, P., Regnier, M.: Towards 2D Pattern Matching Complexity, manuscript (1992)
12. Rosenfeld, A., Kak, A.C.: Digital Picture Processing. Academic Press 1982
13. Regnier, M., Rostami, L.: A Unifying Look at d-Dimensional Periodicities and Space Coverings. Proc. 4th Symposium on Combinatorial Pattern Matching (1993) 215–227

Probabilistic Domains

Reinhold Heckmann

FB 14 – Informatik, Prof. Wilhelm
Universität des Saarlandes, Postfach 151150
D-66041 Saarbrücken, Germany
e-mail: heckmann@cs.uni-sb.de

Abstract

We show the equivalence of several different axiomatizations of the notion of (abstract) *probabilistic domain* in the category of dcpo's and continuous functions. The axiomatization with the richest set of operations provides probabilistic selection among a finite number of possibilities with arbitrary probabilities, whereas the poorest one has binary choice with equal probabilities as the only operation. The remaining theories lie in between; one of them is the theory of binary choice by Graham [1].

1 Introduction

A probabilistic programming language could contain different kinds of language constructs to express probabilistic choice. In a rather poor language, there might be a construct $x \oplus y$, whose semantics is a choice between the two possibilities x and y with equal probabilities 1/2. The 'possibilities' x and y can be statements in an imperative language or expressions in a functional language. A quite rich language could contain a construct $[p_1 : x_1, \ldots, p_n : x_n]$, where p_i are real numbers between 0 and 1 whose sum is 1. The semantics would be to select one of the possibilities x_i with probability p_i.

Graham [1], Jones [3], and Jones / Plotkin [4] consider an intermediate language with a construct $x \stackrel{p}{—} y$, which is written as $p \rightarrow x, y$ by Graham and $x +_p y$ by Jones, where p is a real number between 0 and 1. The semantics of this construct is to select x with probability p and y with probability $1 - p$.

The notion of an (abstract) *probabilistic domain* was introduced by Graham [1] and further elaborated by Jones [3, 4] to describe the denotational semantics of a probabilistic language with the construct $x \stackrel{p}{—} y$. A probabilistic domain is a dcpo together with a continuous operation satisfying several axioms, which is used to model the choice construct semantically. For reasons of simplicity, we denote the results of this semantic operation by $x \stackrel{p}{—} y$ as well, where x and y are no longer language constructs, but members of the underlying dcpo.

Jones and Plotkin define a *probabilistic power domain construction* which produces the free probabilistic domain over a given base domain. This construction is a strong monad in the sense of Moggi [5, 6]. Hence the denotational semantics of probabilistic languages with a construct $x \xrightarrow{p} y$ can be written down schematically using this monad. Such a semantics can be found in [3].

In the paper at hand, we introduce some other notions of probabilistic domain with other semantic operations which describe a whole range of language constructs from the binary choice $x \oplus y$ over $x \xrightarrow{p} y$ till $[p_1 : x_1, \ldots, p_n : x_n]$ with various intermediate steps. Every kind of probabilistic domain is described as a dcpo together with some continuous operations satisfying some axioms, i.e., as a model of some algebraic theory in the category $\mathcal{DCPO}$. Then, we prove that *all these theories are equivalent* in the sense that their categories of models are equivalent. This has several consequences. First, one sees that in the category $\mathcal{DCPO}$, all the probabilistic operations mentioned above are in fact equally expressive; even the multiple choice $[p_1 : x_1, \ldots, p_n : x_n]$ can be defined in terms of binary choice $x \oplus y$ (with the help of fixed point iteration). Next, the probabilistic power construction of [3, 4] not only produces the free probabilistic domain with $x \xrightarrow{p} y$, but free probabilistic domains with all other operations as well because all the categories of probabilistic domains are equivalent. Thus, one power construction can be used to describe the semantics of a whole range of probabilistic languages.

Finding algebraic theories which are equivalent to the probabilistic theory of Graham and Jones also shows how some disadvantages of that theory can be avoided. Their theory refers to the unit interval $\mathbf{I} = [0..1]$ of the reals with the standard Hausdorff topology and thus goes beyond domain theory, and their axiom of associativity (in the version of Jones)

$$\text{if } pq \neq 1, \text{ then } (x \xrightarrow{p} y) \xrightarrow{q} z = x \xrightarrow{pq} (y \xrightarrow{r} z), \text{ where } r = \tfrac{q(1-p)}{1-pq}$$

is a conditional axiom and contains a complex fraction which reflects the recalculation of probabilities when moving the parentheses. The condition is needed to prevent the denominator of this fraction to become zero. The equivalent theories presented in our paper tend to avoid these problems; many of them refer to domains (dcpo's) only, or contain only simple unconditional axioms.

After introducing the mathematical background in Section 2, we present our richest theory, Multiple Choice with Divergence (MCD), in Section 3. Its basic operations are the choice among n possibilities $x_1, \ldots, x_n$ with probabilities $p_1, \ldots, p_n$, where $\sum_{i=1}^{n} p_i \leq 1$, for every finite $n \geq 0$. The difference $1 - \sum_{i=1}^{n} p_i$ is the probability to stay undecisive for ever, i.e., to diverge. The possibility of divergence would be odd in a real programming language, but we need it for the purpose of our equivalence proof.

The theory MCD has particularly neat axioms, which are powerful, simple, algorithmically intuitive, and also algebraically intuitive if the multiple choice is considered as a formal linear combination $\sum_{i=1}^{n} p_i \cdot x_i$. In her thesis [3], Jones derived most parts of MCD from her theory and used this to prove that her probabilistic power domains are free probabilistic domains over the argument domain. However, Jones did not present a complete description of MCD, nor did she work the other way round and prove the equivalence of MCD and her theory.

In Section 4, we restrict multiple choice to binary choice where the sum of the two probabilities is 1. The resulting operation is the original operation $x \xrightarrow{p} y$ of Graham and Jones. We present four versions of the theory of Binary Choice: Theory BC-A (Binary Choice with Associativity) is the original theory in the version of Jones with the complex conditional associativity axiom. In theory BC-R, associativity is replaced by two simpler unconditional axioms, the Rectangle axiom and the axiom of linear combination. Theory BC-P has yet another set of axioms which contains a Product axiom. Theory BC-L has a large axiom set which contains all the three other axiom sets. Because of our main result that all these theories have the same models, a dcpo with binary choice satisfies all the properties listed in theory BC-L once it has been proved that it satisfies one of the three small axiom sets BC-A, BC-R, or BC-P.

In Section 5, we restrict the binary choice between x with probability p and y with probability $1-p$ to two special cases: a binary choice '$\oplus$' between x and y with equal probabilities 1/2, and a choice between x with probability p and $\perp$ with probability $1-p$, which can be seen as multiplication of x by a scalar p drawn from the unit interval (with the Scott topology) and consequently is written as $p \cdot x$. These operations are similar to the operations in a vector space or module, where '$\oplus$' plays the role of addition. Thus, we call the theories with these operations IM for **I**-module. We present two versions of this theory: a theory IM-S with a small axiom set, and IM-L with a large axiom set. The axioms of both theories are simple equality statements. Because of our results, it suffices to verify the axioms of IM-S for a given **I**-module structure, and then all the properties listed in IM-L hold as well.

In Section 6, we even drop multiplication and obtain a theory with binary choice with equal probabilities as the only operation. We call this theory MV (Mean Value algebra) since this kind of choice has the algebraic properties of mean value formation. The theory MV has the advantage of not mentioning real numbers at all, at the expense of a complex axiom, which states that the least fixed point of the function $\lambda x.\, a \oplus x$ is a. Computationally, this axiom reflects the fact that in a recursive program $x = a \oplus x$, the possibility a is chosen with probability $1/2 + 1/4 + 1/8 + \cdots = 1$, whence the program is equivalent to a. The other theories do not need this axiom explicitly since it follows from the structure of the unit interval.

The theory MV was already presented by the author in [2] as an example of a 'power theory', i.e., a theory with a binary operation modeling the binary choice operator of non-deterministic programming languages. In that paper, we did not mention any other probabilistic theory, but only conjectured the equivalence with BC-A, the theory of Jones.

In the course of presenting these more and more restricted theories, we also derive every theory (except for MCD, of course) from a less restricted theory presented earlier. This is done in the following order:

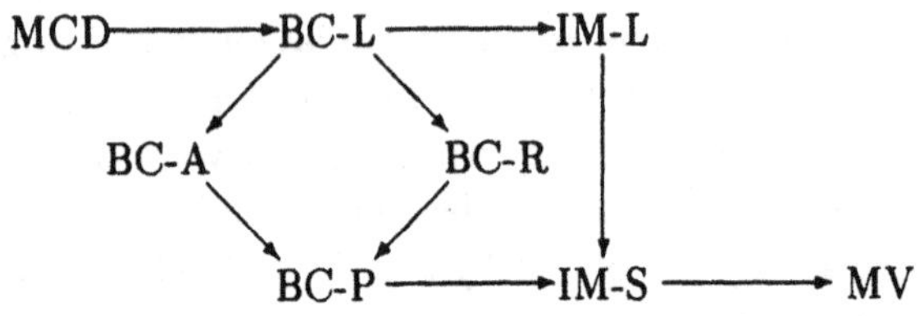

To show equivalence of all theories, we finally have to derive the most powerful theory MCD from the most restricted theory MV, i.e., we have to define multiple choice with arbitrary probabilities in terms of binary choice with equal probabilities 1/2 (and joins of ascending sequences). This is done in Section 7.

2 Mathematical Background

We use the standard definitions of posets, least upper bounds or joins (denoted by $\bigsqcup A$), and directed sets. A *dcpo* is a poset where every directed set has a least upper bound. In this paper, we often call dcpo's *domains*. A function $f : \mathbf{X} \to \mathbf{Y}$ between dcpo's $\mathbf{X}$ and $\mathbf{Y}$ is *continuous* if for all directed subsets D of $\mathbf{X}$, $f(\bigsqcup D) = \bigsqcup f(D)$ holds. The category of dcpo's and continuous functions is called $\mathcal{DCPO}$.

A subset O of a dcpo $\mathbf{X}$ is *Scott open* if it is upper ($x \in O$, $x \sqsubseteq y \Rightarrow y \in O$), and for all directed sets D, $\bigsqcup D \in O$ implies $D \cap O \neq \emptyset$. The Scott open sets of a dcpo $\mathbf{X}$ form a topology on $\mathbf{X}$, the Scott topology. A function $f : \mathbf{X} \to \mathbf{Y}$ between dcpo's is continuous in the sense of the previous paragraph iff $f^{-1}V$ is Scott open in $\mathbf{X}$ for every Scott open set V of $\mathbf{Y}$. Thus, $\mathcal{DCPO}$ can be considered as a full subcategory of the category $\mathcal{TOP}$ of topological spaces, and it makes sense to speak of the continuity of a function from a space to a dcpo, as it will be done in the description of the BC theories.

The *unit interval* $\mathbf{I}$ is the set of real numbers r with $0 \leq r \leq 1$. We can either consider it as a dcpo ordered by '$\leq$' and equip it with the Scott topology, or topologize it by the standard Hausdorff topology. The two possibilities are connected by the following lemma:

Lemma 2.1 A function $f : \mathbf{I} \to Y$ from the unit interval to a dcpo Y is continuous w.r.t. the Scott topology on $\mathbf{I}$ if and only if it is monotonic w.r.t. the standard order of $\mathbf{I}$ and continuous w.r.t. the Hausdorff topology of $\mathbf{I}$.

3 Multiple Choice with Divergence

In this section, we present the probabilistic theory with the most powerful operations: the theory MCD of multiple choice with divergence. The basic operation of MCD is choice between n possibilities $x_1, \ldots, x_n$ with probabilities $p_1, \ldots, p_n$, whose sum is at most 1.

In the following table as well as in all subsequent ones, we assume that the probabilistic domain to be described is a *dcpo* called X.

Operations: Continuous functions $\nabla_n \times X^n \to X$ for every $n \geq 0$, where

$$\nabla_n = \{(p_1, \ldots, p_n) \in \mathbf{I}^n \mid p_1 + \cdots + p_n \leq 1\}$$

are dcpo's, i.e., equipped with the Scott topology. The result of applying the operation of degree n to $(p_1, \ldots, p_n)$ in ∇_n and $(x_1, \ldots, x_n)$ in X^n is written $[p_1 : x_1, \ldots, p_n : x_n]$.

Homomorphisms are continuous functions h with

$$h\,[p_1 : x_1, \ldots, p_n : x_n] = [p_1 : h\,x_1, \ldots, p_n : h\,x_n].$$

Axioms: The axioms are those of linear combinations $\sum_{i=1}^{n} p_i \cdot x_i$, namely:

Permutation P: For every permutation π of $\{1, \ldots, n\}$,

$$[p_{\pi 1} : x_{\pi 1}, \ldots, p_{\pi n} : x_{\pi n}] = [p_1 : x_1, \ldots, p_n : x_n]$$

1 law: $[1 : x] = x$

0 law: $[0 : x, p_1 : y_1, \ldots, p_n : y_n] = [p_1 : y_1, \ldots, p_n : y_n]$

Addition $+$:

$$[p : x, q : x, r_1 : y_1, \ldots, r_n : y_n] = [p + q : x, r_1 : y_1, \ldots, r_n : y_n]$$

Substitution S:

$$[p : [q_1 : x_1, \ldots, q_k : x_k], r_1 : y_1, \ldots, r_n : y_n]$$
$$= [p\,q_1 : x_1, \ldots, p\,q_k : x_k, r_1 : y_1, \ldots, r_n : y_n]$$

For simplicity, we have omitted the universal quantification, which for instance for substitution should be: for all $k \geq 0$ and $n \geq 0$, $x_1, \ldots x_k$, $y_1, \ldots y_n$ in X, $(q_1, \ldots, q_k)$ in ∇_k, and $(p, r_1, \ldots, r_n)$ in ∇_{n+1}. Thus, the axioms are not conditional, although they can be applied only to real numbers satisfying certain conditions.

4 Binary Choice without Divergence

In this section, we present our four versions of the theory of binary choice without divergence BC, and derive them from MCD. The binary choice $x \xrightarrow{p} y$ introduced here corresponds to $[p : x, 1 - p : y]$ from the previous section. Whereas MCD refers to ∇_n with the Scott topology, the BC theories refer to $\mathbf{I}$ with the Hausdorff topology.

Operations: A constant $0 : X$ and an operation $\beta : \mathbf{I} \times X \times X \to X$, which is continuous in each argument separately, if $\mathbf{I}$ is equipped with the standard Hausdorff topology. We write $x \stackrel{p}{-} y$ instead of $\beta(p, x, y)$.

Homomorphisms are continuous functions h with
$h(0) = 0$ and $h(x \stackrel{p}{-} y) = hx \stackrel{p}{-} hy$.

Axioms, version L (large axiom set):

$\perp$ Least element: $0 \sqsubseteq x$ for all x in X.

C Commutativity: $x \stackrel{p}{-} y = y \stackrel{1-p}{-} x$.

0 Zero law: $x \stackrel{0}{-} y = y$.

1 One law: $x \stackrel{1}{-} y = x$.

I Idempotence: $x \stackrel{p}{-} x = x$.

D Distributivity: $x \stackrel{p}{-} (y \stackrel{q}{-} z) = (x \stackrel{p}{-} y) \stackrel{q}{-} (x \stackrel{p}{-} z)$.

P Product law: $(x \stackrel{p}{-} y) \stackrel{q}{-} y = x \stackrel{pq}{-} y$.

L Linear combination:
$(x \stackrel{p}{-} y) \stackrel{r}{-} (x \stackrel{q}{-} y) = x \stackrel{s}{-} y$ where $s = rp + (1-r)q$.

R Rectangle law: $(x \stackrel{q}{-} y) \stackrel{p}{-} (u \stackrel{q}{-} v) = (x \stackrel{p}{-} u) \stackrel{q}{-} (y \stackrel{p}{-} v)$.

A Associativity:
If $pq \neq 1$, then $(x \stackrel{p}{-} y) \stackrel{q}{-} z = x \stackrel{pq}{-} (y \stackrel{r}{-} z)$, where $r = \frac{q(1-p)}{1-pq}$.

Axioms, version A (with associativity):
Axioms $\perp$, C, 1, I, and A from the list above.

Axioms, version R (with rectangle law):
Axioms $\perp$, 0, 1, L, and R from the list above.

Axioms, version P (with product law):
Axioms $\perp$, 0, 1, I, P, $L\frac{1}{2}$, and $R\frac{1}{2}$, where $L\frac{1}{2}$ is the instance of L with $r = 1/2$, and $R\frac{1}{2}$ is the instance of R with $p = q = 1/2$.

The wording 'β is continuous in each argument separately' means that the functions $\lambda p.\, \beta(p, x, y) : \mathbf{I} \to X$ are continuous for every fixed x and y, and analogously for the second and third argument. Within $\mathcal{DCPO}$, such a separate continuity would be equivalent to the continuity of β itself; this is why we did not postulate it explicitly in case of MCD.

Jones [3] has a more complex continuity requirement for β which is more restrictive in general than ours, but equivalent for the important case of a continuous domain X. We relaxed the continuity requirement because with the stronger version, equivalence of BC-A to the other probabilistic theories cannot be proved.

The rectangle law is named because of the following rectangular scheme:

$$\begin{array}{ccc} x & \stackrel{p}{-} & y \\ {\scriptstyle q}| & & |{\scriptstyle q} \\ u & \stackrel{p}{-} & v \end{array}$$

On the left hand side of R, choice is first performed within the two rows, then the results of the rows are combined. On the right hand side, choice is first done in the two columns, then the results of the columns are combined.

We presented theory BC in four versions because the equivalence of the respective sets of axioms is by no means obvious. For instance, we have no idea how to prove associativity from the axioms of BC-R directly, without reconstructing MCD as we have done in the paper at hand.

Theory BC-L comprises all interesting equalities we know of, BC-A is the theory of Graham and Jones, BC-R is the nicest theory in our view since it consists of simple unconditional axioms only, and BC-P consists of just the properties we need to derive IM-S in the next section (which in turn consists of just the properties we need to derive MV).

Derivation of BC-L from MCD

The constant 0 of BC is case $n = 0$ of MCD, i.e., $0 = []$; and $\beta(p, x, y) = x \xrightarrow{p} y$ is defined by $[p : x,\ 1-p : y]$. Continuity of β in the second and third argument is immediate, and continuity in the first argument holds since $\varphi : \mathbf{I}_H \to \nabla_2$ with $\varphi(p) = (p,\ 1-p)$ is continuous, where $\mathbf{I}_H$ is the unit interval with the Hausdorff topology, and ∇_2 has the Scott topology.

Next, we show that 0 is the least element: $0 = [\,] = [0 : x]$ holds by the 0 law of MCD. By continuity and hence monotonicity of the operation of MCD, $[0 : x] \sqsubseteq [1 : x]$ follows. By the 1 law, the latter term equals x.

The equational axioms of BC-L can be shown by the following strategy: translate both sides into MCD by $x \xrightarrow{p} y = [p : x,\ 1-p : y]$, then flatten them using substitution, delete entries $0 : x$ using the 0 axiom of MCD, combine multiple entries with the same dcpo element using the + axiom, and then compare both sides of the equality. For instance, the proof of L looks as follows:

We have to show $(x \xrightarrow{p} y) \xrightarrow{r} (x \xrightarrow{q} y) = x \xrightarrow{s} y$ where $s = rp + (1-r)q$. Translating the left hand side into MCD yields:

$$(x \xrightarrow{p} y) \xrightarrow{r} (x \xrightarrow{q} y) = [r : [p : x,\ 1-p : y],\ 1-r : [q : x,\ 1-q : y]]$$

With substitution and addition, we obtain $[s : x,\ s' : y]$, where $s = rp + (1-r)q$ as required, and $s' = r(1-p) + (1-r)(1-q)$, which is $1-s$ as required (check $s + s' = 1$).

Derivation of BC-P from BC-R

We have to deduce I and P from 0, 1, L, and R.

I: $x \xrightarrow{p} x \overset{1}{=} (x \xrightarrow{1} x) \xrightarrow{p} (x \xrightarrow{1} x) \overset{L}{=} x \xrightarrow{s} x$
where $s = p \cdot 1 + (1-p) \cdot 1 = 1$. By 1, $x \xrightarrow{s} x = x$ follows.

P: $(x \xrightarrow{p} y) \xrightarrow{q} y \overset{0}{=} (x \xrightarrow{p} y) \xrightarrow{q} (x \xrightarrow{0} y) \overset{L}{=} x \xrightarrow{s} y$
where $s = q \cdot p + (1-q) \cdot 0 = pq$.

Derivation of BC-P from BC-A

We have to deduce 0, P, $L\frac{1}{2}$, and $R\frac{1}{2}$ from C, 1, I, and A.

Axiom 0: $x \xrightarrow{0} y \stackrel{C}{=} y \xrightarrow{1} x \stackrel{1}{=} y$

For P, we have to distinguish two cases: if $pq = 1$, then $p = q = 1$, and $(x \xrightarrow{1} y) \xrightarrow{1} y = x = x \xrightarrow{1} y$ holds by the 1 law. Otherwise, axiom A can be applied:

$$(x \xrightarrow{p} y) \xrightarrow{q} y \stackrel{A}{=} x \xrightarrow{pq} (y \xrightarrow{r} y) \stackrel{I}{=} x \xrightarrow{pq} y$$

For $L\frac{1}{2}$, we have to show $(x \xrightarrow{p} y) \xrightarrow{1/2} (x \xrightarrow{q} y) = x \xrightarrow{(p+q)/2} y$. Applying A to the left hand side, we obtain $x \xrightarrow{p/2} (y \xrightarrow{r} (x \xrightarrow{q} y))$ with $r = \frac{(1-p)/2}{1-p/2} = \frac{1-p}{2-p}$. Applying C yields $x \xrightarrow{p/2} ((x \xrightarrow{q} y) \xrightarrow{r'} y)$ with $r' = 1 - r = \frac{1}{2-p}$. Applying P (which is already proved) yields $x \xrightarrow{p/2} (x \xrightarrow{qr'} y)$. Now, we apply C twice, then P, and finally C again, which gives $x \xrightarrow{s} y$ with $s = 1 - (1 - \frac{q}{2-p})(1 - \frac{p}{2}) = 1 - \frac{2-p-q}{2-p} \cdot \frac{2-p}{2} = (p+q)/2$.

For $R\frac{1}{2}$, we have to show $(x \xrightarrow{1/2} y) \xrightarrow{1/2} (u \xrightarrow{1/2} v) = (x \xrightarrow{1/2} u) \xrightarrow{1/2} (y \xrightarrow{1/2} v)$. This is done by the following chain of equations:

$$(x \xrightarrow{1/2} y) \xrightarrow{1/2} (u \xrightarrow{1/2} v) \stackrel{A}{=} x \xrightarrow{1/4} (y \xrightarrow{1/3} (u \xrightarrow{1/2} v)) \stackrel{C}{=} x \xrightarrow{1/4} ((u \xrightarrow{1/2} v) \xrightarrow{2/3} y)$$
$$\stackrel{A}{=} x \xrightarrow{1/4} (u \xrightarrow{1/3} (v \xrightarrow{1/2} y)) \stackrel{A}{=} (x \xrightarrow{1/2} u) \xrightarrow{1/2} (v \xrightarrow{1/2} y) \stackrel{C}{=} (x \xrightarrow{1/2} u) \xrightarrow{1/2} (y \xrightarrow{1/2} v)$$

5 I-Modules

In this section, we introduce the theory IM of **I**-modules. Its 'addition' is binary choice with equal probabilities 1/2, and its 'multiplication' is choice between a point and 0. The axioms are very much like those of a module, hence the name.

Theory IM comes up in two versions: IM-L has a large set of axioms which includes all useful properties we know of, and IM-S has a small subset thereof, just enough to derive theory MV in the next section.

Again, we do not know how all axioms of IM-L can be proved from those of IM-S directly, without reconstructing MCD as done in this paper.

Operations: A constant $0 : X$, a continuous operation $\oplus : X \times X \to X$, and a continuous operation $\cdot : \mathbf{I} \times X \to X$, where $\mathbf{I}$ is considered as a dcpo (Scott topology).

Homomorphisms are continuous functions h with
$h(0) = 0$, $h(x \oplus y) = hx \oplus hy$, and $h(p \cdot x) = p \cdot hx$.

Axioms, version L (large axiom set):

$\bot$ Least element: $0 \sqsubseteq x$ for all x in X.

C Commutativity: $x \oplus y = y \oplus x$.

I Idempotence: $x \oplus x = x$.

R Rectangle law: $(x \oplus y) \oplus (u \oplus v) = (x \oplus u) \oplus (y \oplus v)$.

$R0$ Right zero: $p \cdot 0 = 0$.

RD Right distributivity: $p \cdot (x \oplus y) = p \cdot x \oplus p \cdot y$.

$L0$ Left zero: $0 \cdot x = 0$.

LD Left distributivity: $(p \oplus q) \cdot x = p \cdot x \oplus q \cdot x$, where $p \oplus q = (p+q)/2$ in **I**.

1 One law: $1 \cdot x = x$.

PA Product associativity: $p \cdot (q \cdot x) = (p \cdot q) \cdot x$.

Axioms, version S (small axiom set):
Axioms R, $L0$, LD, and 1 from the list above.

Surprisingly, idempotence and commutativity of '$\oplus$' do not show up as axioms of IM-S. Nevertheless, they hold in every IM-S algebra by the main result of our paper.

Derivation of IM-S from BC-P

We define: $x \oplus y \;=\; x \xrightarrow{1/2} y$, and $p \cdot x \;=\; x \xrightarrow{p} 0$.

The operation $\oplus = \lambda(x, y).\, \beta(1/2, x, y) : X \times X \to X$ is continuous in its two arguments separately, since β is continuous in its second and third argument separately. Within $\mathcal{DCPO}$, this separate continuity is equivalent to the continuity of '$\oplus$' itself.

The function $\cdot \;=\; \lambda(p, x).\, \beta(p, x, 0) : \mathbf{I} \times X \to X$ is continuous in its second argument since β is. For continuity in the first argument, we apply Lemma 2.1, i.e., we have to show that for fixed x, the function $\lambda p.\, p \cdot x$ is monotonic.

Let $p \leq q$ in **I**. We have to show $x \xrightarrow{p} 0 \sqsubseteq x \xrightarrow{q} 0$. Because of $p \leq q$, there is r in **I** such that $p = r \cdot q$. Applying the product law P of BC-P, we obtain $x \xrightarrow{p} 0 = (x \xrightarrow{r} 0) \xrightarrow{q} 0$. From $0 \sqsubseteq x$, $x \xrightarrow{r} 0 \sqsubseteq x \xrightarrow{r} x \stackrel{I}{=} x$ follows, whence $x \xrightarrow{p} 0 \sqsubseteq x \xrightarrow{q} 0$.

R: The rectangle law of IM is $R\frac{1}{2}$ of BC-P.

$L0$: $0 \cdot x \;=\; x \xrightarrow{0} 0 \stackrel{0}{=} 0$.

LD: Left distributivity of IM is the instance of $L\frac{1}{2}$ of BC-P with $y = 0$.

1: $1 \cdot x \;=\; x \xrightarrow{1} 0 \stackrel{1}{=} x$.

Derivation of IM-L from BC-L

When expressed in the language of BC, all the axioms of IM-L but RD become instances of axioms of BC-L. Right distributivity becomes

$$(x \xrightarrow{1/2} y) \xrightarrow{p} 0 \;=\; (x \xrightarrow{p} 0) \xrightarrow{1/2} (y \xrightarrow{p} 0),$$

with follows from distributivity D of BC-L with commutativity.

6 Mean Values

The probabilistic theory with the weakest operations is MV, the theory of mean values. It results from IM by dropping multiplication. Thus, MV does not mention real numbers explicitly.

Operations: A constant $0 : X$, and a continuous operation $\oplus : X \times X \to X$.

Homomorphisms are continuous functions h with

$h(0) = 0$ and $h(x \oplus y) = hx \oplus hy$.

Axioms: Commutativity: $x \oplus y = y \oplus x$,

Rectangle law: $(x \oplus y) \oplus (u \oplus v) = (x \oplus u) \oplus (y \oplus v)$,

Least element: $0 \sqsubseteq x$,

Fixed point axiom: The least fixed point of $\lambda x.\, a \oplus x$ is a.

For the fixed point axiom, remember that the carrier X is a dcpo. The fixed point axiom may alternatively be written as idempotence $a \oplus a = a$, which means that a is a fixed point of $\lambda x.\, a \oplus x$, plus the conditional axiom $a \oplus b = b \Rightarrow a \sqsubseteq b$, which means that a is the least fixed point. Yet another formulation follows from making the fixed point iteration explicit: if $a_0 = 0$ and $a_{n+1} = a \oplus a_n$, then $\bigsqcup_{n \geq 0} a_n = a$. From this statement, a slightly stronger one can be easily deduced: if $b_0 \sqsubseteq a$ and $b_{n+1} = a \oplus b_n$, then $\bigsqcup_{n \geq 0} b_n = a$. It is this last version which is needed for the derivation of MCD from MV at the end of this paper.

Now let us derive the axioms of MV from those of IM-S. The rectangle law is immediate. The least element property of 0 holds since $0 = 0 \cdot x \sqsubseteq 1 \cdot x = x$. For the fixed point axiom, we have to consider the sequence defined by $a_0 = 0$ and $a_{n+1} = a \oplus a_n$. We claim $a_n = (1 - 2^{-n}) \cdot a$ for all n; the equation $\bigsqcup_{n \geq 0} a_n = a$ then follows from continuity of multiplication and the property $1 \cdot a = a$. The equality $a_0 = (1 - 2^{-0}) \cdot a$ holds since $0 \cdot a = 0$. For the inductive step, we have $a_{n+1} = a \oplus a_n = 1 \cdot a \oplus (1 - 2^{-n}) \cdot a = (1 + 1 - 2^{-n})/2 \cdot a = (1 - 2^{-(n+1)}) \cdot a$.

For commutativity, fix two members a and b of X. We start with some auxiliary statements. In the proof of the third, we may use idempotence because it follows from the fixed point axiom, which is already validated. (It could also be shown directly by $x \oplus x = 1 \cdot x \oplus 1 \cdot x = 1 \cdot x = x$.)

(1) $a \oplus p \cdot a = p \cdot a \oplus a$

Proof: $a \oplus p \cdot a = 1 \cdot a \oplus p \cdot a = (p+1)/2 \cdot a$, and same for $p \cdot a \oplus a$.

(2) $a \oplus 0 = 0 \oplus a$

Proof: From (1) with $p = 0$.

(3) $a \oplus c = c \oplus a \Rightarrow a \oplus (b \oplus c) = (c \oplus b) \oplus a$

Proof: $a \oplus (b \oplus c) \stackrel{I}{=} (a \oplus a) \oplus (b \oplus c) \stackrel{R}{=} (a \oplus b) \oplus (a \oplus c) = (a \oplus b) \oplus (c \oplus a) \stackrel{R}{=} (a \oplus c) \oplus (b \oplus a) = (c \oplus a) \oplus (b \oplus a) \stackrel{R}{=} (c \oplus b) \oplus (a \oplus a) \stackrel{I}{=} (c \oplus b) \oplus a$.

Now we define $c_0 = 0$ and $c_{n+1} = b \oplus c_n$. From the proof of the fixed point axiom, we know $c_n = (1 - 2^{-n}) \cdot b$. By (1), $b \oplus c_n = c_n \oplus b$ follows. Thus,

$c_{n+1} = c_n \oplus b$ also holds. By induction, we can show $a \oplus c_n = c_n \oplus a$ for all n; the start holds by (2), and the inductive step follows from (3). We already know $\bigsqcup_{n \geq 0} c_n = b$. Continuity of '$\oplus$' yields $a \oplus b = b \oplus a$ as required.

7 The Big Step: From MV to MCD

In the previous sections, we started from the theory MCD, which has a rich set of operations, and restricted its operations until only binary choice with equal probabilities was left. In this section, we go all the way back: we assume an MV algebra X as given, and prove that it is an MCD algebra as well. To this end, we have to reconstruct multiple choice with arbitrary probabilities from binary choice with probabilities 1/2. We first consider multiple binary choice, then multiple choice with dyadic rationals as probabilities, and finally apply directed joins and continuity arguments to reach all reals in the unit interval.

Multiple Binary Choice

Let X be an MV algebra. For every n, we define an operator $\bigoplus_n : X^{2^n} \to X$ which takes 2^n arguments from X.

- $\bigoplus_0(x) = x$.
- $\bigoplus_{n+1}(x_i \mid i = 1..2^{n+1}) = \bigoplus_n(x_i \mid i = 1..2^n) \oplus \bigoplus_n(x_i \mid i = 2^n+1..2^{n+1})$.

Thus, $\bigoplus_n(x_1, \ldots, x_{2^n})$ is obtained by evaluating a complete binary tree of depth n, whose inner nodes are marked by '$\oplus$' and whose leaves are x_1 through x_{2^n}. Complete binary trees can be pasted into each other:

Proposition 7.1
$\bigoplus_n(\bigoplus_m(x_{ij} \mid j = 1..2^m) \mid i = 1..2^n) = \bigoplus_{n+m}(x_{ij} \mid i = 1..2^n, j = 1..2^m)$
(The 2^n sequences $(x_{ij} \mid j = 1..2^m)$ are concatenated.)

Proof: Induction by n. □

From commutativity and the rectangle law, we can conclude:

Proposition 7.2 The operands of $\bigoplus_n$ can be arbitrarily permuted.

Proof: Induction on n. Case $n = 0$ is obvious, and case $n = 1$ holds by commutativity. For $n > 1$, let $\xi = (x_i \mid i = 1..2^n)$ be the sequence of arguments, and let α be its first quarter, β the second, γ the third, and δ the last.

It suffices to show that two adjacent operands x_k and x_{k+1} can be transposed. If $k \neq 2^{n-1}$, then the pair to be transposed is contained in the first half $\alpha\beta$ or in the second $\gamma\delta$. Because of $\bigoplus_n(\xi) = \bigoplus_{n-1}(\alpha\beta) \oplus \bigoplus_{n-1}(\gamma\delta)$, the pair can be transposed by induction.

The difficult case is $k = 2^{n-1}$, i.e., the last item of β has to be transposed with the first item of γ. By definition,

$$\bigoplus_n(\xi) = (\bigoplus_{n-2}(\alpha) \oplus \bigoplus_{n-2}(\beta)) \oplus (\bigoplus_{n-2}(\gamma) \oplus \bigoplus_{n-2}(\delta))$$

holds. Applying commutativity to the right subexpression and then the rectangle law to the whole expression yields

$$(\bigoplus_{n-2}(\alpha) \oplus \bigoplus_{n-2}(\delta)) \oplus (\bigoplus_{n-2}(\beta) \oplus \bigoplus_{n-2}(\gamma)) = \bigoplus_{n-1}(\alpha\delta) \oplus \bigoplus_{n-1}(\beta\gamma)$$

Then the induction hypothesis can be applied, and the expression can be transformed back. □

In the sequel, we shall use an abbreviation: if an argument of $\bigoplus_n$ occurs k times, we shall write $k \cdot x$, e.g., $\bigoplus_2(3 \cdot x,\ 1 \cdot y,\ 0 \cdot z) = \bigoplus_2(x,\ x,\ x,\ y)$.

Multiple Choice with Dyadic Rationals

Now, we construct values corresponding to multiple choice $[p_1 : x_1, \ldots, p_r : x_r]$ with $p_i = k_i/2^n$ where k_i and n are non-negative integers. For simplicity, the exponent of the denominator is written as an index, i.e., we define values

$$\langle k_1 : x_1, \ldots, k_r : x_r \rangle_n$$

where $r \geq 0$, x_i in X, n and k_i are non-negative integers with $k_1 + \cdots + k_r \leq 2^n$. The definition of these values is in terms of $\bigoplus_n$, where the necessary number of arguments is obtained by filling up with 0.

$$\langle k_1 : x_1, \ldots, k_r : x_r \rangle_n = \bigoplus_n(k_1 \cdot x_1, \ldots, k_r \cdot x_r, (2^n - \sum_{i=1}^{r} k_i) \cdot 0)$$

In the sequel, we show that the dyadic choice expressions defined above satisfy close analogues of the axioms of MCD. For simplicity, we shall often use abbreviations such as $\langle k_i : x_i,\ l : y,\ m_j : z_j \rangle_n$
for $\langle k_1 : x_1, \ldots, k_r : x_r,\ l : y,\ m_1 : z_1, \ldots, m_s : z_s \rangle_n$.

Proposition 7.3

(1) The entries in a dyadic choice expression may be arbitrarily permuted.

(2) For k_i with $\sum_i k_i \leq 2^n$: $\quad \langle 0 : x,\ m_i : y_i \rangle_n = \langle m_i : y_i \rangle_n$

(3) For k, l, and m_i with $k + l + \sum_i m_i \leq 2^n$:

$$\langle k : x,\ l : x,\ m_i : y_i \rangle_n = \langle k + l : x,\ m_i : y_i \rangle_n$$

(4) For k_i and l_i with $\sum_i k_i \leq 2^n$ and $\sum_i l_i \leq 2^n$:

$$\langle k_i : x_i \rangle_n \oplus \langle l_i : x_i \rangle_n = \langle k_i + l_i : x_i \rangle_{n+1}$$

(5) For k_i with $\sum_i k_i \leq 2^n$: $\langle k_i : x_i \rangle_n = \langle 2k_i : x_i \rangle_{n+1}$

(6) For k and s_i with $k + \sum_i s_i \leq 2^n$ and l_j with $\sum_j l_j \leq 2^m$:

$$\langle k : \langle l_j : x_j \rangle_m,\ s_i : y_i \rangle_n = \langle k\, l_j : x_j,\ 2^m s_i : y_i \rangle_{n+m}$$

(7) For k and l_i with $k + 1 + \sum_i l_i \leq 2^n$:

$$\langle k : x,\ l_i : y_i \rangle_n \sqsubseteq \langle k + 1 : x,\ l_i : y_i \rangle_n$$

Proof: Most proofs are straightforward. We give a few hints:

(5) follows from (4) and idempotence.

(6) is shown by applying Prop. 7.1 and the fact $y_i = \bigoplus_m(2^m \cdot y_i)$.

(7) After the transformation into $\bigoplus_n$ expressions, the two sides only differ in that one of the 2^n operands is 0 on the left hand side, and x on the right hand side. The operation '$\oplus$' is continuous, whence monotonic, and $0 \sqsubseteq x$ holds in every MV algebra. □

Multiple Choice with Real Coefficients

In this subsection, we use the dyadic choice expressions of the previous subsection to define choice expressions with real numbers as coefficients.

The unit interval **I** is a *continuous domain*, and the dyadic rationals form a basis of this domain. The way-below relation on **I** is given by $p \ll q$ iff $p = 0$ or $p < q$. It has the property that for all directed sets D of **I**, $p \ll \bigsqcup D$ holds iff there is d in D with $p \ll d$. Every p in **I** is a directed join of all dyadic rationals d with $d \ll p$.

For every p in **I**, we define $p^{(n)}$ to be the greatest non-negative integer k with $k/2^n \ll p$. We show several properties of this notion:

Proposition 7.4

(1) $0^{(n)} = 0$ for all n.

(2) If $p \leq q$, then $p^{(n)} \leq q^{(n)}$.

(3) $2p^{(n)} \leq p^{(n+1)}$.

(4) If $k \neq 0$ and $m \geq n$, then $(k/2^n)^{(m)} = 2^{m-n} \cdot k - 1$.

Proof:

(1) is obvious, and (2) holds since $p^{(n)}/2^n \ll p \leq q$.

(3) $p^{(n)}/2^n \ll p$ implies $2p^{(n)}/2^{n+1} \ll p$, whence $2p^{(n)} \leq p^{(n+1)}$.

(4) The statement $l/2^m \ll k/2^n$ is equivalent to $l \ll 2^{m-n} \cdot k$. Since the right hand side is not 0, this is in turn equivalent to $l < 2^{m-n} \cdot k$, or $l \leq 2^{m-n} \cdot k - 1$. □

We now define arbitrary choice as follows:

$$[p_1 : x_1, \ldots, p_r : x_r] = \bigsqcup_{n \geq 0} \langle p_1^{(n)} : x_1, \ldots, p_r^{(n)} : x_r \rangle_n$$

The dyadic choice expressions in this definition are well-defined since $\sum_i p_i \leq 1$ implies $\sum_i p_i^{(n)} \leq \sum_i p_i \cdot 2^n \leq 2^n$. The join is well-defined because it is directed. For, $\langle p_i^{(n)} : x_i \rangle_n$ equals $\langle 2p_i^{(n)} : x_i \rangle_{n+1}$ by Prop. 7.3 (5), which by Prop. 7.4 (3) and Prop. 7.3 (7) is below $\langle p_i^{(n+1)} : x_i \rangle_{n+1}$.

By Prop. 7.3 (1), the entries in a multiple choice expression may be arbitrarily permuted, i.e., the permutation axiom of MCD is satisfied. By Prop. 7.4 (1) and Prop. 7.3 (2), the expressions satisfy the 0 axiom of MCD. The proof of the remaining MCD axioms is postponed.

The expressions $[p_i : x_i]$ are continuous in every argument x_i as a directed join of continuous functions. Continuity in p_i is a bit more complex. Thanks to the permutation rule, it suffices to show continuity in the first argument. We claim: If D is a directed set in $\mathbf{I}$ with $\bigsqcup D = p$, then $\bigsqcup_{d \in D}[d : x,\ q_i : y_i] = [p : x,\ q_i : y_i]$.

The relation '$\sqsubseteq$' holds by monotonicity (Prop. 7.4 (2) and Prop. 7.3 (7)). For the opposite relation, $p^{(n)}/2^n \ll p = \bigsqcup D$ implies the existence of some d_n in D such that $p^{(n)}/2^n \ll d_n$, whence $p^{(n)} \leq d_n^{(n)}$. Then

$$\begin{aligned}
[p : x,\ q_i : y_i] &= \textstyle\bigsqcup_n \langle p^{(n)} : x,\ q_i^{(n)} : y_i\rangle_n \\
&\sqsubseteq \textstyle\bigsqcup_n \langle d_n^{(n)} : x,\ q_i^{(n)} : y_i\rangle_n \\
&\sqsubseteq \textstyle\bigsqcup_n \bigsqcup_{d \in D} \langle d^{(n)} : x,\ q_i^{(n)} : y_i\rangle_n \\
&= \textstyle\bigsqcup_{d \in D} \bigsqcup_n \langle d^{(n)} : x,\ q_i^{(n)} : y_i\rangle_n \\
&= \textstyle\bigsqcup_{d \in D}[d : x,\ q_i : y_i]
\end{aligned}$$

This completes the proof of the continuity of the multiple choice operation.

Finally, we show that a multiple choice with coefficients which happen to be dyadic rationals coincides with the dyadic choice introduced earlier.

Proposition 7.5 $\quad [k_1/2^n : x_1, \ldots, k_r/2^n : x_r] = \langle k_1 : x_1, \ldots, k_r : x_r\rangle_n$

Proof: By applying Prop. 7.3 (2), we may assume without restriction that all k_i are strictly positive. Using Prop. 7.4 (4), we have to show

$$\bigsqcup_{m \geq n} \langle 2^{m-n} \cdot k_i - 1 : x_i\rangle_m = \langle k_i : x_i\rangle_n.$$

Renaming $m - n$ into m, this is equivalent to $\bigsqcup_{m \geq 0} \langle 2^m \cdot k_i - 1 : x_i\rangle_{n+m} = \langle k_i : x_i\rangle_n$.

We apply the last version of the fixed point axiom of MV (Section 6), which says: if $b_0 \sqsubseteq a$ and $b_{m+1} = b_m \oplus a$, then $\bigsqcup_{m \geq 0} b_m = a$. Of course, we set $a = \langle k_i : x_i\rangle_n$ and $b_m = \langle 2^m k_i - 1 : x_i\rangle_{n+m}$. The relation $b_0 \sqsubseteq a$ holds by Prop. 7.3 (7) and (5). Next, we compute $b_m \oplus a$.

$$\begin{aligned}
b_m \oplus a &= \langle 2^m k_i - 1 : x_i\rangle_{n+m} \oplus \langle k_i : x_i\rangle_n \\
&\overset{7.3\,(5)}{=} \langle 2^m k_i - 1 : x_i\rangle_{n+m} \oplus \langle 2^m k_i : x_i\rangle_{n+m} \\
&\overset{7.3\,(4)}{=} \langle 2^m k_i - 1 + 2^m k_i : x_i\rangle_{n+m+1} = b_{m+1} \qquad \square
\end{aligned}$$

Now we are ready to prove the axioms of MCD. Permutation and the 0 law were already handled above. The 1 law holds, since $[1 : x]$ equals $\langle 1 : x\rangle_0$ by Prop. 7.5, which in turn equals x by definition. The addition law is left to the reader. For substitution, we have to show $[p : [r_j : x_j],\ q_i : y_i] = [p\, r_j : x_j,\ q_i : y_i]$.

Because of continuity of multiple choice, it suffices to prove this equation for dyadic rationals.

$$\begin{aligned}
[p/2^n : [r_j/2^m : x_j],\ q_i/2^n : y_i] &\overset{7.5}{=} \langle p : \langle r_j : x_j\rangle_m,\ q_i : y_i\rangle_n \\
&\overset{7.3\,(6)}{=} \langle p\, r_j : x_j,\ 2^m q_i : y_i\rangle_{n+m} \\
&\overset{7.5}{=} [(p/2^n)(r_j/2^m) : x_j,\ q_i/2^n : y_i]
\end{aligned}$$

This completes the derivation of MCD from MV.

Going Back and Forth

The derivation of MV from MCD and vice versa are inverse to each other. If we start with an MV algebra and construct multiple choice, then $[1/2 : x,\ 1/2 : y]$ equals $\langle 1 : x,\ 1 : y\rangle_1$ by Prop. 7.5, which in turn equals $\bigoplus_1(x,\ y) = x \oplus y$ by definition. This means that we get back the original MV algebra by restriction.

Conversely, if we start with a multiple choice operator, restrict it to the special case $x \oplus y = [1/2 : x,\ 1/2 : y]$, and then reconstruct multiple choice following the lines of this section, then we obtain the original multiple choice back. The proof of this fact is not particularly difficult and hence omitted.

Also, we never considered homomorphisms. The proofs that the homomorphisms of one theory are also homomorphisms of all other theories are straightforward and omitted.

Acknowledgements

This work was begun during my visit at the Theory and Formal Methods Section of Imperial College, London. This visit was made possible by a grant of the Deutsche Forschungsgemeinschaft. The work was continued at Universität des Saarlandes, Saarbrücken, and finished when I stayed with family Nomine as a guest in their home at Lübben, Brandenburg. I like to thank all the people at these different places for their stimulating environment, and all the people who commented upon a draft version of this paper.

References

[1] S.K. Graham. Closure properties of a probabilistic domain construction. In Michael G. Main, A. Melton, Michael Mislove, and D. Schmidt, editors, *Mathematical Foundations of Programming Language Semantics (MFPLS '87)*, pages 213–233. *Lecture Notes in Computer Science 298*, Springer-Verlag, 1988.

[2] R. Heckmann. Product operations in strong monads. In G.L. Burn, S.J. Gay, and M.D. Ryan, editors, *Proceedings of the First Imperial College, Department of Computing, Workshop on Theory and Formal Methods*, Workshops in Computing, pages 159–170. Springer-Verlag, 1993.

[3] C.J. Jones. *Probabilistic Non-Determinism*. PhD thesis, Univ. of Edinburgh, 1990.

[4] C.J. Jones and G.D. Plotkin. A probabilistic powerdomain of evaluations. In *LICS '89*, pages 186–195. IEEE Computer Society Press, 1989.

[5] E. Moggi. Computational lambda-calculus and monads. In *4th LICS Conference*, pages 14–23. IEEE, 1989.

[6] E. Moggi. Notions of computation and monads. *Information and Computation*, 93:55–92, 1991.

Some Results on Top-context-free Tree Languages

Dieter Hofbauer[1] * Maria Huber[2] ** Gregory Kucherov[2]

[1] Technische Universität Berlin, Franklinstraße 28/29, FR 6-2
D - 10587 Berlin, Germany, e-mail: dieter@cs.tu-berlin.de
[2] CRIN & INRIA-Lorraine, 615, rue du Jardin Botanique
54602 Villers-lès-Nancy, France, e-mail: {huber,kucherov}@loria.fr

Abstract. Top-context-free tree languages (called *corégulier* by Arnold and Dauchet [1, 2]) constitute a natural subclass of context-free tree languages. In this paper, we give further evidence for the importance of this class by exhibiting certain closure properties. We systematically treat closure under the operations *replacement* and *substitution* as well as under the corresponding *iteration* operations. Several other well-known language classes are considered as well. Furthermore, various characterizations of the regular top-context-free languages are given, among others by means of restricted regular expressions.

1 Introduction

This paper is motivated by our previous work on tree languages related to term-rewriting systems [11, 7, 10]. It is well-known that for a left-linear term-rewriting system R, the set $Red(R)$ of ground terms reducible by R is a regular tree language. Conversely, if $Red(R)$ is regular, then R can effectively be "linearized", i.e., a finite language can be substituted for its non-linear variables without changing the set of reducible ground terms [7, 10, 14]. However, little is known about conditions on which $Red(R)$ is context-free. Here again, non-linear variables play a crucial role.

This motivation led us to study the class of *top-context-free* languages, which turned out to be of special importance. Top-context-free tree languages are languages generated by context-free tree grammars in which right-hand sides of production rules contain non-terminal symbols, if at all, only at the top position. This class has been studied by Arnold and Dauchet [1, 2] who proved in particular the following result.

Theorem 1 *The language* $L = \{f(t,t) \,|\, t \in L'\}$ *is context-free iff* L' *is top-context-free iff* L *itself is top-context-free.*

The theorem remains true if "context-free" and "top-context-free" are replaced by "regular" and "finite" respectively. We conjecture that this analogy

* Partially supported by a post-doc grant of the M.E.N.
** Supported by the M.E.S.R.

can also be drawn for the language $Red(R)$ mentioned above: It is context-free iff a top-context-free language can be substituted for the non-linear variables in R without changing the set of reducible ground terms. This paper is devoted to the study of some related topics that could serve as a basis for further investigations.

The class of top-context-free languages is in a sense orthogonal to that of regular languages. Though these two classes intersect, there are very simple languages that are top-context-free but not regular and vice versa. For example, the language $\{f(g^i(a), g^i(a)) \mid i \geq 0\}$ is top-context-free but not regular. Conversely, Arnold and Dauchet showed that the language of all terms over a signature of one binary and one constant symbol is not top-context-free. In order to obtain a criterion that a language is not top-context-free we, more generally, prove that every top-context-free language is *slim*, a simple syntactic property.

We further study the class of languages that are both top-context-free and regular. We propose a number of equivalent characterizations of this class in terms of grammars (linear top-context-free, non-branching regular), linear regular expressions, and more syntactic properties (slim, passable, polynomially size-bounded).

Closure properties play an important role in all branches of formal language theory. A detailed analysis of closure properties for the class of regular tree languages can be found in [6]. In this paper we continue this topic, analyzing closure of different classes under the operations *replacement*, *substitution*, and their iterations. Replacement and substitution, considered also in [5], are two possible extentions of the string product to the tree case. In contrast to replacement, substitution replaces equal symbols by equal terms. We make an exhaustive study of closure properties under these operations for six classes of tree languages: finite, regular, linear top-context-free, top-context-free, linear context-free, and context-free.

2 Notations

We assume the reader to be familiar with basic definitions in term rewriting [4] and formal language theory [9, 6]. A signature Σ is a finite set of function symbols of fixed arity; for $n \geq 0$, Σ_n denotes the set of symbols in Σ of arity n. $\mathcal{T}_\Sigma(X)$ is the set of (finite) terms over Σ and a set of variables X. The set of ground terms, i.e., terms without variables, over Σ is denoted by $\mathcal{T}_\Sigma$. For $t \in \mathcal{T}_\Sigma(X)$, $\mathcal{P}os(t)$ is the set of positions in t, defined in the usual way as sequences of natural numbers. We write $p \leq q$ if p is a prefix of q. The subterm of t at position p is $t|_p$. For $p \in \mathcal{P}os(t)$, $t|_p$ is a principal subterm of t if $|p| = 1$, and it is a proper subterm of t if $|p| \geq 1$. Here, $|p|$ denotes the length of p. The depth of t is $|t| = max\{|p| \mid p \in \mathcal{P}os(t)\}$, its size is $size(t) = |\mathcal{P}os(t)|$. If t' is a subterm of t, then t can be written as $c[t']$ where $c[\ ]$ is a context. A context is called Σ-context in case it contains only symbols from Σ.

A variable x is said to be linear in t if there is only one position $p \in \mathcal{P}os(t)$ such that $t|_p = x$, and is said to be non-linear in t otherwise. A term is linear if all its variables are linear and is non-linear otherwise.

If unambiguous, we sometimes prefer vector notation to "three dots notation". For example, $f(\vec{t})$ abbreviates $f(t_1, \ldots, t_n)$ (n and t_i will be clear from the context), and $f(\vec{x})$ stands for $f(x_1, \ldots, x_n)$. For $f \in \Sigma_n$ and $L_1, \ldots, L_n \subseteq \mathcal{T}_\Sigma$ let $f(L_1, \ldots, L_n) = \{f(t_1, \ldots, t_n) \mid t_1 \in L_1, \ldots, t_n \in L_n\}$. The cardinality of a finite (multi-)set S is denoted by $|S|$.

3 Context-free languages, Replacement, and Substitution

Definition 2 *A* context-free tree grammar $G = (N, \Sigma, P, S)$ *consists of disjoint signatures* N (nonterminals) *and* Σ (terminals), *a finite rewrite system* P *over* $N \cup \Sigma$*, and a distinct constant symbol* $S \in N_0$ (initial symbol)*; all rules in* P *are of the form*

$$A(x_1, \ldots, x_n) \rightarrow t$$

where $A \in N_n$, $n \geq 0$, $x_1, \ldots, x_n$ *are pairwise different variables, and* $t \in \mathcal{T}_{N \cup \Sigma}(\{x_1, \ldots, x_n\})$.

- *G is said to be* regular *if N contains only constant symbols.*
- *G is said to be* top-context-free *if all proper subterms of right-hand sides of rules are in $\mathcal{T}_\Sigma(\{x_1, \ldots, x_n\})$.*
- *G is said to be* linear *if all right-hand sides of rules in P are linear.*

The language generated by a grammar $G = (N, \Sigma, P, S)$ is

$$\mathcal{L}(G) = \{t \in \mathcal{T}_\Sigma \mid S \rightarrow_P^* t\}.$$

A language $L \subseteq \mathcal{T}_\Sigma$ is called (linear) context-free (regular, ...) if there is a (linear) context-free (regular, ...) grammar generating L. For $A \in N_n$ we also use the more general notation

$$\mathcal{L}(G, A(x_1, \ldots, x_n)) = \{t \in \mathcal{T}_\Sigma(X) \mid A(x_1, \ldots, x_n) \rightarrow_P^* t\}.$$

Thus $\mathcal{L}(G) = \mathcal{L}(G, S)$.

FIN (REG, LINTOPCF, TOPCF, LINCF, CF) will denote the class of finite (regular, linear top-context-free, top-context-free, linear context-free, context-free) languages. By definition we have the inclusions FIN $\subseteq$ REG $\subseteq$ LINCF $\subseteq$ CF, FIN $\subseteq$ LINTOPCF $\subseteq$ TOPCF $\subseteq$ CF and LINTOPCF $\subseteq$ LINCF. All inclusions are proper and both LINTOPCF and TOPCF are incomparable with REG.

Top-context-free languages were studied by Arnold and Dauchet [1, 2] under the name of *langages coréguliers.* In [1] they showed that TOPCF coincides with the class of languages obtained by deterministic top-down tree transformations on monadic regular languages. It can even be shown that it is sufficient to consider a single monadic language, e.g., $\mathcal{T}_{\{0,1,\lambda\}}$ where 0 and 1 are symbols of arity 1 and λ is a constant symbol.

Regular tree languages have been extensively studied, e.g., in [6]. For context-free tree languages see, e.g., [12]. Several normal forms have been defined for regular and context-free grammars. In this paper we will use the fact that for each grammar there is a *reduced* grammar of the same type, generating the same language. A grammar is said to be reduced if all nonterminals A in N_n, $n \geq 0$, are

- *reachable*, i.e., $S \rightarrow_P^* c[A(t_1, \ldots, t_n)]$ for some term $c[A(t_1, \ldots, t_n)] \in \mathcal{T}_{\Sigma \cup N}$, and
- *productive*, i.e., $\mathcal{L}(G, A(x_1, \ldots, x_n)) \neq \emptyset$.

It is well-known that such a normal form always exists. For top-context free grammars we will use another normal form. We call a context-free grammar *slow* if all right-hand sides of its rules contain exactly one Σ-symbol. Thus, slow top-context-free grammars contain only rules of the form

$$A(x_1, \ldots, x_n) \rightarrow f(y_1, \ldots, y_m)$$
$$A(x_1, \ldots, x_n) \rightarrow B(z_1, \ldots, f(y_1, \ldots, y_m), \ldots, z_k),$$

where $B \in N_k$, $k \geq 1$, $f \in \Sigma_m$, $m \geq 0$, $\{y_1, \ldots, y_m, z_1, \ldots, z_k\} \subseteq \{x_1, \ldots, x_n\}$. Whereas not all context-free languages can be generated by slow grammars (for an example see [3], exercise 17), for each (linear) top-context-free language there is a slow reduced (linear) top-context-free grammar generating this language. A proof can be found in [8].

The operations c-replacement and c-substitution constitute two different ways of "replacing" a constant c in all terms of a language L by terms of a language L'. The c-substitution operation substitutes all occurrences of c in a term of L by the same term of L'. When applying the c-replacement operation, all c's in terms of L are replaced independently by possibly different terms of L'. Thus the c-substitution corresponds to the usual substitution, if c is treated as a variable. The c-replacement corresponds to a substitution, where all c's are considered as different (linear) variables. In [5] c-replacement and c-substitution are called OI- and IO-substitution respectively.

Definition 3 *For languages L, L' and a constant symbol c, the* c-replacement of L' into L *is* $L \cdot_c L' = \bigcup_{t \in L} t \cdot_c L'$, *where $t \cdot_c L'$ is defined by (for $n \geq 0$)*

$$f(t_1, \ldots, t_n) \cdot_c L' = \begin{cases} L' & \text{if } f = c, \\ f(t_1 \cdot_c L', \ldots, t_n \cdot_c L') & \text{otherwise.} \end{cases}$$

The c-substitution of L' into L *is* $L \diamond_c L' = \bigcup_{t \in L} \bigcup_{t' \in L'} \{t \diamond_c t'\}$, *where $t \diamond_c t'$ is defined by (for $n \geq 0$)*

$$f(t_1, \ldots, t_n) \diamond_c t' = \begin{cases} t' & \text{if } f = c, \\ f(t_1 \diamond_c t', \ldots, t_n \diamond_c t') & \text{otherwise.} \end{cases}$$

When c is clear from the context or arbitrary, we will not mention it. Given classes of languages $\mathcal{C}$ and $\mathcal{C}'$, $\mathcal{C}$ is said to be *closed under replacement (substitution)* by $\mathcal{C}'$, if $L \cdot_c L' \in \mathcal{C}$ ($L \diamond_c L' \in \mathcal{C}$ respectively) holds for all $L \in \mathcal{C}$, $L' \in \mathcal{C}'$ and all constant symbols c. We will also write $\mathcal{C} \cdot \mathcal{C}' \subseteq \mathcal{C}$ ($\mathcal{C} \diamond \mathcal{C}' \subseteq \mathcal{C}$). $\mathcal{C}$ is said to be closed under replacement (substitution) if it is closed under replacement (substitution) by $\mathcal{C}$ (cf. Gécseg and Steinby [6], III.3.6 and II.4.3).

The replacement and the substitution operations for tree languages give rise to two types of star operations, the replacement iteration and the substitution iteration. For a language L and a constant c, the *c-replacement iteration* is defined by $L^{*_c} = \bigcup_{n \geq 0} L_n$, where

$$L_0 = \{c\} \text{ and } L_{n+1} = L_n \cdot_c (L \cup \{c\}).$$

The *c-substitution iteration* is defined by $L^{\diamond_c} = \bigcup_{n \geq 0} L^{\diamond_{n,c}}$, where

$$L_0 = \{c\} \text{ and } L_{n+1} = L_n \diamond_c L$$

The c-replacement iteration (called *c-iteration* in [6]) generalizes the star operation for word languages to trees. Given a class $\mathcal{C}$ of languages, $\mathcal{C}$ is said to be closed under replacement iteration (substitution iteration), if $L^{*_c} \in \mathcal{C}$ ($L^{\diamond_c} \in \mathcal{C}$ respectively) holds for all $L \in \mathcal{C}$ and all constant symbols c. We will also write $\mathcal{C}^* \subseteq \mathcal{C}$ ($\mathcal{C}^\diamond \subseteq \mathcal{C}$).

4 Top-context-free Languages Are Slim

In this section we give a a criterion for showing that certain languages are not top-context-free. It can be seen as a generalization of a proof method used by Arnold and Dauchet in [1]. We prove that every top-context-free language is *slim*. Intuitively, a term is slim if it can be "decomposed" in a top-down way such that at each intermediate step only a bounded number of different subterms occur. If there is such a bound, uniform for all terms in the language, then the language is said to be slim. Formally:

Definition 4 (slim) *A* decomposition *of $t \in T_\Sigma$ is a finite sequence $D_0, \ldots, D_m$ of subsets of T_Σ where $D_0 = \{t\}$, $D_m = \emptyset$, and for all i, $0 \leq i < m$, there is some term $f(t_1, \ldots, t_n) \in D_i$, $n \geq 0$, such that*

$$D_{i+1} = (D_i \setminus \{f(t_1, \ldots, t_n)\}) \cup \{t_1, \ldots, t_n\}.$$

t is k-slim *for $k \in I\!N$ if t has a decomposition $D_0, \ldots, D_m$ where $|D_i| \leq k$ for all i, $0 \leq i \leq m$. A language is k-slim if it contains only k-slim terms; it is said to be* slim *if it is k-slim for some k.*

EXAMPLE 5. All terms $f(a, f(a, \ldots f(a, a) \ldots))$ are 2-slim. The same is true, more generally, for all terms $f(g^{i_1}(a), f(g^{i_2}(a), \ldots f(g^{i_m}(a), a) \ldots)))$, $i_j \in I\!N$.

EXAMPLE 6. Define $t_0 = a$, $t_{i+1} = f(t_i, t_i)$. The sequence $\{t_i\}, \{t_{i-1}\}, \ldots, \{t_0\}, \emptyset$ is a decomposition of t_i, therefore t_i is 1-slim.

Note that every subterm of a k-slim term is also k-slim. Note also that all languages over a signature containing only symbols of arity at most one are 1-slim. Hence there are slim languages which are not top-context-free – not even recursively enumerable.

Lemma 7 *Top-context-free languages are slim.*

Proof. Let $G = (N, \Sigma, P, S)$ be a slow top-context-free grammar and let k be the maximal arity of symbols in $N \cup \Sigma$. We will show that $\mathcal{L}(G)$ is k-slim. Consider a derivation $S = t_0 \rightarrow_P \ldots \rightarrow_P t_m = t$ of a term $t \in \mathcal{T}_\Sigma$. Define sets D_i, $1 \leq i \leq m$, by $D_m = \{t_m\}$, $D_{m-1} = \{s \mid s \text{ a principal subterm of } t_m\}$, and, for $0 < i < m$,

$$D_{i-1} = \begin{cases} (D_i \cap (\{y_1\gamma, \ldots, y_p\gamma\} \setminus \{f(z_1, \ldots, z_q)\gamma\})) \cup \{z_1\gamma, \ldots, z_q\gamma\} \\ \quad \text{if } f(z_1, \ldots, z_q)\gamma \in D_i, \\ D_i \text{ else.} \end{cases}$$

where $t_{i-1} = l\gamma$ and $t_i = r\gamma$ for a rule

$$l = A(x_1, \ldots, x_n) \rightarrow B(y_1, \ldots, f(z_1, \ldots, z_q), \ldots, y_p) = r$$

from P. If now in the sequence $D_m, \ldots, D_0$ repetitions of sets are eliminated we obtain a decomposition of t. Clearly $|D_i| \leq k$, thus t is k-slim. □

The next – somewhat technical – lemma gives sufficient conditions for a term to be *not* k-slim. Define $B_k = \mathcal{P}os(t_k)$, t_k from example 6, and $b_k = \{p \in B_k \mid |p| = k\}$. An injective function $h : B_k \rightarrow D$ is a *(homeomorphic) embedding* from B_k into a tree domain D, if different edges in B_k – seen as a directed graph – map to disjoint paths in D. Note that $h(B_k)$ is uniquely determined by $h(b_k) \subseteq D$.

Lemma 8 *Let $t \in \mathcal{T}_\Sigma$ and $h : B_k \rightarrow \mathcal{P}os(t)$ be an embedding. Suppose $t|_q \neq t|_{\bar{q}}$ for all $p, \bar{p} \in h(b_k)$ and all $q, \bar{q}$ with $q \leq p$, $\bar{q} \leq \bar{p}$, $q \neq \bar{q}$. Then t is not k-slim.*

We conclude this section with some immediate corollaries to lemma 8. Let us mention, however, the limitations of this simple criterion. The term $h(h(a, b, c), h(b, c, a), h(c, a, b))$, e.g., is not 4-slim, but this is not provable using lemma 8.

EXAMPLE 9. The language $\mathcal{T}_\Sigma$ of all ground terms over signature Σ is not slim if, and only if, $\Sigma_n \neq \emptyset$ for some $n \geq 2$, and $\Sigma_0 \neq \emptyset$. Clearly terms built up using only unary symbols and constants are 1-slim, also the empty set is slim. Conversely, given a symbol $h \in \Sigma_n$, $n \geq 2$, and $a \in \Sigma_0$, for each k there are terms which are not k-slim. Define terms $t[i, j]$ inductively by

$$\begin{aligned} t[0, 0] &= h(a, a, \ldots), \\ t[0, j + 1] &= h(a, t[0, j], \ldots), \\ t[i + 1, j] &= h(t[i, 2j], t[i, 2j + 1], \ldots) \end{aligned}$$

where $\ldots$ is filled with a's. Now $t[k, 0]$ is not k-slim by lemma 8 using an embedding where $h(b_k) = \{1, 2\}^k$.

Corollary 10 *$\mathcal{T}_\Sigma$ is top-context-free iff Σ contains only symbols of arity at most one or no constant symbol.*

This is obvious from example 9 and the fact that, in case Σ has only symbols of arity at most one, $\mathcal{T}_\Sigma$ is generated by the top-context-free grammar

$$\begin{aligned} S &\to A(c) \text{ for all constant symbols } c \in \Sigma, \\ A(x) &\to A(f(x)) \text{ for all unary symbols } f \in \Sigma, \\ A(x) &\to x. \end{aligned}$$

By a simple generalization of example 9 we can prove the following lemma which will be used in the next section.

Definition 11 (branching) *A regular grammar $G = (N, \Sigma, P, S)$ is said to be* branching *if $A \to_P^* c[A, A]$ for some $A \in N$ and some term $c[A, A] \in \mathcal{T}_{N \cup \Sigma}$ containing A at more than one occurrence. Otherwise G is* non-branching.

Lemma 12 *If G is a branching reduced regular grammar, then $\mathcal{L}(G)$ is not slim, hence not top-context-free.*

5 Regular Top-context-free Languages

In this section we study the class of languages that are both regular and top-context-free.

5.1 Linear Top-context-free Languages

For strings, a right-regular grammar (rules of the form $A \to wB$) can always be transformed into an equivalent left-regular one (rules of the form $A \to Bw$), and vice versa. When regarding string grammars as tree grammars – map letters to unary function symbols – this means transforming a regular tree grammar into an equivalent top-context-free tree grammar and vice versa. This is not possible in general. The following lemma, however, allows to go from regular grammars to (linear) top-context-free ones and vice versa under additional assumptions.

Lemma 13 *For a language L the following statements are equivalent:*

(1) L is generated by a regular grammar where no right-hand side of a rule contains more than one nonterminal.
(2) L is generated by a linear top-context-free grammar where each nonterminal has arity at most one.
(3) L is generated by a top-context-free grammar where the right-hand side of every rule contains at most one variable position.

Using lemma 13 we prove now the converse to lemma 12.

Lemma 14 *A language generated by a non-branching regular grammar is linear top-context-free.*

Proof. Let $G = (N, \Sigma, P, S)$ be a non-branching regular grammar that we suppose to be reduced. We will show that $\mathcal{L}(G)$ is linear top-context-free by induction on $|N|$. Clearly for $N = \{S\}$, $\mathcal{L}(G)$ is linear top-context-free by lemma 13. For $|N| > 1$ we define

$$N' = \{A \in N \mid A \rightarrow_P^* c[S] \text{ for some context } c[\,]\},$$

$N'' = N \setminus N'$, $P' = P \cap \{A \rightarrow t \mid A \in N'\}$, and $G' = (N', \Sigma \cup N'', P', S)$.

First observe that $\mathcal{L}(G')$ is linear top-context-free by lemma 13. Indeed, suppose $A \rightarrow c[B, B']$ is a rule in P' where $B, B' \in N'$ occur at different positions in the term $c[B, B']$. Then by definition of N' and since G is reduced, we have

$$S \rightarrow_P^* a[A] \rightarrow_P a[c[B, B']] \rightarrow_P^* a[c[b[S], b'[S]]]$$

for some contexts $a[\,]$, $b[\,]$, $b'[\,]$, contradicting the assumption that G is non-branching.

For $A \in N''$ define $G_A = (N_A, \Sigma, P_A, A)$ where $N_A = \{B \in N \mid A \rightarrow_P^* c[B]$ for some context $c[\,]\}$ and $P_A = P \cap \{B \rightarrow t \mid B \in N_A\}$. Note that $N_A \subseteq N''$ and that G_A is reduced and non-branching. From $S \notin N''$ we get $|N_A| \leq |N''| < |N|$, thus by induction hypothesis, $\mathcal{L}(G_A)$ is linear top-context-free.

Let $N'' = \{A_1, \ldots, A_n\}$. As is easily seen, $\mathcal{L}(G_{A_i}) = \mathcal{L}(G, A_i)$ for $1 \leq i \leq n$ and

$$\mathcal{L}(G) = \mathcal{L}(G') \cdot_{A_1} \mathcal{L}(G_{A_1}) \cdots \cdot_{A_n} \mathcal{L}(G_{A_n}).$$

Since $\mathcal{L}(G')$ as well as $\mathcal{L}(G_{A_1}), \ldots, \mathcal{L}(G_{A_n})$ are linear top-context-free, $\mathcal{L}(G)$ is linear top-context-free, too, by lemma 23. □

We conclude this section with a criterion allowing to prove that certain languages are not linear top-context-free. In close analogy to the result that every top-context-free language is slim, we will show that every linear top-context-free language is *passable*, a notion defined by K. Salomaa [13]. The definition of "k-passable" is just the definition of "k-slim" if sets are treated as *multisets*. Salomaa also showed that passability of a language implies a uniform polynomial size-bound, i.e., the size of terms in the language is polynomially bounded by their depth.

Definition 15 (passable) *A* multi-decomposition *of $t \in \mathcal{T}_\Sigma$ is a finite sequence $D_0, \ldots, D_m$ of multisets over $\mathcal{T}_\Sigma$ where $D_0 = \{t\}$, $D_m = \emptyset$, and for all i, $0 \leq i < m$, there is some term $f(t_1, \ldots, t_n) \in D_i$, $n \geq 0$, such that*

$$D_{i+1} = (D_i \setminus \{f(t_1, \ldots, t_n)\}) \cup \{t_1, \ldots, t_n\}$$

where all sets and operations are interpreted as multisets and multiset operations. t is k-passable *for $k \in N$, if t has a multi-decomposition $D_0, \ldots, D_m$ where $|D_i| \leq k$ for all i, $0 \leq i \leq m$. A language is k-passable if it contains only k-passable terms; it is said to be* passable *if it is k-passable for some k.*

Salomaa [13] defines k-passability in a slightly different way – using tree automata – which, however, is easily seen to be equivalent to the definition given above. Note that only the empty set is 0-passable.

Let us call a language L *polynomially size-bounded* if there is a polynomial p over $\mathbb{N}$ with one argument such that $size(t) \leq p(|t|)$ for all $t \in L$. Lemma 3.2 in [13] states that $size(t) \leq k \cdot |t|^k + 1$ for all $t \in L$, provided that L is k-passable. Together with the following result this can be used to prove that a language is not linear top-context-free.

Lemma 16 *Linear top-context-free languages are passable.*

Proof. Let G be a linear top-context-free grammar where nonterminals have arity at most k; without loss of generality we assume that G is slow. A straightforward induction on the length of a derivation then shows that $\mathcal{L}(G)$ is $\max\{1,k\}$-passable. □

EXAMPLE 17. The top-context-free language $L = \{t_k \mid k \geq 0\}$ from example 6 is not linear top-context-free, since it is not polynomially size-bounded.

5.2 Linear Regular Expressions

The class REG of regular languages is closed under replacement and replacement iteration. Moreover, according to Kleene's theorem for tree languages, REG is the smallest class containing all finite sets and closed under union, replacement and replacement iteration (cf [6]). In other words, every regular language can be represented by a *regular expression*, constructed from finite sets by using union, replacement and replacement iteration. On the other hand, REG is not closed under substitution and substitution iteration (cf section 6). The situation is inverse for top-context-free languages. We will show in section 6 that this class is closed under substitution and substitution iteration and is not closed under replacement and replacement iteration.

Nevertheless, the subclass of top-context-free languages which are also regular can be represented by regular expressions with restricted use of replacement and replacement iteration.

Definition 18 *Let $\alpha \notin \Sigma$ be a new constant symbol. We inductively define a set of* linear regular expressions $\mathcal{E}$, *an auxiliary set of* contextual linear regular expressions $\mathcal{CE}$, *and the language $\mathcal{L}(e) \subseteq T_\Sigma$ ($\mathcal{L}(e) \subseteq T_{\Sigma\cup\{\alpha\}}$ resp.) represented by $e \in \mathcal{E}$ ($e \in \mathcal{CE}$ resp.) as follows:*

- *for every $a \in \Sigma_0$: $a \in \mathcal{E}$; $\mathcal{L}(a) = \{a\}$; $\alpha \in \mathcal{CE}$; $\mathcal{L}(\alpha) = \{\alpha\}$.*
- *for every $f \in \Sigma_n$: if $e_1,\ldots,e_n \in \mathcal{E}$, then $f(e_1,\ldots,e_n) \in \mathcal{E}$;*
  if $\bar{e} \in \mathcal{CE}$, and $1 \leq i \leq n$, then $f(e_1,\ldots,e_{i-1},\bar{e},e_{i+1},\ldots,e_n) \in \mathcal{CE}$;
  in either case $\mathcal{L}(f(e_1,\ldots,e_n)) = f(\mathcal{L}(e_1),\ldots,\mathcal{L}(e_n))$.
- *if $e_1,e_2 \in \mathcal{E}$, then $e_1 \cup e_2 \in \mathcal{E}$; if $e_1,e_2 \in \mathcal{CE}$, then $e_1 \cup e_2 \in \mathcal{CE}$;*
  in either case $\mathcal{L}(e_1 \cup e_2) = \mathcal{L}(e_1) \cup \mathcal{L}(e_2)$.

- *if* $e_1, e_2 \in \mathcal{CE}$, *then* $e_1 \cdot_\alpha e_2 \in \mathcal{CE}$, *and* $e_1{}^{*\alpha} \in \mathcal{CE}$;
  $\mathcal{L}(e_1 \cdot_\alpha e_2) = \mathcal{L}(e_1) \cdot_\alpha \mathcal{L}(e_2)$; $\mathcal{L}(e_1{}^{*\alpha}) = \mathcal{L}(e_1)^{*\alpha}$.
- *if* $\bar{e} \in \mathcal{CE}$, $e \in \mathcal{E}$, *then* $\bar{e} \cdot_\alpha e \in \mathcal{E}$; $\mathcal{L}(\bar{e} \cdot_\alpha e) = \mathcal{L}(\bar{e}) \cdot_\alpha \mathcal{L}(e)$.

Obviously, for every $e \in \mathcal{E} \cup \mathcal{CE}$, $\mathcal{L}(e)$ is a regular language, since e is a regular expression. For $e \in \mathcal{CE}$, it is easy to see by induction that α occurs exactly once in each term of $\mathcal{L}(e)$. Therefore, if $e \in \mathcal{CE}$, then $\mathcal{L}(e)^{*\alpha} = \mathcal{L}(e)^{\diamond_\alpha}$ and $\mathcal{L}(e) \cdot_\alpha L = \mathcal{L}(e) \diamond_\alpha L$ for every $L \subseteq \mathcal{T}_\Sigma$.

Proposition 19 *A language represented by a linear regular expression is top-context-free.*

Proof. According to the remark above, every replacement (replacement iteration resp.) in e can be interpreted as a substitution (substitution iteration resp.) without changing $\mathcal{L}(e)$. TOPCF is closed under union, substitution and substitution iteration (see section 6). Closure under substitution implies that $f(L_1, \ldots, L_n)$ is top-context-free if $L_1, \ldots, L_n$ are top-context-free. Thus every operation in linear regular expressions preserves top-context-freeness. □

The proof of the following lemma (see [8]) uses a standard technique for constructing regular expressions from automata (or grammar) representations. It is somewhat a mixture of that for words (cf [9]) and that for trees (cf [6]).

Lemma 20 *A language generated by a non-branching regular grammar can be represented by a linear regular expression.*

5.3 Characterizations of Regular Top-context-free Languages

Collecting together all results on regular top-context-free languages obtained so far, we can state the following

Theorem 21 *For a regular language L the following statements are equivalent:*

(1) L is linear top-context-free.
(2) L is top-context-free.
(3) L is slim.
(4) L can be generated by a non-branching regular grammar. Moreover, every reduced regular grammar generating L is non-branching.
(5) L can be represented by a linear regular expression.
(6) L is passable.
(7) L is polynomially size-bounded.

Proof. Trivially (1) ⇒ (2), and (2) ⇒ (3) by lemma 7. (3) ⇒ (4) is lemma 12 and (4) ⇒ (1) by lemma 14. (4) ⇒ (5) by lemma 20 and (5) ⇒ (2) by proposition 19. (1) ⇒ (6) by lemma 16 and (6) ⇒ (7) by lemma 3.2 in [13]. Finally, (7) ⇒ (4) is easy to show. Indeed, if L is generated by a reduced branching regular grammar, a sequence of terms of L can be constructed in an obvious way such that their size grows exponentially with respect to their depth. □

Conditions (4) and (5) can be seen as syntactic characterizations of REG ∩ TOPCF = REG ∩ LINTOPCF.

6 Closure Properties

In this chapter we study some closure properties of classes of tree languages. First we just mention a few well-known properties, then concentrate on studying closure of the classes FIN, REG, LINTOPCF, TOPCF, LINCF, CF under replacement, substitution and their iterations. We summarize positive and negative results in tables.

We define (linear) homomorphisms on $\mathcal{T}_\Sigma$ as (linear) *tree homomorphisms* in the usual way [6].

Lemma 22 FIN, REG, LINTOPCF, TOPCF, LINCF, *and* CF *are closed under union, under intersection with regular languages, and under linear homomorphisms.*

TOPCF is even closed under arbitrary homomorphisms, and a proof of its closure properties can be found in [1].

Lemma 23 (Closure under Replacement) *(1)* FIN, REG, LINTOPCF, TOPCF, LINCF, *and* CF *are closed under replacement by* FIN.
(2) LINTOPCF·LINTOPCF = LINTOPCF *and* LINTOPCF·TOPCF = TOPCF.
(3) REG, LINCF, *and* CF *are closed under replacement.*
(4) TOPCF·LINTOPCF $\not\subseteq$ TOPCF.

Proof. (1) Let $G = (\Sigma, N, P, S)$ be a context-free grammar and let L' over Σ' be finite. Then the grammar $(\Sigma \cup \Sigma',\ N,\ \{A(\vec{x}) \to t' \mid A(\vec{x}) \to t \in P,\ t' \in t \cdot_c L'\},\ S)$ generates $\mathcal{L}(G)\cdot_c L'$. This grammar is of the same type as G.

(2) Let $G = (N, \Sigma, P, S)$ be linear top-context-free and $G' = (N', \Sigma', P', S')$ be top-context-free. Without loss of generality let G be slow; this is crucial for the proof, since it guarantees that, if $t \in \mathcal{T}_{N \cup \Sigma}(X)$ is the right-hand side of a rule in a slow linear grammar and y is a variable not occuring in t, then $t \cdot_c y$ is linear.

A top-context-free grammar $\bar{G}$ generating $\mathcal{L}(G)\cdot_c\mathcal{L}(G')$ is constructed as follows: The set of nonterminals in $\bar{G}$ is $N \times (N' \cup \{\text{done}\})$ where "done" is a new unary nonterminal; if A has arity n and A' has arity m, then (A, A') has arity $n+m$. The initial symbol of $\bar{G}$ is (S, S') and $\bar{G}$ contains the following rules:

$$
\begin{array}{rll}
(A,A')(\vec{x},\vec{y}) \to (A,B')(\vec{x},\vec{t}) & \text{if } A'(\vec{y}) \to B'(\vec{t}) \text{ is in } P', A \in N,\\
(A,A')(\vec{x},\vec{y}) \to (A,\text{done})(\vec{x},t) & \text{if } A'(\vec{y}) \to t \text{ is in } P', t \in \mathcal{T}_{\Sigma'}, A \in N,\\
(A,\text{done})(\vec{x},y) \to (B,\text{done})(\vec{t},y) & \text{if } A(\vec{x}) \to B(\vec{t}) \text{ is in } P, \vec{t} \text{ does not contain } c,\\
(A,\text{done})(\vec{x},y) \to (B,S')(\vec{t}\cdot_c\{y\}) & \text{if } A(\vec{x}) \to B(\vec{t}) \text{ is in } P, \vec{t} \text{ contains } c,\\
(A,\text{done})(\vec{x},y) \to t\cdot_c\{y\} & \text{if } A(\vec{x}) \to t \text{ is in } P, t \in \mathcal{T}_\Sigma.
\end{array}
$$

In order to proof that $\bar{G}$ generates $\mathcal{L}(G)\cdot_c\mathcal{L}(G')$ use the fact that $(A, S')(\vec{t}) \to^*_{\bar{G}} (A, \text{done})(\vec{t}, t')$ implies $t' \in \mathcal{L}(G')$. Moreover, as G is linear, there are no copies of subterms, which could cause c's at different positions to be always instantiated by the same terms. Note also that $\bar{G}$ is linear if G' is linear.

(3) Let $G = (\Sigma, N, P, S)$ and $G' = (\Sigma', N', P', S')$ be context-free grammars with $N \cap N' = \emptyset$. Then the context-free grammar

$$(\Sigma \cup \Sigma',\ N \cup N',\ \{A(\vec{x}) \to t \cdot_c \{S'\} \mid A(\vec{x}) \to t \in P\} \cup P',\ S)$$

generates $\mathcal{L}(G) \cdot_c \mathcal{L}(G')$. It is regular (linear), if both G and G' are regular (linear).

(4) Let L be generated by $\{S \to A(c),\ A(x) \to A(f(x,x)),\ A(x) \to x\}$. Let $L' = \{g^i(a) \mid i \geq 0\}$ be generated by $\{S \to A(c),\ A(x) \to A(g(x)),\ A(x) \to x\}$. Then $L \cdot_c L'$ is not slim, thus not top-context-free, as is easily shown using results of section 4. □

Lemma 24 (Closure under Substitution) *(1)* FIN, REG, LINTOPCF, TOPCF, LINCF, *and* CF *are closed under substitution by* FIN.
(2) TOPCF$\diamond$TOPCF = TOPCF *and* CF$\diamond$TOPCF = CF.
(3) FIN$\diamond$LINTOPCF = LINTOPCF.
(4) FIN$\diamond$REG $\not\subseteq$ CF.
(5) LINTOPCF$\diamond$LINTOPCF $\not\subseteq$ LINTOPCF.
(6) REG$\diamond$LINTOPCF $\not\subseteq$ LINCF *and* REG$\diamond$LINTOPCF $\not\subseteq$ TOPCF.

Proof. (1) First observe that for a ground term t, $\diamond_c\{t\}$ is a linear homomorphism. Hence by lemma 22, $L \in \mathcal{C}$ implies $L \diamond_c \{t\} \in \mathcal{C}$. Now (1) follows from $L \diamond_c L' = \bigcup_{t \in L'} (L \diamond_c \{t\})$ and from the closure under union (lemma 22).

(2) From a context-free grammar G and a top-context-free grammar G' with disjoint sets of nonterminals, a context-free grammar $\bar{G}$ generating $\mathcal{L}(G) \diamond_c \mathcal{L}(G')$ can be constructed as follows: Nonterminals in $\bar{G}$ are the nonterminals of G' together with a nonterminal $\bar{A}$ of arity $n+1$ for each nonterminal A in G of arity n; hence $\bar{S}$ is unary for S, the initial symbol of G. The initial symbol of $\bar{G}$ is S', the initial symbol of G'. The rules of $\bar{G}$ are:

$$
\begin{array}{rll}
A'(\vec{x}) \to t & \text{if } A'(\vec{x}) \to t \text{ is a rule in } G', & \text{t contains a nonterminal,} \\
A'(\vec{x}) \to \bar{S}(t) & \text{if } A'(\vec{x}) \to t \text{ is a rule in } G', & \text{t contains no nonterminal,} \\
\bar{A}(\vec{x}, y) \to h(t) \diamond_c y & \text{if } A(\vec{x}) \to t \text{ is a rule in } G, &
\end{array}
$$

where h is the (linear) homomorphism defined by

$$h(A(t_1, \ldots, t_n)) = \bar{A}(h(t_1), \ldots, h(t_n), c) \text{ for all nonterminals } A \text{ and}$$
$$h(f(t_1, \ldots, t_n)) = f(h(t_1), \ldots, h(t_n)) \text{ for all terminals } f.$$

In the special case where G is top-context-free this yields:

$$
\begin{array}{ll}
\bar{A}(\vec{x}, y) \to \bar{B}(\vec{t} \diamond_c y, y) & \text{if } A(\vec{x}) \to B(\vec{t}) \text{ is a rule in } G, \\
\bar{A}(\vec{x}, y) \to t \diamond_c y & \text{if } A(\vec{x}) \to t \text{ is a rule in } G, \text{ t contains no nonterminal.}
\end{array}
$$

Thus $\bar{G}$ is top-context-free in case G is top-context-free.

(3) Let G be a linear top-context-free grammar, and s a term. Since LINTOPCF is closed under union, it is sufficient to show that $s \diamond_c \mathcal{L}(G)$ is generated by a

linear top-context-free grammar $\bar{G}$. $\bar{G}$ is constructed as follows: Let s contain m occurrences of the symbol c. For each nonterminal A in G of arity n we have a nonterminal $\bar{A}$ of arity $m \cdot n$ in $\bar{G}$. If $\vec{x}$ is $x_1, \ldots, x_n$ then let $\pi_1, \ldots, \pi_m$ be variable renamings such that all variables $x_i\pi_j$ are pairwise distinct. Let $\vec{x}\pi_i$ denote $x_1\pi_i, \ldots, x_n\pi_i$, for $\vec{t}$ similarly.

Now, if $A(\vec{x}) \rightarrow B(\vec{t})$ is a rule in G, then $\bar{A}(\vec{x}\pi_1, \ldots, \vec{x}\pi_m) \rightarrow \bar{B}(\vec{t}\pi_1, \ldots, \vec{t}\pi_m)$ is a rule in $\bar{G}$.

If $A(\vec{x}) \rightarrow t$ is a rule in G where t contains no nonterminal, then $\bar{A}(\vec{x}\pi_1, \ldots, \vec{x}\pi_m) \rightarrow s'$ is a rule in $\bar{G}$, where s' is obtained from s by replacing the m symbols c successively by $t\pi_1, \ldots, t\pi_m$.

(4) Consider $\mathcal{T}_{\{f,a\}}$. This language is not top-context-free by corollary 10, hence by theorem 1 the language $\{f(c,c)\}\diamond_c\mathcal{T}_{\{f,a\}}$ is not context-free.

(5) Let L be generated by $\{S \rightarrow A(c),\ A(x) \rightarrow A(f(c,x)),\ A(x) \rightarrow x\}$. Let $L' = \{g^i(a) \mid i \geq 0\}$ be generated by $\{S \rightarrow A(c),\ A(x) \rightarrow A(g(x)),\ A(x) \rightarrow x\}$. Then $L\diamond_c L'$ is not linear top-context-free. To show this, an appropriate pumping lemma for linear top-context-free languages can be used, see [8].

(6) Consider $\mathcal{T}_{\{f,c\}}\diamond_c\{g^i(a) \mid i \geq 0\}$. It is neither linear context-free (by a pumping lemma for linear context-free languages given in [8]) nor top-context-free (using results from section 4). □

Lemma 25 (Closure under Replacement Iteration) *(1)* Reg, LinCf, *and* Cf *are closed under replacement iteration.*
(2) $\text{Fin}^* \not\subseteq$ TopCf.

Proof. (1) Let G be a context-free grammar. A context-free grammar $\bar{G}$ generating $\mathcal{L}(G)^{*_c}$ is constructed as follows: $\bar{G}$ has the same nonterminals and the same initial symbol S as G, and the rules of $\bar{G}$ are:

$$\begin{aligned} A(\vec{x}) &\rightarrow t\cdot_c\{S\} \quad \text{if } A(\vec{x}) \rightarrow t \text{ is a rule in G,} \\ S &\rightarrow c. \end{aligned}$$

If G is regular or linear then $\bar{G}$ is so.

(2) Consider $\{f(c,c)\}^{*_c} = \mathcal{T}_{\{c,f\}}$; it is not top-context-free by corollary 10. □

Lemma 26 (Closure under Substitution Iteration) *(1)* TopCf *is closed under substitution iteration.*
(2) $\text{Reg}^\diamond \not\subseteq$ Cf.
(3) $\text{Fin}^\diamond \not\subseteq$ LinTopCf.

Proof. (1) Given a top-context-free grammar $G = (N, \Sigma, P, S)$, in order to get a top-context-free grammar $\bar{G}$ generating $\mathcal{L}(G)^{\diamond_c}$ we can use a construction analogous to that given in the proof of lemma 24(2). Just the following rules have to be added. If $A(\vec{x}) \to t$ is a rule in G, $t \in \mathcal{T}_\Sigma(X)$, we have in $\bar{G}$ not only the rule $\bar{A}(\vec{x}, y) \to t\diamond_c y$, but also the rule

$$\bar{A}(\vec{x}, y) \to \bar{S}(t\diamond_c y).$$

(2) Consider the regular language $L = \{f(c,c)\} \cup \mathcal{T}_\Sigma$ over $\Sigma = \{a, h\}$, where a is a constant and h is binary. We have $L^{\diamond_c} = \{f(c,c)\}^{\diamond_c} \cup (\{f(c,c)\}^{\diamond_c}\diamond_c\mathcal{T}_\Sigma)$. Thus $L^{\diamond_c} \cap \{f(t,t') \mid t,t' \in \mathcal{T}_\Sigma\} = \{f(t,t) \mid t \in \mathcal{T}_\Sigma\}$, which is not context-free by theorem 1 and corollary 10. As $\{f(t,t') \mid t,t' \in \mathcal{T}_\Sigma\}$ is regular and Cf is closed under intersection with regular languages, $L^{\diamond_c}$ is not context-free.

(3) For $L = \{f(c,c)\}$, $L^{\diamond_c}$ is the set of complete binary trees over $\{c, f\}$. Thus, by example 17, $L^{\diamond_c} \not\subseteq$ LinTopCf. □

Closure by Replacement: $\mathcal{C}\cdot\mathcal{C}'$

$\mathcal{C}$ \ $\mathcal{C}'$	Fin	Reg	LinTopCf	TopCf	LinCf	Cf
Fin	= Fin 23(1)	= Reg 23(3)	= LinTopCf 23(2)	= TopCf 23(2)	= LinCf 23(3)	= Cf 23(3)
Reg	= Reg 23(1)	= Reg 23(3)	⊆ LinCf 23(3)	⊆ Cf 23(3)	= LinCf 23(3)	= Cf 23(3)
LinTopCf	= LinTopCf 23(1)	⊆ LinCf 23(3)	= LinTopCf 23(2)	= TopCf 23(2)	= LinCf 23(3)	= Cf 23(3)
TopCf	= TopCf 23(1)	⊆ Cf 23(3)	⊆ Cf 23(3), 23(4)	⊆ Cf 23(3), 23(4)	⊆ Cf 23(3)	= Cf 23(3)
LinCf	= LinCf 23(1)	= LinCf 23(3)	= LinCf 23(3)	⊆ Cf 23(3)	= LinCf 23(3)	= Cf 23(3)
Cf	= Cf 23(1), 23(3)	= Cf 23(3)	= Cf 23(3)	= Cf 23(3)	= Cf 23(3)	= Cf 23(3)

Closure by Substitution: $\mathcal{C}\diamond\mathcal{C}'$

$\mathcal{C}$ \ $\mathcal{C}'$	Fin	Reg	LinTopCf	TopCf	LinCf	Cf
Fin	= Fin 24(1)	⊈ Cf 24(4)	= LinTopCf 24(3)	= TopCf 24(2)	⊈ Cf 24(4)	⊈ Cf 24(4)
Reg	= Reg 24(1)	⊈ Cf 24(4)	⊆ Cf 24(2), 24(6)	⊆ Cf 24(2), 24(6)	⊈ Cf 24(4)	⊈ Cf 24(4)
LinTopCf	= LinTopCf 24(1)	⊈ Cf 24(4)	⊆ TopCf 24(2), 24(5)	= TopCf 24(2)	⊈ Cf 24(4)	⊈ Cf 24(4)
TopCf	= TopCf 24(1)	⊈ Cf 24(4)	= TopCf 24(2)	= TopCf 24(2)	⊈ Cf 24(4)	⊈ Cf 24(4)
LinCf	= LinCf 24(1)	⊈ Cf 24(4)	⊆ Cf 24(2), 24(6)	⊆ Cf 24(2), 24(6)	⊈ Cf 24(4)	⊈ Cf 24(4)
Cf	= Cf 24(1)	⊈ Cf 24(4)	= Cf 24(2)	= Cf 24(2)	⊈ Cf 24(4)	⊈ Cf 24(4)

$\mathcal{C}$	Closure by Replacement Iteration: $\mathcal{C}^*$	Substitution Iteration: $\mathcal{C}^\diamond$
Fin	$\subseteq$ Reg 25(1), 25(2)	$\subseteq$ TopCf 26(1), 26(3)
Reg	$=$ Reg 25(1)	$\not\subseteq$ Cf 26(2)
LinTopCf	$\subseteq$ LinCf 25(1), 25(2)	$\subseteq$ TopCf 26(1), 26(3)
TopCf	$\subseteq$ Cf 25(1), 25(2)	$=$ TopCf 26(1)
LinCf	$=$ LinCf 25(1)	$\not\subseteq$ Cf 26(2)
Cf	$=$ Cf 25(1)	$\not\subseteq$ Cf 26(2)

References

1. A. Arnold and M. Dauchet. Transductions de Forêts Reconnaissables Monadiques. Forêts Corégulières. *RAIRO Informatique Théorique et applications*, 10(3):5–28, 1976.
2. A. Arnold and M. Dauchet. Un Théorème de Duplication pour les Forêts Algébriques. *JCSS*, 13:223–244, 1976.
3. M. Dauchet and S. Tison. Structural Complexity of Classes of Tree Languages. In *Tree Automata and Languages*, pp. 327–353. Elsevier (North-Holland), 1992.
4. N. Dershowitz and J.-P. Jouannaud. Rewrite Systems. In *Handbook of Theoretical Computer Science*, vol. B, pp. 243–320. Elsevier, 1990.
5. J. Engelfriet and E. Schmidt. IO and OI. I. *JCSS*, 15:329–353, 1977.
6. F. Gécseg and M. Steinby. *Tree automata*. Akadémiai Kiadó, Budapest, 1984.
7. D. Hofbauer and M. Huber. Computing linearizations using test sets. In *3rd International Workshop on Conditional Term Rewriting Systems*, LNCS 656, pp. 287–301. Springer-Verlag, 1992.
8. D. Hofbauer, M. Huber, and G. Kucherov. Some Results on Top-context-free Tree Languages. Centre de Recherche en Informatique de Nancy, Technical Report, to appear, 1993.
9. J. Hopcroft and J. Ullman. *Introduction to Automata Theory. Languages and Computation*. Addison-Wesley, 1979.
10. G. Kucherov and M. Tajine. Decidability of regularity and related properties of ground normal form languages. In *3rd International Workshop on Conditional Term Rewriting Systems*, LNCS 656, pp. 272–286. Springer-Verlag, 1992.
11. G. A. Kucherov. On relationship between term rewriting systems and regular tree languages. In *4th Conference on Rewriting Techniques and Applications*, LNCS 488, pp. 299–311. Springer-Verlag, 1991.
12. T. S. E. Maibaum. Pumping lemmas for term languages. *JCSS*, 17:319–330, 1978.
13. K. Salomaa. Deterministic Tree Pushdown Automata and Monadic Tree Rewriting Systems. *JCSS*, 37:367–394, 1988.
14. S. Vágvölgyi and R. Gilleron. For a rewriting system it is decidable whether the set of irreducible ground terms is recognizable. *Bulletin of the European Association for Theoretical Computer Science*, 48:197–209, 1992.

On Higher Order Recursive Program Schemes

Zurab Khasidashvili

School of Information Systems, UEA
Norwich NR4 7TJ England
zurab@sys.uea.ac.uk

Abstract. We define *Higher Order Recursive Program Schemes* (HRPSs) by allowing metasubstitutions (as in the λ-calculus) in right-hand sides of function and quantifier definitions. A study of several kinds of *similarity* of redexes makes it possible to lift properties of (first order) Recursive Program Schemes to the higher order case. The main result is the decidability of weak normalization in HRPSs, which immediately implies that HRPSs do not have full computational power. We analyze the structural properties of HRPSs and introduce several kinds of *persistent* expression reduction systems (PERSs) that enjoy similar properties. Finally, we design an optimal evaluation procedure for PERSs.

1 Introduction

Higher Order Recursive Program Schemes (HRPSs) are recursive definitions of functions, predicates, and quantifiers, considered as rewriting systems. Similar definitions are used when one extends a theory by introducing new symbols [16]. $\exists aA \Leftrightarrow (\tau a(A)/a)A$ and $\exists! aA \Leftrightarrow \exists aA \wedge \forall a \forall b(A \wedge (b/a)A \Rightarrow a = b)$ are examples of such definitions. Definitions of new symbols are added to the theory as axioms, and weak normalization of the system of definitions considered as a rewriting system ensures that the enriched theory is a conservative extension of the original one.

The main result of the paper — decidability of weak normalization (that is, existence of a normal form) in HRPSs — implies that HRPSs do not have full computational power: the existence of an interpreter for, say λ-calculus, in an HRPS would imply decidability of weak normalization for λ-terms, which is not valid [2]. Note that rewrite rules for the conditional cannot be used for evaluating expressions on the syntactic level, since they do not fall into the scope of our HRPSs. Indeed, it is well-known that addition of $if - then - else$ yields full computational power [3]. The deep reason for Turing incompleteness of HRPSs is the restricted possibility for redex creation compared to languages with full computational power, the λ-calculus and Combinatory Logic, for example. This paper is a part of a general study of how various kinds of redex creation are reflected in syntactic properties of rewriting systems such as normalization, perpetuality, expressive power, etc. Some results in this direction are obtained in [7, 8, 10].

In [6], we introduced a formalism for higher order rewriting (i.e., term rewriting systems (TRSs) with bound variables and substitution mechanism) which is close to the Combinatory Reduction Systems (CRSs) of Klop [11]. The syntax of our *Expression Reduction Systems* (ERSs, called CRSs in [6]) is closer to the syntax of λ-calculus and First Order Logic. For example, the β-rule is written as $\beta : Ap(\lambda aA, B) \rightarrow (B/a)A$, where a is to be instantiated by a variable and A and B are to be instantiated by terms; an instance $(t/x)s$ of $(B/a)A$ denotes the result of substitution of the term t for x in the term s. To express "pure" substitutions syntactically we introduced S-reduction rules $S^{n+1}a_1 \ldots a_n A_1 \ldots A_n A_0 \rightarrow (A_1/a_1, \ldots, A_n/a_n)A_0$, $n = 1, 2, \ldots$.

HRPSs are OERSs where left-hand sides of rewrite rules contain exactly one function or quantifier symbol. In order to construct an interpretation of HRPSs in (first order) Recursive Program Schemes (RPSs), we split an HRPS R into a "first order part" R_f, which delays substitutions, and a "substitution part" $\underline{S}$. (The method was originally used in [11] to prove the Church-Rosser property.) For example, a β-reduction step $(\lambda x\, t)s \rightarrow (s/x)t$ *expands* to a β_f-reduction step $(\lambda x\, t)s \rightarrow \underline{S}x\, s\, t$ and an $\underline{S}$-step $\underline{S}x\, s\, t \rightarrow (s/x)t$ (underlining of S-symbols is used to distinguish S-redexes created during R_f-reduction steps). Then the interpretation of HRPSs in RPSs, in which $\underline{S}$-reductions play the role of projection functions, can (roughly) be expressed by the following *Representation Lemma:* for any R-reduction $P : t \twoheadrightarrow s$, where R is an HRPS, there is an R_f-reduction $P_f : t \twoheadrightarrow o$ such that s is obtained from o by any normalizing $\underline{S}$-reduction $P_{\underline{S}}$; and conversely.

As in the case of orthogonal TRSs (OTRSs), we say that a subterm s of a term t in an orthogonal ERS (OERS) is *inessential* if there is a reduction P starting from t such that s does not have *descendants* under P; we call s *essential* otherwise [7]. The notion of descendant is a generalization of the usual notion of *residual* of a redex to all subterms in a way that makes it possible to trace contracted redexes: the descendant of a contracted redex is its contractum, while it does not have residuals. The descendant notion allows us to introduce the key concepts of this paper: several kinds of *similarity* of redexes. We explain the notion informally in terms of β-redexes. Let us consider the redexes $u = (\lambda x.x)s$, $v = (\lambda x.(\lambda y.z)x)o$, $w = (\lambda x.xx)e$, and $u' = (\lambda x.y)t$. We call u and v *similar* (written $u \sim v$) because the binding variable x occurs free both in the bodies of u and v. In contrast, we have $u \not\sim u'$. We call u and w *essentially similar* (written $u \approx w$) because the binding variable x has essential occurrences in bodies of both redexes. Similarly, $v \approx u'$, because the occurrence of x in the body $(\lambda y.z)x$ of v is inessential — it does not have descendants in the contractum of $(\lambda y.z)x$. Similarity and essential similarity of terms obtained one from another by replacing some proper subterms are defined analogously.

The crucial property of essentially similar terms is the following *Essential Similarity Lemma:* corresponding subterms of essentially similar terms are either both essential or both inessential. A consequence is that corresponding arguments of essentially similar redexes are either both essential or both inessential. Hence, for any redex u, its *essential similarity class* $\langle u\rangle_e$, consisting of all redexes essentially similar to u, has an *essentiality indicator* which indicates which arguments of any $v \in \langle u\rangle_e$ are essential. Another consequence of the Essential

Similarity Lemma is that essentially similar redexes create essentially similar redexes, i.e., one can define an *essential chain* to be a sequence $\langle u_0\rangle_e, \langle u_1\rangle_e, \ldots$ such that any $v_i \in \langle u_i\rangle_e$ creates an essential redex $v_{i+1} \in \langle u_{i+1}\rangle_e$. Then a term t in an HRPS R is weakly normalizable iff any essential chain of the essential similarity class of any essential redex of t is finite. So, in order to prove decidability of weak normalization in HRPSs, we need an algorithm for finding all essential (and inessential) subterms in a given term, and an algorithm for finding essentiality indicators of all redexes. Complete descriptions of the algorithms are presented in the body of the paper; we only note that our algorithm can also find essentiality indicators of redexes that do not have normal forms.

The above properties of HRPSs are due to the fact that each subterm s of a term t is *free*: if s is inside a redex u, then it is either inside an argument of u or coincides with u. We introduce *persistent* ERSs (PERSs), where not all subterms are free but all free subterms remain free under any reduction. This persistency property of free subterms is due to the fact that PERSs are the systems where only a special kind of redex creation — *generation* — is possible: all new redexes are actually present in right-hand sides of rewrite rules. For example, in the step $\sigma x(x) \to f((\sigma x(x)/x)x) = f(\sigma x(x))$, which corresponds to a rule $\sigma a(A) \to f((\sigma a(A)/a)A)$ and an assignment $\theta(a) = \theta(A) = x$, the created redex $\sigma x(x)$ is an instance of the metaterm $\sigma a(A)$ present in the right-hand side of the rewrite rule. We have generation here because $\theta(a)$ has an occurrence in $\theta(A)$. Therefore, the generation is not *uniform* — uniformly generated redexes are present in right-hand sides of rules outside "mobile" arguments of metasubstitutions. During the reduction step $\sigma x(x) \to f((d/x)x) = f(d)$ in the system $\{r_1 : \sigma a(A) \to f((d/a)A),\ r_2 : f(d) \to c\}$, where d and c are constants, we have *quasi-generation* in the sense that all symbols needed to create the new redex $f(d)$ are present in the right-hand side of r_1. The Essential Similarity Lemma remains valid in PERSs if the replaced subterms are free. Therefore, all the results obtained for HRPSs, the decidability of weak normalization in particular, remain valid for PERSs in general. Similar reasoning shows that strong normalization (that is, termination of all reductions) also is decidable in PERSs.

For uniformly persistent systems, we show that the strategy that in each step contracts an innermost essential redex is optimal. For PERSs in general, sharing of redexes of the same origin [14] is necessary. Alternatively, one can define an *irreducible* version of the PERS and use the innermost essential strategy without sharing in the irreducible system. As a corollary, we have an algorithm for optimal S-reductions and, in general, algorithms for optimal developments in OERSs, since developments are (up to isomorphism) reductions in non-creating HRPSs (where no redex-creation is possible). The above results cannot be generalized to *quasi-persistent* ERSs, where quasi-generation of redexes is possible.

The paper is organized as follows. In section 2, the review ERSs; in section 3, we study similarity of redexes; the main results are obtained in section 4 and are generalized to PERSs in section 5; we study optimal reductions in PERSs in section 6. Complete proofs of the results are reported in [9].

2 Orthogonal Expression Reduction Systems

Combinatory Reduction Systems have been introduced in Klop [11] to provide a uniform framework for reductions with substitutions (referred to also as higher order rewriting) as in the λ-calculus [2]. Several other formalisms have been introduced later. We refer to Klop et al. [13] for further information. Here we describe a system for higher order rewriting, called *Expression Reduction Systems*, as defined in [6] (under the name of CRSs).

Definition 2.1 (1) Let Σ be an *alphabet*, comprising *variables* $v_0, v_1, \ldots$; *function symbols*, also called *simple operators*; and *operator signs* or *quantifier signs*. Each function symbol has an *arity* $k \in N$, and each operator sign σ has an *arity* (m, n) with $m, n \neq 0$ such that, for any sequence $x_1, \ldots, x_m$ of pairwise distinct variables, $\sigma x_1 \ldots x_m$ is a *compound operator* or a *quantifier* with *arity* n. Occurrences of $x_1, \ldots, x_m$ in $\sigma x_1 \ldots x_m$ are called *binding variables*. Each quantifier $\sigma x_1 \ldots x_m$, as well as the corresponding quantifier sign σ and binding variables $x_1 \ldots x_m$, has a *scope indicator* $(k_1, \ldots, k_l)$ to specify the arguments in which $\sigma x_1 \ldots x_m$ binds all free occurrences of $x_1, \ldots, x_m$. *Terms* are constructed from variables using functions and quantifiers in the usual way.

(2) *Metaterms* are constructed from *terms*, *term metavariables*, which range over terms, and *object metavariables*, which range over variables. Apart from the usual rules for term-formation, one is allowed to have *metasubstitutions* — expressions of the form $(A_1/a_1, \ldots, A_n/a_n)A_0$, where a_i are object metavariables and A_j are metaterms. Metaterms that do not contain metasubstitutions are called *simple metaterms*. An *assignment* maps each object metavariable to a variable and each term metavariable to a term over Σ. If t is a metaterm and θ is an assignment, then the *θ-instance* $t\theta$ of t is the term obtained from t by replacing metavariables with their values under θ, and by replacement of subterms of the form $(t_1/x_1, \ldots, t_n/x_n)t$ by the result of substitution of terms $t_1, \ldots, t_n$ for free occurrences of $x_1, \ldots, x_n$ in t.

Definition 2.2 (1) An *Expression Reduction System* (ERS) is a pair (Σ, R), where Σ is an alphabet, described in Definition 2.1, and R is a set of rewrite rules $r : t \to s$, where t and s are metaterms such that t is a simple metaterm and is not a metavariable, and each term metavariable which occurs in s occurs also in t. Further,

(a) The metaterms t and s do not contain variables, and each occurrence of an object metavariable in t and s is bound.

(b) An occurrence of a term-metavariable A in s is in the scope of an occurrence of an object metavariable a in s iff any occurrence of A in t is in the scope of an occurrence of a in t.

(2) An assignment θ is *admissible* for a rule $r : t \to s$ if occurrences of binding variables in $s\theta$ corresponding to object metavariables of s not occurring in t do not bind variables in subterms corresponding to term metavariables of s. For any admissible assignment θ', $t\theta'$ is an *r-redex*, and $s\theta$ is the *contractum* of $t\theta$. Redexes that are instances of the left-hand side of the same rule are called *weakly similar*.

(3) R is *simple* if right-hand sides of R-rules are simple.

Below we ignore questions relating to renaming of bound variables.

Notation We use a, b for object metavariables, A, B for term metavariables, c, d for constants, t, s, e, o for terms and metaterms, u, v, w for redexes, σ, δ, ε for operators and operator signs, and P, Q for reductions. We write $s \subseteq t$ if s is a subterm of t. A one-step reduction in which a redex u in a term t is contracted is written as $t \xrightarrow{u} s$ or $t \rightarrow s$. We write $P : t \twoheadrightarrow s$ if P denotes a reduction of t to s. $|P|$ denotes the length of P. $P + Q$ denotes the concatenation of P and Q.

The ERS S consists of the rules of the form $S^{n+1}a_1 \ldots a_n A_1 \ldots A_n A \rightarrow (A_1/a_1, \ldots, A_n/a_n)A$, $n = 1, 2 \ldots$, where S^{n+1} is the *operator sign of substitution* with arity $(n, n+1)$ and scope indicator $(n+1)$, and $a_1, \ldots, a_n$ and $A_1, \ldots, A_n, A$ are pairwise distinct object and term metavariables, respectively. For any ERS R, R_f is the ERS obtained from R by adding symbols $\underline{S}^{n+1}$ in the alphabet and by replacing in right-hand sides of the rules all metasubstitutions of the form $(t_1/a_1, \ldots, t_n/a_n)t$ with $\underline{S}^{n+1}a_1 \ldots a_n t_1 \ldots t_n, t$, respectively. If R is simple, then $R_{fS} =_{def} R_f =_{def} R$. Otherwise $R_{fS} =_{def} R_f \cup \underline{S}$, where $\underline{S}$-rules are obtained from S-rules by underlining the S-symbols. For each step $e = C[t_i\theta] \xrightarrow{u} C[s_i\theta] = o$ in R there is a reduction $P : e = C[t_i\theta] \rightarrow C[s_i'\theta] \twoheadrightarrow C[s\theta] = o$ in R_{fS}, where $C[s'\theta] \twoheadrightarrow C[s\theta]$ is the rightmost innermost normalizing $\underline{S}$-reduction. We call P the *expansion* of u. The notion of *expansion* generalizes naturally to R-reductions with 0 or more steps.

Let $t \xrightarrow{u} s$ be an R_f-reduction step and let e be the contractum of u in s. For each argument o of u there are 0 or more arguments of e. We call them (u-)*descendants* of o. Correspondingly, subterms of o have 0 or more *descendants*. The *descendant* of each pattern-subterm (i.e., a subterm headed at the pattern) of u is e. It is clear what is to be meant by *descendants* of a subterm that is not in u. In an S-reduction step $C[S^{n+1}x_1 \ldots x_n\, t_1 \ldots t_n t_0] \xrightarrow{u} C[(t_1/x_1, \ldots, t_n/x_n)t_0]$, the argument t_i and subterms in t_i have the same number of *descendants* as the number of free occurrences of x_i in t_0. All subterms of t_0, including free occurrences of $x_1, \ldots, x_n$, have exactly one *descendant*. The *descendant* of the contracted redex u itself is its contractum. The notion of *descendant* extends by transitivity to arbitrary R_{fS}-reductions. If P is an R-reduction, then P-*descendants* are defined to be the descendants under the expansion of P. The *ancestor* relation is converse to that of descendant. If $t \xrightarrow{u} s$ in R, then a redex in s is called a *new* redex or a *created* redex if it is not a residual of a redex of t (descendants of all redexes except the contracted redex are *residuals*).

We call the co-initial reductions $P : t \twoheadrightarrow s$ and $Q : t \twoheadrightarrow e$ *strictly equivalent* (written $P \approx_{st} Q$) if $s = e$ and P-descendants and Q-descendants of any subterm of t are the same in s and e.

The definition of *orthogonality* in ERSs is similar to the case of TRSs: all the rules are left-linear and in no term redex-patterns can overlap (*redex-pattern* in ERSs and *contractum-pattern* in simple ERSs are defined similarly to the case of TRSs, see [11, 6]). As in the case of the λ-calculus [2], for any co-initial reductions P and Q, one can define in OERSs the notion of *residual of P under Q*, written P/Q, due to Lévy [14]. Below, we use the following properties of /:

Theorem 2.1 [6] Let P, P', Q and Q' be co-initial reductions in an OERS.
(1) (**Strict Church-Rosser**) $P + Q/P \approx_{st} Q + P/Q$.
(2) $(P + P')/Q \approx_{st} P/Q + P'/(Q/P)$, $P/(Q + Q') \approx_{st} (P/Q)/Q'$.

3 Similarity of redexes

In this section, we study some properties of substitutions and similarity of terms in HRPSs. In particular we prove the Replacement Lemma, the Essential Similarity Lemma, and the Uniform Generation Lemma.

We call a subterm s in t *essential* (written $ES(s,t)$) if s has at least one descendant under any reduction starting from t and call it *inessential* (written $IE(s,t)$) otherwise [7]. We say that $P : t \twoheadrightarrow s$ *erases* a subterm $s \subseteq t$ if s does not have descendants under P. The notion of essentiality is a generalization of the notion of *neededness* [5, 15] in a way that it works for all subterms, bound variables in particular.

The following lemma is valid for all OERSs; the proof is the same as in the case of OTRSs [7] and follows easily from the strict CR theorem.

Lemma 3.1 (1) Let $s_0, \ldots, s_k \subseteq t$ be inessential in t. Then there is a reduction starting from t that erases them.
(2) Let $P : t \twoheadrightarrow t'$ and $s \subseteq t$. Then $IE(s,t)$ iff any P-descendant of s is inessential in t'.

Definition 3.1 We call an ERS R' a *subsystem* of an ERS R if the alphabet and the set of rules of R' are subsets of those of R.

Notation Below $FV(t)$ (resp. $EFV_R(t)$) denotes the set of variables having (R-essential) free occurrences in t. For any subsystems R_1 and R_2 of R and any $s \subseteq t$, $EBV_{R_1,R_2}(s)$ is the set of variables having such free occurrences in s that are R_2-essential in s and are bound by quantifiers belonging to patterns of R_1-redexes that are outside s. We write $BV_R(s)$ for $EBV_{R,\emptyset}(s)$ and $EBV_R(s)$ for $EBV_{R,R}(s)$. We write $t = (t_1//e_1, \ldots, t_n//e_n)e$ if t is obtained from e by replacing non-overlapping proper subterms $e_1, \ldots, e_n$ in e with $t_1, \ldots, t_n$, respectively.

Definition 3.2 We call an OERS R a *Higher Order Recursive Program Scheme* (HRPS) if, for any rule $t \to s$, pattern of t consists of one operator, i.e., t has the form $\sigma a_1 \ldots a_m(A_1, \ldots, A_n)$, where σ is an operator sign with arity (m, n).

Definition 3.3 (1) Let $\sigma a_1 \ldots a_n A_1 \ldots A_m$ be the left-hand side of a rewrite rule r in an HRPS R and let $u = \sigma x_1 \ldots x_n t_1 \ldots t_m$ be an r-redex. The *characteristic system* of u (written $CS(u)$) is the set of pairs (a_j, A_i) such that t_i is in the scope of σ and $x_j \in FV(t_i)$ ($i = 1, \ldots, m$, $j = 1, \ldots, n$). We call u an $\langle r\rangle$*-redex*, where $\langle r\rangle = (r, CS(u))$ is a *characterized rule* (*C-rule* for short). For any subsystem R' of R, an R'*-essential characteristic system* of u (written $ECS_{R'}(u)$) is the set of pairs (a_j, A_i) such that t_i is in the scope of σ and $x_j \in EFV_{R'}(t_i)$. We call u an $\langle r\rangle_e$*-redex*, where $\langle r\rangle_e = (r, ECS_{R'}(u))$ is an R'*-essentially characterized rule* ($EC_{R'}$*-rule* for short). (We omit the subscript R' if $R = R'$.)

(2) Let $t = (t_1//e_1, \ldots, t_k//e_k)e$. We write $e \prec_{R_1,R_2} t$ if $EBV_{R_1,R_2}(e_i) \subseteq EBV_{R_1,R_2}(t_i)$ for all $i = 1, \ldots, k$, and write $e \sim_{R_1,R_2} t$ if $e \prec_{R_1,R_2} t$ and $t \prec_{R_1,R_2} e$. We abbreviate $\prec_{R,\emptyset}$ to $\prec_R$ and $\prec_{R,R}$ to $\prec\!\!\prec_R$. We call t and e *R-similar* (resp. *R-essentially similar*), written $e \sim_R t$ (resp. $e \approx_R t$), if $s \prec_R t$ and $t \prec_R s$ (resp. $s \prec\!\!\prec_R t$ and $t \prec\!\!\prec_R s$).

Of course, (essential) similarity of terms depends on the specification of the replaced subterms. Note that, for any weakly similar R-redexes v and u, if one specifies replaced subterms to be the arguments of the redexes, then $v \prec u$ (resp. $v \prec\!\!\prec u$) iff $CS(v) \subseteq CS(u)$ (resp. $ECS_R(v) \subseteq ECS_R(u)$). Below, when we speak of (essential) similarity of redexes without specifying replaced subterms, we mean that the replaced subterms are the arguments of the redexes; we write $v \overset{r}{\prec} u$, $v \overset{r}{\prec\!\!\prec} u$, $v \overset{r}{\sim} u$, and $v \overset{r}{\approx} u$ for $v \prec u$, $v \prec\!\!\prec u$, $v \sim u$, and $v \approx u$, respectively, to stress the fact that the replaced subterms are specified to be arguments of the redexes. $\langle r \rangle$, as well as $\langle u \rangle$, will also denote the equivalence class of all $\langle r \rangle$-redexes (which are similar to u). $\langle r \rangle_e$, as well as $\langle u \rangle_e$, will also denote the equivalence class of all $\langle r \rangle_e$-redexes.

3.1 The Replacement Lemma

Definition 3.4 Let $u = Sx_1 \ldots x_n t_1 \ldots t_n t_0$ and t_0' be an S-normal form of t_0. A subterm e in u is called *u-inessential* (written $IE_S(u; e)$) if e is in t_i for some $1 \leq i \leq n$ and $x_i \notin FV(t_0')$.

Lemma 3.2 (1) Let $u = Sx_1 \ldots x_n t_1 \ldots t_n t_0 \subseteq t$. Then $IE_S(u; t_i)$ iff $x_i \notin EFV_S(t_0)$.

(2) Let $s \subseteq t$. Then $IE_S(s,t)$ iff $IE_S(u; s)$ for some S-redex u in t.

(3) Let $e \subseteq s \subseteq t$. Then $ES_S(e,t)$ iff $ES_S(e,s)$ and $ES_S(s,t)$.

Proof. (1) From Lemma 3.1.(2). (2) One can take for u the redex whose residual erases all descendants of s in the rightmost innermost normalizing S-reduction. (3) ($\Rightarrow$) From the definition of essentiality. ($\Leftarrow$) By (2), the redex that would make e inessential can neither occur in s nor contain s in its argument.

Lemma 3.3 (Replacement Lemma) Let s be obtained from t by replacing non-overlapping proper subterms $t_1, \ldots, t_n$ with $s_1, \ldots, s_n$, respectively, where s_i and t_i do not contain S-redexes, and let $ES_S(s_i, s) \Rightarrow BV_S(t_i) \subseteq BV_S(s_i)$ $(i = 1, \ldots, n)$. Further, let s' and t' be any corresponding subterms in s and t that are not in replaced subterms. Then $IE_S(s', s) \Rightarrow IE_S(t', t)$.

Proof sketch. By induction on the length of s. It is enough to consider the case when t and s are S-redexes. Let $t = Sx_1 \ldots x_k e_1 \ldots e_k e$, $s = Sx_1 \ldots x_k o_1 \ldots o_k o$, $s' \subseteq o_l$, and $IE_S(s', s)$. If $IE_S(s', o_l)$, then by the induction assumption $IE_S(t', e_l)$ and hence $IE_S(t', t)$. Otherwise, by Lemma 3.2.(3), $IE_S(o_l, s)$; by Lemma 3.2.(2), $IE_S(s; o_l)$; and by Lemma 3.2.(1), $x_l \notin EFV_S(o)$. Therefore, it follows from the induction assumption (which is valid by Lemma 3.2.(2)) that x_l does not have an essential occurrence in e_0 either outside or inside the replaced subterms. Hence, by Lemma 3.2.(1), $IE_S(t; e_l)$ and by Lemma 3.2.(2), $IE_S(t; t')$ and $IE_S(t', t)$.

3.2 The Essential Similarity Lemma

In the rest of this section we only consider HRPSs.

Notation Recall that, if F is a set of R-redexes in a term t, then a *complete F-development of t* is a reduction that contracts residuals of redexes from F as long as possible. Below F_R denotes a complete F-development in R, F_f denotes a complete F-development in R_f, and $F_{\underline{S}}$ denotes a complete development of the set of $\underline{S}$-redexes created during F_f. If F consists of one redex u only, then we write u_R, u_f, and $u_{\underline{S}}$ for F_R, F_f, and $F_{\underline{S}}$, respectively.

Lemma 3.4 Let F be a set of R-redexes in a term t. Then $F_R \approx_{st} F_f + F_{\underline{S}}$.

Proof. By induction on number n of redexes in F. The case $n = 0$ is trivial. So let $F = F' \cup \{u\}$, where u is an outermost among redexes in F. Then $F_R \approx_{st} F'_R + u'_R$ (where $u' = u/F_R$) $\approx_{st}$(by the induction assumption)$\approx_{st} F'_f + F'_{\underline{S}} + u'_R \approx_{st} F'_f + u''_R + F'_{\underline{S}}/u''_R$ (where u'' is the unique ancestor of u') $\approx_{st} F'_f + u''_f + u''_{\underline{S}} + F'_{\underline{S}}/u''_R \approx_{st} F_f + u''_{\underline{S}} + F'_{\underline{S}}/u''_R \approx_{st} F_f + F_{\underline{S}}$.

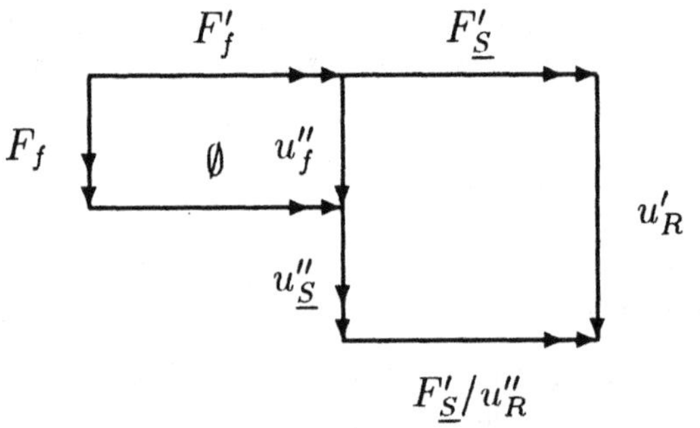

Lemma 3.5 (Representation Lemma) Let R be an HRPS.

(1) For any $P : t \twoheadrightarrow_R s$ there are $Q : s \twoheadrightarrow_R e$ and $P' : t \twoheadrightarrow_{R_f} o$ such that $P + Q \approx_{st} P' + P''$, where P'' is a normalizing $\underline{S}$-reduction starting from o.

(2) If $P_f : t \twoheadrightarrow_{R_f} s$ and $P_{\underline{S}}$ is a normalizing $\underline{S}$-reduction starting from s, then there is an R-reduction P_R such that $P_f + P_{\underline{S}} \approx_{st} P_R$.

Proof. (1) By induction on $|P|$. Let $P = P^* + u$. By the induction assumption, there are R-reduction Q^*, R_f-reduction P_1, and a normalizing $\underline{S}$-reduction Q_1 such that $P^* + Q^* \approx_{st} P_1 + Q_1$. Let F be the set of all Q^*-residuals of u and let F' be the set of their Q_1-ancestors for which redexes from F are residuals ($\underline{S}$-reduction steps do not create new redexes). Then, $F'_R + Q_1/F'_R \approx_{st} Q_1 + F_R$. By Lemma 3.4, $F'_R = F'_f + F'_{\underline{S}}$. Thus $P_1 + F'_f + F'_{\underline{S}} + Q_1/F'_R \approx_{st} P_1 + Q_1 + F_R \approx_{st} P^* + Q^* + F_R \approx_{st} P^* + u + Q^*/u = P + Q^*/u$ and we can take $Q = Q^*/u$, $P' = P_1 + F'_f$, and $P'' = F'_{\underline{S}} + Q_1/F'_R$. (Note that Q contracts the redexes that belong to the families [14, 1] of redexes contracted by P.)

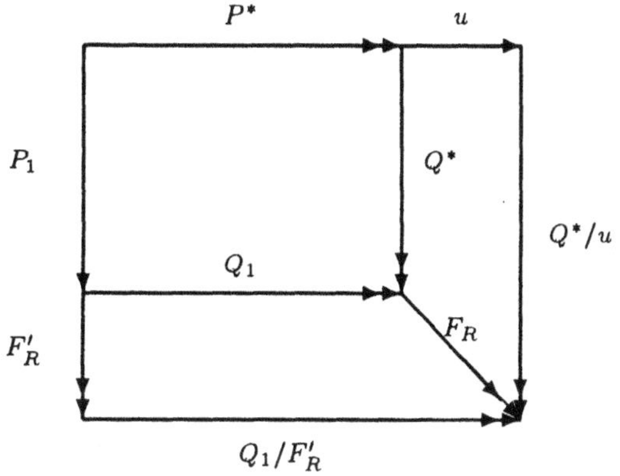

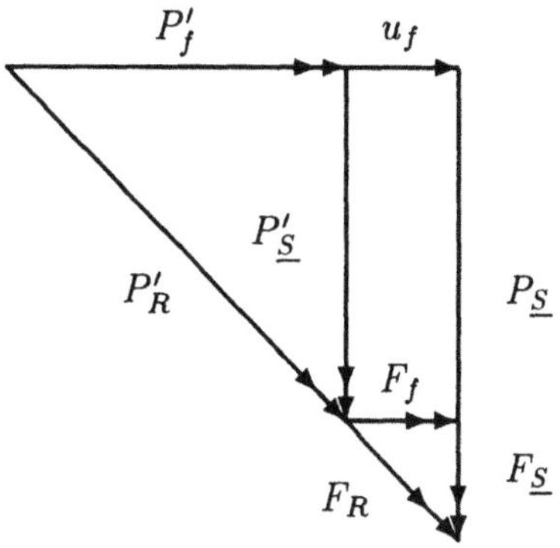

(2) By induction on $|P_f|$. The case $|P_f| = 1$ is immediate. So let $P_f : t \twoheadrightarrow e \xrightarrow{u} s$ and let $P'_f : t \twoheadrightarrow e$ be the initial part of P_f. By the induction assumption, there is an R-reduction P'_R such that $P'_R \approx_{st} P'_f + P'_{\underline{S}}$. Hence $P_f + P_{\underline{S}} \approx_{st} P'_f + u_f + P_{\underline{S}} \approx_{st} P'_f + P'_{\underline{S}} + F_f + F_{\underline{S}}$ (where F is the set of residuals of u under $P'_{\underline{S}}$) $\approx_{st}$ (by the induction assumption) $\approx_{st} P'_R + F_f + F_{\underline{S}} \approx_{st}$ (by Lemma 3.4)$\approx_{st} P'_R + F_R$, and we can take $P_R = P'_R + F_R$.

Corollary 3.1 Let R be an HRPS. Then $IE_R(s,t)$ iff there is an R_f-reduction $P : t \twoheadrightarrow e$ such that all P-descendants of s in t' are $\underline{S}$-inessential.

Lemma 3.6 (Essential Similarity Lemma) Let $s = (s_1//t_1, \ldots, s_n//t_n)t$, in an HRPS R, let $t \twoheadleftarrow\!\!\prec_R s$, and let s' and t' be any corresponding subterms of s and t that are outside the replaced subterms. Then $IE_R(s', s) \Rightarrow IE_R(t', t)$.

Proof. Let $IE_R(s', s)$. By Lemma 3.1.(1), there are R-reductions $s_i \twoheadrightarrow s_i^*$ and $t_i \twoheadrightarrow t_i^*$ such that none of R-inessential free variables of s_i and t_i that are bound in s and t have descendants in s_i^{*j} and t_i^{*j}. Hence, by Lemma 3.1.(2), it is enough to consider the case then $EBV_R(s_i) = BV(s_i)$ and $EBV_R(t_i) = BV(t_i)$. By Corollary 3.1, there is an R_f-reduction $P : s \twoheadrightarrow e$ such that all P-descendants of s' are $\underline{S}$-inessential. Let $Q : t \twoheadrightarrow o$ be an R_f-reduction that contracts redexes corresponding to the contracted redexes of P that are not inside (the descendants of) $s_1, \ldots s_n$ and omits the steps made inside $s_1, \ldots s_n$. Thus, if $s_i^1, \ldots s_i^{k_i}$ is the enumeration of all P-descendants of s_i from left to right and $t_i^1, \ldots t_i^{k_i}$ is the enumeration of all Q-descendants of t_i from left to right ($i = 1, \ldots, n$), then o is obtained from e by replacing s_i^j with t_i^j (subterms s_i^j and t_i^j are disjoint, $t_i^j = t_i$, and $s_i \twoheadrightarrow s_i^j$). Since $t \twoheadleftarrow\!\!\prec_R s$, it follows from the conditions (a)-(b) in the Definition 2.2 that $o \prec_{R \cup \underline{S}, R} e$; and since $EBV_R(s_i) = BV(s_i)$ and $EBV_R(t_i) = BV(t_i)$, we have that $o \prec_{R \cup \underline{S}, \emptyset} e$, in particular, $o \prec_{\underline{S}} e$. Thus, by Lemma 3.1.(2) and the Replacement Lemma, all descendants of t' in o' are $\underline{S}$-inessential. Hence, by Corollary 3.1, $IE_R(t', t)$.

3.3 The Uniform Generation Lemma

In this subsection, we prove the Uniform Generation Lemma; it establishes a relation between similarity of redexes and generation of redexes in HRPSs.

Lemma 3.7 Let $e_0 \subseteq s_0 \subseteq t_0$, $P : t_0 \xrightarrow{u_0} t_1 \xrightarrow{u_1} \ldots \rightarrow t_n$, and let $s_{i+1} \subseteq t_{i+1}$ be a u_i-descendant of $s_i \subseteq t_i$ $(i = 0, \ldots, n-1)$. Then there is a reduction $Q : o_0 = s_0 \xrightarrow{v_0} o_1 \xrightarrow{v_1} \ldots \rightarrow o_n$ such that $s_i = o_i\theta_i$ for some substitution θ_i and the descendants of e_0 in s_i and o_i are corresponding occurrences.

Proof sketch. By induction on $|P|$, considering relative positions of u_i and s_i.

Lemma 3.8 (1) Each outermost redex in a term t is essential.
(2) $ES(e,t)$ iff $ES(s,t)$ and $ES(e,s)$.
(3) $IE(e,t)$ iff e is in an inessential argument of an essential redex u of t.

Proof sketch. Similarly to the case of OTRSs [7], using Lemma 3.7.

Lemma 3.9 Let $t \xrightarrow{w} s$ and let $v \subseteq s$ be a residual of a redex $u \subseteq t$. Then $u \overset{r}{\approx}_R v$.

Proof. If $u \subseteq w$, then by Lemma 3.7, $v = u\theta$ for some substitution θ and $u \overset{r}{\approx}_R v$ follows from the Essential Similarity Lemma. If u and w do not overlap, then $u = v$. Otherwise, if $w \subseteq u$, then $u \overset{r}{\approx}_R v$ follows from Lemma 3.1.(2).

Lemma 3.10 (Uniform Generation Lemma) Let R be an HRPS, R' be a subsystem of R, u and v be R-redexes, $u \overset{r}{\twoheadleftarrow\!\!\!<}_{R'} v$, $u \xrightarrow{u} o$, and $v \xrightarrow{v} e$. If there is an R'-essential R-redex w in o created by u, then e contains an R'-essential R-redex w', created by v, such that $w \overset{r}{\twoheadleftarrow\!\!\!<}_{R'} w'$.

Proof. Let o' and e' be contracta of u and v in R_f. Then e' is obtained from o' by replacing the descendants of arguments of u with corresponding descendants of arguments of v. Since the replaced subterms do not contain $\underline{S}$-redexes (and R'-essentiality coincides with $R' \cup \underline{S}$-essentiality), it follows from conditions (a)-(b) of Definition 2.2 that $o' \twoheadleftarrow\!\!\!<_{\underline{S} \cup R'} e'$. Let w_1 be the ancestor of w in o' and w_2 be the corresponding redex of w_1 in e'. Then $ES_{\underline{S} \cup R'}(w_1, o')$ and, by Lemma 3.6, $ES_{\underline{S} \cup R'}(w_2, e')$. Therefore, w_2 has an R'-essential residual w' in e'.

Let $w_1 = \sigma x_1 \ldots x_k(o_1, \ldots, o_m)$ and $w_2 = \sigma y_1 \ldots y_k(e_1, \ldots, e_m)$. Let o_j be in the scope of σ and x_i' be an occurrence of x_i in o_j that is $R' \cup \underline{S}$-essential in o_j. If x_i' is outside the replaced subterms, then its corresponding occurrence of y_i in e_j is $R' \cup \underline{S}$-essential in e_j by Lemma 3.6. If x_i' is in a replaced subterm t^*, then, by Lemma 3.8.(2), t^* is $R' \cup \underline{S}$-essential in o_j, its corresponding replaced subterm s^* is $R' \cup \underline{S}$-essential in e_j by Lemma 3.6, and, again by Lemma 3.8.(2), each occurrence of y_i in s^* that is $R' \cup \underline{S}$-essential in s^* (there exists one because $o' \twoheadleftarrow\!\!\!<_{\underline{S} \cup R'} e'$) is $R' \cup \underline{S}$-essential in e_j as well. Thus $w_1 \overset{r}{\twoheadleftarrow\!\!\!<}_{\underline{S} \cup R'} w_2$. Hence, by Lemma 3.9, $w \overset{r}{\twoheadleftarrow\!\!\!<}_{R'} w'$.

Remark 3.1 It follows easily from Lemmas 3.8 and 3.6 that the latter remains valid if the condition $t \twoheadleftarrow\!\!\!<_R s$ is replaced by a (strictly) weaker condition that, for any corresponding redexes w and w' in t and s, $w \overset{r}{\twoheadleftarrow\!\!\!<}_R w'$.

4 Decidability of weak normalization in HRPSs

In this section, we prove decidability of weak and strong normalization in HRPSs. The following definition is crucial; its correctness follows from the Essential similarity Lemma and the Uniform Generation Lemma.

Definition 4.1 (1) We call a sequence $\langle r_0\rangle_e, \langle r_1\rangle_e, \ldots$ an *essential* $\langle r_0\rangle_e$*-chain* or an *essential* u_0*-chain*, where $u_0 \in \langle r_0\rangle_e$, if an essential $\langle r_{i+1}\rangle_e$-redex is created by contraction of any $\langle r_i\rangle_e$-redex.

(2) We call the sequence of numbers of essential arguments of u the *essentiality indicator* of $\langle u\rangle_e$ and of u.

(3) We call a sequence $\langle r_0\rangle, \langle r_1\rangle, \ldots$ an $\langle r_0\rangle$*-chain* or a u_0*-chain*, where $u_0 \in \langle r_0\rangle$, if an $\langle r_{i+1}\rangle$-redex is generated by contraction of any $\langle r_i\rangle$-redex .

Lemma 4.1 (1) A term t in an HRPS is weakly normalizable iff all essential chains of essential redexes in t are finite.

(2) A term t in an HRPS R is strongly normalizable iff all chains of redexes in t are finite.

Proof sketch. (1) Similarly to the case of OTRSs [7]. (2) ($\Rightarrow$) Immediate. ($\Leftarrow$) Existence of an infinite reduction would imply existence of an infinite sequence $u_0, v_0, u_1, v_1, \ldots$, such that v_i is a contracted residual of u_i and v_i generates u_{i+1}, $i = 0, 1, \ldots$; therefore, by Lemma 3.10, there would exist an infinite chain $\langle u_0\rangle = \langle w_0\rangle, \langle w_1\rangle, \ldots$ (such that $u_i \overset{r}{\prec} w_i$), a contradiction.

Lemma 4.2 Let essentiality indicators of all EC-rules in an HRPS R be known. Then one can find all inessential subterms of a term t in R as follows:

Algorithm 4.1 Choose in t an innermost redex; find its essential characteristic system (which coincides with its characteristic system); underline its inessential arguments; and mark the redex itself. Now choose in t an unmarked redex that only contains marked redexes; find its essential characteristic system (only occurrences that are in the underlined subterms are inessential); underline its inessential arguments; mark the redex itself; and so on, as long as possible. Then exactly occurrences that are in underlined subterms are inessential in t.

Proof. From Lemma 3.8.

Definition 4.2 Let $r : t = \sigma a_1 \ldots a_n A_1 \ldots A_m \to B$, and let θ be an admissible assignment such that $A_i\theta$ are in R-normal form and $t\theta \in \langle r\rangle_e$. Then we call $r\theta : t\theta \to s\theta$ a *trivial* $\langle r\rangle_e$*-instance* of r.

Lemma 4.3 Let $\langle r_1\rangle_e, \ldots, \langle r_l\rangle_e$ be all EC-rules in an HRPS R and $r_i\theta_i : t_i\theta \to s_i\theta$ be a trivial $\langle r_i\rangle_e$-instance of $r_i : t_i \to s_i$ $(i = 1, \ldots, l)$. Then the essentiality indicators of the EC-rules in R can be found using the following

Algorithm 4.2 Find, for each i, all arguments of $t_i\theta_i$ that do not have descendants in $s_i\theta_i$. Let the corresponding arguments of any $\langle r_i\rangle_e$-redex be 0-*inessential*. Let the 0-*essentiality indicator* of $\langle r_i\rangle_e$ be the list of numbers of arguments of any $\langle r_i\rangle_e$-redex that are not 0-inessential. Apply Algorithm 4.1 to the right-hand sides of all EC-rules of R using 0-essentiality indicators of EC-rules instead of essentiality indicators. Let the 1-*inessential* arguments of $t_i\theta_i$ be all arguments whose descendants in $s_i\theta_i$ are in underlined subterms. Let the corresponding arguments of any $\langle r_i\rangle_e$-redex be 1-*inessential*, and let the 1-*essentiality indicator* of $\langle r_i\rangle_e$ be the list of numbers of arguments of any $\langle r_i\rangle_e$-redex that are not 1-inessential. Apply again Algorithm 4.1 to the right-hand sides of all EC-rules of R using 1-essentiality indicators of EC-rules instead of essentiality indicators; and so on. The algorithm stops after n_0 steps if n_0-essentiality indicator of each EC-rule in R coincides with its $(n_0 - 1)$-essentiality indicator. Let the n_0-inessential arguments of R-redexes be *inessential**. Then the essentiality indicator of $\langle r_i\rangle_e$ coincides with the list of non-inessential* arguments of $t_i\theta_i$.

Proof. An easy induction on n shows that n-inessential arguments of each redex are inessential; the case $n = 0$ follows from Lemma 3.6, and the induction step follows from Lemmas 4.2 and 3.1.(2). Now let us prove by induction on k that if, for an EC-rule $\langle r_i\rangle_e$, there is an $\langle r_i\rangle_e$-redex u whose j-th argument s_j (is inessential and) is erased by some reduction P with a length $|P| \le k$, then the j-th argument e_j of $t_i\theta_i$ is inessential*. The case $k = 1$ is obvious. So suppose $P : u \xrightarrow{u} o \twoheadrightarrow e$. Let s'_j be a descendant of s_j in o, and let v be the minimal redex that contains s'_j and has a descendant in e. Suppose that $v \in \langle r_m\rangle_e$ and s'_j is in its p-th argument. By Lemma 3.7, there is a reduction Q starting from v with a length less than k, such that the p-th argument of v does not have Q-descendants. Hence, by the induction assumption, the p-th argument of $t\theta_m$ is inessential*. Similarly, any descendant of s_j in o is in an inessential* argument of some redex. Since $CS(t_i\theta_i) = ECS(t_i\theta_i) = ECS(u) \subseteq CS(u)$, for any descendant e'_j of e_j there is a descendant s^*_j of s_j in o that is not in an inessential argument of a non-created redex and such that, for any $q = 1, \ldots, l$, e'_j is in an argument of an $\langle r_q\rangle_e$-redex iff s^*_j is in the corresponding argument of a created $\langle r_q\rangle_e$-redex. Hence, any descendant of e_j in $s_i\theta_i$ is in an inessential* argument of some redex, and e_j itself is inessential*.

Example 4.1 In order to illustrate Algorithm 4.2, let us consider the following HRPS $R = \{\sigma a(A, B) \to (\varepsilon a(A)/a)B,\ \delta a(A) \to \sigma a(A, f(A)),\ f(A) \to g(A, A),\ g(A, B) \to const\}$, where a is an object metavariable, A, B are term metavariables, f, g are function symbols, σ, ε, and δ are quantifier signs with arities $(1,2)$, $(1,1)$, and $(1,1)$, and scope indicators $(1,2)$, (1), and (1), respectively. The rule for σ has four trivial instances $r_1 : \sigma x(x, x) \to (\varepsilon x(x)/x)x = \varepsilon x(x)$, $r_2 : \sigma x(x, y) \to (\varepsilon x(x)/x)y = y$, $r_3 : \sigma x(y, x) \to (\varepsilon x(y)/x)x = \varepsilon x(y)$, and $r_4 : \sigma x(y, y) \to (\varepsilon x(y)/x)y = y$ with $ECSs$ $\{(a, A), (a, B)\}, \{(a, A)\}, \{(a, B)\}$, and $\{\}$, respectively. Similarly, we can choose trivial instances of the rules for δ, f, and g: $r_5 : \delta x(x) \to \sigma x(x, f(x))$, $r_6 : \delta x(y) \to \sigma x(y, f(y))$, $r_7 : f(x) \to g(x, x)$, and $r_8 : g(x, y) \to const$. The result of Algorithm 4.2 is then as follows:

$$r_1 : \sigma x(x, x) \to (\varepsilon x(x)/x)x = \varepsilon x(x) \qquad r_5 : \delta x(\overbrace{\ x\ }^{2}) \to \sigma x(\underline{x}_{2,3}, f(\underline{x}_{2,3}))$$

$$r_2 : \sigma x(\overbrace{\ x\ }^{0}, y) \to (\varepsilon x(x)/x)y = y \qquad r_6 : \delta x(\overbrace{\ y\ }^{2}) \to \sigma x(\underline{y}_{1,2,3}, f(\underline{y}_{2,3}))$$

$$r_3 : \sigma x(y, x) \to (\varepsilon x(y)/x)x = \varepsilon x(y) \qquad r_7 : f(\overbrace{\ x\ }^{1}) \to g(\underline{x}_{1,2,3}), \underline{x}_{1,2,3}))$$

$$r_4 : \sigma x(\overbrace{\ y\ }^{0}, y) \to (\varepsilon x(y)/x)y = y \qquad r_8 : g(\overbrace{\ x\ }^{0}, \overbrace{\ y\ }^{0}) \to const$$

where $\overbrace{\quad}^{i}$ indicates that the subterm is i-inessential and $\underline{\ }_j$ indicates that the underlining was made in j-th running of Algorithm 4.1 (we have $j \leq 3$). Note that, for example, the ECS of the right-hand side $\sigma x(x, f(x))$ of r_5 used in the second running is a proper subset of ECS of $\sigma x(x, f(x))$ used in the first running, and this makes it possible to determine that the argument x of the left-hand side $\delta x(x)$ of r_5 is 2-inessential, and hence inessential.

Theorem 4.1 (1) Weak normalization is decidable in HRPSs.
(2) HRPSs do not have full computational power.
(3) Strong normalization is decidable in HRPSs.

Proof. (1) From Lemmas 4.1-4.3. (2) From (1). (3) From Lemmas 4.1.

5 Persistent systems

Without restricting the class of OERSs we can assume that in right-hand sides of rewrite rules the last argument of each metasubstitution is a term-metavariable or a metasubstitution.

Definition 5.1 Let R be an orthogonal ERS.
(1) Let $t \stackrel{u}{\to} s$, let $t \to t' \twoheadrightarrow s$ be its expansion, let $o \subseteq t'$ be the contractum of u in R_f, and let v be a new redex in s. We call v *generated* if v is a residual of a redex w of t' whose pattern is in the pattern of o. We call v *uniformly generated* if the pattern of w is in the pattern of o and is not inside an $\underline{S}$-redex. We call v *quasi-generated* if any of its pattern-subterms is a descendant of a pattern-subterm of o that is not an $\underline{S}$-redex.
(2) We call R respectively *persistent* (PERS), *uniformly persistent*, or *quasi-persistent* if, for any R-reduction step, each created redex is generated, uniformly generated, or quasi-generated.

A quasi-persistent ERS that is not persistent was considered in the introduction. It is easy to see that a non-simple OERS R is an HRPS iff R_{fS} is persistent. Obviously, a PERS need not be an HRPS.

We call a subterm s in t *free* if s is not a proper pattern-subterm of a redex in t. It is easy to see that all free subterms remain free under any reduction in PERSs. This fails already for quasi-persistent systems. All properties of similar and essentially similar terms in HRPSs are valid because all subterms are free in HRPSs. Therefore, it is not difficult to check that this properties remain valid for all PERSs if in the definition of similarity and essential similarity one requires the replaced subterms to be free; Theorem 4.1 generalizes to PERSs as well.

Obviously, a PERS R is weakly (resp. strongly) normalizing iff all essential chains (resp. all chains) in R are finite. For any subsystem R' of R, we call an R-redex u *$ECS_{R'}$-complete* if each binding variable of a pattern quantifier of u has an R'-essential free occurrence in each argument that belongs to its binding scope. It can be shown that any R-essential chain (resp. any chain) of a redex w is a subsequence of an R-essential chain (resp. chain) of an ECS_R-complete (resp. $ECS_\emptyset$-complete) redex that is weakly similar to w. Thus, in order to establish weak (strong) normalization of a PERS, it is enough to check essential chains (chains) of ECS_R-complete ($ECS_\emptyset$-complete) redexes only.

6 Optimal normalization in persistent ERSs

Theorem 6.1 Let t be a term in a uniformly persistent ERS. Contraction of innermost essential redexes gives a reduction of t to normal form with the least number of steps, whenever the normal form exists.

Proof sketch. Let $P : t = t_0 \xrightarrow{u_0} \ldots \to t_n$ be a normalizing reduction starting from t and $Q : t = s_0 \xrightarrow{v_0} s_1 \xrightarrow{v_1} \ldots$ be an innermost essential reduction. It can be shown by induction on i that, for each $i < |Q|$, there is a number $n_i < n$ such that $ES(u_{n_i}, t_{n_i})$, $u_{n_i} \approx v_i$, and $i \neq j$ implies $n_i \neq n_j$. Therefore $|Q| \leq |P|$.

Thus, one can construct optimal sequential normalizing reductions in uniformly persistent ERSs. For PERSs in general, sharing of redexes of the same family [14, 1] is necessary. For example, one can check that all normalizing reductions starting from a term $\sigma x(f(x))$ in the following PERS $R = \{\sigma a(A) \to (\varepsilon a(A)/a)A, \varepsilon a(A) \to (\tau a(A)/a)A, f(A) \to g(A, A)\}$ must contract two copies of at least one generated redex. Alternatively, for each PERS one can construct its *irreducible* version, by eliminating all defined symbols in the right-hand sides of rules. To avoid (sometimes vain) substitutions during reduction steps, one can instead use trivial instances of the rules in the following way (we consider only the case of HRPSs). Let $r : t = \sigma a_1 \ldots a_n A_1 \ldots A_m \to s$ and let θ be an admissible assignment such that $t\theta \in \langle r \rangle_e$ and $A_i\theta = f_l(x_{i_1}, \ldots, x_{i_k})$, where $x_{i_j} = \theta(a_{i_j})$ and f_l is a fresh function symbol, chosen different for each EC-rule $\langle r \rangle_e$ and each i. By Theorem 4.1, one can decide wheither $t\theta$ has a normal form t' and find it. Let us call $t\theta \to t'$ the *irreducible $\langle r \rangle_e$-rule* (it is not an ERS rule, but represents the irreducible rule whose admissible assignments are all assignments θ' such that $t\theta' \in \langle r \rangle_e$). Then, for any $\langle r \rangle_e$-redex $u = \sigma x_1, \ldots, x_n s_1 \ldots s_m$, one defines its *contractum according to $t\theta \to t'$* to be the normal form of t' with respect to the rules $f_l(x_{i_1}, \ldots, x_{i_k}) \to s_i$. Now an optimal normalizing reduction of a normalizable term o in an HRPS R consists of execution of essential redexes in an inside out order according to the irreducible EC-rules; and the length of the reduction coincides with the number of essential redexes in o.

Acknowledgments I thank G. Gonthier and L. Maranget for many suggestions, R. Kennaway, B. Pierce, and F. J. de Vries for careful reading, and J.W. Klop and J.-J. Lévy for their support during my stay at CWI and INRIA.

References

1. Asperti A, Laneve C. Interaction Systems 1. The theory of optimal reductions. INRIA Report 1748, 1992.
2. Barendregt H. P. The Lambda Calculus, its Syntax and Semantics. North-Holland, 1984.
3. Courcelle B. Recursive Applicative Program Schemes. In: J. van Leeuwen ed. Handbook of Theoretical Computer Science, Chapter 9, vol.B, 1990, p. 459-492.
4. Dershowitz N., Jouannaud J.-P. Rewrite Systems. In: J.van Leeuwen ed. Handbook of Theoretical Computer Science, Chapter 6, vol. B, 1990, p. 243-320.
5. Huet G., Lévy J.-J. Computations in Orthogonal Rewriting Systems. In Computational Logic, Essays in Honour of Alan Robinson, ed. by J.-L. Lassez and G. Plotkin, MIT Press, 1991.
6. Khasidashvili Z. The Church-Rosser theorem in Orthogonal Combinatory Reduction Systems. INRIA Report 1825, 1992.
7. Khasidashvili Z. Optimal normalization in orthogonal term rewriting systems. In: Proc. of the fifth International Conference on Rewriting Techniques and Applications, Springer LNCS, vol. 690, C. Kirchner, ed. Montreal, 1993, p. 243-258.
8. Khasidashvili Z. Perpetuality and strong normalization in orthogonal term rewriting systems. CWI report CS-R9345, 1993. To appear in: Proc. of 11-th Symposium on Theoretical Aspects of Computer Science, Springer LNCS, Caen, 1994.
9. Khasidashvili Z. Higher order recursive program schemes are Turing incomplete. CWI report CS-R9348, 1993.
10. Khasidashvili Z. Perpetual reductions in orthogonal combinatory reduction systems. CWI report CS-R9349, 1993.
11. Klop J. W. Combinatory Reduction Systems. Mathematical Centre Tracts n.127, CWI, Amsterdam, 1980.
12. Klop J. W. Term Rewriting Systems. In: S. Abramsky, D. Gabbay, and T. Maibaum eds. Handbook of Logic in Computer Science, vol. II, Oxford University Press, 1992, p. 1-116.
13. Klop J. W., van Oostrom V., van Raamsdonk F. Combinatory reduction Systems: introduction and survey. In: To Corrado Böhm, J. of Theoretical Computer Science 121, 1993, p. 279-308.
14. Lévy J.-J. Optimal Reduction in the Lambda-Calculus. In: To H. B. Curry Essays on Combinatory Logic, Lambda Calculus and Formalism, J. P. Seldin and J. R. Hindley eds, Academic Press, 1980.
15. Maranget L. "La stratégie paresseuse", These de l'Université' de Paris VII, 1992.
16. Pkhakadze Sh. Some problems of the Notation Theory (in Russian). Proceedings of I. Vekua Institute of Applied Mathematics of Tbilisi State University, 1977.

Graphs and Decidable Transductions Based on Edge Constraints
(Extended Abstract)

Nils Klarlund* & Michael I. Schwartzbach**

Aarhus University, Department of Computer Science,
Ny Munkegade, DK-8000 Århus, Denmark
{klarlund,mis}@daimi.aau.dk

Abstract. We give examples to show that not even **c-edNCE**, the most general known notion of context-free graph grammar, is suited for the specification of some common data structures.
To overcome this problem, we use monadic second-order logic and introduce *edge constraints* as a new means of specifying a large class of graph families. Our notion stems from a natural dichotomy found in programming practice between ordinary pointers forming spanning trees and auxiliary pointers cutting across.
Our main result is that for certain transformations of graphs definable in monadic second-order logic, the question of whether a graph family given by a specification $\mathcal{A}$ is mapped to a family given by a specification $\mathcal{B}$ is decidable. Thus a decidable Hoare logic arises.

1 Introduction

Graphs are complicated objects to describe. Thus various grammars and logics have emerged for their representation, see the chapter by Courcelle [1]. The *monadic second-order logic of graphs* (M2L-G) allows a very large class of graph families to be described. The first-order terms of the logic denote nodes. The second-order terms denote sets of nodes. Nodes and edges are related by built-in predicates. The M2L-G formalism is very well-suited for describing properties of some common data structures, see our earlier paper [5].

Some authors consider logics that comprise quantification over edges. For these logics, a fundamental result is that a family of graphs allows a decidable M2L if and only if the family is specified by a *hyperedge-replacement grammar* [2]. Such grammars constitute a natural generalization of context-free grammars for string languages.

An even larger class of context-free grammars is known as **c-edNCE**. The monadic logic of graph families thus given is undecidable, but certain other questions, such a non-emptiness of a specification, are decidable, see [4].

* The author is supported by a fellowship from the Danish Research Council.

** The author is partially supported by the BRICS Center under the Danish Research Foundation.

For programming purposes, we would like to describe common data structures found in the store such as trees and doubly-linked lists. Indeed, this is possible within the framework of decidable formalisms as e.g. hyperedge-replacement grammars. Many other graph shapes are not representable. But whatever specification formalism we choose, we should be able to represent trees with additional, unconstrained pointers—reflecting a situation where almost nothing is said about the store, as is the case with type systems of most imperative programming languages.

We show in this paper that not even **c-edNCE** grammars are able to define such families of graphs.

To reason about data structures, it is vital to model the execution of programs. Therefore, we must formulate ways of transforming graphs corresponding to statements in a programming language. For program correctness, we would use Hoare logic to show that the store transformations leave the graph specifications satisfied.

In this paper we consider restricted graph transformations, called *transductions*, which are based on the method of *semantic interpretation* [7] and studied in [3]. Given logical graph specifications $\mathcal{A}$ and $\mathcal{B}$ and a transduction, we address the problem of verifying what we call *transductional correctness*: for any graph satisfying $\mathcal{A}$, any graph resulting from the transduction satisfies $\mathcal{B}$. This informal definition omits the difficulty of having shared logical variables in $\mathcal{A}$ and $\mathcal{B}$—a problem that is explicitly solved in this paper. Decidability of transductional correctness amounts to decidability of the corresponding Hoare logic.

Contributions of this paper

We devise a class of graph specifications

- that may model loosely restrained edges, and
- for which transductional correctness is decidable.

Our graphs consist of *ordinary edges* constituting an underlying spanning forest, called the *backbone*, and *auxiliary edges* cutting across the backbone.

These notions stem from a natural dichotomy found in programming practice between ordinary pointers forming spanning trees and auxiliary pointers cutting across as used for short-cuts (such as extra links pointing backward to previous elements) or for indexing into other data structures using unrestrained pointers.

Our graph specifications are based on combining the full M2L in form of a *backbone formula* for specifying ordinary edges together with a special M2L syntax, called *edge constraints*, for specifying auxiliary edges. The formulas in an edge constraint involve only the backbone to specify the sources and destinations of auxiliary edges. The resulting class of graph families thus definable is called **EC**. We show that the classes **c-edNCE** and **EC** are incomparable.

We next introduce a class of transductions. They are formulated in M2L and are similar to the ones considered in [3]. We use extra logical variables to model edges that are followed, deleted, or added during the transformation of the graph.

Our main result is that the transduction problem is decidable for **EC**. This result is based on a rather complicated encoding of the effects of the transduction within M2L on the backbone alone. The obstacle that we overcome is that it is impossible to directly represent all auxiliary edges in the logic of the backbone. The key idea is to distinguish between the bounded number of auxiliary edges that are explicitly manipulated by the transduction and the others, which are represented by a universal quantification in the logic.

Our other work

In an accompanying paper [6], we outline a typing system for data structures and define a programming language. The typing information is expressed in a logic on the underlying recursive data types. The programming language provides assignment, dereference, allocation, deallocation, and limited forms of iterations based on regular walks. We show in [6] that the operational semantics is captured by transductions and that by the results in this paper the resulting Hoare logic on data structures is decidable.

In [5], we also used monadic second-order logic to reason about data structures as graphs, but we restricted ourselves to trees with auxiliary edges that are functionally determined by the backbone in terms of regular walks.

2 Rooted Graphs

A *graph alphabet* Λ consists of a finite set $\Lambda^{\mathbf{V}}$ of node labels (which include a special label **spare**) and a finite set $\Lambda^{\mathbf{E}}$ of edge labels. Usually, we denote a node label by v. There are two kinds of edge labels: *ordinary* and *auxiliary*. Usually, an ordinary edge label is denoted f and an auxiliary edge label is denoted a. An edge label that is either ordinary or auxiliary is denoted n.

A *rooted graph* G over Λ consists of a finite set $G^{\mathbf{V}}$ of labeled nodes; a finite set $G^{\mathbf{E}}$ of labeled edges; and a finite set of node variables x, called *roots*, denoting nodes in GThe label of node $v \in G^{\mathbf{V}}$ is denoted $G^{\mathbf{L}}(v)$. Nodes are either *ordinary* or *spare* according to their label. An edge from v to w labeled n is denoted (v, n, w). For each v and n, there is at most one such edge. Loops are allowed. The edges of G are divided into *ordinary* and *auxiliary* ones according to their label. The node denoted by root x is written x^G.

The set of all graphs over Λ is denoted $\mathbf{GR}(\Lambda)$. An *edge set* $\mathcal{E}$ is a set of edges such that $(v, \mathsf{n}, w) \in \mathcal{E}$ and $(v, \mathsf{n}, u) \in \mathcal{E}$ implies $w = u$.

We sometimes view G as consisting of $\overline{G}$, called the *backbone*, which is all of G except for the auxiliary edges, and $\overline{\overline{G}}$, which is the edge set of auxiliary edges in G. Thus, G may be written as $(\overline{G}, \overline{\overline{G}})$.

The spare nodes model free memory cells in programming language applications. They are essential to allow addition and deletion of nodes by transductions.

Figure 1 shows a sketch of a rooted graph. The ordinary edges are drawn as solid arrows, whereas the auxiliary edges are dashed; spare nodes are black; the roots are called x_1, x_2, and x_3.

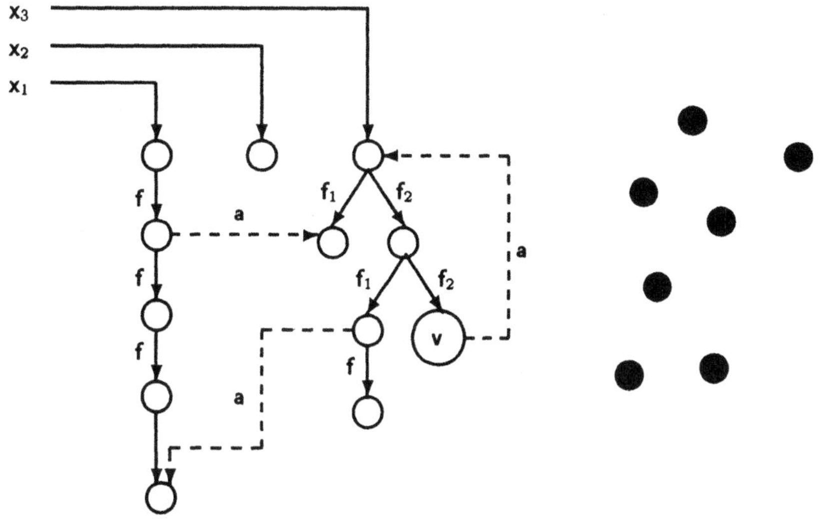

Fig. 1. A rooted graph.

3 The Logic M2L-BB

The key to specifying data structures is the *Monadic Second-Order of Backbones*, abbreviated *M2L-BB*. First-order terms range over nodes in the graph. Second-order terms range over *sets* of nodes.

Syntax

Assume a graph alphabet Λ. The logic of rooted graphs over Λ is denoted M2L-BB(Λ). Its syntax is as follows.

Address terms $\boldsymbol{A}$ denote nodes in the graph.

$\boldsymbol{A}$	$::=$	x	root
		src	source
		dst	destination
		$\alpha, \beta, \ldots$	first-order variable

The terms **src** and **dst** are special variables used in certain assertions. *Address set terms* $\boldsymbol{\Sigma}$ denote sets of nodes.

$\boldsymbol{\Sigma}$	$::=$	$\emptyset$	empty set
		$\boldsymbol{\Sigma}_1 \cup \boldsymbol{\Sigma}_2$	set union
		$\boldsymbol{\Sigma}_1 \setminus \boldsymbol{\Sigma}_2$	set difference
		$S, T, \ldots$	second-order variable

Formulas $\boldsymbol{\Phi}$ denote **true** or **false**.

$\boldsymbol{\Phi}$	$::=$	$\boldsymbol{A}_1 = \boldsymbol{A}_2$	equality

$\boldsymbol{A} \in \boldsymbol{\Sigma}$	set membership
$\boldsymbol{\Sigma}_1 \subseteq \boldsymbol{\Sigma}_2$	set inclusion
$\boldsymbol{A}_1 \xrightarrow{\mathsf{f}} \boldsymbol{A}_2$	successor relation, where $\mathsf{f} \in \Lambda^{\mathbf{E}}$ is ordinary
$\mathsf{v}?\boldsymbol{A}$	test for node label, where $\mathsf{v} \in \Lambda^{\mathbf{V}}$
$\neg\boldsymbol{\Phi}$	negation
$\boldsymbol{\Phi}_1 \wedge \boldsymbol{\Phi}_2$	conjunction
$\exists^0\alpha : \boldsymbol{\Phi}$	first-order quantification over all nodes
$\exists^0 S : \boldsymbol{\Phi}$	second-order quantification over all nodes

Note that the syntax does not allow references to auxiliary edges. We also use unmarked quantifiers that range only over ordinary nodes. They can be viewed as abbreviations according to the following.

$$\exists\alpha : \boldsymbol{\Phi} \equiv \exists^\circ\alpha : \neg\mathbf{spare?}\alpha \wedge \boldsymbol{\Phi}$$
$$\exists S : \boldsymbol{\Phi} \equiv \exists^\circ S : (\neg\exists^\circ\alpha : \alpha \in S \wedge \mathbf{spare?}\alpha) \wedge \boldsymbol{\Phi}$$

We also assume abbreviations $\forall$, $\Rightarrow$, $\vee$, etc.

Semantics

M2L-BB is interpreted relative to a backbone $\overline{G}$. The interpretation of x is given by $\overline{G}$ as $\mathsf{x}^{\overline{G}}$. The constants **dst** and **src** are used as variables. The semantics of variables is formulated below by substitution for values in $\overline{G}^{\mathbf{V}}$. A value v is interpreted as itself, i.e. $v^{\overline{G}} = v$. A non-variable address set term $\boldsymbol{\Sigma}$ is interpreted as follows.

$$\emptyset^{\overline{G}} = \emptyset$$
$$(\boldsymbol{\Sigma}_1 \cup \boldsymbol{\Sigma}_2)^{\overline{G}} = \boldsymbol{\Sigma}_1^{\overline{G}} \cup \boldsymbol{\Sigma}_2^{\overline{G}}$$
$$(\boldsymbol{\Sigma}_1 \backslash \boldsymbol{\Sigma}_2)^{\overline{G}} = \boldsymbol{\Sigma}_1^{\overline{G}} \backslash \boldsymbol{\Sigma}_2^{\overline{G}}$$

The semantics of formulas is as follows.

$\overline{G} \models \boldsymbol{A}_1 = \boldsymbol{A}_2$	if $\boldsymbol{A}_1^{\overline{G}} = \boldsymbol{A}_2^{\overline{G}}$
$\overline{G} \models \boldsymbol{A} \in \boldsymbol{\Sigma}$	if $\boldsymbol{A}^{\overline{G}} \in \boldsymbol{\Sigma}^{\overline{G}}$
$\overline{G} \models \boldsymbol{\Sigma}_1 \subseteq \boldsymbol{\Sigma}_2$	if $\boldsymbol{\Sigma}_1^{\overline{G}} \subseteq \boldsymbol{\Sigma}_2^{\overline{G}}$
$\overline{G} \models \boldsymbol{A}_1 \xrightarrow{\mathsf{f}} \boldsymbol{A}_2$	if $(\boldsymbol{A}_1^{\overline{G}}, \mathsf{f}, \boldsymbol{A}_2^{\overline{G}}) \in \overline{G}^{\mathbf{E}}$
$\overline{G} \models \mathsf{v}?\boldsymbol{A}$	if $\overline{G}^{\mathbf{L}}(\boldsymbol{A}^{\overline{G}}) = \mathsf{v}$
$\overline{G} \models \neg\boldsymbol{\Phi}$	if not $\overline{G} \models \boldsymbol{\Phi}$
$\overline{G} \models \boldsymbol{\Phi}_1 \wedge \boldsymbol{\Phi}_2$	if $\overline{G} \models \boldsymbol{\Phi}_1$ and $\overline{G} \models \boldsymbol{\Phi}_2$
$\overline{G} \models \exists^\circ\alpha : \boldsymbol{\Phi}$	if there is $v \in \overline{G}^{\mathbf{V}}$ such that $\overline{G} \models \boldsymbol{\Phi}(\alpha \mapsto v)$
$\overline{G} \models \exists^\circ S : \boldsymbol{\Phi}$	if there is $V \subseteq \overline{G}^{\mathbf{V}}$ such that $\overline{G} \models \boldsymbol{\Phi}(S \mapsto V)$,

If $\boldsymbol{\Phi}$ has free variables $\mathfrak{F}$ and $\mathfrak{I}$ is an interpretation of these variables in $\overline{G}^{\mathbf{V}}$, then

$$\overline{G}, \mathfrak{I} \models \boldsymbol{\Phi} \text{ if } \overline{G} \models \boldsymbol{\Phi}(\mathfrak{F} \mapsto \mathfrak{I}).$$

If $\overline{G} \models \boldsymbol{\Phi}$ holds for all $\overline{G}$, then we say that $\boldsymbol{\Phi}$ is *valid* and we write $\models \boldsymbol{\Phi}$. A graph G is *tree-formed* if

- all edges are between ordinary nodes; and
- the graph induced by ordinary nodes and ordinary edges is a directed forest such that each root is the value of some root variable.

Note that the graph depicted in Figure 1 is tree-formed.

Lemma 1. *There is a formula Φ such that G is tree-formed if and only if $G \models \Phi$.*

Proof Among other conditions, acyclicity and reachability can be encoded in M2L-BB. □

We say that Φ is *tree-valid* and we write $\Vdash \Phi$ if $\overline{G} \models \Phi$ holds for all tree-formed $\overline{G}$.

Theorem 2. *Validity is undecidable, but tree-validity is decidable.*

Proof The first result follows from the undecidability of the first-order logic of finite graphs. The second result follows from the decidability of the monadic second-order logic of finite trees. □

Edge Constraints and Assertions

Constraints on auxiliary edges cannot just be formulas, since the logic refers only to ordinary edges. Instead, an *edge constraint* is of the form $[\sigma \xrightarrow{\mathsf{a}} \delta]$, where σ is a formula involving **src** as a free variable, and δ is a formula with free variables **src** and **dst**. The edge constraint is *valid* for a given graph if whenever σ is valid with a node v in place of **src**, then there is an a-edge (which is unique by definition of a rooted graph) from v to some node w and δ is valid with v and w in place of **src** and **dst**. Note that the edge constraint does not describe any a-edges outside where σ holds.

Formally, let $[\sigma \xrightarrow{\mathsf{a}} \delta]$ be an edge constraint with free variables $\mathfrak{F}$. We say that G and $\mathfrak{F}$ *satisfy* $[\sigma \xrightarrow{\mathsf{a}} \delta]$, and we write $G, \mathfrak{F} \models [\sigma \xrightarrow{\mathsf{a}} \delta]$ if:

for all $v \in G^{\mathsf{V}}$, $G, \mathfrak{F} \models \sigma(\mathbf{src} \mapsto v)$ implies
for some $(v, \mathsf{a}, w) \in \overline{G}$, $G, \mathfrak{F} \models \delta(\mathbf{src} \mapsto v, \mathbf{dst} \mapsto w)$.

An *assertion* $\mathcal{A} = \Phi[\sigma_1 \xrightarrow{\mathsf{a}_1} \delta_1] \ldots [\sigma_n \xrightarrow{\mathsf{a}_n} \delta_n]$ consists of a formula Φ, called the *backbone formula*, and a number of edge constraints $[\sigma_i \xrightarrow{\mathsf{a}_i} \delta_i]$. These components are connected through free variables, which are implictly existentially quantified.

Let $\mathfrak{F}$ be a list containing the free variables and let $\mathfrak{F}$ be a value assignment to these variables. An assertion $\mathcal{A}$ is *satisfied* in G with $\mathfrak{F}$, and we write $G, \mathfrak{F} \models \mathcal{A}$, if $\overline{G}, \mathfrak{F} \models \Phi$ and for all i, $G, \mathfrak{F} \models [\sigma_i \xrightarrow{\mathsf{a}_i} \delta_i]$.

An assertion $\mathcal{A}$ specifies the language of graphs

$$\{G \mid G \text{ is tree-formed and for some } \mathfrak{F},\ G, \mathfrak{F} \models \mathcal{A}\}$$

The class of such graph languages is called **EC**.

Example

Consider the common data structure, shown in Figure 2, of linked lists with a head node that points both to the first element of the list and to some designated element. The f- and n-edges are ordinary; the s-edge is auxiliary.

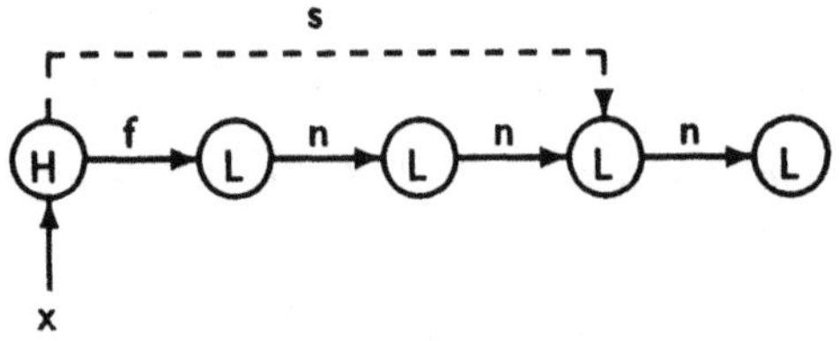

Fig. 2. A list structure

The corresponding backbone formula contains these clauses.

$\mathsf{H}?\mathsf{x}$	*The head node has label* H
$\exists\alpha : \mathsf{x} \xrightarrow{\mathsf{f}} \alpha$	*and an outgoing* f*-edge;*
$\forall\beta,\beta' : \beta \xrightarrow{\mathsf{f}} \beta' \Rightarrow \beta = \mathsf{x}$	*no other node has an outgoing* f*-edge;*
$\forall\beta : \neg\beta{=}\mathsf{x} \Rightarrow \mathsf{L}?\beta$	*all other nodes have label* L*;*
$\forall\beta,\beta' : \beta \xrightarrow{\mathsf{n}} \beta' \Rightarrow \beta \neq \mathsf{x}$	*the head node has no outgoing* n*-edge;*
$\mathsf{L}?\gamma$	*and there is a designated* L*-node...*

Note that we quantify only over ordinary nodes. There is only a single edge constraint.

$[\mathsf{H}?\mathbf{src} \xrightarrow{\mathsf{s}} \gamma{=}\mathbf{dst}]$ *that is the destination of the* s*-edge.*

Here the free variable γ connects the backbone formula and the edge constraint. In conjunction with the general requirement of tree-formedness, this assertion describes backbones that are lists with a head node. Note that the assertion does not eliminate extraneous s-edges from nodes other than the one marked H. In a programming language application these are avoided through elementary type-checking of the transductions that build graphs [6].

4 Relations to Other Formalisms

It is interesting to compare the expressive power of this graph specification formalism with those of other proposals. In particular we show in this section that the set of trees with unrestrained auxiliary edges is not representable as a context-free graph grammar.

We look at the most general class known of context-free graphs languages: **c-edNCE**, which stands for "confluent edge and node labeled,directed graphs given by **N**eighborhood **C**ontrolled **E**mbedding." The grammars that define such languages are complicated. Instead we shall use a result by Engelfriet that these languages are exactly the images of trees under functions definable in monadic second-order logic [4]. The following definition is from [4] (but changed as to allow loops in graphs):

Let Λ_1 and Λ_2 be alphabets. An *M2L-definable function* $f : \mathbf{GR}(\Lambda_1) \to \mathbf{GR}(\Lambda_2)$ is given by the following formulas in M2L-BB(Λ_1):

- a closed formula ϕ_{dom}, called the *domain formula*;
- for every $\mathsf{v} \in \Lambda_2^{\mathbf{V}}$, a formula ϕ_{v}, called a *node formula*, with one free variable **src**; and
- for every $\mathsf{n} \in \Lambda_2^{\mathbf{E}}$, a formula ϕ_{n}, called an *edge formula*, with two free variables **src** and **dst**.

The domain of f is $\{G \in \mathbf{GR}(\Lambda_1) \mid G \models \phi_{dom}\}$. For every $G \in \text{dom}(f)$, the graph $G' = f(G) \in \mathbf{GR}(\Lambda_2)$ is given by

$$G'^{\mathbf{V}} = \{v \in G^{\mathbf{V}} \mid \text{there is exactly one } \mathsf{v} \in \Lambda_1^{\mathbf{V}} \text{such that } G \models \phi_{\mathsf{v}}(\mathbf{src} \mapsto v)\}$$
$$G'^{\mathbf{E}} = \{(v, \mathsf{n}, w) \mid v, w \in G^{\mathbf{V}} \text{and } G \models \phi_{\mathsf{n}}(\mathbf{src} \mapsto v, \mathbf{dst} \mapsto w)\}.$$

(For simplicity, we ignore roots in this section.)

Theorem 3. *[4] A language of graphs is* **c-edNCE** *if and only if it is the image of an M2L-definable function* $f : \mathbf{GR}(\Lambda_1) \to \mathbf{GR}(\Lambda_2)$ *applied to the set of directed trees over* Λ_1.

Such a language is then said to be *f-definable.*

Theorem 4. *[4] It is decidable whether a function f defines a finite language of graphs.*

Lemma 5. *[4] The class of M2L-definable functions is closed under composition.*

Now fix $\Lambda_T^{\mathbf{V}} = \{\mathsf{v}\}$, $\Lambda_T^{\mathbf{E}} = \{\mathsf{f}_1, \mathsf{f}_2, \mathsf{a}\}$. A *tree with equi-level edges* is a graph G over Λ_T such that G restricted to f-edges is a directed tree and such that $(v, \mathsf{a}, w) \in G^{\mathbf{E}}$ if and only if w is the left-most node to the right of v at the same level as v, as shown in Figure 3.

Lemma 6. *The set of trees over* Λ_T *with equi-level edges is not* **c-edNCE**.

Proof Suppose for a contradiction that the set is **c-edNCE** by means of an M2L-definable function f. Then there would be a uniform way of obtaining an M2L-definable function f_i whose graph language represents all finite sequences of configurations that TM (Turing Machine) i may produce with an empty input tape. In fact we may choose $\Lambda^{\mathbf{V}} = \{0, 1, \#\}$ and construct f_i' such that it maps trees with equi-level edges into trees whose $\Lambda^{\mathbf{V}}$ labels at level k encode the configuration of TM i after the k'th step (details are omitted). By Lemma 5, the set of graphs representing finite configuration sequences is then definable by a function $f_i = f_i' \circ f$. But then the Halting Problem would be decidable by Theorem 4, which is a contradiction. □

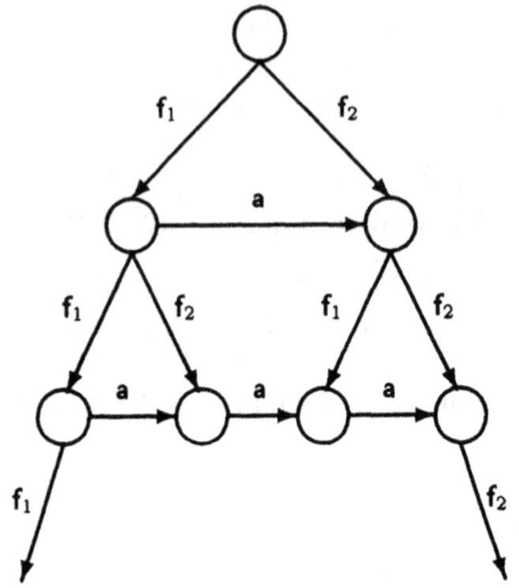

Fig. 3. A tree with equi-level edges.

Lemma 7. *The set of trees over* Λ_T *with unrestrained* a*-edges is not* **c-edNCE**.

Proof If it was we could use Lemmas 5 and 6 to show that also the set of trees with equi-level edges is **c-edNCE**. (We would construct a domain formula checking, among other things, that whenever (v, a, w) and (v', a, w') are edges and v' is a child of v, then w' is a child of w.) □

Theorem 8. **c-edNCE** *and* **EC** *are incomparable.*

Proof EC $\not\subseteq$ **c-edNCE**: The set of trees with unrestrained a-edges is certainly **EC**, but not **c-edNCE** by Lemma 7.

c-edNCE $\not\subseteq$ **EC**: The set of cyclic graphs over singleton node and edge alphabets is **c-edNCE**, but not **EC** (in fact, since the edge label determines whether an edge is ordinary or auxiliary, only list-like structures and certain degenerate structures can be described with singleton edge alphabets). □

5 Transductions

We are interested in graph transformations that model pointer manipulations in programs. These can be specified through a *transduction*, which is defined to be of the form $\mathcal{T} =< L, \mathcal{E}, \rho >$. The component L is a list of labeled *entries*. An entry t defines one or two first-order variables, called *transduction variables*, according to its label as follows.

- **add**-n: this indicates the creation of an n-edge between two nodes denoted by first-order terms **src**(t) and **dst**(t); an existing n-edge from the source is deleted.

- **del-n**: this indicates the deletion of the n-edge whose origin is denoted by the first-order term **src**(t).
- **foll-a**: this indicates the existence of an a-edge which has been followed between two cells denoted by first-order terms **src**(t) and **dst**(t); this makes for an explicit representation of auxiliary edges that are followed and, therefore, known to exist in the original graph.
- v: this indicates that a node denoted by the first-order logical variable **src**(t) is marked with label v (which may be **spare**); if an ordinary node is marked **spare**, then its outgoing and incoming edges are deleted.

The component $\mathcal{E}$ is an environment, which maps root variables to address terms denoting their values. The component ρ is a formula which must hold in order for the free variables in L and $\mathcal{E}$ to denote a transformation. The formula ρ may contain other transduction variables than those defined by L. Together they are designated $\boldsymbol{\mu}$.

The formula ρ must ensure that the entries are consistent with each other. Thus if a graph G and a value assignment $\underline{\boldsymbol{\mu}}$ are such that $G, \underline{\boldsymbol{\mu}} \models \rho$, then some examples of technical relationsships that most hold are:

- given any v and a, there are at most one **foll-a** entry t such that $G, \underline{\boldsymbol{\mu}} \models$ **src**(t) $= v$; and
- given any (v, a, w) that is marked by a **del-a** entry before any **add-a** entry, there is a **foll-a** entry, which makes explicit the assumption that (v, a, w) is an edge in G.

6 Predicate Transformers

Each transduction $\mathcal{T}$ determines a predicate transformer $\mathbf{Tr}_{\mathcal{T}}$. A formula $\boldsymbol{\Phi}$ is translated into $\mathbf{Tr}_{\mathcal{T}}\boldsymbol{\Phi}$ according to the following rules.

$$\begin{aligned}
\mathbf{Tr}_{\mathcal{T}}(\mathsf{x}) &= \mathcal{T}.\mathcal{E}(\mathsf{x}) \\
\mathbf{Tr}_{\mathcal{T}}(\alpha) &= \alpha \\
\mathbf{Tr}_{\mathcal{T}}(\boldsymbol{A}_1 = \boldsymbol{A}_2) &= \mathbf{Tr}_{\mathcal{T}}(\boldsymbol{A}_1) = \mathbf{Tr}_{\mathcal{T}}(\boldsymbol{A}_2)
\end{aligned}$$

$$\mathbf{Tr}_{\mathcal{T}}(\alpha \xrightarrow{\mathsf{f}} \beta) = \begin{cases} \beta = \mathbf{dst}(t) & \text{if } t \text{ is an } \mathbf{add}\text{-f entry in } \mathcal{T}.L, \alpha = \mathbf{src}(t), t \text{ is the last such entry, and no later } \mathbf{spare} \text{ entry } t' \text{ is such that } \mathbf{src}(t') \in \{\alpha, \beta\} \text{ and no later } \mathbf{del}\text{-f entry } t' \text{ is such that } \mathbf{src}(t') = \alpha \\ \mathbf{false} & \text{if there is a } \mathbf{spare} \text{ entry } t \text{ with } \mathbf{src}(t) \in \{\alpha, \beta\} \text{ or there is a } \mathbf{del}\text{-f entry } t \text{ with } \mathbf{src}(t) = \alpha, \text{ and no later } \mathbf{add}\text{-f entry } t' \text{ is such that } \mathbf{src}(t') = \alpha\} \\ \alpha \xrightarrow{\mathsf{f}} \beta & \text{otherwise} \end{cases}$$

$$\mathbf{Tr}_{\mathcal{T}}(\mathsf{v}?\alpha) = \begin{cases} \mathbf{true} & \text{if there is an v-entry } t \text{ in } \mathcal{T}.L \text{ such that } \mathbf{src}(t) = \alpha \text{ and no later v}'\text{-entry } t' \text{ is such that } \mathbf{src}(t') = \alpha \\ \mathsf{v}?\alpha & \text{otherwise} \end{cases}$$

$$\begin{aligned}
\mathbf{Tr}_{\mathcal{T}}(\boldsymbol{A} \in \boldsymbol{\Sigma}) &= \mathbf{Tr}_{\mathcal{T}}(\boldsymbol{A}) \in \boldsymbol{\Sigma} \\
\mathbf{Tr}_{\mathcal{T}}(\boldsymbol{\Sigma}_1 \subseteq \boldsymbol{\Sigma}_2) &= \boldsymbol{\Sigma}_1 \subseteq \boldsymbol{\Sigma}_2 \\
\mathbf{Tr}_{\mathcal{T}}(\neg\boldsymbol{\Phi}) &= \neg\mathbf{Tr}_{\mathcal{T}}\boldsymbol{\Phi} \\
\mathbf{Tr}_{\mathcal{T}}(\boldsymbol{\Phi}_1 \wedge \boldsymbol{\Phi}_2) &= \mathbf{Tr}_{\mathcal{T}}(\boldsymbol{\Phi}_1) \wedge \mathbf{Tr}_{\mathcal{L}}(\boldsymbol{\Phi}_2) \\
\mathbf{Tr}_{\mathcal{T}}(\exists^\circ \alpha : \boldsymbol{\Phi}) &= \exists^\circ \alpha : \mathbf{Tr}_{\mathcal{T}}\boldsymbol{\Phi} \\
\mathbf{Tr}_{\mathcal{T}}(\exists^\circ S : \boldsymbol{\Phi}) &= \exists^\circ S : \mathbf{Tr}_{\mathcal{T}}\boldsymbol{\Phi}
\end{aligned}$$

The *transformed backbone*, denoted $\mathbf{BB}_{\mathcal{T}}(\overline{\mathcal{G}}, \boldsymbol{\mu})$, according to $\mathcal{T}$ on $\overline{G}$ with transduction values $\boldsymbol{\mu}$ is the graph $\overline{G}'$ defined as follows.

- $\overline{G}'^{\mathbf{V}} = \overline{G}^{\mathbf{V}}$;
- $(v, \mathsf{f}, w) \in \overline{G}'^{\mathbf{E}}$ iff $\overline{G}, \boldsymbol{\mu} \models \mathbf{Tr}_{\mathcal{T}}(v \xrightarrow{\mathsf{f}} w)$;
- $\overline{G}'^{\mathbf{L}}(v) = \mathsf{v}$ iff $\overline{G}, \boldsymbol{\mu} \models \mathbf{Tr}_{\mathcal{T}}(\mathsf{v}?v)$; and
- $\mathsf{x}^{\overline{G}'}$ is the node v such that $\overline{G}, \boldsymbol{\mu} \models v = \mathbf{Tr}_{\mathcal{T}}(\mathcal{T}.\mathcal{E}(\mathsf{x}))$.

Lemma 9. *(Faithfulness) Let $\overline{G}' = \boldsymbol{BB}_{\mathcal{T}}(\overline{G}, \boldsymbol{\mu})$ and let $\boldsymbol{\mathfrak{F}}$ be a value assignment to the free variables of $\boldsymbol{\Phi}$. Then,*

$$\overline{G}', \boldsymbol{\mathfrak{F}} \models \boldsymbol{\Phi}$$

if and only if

$$\overline{G}, \boldsymbol{\mathfrak{F}}, \boldsymbol{\mu} \models \boldsymbol{Tr}_{\mathcal{T}}\boldsymbol{\Phi}$$

Proof (Sketch) By a straightforward structural induction. □

We say that $\overline{G}$, $\boldsymbol{\mu}$, and $\mathcal{T}$ determine a *transformation.* In addition to the transformed backbone, the transformation also determines:

- $\mathbf{Foll}_{\mathcal{T}}\text{-}\mathsf{a}(\overline{G}, \boldsymbol{\mu})$, the set of a-edges in the old graph G that were followed;
- $\mathbf{Del}_{\mathcal{T}}\text{-}\mathsf{a}(\overline{G}, \boldsymbol{\mu})$, the set of a-edges in the old graph G that were both followed and deleted; and
- $\mathbf{Add}_{\mathcal{T}}\text{-}\mathsf{a}(\overline{G}, \boldsymbol{\mu})$, the set of a-edges in the new graph G' that were added.

To specify $\mathbf{Foll}_{\mathcal{T}}\text{-}\mathsf{a}(\overline{G}, \boldsymbol{\mu})$, we define a predicate $\mathbf{Foll}_{\mathcal{T}}\text{-}\mathsf{a}$ with free variables **src** and **dst** expressing that an a-edge from **src** to **dst** was followed. Informally,

$\mathbf{Foll}_{\mathcal{T}}\text{-}\mathsf{a} \equiv$ "for some **foll-a** entry in $\mathcal{T}.L$, $\mathbf{src} = \mathbf{src}(t)$ and $\mathbf{dst} = \mathbf{dst}(t)$,"

which can be encoded as a formula. Now,

$$\mathbf{Foll}_{\mathcal{T}}\text{-}\mathsf{a}(\overline{G}, \boldsymbol{\mu}) = \{(v, \mathsf{a}, w) \mid \overline{G}, \boldsymbol{\mu}, \mathbf{src} \mapsto v, \mathbf{dst} \mapsto w \models \mathbf{Foll}_{\mathcal{T}}\text{-}\mathsf{a}\}.$$

Similarly, we define the two other sets by defining predicates $\mathbf{Del}_{\mathcal{T}}\text{-}\mathsf{a}$ and $\mathbf{Add}_{\mathcal{T}}\text{-}\mathsf{a}$:

$\mathbf{Del}_{\mathcal{T}}$-a $\equiv$ "$\mathbf{Foll}_{\mathcal{T}}$-a and there is some **spare** entry with **src** = **src**(t) or **dst** = **src**(t), or some **del-a** or **add-a** entry t with **src** = **src**(t)."

$\mathbf{Add}_{\mathcal{T}}$-a $\equiv$ "if there is an **add-a** entry t such that **src**(t) = **src** and **dst**(t) = **dst**, and no later entries delete this edge."

Lemma 10. $\mathbf{Del}_{\mathcal{T}}\text{-}a(\overline{G}, \underline{\mu}) \subseteq \mathbf{Foll}_{\mathcal{T}}\text{-}a(\overline{G}, \underline{\mu})$ *if* $G, \underline{\mu} \models \rho$.

Proof By the definitions and imposed technical relationships. □

The *transformation relation* induced by $\mathcal{T}$ is:

$$G \longrightarrow_{\mathcal{T}} G'$$

if and only if

for some $\underline{\mu}$:

$$\overline{G}, \underline{\mu} \models \mathcal{T}.\rho,$$
$$\mathbf{Foll\text{-}a}_{\mathcal{T}}(\overline{G}, \underline{\mu}) \subseteq \overline{\overline{G}},$$
$$\overline{G}' = \mathbf{BB}_{\mathcal{T}}(\overline{G}, \underline{\mu}), \text{ and}$$
$$\overline{\overline{G}}' = (\overline{\overline{G}} \backslash \mathbf{Del\text{-}a}_{\mathcal{T}}(\overline{G}, \underline{\mu})) \cup \mathbf{Add\text{-}a}_{\mathcal{T}}(\overline{G}, \underline{\mu})$$

Example (continued)

Consider the linked list with a designated element from Section 4. A common transduction on such structures is the insertion of an new element just before the head. This is realized by the following transduction.

$\mathcal{L}$: $\mathsf{L}(\mu')$.**del**-$\mathsf{f}(\mathsf{x}, \mu)$.**add**-$\mathsf{f}(\mathsf{x}, \mu')$.**add**-$\mathsf{n}(\mu', \mu)$
$\mathcal{E}$: $\mathsf{x} \mapsto \mathsf{x}$
ρ: $\mathsf{x} \xrightarrow{\mathsf{f}} \mu \wedge \mathbf{spare?}\mu'$

Notice how this closely mimics the code that one would write in a conventional programming language. The expressive power of transductions goes beyond mere straight-line code, since regular control structures can be encoded in formulas [5].

7 Transductional Invariance

Let $\mathfrak{A}$ be the free variables in the assertion $\mathcal{A}$ and let $\mathfrak{B}$ be the free variables in the assertion $\mathcal{B}$ that are not already free in $\mathcal{A}$. The problem of transductional correctness is:

> Given assertions $\mathcal{A}$, $\mathcal{B}$, and a transduction $\mathcal{T}$. Does it hold for all G, G', and $\underline{\mathfrak{A}}$ that if G is tree-formed and satisfies $\mathcal{A}$ with $\underline{\mathfrak{A}}$, and if $G \longrightarrow_{\mathcal{T}} G'$, then G' is tree-formed and satisfies $\mathcal{B}$ for some $\underline{\mathfrak{B}}$?

Since tree-formedness by Lemma 1 can be encoded as a backbone formula, we can without loss of generality rephrase the question as follows. We say that the triple $\mathcal{A}\{\mathcal{T}\}\mathcal{B}$ is *tree-valid*, and write $\Vdash \mathcal{A}\{\mathcal{T}\}\mathcal{B}$, if:

$$\text{for all tree-formed } G, \text{all } G', \text{ and all } \underline{\mathfrak{A}},\ G, \underline{\mathfrak{A}} \models \mathcal{A} \text{ and } G \longrightarrow_{\mathcal{T}} G' \text{ implies there is } \underline{\mathfrak{B}} \text{ such that } G', \underline{\mathfrak{B}} \models \mathcal{B}$$

Note that triple tree-validity concerns only transformations of tree-formed graphs.

Our main result is to demonstrate that tree triple validity can be encoded in M2L-BB. For simplicity we assume in what follows that an assertion now contains only one edge constraint, and that $\mathcal{A} = \Phi[\sigma \xrightarrow{\mathsf{a}} \delta]$ and $\mathcal{B} = \Phi'[\sigma' \xrightarrow{\mathsf{a}} \delta']$. Then we say that triple $\mathcal{A}\{\mathcal{T}\}\mathcal{B}$ is *provable* and write $\vdash \mathcal{A}\{\mathcal{T}\}\mathcal{B}$ if

$$\begin{array}{l} \Vdash \forall^\circ \mathfrak{A} : \forall^\circ \boldsymbol{\mu} : \\ \quad (\Phi \ \wedge\ \rho \ \wedge\ \forall^\circ \mathbf{src} \exists^\circ \mathbf{dst} : (\sigma \Rightarrow\ (\delta \ \wedge\ (\neg \mathbf{Foll}_{\mathcal{T}} \Rightarrow (\forall^\circ \mathbf{dst} : \neg \mathbf{Foll}_{\mathcal{T}})))) \\ \quad\quad \Rightarrow \exists^\circ \mathfrak{B} : (\mathbf{Tr}_{\mathcal{T}} \Phi' \\ \quad\quad\quad\quad \wedge\, \forall^\circ \mathbf{src} : \mathbf{Tr}_{\mathcal{T}} \sigma' \ \Rightarrow \\ \quad\quad\quad\quad\quad\quad ((\exists^\circ \mathbf{dst} : \mathbf{Add}_{\mathcal{T}} \ \wedge\ \mathbf{Tr}_{\mathcal{T}} \delta') \\ \quad\quad\quad\quad\quad\quad \vee (\exists^\circ \mathbf{dst} : \mathbf{Foll}_{\mathcal{T}} \ \wedge\ \neg \mathbf{Del}_{\mathcal{T}} \ \wedge\ \mathbf{Tr}_{\mathcal{T}} \delta') \\ \quad\quad\quad\quad\quad\quad \vee (\sigma \ \wedge\ \forall^\circ \mathbf{dst} : \neg \mathbf{Add}_{\mathcal{T}} \wedge \neg \mathbf{Foll}_{\mathcal{T}} \wedge\ (\delta \Rightarrow \mathbf{Tr}_{\mathcal{T}} \delta')))) \end{array}$$

8 Soundness, Completeness, and Decidability

Theorem 11. *(Soundness)* $\vdash \mathcal{A}\{\mathcal{T}\}\mathcal{B}$ *implies* $\Vdash \mathcal{A}\{\mathcal{T}\}\mathcal{B}$.

Proof Assume

(1) $\vdash \mathcal{A}\{\mathcal{T}\}\mathcal{B}$.

Fix a tree-formed G, a G', and a value assignment $\underline{\mathfrak{A}}$ to the free variables $\mathfrak{A}$ of $\mathcal{A}$ such that

(2) $G, \underline{\mathfrak{A}} \models \mathcal{A}$, and

(3) $G \longrightarrow_{\mathcal{T}} G'$.

To establish $\Vdash \mathcal{A}\{\mathcal{T}\}\mathcal{B}$, we only need to find a value assignment $\underline{\mathfrak{B}}$ to the remaining free variables $\mathfrak{B}$ such that

(4) $G', \underline{\mathfrak{A}}, \underline{\mathfrak{B}} \models \mathcal{B}$.

Now by (3) and the definition of transductions, there is a value assignment $\underline{\boldsymbol{\mu}}$ to the transduction variables $\boldsymbol{\mu}$ of $\mathcal{T}$ such that

(5) $\overline{G}, \underline{\boldsymbol{\mu}} \models \mathcal{T}.\rho$

(6) $\mathbf{Foll}_{\mathcal{T}}(\overline{S}, \underline{\boldsymbol{\mu}}) \subseteq \overline{\overline{G}}$,

(7) $\overline{G}' = \mathbf{BB}_{\mathcal{T}}(\overline{G}, \underline{\boldsymbol{\mu}})$, and

(8) $\overline{\overline{G}}' = (\overline{\overline{G}} \backslash \mathbf{Del}_{\mathcal{T}}(\overline{G}, \underline{\boldsymbol{\mu}})) \cup \mathbf{Add}_{\mathcal{T}}(\overline{G}, \underline{\boldsymbol{\mu}})$

In order to apply (1), we would like to show that

(9) $\overline{G}, \underline{\mathfrak{A}}, \underline{\boldsymbol{\mu}} \models \boldsymbol{\Phi} \wedge \rho \wedge \forall^{\circ}\mathbf{src}\exists^{\circ}\mathbf{dst} : \boldsymbol{\sigma} \Rightarrow (\boldsymbol{\delta} \wedge (\neg\mathbf{Foll}_{T} \Rightarrow (\forall^{\circ}\mathbf{dst} : \neg\mathbf{Foll}_{T})))$

holds. Now by (2), we have $\overline{G}, \underline{\mathfrak{A}} \models \boldsymbol{\Phi}$ and $\overline{G}, \underline{\mathfrak{A}} \models [\boldsymbol{\sigma} \xrightarrow{a} \boldsymbol{\delta}]$. Thus it is sufficient to find for each v such that $\overline{G}, \underline{\mathfrak{A}}, \mathbf{src} \mapsto v \models \boldsymbol{\sigma}$ some w satisfying

(10) $\overline{G}, \underline{\mathfrak{A}}, \mathbf{src} \mapsto v, \mathbf{dst} \mapsto w \models \boldsymbol{\delta} \wedge (\neg\mathbf{Foll}_{T} \Rightarrow (\forall^{\circ}\mathbf{dst} : \neg\mathbf{Foll}_{T}))$

The w we choose is the one such that $(v, \mathsf{a}, w) \in \overline{\overline{G}}$. This w exists by virtue of (2) and the definition of edge constraint satisfaction. Moreover, $\overline{G}, \underline{\mathfrak{A}}, \mathbf{src} \mapsto v, \mathbf{dst} \mapsto w \models \boldsymbol{\delta}$. Thus in order to establish (10), it suffices to suppose that

(11) $\overline{G}, \underline{\mathfrak{A}}, \mathbf{src} \mapsto v, \mathbf{dst} \mapsto w \models \neg\mathbf{Foll}_{T}$

and to prove that no u exists such that

(12) $\overline{G}, \underline{\mathfrak{A}}, \mathbf{src} \mapsto v, \mathbf{dst} \mapsto u \models \mathbf{Foll}_{T}$.

For a contradiction, assume that some u does satisfy (12). Then $(v, \mathsf{a}, u) \in \mathbf{Foll}_{T}(\overline{G}, \underline{\boldsymbol{\mu}})$. But by (5), $\mathbf{Foll}_{T}(\overline{G}, \underline{\boldsymbol{\mu}}) \subseteq \overline{\overline{G}}$, and thus $u = w$, which contradicts our supposition (11). It follows that (9) holds, and by (1) we then obtain a $\underline{\mathfrak{B}}$ such that

$$
(13)\quad
\begin{array}{l}
\overline{G}, \underline{\mathfrak{A}}, \underline{\mathfrak{B}}, \underline{\boldsymbol{\mu}} \models \mathbf{Tr}_{T}\boldsymbol{\Phi}' \\
\qquad \wedge \forall^{\circ}\mathbf{src} : \mathbf{Tr}_{T}\boldsymbol{\sigma}' \Rightarrow \\
\qquad\qquad ((\exists^{\circ}\mathbf{dst} : \mathbf{Add}_{T} \wedge \mathbf{Tr}_{T}\boldsymbol{\delta}') \\
\qquad\qquad \vee(\exists^{\circ}\mathbf{dst} : \mathbf{Foll}_{T} \wedge \neg\mathbf{Del}_{T} \wedge \mathbf{Tr}_{T}\boldsymbol{\delta}') \\
\qquad\qquad \vee(\boldsymbol{\sigma} \wedge \forall^{\circ}\mathbf{dst} : \neg\mathbf{Add}_{T} \wedge \neg\mathbf{Foll}_{T} \wedge (\boldsymbol{\delta} \Rightarrow \mathbf{Tr}_{T}\boldsymbol{\delta}')))
\end{array}
$$

holds. From (13) and Lemma 9 (Faithfulness), it follows that

(14) $\overline{G}, \underline{\mathfrak{A}}, \underline{\mathfrak{B}} \models \boldsymbol{\Phi}'$

We thus only need to show that also the edge constraint $[\boldsymbol{\sigma}' \xrightarrow{\mathsf{a}} \boldsymbol{\delta}']$ holds. To do this, we consider $v \in \overline{G}'$ such that

(15) $\overline{G}, \underline{\mathfrak{A}}, \underline{\mathfrak{B}}, \mathbf{src} \mapsto v \models \boldsymbol{\sigma}'$.

We must then prove that there is w such that $(v, \mathsf{a}, w) \in \overline{\overline{G}}'$ and

(16) $\overline{G}, \underline{\mathfrak{A}}, \underline{\mathfrak{B}}, \mathbf{src} \mapsto v, \mathbf{dst} \mapsto w \models \boldsymbol{\delta}'$.

Now by (15) and Lemma 9 (Faithfulness), we have

(17) $\overline{G}, \underline{\mathfrak{A}}, \underline{\mathfrak{B}}, \underline{\boldsymbol{\mu}}, \mathbf{src} \mapsto v \models \mathbf{Tr}_{T}\boldsymbol{\sigma}'$.

Discharging the hypothesis in (13) by means of (17) gives us three cases:

(18) $\overline{G}, \underline{\mathfrak{A}}, \underline{\mathfrak{B}}, \underline{\boldsymbol{\mu}}, \mathbf{src} \mapsto v \models \exists^{\circ}\mathbf{dst} : \mathbf{Add}_{T} \wedge \mathbf{Tr}_{T}\boldsymbol{\delta}'$

(19) $\overline{G}, \underline{\mathfrak{A}}, \underline{\mathfrak{B}}, \underline{\boldsymbol{\mu}}, \mathbf{src} \mapsto v \models \exists^{\circ}\mathbf{dst} : \mathbf{Foll}_{T} \wedge \neg\mathbf{Del}_{T} \wedge \mathbf{Tr}_{T}\boldsymbol{\delta}'$

(20) $\overline{G}, \underline{\mathfrak{A}}, \underline{\mathfrak{B}}, \underline{\boldsymbol{\mu}}, \mathbf{src} \mapsto v \models \boldsymbol{\sigma} \wedge \forall^{\circ}\mathbf{dst} : \neg\mathbf{Add}_{T} \wedge \neg\mathbf{Foll}_{T} \wedge (\boldsymbol{\delta} \Rightarrow \mathbf{Tr}_{T}\boldsymbol{\delta}'))$

In case (18) there is a w such that

$$(21)\overline{G}, \underline{\mathfrak{A}}, \underline{\mathfrak{B}}, \underline{\mu}, \mathbf{src} \mapsto v, \mathbf{dst} \mapsto w \models \mathbf{Add}_{\mathcal{T}} \ \wedge \ \mathbf{Tr}_{\mathcal{T}}\delta'$$

By (8), $(v, \mathsf{a}, w) \in \overline{G}'$, and by Lemma 9 (Faithfulness) (16) holds. Case (19) is handled by a similar argument. Finally, in Case (20) we have by Lemma 9 (Faithfulness) that $\overline{G}, \underline{\mathfrak{A}}, \underline{\mathfrak{B}}, \mathbf{src} \mapsto v \models \sigma$ and $\overline{G}, \underline{\mathfrak{A}}, \underline{\mathfrak{B}}, \mathbf{src} \mapsto v, \mathbf{dst} \mapsto w \models \neg\mathbf{Add}_{\mathcal{T}} \wedge \neg\mathbf{Foll}_{\mathcal{T}} \wedge (\delta \Rightarrow \mathbf{Tr}_{\mathcal{T}}\delta')$, where w is the node such that $(v, \mathsf{a}, w) \in \overline{G}$ (this node exists by virtue of (2)). By (8), (20), and Lemma 10, we infer that $(v, \mathsf{a}, w) \in \overline{G}'$ and by (2) that $\overline{G}, \underline{\mathfrak{A}}, \underline{\mathfrak{B}}, \mathbf{src} \mapsto v, \mathbf{dst} \mapsto w \models \mathbf{Tr}_{\mathcal{T}}\delta$. Thus $\overline{G}, \underline{\mathfrak{A}}, \underline{\mathfrak{B}}, \mathbf{src} \mapsto v, \mathbf{dst} \mapsto w \models \mathbf{Tr}_{\mathcal{T}}\delta'$ holds, whence (16) holds by Lemma 9 (Faithfulness). □

Theorem 12. *(Completeness)* $\Vdash \mathcal{A}\{\mathcal{T}\}\mathcal{B}$ *implies* $\vdash \mathcal{A}\{\mathcal{T}\}\mathcal{B}$.

Proof Proof can be found in full paper. □

Theorem 13. *Transductional correctness is decidable for* **EC**.

Proof By Theorems 2, 11, and 12. □

References

1. B. Courcelle. Graph rewriting: an algebraic and logic approach. In J. van Leeuwen, editor, *Handbook of Theoretical Computer Science*, volume B, pages 193–242. Elsevier Science Publishers, 1990.
2. B. Courcelle. The monadic second-order logic of graphs I. Recognizable sets of finite graphs. *Information and computation*, 85:12–75, 1990.
3. B. Courcelle. Monadic second-order definable graph transductions. In J.C. Raoult, editor, *CAAP '92, Colloquium on Trees in Algebra and Programming, LNCS 581*, pages 124–144. Springer Verlag, 1992.
4. J. Engelfriet. A characterizarion of context-free NCE graph languages by monadic second-order logic on trees. In H. Ehrig, H.J. Kreowski, and G. Rozenberg, editors, *Graph grammars and their applications to computer science, 4th International Workshop, LNCS 532*, pages 311–327. Springer Verlag, 1990.
5. N. Klarlund and M. Schwartzbach. Graph types. In *Proc. 20th Symp. on Princ. of Prog. Lang.*, pages 196–205. ACM, 1993.
6. N. Klarlund and M. Schwartzbach. Invariants as data types. Unpublished, 1993.
7. M. Rabin. A simple method for undecidability proofs and some applications. In *Logic, Methodology and Philosophy of Science II*, pages 58–68. North-Holland, 1965.

Nondeterministic Automata with Concurrency Relations and Domains

Dietrich Kuske

Fachbereich Mathematik und Informatik, Universität GHS Essen, D–45117 Essen
E-mail: mem080@vm.hrz.uni-essen.de

Abstract. We introduce an operational model of concurrent systems, called nondeterministic automata with concurrency relations. These are nondeterministic labelled transition systems where the event set is endowed with a system of symmetric irreflexive binary relations which describe when two events in a particular state commute. This model generalizes the recent concept of Droste's automata with concurrency relations which are based on deterministic labelled transition systems. A permutation equivalence of computation sequences arises canonically, and we obtain a natural domain comprising the induced equivalence classes. We give a complete characterization of all such partial orders. Then we consider certain subclasses of all nondeterministic automata with concurrency relations and characterize the partial orders generated by them. Surprisingly, those automata which satisfy the cube axiom generate particular L–domains, and so called stable automata which satisfy the cube and the inverse cube axiom generate particular distributive L–domains. Restricting to the case of deterministic automata we finally give a representation theorem for dI–domains with particular stable deterministic automata.

1 Introduction

In the study of concurrent processes labelled transition systems have been used frequently as a model for an operational semantics ([Ho78, Mi80, NW91]). A labelled transition system may be defined to be a tupel $\mathcal{T} = (S, E, T, \star)$ where S is a set of states, E a set of events (or actions or symbols), $T \subseteq S \times T \times S$ a set of transitions and $\star \in S$ a distinguished initial state. The deterministic labelled transition systems are a subclass of all labelled transition systems: $\mathcal{T}$ is deterministic iff $(p, a, q), (p, a, r) \in T$ imply $q = r$. One can define a finite computation sequence of $\mathcal{T}$ to be a sequence of the form $(q_0, a_1, q_1)(q_1, a_2, q_2) \ldots (q_{n-1}, a_n, q_n)$ with $(q_{i-1}, a_i, q_i) \in T$ for $i = 1, \ldots n$. Several attempts have been done to incorporate direct information about concurrency into such a model. Stark ([Sta89]) introduced a symmetric irreflexive binary relation $\|$ on the events to describe when two events can occure concurrently. A deterministic labelled transition system with such a relation is called trace automaton. Droste ([Dro90, Dro92]) replaced this one global concurrency relation by a family of concurrency relations indexed by the states. In his model, called automaton with concurrency relations, two events can occur concurrently in one state while this may not be possible in another one. Two transitions (p, a, q) and (p, b, r) are defined to commute whenever a and b are concurrent in state p, i.e. $a \parallel_p b$. Similarly as in trace theory, this yields a natural definition of permutation equivalence for computation sequences of $\mathcal{T}$. Intuitively, two computation sequences are equivalent, if they represent "interleaved views" of a single computation. The set of equivalence classes of computation sequences, called computations, carries an interesting partial order which is naturally induced by the prefix–ordering of computation sequences. Droste [Dro90, Dro92] gave a complete characterization of these partial orders.

The previous models were nondeterministic in the sense that there was indeterminacy in the choice of an event or action that occurs in a certain state, while they were deterministic in the sense that an event or action occuring in a state determines completely the new state. Here we introduce a model which is nondeterministic in both senses, i.e. we start with a nondeterministic labelled transition system and endow it with a family of concurrency relations as introduced by Droste. Similarly as before we obtain a natural equivalence relation for computation sequences of a nondeterministic automaton with concurrency relations $\mathcal{A} = (S, E, T, \star, (\parallel_q)_{q \in S})$ and a nontrivial partial order on the set $D(\mathcal{A})$ comprising the induced equivalence classes of computation sequences which start in the initial state $\star$. In this paper we wish to study the structure of these partial orders.

Using ideas from [Dro90, Dro92] we derive a complete characterization of all partial orders $(D(\mathcal{A}), \leq)$ where $\mathcal{A}$ is a nondeterministic automaton with concurrency relations. Unfortunately, it is impossible in general to reconstruct, conversely, the concurrency relations from the partial order $(D(\mathcal{A}), \leq)$. Therefore we define a class of nondeterministic automata with concurrency relations, called nondeterministic automata with observable concurrency, such that this is possible. These automata are a direct generalization of the cancellative automata with concurrency relations investigated in [BD93, BD94]. In contrary to the deterministic case there are partial orders $(D(\mathcal{A}), \leq)$ with $\mathcal{A}$ a nondeterministic automaton with concurrency relations which cannot be generated by a nondeterministic automaton with observable concurrency. In Sect. 3 we give a complete characterization of the partial orders generated by nondeterministic automata with observable concurrency.

Another possibility to incorporate direct information about concurrency was introduced by Stark in [Sta89]. He endowed a (deterministic) labelled transition system with a residuum operation. This is a partial function $\uparrow$ from the pairs of transitions to transitions and describes what remains of a transition s after performing a transition t. A labelled transition system together with such a residuum operation is called automaton with residuum operation. The transformation process ([Dro92, 3.3(a)]) applied to an automaton with concurrency relations constructs a partial function from $T \times T$ to T. Droste [Dro92] defines a class of automata with concurrency relations (called concurrent automata) for which this transformation process yields an automaton with residuum operation. The converse holds as well: If $\mathcal{A}$ is an automaton with concurrency relations which yields an automaton with residuum operation under the transformation process then $\mathcal{A}$ is a concurrent automaton. We will use this second property of the transformation process to define nondeterministic concurrent automata. Since our automata are a nondeterministic version of the automata with concurrency relations we have to construct a nondeterministic version of the residuum operation of Stark. This will be a total function – from $T \times T$ into the powerset of T. This function can be extended to computation sequences. If it satisfies the cube axiom, we call the nondeterministic automaton with concurrency relations nondeterministic concurrent automaton. In this case the permutation equivalence is a congruence relation with respect to the residuum operation. Thus it is possible to define a similar function on the computations. As in the deterministic case this function enables us to characterize the partial orders $(D(\mathcal{A}), \leq)$ where $\mathcal{A}$ is a nondeterministic concurrent automaton. Surprisingly, it turns out that they are L–domains. L–domains are used in denotational semantics to model indeterminacy. They have been investigated intensively, cf. [Gun85, Coq88, Jun88, GJ88].

In [Dro93] Droste defined stably concurrent automata. i.e. concurrent automata satisfying an "inverse cube axiom". He characterizes the recognizable languages in the monoid consisting of all finite computations of such an automaton. We consider nondeterministic stably concurrent automata and show that the partial orders $(D(\mathcal{A}), \leq)$ are certain distributive L–domains if $\mathcal{A}$ is a nondeterministic stably concurrent automaton. Restricting to the case of deterministic stably concurrent automata we thus find a representation theorem for dI–domains. DI–domains have been much studied in connection with denotational semantics of programming languages. With stable functions as morphisms, they form a cartesian closed category ([Ber78]). They are precisely the distributive event domains ([Win87]). Zhang [Zha89] characterized them in terms of information systems. Droste [Dro92] presented a representation theorem of dI–domains using particular concurrent automata. But these automata where characterized in terms of computation sequences of arbitrary length while our characterization with the inverse cube axiom only needs computation sequences of length two.

2 Nondeterministic Automata with Concurrency Relations

A nondeterministic automaton with concurrency relations is a quintupel $\mathcal{A} = (S, E, T, \star, \|)$ where

1. S and E are countable disjoint nonempty sets, $\star \in S$ is a distinguished element.
2. T is a subset of $S \times E \times S$ such that for any $a \in E$ there exist $p, q \in S$ with $(p, a, q) \in T$.
3. $\| = (\|_q)_{q \in S}$ is a family of irreflexive, symmetric binary relations on E such that whenever $a \|_p b$ there exist states $q, q', r \in S$ and transitions $(p, a, q), (p, b, q'), (q, b, r), (q', a, r) \in T$.

The elements of S are called *states*, the elements of E are *events* and those of T are *transitions*. Intuitively, a transition $s = (p, a, q)$ represents a potential computational step in which event a happens in state p of $\mathcal{A}$ and $\mathcal{A}$ changes to state q. In generalization of [Dro90, Dro92], we do not require that this change is deterministic. We write $\mathrm{ev}(s) = a$ for the event of s. The element $\star$ is the *initial state* of $\mathcal{A}$. The *concurrency relations* $\|_q$ describe the concurrency information for pairs of events at state q. A *finite computation sequence* in $\mathcal{A}$ is either empty (denoted by ϵ) or a finite sequence $\gamma = s_1 s_2 \ldots s_n$ of transitions $s_i = (q_i, a_i, q_{i+1})$ for $i = 1, \ldots n$. q_1 is called *domain* (dom (γ)), q_{n+1} *codomain* (cod (γ)), and n is the *length* of γ ($|\gamma|$). Likewise, an infinite sequence $(s_i)_{i \in \mathbb{N}}$ of transitions $s_i = (q_i, e_i, q_{i+1})$ $(i \in \mathbb{N})$ is called an *infinite computation sequence*, its domain is q_1. A computation sequence is called *initial* if its domain is $\star$. Let $\mathrm{CS}(\mathcal{A})$ ($\mathrm{CS}^0(\mathcal{A})$, $\mathrm{CS}_\star(\mathcal{A})$, $\mathrm{CS}^0_\star(\mathcal{A})$) denote the sets, respectively, of all (all finite, all initial, all finite initial) computation sequences of $\mathcal{A}$. The *composition* $\gamma\delta$ of a finite computation sequence γ and an arbitrary computation sequence δ with cod $\gamma =$ dom δ is defined in the natural way by concatenating γ and δ. If cod γ and dom δ are different we write $\gamma\delta = 0$. A finite computation sequence γ is called *prefix* of an arbitrary computation sequence δ if there exists $\eta \in \mathrm{CS}(\mathcal{A})$ with $\gamma\eta = \delta$.

Now we want the concurrency relations on $\mathcal{A}$ to induce an equivalence relation on $\mathrm{CS}(\mathcal{A})$. This construction is similar to that of traces. We call two finite computation sequences $\gamma = s_1 s_2 \ldots s_n$ and $\delta = t_1 t_2 \ldots t_m$ *strongly equivalent* ($\gamma \approx \delta$) if we obtain γ from δ by replacing an occurence $t_i t_{i+1}$ of the form $(p, a, q)(q, b, r)$ by $s_i s_{i+1} = (p, b, q')(q', a, r)$ for some $1 \leq i < n$ with $a \|_p b$ in $\mathcal{A}$. We then let $\sim$ denote the reflexive and transitive closure of $\approx$ on $\mathrm{CS}^0(\mathcal{A})$. Obviously, $\sim$ is a congruence relation with respect to concatenation and any two equivalent computation sequences have the same length, domain and codomain. Thus, we can define the concatenation of equivalence classes $[\gamma]$ and $[\delta]$ of finite computation sequences γ and δ by $[\gamma] \cdot [\delta] = [\gamma\delta]$ whenever $\gamma\delta$ is defined. Otherwise, $[\gamma] \cdot [\delta]$ is undefined.

Now we define a preorder relation on $\mathrm{CS}^0(\mathcal{A})$ by $\gamma \lesssim \delta$ iff there exists $\eta \in \mathrm{CS}^0(\mathcal{A})$ with $\gamma\eta \sim \delta$. This gives rise to a preorder $\lesssim$ on $\mathrm{CS}(\mathcal{A})$ where for $\gamma, \delta \in \mathrm{CS}(\mathcal{A})$ we let $\gamma \lesssim \delta$ iff for any prefix γ' of γ there exists a prefix δ' of δ with $\gamma' \lesssim \delta'$. Then put $\gamma \sim \delta$ iff $\gamma \lesssim \delta \lesssim \gamma$ and let $[\gamma]$ denote the equivalence class with respect to $\sim$. We order these classes by $[\gamma] \leq [\delta]$ iff $\gamma \lesssim \delta$. Finally we call $D(\mathcal{A}) = \{[\gamma] \mid \gamma \in \mathrm{CS}_\star(\mathcal{A})\}$ the *domain generated by* $\mathcal{A}$. As for deterministic automata with concurrency relations this is indeed a domain (i.e. an algebraic cpo) where the compact elements are given by $D^0(\mathcal{A}) = \{[\gamma] \mid \gamma \in \mathrm{CS}^0_\star(\mathcal{A})\}$ (cf. [Dro90]).

Let us now turn to the domains that are generated by these automata. To do this we introduce some notation. Let $(D, \leq)$ be a domain. D^0 denotes the compact elements of D. $(D, \leq)$ is called ω*-domain* if D^0 is countable. A maximal linearly ordered set $X \subseteq D$ with $x \leq X \leq y$ for $x, y \in D$ is called *chain from x to y*. We call $(D, \leq)$ *domain with finite chains* iff any chain $X \subseteq D$ dominated by a compact element $x \in D^0$ (i.e. $X \leq x$) is finite. For $x, y \in D^0$ we write

$x \multimap y$ if $x < y$ and $x \leq z < y$ implies $x = z$. Such a pair is called *prime interval* and denoted by $\langle x, y \rangle$. Let I_D denote the set of all prime intervals of $(D, \leq)$. Now let $\succ\!\!\multimap$ be an equivalence relation on I_D. Two chains $X = (x_1 \multimap x_2 \multimap x_3 \ldots \multimap x_n)$ and $Y = (y_1 \multimap y_2 \multimap y_3 \ldots \multimap y_n)$ are called *strongly equivalent* iff there exists $1 < i < n$ with $x_j = y_j$ for all $j \neq i$, $x_i \neq y_i$ and $\langle y_i, x_{i+1} \rangle \succ\!\!\multimap \langle x_{i-1}, x_i \rangle \not\succ\!\!\multimap \langle x_{i-1}, y_i \rangle \succ\!\!\multimap \langle x_i, x_{i+1} \rangle$. Let the *equivalence* of chains be the reflexive and transitive closure of this strong equivalence.

A *weak nondeterministic concurrency domain* is a tripel $(D, \leq, \succ\!\!\multimap)$ where $(D, \leq)$ is an ω–domain with finite chains and $\succ\!\!\multimap$ is an equivalence relation on I_D satisfying:
(E) For any $x \in D^0$ any two chains from $\perp$ to x are equivalent.

We turn back to the consideration of the domain generated by a nondeterministic automaton with concurrency relations. For finite initial computation sequences $[\gamma] \multimap [\delta]$ holds iff there exists a transition s with $\gamma s \sim \delta$. This transition is unique. Thus we can define an equivalence on the prime intervals of $(D(\mathcal{A}), \leq)$ by $\langle [\gamma], [\gamma s] \rangle \overset{E}{\succ\!\!\multimap} \langle [\delta], [\delta t] \rangle$ iff $\mathrm{ev}(s) = \mathrm{ev}(t)$, and we call this relation *event equivalence*.

Theorem 1 Let $(D, \leq)$ be a partially ordered set and $\succ\!\!\multimap$ an equivalence relation on I_D. Then the following statements are equivalent:

(i) $(D, \leq, \succ\!\!\multimap)$ is a weak nondeterministic concurrency domain.

(ii) There exists a nondeterministic automaton with concurrency relations $\mathcal{A}$ such that $(D, \leq, \succ\!\!\multimap)$ and $(D(\mathcal{A}), \leq, \overset{E}{\succ\!\!\multimap})$ are isomorphic.

Proof $(ii) \Rightarrow (i)$ Let $\mathcal{A}$ be a nondeterministic automaton with concurrency relations. For any compact element $x \in D^0(\mathcal{A})$ there exists a finite and initial computation sequence γ with $x = [\gamma]$. Now let X be a chain dominated by x. Obviously the lengths of the elements of X strictly increase and are dominated by the (finite) length of γ. Thus X is finite. The proof can be proceeded as the proof of axiom (E) in [Dro92, Theorem 2.6].

$(i) \Rightarrow (ii)$ Let $(D, \leq, \succ\!\!\multimap)$ be a nondeterministic concurrency domain. Then there exists a nondeterministic automaton with concurrency relations $\mathcal{A}$ such that $(D(\mathcal{A}), \leq, \overset{E}{\succ\!\!\multimap})$ and $(D, \leq, \succ\!\!\multimap)$ are isomorphic. In this automaton the states are precisely the compact elements of $(D, \leq)$, the events are the equivalence classes with respect to $\succ\!\!\multimap$, the transitions are given by the set of all tripels $(x, [\langle x, y \rangle], y)$ with $x, y \in D^0$ and $x \multimap y$. The initial state is the smallest element of D. Two different events a and b are concurrent in a state x iff there exists $y, y', z \in D^0$ with $x \multimap y \multimap z$, $x \multimap y' \multimap z$, $a = [\langle x, y \rangle]$ and $b = [\langle x, y' \rangle]$. We call this automaton $\mathcal{A}$ the *automaton induced by* $(D, \leq, \succ\!\!\multimap)$. Observe that the codomain of any finite computation sequence in $\mathcal{A}$ is a compact element of $(D, \leq)$. Thus the mapping $f : D^0(A) \longrightarrow D^0$ with $f([\gamma]) = \mathrm{cod}\ \gamma$ is welldefined. Furthermore this mapping is order–preserving. One can show that the continuous extension is an isomorphism from $(D(\mathcal{A}), \leq, \overset{E}{\succ\!\!\multimap})$ to $(D, \leq, \succ\!\!\multimap)$. □

3 Nondeterministic Automata with Observable Concurrency

From the domain $(D(\mathcal{A}), \leq)$ generated by a nondeterministic automaton with concurrency relations $\mathcal{A}$ and the event equivalence $\stackrel{E}{\succ\!\!-\!\!\prec}$ it is in general impossible to reconstruct the concurrency relations. However, this is possible for the nondeterministic automata with observable concurrency which are considered in this section.

A *nondeterministic automaton with observable concurrency* is a nondeterministic automaton with concurrency relations $\mathcal{A} = (S, E, T, \star, \|)$ such that $\gamma s_1 t_1 \sim \gamma s_2 t_2$ implies $s_1 t_1 \sim s_2 t_2$ for any finite initial computation sequence γ and any transitions s_1, t_1, s_2 and t_2.

The following theorem completely characterizes the weak nondeterministic concurrency domains generated by nondeterministic automata with observable concurrency.

Theorem 2 Let $(D, \leq, \succ\!\!-\!\!\prec)$ be a weak nondeterministic concurrency domain. Then the following statements are equivalent:

(i) $(D, \leq, \succ\!\!-\!\!\prec)$ satisfies the axiom (U):
For any $x, y_1, y_2, z \in D^0$ with $x \multimap y_i \multimap z$ $(i = 1, 2)$, the chains $\{x, y_1, z\}$ and $\{x, y_2, z\}$ are equivalent.

(ii) There exists a nondeterministic automaton with observable concurrency $\mathcal{A}$ such that $(D, \leq, \succ\!\!-\!\!\prec)$ and $(D(\mathcal{A}), \leq, \stackrel{E}{\succ\!\!-\!\!\prec})$ are isomorphic.

Proof *(ii)* $\Rightarrow$ *(i)* Let $\mathcal{A}$ be a nondeterministic automaton with observable concurrency. Then $(D(\mathcal{A}), \leq, \stackrel{E}{\succ\!\!-\!\!\prec})$ is a weak nondeterministic concurrency domain. Suppose $x, y_1, y_2, z \in D^0(A)$ with $x \multimap y_i \multimap z$ $(i = 1, 2)$ and $y_1 \neq y_2$. Then there exist $\gamma \in \mathrm{CS}^0_\star(\mathcal{A})$ and $s_1, s_2, t_1, t_2 \in T$ with $x = [\gamma]$, $y_i = [\gamma s_i]$ $(i = 1, 2)$ and $z = [\gamma s_1 t_1] = [\gamma s_2 t_2]$. Since $\mathcal{A}$ has observable concurrency this implies $s_1 t_1 \sim s_2 t_2$. Suppose $\mathrm{ev}(s_1) \neq \mathrm{ev}(s_2)$. Then the two chains $\{x, y_1, z\}$ and $\{x, y_2, z\}$ are strongly equivalent. Now suppose $\mathrm{ev}(s_1) = \mathrm{ev}(s_2)$. Because of $s_1 t_1 \sim s_2 t_2$ there exist transitions t_3 and s_3 with $s_1 t_1 \approx t_3 s_3 \approx s_2 t_2$, thus $\mathrm{ev}(s_3) = \mathrm{ev}(s_i) \|_{\mathrm{dom}\, s_i} \mathrm{ev}(t_3) = \mathrm{ev}(t_i)$ $(i = 1, 2)$. This implies that the chains $\{[\gamma], [\gamma t_3], [\gamma t_3 s_3]\}$ and $\{[\gamma], [\gamma s_i], [\gamma s_i t_i]\}$ for $i = 1, 2$ are strongly equivalent. Thus $\{x, y_1, z\}$ and $\{x, y_2, z\}$ are equivalent.

(i) $\Rightarrow$ *(ii)* For this implication we only remark that the nondeterministic automaton with concurrency relations induced by such a domain has observable concurrency. □

4 Nondeterministic Concurrent Automata

In a nondeterministic automaton with concurrency relations the concurrency relations $\|_p$ and $\|_q$ for states p and q are completely independent from each other. In the deterministic case Droste [Dro90, Dro92] introduced concurrent automata, a special kind of automata with concurrency relations where the relations $\|_p$ and $\|_q$ are locally dependent. He describes two transformation processes of a concurrent automaton into a residuum automaton as introduced by Stark and vice versa which are inverse to each other. In our case we construct a residuum operation on a nondeterministic automaton with concurrency relations and define a nondeterministic concurrent automaton in terms of this residuum operation rather than in terms of the concurrency relations.

Let $\mathcal{A} = (S, E, T, \star, \|)$ be a nondeterministic automaton with concurrency relations. We define a function $- : (T \cup \{\epsilon\})^2 \longrightarrow \mathfrak{P}(T \cup \{\epsilon\})$ by

$$s - t = \begin{cases} \{s' \in T \cup \{\epsilon\} \mid \exists t' \in T \cup \{\epsilon\} : st' \sim ts'\} & \text{if } s \neq t \\ \{\epsilon\} & \text{otherwise} \end{cases}$$

for $s, t \in T \cup \{\epsilon\}$. This function is called ***residuum***. The residuum of s and t describes what remains of s after performing t. It can be extended inductively to a function $- : \mathrm{CS}^0(\mathcal{A}) \times \mathrm{CS}^0(\mathcal{A}) \longrightarrow \mathfrak{P}(\mathrm{CS}^0(\mathcal{A}))$ by

$$s\gamma - t\delta = \bigcup\{s'\gamma' - \delta \mid \exists t' \in t - s : ts' \sim st',\ \gamma' \in \gamma - t'\}$$

for $s, t \in T$ and $\gamma, \delta \in \mathrm{CS}^0(\mathcal{A})$ with cod s = dom γ and cod t = dom δ. Using the abbreviation $M - \gamma$ for $\bigcup_{\mu \in M} \mu - \gamma$ this can be written as

$$\begin{aligned} s\gamma - t\delta &= \{s'\gamma' \mid \exists t' \in t - s : ts' \sim st',\ \gamma' \in \gamma - t'\} - \delta \\ &= (s\gamma - t) - \delta. \end{aligned}$$

Now we are able to define nondeterministic concurrent automata:

Definition A nondeterministic automaton with concurrency relations $\mathcal{A}$ is called *nondeterministic concurrent automaton* if for any transitions s, t, u, t', u' the following *cube axiom* holds:

$$tu \sim t'u' \implies s - tu = s - t'u'.$$

$s = \epsilon$ implies $s - tu = \{\epsilon\} = s - t'u'$. For $\epsilon \in \{t, u, t', u'\}$ or $t = t'$ we get $tu = t'u'$ from $tu \sim t'u'$ and thus $s - tu = s - t'u'$. Thus the cube axiom holds for elements of $T \cup \{\epsilon\}$, too. Because of $s - t'u' = (s - t') - u'$ the cube axiom can be reformulated as

$$tu \sim t'u' \text{ and } s' \in s - tu \Longrightarrow \exists s'' \in s - t' : s' \in s'' - u'.$$

This can be visualized as shown in the following picture which explains the name "cube axiom".

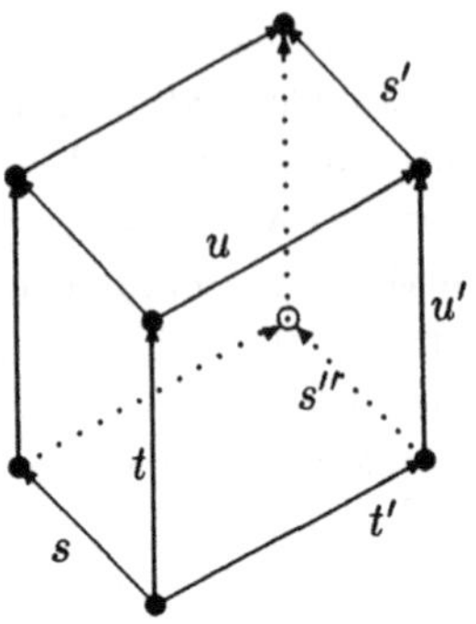

The residuum which is defined for finite computation sequences determines in a natural way a residuum on the equivalence classes of finite computation sequences with respect to $\sim$:

Theorem 3 Let $\mathcal{A}$ be a nondeterministic concurrent automaton. Then the residuum $-$ on finite computations defined by $[\gamma] - [\delta] = \{[\eta] \mid \eta \in \gamma - \delta\}$ is welldefined.

The proof, which exploits the cube axiom, can be found in [Kus94, Satz 6.3.12]. Since it is rather technical, we omit it here.

This residuum operation enjoys some very important properties which are listed in the following proposition. [Kus94, Sect. 6.3] deals with the proof of them which is omitted here. These properties will be used throughout subsequently without mentioning them again.

Proposition 4 Let $\mathcal{A} = (S, E, T, \star, \|)$ be a nondeterministic concurrent automaton and $\gamma, \delta, \eta \in \mathrm{CS}^0(\mathcal{A})$. Then the following statements are satisfied:

1. If cod γ = dom δ and cod γ = dom η then $\gamma\delta - \gamma\eta = \delta - \eta$.
2. If cod δ = dom η then $[\gamma] - [\delta\eta] = ([\gamma] - [\delta]) - [\eta]$.
3. The set $[\gamma] \cdot ([\delta] - [\gamma])$ is the set of all minimal upper bounds of $\{[\gamma], [\delta]\}$ in $(D(\mathcal{A}), \leq)$ if dom γ = dom $\delta = \star$.
4. $[\gamma] \leq [\delta] \iff 1 := [\epsilon] \in [\gamma] - [\delta] \iff \{1\} = [\gamma] - [\delta]$

Property 2 claims that the cube axiom is valid for computations as well as for transitions.

Since $(D(\mathcal{A}), \leq)$ is Mub–complete (i.e. below any upper bound of a subset A of $D(\mathcal{A})$ there exists a minimal upper bound of A) for any nondeterministic automaton with concurrency relations, property 3 implies that $\{[\gamma], [\delta]\} \subseteq D^0(\mathcal{A})$ is bounded if and only if $\gamma - \delta$ is not empty.

Property 1 and 4 imply that any nondeterministic concurrent automaton has observable concurrency: Let $\gamma \in \mathrm{CS}^0_\star(\mathcal{A})$ and $s_1, s_2, t_1, t_2 \in T$ with $\gamma s_1 t_1 \sim \gamma s_2 t_2$. Then $[\gamma s_1 t_1] = [\gamma s_2 t_2]$ and thus $\{1\} = [\gamma s_1 t_1] - [\gamma s_2 t_2] = [s_1 t_1] - [s_2 t_2]$. Analogously we get $\{1\} = [s_2 t_2] - [s_1 t_1]$ and thus $[s_1 t_1] = [s_2 t_2]$, i.e. $s_1 t_1 \sim s_2 t_2$.

We come to a characterization of the domains generated by a nondeterministic concurrent automaton.

Definition Let $(D, \leq)$ be an ω–domain with finite chains and $>\!\!-\!\!<$ an equivalence relation on I_D. We call $(D, \leq, >\!\!-\!\!<)$ *nondeterministic concurrency domain* if the axioms (U), (L) and (C) are satisfied.

(L) For any compact element x the set $\{y \in D \mid a \leq x\}$ is a lattice.
(C) If x, y_1, y_2, b are elements of D^0 with $x -\!\!< y_1, y_2$ and $\{y_1, y_2\} < b$, then there exists $z \in D^0$ with $y_1, y_2 -\!\!< z \leq b$.

Domains which satisfy axiom (L) are known as *L–domains.* L–domains have been studied intensively in denotational semantics [Gun85, Coq88, Jun88, GJ88]. They form a maximal cartesian closed full subcategory of the category of all domains with continuous functions as morphisms.

Axiom (C) is a wellknown axiom in denotational semantics, cf. [Win87, Dro90, Dro92]. A lattice is said to be *upper–semimodular* iff $y_1 -\!\!< \sup(y_1, y_2)$ for any elements x, y_1 and y_2 with $x -\!\!< y_1, y_2$ ([Grä78]). Thus we can combine the axioms (L) and (C): For any compact element x the set $\{a \in D \mid a \leq x\}$ is an upper–semimodular lattice.

It can be shown that a nondeterministic concurrency domain is a weak nondeterministic concurrency domain. Since it satisfies axiom (U), Theorem 2 can be applied. This theorem is sharpend by the following one.

Theorem 5 Let $\mathcal{A}$ be a nondeterministic automaton with observable concurrency. Then the following statements are equivalent:

(i) $(D(\mathcal{A}), \leq, \overset{E}{>\!\!-\!\!<})$ is a nondeterministic concurrency domain.
(ii) $\mathcal{A}$ is a nondeterministic concurrent automaton.

Proof Let $\mathcal{A} = (S, E, T, \star, \|)$ be a nondeterministic concurrent automaton. Then $\mathcal{A}$ has observable concurrency. Thus $(D(\mathcal{A}), \leq, \overset{E}{>\!\!-\!\!<})$ satisfies axiom (U) by Theorem 2. Suppose $x, y_1, y_2 \in D^0(\mathcal{A})$ with $x -\!\!< y_1, y_2$ and $y_1 \neq y_2$. Then there exist $\gamma \in \mathrm{CS}^0_\star(\mathcal{A})$ and transitions s_1 and s_2 with $x = [\gamma]$ and $y_i = [\gamma s_i]$ for $i = 1, 2$. Moreover let z be a minimal upper bound of $\{y_1, y_2\}$. Since $[\gamma s_1] \cdot ([\gamma s_2] - [\gamma s_1])$ is the set of all minimal upper bounds of $\{y_1, y_2\}$, there exists $t \in \gamma s_2 - \gamma s_1 = s_2 - s_1 \subseteq T \cup \{\epsilon\}$ with $z = [\gamma s_1 t]$. $s_1 \neq s_2$ follows from $y_1 \neq y_2$. Thus $t \neq \epsilon$ and therefore $y_1 = [\gamma s_1] -\!\!< [\gamma s_1 t] = z$. It remains to show that $(D(\mathcal{A}), \leq)$ is an L–domain.

Let x, y, b be in $D^0(\mathcal{A})$ with $x, y \leq b$. It will be shown that $x \cdot (y - x)$ contains one and only one element below b. This implies, since $x \cdot (y - x)$ is the set of all minimal upper bounds of $\{x, y\}$, by a result of Jung ([Jun88]), that $(D(\mathcal{A}), \leq)$ is an L–domain.

Since $(D(\mathcal{A}), \leq)$ is a domain with finite chains there exists a minimal upper bound of $\{x, y\}$ below b. Suppose $u, v \in y - x$ with $x \cdot u \leq b$ and $x \cdot v \leq b$. Because of $y \leq x \cdot v$ the set $y - x \cdot v$ equals $\{1\}$. Prop. 4 (2) implies $\{1\} = (y - x) - v$. This is a superset of $u - v = x \cdot u - x \cdot v$ because u is an element of $y - x$. Since the set $\{x \cdot u, x \cdot v\}$ is dominated by b, the residuum of $x \cdot u$ and $x \cdot v$ is not empty. Thus $u - v$ is a nonempty subset of $\{1\}$, i.e. $u - v = \{1\}$. Analogously we get $v - u = \{1\}$. These equalities imply $u \leq v \leq u$, i.e. $u = v$.

The proof of the other implication is omitted (it can be found in [Kus94, Satz 6.4.5]). □

5 The Inverse Cube Axiom

Droste ([Dro93]) defined an inverse cube axiom for deterministic concurrent automata. Then he investigated the recognizable languages in the monoid consisting of all finite computations of a concurrent automaton satisfying this inverse cube axiom. Here we will consider a more general inverse cube axiom and determine the domains generated by a nondeterministic concurrent automaton which satisfies this axiom. The restriction to the case of deterministic concurrent automata will yield a representation theorem for dI–domains. Such a representation by particular deterministic concurrent automata is already known ([Dro92]). But they are defined in terms of computation sequences of arbitrary length while the inverse cube axiom only needs computation sequences of length two, thus it is a much simpler "local" axiom.

Definition A nondeterministic concurrent automaton $\mathcal{A} = (S, E, T, \star, \|)$ satisfies the *inverse cube axiom* if for any transitions $s_i, t_i, u_i \in T$ $(i = 1, 2)$ with $t_1 \neq t_2$ and $t_1 u_1 \sim t_2 u_2$ the following holds:
If there exists a transition $s' \in (s_1 - u_1) \cap (s_2 - u_2)$ then a transition s exists with $s_i \in s - t_i$ for $i = 1, 2$.

We call $\mathcal{A}$ a *stable automaton* if it satisfies the inverse cube axiom and if $s_1 = s_2$ holds for any $s_1, s_2, t \in T$ with $((s_1 - t) \cap (s_2 - t)) \setminus \{\epsilon\} \neq \emptyset$.

The following picture depicts the inverse cube axiom. There the solid lines depict the premisses while the dotted lines are those transitions which exist by the inverse cube axiom.

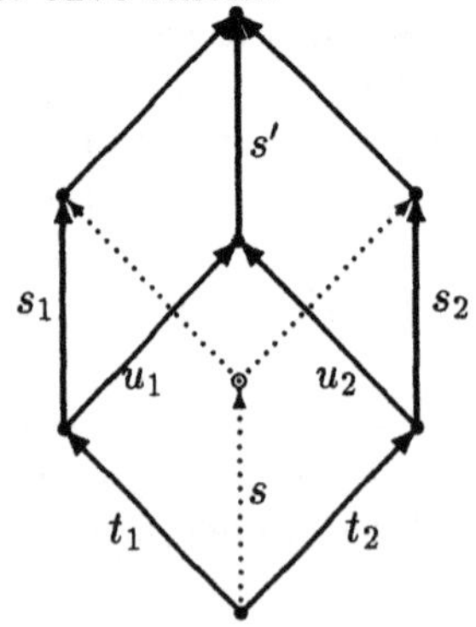

The second axiom implies that the situation depicted in the following picture can not occure in a stable automaton.

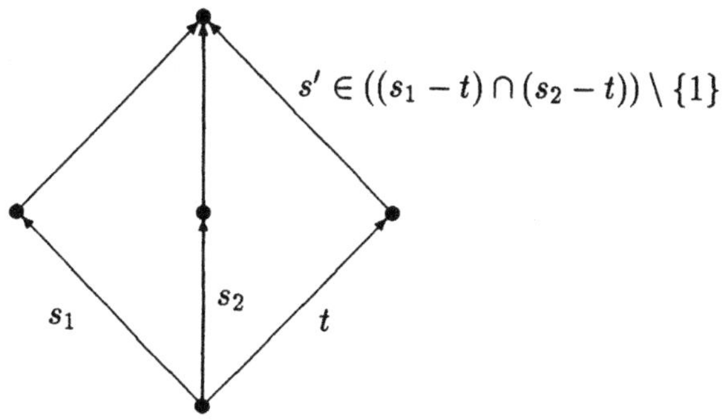

Proposition 6 Let $\mathcal{A} = (S, E, T, \star, \|)$ be a nondeterministic concurrent automaton satisfying the inverse cube axiom. Let $\gamma \in \mathrm{CS}^0(\mathcal{A})$, $t \in T$, $\gamma' \in \gamma - t$ and $s' \in T$ with $s' \lesssim \gamma'$. Additionally, suppose $t \not\lesssim \gamma$. Then a transition s exists with $s' \in s - t$ and $s \lesssim \gamma$.

This proposition can be visualized by the following picture. As usually the solid lines are the premisses while the dotted lines are the conclusion of the

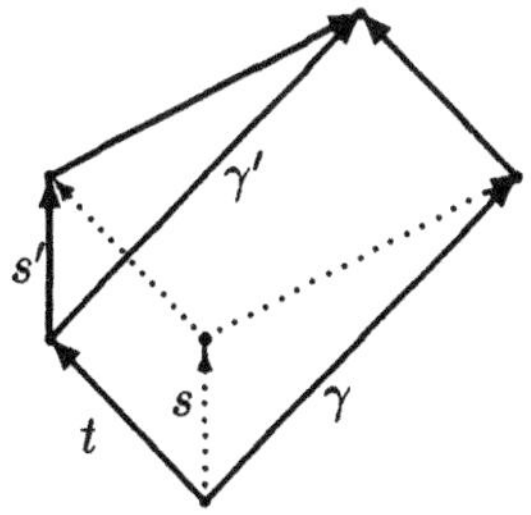

proposition.

The proof is done by induction on the length $|\gamma|$ of γ, i.e. the number of transitions occurring in γ. Here we only show how the inverse cube axiom comes into play for $|\gamma| = 2$, i.e. for $\gamma = u_1 u_2$ with $u_i \in T$ $(i = 1, 2)$. Since $\gamma' \in \gamma - t$ there exist elements of $T \cup \{\epsilon\}$ u_1', u_2' and t' with $tu_1' \sim u_1 t'$, $u_2' \in u_2 - t'$ and $\gamma' = u_1' u_2'$. This situation can be visualized as follows:

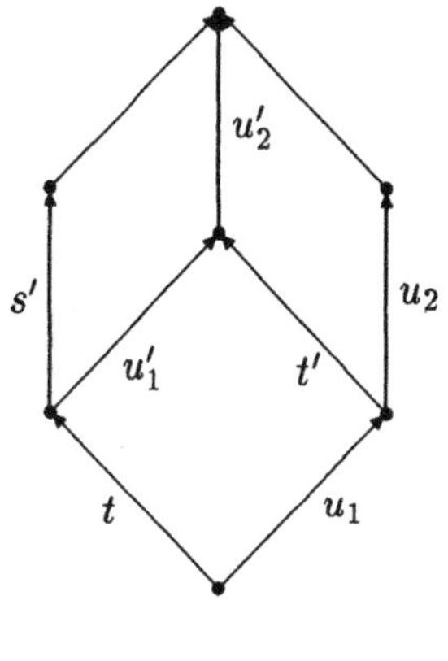

Since t is not dominated by $u_1 u_2$ (with respect to $\lesssim$), γ' has length two, i.e. $u_1', u_2', t' \in T$. Thus we have $u_2' \in s' - u_1'$ and $\epsilon \neq u_2'$. The application of the inverse cube axiom yields the existance of a transition s with the properties stated in the proposition (for a complete proof see [Kus94, Prop. 6.4.7]).

With the help of this proposition we are in the position to characterize those domains which are generated by stable automata. We call an ω–domain *dLI–domain* if the set of all elements below a given compact element is a finite and distributive lattice.

Theorem 7 Let $\mathcal{A} = (S, E, T, \star, \|)$ be a nondeterministic concurrent automaton. Then the following statements are equivalent.

(i) $(D(\mathcal{A}), \leq)$ is a dLI–domain.
(ii) $\mathcal{A}$ is a stable automaton.

Proof *(ii)* $\Rightarrow$ *(i)* Suppose $\mathcal{A}$ is a stable automaton. Then $(D(\mathcal{A}), \leq)$ is an L–domain with finite chains, thus the set of all elements dominated by a given compact element is a lattice of finite height. It remains to show that this lattice is distributive since any distributive lattice of finite height is finite.

It has to be shown that the following two finite partial orders cannot be embedded into $(D(\mathcal{A}), \leq)$.

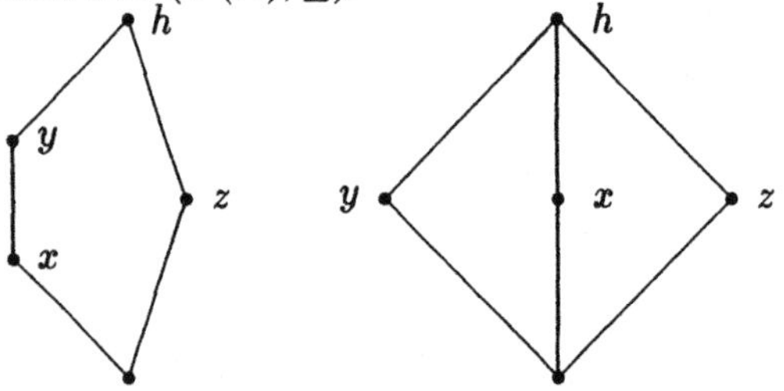

Thus let $h, x, y, z \in D^0(\mathcal{A})$ such that $\{x, y, z\} \leq h$. The set $\{a \in D(\mathcal{A}) \mid a \leq h\}$ is a lattice. Denote the supremum (infimum) in this lattice by $\vee$ ($\wedge$). Suppose furthermore $x > y \wedge z$ and define $w := (x \vee y) \wedge (x \vee z)$. Obviously we have $w \geq x$. Suppose $w > x$. The distributivity will be shown by the proof that this contradicts the assumptions. Let $y \wedge z = [\delta]$ with $\delta \in \mathrm{CS}^0_\star(\mathcal{A})$. Then there exist $\nu, \gamma_y, \gamma_z \in \mathrm{CS}^0(\mathcal{A})$ with $x = [\delta\nu]$, $y = [\delta\gamma_y]$ and $z = [\delta\gamma_z]$. Since $w > x$ there exists a transition s' with $[\delta\nu s'] \leq w$. Since $[\delta\nu] \cdot ([\delta\gamma_y] - [\delta\nu])$ is the set of all minimal upper bounds of $\{[\delta\gamma_y], [\delta\nu]\}$ and $\delta\gamma_y - \delta\nu = \gamma_y - \nu$ there exists $\gamma_y' \in \gamma_y - \nu$ with $x \vee y = [\delta\nu\gamma_y']$. Analogously we find $\gamma_z' \in \gamma_z - \nu$ with $x \vee z = [\delta\nu\gamma_z']$. Since $[\delta\nu s'] \leq w \leq x \vee y$ we have $s' \lesssim \gamma_y'$ and analogously $s' \lesssim \gamma_z'$. The proof proceeds by induction on the length of ν. Let $t := \nu \in T$. If $t \not\lesssim \gamma_y$ then Proposition 6 implies that there exists a transition s_y with $s_y \lesssim \gamma_y$ and $s' \in s_y - t$. If $t \not\lesssim \gamma_z$ we find a transition s_z with $s_z \lesssim \gamma_z$ and $s' \in s_z - t$. We now have to distinguish three cases.

1. Suppose $t \lesssim \gamma_y, \gamma_z$. This implies $\delta t \lesssim \delta\gamma_y, \delta\gamma_z$ contradicting the assumption $x > y \wedge z$.
2. Suppose $t \not\lesssim \gamma_y$ and $t \not\lesssim \gamma_z$. Then the second axiom of stability yields (since $s' \neq \epsilon$) $s_y = s_z$. This implies $y \wedge z = [\delta] < [\delta s_y] \leq y, z$, a contradiction.
3. Finally suppose $t \lesssim \gamma_y$ and $t \not\lesssim \gamma_z$. Then $s' \in s_z - t$ implies $s_z \lesssim ts'$. Since

$t \lesssim \gamma_z$ we have $\{\epsilon\} = t - \gamma_z$ and thus $[t\gamma'_y] \in [t] \cdot ([\gamma_y] - [t]) = [\gamma_y] \cdot ([t] - [\gamma_y]) = \{[\gamma_y]\}$. Therefore we can proceed with $s_z \lesssim ts' \lesssim t\gamma'_y \sim \gamma_y$. Thus we found a transition s_z which is dominated by γ_y and γ_z, i.e. $x < [\delta s_z] \leq y \wedge z$, contradicting $x > y \wedge z$.

The induction step remains to be shown. Let $x = [\delta t \gamma]$ with $t \in T$. As abbreviation we write a for $[\delta t]$. Furthermore let $y' = a \vee y$ and $z' = a \vee z$. Then we have $x \vee y = x \vee a \vee y = x \vee y'$ and $x \vee z = x \vee z'$ since $x \geq a$. Moreover the infimum of y' and z' is a. The induction hypothesis yields
$x \vee (y' \wedge z') = (x \vee y') \wedge (x \vee z')$. The first step of the induction can be applied to the tripel (a, y, z): $a \vee (y \vee z) = (a \vee y) \wedge (a \vee z) = y' \vee z'$. Thus we get $x \vee (y \wedge z) = x \vee a \vee (y \wedge z) = x \vee (y' \wedge z') = (x \vee y') \wedge (x \vee z') = (x \vee y) \wedge (x \vee z)$ which concludes the proof of the first implication.

(i) $\Rightarrow$ *(ii)* For this implication we only give the idea of the proof: The following picture depicts the premisses of the inverse cube axiom. Since the order marked by thick lines and filled circles can not be embedded into a distributive lattice there must exist an element $a = y \wedge z$ with $x -\!\!< a$. This implies the validity of the inverse cube axiom.

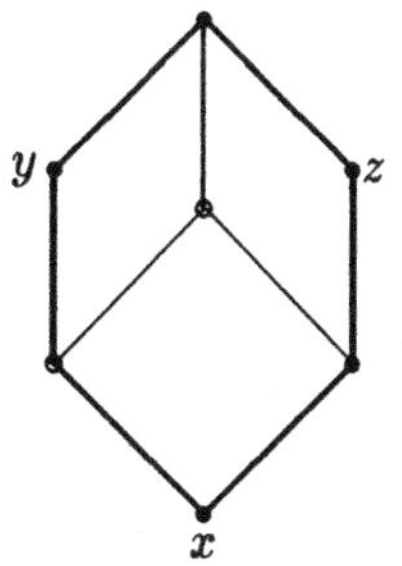

Analogously the order depicting the second axiom of stablity can not be embedded into a distributive lattice. Thus we have that a nondeterministic automaton with observable concurrency generating a dLI–domain is stable. □

Up to now we have that any stable automaton generates a dLI–domain and that any nondeterministic concurrency domain $(D, \leq, >\!\!-\!\!<)$ satsfying axiom (U) such that $(D, \leq)$ is a dLI–domain can be generated by a nondeterministic automaton with observable concurrency which is (by Theorem 7) stable. Our next aim is to show that any dLI–domain $(D, \leq)$ can be generated by a stable automaton. To do this we construct an equivalence relation $>\!\!-\!\!<_d$ on the prime intervals such that $(D, \leq, >\!\!-\!\!<_d)$ satisfies axiom (U).

A prime interval $\langle\, x', y' \,\rangle$ is a *direct cover* of a prime interval $\langle\, x, y \,\rangle$ (denoted by $\langle\, x, y \,\rangle -\!\!<_d \langle\, x', y' \,\rangle$) if $x -\!\!< x' \neq y -\!\!< y'$ holds. Let the *direct equivalence* $>\!\!-\!\!<_d$ be the least equivalence relation containing $-\!\!<_d$. A *dI–domain* is a bounded–complete dLI–domain. It is wellknown that a dI–domain $(D, \leq)$ satisfies axiom (R):

$$\forall x, y, z \in D^0 : \langle\, x, y \,\rangle >\!\!-\!\!<_d \langle\, x, z \,\rangle \implies y = z.$$

The following picture shows that this is not true anymore for dLI–domains since $\langle\, x, y \,\rangle$ and $\langle\, x, z \,\rangle$ are direct covers of $\langle\, \bot, a \,\rangle$.

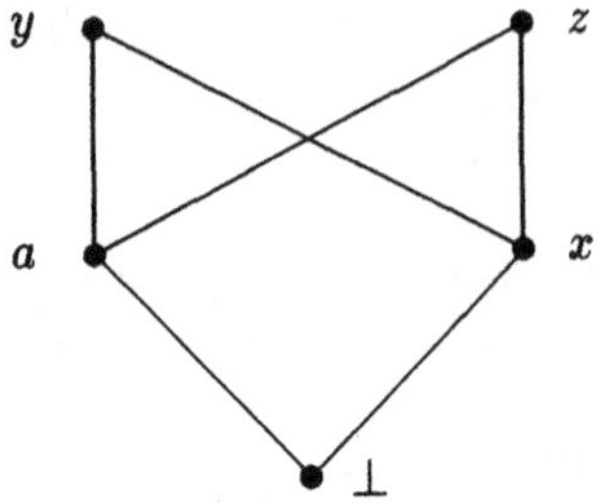

But a slightly weaker property holds in a dLI–domain for any compact elements x, y and z:
$\langle\, x, y \,\rangle \succ\!\!\!-\!\!\!\prec_d \langle\, x, z \,\rangle$ and $\{y, z\}$ is bounded in $(D, \leq) \implies y = z$.

The proof ([Kus94, Prop. 6.4.11]) is based on the fact that for any prime interval $\langle\, x, y \,\rangle$ there exists exactly one prime interval $\langle\, a, b \,\rangle$ with $\langle\, x, y \,\rangle \succ\!\!\!-\!\!\!\prec_d \langle\, a, b \,\rangle$ such that $a \leq x'$, $b \leq y'$ and $b \not\leq x'$ holds for any prime interval $\langle\, x', y' \,\rangle$ with $\langle\, x, y \,\rangle \succ\!\!\!-\!\!\!\prec_d \langle\, x', y' \,\rangle$. (For dI–domains this has been proved by Curien in [Cur86, Lemma 2.2.14].)

Now we are able to prove the following representation theorem for dLI–domains.

Theorem 8 An ω–domain $(D, \leq)$ is a dLI–domain if and only if there exists a stable automaton $\mathcal{A}$ with $(D, \leq) \cong (D(\mathcal{A}), \leq)$.

Proof Let $(D, \leq)$ be a dLI–domain. It is sufficient to show that $(D, \leq, \succ\!\!\!-\!\!\!\prec_d)$ satisfies axiom (U). Thus suppose $x, y_1, y_2, z \in D^0$ with $x -\!\!\!< y_i -\!\!\!< z$ for $i = 1, 2$ and $y_1 \neq y_2$. Since $\{y_1, y_2\}$ is bounded by z, by the fact mentioned above the prime intervals $\langle\, x, y_1 \,\rangle$ and $\langle\, x, y_2 \,\rangle$ are not equivalent with respect to $\succ\!\!\!-\!\!\!\prec_d$. The construction of the direct equivalence yields $\langle\, x, y_i \,\rangle \succ\!\!\!-\!\!\!\prec_d \langle\, y_{3-i}, z \,\rangle$ for $i = 1, 2$. Thus the chains $\{x, y_1, z\}$ and $\{x, y_2, z\}$ are equivalent with respect to the direct equivalence. Hence $(D, \leq, \succ\!\!\!-\!\!\!\prec_d)$ is a nondeterministic concurrency domain with axiom (U). Thus there exists a nondeterministic automaton with observable concurrency which generates an isomorphic domain. By Theorem 7 this automaton is stable.

The other implication is part of Theorem 7. □

Finally we present a representation theorem for dI–domains by our automata. We call a nondeterministic concurrent automaton $\mathcal{A} = (S, E, T, \star, \|)$ *deterministic* if $(p, a, q), (p, a, r) \in T$ imply $q = r$. In a deterministic concurrent automaton the residuum of two transitions contains at most one element. It can be shown inductively that the residuum of two computation sequences contains at most one element as well. Thus the set of all minimal upper bounds of any two compact elements of $(D(\mathcal{A}), \leq)$ is at most a singleton, i.e. $(D(\mathcal{A}), \leq)$ is a Scott–domain. Thus any stable deterministic automaton generates a dI–domain. Since $(D, \leq, \succ\!\!\!-\!\!\!\prec_d)$ satisfies axiom (R) if $(D, \leq)$ is a dI–domain the nondeterministic concurrent automaton induced by $(D, \leq, \succ\!\!\!-\!\!\!\prec_d)$ is deterministic. Therefore any dI–domain can be generated by a deterministic concurrent automaton which is stable by Theorem 6. Thus we proved

Theorem 9 An ω–domain $(D, \leq)$ is a dI–domain if and only if there exists a stable deterministic automaton $\mathcal{A}$ with $(D, \leq) \cong (D(\mathcal{A}), \leq)$.

References

[BCS93] BOLDI, P., F. CARBONE and N. SABADINI: *Concurrent automata, prime event structures and universal domains*, In: Semantics of Programming Languages and Model Theory, (M. Droste, Y. Gurevich, eds.), Gordon and Breach Publ., OPA Amsterdam, 1993, pp. 89–108.

[BD93] BRACHO, F. and M. DROSTE: *From domains to automata with concurrency.* In: 20th ICALP, Lecture Notes in Computer Science vol. 700, Springer, 1993, pp. 669–681.

[BD94] BRACHO, F. and M. DROSTE: *Labelled domains and automata with concurrency.* To appear in Theoretical Computer Science, 1994.

[Ber78] BERRY, G.: *Stable models of typed λ-calculi.* In: 5th ICALP, Lecture Notes in Computer Science vol. 62, Springer, 1978, pp. 72–89.

[Coq88] COQUAND, T.: *Categories of embeddings.* In: *3rd Annual Symposium on Logic in Computer Science* (Y. Gurevich, ed.), IEEE Computer Society, 1988.

[Cur86] CURIEN, P.L.: *Categorical Combinators, Sequential Algorithms and Functional Programming.* Research Notes in Theoretical Computer Science, Pitman, London, 1986.

[Die90] DIEKERT, V.: *Combinatorics on Traces.* Lecture Notes in Computer Science vol. 454, Springer, 1990.

[Dro90] DROSTE, M.: *Concurrency, Automata and Domains.* In: *17th ICALP*, Lecture Notes in Computer Science vol. 443, Springer, 1990, pp. 195–208.

[Dro92] DROSTE, M.: *Concurrent Automata and Domains.* Intern. J. of Found. of Comp. Science 3 (1992), 389–418.

[Dro93] DROSTE, M.: *A Kleene theorem for recognizable languages over concurrency monoids.* 1993.

[Grä78] GRÄTZER, G.: *General Lattice Theory.* Birkhäuser, 1978.

[Gun85] GUNTER, C.: *Profinite Solutions for Recursive Domain Equations.* PhD–Thesis, Univ. of Wisconsin, Madison, 1985.

[GJ88] GUNTER, C. and A. JUNG: *Coherence and consistency in domains.* In: *3rd Annual Symposium on Logic in Computer Science* (Y. Gurevich, ed.), IEEE Computer Society, 1988, pp. 309–317.

[Ho78] HOARE, C.A.R.: *Communicating sequential Processes.* Commun. ACM 21 (1978), 666–676.

[Jun88] JUNG, A.: *Cartesian Closed Categories of Domains.* Dissertation, TH Darmstadt, 1988.

[Kus94] KUSKE, D.: *Modelle nebenläufiger Prozesse – Monoide, Residuensysteme und Automaten.* Dissertation, Universität GHS Essen, 1994.

[Mi80] MILNER, R.: *Calculus of Communicating Processes.* Lecture Notes in Computer Science vol. 92, Springer, 1980.

[NW91] NIELSEN, M. and G. WINSKEL: *Models for concurrency.* In: *Handbook of Logic in Computer Science* (S. Abramsky, D.M. Gabbay, T.S.E. Maibaum, eds.), preliminary version, October 1991.

[PS88] PANANGADEN, P. and E.W. Stark: *Computations, residuals and the power of indeterminacy.* In: *Automata, Languages and Programming,* Lecture Notes in Computer Science vol. 317, Springer 1988, pp. 439–454.

[Per90] PERRIN, D.: *Finite automata.* In: *Handbook of Theoretical Computer Science: Formal Models and Semantics, vol. B* (J. van Leeuwen, ed.), Elsevier, 1990, pp. 1-57.

[Sta89] STARK, E.W.: *Connections between a concrete and an abstract model of concurrent systems.* In: *Proceedings of the 5th Conf. on the Mathematical Foundations of Programming Sematics*, Lecture Notes in Computer Science vol. 389, Springer, 1989, pp. 52–74.

[Win87] WINSKEL, G.: *Event structures.* In: *Petri Nets: Applications and Relationships to Other Models of Concurrency* (W. Brauer, W. Reisig, G. Rozenberg, eds.), Lecture Notes in Computer Science vol. 255, 1987, pp. 325–392.

[Zha89] ZHANG, G.Q.: *DI–domains as information systems.* In: 16th ICALP, Lecture Notes in Computer Science vol. 372, Springer, 1989, pp. 773–788.

Algebraic and combinatorial properties of simple, coloured walks

Donatella Merlini, Renzo Sprugnoli, M. Cecilia Verri

Dipartimento di Sistemi e Informatica
Via Lombroso 6/17 - Firenze - Italy
e-mail: est@ifiidg.bitnet

Abstract. We investigate the algebraic rules for functionally inverting a Riordan array given by means of two analytic functions. In this way, we find an extension of the Lagrange Inversion Formula and we apply it to some combinatorial problems on simple coloured walks. For some of these problems we give both an algebraic and a combinatorial proof.

1 Introduction

Shapiro et al. [15] introduced the concept of a *Riordan array* in 1991. Their aim was to generalize the concept of *renewal array* as defined by Rogers [11] as far back as 1978, in an attempt to define a class of infinite low triangular arrays having properties similar to those of the Pascal triangle. As a matter of fact, similar concepts had been introduced in the literature several years earlier. For example, Hoggatt and Bicknell published a series of papers in the "Fibonacci Quarterly" dealing with what they called *convolutory array* or *convolution triangles* (see, e.g., [1, 6]), which are actually renewal arrays. Even before that, Jabotinsky [7, 8] had introduced an analogous concept, later "re-invented" by Carlitz [2]. This concept was used in the theory of Umbral Calculus [12, 13] and, more recently, it was discussed by Knuth [9] who called it *convolution matrices*. The only difference between this concept and renewal arrays is that it uses exponential generating functions instead of ordinary ones. When dealing with combinatorial sums, Riordan arrays seem to be a very powerful tool (see Theorem 2.1 below and Sprugnoli [16]). Furthermore, it is obvious that every convolution array $\{f_{n,k}\}_{n,k\in N}$ can be trasformed into an equivalent Riordan array when we consider the array $\{\frac{k!}{n!}f_{n,k}\}_{n,k\in N}$.

In the present paper we consider the class of simple coloured walks, i.e., walks on the integral lattice Z^2 made up of unitary steps (hence we call them *simple*) in three directions: east, north-east, north. Furthermore, we can have different kinds of steps in each direction, and each kind is conventionally distinguished by a different colour. Some well-known combinatorial structures, such as binary trees, Motzkin trees and parenthesized expressions, correspond to some particular cases of simple coloured walks. Coloured walks are also a way for dealing with simple walks in which the three kinds of steps can occur with different probabilities.

We show that simple coloured walks correspond to some particular Riordan arrays, and that therefore many combinatorial problems concerning these walks can be algebraically solved by using the corresponding Riordan array and the relative method of performing sums. Many of these problems are very difficult from a combinatorial point of view, so we have tried to give bijective proofs as well, at least for the simplest cases.

In Section 2, we summarize the main properties of Riordan arrays used in our paper: the explicit form of an element in the inverse of a Riordan array is new, although some similar properties are present in the Umbral Calculus theory. In Section 3, we define various kinds of simple coloured walks and prove some basic properties for them. Finally, in Section 4, we give the algebraic proof of many complicated identities on simple coloured walks and a combinatorial proof of some of them in order to evidence the difference between the two approaches.

2 Riordan Arrays

Let $\{f_k\}_{k\in N}$ be a sequence of (real) numbers. The generating function $f(t)$ of the sequence is defined as $f(t) = \mathcal{G}_t\{f_k\}_{k\in N} = \sum_{k=0}^{\infty} f_k t^k$ (the subscript t in $\mathcal{G}_t$ binding the indeterminate t, will almost always be understood). Moreover, given an analytic function $f(t)$, the notation $[t^n]f(t)$ will denote the coefficient of t^n in the Taylor development of $f(t)$ around $t = 0$. The same notation will be applied to formal power series. A *Riordan array* is an infinite low triangular array $\{d_{n,k} | n, k \in N\}$ defined by a couple $(d(t), h(t))$ of formal power series in the sense that $d_{n,k} = [t^n]d(t)(th(t))^k$. As we shall see, $(d(t), h(t))$ is a sort of "generating function" that defines the Riordan array. We are interested in extracting the coefficient $[t^n]$ from some generating function depending on $d(t)$ and $h(t)$. When we are able to find the exact value of the coefficient, $d(t)$ and $h(t)$ can be considered as general formal power series. However, we are sometimes unable to extract the coefficient and may be satisfied with an asymptotic value. In this case, we should use analytic considerations and therefore require that $d(t)$ and $h(t)$ be analytic functions. We usually assume that $d(0) \neq 0$; when we also have $h(0) \neq 0$, the Riordan array is called *proper*. Another way of characterizing Riordan arrays is to consider their corresponding bivariate generating functions. We can easily prove that:

$$d(t, w) = \frac{d(t)}{1 - twh(t)}.$$

The fundamental property of Riordan arrays is given by the following result:

Theorem 2.1 *Let $D = (d(t), h(t))$ be a Riordan array and let $f(t)$ be the generating function of the sequence $\{f_n\}_{n\in N}$. Then:*

$$\sum_{k=0}^{\infty} d_{n,k} f_k = [t^n]d(t)f(th(t)).$$

Conversly, if $\{d_{n,k} | n, k \in N\}$ is an infinite triangle such that for every sequence $\{f_k\}_{k\in N}$ we have:

$$\mathcal{G}\left\{\sum_{k=0}^{\infty} d_{n,k} f_k\right\} = d(t)f(th(t)),$$

where $f(t)$ is the generating function of the sequence f_k, and $d(t)$, $h(t)$ are two analytic functions not depending on $f(t)$, then the triangle defined by the Riordan array $D = (d(t), h(t))$ coincides with $\{d_{n,k}\}$.

The reader is referred to Sprugnoli [16] for the proof. Proper Riordan arrays are further characterized by the following property, proved in Rogers [11].

Theorem 2.2 *Let $(d(t), h(t))$ be a proper Riordan array; then a sequence $A = \{a_k\}_{k \in N}$ exists such that $\forall n \in N$*

$$d_{n+1,k+1} = a_0 d_{n,k} + a_1 d_{n,k+1} + \dots$$

and the generating function $A(t)$ of the sequence A is uniquely determined by the relation $h(t) = A(th(t))$.

The usual row-by-column product of two Riordan arrays is a Riordan array. This can be proved in the following way; if $D = (d(t), h(t)) = \{d_{n,k}\}$ and $F = (f(t), g(t)) = \{f_{n,k}\}$ then:

$$D * F = \{\sum_j d_{n,j} f_{j,k}\} = \{\sum_j [t^n] d(t)(th(t))^j [y^j] f(y)(yg(y))^k\} =$$

$$= \{[t^n] d(t) \sum_j ([y^j] f(y)(yg(y))^k)(th(t))^j\} =$$

$$= \{[t^n] d(t) f(th(t))(th(t)g(th(t)))^k\} = (d(t)f(th(t)), h(t)g(th(t))).$$

Obviously, the Riordan array $I = (1, 1)$ is the only identity. So, if $D = (d(t), h(t))$, is a proper Riordan array, it has an inverse $D^{-1} = (\bar{d}(t), \bar{h}(t))$

$$(d(t), h(t)) * (\bar{d}(t), \bar{h}(t)) = (d(t)\bar{d}(th(t)), h(t)\bar{h}(th(t))) = (1, 1)$$

and therefore

$$\bar{d}(y) = \left[\frac{1}{d(t)} \middle| y = th(t)\right], \qquad \bar{h}(y) = \left[\frac{1}{h(t)} \middle| y = th(t)\right].$$

The existence and uniqueness of $\bar{d}(t)$, $\bar{h}(t)$ is guaranteed by the Lagrange Inversion Formula (LIF). There is a striking relationship between the function $\bar{h}(t)$ and the A-sequence for D, and, conversely, between $h(t)$ and the A-sequence for D^{-1}. By Theorem 2.2 we have:

$$\bar{h}(y) = \bar{h}(th(t)) = \frac{1}{h(t)} = \frac{1}{A(th(t))} = \frac{1}{A(y)}.$$

In general, no simple relationship exists between $d(t)$, $\bar{d}(t)$ and the other quantities. A fine property of coloured walk arrays is that a simple connection can be found between all the functions involved in any array and their inverse.

The Lagrange Inversion Formula can be further used to find an explicit formula for the elements of D^{-1} as a function of the proper Riordan array $D = (d(t), h(t))$, as follows:

Theorem 2.3 *Let $D = (d(t), h(t))$ be any proper Riordan array. Then the elements $\bar{d}_{n,k}$ of the inverse Riordan array $D^{-1} = (\bar{d}(t), \bar{h}(t))$ are given by the formula*

$$\bar{d}_{n,k} = \frac{1}{n}[y^{n-k}]\left(k - \frac{yd'(y)}{d(y)}\right)\frac{1}{d(y)h(y)^n}.$$

Proof. We have

$$\bar{d}_{n,k} = [t^n][w^k]\frac{\bar{d}(t)}{1 - tw\bar{h}(t)} = [t^n][w^k]\left[\frac{\bar{d}(t)}{1-wy}\middle| y = t\bar{h}(t)\right].$$

We now observe that $h(y)\bar{h}(yh(y)) = 1$ and $\bar{h}(t)h(t\bar{h}(t)) = 1$; consequently $y = t\bar{h}(t)$ if and only if $t = yh(y)$ and therefore:

$$\bar{d}_{n,k} = [w^k][t^n]\left[\frac{\bar{d}(t)}{1-wy}\middle| t = yh(y)\right] = [w^k][t^n]\left[\frac{1}{d(y)(1-wy)}\middle| y = th^{-1}(y)\right].$$

By applying the LIF, we now obtain:

$$\bar{d}_{n,k} = [w^k]\frac{1}{n}[y^{n-1}]\left(\frac{\partial}{\partial y}\frac{1}{d(y)(1-wy)}\right)h^{-n}(y) =$$

$$= [w^k]\frac{1}{n}[y^{n-1}]\left(\sum_{r=0}^{\infty} w^{r+1}y^r(r+1) - \frac{d'(y)}{d(y)}\sum_{r=0}^{\infty} w^r y^r\right)\frac{1}{d(y)h(y)^n} =$$

$$= \frac{1}{n}[y^{n-k}]\left(k - \frac{yd'(y)}{d(y)}\right)\frac{1}{d(y)h(y)^n}.$$

■

Obviously, when $k = 0$, Theorem 2.2 reduces to the LIF. Moreover, whenever we find an identity like

$$\sum_{k=0}^{\infty} d_{n,k} f_k = g_n,$$

by Theorem 2.1, we can immediately conclude that the inverse identity

$$\sum_{k=0}^{\infty} \bar{d}_{n,k} g_k = f_n$$

also holds. See [4, 10] for some significant examples treated by other methods.

3 The Riordan Arrays for Coloured Walks

Let us consider the Z^2 lattice and the finite walks starting from the origin O and composed by:

i) *east* steps, i.e., steps from (x, y) to $(x+1, y)$; these steps can be distinguished by their colour, which is chosen from a set of a different colours;
ii) *north-east* steps, i.e., steps from (x, y) to $(x+1, y+1)$; these steps can be distinguished by their colour, which is chosen from a set of b different colours;
iii) *north* steps, i.e., steps from (x, y) to $(x, y+1)$; these steps can be distinguished by their colour, which is chosen from a set of c different colours.

Since each step is unitary, i.e., x and/or y are only incremented by 1, the walks are called *simple*; they are also called *coloured* because of the different colours each step can take on. We are interested in *weakly underdiagonal walks*, that is, walks whose ending point (x, y) is such that $x \geq y$; in other words, the ending point is not situated above the main diagonal $x = y$. When the walk never goes above this diagonal, we simply call it an *underdiagonal walk*. We are interested in simple coloured (weakly) underdiagonal walks and, for simplicity's sake, the term *walk* will henceforth refer to this kind of walk. In Table 1, we give the number of underdiagonal and weakly underdiagonal walks when $a = 1, b = 2, c = 1$, i.e., when there only is one colour for the east and north steps, but two colours (for ex., black and red) for the diagonal, or north-east, steps. In Table 1, n refers to the total number of steps which make up the walks and k refers to the distance of the ending point of the walk from the main diagonal; the distance is measured along the $x-$ or $y-$axis. So, for example, there are 48 underdiagonal walks of length 4 ending just one position below the main diagonal, while there are 56 analogous weakly underdiagonal walks. In Figure 1, we show the 5 underdiagonal walks corresponding to $n = 2$, $k = 0$, and, on the right, we indicate the only walk to be added to obtain the corresponding weakly underdiagonal walks. It

n/k	0	1	2	3	4	5	n/k	0	1	2	3	4	5
0	1						0	1					
1	2	1					1	2	1				
2	5	4	1				2	6	4	1			
3	14	14	6	1			3	20	15	6	1		
4	42	48	27	8	1		4	70	56	28	8	1	
5	132	165	110	44	10	1	5	252	210	120	45	10	1

Table 1. Number of underdiagonal and weakly underdiagonal walks for $a = 1, b = 2, c = 1$

is a simple matter to prove the following:

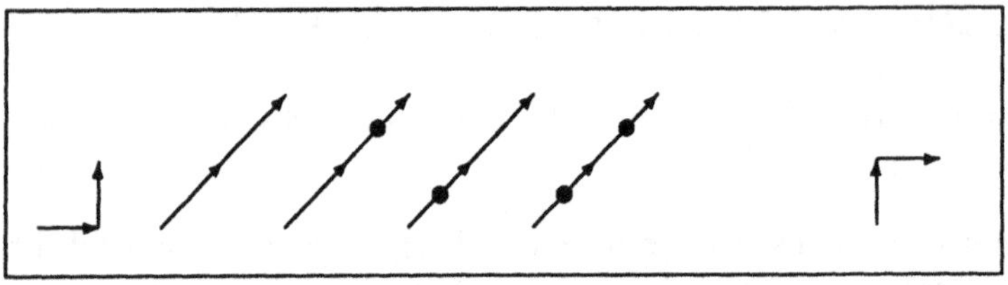

Fig. 1. Underdiagonal and weakly underdiagonal walks for $n = 2, k = 0$

Theorem 3.1 *The infinite arrays $\{p_{n,k}\}$ and $\{q_{n,k}\}$, where $p_{n,k}$ are the n-long underdiagonal walks ending at a distance k from the main diagonal, and $q_{n,k}$ are the corresponding weakly underdiagonal walks, are two Riordan arrays having (a, b, c) as their A-sequence.*

Proof. For $k > 0$, the walks counted by $p_{n,k}$ are made up of:

i) the walks of length $n-1$ ending at distance $k-1$ from the main diagonal, followed by any one of the a coloured east steps;
ii) the walks of length $n-1$ ending at distance k from the main diagonal, followed by any one of the b coloured north-east steps;
iii) the walks of length $n-1$ ending at distance $k+1$ from the main diagonal, followed by any one of the c coloured north steps.

Since the numbers in the column $k = 0$ are arbitrary, we are able to prove our statement by means of Theorem 2.2. ∎

Theorem 2.2 also allows us to find the h-function, common to the two Riordan arrays. In fact, the relation $h(t) = A(th(t))$ becomes

$$h(t) = at^2h(t)^2 + bth(t) + c$$

and the solution having $h(0) \neq 0$ is:

$$h(t) = \frac{1 - bt - \sqrt{\Delta}}{2ct^2},$$

where $\Delta = 1 - 2bt + (b^2 - 4ac)t^2$.

Theorem 3.2 *The explicit forms of the two Riordan arrays for the underdiagonal and weakly underdiagonal walks are, respectively:*

$$\{p_{n,k}\} = \left(\frac{1 - bt - \sqrt{\Delta}}{2act^2}, \frac{1 - bt - \sqrt{\Delta}}{2ct^2}\right), \qquad \{q_{n,k}\} = \left(\frac{1}{\sqrt{\Delta}}, \frac{1 - bt - \sqrt{\Delta}}{2ct^2}\right).$$

Proof. A reasoning analogous to the one in the proof of Theorem 3.1 allows us to express the generating function for the sequence $\{p_{n+1,0}\}_{n\in N}$ in terms of $h(t)$, as follows

$$\frac{d(t)-1}{t} = bd(t) + ctd(t)h(t).$$

This equation can be solved with respect to $d(t)$ by giving the d-function for the underdiagonal walks. As far as weakly underdiagonal walks are concerned, let us first consider the ones corresponding to the A-sequence (c,b,a); the discriminant Δ is the same as before and therefore the h-function is $\tilde{h}(t) = (1-bt-\sqrt{\Delta})/(2at^2)$. We can now observe that $q_{n+1,0}$ is obtained by summing b times $q_{n,0}$, c times the column $k=1$ and a times the column $k=1$ in the (c,b,a) case, which is column $k=-1$ in our case. Consequently, we get the following relation:

$$\frac{d(t)-1}{t} = bd(t) + ctd(t)h(t) + atd(t)\tilde{h}(t).$$

By using the expression found for $\tilde{h}(t)$ and solving for $d(t)$, we find the formula in the statement of the Theorem. ■

Another interesting kind of walks are *Shapiro's walks* [14], which are characterized by the fact that the north-east steps on the main diagonal may have different colours from the north-east steps on the other diagonals. In other words, we have (a,b,c) colours as in the walks above, but on the main diagonal b' colours $(b' \neq b)$ are used for north-east steps. In Table 2, we illustrate the triangles for Shapiro's underdiagonal and weakly underdiagonal walks when $a=1, b=2, c=1$ (as in Table 1), but $b'=1$. We can apply Theorem 3.2's proof to Shapiro's arrays:

n/k	0	1	2	3	4	5	n/k	0	1	2	3	4	5
0	1						0	1					
1	1	1					1	1	1				
2	2	3	1				2	3	3	1			
3	5	9	5	1			3	9	10	5	1		
4	14	28	20	7	1		4	29	34	21	7	1	
5	42	90	75	35	9	1	5	97	117	83	36	9	1

Table 2. Number of Shapiro's underdiagonal and weakly underdiagonal walks for $a=1, b=2, c=1, b'=1$

Theorem 3.3 *The explicit forms of the two Riordan arrays of underdiagonal and weakly underdiagonal Shapiro's walks are, respectively:*

$$\{s_{n,k}\} = \left(\frac{1-(2b'-b)t-\sqrt{\Delta}}{2t(b-b'+(ac+b'^2-bb')t)}, \frac{1-bt-\sqrt{\Delta}}{2ct^2}\right)$$

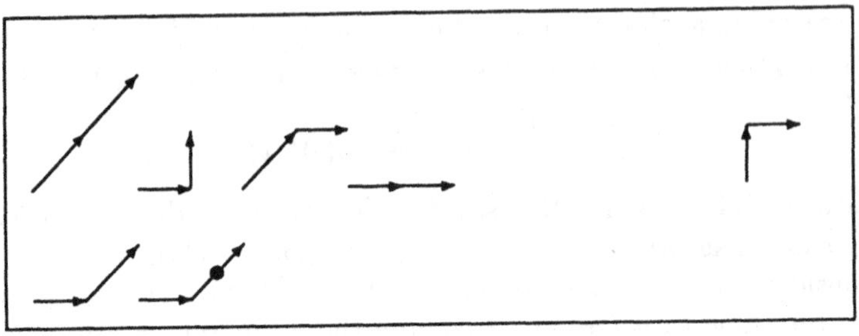

Fig. 2. Shapiro's underdiagonal and weakly underdiagonal walks for $n = 2$

$$\{r_{n,k}\} = \left(\frac{(b-b')t - \sqrt{\Delta}}{t(2b + t(b'^2 - 2bb' + 4ac)) - 1}, \frac{1 - bt - \sqrt{\Delta}}{2ct^2} \right).$$

Proof. The function $h(t)$ is only determined by the three values a, b, c and therefore coincides with the previous case. To compute the function $d(t)$, we observe that $s_{n+1,0} = b's_{n,0} + cs_{n,1}$. Therefore, we have the relation

$$\frac{d(t) - 1}{t} = b'd(t) + cth(t)d(t).$$

By solving for $d(t)$, we obtain our result. In a similar way, we obtain the function $d(t)$ for weakly underdiagonal walks. ∎

From an algebraic point of view, it is important to determine the Riordan arrays which are the inverse of the above walk arrays. As we observed at the end of Section 2, every combinatorial sum $\sum_{k=0}^{\infty} d_{n,k} f_k = g_n$ involving the number of (weakly) underdiagonal walks can be trasformed into another combinatorial sum $\sum_{k=0}^{\infty} \bar{d}_{n,k} g_k = f_n$. Moreover, as will be shown further on, the inverse arrays can be useful for finding formulas relative to the single elements of the original arrays. Unfortunately, there is no simple way (as far as we know) to attach a combinatorial meaning to the numbers appearing in the inverse arrays.

Theorem 3.4 *The inverse of the four kinds of walk arrays considered above are:*

$$\{\bar{p}_{n,k}\} = \left(\frac{a}{a + bt + ct^2}, \frac{1}{a + bt + ct^2} \right), \quad \{\bar{q}_{n,k}\} = \left(\frac{a - ct^2}{a + bt + ct^2}, \frac{1}{a + bt + ct^2} \right),$$

$$\{\bar{s}_{n,k}\} = \left(\frac{a + (b - b')t}{a + bt + ct^2}, \frac{1}{a + bt + ct^2} \right),$$

$$\{\bar{r}_{n,k}\} = \left(\frac{a + (b - b')t - ct^2}{a + bt + ct^2}, \frac{1}{a + bt + ct^2} \right).$$

Proof. As a consequence of Theorem 2.2, we have:

$$\bar{h}(t) = \frac{1}{A(t)} = \frac{1}{a + bt + ct^2},$$

which is the h-function common to the four cases. Let us now consider the underdiagonal walks $\{p_{n,k}\}$:

$$\bar{d}(t) = \left[\frac{1}{d(y)} \middle| t = yh(y) \right].$$

We can obtain an explicit value for $y = y(t)$ having $y(0) = 0$ because the relation between y and t is a second order equation. Thus, we find:

$$y = \frac{t}{a + bt + ct^2},$$

and by substituting this value in $1/d(y)$ we immediately obtain the result desired. The other expressions are found in the same way. ∎

In a sense, these inverse arrays are simpler than the original ones and allow us to apply Theorem 2.3 to look for an explicit form relative to the number of walks. The simplest case is given by the underdiagonal walks.

Theorem 3.5 *The number $\{p_{n,k}\}$ of n-length underdiagonal walks ending at a distance k from the main diagonal is:*

$$p_{n,k} = \frac{k}{na}[y^{n-k}](a + by + cy^2)^{n+1} + \frac{1}{na}[y^{n-k-1}](b + 2cy)(a + by + cy^2)^n.$$

Proof. By applying Theorem 2.3, we immediately obtain:

$$p_{n,k} = \frac{1}{n}[y^{n-k}] \left(k - \frac{yd'(y)}{d(y)} \right) \frac{1}{d(y)h(y)^n} =$$

$$= \frac{1}{n}[y^{n-k}] \left(k + y\frac{b + 2cy}{a + by + cy^2} \right) \frac{a + by + cy^2}{a}(a + by + cy^2)^n.$$

Then, by developing this expression, we easily obtain the result desired. ∎

Obtaining the result desired for other kinds of walks is not difficult from a conceptual point of view but it requires several computations, which the reader can easily do by himself.

When $b^2 - 4ac = 0$, the trinomial $a + bt + ct^2$ can be expressed as the square of a binomial, and we get the following result:

Theorem 3.6 *For the underdiagonal walks corresponding to a, b, c, such that $b^2 - 4ac = 0$, we have the following explicit formulas:*

$$p_{n,k} = a^n \frac{k+1}{n+1} \left(\frac{2c}{b}\right)^{n-k} \binom{2n+2}{n-k}$$

$$\bar{p}_{n,k} = \left(\frac{2c}{b}\right)^{n-k} \frac{1}{a^k} \binom{n+k+1}{n-k} (-1)^{n-k}.$$

Proof. The formula of Theorem 3.5 reduces to:

$$p_{n,k} = \frac{k}{na}[y^{n-k}]a^n(\frac{2c}{b}y+1)^{2n+2} + \frac{1}{na}[y^{n-k-1}](b+2cy)a^n(\frac{2c}{b}y+1)^{2n} =$$

$$= \frac{a^n}{n}\left[[y^{n-k}]k(\frac{2c}{b}y+1)^{2n+2} + [y^{n-k-1}](b+2cy)\frac{4c}{b}(\frac{2c}{b}y+1)^{2n+1}\right] =$$

$$= \frac{a^n}{n}\left[k\binom{2n+2}{n-k}\left(\frac{2c}{b}\right)^{n-k} + \frac{4c}{b}\binom{2n+1}{n-k-1}\left(\frac{2c}{b}\right)^{n-k-1}\right].$$

By developing this expression, we easily get the first result desired and from the Riordan array definition, we obtain:

$$\bar{p}_{n,k} = [t^n]\frac{at^k}{a^{k+1}\left(\frac{2c}{b}t+1\right)^{2k+2}} = \frac{1}{a^k}\binom{-2k-2}{n-k}\left(\frac{2c}{b}\right)^{n-k}$$

and this proves the second result. ■

4 Identities on symmetric walks

In this section, we investigate *symmetric* walks, i. e., walks having $A = (a, b, a)$ as their A–sequence. Symmetric coloured walks are characterized by a large number of combinatorial identities. The concept of Riordan arrays allows us to give almost immediate proofs of these identities. However, when we also try to derive a combinatorial proof, we frequently encounter difficulties and have rarely obtained positive results. Consequently, the aim of this section is to give several examples of combinatorial identities for which we can provide both an algebraic and a combinatorial proof, and to illustrate some other examples for which only algebraic proofs are available.

Let us denote by $q_{n,k}^{[a,b]}$ the number of symmetric weakly underdiagonal walks of length n ending at a distance k from the main diagonal, by $p_{n,k}^{[a,b]}$ and $s_{n,k}^{[a,b,b']}$ the corresponding underdiagonal walks and Shapiro's underdiagonal walks, and by $\beta^{[a,b]}$, $\mu^{[a,b]}$ and $\sigma^{[a,b,b']}$ the following functions:

$$\beta^{[a,b]}(t) = \frac{1}{\sqrt{\Delta}}, \qquad \mu^{[a,b]}(t) = \frac{1 - bt - \sqrt{\Delta}}{2at^2}$$

and

$$\sigma^{[a,b,b']}(t) = \frac{1-(2b'-b)t-\sqrt{\Delta}}{t(b-b'+(ac+b'^2-bb')t)},$$

where, $\Delta = 1-2bt+(b^2-4a^2)t^2$. According to Theorems 3.2 and 3.3, the Riordan arrays associated to the walks above are

$$\left\{q_{n,k}^{[a,b]}\right\} = \left(\beta^{[a,b]}(t), \mu^{[a,b]}(t)\right), \qquad \left\{p_{n,k}^{[a,b]}\right\} = \left(\frac{\mu^{[a,b]}(t)}{a}, \mu^{[a,b]}(t)\right)$$

and

$$\left\{s_{n,k}^{[a,b,b']}\right\} = \left(\sigma^{[a,b,b']}(t), \mu^{[a,b]}(t)\right).$$

By using the Darboux method [3, 5], we can evaluate the following asymptotic approximation:

Theorem 4.1 *The total number of symmetric weakly underdiagonal walks is approximated by:*

$$\sum_{k=0}^{n} q_{n,k}^{[a,b]} \approx \frac{1}{2}(b+2a)^n + \sqrt{\frac{b+2a}{a}}\binom{2n}{n}\frac{(b+2a)^n}{4^{n+1}}\left(\frac{b-2a}{8a(2n-1)}-1\right).$$

We can now prove some relationships among the elements of the above-mentioned families of walks having both an algebraic and a combinatorial proof:

Theorem 4.2 *We have:*

$$q_{n,k}^{[a,b+h]} = \sum_{i=0}^{n}\binom{n}{i}h^{n-i}q_{i,k}^{[a,b]}, \qquad p_{n,k}^{[a,b+h]} = \sum_{i=0}^{n}\binom{n}{i}h^{n-i}p_{i,k}^{[a,b]}.$$

Proof. By applying Theorem 2.1 to the Pascal triangle, we get:

$$\sum_{i=0}^{\infty}\binom{n}{i}f_i = [t^n]\frac{1}{1-t}f\left(\frac{t}{1-t}\right) = [t^n]\Omega(f(t))$$

and by iterating the application, we obtain:

$$\sum_{i=0}^{\infty}\binom{n}{i}h^{n-i}f_i = [t^n]\frac{1}{1-ht}f\left(\frac{t}{1-ht}\right) = [t^n]\Omega^h(f(t)).$$

From the previous relation we have:

$$\Omega^h(\beta^{[a,b]}(t)) = \beta^{[a,b+h]}(t) \qquad \text{and} \qquad \Omega^h(\mu^{[a,b]}(t)) = \mu^{[a,b+h]}(t);$$

therefore, for underdiagonal walks, we obtain:

$$q_{n,k}^{[a,b+h]} = [t^n]\beta^{[a,b+h]}(t)(t\mu^{[a,b+h]}(t))^k = [t^n]\Omega^h(\beta^{[a,b]}(t)(t\mu^{[a,b]}(t))^k) =$$

$$= \sum_{i=0}^{n}\binom{n}{i}h^{n-i}q_{i,k}^{[a,b]}.$$

The combinatorial explanation trivially follows by observing that the coefficient $\binom{n}{i} h^{n-i}$ represents the number of ways to insert $n-i$ north-east steps with h colours into an i-length walk. The corresponding identity for weakly underdiagonal walks is found in the same way. ■

Theorem 4.3 *If* $\{f_k\} = \{1, 0, -1, 0, 1, 0, -1, 0, 1, 0, \ldots\}$, *then*

$$\sum_{k=0}^{n} p_{n,k}^{[a,b]} f_k = b^n.$$

Proof. Let us start with the algebraic proof. The generating function of the sequence f_k is:

$$f(t) = \frac{1}{1+t^2}.$$

Then, by Theorem 2.1, we obtain:

$$\sum_{k=0}^{n} p_{n,k}^{[a,b]} f_k = [t^n] \frac{1}{a} \mu^{[a,b]}(t) f(t \mu^{[a,b]}(t)) =$$

$$= [t^n] \frac{1 - bt - \sqrt{\Delta}}{2a^2t^2} f\left(\frac{1 - bt - \sqrt{\Delta}}{2at}\right) = [t^n] \frac{1}{1-bt} = b^n.$$

Now let us discuss the combinatorial interpretation: if we multiply the numbers $p_{n,k}^{[a,b]}$ by the sequence f_k, we exclude the walks ending at an odd distance from the main diagonal because $f_{2k+1} = 0$; we assign *weight* $+1$ or -1 to the walks ending at an even distance. The theorem asserts that this weighted sum has value b^n, which corresponds to the number of walks made up of a north-east step only. There is a bijection between the walks ending at distance k whose last non-north-east step is north, and the walks ending at distance $k+2$ whose last non-north-east step is east. By transforming the last north step into an east step, the distance from the main diagonal increases by two. This bijection does not concern the b^n walks made up of north-east steps only and, therefore, if we give weight $+1$ and -1 alternatively to the sets in bijection, we get the proof. For example, if $A = (1, 1, 1)$, $n = 4$ and $k = 0$, the walk

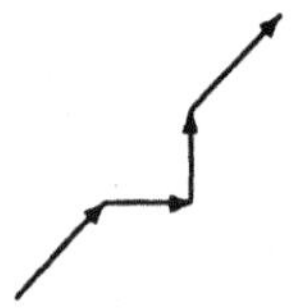

corresponds to the walk

having $n = 4$ and $k = 2$. The b^n excluded walks made up of north-east steps only are the following if $A = (1, 2, 1)$ and $n = 2$:

■

The following identity concerns the underdiagonal walks not having north-east steps and has both an algebraic and a combinatorial proof.

Theorem 4.4 *If* $\{f_k\} = \{1, 1, 0, -1, -1, 0, 1, 1, 0, -1, -1, 0, \ldots\}$, *then*

$$\sum_{k=0}^{n} p_{n,k}^{[a,0]} f_k = a^n.$$

Proof. The algebraic proof is the same as the one given in Theorem 4.3, with $f(t) = (1-t+t^2)^{-1}$. The combinatorial proof, however, is more complicated. We only take into consideration walks made up of east and north steps: obviously they exist only if n and k are both even or both odd. If we multiply the number of these walks by the sequence f_k, we only consider the walks ending at a distance $k \neq 2+3i$ from the main diagonal, for some positive integer i because $f_{2+3i} = 0$. In particular, if n is even (odd), the value of k must be even (odd), too, and different from $2+3i$. We define as *even*, diagonals at an even distance from the main diagonal and *odd*, the ones at an odd distance; once again the distance is measured along the $x-$ or $y-$axis. According to this definition, the main diagonal is even. Let us first examine an even integer n. Our aim is to establish a bijection between the walks ending at distance k from the main diagonal and either the walks ending at distance $k+2$ if $k \neq 3i$ or the ones ending at distance $k+4$ if $k = 3i$. In the first case, if we want to transform a walk ending at distance k into a walk ending at distance $k+2$, we need to move its ending point from the even diagonal k to the following even diagonal $k+2$. In order to do this, we take the point P having the highest coordinates among the points of the walk that intersect the odd diagonal $k+1$. Then we consider the walk made up of the same steps up to P and we add the remaining piece of walk specular with respect to the odd diagonal. The walk obtained is the corresponding walk ending at distance $k+2$. In the second case, we consider the point P having the highest coordinates among the points of the walk that intersect the even diagonal $k+2$. Then we take the walk made up of the same steps up to P and we add the remaining piece of walk specular with respect to the even diagonal. For example, the walk corresponding to $n = 6$ and $k = 0$

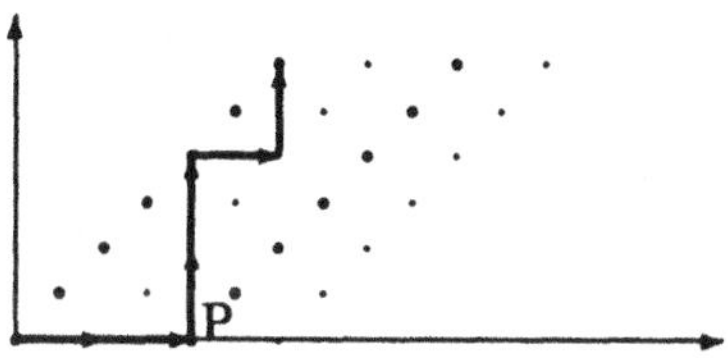

is transformed into the walk

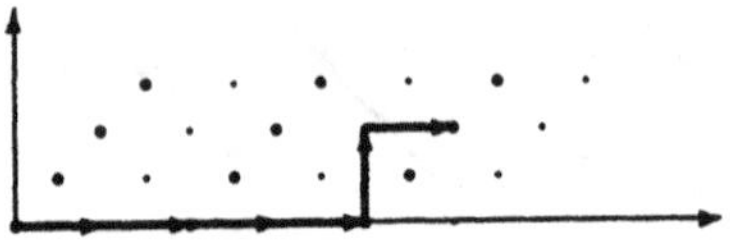

which corresponds to $n = 6$ and $k = 4$. The latter walk is obtained from the previous one by considering the symmetric piece of the walk (with respect to the even diagonal at distance two) contained between point $(2,0)$ and point $(3,3)$. If n is odd, we only need to change *even* with *odd*. For example, the walk corresponding to $n = 5$ and $k = 1$

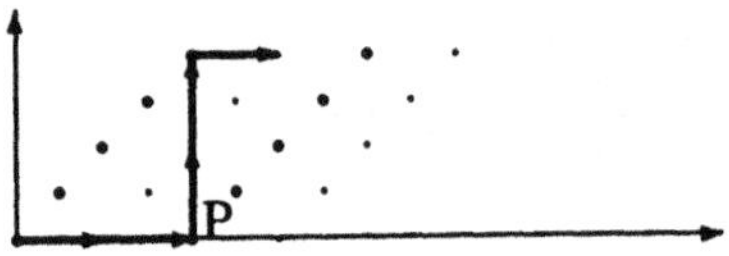

is trasformed into the walk

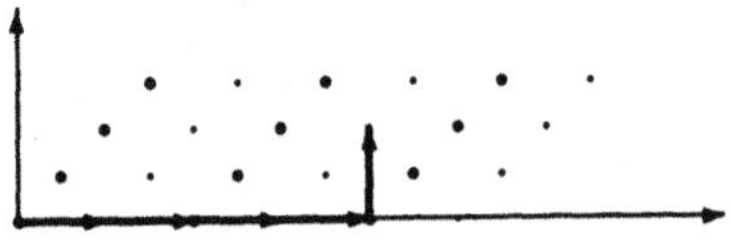

and this corresponds to $n = 5$ and $k = 3$. The *stair walks* are not involved if we apply the previous transformation for the increasing values of k, since they are always situated between the first and second diagonals. In fact, if n is even, we have $k = 0$ and are not able to find any point of the walk on the even diagonal at distance two. The same is true when n is odd. Finally, if we give weight $+1$ and -1 to the $\mu_{n,k}^{[a,0]}$, we can conclude our proof because the number of *stair walks* is exactly a^n. For example, if $A = (1,0,1)$ and $n = 2,3,4$, the uninvolved stair walks are the following:

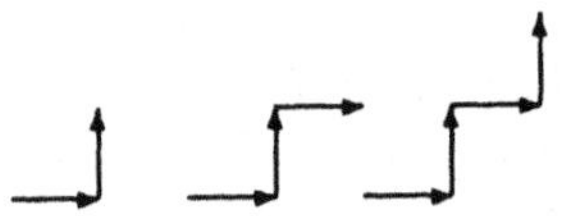

■

Let us now examine another identity involving Shapiro's symmetric underdiagonal walks. To this purpose, we expand the Z^2 lattice so that every east and north step can have a general length, say z. We can prove the following theorem:

Theorem 4.5 *(Shapiro's identity) If $b' = b - a(z-1)$ we have:*

$$\sum_{k=0}^{n} s_{n,k}^{[a,b,b']}(zk+1) = (b+2a)^n.$$

Proof. The algebraic proof can be obtained by applying Theorem 2.1, if we consider that the generating function of the sequence $\{zk+1\}_{k\in N}$ is $f(t) = (1+(z-1)t)/((1-t)^2)$. As far as the combinatorial proof of Shapiro's identity is concerned, let us consider a line λ parallel to the main diagonal and at distance 1 from it. We define the weight of a walk as the distance of its ending point from λ; clearly, all the walks counted by $s_{n,k}^{[a,b,b']}$ have a weight of $zk+1$. The total weight of all of Shapiro's symmetric underdiagonal walks is therefore:

$$W_n = \sum_{k=0}^{n} s_{n,k}^{[a,b,b']}(zk+1),$$

and the theorem identity is proved if we prove that $W_n = (b+2a)^n$. Let us proceed by induction on n. The initial cases $W_0 = 1$ and $W_1 = b+2a$ are trivial and can be checked by inspection. Now, let us assume $W_n = (b+2a)^n$ and take a walk not ending on the main diagonal. Let w be its weight; the walk generates the following walks of length $n+1$: a walks of weight $(w+z)$, b walks of weight w and a walks of weight $(w-z)$. Clearly, the total balance for these walks is $(b+2a)w$. When we have a walk ending on the main diagonal, its weight is $w=1$ and it can only produce b' walks of length w and a walks of length $(w+z)$. The total balance is again $b'w + a(w+z) = (b+2a)w$ because $b' = b - a(z-1)$. Hence, every walk of length n and weight w produces some walks of length $n+1$ and a total weight of $(b+2a)w$. Since all the walks are obtained in this way, we conclude that $W_{n+1} = (b+2a)W_n = (b+2a)^{n+1}$. ∎

The following identities will only be proved algebraically. The first one is represented by a relation in which Fibonacci's number sequence F_n appear.

Theorem 4.6 *If* $\{f_k\} = \{0,1,1,0,0,0,-1,-1,0,0,0,1,1,0,0,0,-1,-1,\ldots\}$, *then*

$$\sum_{k=0}^{n} \mu_{n,k}^{[a,0]} f_k = F_n a^n.$$

Proof. The generating function of the sequence f_k is $f(t) = t/(1-t+t^2-t^3+t^4)$, and so for Theorem 2.1 the proof is complete. ∎

The last two identities concern the symmetric underdiagonal walks corresponding to values of a, b, c such that $b^2 - 4ac = 0$, and for this reason they represent an application of Theorem 3.6; in particular they correspond to the sequence $A = (1,2,1)$. These results are probably not very significant from a combinatorial point of view, but they evidence the validity of an algebraic approach in the search of closed forms for combinatorial sums.

Theorem 4.7 *If* $\{f_k\} = \{1,-1,0,1,-1,0,1,-1,0,1,-1\ldots\}$ *and* $\{g_k\} = \{0,1,$ $-2,1,2,-4,2,3,-6,3,4,-8,4\ldots\}$, *then*

$$\sum_{k=0}^{n} p_{n\,k}^{[1,2]} f_k = 1, \qquad \sum_{k=0}^{n} (-1)^{n-k}\binom{n+k-1}{2k+1} = f_n$$

and

$$\sum_{k=0}^{n} p_{n,k}^{[1,2]} g_k = n, \qquad \sum_{k=0}^{n} (-1)^{n-k} \binom{n+k-1}{2k+1} k = g_n.$$

Proof. The first identity derives from Theorem 2.1, with $f(t) = (t^2 + t + 1)^{-1}$. The second identity derives from Theorem 3.6, for which we have:

$$\bar{p}_{n,k}^{[1,2]} = (-1)^{n-k} \binom{n+k-1}{2k+1}.$$

The other identities are proved in an analogous way, if we consider that the generating function of the sequence g_k is $g(t) = t/(t^2 + t + 1)^2$. ■

References

1. M. Bicknell, V. E. Hoggatt: Unit determinants in generalized Pascal triangles, *Fibonacci Quarterly*, 11 (Apr. 1973), 131-144.
2. L. Carlitz: Generalized Stirling and related numbers, *Rivista di Matematica della Università di Parma*, serie 4, 4, 79-99, 1978.
3. L. Comtet: *Advanced Combinatorics*, Reidel, Dordrecht, 1974.
4. G.P. Egorychev: *Integral representation and the computation of combinatorial sums*, Translations of mathematical monographs 59, American Mathematical Society, 1984.
5. D.H. Greene, D.E. Knuth: *Mathematics for the Analysis of Algorithms*, Birkäuser, 1982.
6. V. E. Hoggatt, M. Bicknell-Johnson: Numerator polynomial coefficient arrays for Catalan and related sequence convolution triangles, *Fibonacci Quarterly*, 15 (Feb. 1977), 30-34.
7. E. Jabotinsky, Sur la représentation de la composition de fonctions par un produit de matrices. Application à l'itération de e^x et de $e^x - 1$, *Comptes Rendus Hebdomadaires des Sciences de L'Academie des Sciences*, 224, 323-324, 1947.
8. E. Jabotinsky, Representation of functions by matrices. Application to Faber polynomials, *Proceedings of the American Mathematical Society*, 4, 546-553, 1953.
9. D. E. Knuth, Convolution polynomial, *The Mathematica Journal*, 2, 4, 67-78, 1992.
10. J. Riordan: *Combinatorial identities*, Wiley, New York, 1968.
11. D. G. Rogers, Pascal triangles: Catalan numbers and renewal arrays, *Discrete Mathematics*, 22, 301-310, 1978.
12. S. Roman: *The Umbral Calculus*, Academic Press, Orlando, 1978.
13. S. Roman, G. C. Rota: The umbral calculus, *Advances in Mathematics*, 27, 95-188, 1978.
14. L.V. Shapiro: Private Communication.
15. L.V. Shapiro, S. Getu, W.-J. Woan, L. Woodson: The Riordan group. *Discrete Applied Mathematics*, 34, 229-239, 1991.
16. R. Sprugnoli, Riordan arrays and combinatorial sums, to appear in *Discrete Mathematics*.

Probabilistic Analysis of an Election Algorithm in a Tree

Yves Métivier and Nasser Saheb

LaBRI, Université Bordeaux I, ENSERB,
351 cours de la Libération, 33405 Talence, France

Abstract. In this paper we consider the well-known case of election in a tree, and we study the probability for any vertex of a given tree to be elected. In particular, we show that if we consider the probability distribution based on the comparison of the election probabilities of neighbour vertices, there is one or two vertices having the highest probability of being elected. We give a very simple algorithm to compute these vertices, and we prove that in fact they are the medians.
Exact computations are done for special families of trees as filiform trees, wheels and crystals.

Keywords : Election, Labelled Graphs, Median, Probabilistic analysis, Tree.

1 Introduction

The aim of an election is to choose exactly one element in a set : this element is called elected or leader. The leader can be used subsequently to make decisions in a distributed system or to centralize some information. The election problem is standard in the domain of distributed algorithms, and many solutions are known [1], [7], [10], [12]. In this paper we consider the well-known case of election in a tree, and study the probability for any vertex of a given tree to be elected.

Election algorithms can be conveniently described by means of graph rewriting systems [10]. We suppose that initially every vertex and every edge has the same label - this assumption reflects the initial homogeneity of the distributed system, all processes and chanels are initially undistinguishable. Now we look for a noetherian graph rewriting system such that when, after some number of rewriting steps, we get an irreducible labelled graph then there is a special label that is attached to exactly one vertex; this vertex is considered as elected.

In the case of trees we consider the following one. The set L of labels is equal to $\{\mathbf{N}, \mathbf{F}, \mathbf{T}\}$.

* This research was supported by EC Cooperative Action IC-1000 (project ALTEC: *Algorithms for Future Technologies*).

Initially every vertex of the tree is labelled with **N**. The rewriting system $\mathcal{R}$ has two rules:

(1) if an **N**–labelled vertex x, is linked to exactly one **N**–labelled vertex then x can be relabelled **F**,

(2) if an **N**–labelled vertex has no **N**–labelled vertices in its neighbourhood then it can be relabelled **T**.

We have :

Proposition 1. *If the graph rewriting system $\mathcal{R}$ works on a tree with n vertices, such that initially every vertex is labelled* **N** *then after n rewriting steps we get an irreducible graph, with exactly one* **T***-labelled vertex; this vertex is the elected vertex. Moreover, any vertex may be elected.*

In this work we study the probability for any vertex of a given tree to be elected. In particular, we show that if the probability distribution is based on the number of leaf-removal processes leading to the election of a given vertex, there is one or two vertices having the highest probability of being elected. We give a very simple algorithm to compute these vertices, and we prove that in fact they are the medians.

Some regular shaped trees are analyzed more precisely.

The study of the election algorithm is restricted to the cases of trees. Its generalization for more complex graphs is quite complicated. We hope, however, that this first step sheds some light on the quantitative behaviour of election algorithms and motivates further studies in this direction. The techniques used here are based on the comparison of probabilities for various vertices and avoid a direct counting by means of combinatorial methods.

The paper is organized as follows. Section 1 concerns basic definitions and results about trees. In Section 2, the election is introduced, and basic properties are given. Section 3 provides an effective computation and links with median. Another interesting result obtained in this section is a comparison between the probabilistic behaviour of the election process in a tree and that of a random walk on this tree. Section 4 presents the calculus for special families of trees having a 'natural' centre.

It is possible to introduce other probability distributions leading to different results. For a more detailed version with illustrative examples the reader is referred to "Y. Métivier and N. Saheb. *Probabilistic analysis of an election algorithm in a tree,* Report 92-47 of LaBRI, Bordeaux I University, (1992)."

2 Basic notions and notation

A *simple graph* $G = (V, E)$ is defined as a finite set V of *vertices* together with a set E of *edges* which is a set of pairs of vertices, $E \subseteq \{\{v, v'\} \mid v, v' \in V\}$. The cardinality of V is called the *size* of the graph. We suppose that for each edge $e = \{v, v'\}$, $v \neq v'$, that is we consider graphs which contain no self-loop. Let $e = \{v, v'\}$ be an edge, then we say that v' is adjacent to v, or v' is a *neighbour* of v and that e is *incident* with v. For short, the edge $\{v, v'\}$ will be denoted vv'.

The *degree* of a vertex v, $deg(v)$, is the number of adjacent vertices to v. Any vertex of degree one is called a *leaf.* A *path* P from v_1 to v_i in G is a sequence

$P = v_1, e_1, v_2, e_2, ..., e_{i-1}, v_i$ of vertices and edges such that for $1 \leq j < i$, e_j is an edge incident with vertices v_j and v_{j+1}; $i-1$ is the *length* of P. If $v_1 = v_i$ then P is said to be a *cycle*.

Two vertices v and w are *connected* if there is a path from v to w. A graph is said to be connected if any two vertices are connected.

A *tree* is a connected graph containing no cycles. In a tree any two vertices v and v' are connected by precisely one path; the length of this path is the distance between v and v', it will be denoted by $D(v, v')$. From this property we deduce :

Proposition 2. *Let $T = (V, E)$ be a tree; then there exists at least one leaf v_f in V. Moreover if V contains more than one element, let e be the edge incident with v_f, then $(V \setminus \{v_f\}, E \setminus \{e\})$ is still a tree.*

From this proposition, we deduce that the algorithm given in the introduction elects a vertex in a tree. At each step we remove a leaf, until the tree contains exactly one vertex.

A tree T' is said to be a *factor* of a tree T if T' is equal to T or T' is a factor of a tree obtained by the removal of a leaf of T.

Let $T = (V, E)$ be a tree, let v be a vertex, we define Dist(v,T) by :

$$Dist(v, T) = \sum_{w \in T} D(v, w),$$

a vertex of V is said to be a *median* if it is an element of the set $m(T)$ defined by

$$m(T) = \{v \mid Dist(v, T) = min_{w \in V} Dist(w, T)\}.$$

A tree has one or two medians [15].

3 Probability of electing of a vertex in a tree

In this section, we consider a tree $T = (V, E)$ of size n with the set V of vertices identified with the integers $1, .., n$. According to the introductive proposition, whenever the rewriting system $\mathcal{R}$ is applied to T, whose vertices are initially labelled **N**, after n rewriting steps we get an irreducible tree with exactly one **T**-labelled vertex which is the elected vertex. Clearly, one may consider the first $n-1$ steps as a leaf-removal sequence; the remaining leaf is then the elected vertex. From now on, we identify the electing algorithm with a leaf-removal process leaving a vertex :

to any tree T as above it corresponds a leaf removal sequence of length $n-1$ and vice versa.

At each step of the leaf-removal process there are at least two nondeterministic choices, supposing that $n \geq 2$. The goal of this study is to evaluate the probability of election for vertices in a given tree, whenever probabilities are assigned to nondeterministic choices. Here, as in other similar problems, it is possible to develop several different points of view. In this paper we assume :

All leaf-removal sequences are of the same probability and, therefore, the probability $p_x(T)$ (or simply p_x, whenever T is understood from the context) of electing of a vertex x is the ratio between the number of those which leave this vertex and the number of all leaf-removal ones.

3.1 The poset of the set of factors

For a given tree T of size n, the class $\mathcal{T}$ of factors of T equipped with the binary relation 'factor of', denoted by $\sqsubseteq$, is a poset. It is easy to see that $(\mathcal{T}, \sqsubseteq)$ is a graded lattice, see [14, Chapter 3]. Let C_u^v be the number of all saturated chains from v to u, for $u, v \in \mathcal{T}$; it denotes then the number of all leaf-removal sequences which, applied to u, yield v.

Using this notation, the probability of electing a vertex x in the tree T, is given by

$$p_x(T) = \frac{C_T^x}{C_T^\emptyset}. \tag{1}$$

On the other hand, one may use the function ζ on the incidence algebra of $\mathcal{T}$ over the set of reals to compute C_u^v, see [14]; ζ is defined by

$$\zeta(v, u) = \begin{cases} 1, & \text{if } v \sqsubseteq u \\ 0, & \text{otherwise.} \end{cases} \tag{2}$$

The probability $p_x(T)$ is then

$$p_x(T) = \frac{(\zeta - 1)^{n-1}(x, T)}{(\zeta - 1)^n(\emptyset, T)}, \tag{3}$$

where $(\zeta - 1)(x, y) = \zeta(x, y) - \delta(x, y)$, with δ the Kronecker symbol, and the multiplication (or convolution) is defined by

$$fg(x, y) = \sum_{x \leq z \leq y} f(x, z) g(z, y).$$

3.2 Matrix form

It is convenient to introduce the square matrix A whose rows and columns are identified with factors of T. For two factors u and v of T, the element A_u^v in row u and column v is defined by

$$A_u^v = \begin{cases} 1, & \text{if } v \sqsubset u \\ 0 & \text{otherwise.} \end{cases} \tag{4}$$

The number of chains of length k from a factor v to a factor u is then clearly the element of row u and column v in A^k. In particular, we have

$$p_x(T) = \frac{(A^{n-1})_T^x}{(A^n)_T^\emptyset}. \tag{5}$$

3.3 Relation with partially commutatitve monoids

Let T be a tree of size n whose vertices are identified with the integers $1, ..., n$. To T corresponds a commutation system $S = (V, \theta)$ as follows. The alphabet V is the set $1, 2, ..., n$ and $(i, j) \in \theta$ if and only if i and j are not adjacent; the tree T is, therefore, the conflict graph of S, see [4].

To any leaf-removal sequence leading, to the election of a vertex $x \in V$, corresponds a word $w = i_1 i_2 ... i_{n-1} x$ of length n on V, where i_k is the kth removed leaf, $k = 1, ..., n-1$. This word is called *representation*. The representation of a leaf-removal sequence then must be a word $w = i_1..i_{n-1} i_n$ having exactly one occurrence of each letter of V, such that, for any $k = 1, ..., n$, $i_k ... i_n$ is a factor of T. Let $W(x)$ be the set of representations of all leaf-removal sequences leading to the election of x.

The next proposition provides a counting method in terms of cardinality of traces in a commutation system.

Proposition 3. *The set $W(x)$ is a trace in the commutation system S. The number of leaf-removal sequences leading to the election of a vertex x is, therefore, the cardinality of the trace in which the word w is situated, where w represents a leaf-removal sequence leading to the election of x.*

4 Effective computation

We introduce here a simple method for computing the probability distribution p for a given tree; it is based on the comparison of the election probabilities of neighbour vertices. On the other hand, these comparisons suggest introducing one or two vertices, which are said commanding, having the highest probability of being elected.

Throughout this section $T = (V, E)$ is a fixed tree of size $n \geq 2$.

For a pair (x, y) of adjacent vertices let $N_x(xy)$ be the size of the connected component in which x is situated, whenever one removes the edge (xy). A vertex x is said *commanding* if, for any adjacent vertex y, we have $N_x(xy) \geq N_y(xy)$. It is easy to see that any tree has one or two commanding vertices.

The following algorithm yields a commanding vertex of a tree T. To every vertex is assigned a weight; initially, its value is one.

for all $x \in V$ **do** $weight(x) := 1$ **od** ;
while $Card(V) > 1$ **do**
  choose a leaf a with minimal *weight* ;
  $V := V \setminus \{a\}$;
  for the vertex b adjacent to a **do**
  $weight(b) := weight(b) + weight(a)$;
  $E := E \setminus \{a, b\}$
   od
  od;

Let a be a leaf, and let b the vertex adjacent to a; if we remove a then the weight of a is $N_a(ab)$ in the initial tree T.

Lemma 4. *For any pair (x, y) of adjacent vertices of T, we have*

$$\frac{C_T^{xy}}{C_T^{y}} = \frac{N_x(xy)}{n-1}. \tag{6}$$

The next proposition provides a powerful tool to calculate the probability distribution p by comparing the probabilities of election for two adjacent vertices.

Proposition 5. *For any pair of adjacent vertices (x, y), we have :*

$$\frac{p_x}{p_y} = \frac{N_x(xy)}{N_y(xy)}. \tag{7}$$

Proof. Lemma 4 gives C_T^y and similarly C_T^x in terms of C_T^{xy} and $N_x(xy)$. On the other hand, the ratio p_x/p_y is the same as C_T^x/C_T^y. The proof follows.

From this proposition we deduce easily :

Corollary 6. *In any tree, the commanding vertices have the highest probability of being elected.*

Proposition 5 allows to get an explicit expression for the probability p_x. Let x be a given vertex in the tree T. For any edge e, let

$$\theta_x(e) = \frac{n - N_x(e)}{N_x(e)}.$$

$\theta_x(e)$ is thus the ratio between the sizes of the two connected components whenever one removes the edge e, the denominator being the size of the component in which x is situated and the numerator the size of the other one. With this notations :

Proposition 7. *We have*

$$p_x = \left[\sum_{y \in V} \prod_{e \in c(x,y)} \theta_x(e)\right]^{-1}, \tag{8}$$

where $c(x, y)$ is the unique path from x to y.

We end this section proving that a vertex is a commanding vertex if and only if it is a median. Various characterizations of a median have been obtained [8], [13], [15]. Here we use the following result see [15].

Theorem 8. *Let $T = (V, E)$ be a tree; a vertex v is a median if and only if for every neighbour w of v, $N_w(vw) \leq Card(V)/2$.*

From this theorem we deduce immediately :

Proposition 9. *A vertex is a commanding vertex if and only if it is a median.*

Proof. Since we remove the neighbours of the commanding vertex before it, when a neighbour is removed its weight is necessarily smaller than $Card(V)/2$. Conversely, if we consider a median a and if it is removed before a neighbour b which is not median then $N_a(ab) \leq Card(V)/2$ and $N_b(ba) \geq Card(V)/2$. The result follows from the previous theorem.

4.1 The election process and Markov chains

In the following section we introduce two random walks on the vertices of T. We prove then that the probability distribution p is the stationary probability distribution for each of the random walks.

Let $T = (V, E)$ be a tree of size $n \geq 2$. We introduce two Markov chains $X^{(t)}$ and $Y^{(t)}$ on V, considered as the set of states.

They are characterized by their matrices of transition probabilities P and Q as follows.

$$P_x^y = \begin{cases} \frac{N_y(xy)}{n-1}, & \text{if x and y are adjacent} \\ 0, & \text{otherwise} \end{cases} \tag{9}$$

and

$$Q_x^y = \begin{cases} \frac{N_y(xy)}{n}, & \text{if x and y are adjacent} \\ \frac{1}{n}, & \text{if x=y} \\ 0, & \text{otherwise.} \end{cases} \tag{10}$$

P and Q are obviously stochastic matrices.

Proposition 10. *In any tree $T = (V, E)$, the vector $p = (p_x : x \in V)$ is the eigenvector of P with respect to the eigenvalue 1, i.e. p is the stationary distribution of $X^{(t)}$.*

Proof. We have

$$C_T^x = \sum_{\text{y adjacent to x}} C_T^{xy}.$$

Using Lemma 4 to calculate C_T^{xy}, we get

$$C_T^x = \sum_{\text{y adjacent to x}} \frac{N_y(xy)}{n-1} C_T^y, \tag{11}$$

which proves that p is stationary for the Markov chain $X^{(t)}$.

Proposition 11. *In any tree T, the vector p is the eigenvector of Q with respect to the eigenvalue 1, i.e. p is the stationary distribution of $Y^{(t)}$.*

Proof. Multiply the members of (11) by $n - 1$ and, then, divide them by n.

Remark. The chains $X^{(t)}$ and $Y^{(t)}$ are both irreducible, the second one has the advantage of being aperiodic; we deduce, therefore, from Proposition 11 the following surprising property. Suppose that a particle moves at times $t = 1, 2, ...$ from a vertex to one of its neighbours or to this same vertex according to the probabilistic rules of the matrix Q. Then, the probability of finding the particle on a given vertex x at time t, as $t \to \infty$, is the same as the probability of the election of the vertex, whatever is the starting situation of the particle.

5 Study of a special class of trees

We consider here a very special family of symmetric trees. The asymptotic study of the election probabilities for these trees seems interesting since it is related to the combinatorial problem of partitions.

A *crystal* is a tree with a distinguished vertex c of degree ≥ 2, called *centre*, such that all vertices of distance d from c have the same degree. A crystal may be characterized by a sequence $a_0, a_1, ..., a_r$ of positive integers, where r is its *radius*, a_0 the degree of c and conventionally a_{i+1} the common degree of all vertices of distance i, $i = 1, ..., r$. We have then $a_0 \geq 2$, $a_i \geq 1$ and $a_r = 0$. We refer to a_i as the *arity* of distance i. In this section p_i denotes the probability that elected vertex has the distance i from the centre.

If $a_1 = a_2 = ... = a_{r-1} = 1$, then the crystal is called a *wheel*. A *filiform tree* is a wheel such that $a_0 = 2$.

Filiform trees constitute simplest instances of the category. So they are the first subject of this study.

5.1 The case of filiform trees

Let a crystal be defined by its arity sequence :

$$a_0 = 2, a_1 = a_2 = ... = a_{r-1} = 1, a_r = 0. \tag{12}$$

Then the size of the tree is $n = 2r + 1$. A very simple computation based on Proposition 5 proves that the probability distribution for the election is binomial. The probability of getting an elected vertex of distance i is

$$p_i = \begin{cases} \frac{\binom{2r}{r-i}}{2^{2r-1}}, & \text{if } i \geq 1 \\ \frac{\binom{2r}{r}}{2^{2r}}, & \text{if } i = 0. \end{cases} \tag{13}$$

Let the random variable D_r denote the distance of the elected vertex from the centre. Then, by the central limit theorem, see [6, Chapter 10], as $r \to \infty$

$$Pr(D_r \leq \alpha\sqrt{r}) \to \sqrt{\frac{2}{\pi}} \int_0^{\alpha/\sqrt{2}} e^{-\frac{1}{2}t^2} dt. \tag{14}$$

This result asserts roughly that, whenever the size of a filiform tree grows to infinity, then, with a significant probability, the elected vertex can have a distance of the same order as the square root of the size from the centre. As we shall see, in all other instances of crystals, with probability 1, the elected vertex has a finite distance from the centre.

5.2 The case of wheels

Let $a_0 \geq 3, a_1 = a_2 = ... = a_{r-1} = 1, a_r = 0$. The size of the wheel will be $n = ra_0+1$. Let p_k denote the probability of getting a vertex of distance k from the centre as the elected vertex. Proposition 5 allows to calculate the ratio p_{k+1}/p_k :

$$\frac{p_{k+1}}{p_k} = \frac{r-k}{n-r+k}, \quad \text{for } k = 1, 2, ..., r-1 \tag{15}$$

and

$$\frac{p_1}{p_0} = \frac{ra_0}{n-r}. \tag{16}$$

Hence

$$p_k = p_0 a_0 \frac{r!(n-r-1)!}{(n-r+k-1)!(r-k)!}. \tag{17}$$

We have consequently

$$p_0 = \left[1 + a_0 r! \sum_{k=1}^{r} \frac{(n-r-1)!}{(n-r+k-1)!(r-k)!}\right]^{-1}. \tag{18}$$

Thus the probability distribution p_k, $k = 0, 1, ..., r$, is obtained from (17) and (18).

More interesting is the asymptotic behaviour of p_k. As the size of the wheel approaches infinity, one of the following states holds :

(i) The perimeter a_0 becomes large. Then, by (15) the ratio $p_{k+1}/p_k, k = 1, 2, ...,$ tends to zero. On the other hand, by (16), p_1/p_0 approaches 1 and hence

$$p_0 \text{ and } p_1 \longrightarrow \frac{1}{2}, \qquad p_2, p_3, \ldots \longrightarrow 0. \tag{19}$$

(ii) The perimeter a_0 remains bounded. Then, by a straightforward computation, using the fact that the sum of the probabilites is 1, we get from (15) and (16)

$$p_0 \longrightarrow \frac{1}{2}(1 - \frac{1}{a_0 - 1}) \tag{20}$$

and

$$p_k \longrightarrow \frac{a_0}{2}[1 - \frac{1}{a_0-1}]\frac{1}{(a_0-1)^k}, \qquad k = 1, 2, 3, ..., \tag{21}$$

which is an almost geometric distribution.

We may thus summarize the asymptotic aspect of the election algorithm in a wheel as follows. If the perimeter grows then, with probability 1, the elected vertex will have a distance ≤ 1 from the centre. If the perimeter remains bounded, when the size tends to ∞, then the elected vertex may have any *finite* distance from the centre, but the probability of the event decreases exponentially as the distance increases.

5.3 The case of crystals

We study here the asymptotic behaviour of the election algorithm in crystals which are not wheel. Given a crystal T, as introduced, let x and y be two vertices of distances k and $k+1$ from the centre respectively. The size of the crystal will be $n = \sum_{0\leq i\leq r}\prod_{0\leq j<i} a_j$, and we have clearly :

$$N_y(xy) = \sum_{k+1\leq i\leq r} \prod_{k+1\leq j<i} a_j \tag{22}$$

and

$$N_x(xy) = n - N_y(xy). \tag{23}$$

On the other hand the number of vertices of distance $k+1$ from the centre is a_k times that of vertices of distance k. Putting together this fact, (22), (23) and Proposition 5, we get the ratio p_{k+1}/p_k, which allows in turn to compute the probability distribution p in terms of p_0. Finally summing over k, a close formula is obtained for p_0 and consequently for each p_k.

Consider now an infinite crystal given by its infinite arity sequence $a_0, a_1, a_2, ...$ such that $a_0 \geq 2$ and $a_k \geq 2$ at least for one $k \geq 1$. This infinite crystal is regarded as the 'limit' of the sequence of finite crystals $T_n, n = 0, 1, 2, ...$, where T_n is characterized by the truncated finite sequence $a_0, a_1, ..., a_n, 0$. The probability distribution p for the infinite crystal is then naturally approximated by the sequence of probability distributions related to the election in $T_r, r = 0, 1, 2, ...$

It is easy to see that as $r \to \infty$,

$$p_k/p_{k-1} \quad \longrightarrow \quad \frac{a_{k-1}}{a_0 a_1 ... a_{k-1} - 1}, \qquad k = 1, 2, 3, ... \tag{24}$$

Identifying these probabilities with their limits, we get

$$p_k = p_0 \frac{a_0 a_1 ... a_{k-1}}{(a_0 - 1)(a_0 a_1 - 1)...(a_0 a_1 ... a_{k-1} - 1)}. \tag{25}$$

We have therefore

$$\begin{cases} p_0 = \left[\sum_{j\geq 0}\prod_{0\leq i\leq j-1}\alpha_i\right]^{-1} \\ p_k = p_0 \prod_{0\leq i\leq k-1}\alpha_i, \qquad k = 1, 2, 3, ... \end{cases} \tag{26}$$

with

$$\alpha_i = \frac{a_i}{a_0 a_1 ... a_i - 1}.$$

It is easy to see that α_i can be rewritten as

$$\begin{aligned} \alpha_i &= [0.a_i a_i a_i ...]_{a_0 a_1 ... a_i} \\ &= \text{the real number whose } a_0 a_1 ... a_i \text{ary expansion is } \quad 0.a_i a_i a_i ..., \end{aligned} \tag{27}$$

with the exception that $\alpha_0 = a_0/(a_0 - 1)$.

Consider now the special case of fixed arities :

$$a_0 = a_1 = a_2 = ... = a \geq 2. \tag{28}$$

Letting $u = a$ and $t = a^{-1}$, we get from (25)

$$p_k = p_0 \frac{u^k t^{\binom{k+1}{2}}}{(1-t)(1-t^2)...(1-t^k)}. \tag{29}$$

Hence

$$p_0 = \left[1 + \sum_{n \geq 1} \frac{u^n t^{\binom{n+1}{2}}}{(1-t)(1-t^2)...(1-t^n)} \right]^{-1}. \tag{30}$$

Let, on the other hand $Q(n,m)$ be the number of partitions of n into m unequal summands. It is the same as the number of partitions of $n - \binom{m+1}{2}$ into summands which are all $\leq m$, see [3, pp.105-106]. The generating function $\psi(t,u)$ of $Q(n,m)$ is then written as

$$\begin{aligned} \psi(t,u) &= 1 + \sum_{1 \leq m \leq n} Q(n,m) t^n u^m \\ &= \prod_{i \geq 1} (1 + ut^i) \\ &= 1 + \sum_{m \geq 1} \frac{u^m t^{\binom{m+1}{2}}}{(1-t)(1-t^2)...(1-t^m)}. \end{aligned} \tag{31}$$

This identity allows to simplify (30) into a convergent infinite product :

$$p_0 = \prod_{j \geq 0} \frac{a^j}{a^j + 1}. \tag{32}$$

In the case of infinite crystals with fixed arities, there exists also a simple expression in the form of an infinite product for the generating function of the probability distribution p. Let p_k be the probability of getting an elected vertex of distance k from the centre and let

$$G(z) = \sum_{k \geq 0} p_k z^k. \tag{33}$$

Using the same techniques as above with a different u, we get

$$G(z) = \prod_{j \geq 0} \frac{a^j + z}{a^j + 1}. \tag{34}$$

Morever, a straightforward computation yields the expected distance D of the elected vertex from the centre :

$$E(D) = \sum_{j \geq 0} \frac{1}{1 + a^j}. \tag{35}$$

Acknowledgements. The authors would like to express their gratitude to R.Cori and P.Flajolet for their helpful comments and suggestions.

References

1. D. Angluin. *Local and global properties in networks of processors*, Proceedings of the 12th STOC, (1980) 82–93.
2. C. Berge. *Graphes et Hypergraphes*, Dunod, Paris (1970).
3. L. Comtet. *Advanced combinatorics*, D.Reidel Publishing Company, (1974).
4. R. Cori and Y. Métivier. *Recognizable subsets of free partially commutative monoids*, Theoret. Comput. Sci. **58**, (1988) 201–208.
5. R. Cori and D. Perrin. *Sur la reconnaissabilité dans les monoïdes partiellement commutatifs libres*, RAIRO Inform. Théor. **58**, (1985) 21–32.
6. W. Feller. *Introduction to probability theory and its applications*, Wiley, New York, (1970).
7. H. Garcia-Molina. *Election in a distributed computing system*, IEEE Trans. Comput. **C31**, 1 (1982) 48–59.
8. O. Gerstel and S. Zaks. *A new characterization of tree medians with applications to distributed algorithms*, DAIMI PB-364, Computer Science Department AArhus University (1991).
9. E. Korach, D. Rotem and N. Santoro. *Distributed algorithms for finding centers and medians in network*, ACM Trans. on Programming Languages and Systems **6**, No3 (July 1984) 380–401.
10. I. Litovsky, Y. Métivier and W. Zielonka. *The power and the limitations of local computations on graphs and networks*, In: proceedings of 18th International workshop on Graph-Theoretic Concepts in Computer Science, WG 92, Lecture Notes in Comput. Sci. **657** (1993) 333-345.
11. M. Lothaire. *Combinatorics on words*, Addison-Wesley Publishing Company, (1983).
12. A. Mazurkiewicz. *Solvability of asynchronous ranking problem*, Inform. Proc. Letters **28**, (1988) 221–224.
13. S. Mitchell. *Another characterization of the centroid of a tree*, Discrete Mathematics **24**, (1978) 277–280.
14. R.-P. Stanley. *Enumerative Combinatorics*, Wadsworth and Brooks /Cole (1986).
15. B. Zelinka. *Medians and peripherians of trees*, Arch. Math,. (Brno) (1968) 87–95.

On the First–Order Equivalence of Call–by–Name and Call–by–Value

Thomas Noll

Lehrstuhl für Informatik II, Aachen University of Technology,
Ahornstr. 55, D–52056 Aachen, Germany,
e–mail: noll@zeus.informatik.rwth-aachen.de

Abstract. Within the framework of (first–order) recursive applicative program schemes we prove the parameter–passing mechanisms call–by–name and call–by–value to be of the same computational power, thus solving an open problem in the theory of functional programming. The equivalence proof is given constructively by a detour through flowchart program schemes which operate on pushdown stores. This result is in contrast to the non–deterministic (i.e., language–theoretic) case where the outermost (OI) and the innermost (IO) expansion strategy of macro grammars lead to incomparable classes of string languages.

1 Introduction

Program schemes have been introduced in order to distinguish precisely the control structure of a program from the other aspects, like the semantic domains involved in the computations. Here, we consider the class of *recursive applicative program schemes* (or: *recursive schemes*) of which every member represents a family of corresponding first–order functional programs.

The aim of this paper is to study whether the choice of a particular parameter-passing mechanism has an impact on the computational power of this class. We show that for each recursive scheme S there exists another recursive scheme S' such that S evaluated via call–by–name in any interpretation computes the same function as S' evaluated via call–by–value in the same interpretation (and vice versa). Moreover, S' can be effectively constructed. An *interpretation* specifies the semantic domain in which the computations of S and S' have to be carried out, and it gives a meaning to the basic operations occurring in the schemes. To allow for terminating computations in the presence of recursion, there is always a fixed–interpreted if–then–else–conditional which is strict only in its first component.

Note that this notion of computational power corresponds to the natural notion of *semantical equivalence* of programs, and therefore it captures the "real" computational power of a program in all interpretations. It should not be confused with other (usually stronger) notions of equivalence, e.g. *formal equivalence* (cf. [15, 16]). Program equivalence in the latter sense essentially abstracts from the special meaning of if–then–else; it results in the comparison of certain formal languages associated with program schemes. This aspect will be investigated later in greater detail.

With regard to semantical equivalence, the problem in question was addressed by several authors but not completely solved.

- A proof idea for one inclusion was already proposed in [10]: Every call-by-value scheme is equivalent to a call-by-name scheme which is forced to evaluate its arguments by some trivial test. This approach is described in Section 3.1.
- In the setting of higher-order recursive schemes, Plotkin proved in [20] that call-by-name and call-by-value have the same computational power. Given a call-by-name scheme S, he constructs a call-by-value interpreter which simulates the call-by-name computation of S. However, the evaluation of argument positions is delayed by means of additional λ-abstractions, that is, the functional level of the scheme is raised. Therefore, this approach does not provide a solution for our question.
- De Roever showed in [21] that every call-by-name scheme is equivalent to a non-deterministic call-by-value scheme which guesses which of its arguments it will actually need. (From this result it can be immediately concluded that call-by-name and call-by-value have the same power if a non-deterministic choice operator is available.)
- In [17], Mycroft introduces so-called *oracle functions* which predict whether a function evaluation makes use of a certain argument. Thus, they can be used to replace de Roever's non-deterministic choice by deterministic tests. However, Mycroft extends the underlying signature by additional constants, and he assumes a fixed-interpreted **case** operation to be available.
- Results of Goerdt as well as of Kfoury, Tiuryn and Urzyczyn [12, 14] imply that call-by-name schemes are equivalent to flowcharts with a pushdown store, provided that semantic equality is available in the interpretation. Together with the equivalence of call-by-value schemes and flowcharts with a pushdown store (as established in [3]), this yields a partial answer to our question.
- Albayrak [1] investigated the special class of *monadic recursive schemes* and showed that call-by-name and call-by-value have the same computational power for this class. His proof is based on the fact that strictness of functions becomes decidable in the monadic case.

In this paper we do not only show that the two parameter-passing mechanisms are equally powerful in the above sense but we also give a constructive proof: given a recursive scheme S, an equivalent scheme S' can effectively be constructed, i.e., call-by-name and call-by-value are *intertranslatable*. The basic idea for the simulation of call-by-value in call-by-name is already given above. Proving the reverse inclusion involves a sequence of translations. First, following the technique described in [17], the given call-by-name scheme is transformed into a call-by-value scheme extended by additional fixed-interpreted operation symbols. In the next step, we simulate the latter by means of a flowchart scheme with a pushdown store and labels as values but without use of the additional symbols. The label values can be shown to be redundant (cf. [5, 13]). Thus, the result is a flowchart scheme with a pushdown store which is equivalent to a call-by-value scheme (cf. [3])).

The paper is organized as follows: Section 2 introduces the syntax and semantics of recursive schemes. Section 3 gives the proof of our claim. In Section 4, we examine some aspects of the connections between recursive program schemes and formal languages. Finally, Section 5 draws some conclusions and directs to future research.

2 Mathematical Preliminaries

We start with a description of the syntax and semantics of recursive schemes. A detailed account on this topic and a guide to the literature can be found in [6].

Definition 1 (Syntax of recursive schemes)
A *signature* $\Sigma = (\Omega, \Pi)$ consists of a ranked alphabet $\Omega = \bigcup_{n \in \mathbf{N}} \Omega^{(n)}$ of *operation symbols* and of a ranked alphabet $\Pi = \bigcup_{n \in \mathbf{N}} \Pi^{(n)}$ of *predicate symbols*, n denoting the rank of every symbol. Let $X = \{x_1, x_2, \ldots\}$ be an enumerable set of *variables*. The set $T_\Sigma(X)$ of *Σ-terms over X* is the smallest set T satisfying

- $X \subseteq T$,
- if $f \in \Omega^{(n)}$, and $t_1, \ldots, t_n \in T$, then $f(t_1, \ldots, t_n) \in T$, and
- if $p \in \Pi^{(n)}$, $t_1, \ldots, t_n \in T$, and $u_1, u_2 \in T$, then if $p(t_1, \ldots, t_n)$ then u_1 else $u_2 \in T$.

Moreover, let $\Phi = \{F_1^{(n_1)}, \ldots, F_r^{(n_r)}\}$ be a non-empty ranked alphabet of *function variables*. A *recursive applicative program scheme S over Σ* (for short: *recursive scheme*) is a system of equations $S = (F_k(x_1, \ldots, x_{n_k}) = t_k \mid 1 \leq k \leq r)_c$ where $t_k \in T_{(\Omega \cup \Phi, \Pi)}(\{x_1, \ldots, x_{n_k}\})$ for $1 \leq k \leq r$ and $c \in \{\mathsf{cbn}, \mathsf{cbv}\}$. The set of all recursive schemes over Σ is denoted by RPS_Σ. The annotation c denotes the parameter–passing mechanism to be used. If $c = \mathsf{cbn}$ ($c = \mathsf{cbv}$), the corresponding subclass of RPS_Σ is denoted by CBN_Σ (CBV_Σ). ◇

In the sequel, $\Sigma = (\Omega, \Pi)$, X, and Φ are supposed to be arbitrary but fixed sets.

Definition 2 (Semantics of recursive schemes)
A *Σ-structure* $\mathfrak{A} = (A, \alpha)$ consists of a non-empty set A, called *(semantic) domain*, and of an *interpretation* α assigning strict and total mappings of the type $A^n \to A$ and $A^n \to \{\mathsf{true}, \mathsf{false}\}$ to the symbols in Ω and Π, respectively. Here, true and false denote the boolean constants; they are not necessarily elements of A. The if–then–else is taken with its standard interpretation.
The *semantics* of a recursive scheme $S = (F_k(x_1, \ldots, x_{n_k}) = t_k \mid 1 \leq k \leq r)_c \in RPS_\Sigma$ with respect to $\mathfrak{A}$ is the partial mapping $\mathfrak{A}[\![S]\!] : A^{n_1} \quad A$ assigned to the first equation of S using the parameter–passing mechanism indicated by c.

This mapping can be defined *operationally* (i.e., by means of term rewriting) [6, 18] or *denotationally* (i.e., by naturally extending the interpretation of every symbol over a flat domain $A \cup \{\perp\}$ and by assigning to S the least fixed point of a continuous functional over the associated function space) [2, 4].
Let $\mathfrak{C}_1$ and $\mathfrak{C}_2$ be two classes of (recursive) program schemes over Σ. Two schemes $S_1 \in \mathfrak{C}_1$ and $S_2 \in \mathfrak{C}_2$ are called *equivalent* (denoted by $S_1 \equiv S_2$) iff $\mathfrak{A}[\![S_1]\!] = \mathfrak{A}[\![S_2]\!]$ in every Σ–structure $\mathfrak{A}$. The class $\mathfrak{C}_1$ is *translatable into* $\mathfrak{C}_2$ ($\mathfrak{C}_1 \rightsquigarrow \mathfrak{C}_2$) iff given $S_1 \in \mathfrak{C}_1$ one can effectively construct $S_2 \in \mathfrak{C}_2$ such that $S_1 \equiv S_2$. The classes $\mathfrak{C}_1$ and $\mathfrak{C}_2$ are *intertranslatable* ($\mathfrak{C}_1 \leftrightsquigarrow \mathfrak{C}_2$) iff $\mathfrak{C}_1 \rightsquigarrow \mathfrak{C}_2$ and $\mathfrak{C}_2 \rightsquigarrow \mathfrak{C}_1$. ◇

Note that, since effective constructability is required, the notion of intertranslatability is stronger than the notion of equivalence. In [5, 13] it is shown, for example, that for every flowchart with arrays and labels there exists an equivalent flowchart with arrays only. However, one can show that if there was an effective translation from the first class of schemes to the second, an undecidable property of test–free flowcharts with arrays and labels would be decidable: the convergence property.

The other models of computation involved in the translation from call–by–name to call–by–value will be defined later.

3 The Equivalence of Call–by–Name and Call–by–Value

In this section we will establish the main theorem of this paper.

Theorem 3 (Intertranslatability of call–by–name and call–by–value)

$$CBN_\Sigma \leftrightsquigarrow CBV_\Sigma .$$

The proofs of the two inclusions are carried out in Section 3.1 and Section 3.2, respectively.

3.1 From Call–by–Value to Call–by–Name

Theorem 4 (Translatability of call–by–value into call–by–name)

$$CBV_\Sigma \rightsquigarrow CBN_\Sigma .$$

Proof The idea of the proof is already given in [10]. We will only sketch it; details can be found in [1]. We distinguish two cases concerning the set of predicate symbols Π.

- If $\Pi \setminus \Pi^{(0)} = \emptyset$, that is, Π does not contain any non–constant predicate symbol, the semantics of the given scheme

$$S = (F_k(x_1, \ldots, x_{n_k}) = t_k \mid 1 \leq k \leq r)_{\mathsf{cbv}} \in CBV_\Sigma$$

is either the globally undefined mapping (if recursion occurs) or a polynomial, i.e., the derived operation of a term $t \in T_\Sigma(X)$. Both situations can be distinguished by means of an abstract interpretation of S which additionally yields t in the second case. Hence, $S' = (F_1(x_1,\ldots,x_{n_1}) = F_1(x_1,\ldots,x_{n_1}))_{\mathsf{cbn}}$ and $S' = (F_1(x_1,\ldots,x_{n_1}) = t)_{\mathsf{cbn}}$, respectively, are schemes in CBN_Σ equivalent to S.

- If $p^{(n)} \in \Pi \setminus \Pi^{(0)}$, an equivalent scheme $S' \in CBN_\Sigma$ can be obtained by replacing the right-hand side of every equation in S by a term in which every parameter is forced to be evaluated. For example, the equation $F(x_1, x_2) = t$ is translated into

$$F(x_1,x_2) = \mathsf{if}\ p(\underbrace{x_1,\ldots,x_1}_{n \text{ times}})\ \mathsf{then}\ \begin{array}{l}\mathsf{if}\ p(x_2,\ldots,x_2)\ \mathsf{then}\ t\\ \qquad\qquad\qquad\quad \mathsf{else}\ t\end{array}\ \mathsf{else}\ \begin{array}{l}\mathsf{if}\ p(x_2,\ldots,x_2)\ \mathsf{then}\ t\\ \qquad\qquad\qquad\quad \mathsf{else}\ t\end{array}$$

Note that we consider strict and total interpretations only. Hence, this transformation does not influence the termination property of the evaluation.

◇

3.2 From Call-by-Name to Call-by-Value

Theorem 5 (Translatability of call-by-name into call-by-value)

$$CBN_\Sigma \leadsto CBV_\Sigma.$$

As indicated in the introduction, proving this inclusion involves a sequence of translations.

- The given call-by-name scheme is transformed into a call-by-value scheme extended by additional operation symbols with fixed interpretation (Definition 6, Lemma 7).
- The extended scheme is simulated by means of a flowchart scheme with a pushdown store and labels as values but without use of the additional symbols (Definition 9, Lemma 10).
- The label values are shown to be unnecessary, that is, the call-by-name scheme can be simulated by a flowchart scheme with a pushdown store (Lemma 12).
- Finally, flowcharts with a pushdown store are translatable into call-by-value schemes (Lemma 13).

The first translation was described in [17]. Mycroft introduces so-called *oracle functions* which predict the index of the parameter that a function will use next. To this end, he enlarges the set of operation symbols by additional constants $\bot_1, \bot_2, \ldots$ which "will act as bombs which explode when used in a calculation", and he assumes a **case** operation (which he calls **select**) to be present in the interpretation. Following Mycroft, we denote a call of an n-ary oracle function by $F(\bot_i, t_j \mid i \in I, j \in J)$ which represents the call $F(u_1,\ldots,u_n)$ where $u_i = \bot_i$ if $i \in I$ and $u_i = t_i$ otherwise ($I \cup J = \{1,\ldots,n\}$). This call will

- return $\bot_i$ if F evaluates the ith parameter before evaluating any other parameter indexed by I,
- return a non–$\bot$ value if F returns without evaluating any of the parameters indexed by I, and
- compute forever if F diverges without evaluating any of the parameters indexed by I.

The notion "before" refers to a top–down left–to–right traversal of the right–hand side of F as it is usually followed by stack–oriented implementations of first–order functional languages.

The corresponding class of recursive schemes is given in the following definition.

Definition 6 (Extended call–by–value scheme)
Let $\{\bot_1, \bot_2, \ldots\}$ be an enumerable set of constant operation symbols disjoint from Ω. The set $T^*_{(\Omega\cup\Phi,\Pi)}(X)$ of *extended* $(\Omega\cup\Phi, \Pi)$*–terms over* X is the smallest set T satisfying

- $X \subseteq T$,
- if $\varphi \in \Omega^{(n)} \cup \Phi^{(n)}$, and $t_1, \ldots, t_n \in T$, then $\varphi(t_1, \ldots, t_n) \in T$,
- if $p \in \Pi^{(n)}$, $t_1, \ldots, t_n \in T$, and $u_1, u_2 \in T$, then $\mathsf{if}\ p(t_1, \ldots, t_n)\ \mathsf{then}\ u_1\ \mathsf{else}\ u_2 \in T$, and
- if $F \in \Phi^{(n)}$, $I = \{i_1, \ldots, i_k\} \subseteq \{1, \ldots, n\}$, $J = \{1, \ldots, n\} \setminus I$, $t_j \in T$ for $j \in J$, and $u_0, \ldots, u_k \in T$, then
$\mathsf{case}\ F(\bot_i, t_j \mid i \in I, j \in J)\ \mathsf{of}\ \bot_{i_1} : u_1; \ldots; \bot_{i_k} : u_k\ \mathsf{else}\ u_0 \in T$.

An *extended call–by–value scheme over* Σ is a sequence of equations

$$S = (F_k(x_1, \ldots, x_{n_k}) = t_k \mid 1 \leq k \leq r)_{\mathsf{cbv}}$$

where $t_k \in T^*_{(\Omega\cup\Phi,\Pi)}(\{x_1, \ldots, x_{n_k}\})$ for $1 \leq k \leq r$. The set of all extended call–by–value schemes over Σ is denoted by CBV^*_Σ. Let $\mathfrak{A} = (A, \alpha)$ be a Σ–structure, and let $\{\bot_1, \bot_2, \ldots\}$ be an enumerable set of values disjoint from A. The *extension* of $\mathfrak{A}$, denoted by $\mathfrak{A}^* = (A^*, \alpha^*)$, is given as follows ($\vartheta \in \Omega^{(n)} \cup \Pi^{(n)}$, $a, a_i, b \in A^*$):

$$A^* = A \cup \{\bot_1, \bot_2, \ldots\}$$

$$\alpha^*(\bot_i) = \bot_i$$

$$\alpha^*(\vartheta)(a_1, \ldots, a_n) = \begin{cases} \bot_i & \text{if } a_j = \bot_i \text{ and} \\ & a_k \notin \{\bot_1, \bot_2, \ldots\} \\ & \text{for } 1 \leq k < j \\ \alpha(\vartheta)(a_1, \ldots, a_n) & \text{otherwise} \end{cases}$$

$$\alpha^*(\mathsf{if\,.\,then\,.\,else\,.})(b, a_1, a_2) = \begin{cases} \bot_i & \text{if } b = \bot_i \\ a_1 & \text{if } b = \mathsf{true} \\ a_2 & \text{if } b = \mathsf{false} \end{cases}$$

$$\alpha^*(\mathsf{case\,.\,of}\ \ldots\ \mathsf{else\,.})(a, \bot_{i_1}, a_1, \ldots, \bot_{i_k}, a_k, a_0)$$

$$= \begin{cases} a_1 & \text{if } a = \bot_{i_1} \\ \vdots & \\ a_k & \text{if } a = \bot_{i_k} \\ a_0 & \text{if } a \in A \end{cases}$$

Together with the call–by–value parameter–passing mechanism, this extension $\mathfrak{A}^*$ yields a semantic mapping $\mathfrak{A}^*[\![S]\!] : A^{n_1} \quad A$ for every extended call–by–value scheme $S \in CBV^*_\Sigma$ (cf. Definition 2). ◇

Thus, the extended structure $\mathfrak{A}^*$ enlarges the semantic domain, it fixes the meaning of the **case** operation, and it defines the interpretation of the signature symbols on the larger domain. Note that $CBV_\Sigma \subseteq CBV^*_\Sigma$, and that $\mathfrak{A}^*[\![.]\!]$ is consistent with $\mathfrak{A}[\![.]\!]$, i.e., if $S \in CBV_\Sigma$, then $\mathfrak{A}^*[\![S]\!] = \mathfrak{A}[\![S]\!]$.

In [17], Mycroft gives the meaning of a **case** (**select**) expression by rewriting it into a cascade of if–**then**–**else** operations. However, this technique does not yield a more general solution since semantic equality is needed.

Lemma 7 (Translatability of CBN_Σ into CBV^*_Σ)

$$CBN_\Sigma \rightsquigarrow CBV^*_\Sigma.$$

Proof We will only give a sketch of the proof. Details can be found in [17]. The transformation starts up with a scheme $S \in CBN_\Sigma$ where each parameter is passed by name. Thus, we can represent every call in the form $F(t_1 : \mathsf{cbn}, \ldots, t_n : \mathsf{cbn})$. The translation of S into an equivalent scheme $S' \in CBV^*_\Sigma$ is done by an iterated rewriting process: any call $F(t_i : \mathsf{cbn}, t_j : \mathsf{cbv} \mid i \in I, j \in J)$ is replaced by

$$\begin{array}{l} \textbf{case } F(\bot_i : \mathsf{cbv}, t_j : \mathsf{cbv} \mid i \in I, j \in J) \textbf{ of} \\ \quad \vdots \\ \quad \bot_k : F(t_i : \mathsf{cbn}, t_j : \mathsf{cbv} \mid i \in I \setminus \{k\}, j \in J \cup \{k\}) \\ \quad \vdots \\ \textbf{else } F(u_i : \mathsf{cbv}, t_j : \mathsf{cbv} \mid i \in I, j \in J) \end{array}$$

where k ranges over I, and where u_i stands for any constant term. This rewriting has to be carried out until $I = \emptyset$, resulting in a scheme $S' \in CBV^*_\Sigma$ with $\mathfrak{A}^*[\![S']\!] = \mathfrak{A}[\![S]\!]$ for every Σ–structure $\mathfrak{A}$. ◇

Example 8 Let us consider the following recursive scheme over

$$\Sigma = (\{0^{(0)}, decr^{(1)}, +^{(2)}\}, \{nonnull^{(1)}\})$$

(essentially borrowed from [17]) in which the main function FCT calls a primitive–recursively defined multiplication function MLT with an undefined second argument.

$$S = \begin{pmatrix} FCT(x_1) & = & MLT(x_1, INF(x_1)) \\ MLT(x_1, x_2) & = & \textbf{if } nonnull(x_1) \textbf{ then } x_2 + MLT(decr(x_1), x_2) \textbf{ else } 0 \\ INF(x_1) & = & INF(x_1) \end{pmatrix}_{\mathsf{cbn}}$$

Note that, with the usual interpretation of Σ, $FCT(0) = 0$ whereas a call-by-value evaluation of S would not terminate.
In order to restrict the size of the resulting scheme we exploit the fact that both MLT and INF are strict in their first argument which can therefore safely be passed by value. Hence it suffices to replace every call of the form $MLT(t_1, t_2)$ by **case** $MLT(t_1, \bot_2)$ **of** $\bot_2 : MLT(t_1, t_2)$ **else** $MLT(t_1, 0)$, resulting in the extended call-by-value scheme

$$S' = \left(\begin{array}{rcl} FCT(x_1) & = & \underline{\textsf{case } MLT(x_1, \bot_2) \textsf{ of } \bot_2 :} MLT(x_1, INF(x_1)) \\ & & \qquad\qquad\qquad \underline{\textsf{else } MLT(x_1, 0)} \\ MLT(x_1, x_2) & = & \textsf{if } nonnull(x_1) \textsf{ then} \\ & & \quad x_2 + \underline{\textsf{case } MLT(decr(x_1), \bot_2) \textsf{ of}} \\ & & \qquad\quad \underline{\bot_2 :} MLT(decr(x_1), x_2) \\ & & \qquad\quad \underline{\textsf{else } MLT(decr(x_1), 0)} \\ & & \textsf{else } 0 \\ INF(x_1) & = & INF(x_1) \end{array} \right)_{\textsf{cbv}}$$

where we have underlined the parts which have been added by the transformation. Now, the equation $FCT(0) = 0$ holds as desired. ◇

Now, we define the next class of schemes involved in the translation process, flowchart schemes (sometimes also called *iterative program schemes* or *GOTO schemes*).

Definition 9 (Flowchart scheme)
Let L be a set of *labels*. The set FSP_Σ of *flowchart program schemes over Σ with a pushdown store* (for short: *flowcharts with a pushdown*) is the smallest set T such that if $w \in L^*$, $f \in \Omega^{(n)}$, $p \in \Pi^{(n)}$, $x, x_1, \ldots, x_n \in X$, $l_1, l_2 \in L$, and $S_1, S_2 \in T$, then

- $w : x := f(x_1, \ldots, x_n) \quad \in \quad T$,
- $w : \textsf{if } p(x_1, \ldots, x_n) \textsf{ then } l_1 \textsf{ else } l_2 \quad \in \quad T$,
- $w : \textsf{goto } l_1 \quad \in \quad T$,
- $w : \textsf{return } x \quad \in \quad T$,
- $w : \textsf{push } x \quad \in \quad T$,
- $w : x := \textsf{pop} \quad \in \quad T$, and
- $S_1; S_2 \quad \in \quad T$.

In the set $FSPL_\Sigma$ of *flowchart program schemes over Σ with a pushdown store and labels as values* (for short: *flowcharts with a pushdown and labels*), given $w \in L^*$, $x \in X$, and $l \in L$, the following instructions are additionally allowed:

- $w : \textsf{push } l \quad \in \quad FSPL_\Sigma$,
- $w : x := l \quad \in \quad FSPL_\Sigma$, and
- $w : \textsf{goto } x \quad \in \quad FSPL_\Sigma$.

To every flowchart with a pushdown (and labels) S, a rank is assigned by distinguishing n *input variables* $x_1, \ldots, x_n \in X$ from the other variables. A *computation* of S in a Σ–structure $\mathfrak{A} = (A, \alpha)$ is a sequence of states, each state consisting of a valuation of the variables, a pointer to the next instruction to be executed, and a pushdown over A (i.e., an element of A^*). At the outset of the computation, the pushdown is empty, the first instruction is to be executed next, and all the variables other than the input variables have an undefined value. The instructions have their usual meaning; in particular, the **return** x instruction finishes the computation and yields the value stored in x. Thus, the operational semantics of S just outlined defines a (partial) mapping $\mathfrak{A}[\![S]\!] : A^n \quad A$. ◇

Note that the comparison between call–by–name and call–by–value becomes trivial if we operate on natural numbers, and if elementary arithmetic is part of the interpretation, i.e., if the constant zero, the successor function, and the test for zero are available. In that case, every computable function can be implemented by a flowchart without pushdown, and hence by a call–by–value scheme. However, there are mappings on arbitrary domains which are not "flowchartable" but which can be computed by a call–by–value scheme [19]. In this sense, recursion is stronger than iteration.

The following result is completely new. It says that extended call–by–value schemes can be simulated by flowcharts with a pushdown and labels without using the additional **case** and $\perp_i$ symbols.

Lemma 10 (Translatability of CBV^*_Σ into $FSPL_\Sigma$)

$$CBV^*_\Sigma \rightsquigarrow FSPL_\Sigma.$$

Proof We only describe the basic principle of the translation; it will be illustrated by Example 11. Let $S = (F_k(x_1, \ldots, x_{n_k}) = t_k \mid 1 \le k \le r)_{\mathsf{cbv}} \in CBV^*_\Sigma$. An equivalent flowchart $S' \in FSPL_\Sigma$ is constructed as follows: S' uses $x_1, \ldots, x_{n_1}$ as input variables. When calling a function variable, the following information is transferred onto the pushdown store:

1. the values of local variables which have to be saved,
2. the return label, and
3. the argument values.

Two types of function calls are distinguished: *oracle calls* (i.e., those occurring as the first argument of a **case** operation) and *non–oracle calls* (the remaining ones). Every function definition $F_k(x_1, \ldots, x_{n_k}) = t_k$ in S is translated into 2^{n_k} sequences of flowchart instructions:

- The sequence labelled by l_{F_k} evaluates non–oracle calls.
- For every non–empty index subset $I \subseteq \{1, \ldots, n_k\}$, the sequence labelled by $l^I_{F_k}$ evaluates oracle calls of the form $F_k(\perp_i, t_j \mid i \in I, j \in J)$.

This splitting is necessary since the $\perp_i$ ($i \in I$) arguments are handled in a special way. When executing the oracle call, for each $\perp_i$ a distinguished label, say $l_{\perp_i}$, is pushed instead of a semantic value. This label marks a sequence of instructions which evaluate the $\bot_i$ branch of the **case** expression. On encountering the corresponding parameter x_i in the called oracle, the control is immediately transferred back to $l_{\bot_i}$, and the local variables of the calling function are restored from the pushdown. Thus, the "explosion" of $\bot_i$ results in an instant return to the calling function. If none of the x_i parameters ($i \in I$) is used, execution continues at the return label (pushed by the calling function), and the local variables are also restored. At this return label, the **else** part of the **case** expression has to be evaluated. As one can see, the only task of an oracle function is to simulate the control flow of the **case** operation by handling the labels in an appropriate way.

In contrast, non–oracle calls return a value: when executing the call, the local variable values, the return label, and the argument values are pushed. On finishing the call, the return value is pushed, execution continues at the return label, and the local variables are restored. Thus, non–oracle calls are implemented just as function calls in ordinary call–by–value languages. ◇

Example 11 (continued) Let us consider the flowchart assigned to the extended call–by–value scheme S' from Example 8. The following instruction sequences are (at least in part) presented here:

1. The initial call of the first function variable, FCT, with the supplied input value x_1,
2. the non–oracle version of FCT, labelled by l_{FCT}, and
3. the oracle $MLT(x_1, \bot_2)$, labelled by $l^{\{2\}}_{MLT}$.

For reasons of clarity, we omit the **push** and **pop** instructions for local variable values which have to be saved.

initial call		push l_1;	(* push return label *)
		push x_1;	(* push FCT argument *)
		goto l_{FCT};	(* initial call of FCT *)
	l_1 :	x_2 := pop; return x_2;	(* return result *)
FCT	l_{FCT} :	x_1 := pop;	(* pop argument *)
		push l_3;	(* push return label *)
		push x_1; push l_2;	(* push MLT arguments *)
		goto $l^{\{2\}}_{MLT}$;	(* call oracle $MLT(x_1, \bot_2)$ *)
	l_2 :	...	(* code of $MLT(x_1, INF(x_1))$ *)
	l_3 :	push l_4; push x_1;	(* prepare MLT call *)
		x_2 := 0; push x_2; goto l_{MLT};	(* call $MLT(x_1, 0)$ *)
	l_4 :	x_3 := pop; x_4 := pop;	(* pop result and return label *)
		push x_3; goto x_4;	(* return result *)
MLT oracle	$l^{\{2\}}_{MLT}$:	x_2 := pop; x_1 := pop;	(* pop arguments *)
		if $nonnull(x_1)$ then l_5 else l_6	(* evaluate condition *)
	l_5 :	x_3 := pop; goto x_2;	(* jump to $\bot_2$ branch *)
		...	(* never executed *)
	l_6 :	x_4 := pop; goto x_4;	(* return *)

The working method of the above flowchart is illustrated by the following diagram. It exhibits the relation between the labels of the flowchart and the subexpressions of the scheme as well as the control flow, indicated by arrows.

FCT :			*MLT* oracle :	
l_{FCT} :	**case** $MLT(x_1, \bot_2)$ **of**	$\longrightarrow$	$l^{\{2\}}_{MLT}$:	**if** $nonnull(x_1)$
l_2 :	$\bot_2 : MLT(x_1, INF(x_1))$	$\longleftarrow$	l_5 :	**then** $x_2 + \ldots$
l_3 :	**else** $MLT(x_1, 0)$	$\longleftarrow$	l_6 :	**else** 0

Note that in the *MLT* oracle the code of the **case** expression (which constitutes the second argument of the adding operation) is never executed. This results from the fact that the first summand already yields a $\bot_2$ value (cf. the extended interpretation of operation symbols in Definition 6). $\diamond$

In general, flowcharts with a pushdown and labels are more powerful than flowcharts with a pushdown only [5]. However, if we consider only those flowcharts which result from the translation described in the proof of Lemma 10 (the corresponding class of schemes is denoted by $FSPl_\Sigma$), we are able to show that the use of labels as values is unnecessary.

Lemma 12 (Translatability of $FSPl_\Sigma$ into FSP_Σ)

$$FSPl_\Sigma \rightsquigarrow FSP_\Sigma.$$

Proof A proof of the above lemma is given in [13]. It is based on the observation that the set of labels occurring in a flowchart $S \in FSPl_\Sigma$ can be represented by means of a binary decision tree. Every label corresponds to a path through this tree. Such a path can be characterized by a sequence of **true** and **false** values depending on which decision is made in the inner nodes.
The construction is illustrated by the following example: let $p \in \Pi^{(1)}$ be a monadic predicate, let $\mathfrak{A} = (A, \alpha)$ be a Σ–structure, and let $l_1, \ldots, l_4 \in L$ be labels of S. Furthermore, let $z_1, z_2 \in X$ be variables not occurring in S, and let $x, y \in X$ be variables with values $a, b \in A$, respectively, such that $\alpha(p)(a) =$ **true** and $\alpha(p)(b) =$ **false**. We use the following decision tree:

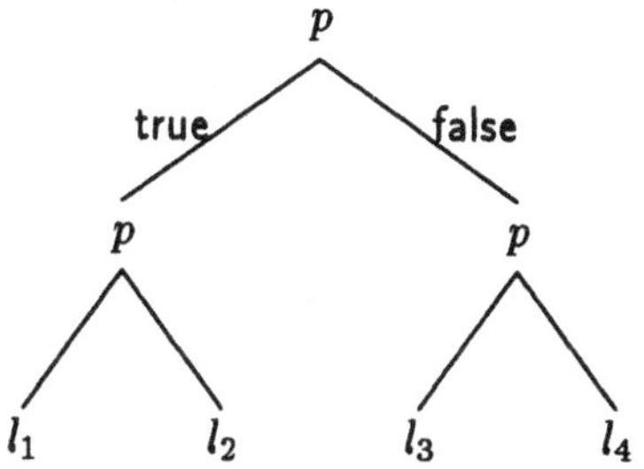

Now, we can simulate the instructions dealing with labels as values in the following way:

Replace	by
push l_2	push x; push y
z := pop	z_2 := pop; z_1 := pop
goto z	if $p(z_1)$ then l_T else l_F; l_T : if $p(z_2)$ then l_{TT} else l_{TF}; l_{TT} : goto l_1; l_{TF} : goto l_2; l_F : if $p(z_2)$ then l_{FT} else l_{FF}; l_{FT} : goto l_3; l_{FF} : goto l_4;

The required predicate p and the variables x, y can be determined by using a concept introduced by Constable and Gries, the *locator scheme* [5]. The basic idea is the following: when the original scheme S executes a recursive call (i.e., the code of a recursive oracle or non–oracle call in the underlying recursive scheme), then it must perform some predicate test twice with opposite results before completing that call or else it is in an infinite loop. This property can be used to provide p, x and y.
Note that this argumentation only holds if the **goto** statements are used in a structured (i.e., procedure–like) way as in the case of $FSPl_\Sigma$ schemes. Thus, S can be simulated by a flowchart with a pushdown store but without labels. Also note that an analogous argumentation holds for non–monadic predicates. ◇

Lemma 13 (Translatability of FSP_Σ into CBV_Σ)

$$FSP_\Sigma \rightsquigarrow CBV_\Sigma.$$

Proof A detailed proof can be found in [3]. The basic idea is the following: the given flowchart $S \in FSP_\Sigma$ is translated into a call–by–value scheme $S' = (F(x_1, \ldots, x_n) = t) \in CBV_\Sigma$ consisting of a single equation. The pushdown store of S is represented by the "runtime stack" of invocations of F. When S executes a push x instruction, S' executes a call of F where the value of x is passed as an argument. Similarly, a pop operation results in the return from F. ◇

4 Recursive Schemes and Macro Grammars

As we mentioned already in the introduction, there are stronger notions of program equivalence, like e.g. *formal equivalence* [15, 16]. The latter takes into account the set of all execution paths which a program can possibly pass through without caring about if–conditions. That is, deterministic decisions are replaced by non–deterministic choices.

Taking this approach within the framework of recursive schemes, an expression of the form if t then u_1 else u_2 has to be interpreted as the union of the sets of values which can be derived from u_1 and by u_2 in the same way, the so–called *syntactic value languages* of u_1 and u_2, respectively. If we now allow for calls of function variables, these syntactic value languages can be described by means of *context–free tree grammars* (cf. [9, 10, 8, 7]) where function variables play the rôle of nonterminal symbols. Then, the reduction relations of the parameter–passing mechanisms call–by–name and call–by–value correspond to the OI and IO derivation relations, respectively. The incomparability of the class of OI languages and of the class of IO languages, which has been proved in [11] (for the corresponding string languages), implies the incomparability of the two parameter–passing mechanisms with respect to formal equivalence.

Note that an analogous argumentation holds if we restrict our attention to the class of *free schemes* [13]. Schemes of this class are characterized by the property that during the execution under any interpretation, no predicate is applied more than once to the same tuple of semantic values. In this case, given an expression of the form if $p(t_1, \ldots, t_n)$ then u_1 else u_2, one can always choice between the left branch u_1 and the right branch u_2 by appropriately defining the interpretation of p. Hence, the syntactic value language of a scheme equals to its (semantic) value language; in other words, freeness corresponds to non–determinism.

The following example shows that call–by–name and call–by–value are incomparable with respect to free schemes also.

Example 14 We consider two free recursive schemes over the signature $\Sigma = (\{0^{(0)}, 1^{(0)}, c^{(0)}, \cdot^{(2)}\}, \{p_1^{(1)}, p_2^{(1)}, p_3^{(1)}\})$, which are interpreted over the domain of strings $\{0, 1, c\}^*$. The symbols 0, 1 and c denote single–letter constants, and the binary infix operator $\cdot$ is interpreted as the string concatenation operator.

$$\left(\begin{array}{rcl} S & = & F(A(1), 1) \\ F(x_1, x_2) & = & \text{if } p_1(x_2) \text{ then } F(x_1 \cdot x_1, 1 \cdot x_2) \text{ else } x_1 \\ A(x_1) & = & \text{if } p_2(x_1) \text{ then} \\ & & \quad \text{if } p_3(x_1) \text{ then } 0 \cdot A(1 \cdot x_1) \text{ else } A(1 \cdot x_1) \cdot 0 \\ & & \text{else} \\ & & \quad 1 \end{array}\right)_{\mathsf{cbn}}$$

and

$$\left(\begin{array}{rcl} S & = & F(1, 1) \\ F(x_1, x_2) & = & \text{if } p_1(x_2) \text{ then } G(F(x_1 \cdot 1, 1 \cdot x_2)) \text{ else } G(x_1) \\ G(x_1) & = & x_1 \cdot c \cdot x_1 \end{array}\right)_{\mathsf{cbv}}$$

Note that the second argument of F (in both schemes) and the first parameter of A (in the first scheme) are only introduced to guarantee the freeness: in any recursive call, the parameter is prefixed by the letter 1. Hence, no predicate tests the same word twice.

For this reason, the value languages of the two schemes are generated by the macro grammars which are obtained from the recursive schemes by dropping the superfluous arguments, and by turning deterministic choice into non–

deterministic union. This results in the OI macro grammar

$$\begin{pmatrix} S & \rightarrow & F(A) \\ F(x) & \rightarrow & F(xx) \mid x \\ A & \rightarrow & 0A \mid A0 \mid 1 \end{pmatrix}_{\text{OI}}$$

which generates a non–IO language [11], and in the IO macro grammar

$$\begin{pmatrix} S & \rightarrow & F(1) \\ F(x) & \rightarrow & G(F(x1)) \mid G(x) \\ G(x) & \rightarrow & xcx \end{pmatrix}_{\text{IO}}$$

which generates a non–OI language [11], respectively. ◇

5 Conclusions and Future Work

In this paper we solved an open problem in the theory of functional programming concerning the computational power of the two parameter–passing mechanisms call–by–name and call–by–value with respect to first–order recursive schemes. The proof was carried out involving a sequence of translation steps in which flowcharts with a pushdown store were used as intermediate representations.

The transformation from call–by–name to call–by–value is such that it does not cause any unbounded increase in either the static program size or in the execution time. Therefore, the use of call–by–name does not add anything to the strict power of the language. However, an exponential blowup at least in the static size is possible. Thus, our techniques do not necessarily lead to more efficient implementations of call–by–name (in contrast to the more pragmatic approach of Mycroft described in [17]).

Currently, we are extending our results to the higher–order setting. Note that the results of Plotkin [20] only yield a partial answer since his simulation techniques raise the functional level of programs. Results of Goerdt as well as of Kfoury, Tiuryn and Urzyczyn [12, 14] stating the equivalence of level–n call–by–name schemes and of flowcharts with level–n pushdowns in the presence of semantic equality seem to imply the equivalence of call–by–name schemes and of call–by–value schemes in the higher–order case under this restriction.

Acknowledgements

I would like to express my thanks to Professor K. Indermark for valuable comments and suggestions. I also wish to thank A. Kindler and M. Mohnen for carefully reading a draft of this paper.

References

1. C.A. Albayrak. Vergleichende Gegenüberstellung der Parameterübergabemechanismen Call–by–name und Call–by–value im Rahmen funktionaler Programme. Master's thesis, Aachen Univ. of Technology, March 1993. In German.

2. J.W. de Bakker. Least fixed points revisited. *Theoretical Computer Science*, 2:155–181, 1976.
3. S. Brown, D. Gries, and T. Szymanski. Program schemes with pushdown stores. *SIAM Journal on Computing*, 1:242–268, 1972.
4. J.M. Cadiou. *Recursive Definitions of Partial Functions and their Computations*. PhD thesis, Stanford University, 1972.
5. R.L. Constable and D. Gries. On classes of program schemata. *SIAM Journal on Computing*, 1:66–118, 1972.
6. B. Courcelle. Recursive applicative program schemes. In J. van Leeuwen, editor, *Handbook of Theoretical Computer Science, Vol. B*, chapter 9, pages 459–492. Elsevier Science Publishers, 1990.
7. W. Damm. The IO– and OI–hierarchies. *Theoretical Computer Science*, 20:95–207, 1982.
8. W. Damm, E. Fehr, and K. Indermark. Higher–type recursion and self–application as control structures. In E.J. Neuhold, editor, *Formal Description of Programming Concepts*, pages 461–487. Elsevier (North–Holland), 1978.
9. J. Engelfriet and E.M. Schmidt. IO and OI. Part I. *Journal of Computer and System Sciences*, 15:328–353, 1977.
10. J. Engelfriet and E.M. Schmidt. IO and OI. Part II. *Journal of Computer and System Sciences*, 16:67–99, 1978.
11. M.J. Fischer. *Grammars with Macro–like Productions*. PhD thesis, Harvard University, Cambridge, 1968.
12. A. Goerdt. Characterizing complexity classes by general recursive definitions in higher types. *Information and Control*, 101(2):202–218, 1992.
13. S.A. Greibach. *Theory of Program Structures: Schemes, Semantics, Verification*, volume 36 of *Lecture Notes in Computer Science*. Springer–Verlag, 1975.
14. A.J. Kfoury, J. Tiuryn, and P. Urzyczyn. On the expressive power of finitely typed and universally polymorphic recursive procedures. *Theoretical Computer Science*, 93:1–41, 1992.
15. H. Langmaack. On procedures as open subroutines. Part I. *Acta Informatica*, 2:311–333, 1973.
16. H. Langmaack. On procedures as open subroutines. Part II. *Acta Informatica*, 3:227–241, 1974.
17. A. Mycroft. *Abstract Interpretation and Optimizing Transformations for Applicative Programs*. PhD thesis, University of Edinburgh, 1981.
18. M. Nivat. On the interpretation of recursive polyadic program schemes. *Symposia Mathematica*, 15:255–281, 1975.
19. M.S. Paterson and C.E. Hewitt. Comparative schematology. In *Record on Project MAC Conference on Concurrent Systems and Parallel Computation*, pages 119–128. ACM, 1970.
20. G.D. Plotkin. Call–by–name, call–by–value, and the λ–calculus. *Theoretical Computer Science*, 1:125–159, 1975.
21. W.-P. de Roever. First–order reduction of call–by–name to call–by–value. In *Proc. 4th MFCS*, volume 32 of *Lecture Notes in Computer Science*, pages 377–398. Springer–Verlag, 1975.

On the Modularity of Confluence of Constructor-Sharing Term Rewriting Systems

Enno Ohlebusch

Universität Bielefeld, 33501 Bielefeld, Germany,
e-mail: enno@techfak.uni-bielefeld.de

Abstract. Toyama's Theorem states that confluence is a modular property of disjoint term rewriting systems. This theorem does not generalize to combined systems with shared constructors. Thus the question arises naturally whether there are sufficient conditions which ensure the modularity of confluence in the presence of shared constructors. In particular, Kurihara and Krishna Rao posed the problem whether there are interesting sufficient conditions independent of termination. This question appeared as Problem 59 in the list of open problems in the theory of rewriting published recently [DJK93]. The present paper gives an affirmative answer to that question. Among other sufficient criteria, it is shown that confluence is preserved under the combination of constructor-sharing systems if the systems are also normalizing. This in conjunction with the fact that normalization is modular for those systems implies the modularity of semi-completeness.

1 Introduction

It is well-known from software engineering that programmers are encouraged to write their programs in a modular way in order to handle large systems. Thus, from a practical point of view, it is worth knowing under what conditions the combined program inherits properties from its constituent modules. For this reason it is not astonishing that the subject of modular properties of term rewriting systems (TRSs) is receiving a lot of attention. The first important result in this area states that confluence is modular for disjoint TRSs. More precisely, the combination $(\mathcal{F}, \mathcal{R}) = (\mathcal{F}_1 \cup \mathcal{F}_2, \mathcal{R}_1 \cup \mathcal{R}_2)$ of two confluent TRSs $(\mathcal{F}_1, \mathcal{R}_1)$ and $(\mathcal{F}_2, \mathcal{R}_2)$ is also confluent if the signatures $\mathcal{F}_1$ and $\mathcal{F}_2$ are disjoint. It was first proved by Toyama [Toy87b] and is by now referred to as Toyama's Theorem. Not long ago a simplified proof of Toyama's Theorem was given by Klop et al. [KMTV91]. In contrast to this encouraging result, termination and completeness turned out to lack a modular behavior (see [Toy87a] and also [Ohl93b]). Thus several sufficient criteria ensuring their modularity have been given (for an overview see e.g. [Mid90, Gra93, Ohl93a]). In order to prove modularity of completeness, one can of course use the confluence of the combined system to show its termination. For example the deep theorem that completeness is modular for left-linear disjoint TRSs [TKB89] crucially depends on Toyama's Theorem.

In recent investigations (cf. [KO92, MT93, Ohl93a, Gra93]), one tries to weaken the disjointness requirement. One way to do it is to allow shared constructors (function symbols that do not occur at the root position of the left-hand side of any rewrite rule). Unfortunately, confluence is not preserved under the combination of constructor-sharing TRSs. In [KO92], Kurihara and Ohuchi gave the following counterexample:

Example 1.1 Consider the TRSs $\mathcal{R}_1 = \{F(x,x) \to A, F(x,c(x)) \to B\}$ and $\mathcal{R}_2 = \{a \to c(a)\}$. Both systems are confluent and they share the constructor c. The term $F(a,a)$ rewrites to A as well as to B, i.e., it has two different normal forms w.r.t. to $\to_{\mathcal{R}_1 \cup \mathcal{R}_2}$. This shows that $\mathcal{R}_1 \cup \mathcal{R}_2$ is not confluent.

In [KO92, MT93], the modularity of completeness for constructor-sharing TRSs (under certain assumptions) is proved as follows: Let $\mathcal{R}_1$ and $\mathcal{R}_2$ be two complete TRS which share at most constructors. First of all their combined system $\mathcal{R} = \mathcal{R}_1 \cup \mathcal{R}_2$ is locally confluent because local confluence is modular (cf. [Mid90]). Moreover, sufficient conditions for the modularity of termination are presupposed. These imply termination of $\mathcal{R}$. Confluence of $\mathcal{R}$ is then concluded from Newman's Lemma. At this point the lack of a sufficient criterion for the modularity of confluence in the presence of shared constructors becomes apparent. If it were the other way round, i.e., if one could conclude that the combined system inherits confluence from its constituent systems, then it would be possible to use the confluence of the combined system to show its termination.

A glance at the previous counterexample reveals that $\mathcal{R}_1$ is not left-linear. This is essential because confluence is a modular property of left-linear TRSs with shared constructors. This result is a consequence of a theorem proved in a different context by Raoult and Vuillemin [RV80] (cf. also [Klo92]). Another observation is that $\mathcal{R}_2$ is not terminating; it is not even normalizing. Moreover, the only rule of $\mathcal{R}_2$ is constructor-lifting, i.e., the root symbol of its right-hand side is a shared constructor. In this paper, it will be proved that all these facts are also essential. More precisely, it will be shown that confluence is modular for TRSs with shared constructors if a certain "collapsing reduction" relation is normalizing. This will be achieved by an extension of the techniques used in [KMTV91]. Consequences of this result are the modularity of confluence for constructor-sharing TRSs without collapsing and constructor-lifting rules and for normalizing constructor-sharing TRSs. The mentioned sufficient criteria solve Problem 59 positively, and it is possible that our approach leads to more such criteria. The most interesting result is certainly the modularity of semi-completeness which follows from the above in conjunction with the fact that normalization is modular for constructor-sharing TRSs. With regard to proving modularity of completeness the result implies that one just has to take care of the termination of the combined system (as in the disjoint union case).

The paper is organized as follows: Section 2 briefly recalls the basic notions of term rewriting. The next section contains required notions of combined systems with shared constructors. Collapsing reduction is introduced in Section 4. Then Section 5 shows that confluence is modular if the collapsing reduction relation is normalizing. Section 6 is dedicated to the modularity of semi-completeness. Finally, the last section contains concluding remarks.

2 Preliminaries

In this section, we briefly recall the basic notions of term rewriting as surveyed in e.g. Dershowitz and Jouannaud [DJ90] and Klop [Klo92].

A *signature* is a countable set $\mathcal{F}$ of *function symbols* or *operators*, where every $f \in \mathcal{F}$ is associated with a natural number denoting its arity. Nullary operators are called *constants*. The set $\mathcal{T}(\mathcal{F},\mathcal{V})$ of *terms* built from a signature $\mathcal{F}$ and a countable set of *variables* $\mathcal{V}$ with $\mathcal{F} \cap \mathcal{V} = \emptyset$ is the smallest set such that $\mathcal{V} \subseteq \mathcal{T}(\mathcal{F},\mathcal{V})$ and if $f \in \mathcal{F}$ has arity n and $t_1,\ldots,t_n \in \mathcal{T}(\mathcal{F},\mathcal{V})$, then $f(t_1,\ldots,t_n) \in \mathcal{T}(\mathcal{F},\mathcal{V})$. We write f instead of $f(\,)$ whenever f is a constant. For $t \in \mathcal{T}(\mathcal{F},\mathcal{V})$ we define $root(t)$ by: $root(t) = t$ if $t \in \mathcal{V}$, and $root(t) = f$ if $t = f(t_1,\ldots,t_n)$.

A *substitution* σ is a mapping from $\mathcal{V}$ to $\mathcal{T}(\mathcal{F},\mathcal{V})$ such that $\{x \in \mathcal{V} \mid \sigma(x) \neq x\}$ is finite. This set is called the *domain* of σ and will be denoted by $\mathcal{D}om(\sigma)$. Occasionally we present a substitution σ as $\{x \mapsto \sigma(x) \mid x \in \mathcal{D}om(\sigma)\}$. Substitutions extend uniquely to morphisms from $\mathcal{T}(\mathcal{F},\mathcal{V})$ to $\mathcal{T}(\mathcal{F},\mathcal{V})$, that is, $\sigma(f(t_1,\ldots,t_n)) = f(\sigma(t_1),\ldots,\sigma(t_n))$ for every n-ary function symbol f and terms $t_1,\ldots,t_n$. We call $\sigma(t)$ an *instance* of t. We also write $t\sigma$ instead of $\sigma(t)$.

Let $\Box$ be a special constant. A *context* $C[,\ldots,]$ is a term in $\mathcal{T}(\mathcal{F} \cup \{\Box\},\mathcal{V})$ which contains at least one occurrence of $\Box$. If $C[,\ldots,]$ is a context with n occurrences of $\Box$ and $t_1,\ldots,t_n$ are terms, then $C[t_1,\ldots,t_n]$ is the result of replacing from left to right the occurrences of $\Box$ with $t_1,\ldots,t_n$. A context containing precisely one occurrence of $\Box$ is denoted by $C[\,]$. A term t is a *subterm* of a term s if there exists a context $C[\,]$ such that $s = C[t]$. A subterm t of s is *proper*, denoted by $s \rhd t$, if $s \neq t$. By abuse of notation we write $\mathcal{T}(\mathcal{F},\mathcal{V})$ for $\mathcal{T}(\mathcal{F} \cup \{\Box\},\mathcal{V})$, interpreting $\Box$ as a special constant which is always available but used only for the aforementioned purpose.

Let $\to$ be a binary relation on terms, i.e., $\to \subseteq \mathcal{T}(\mathcal{F},\mathcal{V}) \times \mathcal{T}(\mathcal{F},\mathcal{V})$. The reflexive transitive closure of $\to$ is denoted by $\to^*$. If $s \to^* t$, we say that s *reduces* to t and we call t a *reduct* of s. We write $s \leftarrow t$ if $t \to s$; likewise for $s \;{}^*\!\!\leftarrow t$. The transitive closure of $\to$ is denoted by $\to^+$, and $\leftrightarrow$ denotes the symmetric closure of $\to$ (i.e., $\leftrightarrow\, = \,\to \cup \leftarrow$). The reflexive transitive closure of $\leftrightarrow$ is called *conversion* and denoted by $\leftrightarrow^*$. If $s \leftrightarrow^* t$, then s and t are *convertible*. Two terms t_1, t_2 are *joinable*, denoted by $t_1 \downarrow t_2$, if there exists a term t_3 such that $t_1 \to^* t_3 \;{}^*\!\!\leftarrow t_2$. Such a term t_3 is called a *common reduct* of t_1 and t_2. The relation $\downarrow$ is called *joinability*. A term s is a *normal form* w.r.t. $\to$ if there is no term t such that $s \to t$. A term s has a normal form if $s \to^* t$ for some normal form t. The set of all normal forms of $\to$ is denoted by $NF(\to)$. The relation $\to$ is *normalizing* if every term has a normal form; it is *terminating*, if there is no infinite reduction sequence $t_1 \to t_2 \to t_3 \to \ldots$. In the literature, the terminology *weakly normalizing* and *strongly normalizing* is often used instead of normalizing and terminating, respectively. The relation $\to$ is *confluent* if for all terms s, t_1, t_2 with $t_1 \;{}^*\!\!\leftarrow s \to^* t_2$ we have $t_1 \downarrow t_2$. It is well-known that $\to$ is confluent if and only if every pair of convertible terms is joinable. The relation $\to$ is *locally confluent* if for all terms s, t_1, t_2 with $t_1 \leftarrow s \to t_2$ we have $t_1 \downarrow t_2$. If $\to$ is confluent and terminating, it is called *complete* or *convergent*. The famous

Newman's Lemma states that termination and local confluence imply confluence. If $\rightarrow$ is confluent and normalizing, then it is called *semi-complete*. Sometimes this property is called *unique normalization* because it is equivalent to the property that every term has a unique normal form. Some of these notions are also used in their specialization to terms; the phrase "t is terminating" means for instance that every reduction sequence starting from t is finite.

A *term rewriting system* (TRS for short) is a pair $(\mathcal{F}, \mathcal{R})$ consisting of a signature $\mathcal{F}$ and a set $\mathcal{R} \subset \mathcal{T}(\mathcal{F}, \mathcal{V}) \times \mathcal{T}(\mathcal{F}, \mathcal{V})$ of *rewrite rules* or *reduction rules*. Every rewrite rule (l, r) must satisfy the following two constraints: (i) the left-hand side l is not a variable, and (ii) variables occurring in the right-hand side r also occur in l. Rewrite rules (l, r) will be denoted by $l \rightarrow r$. A rewrite rule $l \rightarrow r$ is *left-linear* if l does not contain multiple occurrences of the same variable; it is *collapsing* if r is a variable. An instance of a left-hand side of a rewrite rule is a *redex* (reducible expression). The rewrite rules of a TRS $(\mathcal{F}, \mathcal{R})$ define a *rewrite relation* $\rightarrow_{\mathcal{R}}$ on $\mathcal{T}(\mathcal{F}, \mathcal{V})$ as follows: $s \rightarrow_{\mathcal{R}} t$ if there exists a rewrite rule $l \rightarrow r$ in $\mathcal{R}$, a substitution σ and a context $C[\,]$ such that $s = C[l\sigma]$ and $t = C[r\sigma]$. We say that s rewrites to t by *contracting* redex $l\sigma$. We call $s \rightarrow_{\mathcal{R}} t$ a *rewrite step* or *reduction step*. A TRS $(\mathcal{F}, \mathcal{R})$ has one of the above properties (e.g. termination) if its rewrite relation has the respective property. We often simply write $\mathcal{R}$ instead of $(\mathcal{F}, \mathcal{R})$ if there is no ambiguity about the underlying signature $\mathcal{F}$. A reduction step $s \rightarrow_{\mathcal{R}} t$ is *innermost* if no proper subterm of the contracted redex is itself a redex. $\rightarrow_{\mathcal{R}}$ is *innermost normalizing* if every term s rewrites to a term $t \in NF(\rightarrow_{\mathcal{R}})$ such that every reduction step in $s \rightarrow_{\mathcal{R}}^{*} t$ is innermost.

3 Basic Notions of Constructor-Sharing TRSs

Definition 3.1 *Constructors* are function symbols that do not occur at the root position of the left-hand side of any rewrite rule; the others are called *defined symbols*. The union $(\mathcal{F}, \mathcal{R}) = (\mathcal{F}_1 \cup \mathcal{F}_2, \mathcal{R}_1 \cup \mathcal{R}_2)$ of two TRSs $(\mathcal{F}_1, \mathcal{R}_1)$ and $(\mathcal{F}_2, \mathcal{R}_2)$, where

$$\mathcal{C} = \mathcal{F}_1 \cap \mathcal{F}_2 \subseteq (\mathcal{F}_1 \cup \mathcal{F}_2) \setminus \{root(l) \mid l \rightarrow r \in \mathcal{R}_1 \cup \mathcal{R}_2\}$$

is called the *combined TRS of* $(\mathcal{F}_1, \mathcal{R}_1)$ *and* $(\mathcal{F}_2, \mathcal{R}_2)$ *with shared constructors* $\mathcal{C}$. In this case we define $\mathcal{D}_1 = \mathcal{F}_1 \setminus \mathcal{C}$, $\mathcal{D}_2 = \mathcal{F}_2 \setminus \mathcal{C}$, and $\mathcal{D} = \mathcal{D}_1 \uplus \mathcal{D}_2$.
A property $\mathcal{P}$ of TRSs is called *modular* if for all TRSs $\mathcal{R}_1$ and $\mathcal{R}_2$ which share at most constructors, their union $\mathcal{R}_1 \cup \mathcal{R}_2$ has the property $\mathcal{P}$ if and only if both $\mathcal{R}_1$ and $\mathcal{R}_2$ have the property $\mathcal{P}$. From now on $\rightarrow\, = \,\rightarrow_{\mathcal{R}}\, = \,\rightarrow_{\mathcal{R}_1 \cup \mathcal{R}_2}$.

Definition 3.2 In order to enhance readability, function symbols from $\mathcal{D}_1$ are called black, those from $\mathcal{D}_2$ white, and shared constructors as well as variables are called transparent. If a term s does not contain white (black) function symbols, we speak of a *black (white) term*. s is said to be *transparent* if it only contains shared constructors and variables. Consequently, a transparent term may be regarded as black or white, this is convenient for later purposes. s is called *top* *black (top white, top transparent)* if $root(s)$ is black (white, transparent). To emphasize that $\mathcal{F}_i = \mathcal{D}_i \uplus \mathcal{C}$, we write $\mathcal{T}(\mathcal{D}_i, \mathcal{C}, \mathcal{V})$ instead of $\mathcal{T}(\mathcal{F}_i, \mathcal{V})$ at the appropriate places.

In the sequel, we often state definitions and considerations only for one color (the same applies mutatis mutandis for the other color).

Definition 3.3 If s is a top black term such that $s = C^b[s_1, \ldots, s_n]$ for some black context $C^b[, \ldots,] \neq \Box$ and $root(s_j) \in \mathcal{D}_2$ for $j \in \{1, \ldots, n\}$, then we denote this by $s = C^b[\![s_1, \ldots, s_n]\!]$. In this case s is the only *black principal* subterm of s and $s_1, \ldots, s_n$ are the *white principal* subterms of s. If s is a top transparent term such that

$$s = \begin{cases} C^t[s_1, \ldots, s_l] & \text{where } C^t[, \ldots,] \in \mathcal{T}(\mathcal{C}, \mathcal{V})\ ,\ root(s_j) \in \mathcal{D}_1 \uplus \mathcal{D}_2 \\ C^b[t_1, \ldots, t_m] & \text{where } C^b[, \ldots,] \in \mathcal{T}(\mathcal{D}_1, \mathcal{C}, \mathcal{V})\ ,\ root(t_j) \in \mathcal{D}_2 \\ C^w[u_1, \ldots, u_n] & \text{where } C^w[, \ldots,] \in \mathcal{T}(\mathcal{D}_2, \mathcal{C}, \mathcal{V})\ ,\ root(u_j) \in \mathcal{D}_1 \end{cases}$$

then this will be denoted by

$$s = \begin{cases} C^t[\![s_1, \ldots, s_l]\!] & (\text{note that } C^t[, \ldots,] \neq \Box) \\ C^b[\![t_1, \ldots, t_m]\!] & (\text{note that } C^b[, \ldots,] \neq \Box) \\ C^w[\![u_1, \ldots, u_n]\!] & (\text{note that } C^w[, \ldots,] \neq \Box) \end{cases}$$

In this situation, the terms $u_1, \ldots, u_n$ $(t_1, \ldots, t_m)$ are called the *black (white) principal* subterms of s.

Example 3.4 Let $\mathcal{D}_1 = \{F, A\}$, $\mathcal{D}_2 = \{g, b\}$, and $\mathcal{C} = \{c\}$. The term $s = c(F(b), g(A))$ has representations

$$s = \begin{cases} C^t[\![F(b), g(A)]\!] \text{ with } C^t[, \ldots,] = c(\Box, \Box) \\ C^b[\![b, g(A)]\!] \text{ with } C^b[, \ldots,] = c(F(\Box), \Box) \\ C^w[\![F(b), A]\!] \text{ with } C^w[, \ldots,] = c(\Box, g(\Box)) \end{cases}$$

Definition 3.5 For a top black term s, the *rank* of s is defined by

$$rank(s) = \begin{cases} 1 & , \text{if } s \in \mathcal{T}(\mathcal{D}_1, \mathcal{C}, \mathcal{V}) \\ 1 + max\{rank(s_j) \mid 1 \leq j \leq n\}, & \text{if } s = C^b[\![s_1, \ldots, s_n]\!] \end{cases}$$

If s is a top transparent term, then the rank of s is defined by

$$rank(s) = \begin{cases} 0 & , \text{if } s \in \mathcal{T}(\mathcal{C}, \mathcal{V}) \\ max\{rank(t_j) \mid 1 \leq j \leq m\}, & \text{if } s = C^t[\![t_1, \ldots, t_m]\!] \end{cases}$$

Definition 3.6 For a top black term s, the set of *special subterms* of s is defined by

$$S(s) = \begin{cases} \{s\} & , \text{if } s \in \mathcal{T}(\mathcal{D}_1, \mathcal{C}, \mathcal{V}) \\ \{s\} \cup \bigcup_{j=1}^{n} S(s_j), & \text{if } s = C^b[\![s_1, \ldots, s_n]\!] \end{cases}$$

If s is a top transparent term, then the set of special subterms of s is defined by

$$S(s) = \begin{cases} \{s\} & , \text{if } s \in \mathcal{T}(\mathcal{C}, \mathcal{V}) \\ \{s\} \cup \bigcup_{j=1}^{m} S(t_j), & \text{if } s = C^t[\![t_1, \ldots, t_m]\!] \end{cases}$$

Definition 3.7 Let s be a top black term. Let $s = C^b[\![s_1, \ldots, s_n]\!]$ and $s \to_{\mathcal{R}} t$ by an application of a rewrite rule of $\mathcal{R} = \mathcal{R}_1 \cup \mathcal{R}_2$. We write $s \to^i_{\mathcal{R}} t$ if the rule is applied in one of the s_j and we write $s \to^o_{\mathcal{R}} t$ otherwise. The relation $\to^i_{\mathcal{R}}$ is called *inner* reduction and $\to^o_{\mathcal{R}}$ is called *outer* reduction. Now let s be a top transparent term. If $s = C^t[\![s_1, \ldots, s_n]\!]$ and $s \to_{\mathcal{R}} t$, then $t = C^t[s_1, \ldots, s_{j-1}, t_j, s_{j+1}, \ldots, s_n]$ for some $j \in \{1, \ldots, n\}$. In this case we write $s \to^i_{\mathcal{R}} t$ if $s_j \to^i_{\mathcal{R}} t_j$ and $s \to^o_{\mathcal{R}} t$ if $s_j \to^o_{\mathcal{R}} t_j$. In order to indicate which TRS the applied rule stems from, we also use the notation $s \to^o_{\mathcal{R}_1} t$, $s \to^o_{\mathcal{R}_2} t$, $s \to^i_{\mathcal{R}_1} t$, and $s \to^i_{\mathcal{R}_2} t$.

Definition 3.8 Let s be a top black term. A rewrite step $s \to t$ is *destructive at level 1* if the root symbols of s and t have different colors (i.e., $root(t) \in \mathcal{D}_2 \cup \mathcal{C} \cup \mathcal{V}$). A rewrite step $s \to t$ is *destructive at level* $m+1$ (for some $m \geq 1$) if $s = C^b[\![s_1, \ldots, s_j, \ldots, s_n]\!] \to^i C^b[s_1, \ldots, t_j, \ldots, s_n] = t$ with $s_j \to t_j$ destructive at level m. For a top transparent term s a rewrite step $s \to t$ is *destructive at level m* if it is of the form $s = C^t[\![s_1, \ldots, s_j, \ldots, s_n]\!] \to C^t[s_1, \ldots, t_j, \ldots, s_n] = t$ with $s_j \to t_j$ destructive at level m. Note that if a rewrite step is destructive, then the applied rewrite rule is collapsing or constructor-lifting. A rule $l \to r$ is called *constructor-lifting* if $root(r)$ is a shared constructor.

Definition 3.9 As in [Mid90], we introduce some special notations in order to enable a compact treatment of "degenerate" cases of $t = C^b[\![t_1, \ldots, t_n]\!]$. To this end, the notion of context is extended. We write $C^b\langle, \ldots, \rangle$ for a black term containing zero or more occurrences of $\Box$ and $C^b\{, \ldots, \}$ for a black term different from $\Box$ itself, containing zero or more occurrences of $\Box$. If $t_1, \ldots, t_n$ are the (possibly zero) white principal subterms of some term t (from left to right), then we write $t = C^b\{\!\{t_1, \ldots, t_n\}\!\}$ provided that $t = C^b\{t_1, \ldots, t_n\}$. We write $t = C^b\langle\!\langle t_1, \ldots, t_n\rangle\!\rangle$ if $t = C^b\langle t_1, \ldots, t_n\rangle$ and either $C^b\langle, \ldots, \rangle \neq \Box$ and $t_1, \ldots, t_n$ are the white principal subterms of t or $C^b\langle, \ldots, \rangle = \Box$ and $t \in \{t_1, \ldots, t_n\}$.

Definition 3.10 In order to code principal subterms by variables and to cope with outer rewrite steps using non-left-linear rules, the following notation is convenient. For terms $s_1, \ldots, s_n, t_1, \ldots, t_n$ we write $<s_1, \ldots, s_n> \propto <t_1, \ldots, t_n>$ if $t_i = t_j$ whenever $s_i = s_j$, for all $1 \leq i < j \leq n$. If $<s_1, \ldots, s_n> \propto <t_1, \ldots, t_n>$ and $<t_1, \ldots, t_n> \propto <s_1, \ldots, s_n>$, we write $<s_1, \ldots, s_n> \infty <t_1, \ldots, t_n>$.

The following facts will be heavily used in the sequel without being explicitly mentioned. The simple proofs are omitted.

Lemma 3.11 Let $s, t \in \mathcal{T}(\mathcal{F}, \mathcal{V})$. If $s \to^o_{\mathcal{R}_1} t$, then $s = C^b\{\!\{s_1, \ldots, s_n\}\!\}$ for some $C^b\{\!\{, \ldots, \}\!\}$ and $s_1, \ldots, s_n$ with $root(s_j) \in \mathcal{D}_2$. Furthermore, if $x_1, \ldots, x_n$ are fresh variables with $< s_1, \ldots, s_n > \ \infty \ < x_1, \ldots, x_n >$, then $C^b\{x_1, \ldots, x_n\} \to \hat{C}^b\langle x_{i_1}, \ldots, x_{i_m}\rangle$ by the same rule $l \to r$, where $\hat{C}^b\langle, \ldots, \rangle$ is some black context and $i_1, \ldots, i_m \in \{1, \ldots, n\}$. Thus it follows for all terms $t_1, \ldots, t_n$ with $< s_1, \ldots, s_n > \propto < t_1, \ldots, t_n >$ that $C^b\{t_1, \ldots, t_n\} \to \hat{C}^b\langle t_{i_1}, \ldots, t_{i_m}\rangle$ by the same rule $l \to r$. Consequently, $t = \hat{C}^b\langle\!\langle s_{i_1}, \ldots, s_{i_m}\rangle\!\rangle$. If $s \to^o_{\mathcal{R}_1} t$ is not destructive at level 1, then even $t = \hat{C}^b\{\!\{s_{i_1}, \ldots, s_{i_m}\}\!\}$.

Lemma 3.12 Let $s,t \in \mathcal{T}(\mathcal{F},\mathcal{V})$. If $s \to^i t$, then $s = C[\![s_1,\dots,s_j,\dots,s_n]\!]$ and $t = C[s_1,\dots,s'_j,\dots,s_n]$ for some context $C[,\dots,]$ which is either black or white, and terms $s_1,\dots,s_n,s'_j$ with $s_j \to s'_j$ for some $j \in \{1,\dots,n\}$. If $s \to^i t$ is not destructive at level 2, then $t = C[\![s_1,\dots,s'_j,\dots,s_n]\!]$.

Lemma 3.13 If $s \to^* t$, then $rank(s) \geq rank(t)$.

Proposition 3.14 Normalization is modular for constructor-sharing TRSs.
Proof: See [Ohl93a]. □

4 Collapsing Reduction

As noticed in [Toy87b] and [KMTV91], the main difficulties in giving a proof for the modularity of confluence are due to the fact that the black and white layer structure of a term need not be preserved under reduction. That is to say, by a destructive rewrite step a for instance black layer may disappear, thus allowing two originally distinct white layers to merge. Terms with a stable layer structure will be called preserved.

Definition 4.1 A term s is *preserved* if there is no rewrite derivation starting from s that contains a destructive rewrite step. We call s *black (white) preserved* if all its black (white) principal subterms are preserved.

Clearly, a preserved term is both black and white preserved. If a top black (top white) term is black (white) preserved, then it is preserved. Note also that the properties preserved and black (white) preserved are both conserved under reduction.

Definition 4.2 We write $s \to_c t$ if there exists a context $C[\,]$ and terms s_1, t_1 such that $s = C[s_1], t = C[t_1], s_1$ is a special subterm of s, $s_1 \to^+ t_1$ and the root symbols of s_1 and t_1 have different colors. The relation $\to_c$ is called *collapsing reduction* and s_1 is a *collapsing redex*.

Note that every destructive rewrite step is a $\to_c$ step. On the other hand, every $\to_c$ step contains at least one destructive step. Furthermore, $\to_c$ is not closed under contexts in general because the notion "special subterm" depends on the surrounding context.

Lemma 4.3 1. If $s \to_c t$, then $s \to^+ t$.
2. A term is preserved if and only if it contains no collapsing redexes.
Proof: Straightforward. □

Example 4.4 Let $\mathcal{R}_1 = \{F(x,y) \to c(A), G(x) \to x\}$, $\mathcal{R}_2 = \{h(x) \to c(x)\}$. We have the following collapsing reduction sequence:

$$F(A,h(G(h(A)))) \to_c F(A,h(c(A))) \to_c c(A)$$

The first step is valid because $G(h(A))$ is a special subterm of $F(A,h(G(h(A))))$, $G(h(A)) \to^+ c(A)$, and the root symbols of $G(h(A))$ and $c(A)$ have different colors.

5 Confluence is Modular if $\to_c$ is Normalizing

In this section $(\mathcal{F}_1, \mathcal{R}_1)$ and $(\mathcal{F}_2, \mathcal{R}_2)$ are assumed to be confluent constructor-sharing TRSs. First we show that white preserved terms are confluent w.r.t. the combined system $(\mathcal{F}, \mathcal{R})$. If $\to_c$ is normalizing, then this result can be used to show confluence of $(\mathcal{F}, \mathcal{R})$. The next proposition states that monochrome outer reduction is confluent.

Proposition 5.1 The relations $\to^o_{\mathcal{R}_1}$ and $\to^o_{\mathcal{R}_2}$ are confluent.

Proof: It suffices to show the claim for $\to^o_{\mathcal{R}_1}$. Let $t_1 \ {}_{\mathcal{R}_1}\!\overset{*\,o}{\leftarrow} t \overset{o\,*}{\to}_{\mathcal{R}_1} t_2$. If t is an element of $\mathcal{T}(\mathcal{D}_1, \mathcal{C}, \mathcal{V})$, then the claim is true. Therefore, we may assume $t = C^b[\![s_1, \ldots, s_n]\!]$, $t_1 = C^b_1\langle\!\langle s_{i_1}, \ldots, s_{i_m}\rangle\!\rangle$ and $t_2 = C^b_2\langle\!\langle s_{j_1}, \ldots, s_{j_p}\rangle\!\rangle$. We choose fresh variables $x_1, \ldots, x_n$ such that $\langle s_1, \ldots, s_n\rangle \propto \langle x_1, \ldots, x_n\rangle$, and set $t' = C^b[x_1, \ldots, x_n]$, $t'_1 = C^b_1[x_{i_1}, \ldots, x_{i_m}]$, and $t'_2 = C^b_2[x_{j_1}, \ldots, x_{j_p}]$. Repeated application of Lemma 3.11 yields $t'_1 \ {}^{*}_{\mathcal{R}_1}\!\leftarrow t' \to^*_{\mathcal{R}_1} t'_2$. Since this is a conversion in $(\mathcal{F}_1, \mathcal{R}_1)$, there exists a common reduct $\hat{C}^b[x_{k_1}, \ldots, x_{k_l}]$ of t'_1 and t'_2, i.e., $t'_1 \to^*_{\mathcal{R}_1} \hat{C}^b[x_{k_1}, \ldots, x_{k_l}] \ {}^{*}_{\mathcal{R}_1}\!\leftarrow t'_2$. By the special choice of the variables $x_1, \ldots, x_n$, it follows that $t_1 \overset{o\,*}{\to}_{\mathcal{R}_1} \hat{C}^b\langle\!\langle s_{k_1}, \ldots, s_{k_l}\rangle\!\rangle \ {}_{\mathcal{R}_1}\!\overset{*\,o}{\leftarrow} t_2$. □

Definition 5.2 Let S be a set of confluent terms. A set $\hat{S}$ of terms *represents* S if the following two conditions are satisfied:

1. Every term s in S has a unique reduct $\hat{s}$ in $\hat{S}$, called the *representative* of s.
2. Joinable terms in S have the same representative in $\hat{S}$.

Lemma 5.3 Every finite set S of confluent terms can be represented.

Proof: Since S consists of confluent terms, joinability is an equivalence relation on S. Hence we can partition S into equivalence classes $C_1, \ldots, C_n$ of joinable terms. Since these classes are finite, for every $C_j = \{s_1, \ldots, s_m\}$ there exist a common reduct t_j of $s_1, \ldots, s_m$, i.e., $s_l \to^* t_j$ for every $l \in \{1, \ldots, m\}$. Obviously, the set $\{t_1, \ldots, t_n\}$ represents S. □

Lemma 5.4 Preserved terms are confluent.

Proof: We show that every preserved term t is confluent by induction on $rank(t)$. The case $rank(t) = 0$ is trivially true. Let $rank(t) = k > 0$ and suppose that the assertion holds for any term s with $rank(s) < k$. Distinguish the cases:
Case (i): t is top black.
Consider a conversion $t_1 \ {}^{*}\!\leftarrow t \to^* t_2$. Since t is preserved, each term u occurring in the conversion is top black. Let S be the set of all white principal subterms occurring in the conversion. By the induction hypothesis, S consists of confluent terms because every element of S is preserved and has rank less than k. It follows from Lemma 5.3 that S can be represented by a set $\hat{S}$. We write $\tilde{u}$ for the term obtained from u by replacing each white principal subterm with its representative. Note that $u \to^* \tilde{u}$.

We claim that $\tilde{t}_1 \ {}_{\mathcal{R}_1}\!\overset{*\,o}{\leftarrow} \tilde{t} \overset{o\,*}{\to}_{\mathcal{R}_1} \tilde{t}_2$. Let $u_1 \to u_2$ be a step in the conversion $t_1 \ {}^{*}\!\leftarrow t \to^* t_2$. Since u_1 is top black, we may write $u_1 = C^b_1\{\!\{s_1, \ldots, s_n\}\!\}$. The claim will be proved by showing $\tilde{u}_1 \overset{o\,*}{\to}_{\mathcal{R}_1} \tilde{u}_2$. We distinguish the following cases.

1. If $u_1 \to^{o}_{\mathcal{R}_1} u_2$, then $u_2 = C_2^b\{\!\{s_{i_1}, \ldots, s_{i_m}\}\!\}$. It is easy to verify that $\tilde{u}_1 = C_1^b\{\hat{s}_1, \ldots, \hat{s}_n\} \to^{o}_{\mathcal{R}_1} C_2^b\{\hat{s}_{i_1}, \ldots, \hat{s}_{i_m}\} = \tilde{u}_2$ (cf. Def. 5.2 and Lemma 3.11).
2. If $u_1 \to u_2$ is not an outer $\mathcal{R}_1$-rewrite step, then, since u_1 is preserved, we may write $u_1 = C_1^b[\![s_1, \ldots, s_j, \ldots, s_n]\!] \to C_1^b[\![s_1, \ldots, s_j', \ldots, s_n]\!] = u_2$ where $s_j \to s_j'$. Since the terms s_j and s_j' are trivially joinable, we have $\hat{s}_j = \hat{s}_j'$ and therefore $\tilde{u}_1 = C_1^b[\hat{s}_1, \ldots, \hat{s}_j, \ldots, \hat{s}_n] = \tilde{u}_2$.

This shows the claim $\tilde{t}_1 \; {}_{\mathcal{R}_1}\!\overset{*\,o}{\leftarrow} \tilde{t} \overset{o\,*}{\to}_{\mathcal{R}_1} \tilde{t}_2$. Since $\to^{o}_{\mathcal{R}_1}$ is confluent, the terms $\tilde{t}_1$ and $\tilde{t}_2$ have a common reduct, which is also a common reduct of t_1 and t_2.
Case (ii): t is top white. Analogous to case (i).
Case (iii): t is top transparent.
Let $t = C^t[\![s_1, \ldots, s_n]\!]$ and consider a conversion $t_1 \; {}^*\!\!\leftarrow t \to^* t_2$. Clearly, we may write $t_1 = C^t[u_1, \ldots, u_n]$ and $t_2 = C^t[v_1, \ldots, v_n]$ where $u_j \; {}^*\!\!\leftarrow s_j \to^* v_j$. By cases (i) and (ii), there are terms $w_1, \ldots, w_n$ such that $u_j \to^* w_j \; {}^*\!\!\leftarrow v_j$. Obviously, $C^t[w_1, \ldots, w_n]$ is a common reduct of t_1 and t_2. □

Proposition 5.5 White (black) preserved terms are confluent.
Proof: We show that every white preserved term is confluent. So suppose t is a white preserved term and consider a conversion $t_1 \; {}^*\!\!\leftarrow t \to^* t_2$. It has to be shown that the terms t_1 and t_2 are joinable. As in the proof of Lemma 5.4, let S be the set of all white principal subterms occurring in the conversion. Notice that if u is a top white term occurring in the conversion, then u itself belongs to S. By Lemma 5.4, S consists of confluent terms because every element of S is preserved. By Lemma 5.3, S can be represented by a set $\hat{S}$. Recall that $\tilde{u}$ denotes the result of replacing every white principal subterm in u with its representative. Again we claim that $\tilde{t}_1 \; {}_{\mathcal{R}_1}\!\overset{*\,o}{\leftarrow} \tilde{t} \overset{o\,*}{\to}_{\mathcal{R}_1} \tilde{t}_2$. Let $u_1 \to u_2$ be a step in the conversion $t_1 \; {}^*\!\!\leftarrow t \to^* t_2$. The claim will be proved by distinguishing the following cases.

1. Suppose u_1 is a top black or top transparent term, i.e., $u_1 = C_1^b\{\!\{s_1, \ldots, s_n\}\!\}$. If $u_1 \to^{o}_{\mathcal{R}_1} u_2$, then u_2 can be written as $u_2 = C_2^b\langle\!\langle s_{i_1}, \ldots, s_{i_m}\rangle\!\rangle$ and it follows that $\tilde{u}_1 = C_1^b\{\hat{s}_1, \ldots, \hat{s}_n\} \to^{o}_{\mathcal{R}_1} C_2^b\langle\hat{s}_{i_1}, \ldots, \hat{s}_{i_m}\rangle = \tilde{u}_2$. Otherwise $u_1 \to u_2$ is not an outer $\mathcal{R}_1$-rewrite step. Since u_1 is white preserved, $u_1 \to u_2$ can be written as $u_1 = C_1^b[\![s_1, \ldots, s_j, \ldots, s_n]\!] \to C_1^b[\![s_1, \ldots, s_j', \ldots, s_n]\!] = u_2$ where $s_j \to s_j'$. Clearly, $\hat{s}_j = \hat{s}_j'$ and hence $\tilde{u}_1 = C_1^b[\hat{s}_1, \ldots, \hat{s}_j, \ldots, \hat{s}_n] = \tilde{u}_2$.
2. Suppose u_1 is top white. Since u_1 is preserved, u_2 must also be top white and preserved. Hence u_1 and u_2 are both in S. Of course, they must have the same representative. So $\tilde{u}_1 = \hat{u}_1 = \hat{u}_2 = \tilde{u}_2$.

This shows the claim. Since $\to^{o}_{\mathcal{R}_1}$ is confluent, the terms $\tilde{t}_1$ and $\tilde{t}_2$ have a common reduct $\tilde{t}_3$. We conclude that $t_1 \to^* \tilde{t}_3 \; {}^*\!\!\leftarrow t_2$.
□

For the rest of this section, we additionally assume $\to_c$ to be normalizing. Under this condition confluence turns out to be modular.

Lemma 5.6 Every term t has a preserved reduct.
Proof: Since $\to_c$ is normalizing, $t \to_c^* t'$ for some $t' \in NF(\to_c)$. By Lemma 4.3, t' is preserved. □

The idea of the modularity proof of confluence is to project a conversion $t_1 \; {}^*\!\!\leftarrow t \rightarrow^* t_2$ to a conversion involving only white preserved terms (in order to use Proposition 5.5). The projection consists of choosing an appropriate white (black) witness, according to the following definition.

Definition 5.7 Let $s = C^b\langle\langle s_1, \ldots, s_n\rangle\rangle$. A *white witness* of s is a white preserved term $t = C^b\langle t_1, \ldots, t_n\rangle$ which satisfies the following two properties:

1. $s_j \rightarrow^* t_j$ for every $j \in \{1, \ldots, n\}$,
2. $\langle s_1, \ldots, s_n\rangle \propto \langle t_1, \ldots, t_n\rangle$.

Lemma 5.8 Every term has a white (black) witness.
Proof: Let $s = C^b\langle\langle s_1, \ldots, s_n\rangle\rangle$. According to Lemma 5.6, every s_j has a preserved reduct t_j. Evidently, we may assume that $\langle s_1, \ldots, s_n\rangle \propto \langle t_1, \ldots, t_n\rangle$. The term $t = C^b\langle t_1, \ldots, t_n\rangle$ is white preserved. □

In the following $\dot{s}$ denotes an arbitrary white witness of s. Note that $s \rightarrow^* \dot{s}$.

Proposition 5.9 Let $s \rightarrow t$. If all white principal subterms of s are confluent, then $\dot{s} \downarrow \dot{t}$.
Proof: As usual, we prove the proposition by case analysis.
Case (i): s is top black or top transparent.
If $s \in \mathcal{T}(\mathcal{D}_1, \mathcal{C}, \mathcal{V})$, then $\dot{s} = s \rightarrow_{\mathcal{R}_1} t = \dot{t}$ and the assertion follows from the confluence of $\mathcal{R}_1$. So suppose $s = C^b[\![s_1, \ldots, s_n]\!]$ and $\dot{s} = C^b[t_1, \ldots, t_n]$.

1. If $s \rightarrow^o_{\mathcal{R}_1} t$, then $t = \hat{C}^b\langle\langle s_{i_1}, \ldots, s_{i_m}\rangle\rangle$. Hence $\dot{t} = \hat{C}^b\langle u_{i_1}, \ldots, u_{i_m}\rangle$ for respective reducts $u_{i_1}, \ldots, u_{i_m}$ of $s_{i_1}, \ldots, s_{i_m}$. Since $\langle s_1, \ldots, s_n\rangle \propto \langle t_1, \ldots, t_n\rangle$, we obtain $\dot{s} \rightarrow \hat{C}^b\langle t_{i_1}, \ldots, t_{i_m}\rangle$ from Lemma 3.11. It follows from $t_j \; {}^*\!\!\leftarrow s_j \rightarrow^* u_j$ and the confluence of s_j that $t_j \downarrow u_j$ for every index $j \in \{i_1, \ldots, i_m\}$. Thus $\dot{s} \downarrow \dot{t}$.
2. If $s \rightarrow t$ is not an outer $\mathcal{R}_1$-rewrite step, then $t = C^b[s_1, \ldots, s'_j, \ldots, s_n]$ where $s_j \rightarrow s'_j$ for some index $j \in \{1, \ldots, n\}$. Since $C^b[, \ldots,]$ is black, we have $\dot{t} = C^b[u_1, \ldots, u_n]$ for some respective reducts $u_1, \ldots, u_j, \ldots, u_n$ of $s_1, \ldots, s'_j, \ldots, s_n$. The joinability of t_l and u_l for $l \in \{1, \ldots, n\}$ is obtained as in the previous case. Hence $\dot{s} \downarrow \dot{t}$.

Case (ii): s is top white.
In this case s itself is the only white principal subterm of s. From $\dot{s} \; {}^*\!\!\leftarrow s \rightarrow t \rightarrow^* \dot{t}$ and confluence of s it follows that $\dot{s} \downarrow \dot{t}$. □

Theorem 5.10 Confluence is a modular property of constructor-sharing TRSs provided that $\rightarrow_c$ is normalizing.
Proof: By induction on $rank(t)$ we show that every term t is confluent if $\rightarrow_c$ is normalizing. If $rank(t) = 0$, then the assertion holds vacuously. Suppose $rank(t) > 0$ and consider a conversion $t_1 \; {}^*\!\!\leftarrow t \rightarrow^* t_2$.
Case (i): t is top black.
The proof for this case is illustrated in Figure 1. First every term in the conversion (black dots) is reduced to a white witness (white dots). Since all white

principal subterms occurring in the conversion $t_1 \; {}^*\!\!\leftarrow t \rightarrow^* t_2$ have rank less than $rank(t)$, the induction hypothesis implies their confluence. Repeated application of Proposition 5.9 yields a conversion between the white witnesses (upper grey dots). Since white witnesses are white preserved, they are confluent by Proposition 5.5. Hence t_1 and t_2 have a common reduct.
Case (ii): t is top white. Analogous to case (i) (using black witnesses).
Case (iii): t is top transparent. The assertion follows as in Lemma 5.4, case (iii).
□

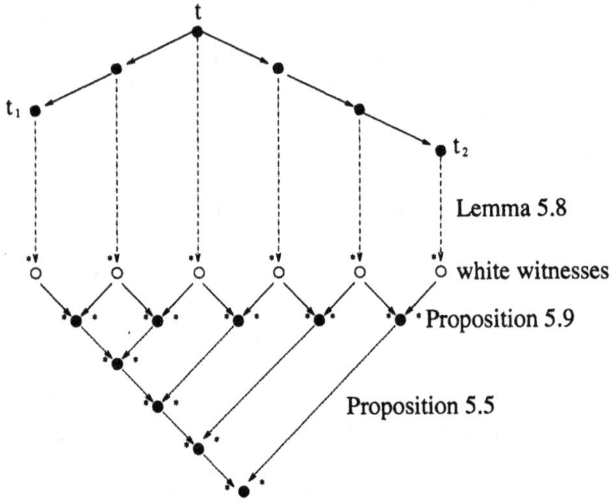

Figure 1

Corollary 5.11 If $\mathcal{R}_1$ and $\mathcal{R}_2$ are confluent and contain neither collapsing nor constructor-lifting rules, then their combined system $\mathcal{R} = \mathcal{R}_1 \cup \mathcal{R}_2$ is confluent.
Proof: This is an immediate consequence of the above theorem because $\rightarrow_c$ is empty for those systems. □

The next example shows why collapsing rules also have to be excluded.

Example 5.12 Consider the TRSs $\mathcal{R}_1 = \{F(x, C(x)) \rightarrow A, F(x,x) \rightarrow B\}$ and $\mathcal{R}_2 = \{a \rightarrow g(C(a)), g(x) \rightarrow x\}$ which share the constructor C. Both are confluent, but the term $F(a,a)$ has two normal forms A and B.

6 Modularity of Semi-Completeness

In Klop et al. [KMTV91], it is shown that for arbitrary disjoint TRSs $\mathcal{R}_1$ and $\mathcal{R}_2$ the relation $\rightarrow_c$ is terminating. Consequently, by Theorem 5.10, confluence is modular for disjoint TRSs. In contrast to the disjoint union case, $\rightarrow_c$ is not even normalizing in the presence of shared constructors. Consider e.g. the TRSs of Example 1.1. The term a has no normal form w.r.t. $\rightarrow_c$ because the derivation

$$a \rightarrow_c C(a) \rightarrow_c C(C(a)) \rightarrow_c C(C(C(a))) \rightarrow_c \cdots$$

is infinite. Replacing $\mathcal{R}_2$ with $\{a \to c(a), a \to b\}$ yields an example which shows that normalization of $\mathcal{R}_1$ and $\mathcal{R}_2$ does not imply normalization of $\to_c$. However, the term rewriting system $\{a \to c(a), a \to b\}$ is not confluent. Our next goal is to show that semi-completeness of $\mathcal{R}_1$ and $\mathcal{R}_2$ ensures normalization of $\to_c$.

Definition 6.1 Let $C^t[,\ldots,] \in \mathcal{T}(\mathcal{C},\mathcal{V})$. Define

$$\|C^t[,\ldots,]\| = \begin{cases} 0 & \text{, if } C^t[,\ldots,] = \Box \\ 1 + \sum_{i=1}^n \|t_i\|, & \text{if } C^t[,\ldots,] = f(t_1,\ldots,t_n),\ f \neq \Box \end{cases}$$

For $s \in \mathcal{T}(\mathcal{D},\mathcal{C},\mathcal{V})$, define

$$\|s\| = \begin{cases} 0 & \text{, if } s \text{ is top black or top white} \\ \|C^t[,\ldots,]\|, & \text{if } s = C^t[\![s_1,\ldots,s_n]\!] \end{cases}$$

That is, $\|s\|$ denotes the number of transparent symbols occurring in the outer transparent context of s.

Lemma 6.2 If $\mathcal{R}_1$ and $\mathcal{R}_2$ are semi-complete, then the collapsing reduction relation $\to_c$ is terminating on $\mathcal{T}(\mathcal{D}_1,\mathcal{C},\mathcal{V}) \cup \mathcal{T}(\mathcal{D}_2,\mathcal{C},\mathcal{V})$.
Proof: W.l.o.g. it suffices to show that each $\to_c$ reduction sequence starting from some term $t \in \mathcal{T}(\mathcal{D}_1,\mathcal{C},\mathcal{V})$ is finite. We prove this by contradiction. Suppose there is an infinite reduction sequence

$$t = t_1 \to_c t_2 \to_c t_3 \to_c \ldots$$

Obviously, $t_j \notin \mathcal{T}(\mathcal{C},\mathcal{V})$ for each $j \in \mathbb{N}$ and $t_j \to_c t_{j+1}$ implies $t_j \to_{\mathcal{R}_1}^+ t_{j+1}$. We first prove that $t_j \to_c t_{j+1}$ implies $\|t_j\| < \|t_{j+1}\|$, considering the following cases.

- If t_j is top black, then t_j is the only special subterm of t_j. According to the definition of $\to_c$, $t_{j+1} = C^t[\![s_1,\ldots,s_n]\!]$ for some context $C^t[,\ldots,] \neq \Box$ and top black terms $s_1,\ldots,s_n$. Consequently, $\|t_j\| = 0 < \|t_{j+1}\|$.
- If $t_j = C^t[\![s_1,\ldots,s_i,\ldots,s_n]\!]$, then the special subterms of t_j, apart from t_j itself, are the top black terms $s_1,\ldots,s_n$. According to the definition of $\to_c$, we have $t_{j+1} = C^t[s_1,\ldots,s_i',\ldots,s_n]$, where $s_i \to_{\mathcal{R}_1}^+ s_i'$ and s_i' is top transparent. Thus $\|t_j\| < \|t_{j+1}\|$.

Hence $t_j \to_c t_{j+1}$ implies $\|t_j\| < \|t_{j+1}\|$, and we obtain an infinite ascending sequence of natural numbers

$$\|t_1\| < \|t_2\| < \|t_3\| < \|t_4\| < \ldots$$

Since $\mathcal{R}_1$ is normalizing, $t \to_{\mathcal{R}_1}^* t'$ for some $t' \in NF(\to_{\mathcal{R}_1})$. Let $\|t'\| = k$. Then there is a $j \in \mathbb{N}$ such that $\|t_j\| > k$. On the other hand, since $t' \ {}_{\mathcal{R}_1}^*\!\!\leftarrow t \to_{\mathcal{R}_1}^* t_j$, the term t' is in normal form w.r.t. $\to_{\mathcal{R}_1}$, and $\mathcal{R}_1$ is confluent, it follows that $t_j \to_{\mathcal{R}_1}^* t'$. Hence we have $t_j = C^t[\![s_1,\ldots,s_n]\!] \to_{\mathcal{R}_1}^* C^t[s_1',\ldots,s_n'] = t'$, where $s_i \to_{\mathcal{R}_1}^* s_i'$, for every $i \in \{1,\ldots,n\}$. In conclusion, $\|t'\| \geq \|t_j\| > k$ yields a contradiction. $\Box$

In order to prove the normalization of $\to_c$ on $\mathcal{T}(\mathcal{D},\mathcal{C},\mathcal{V})$, we actually show the stronger statement that $\to_c$ is innermost normalizing.

Lemma 6.3 Let s be a top white term and let $s \to_c^* s'$ be an innermost derivation such that $s' \in NF(\to_c)$. Then for any black context $C^b[,\dots,]$ it follows $C^b[\dots,s,\dots] \to_c^* C^b[\dots,s',\dots]$

Proof: If all terms in $s \to_c^* s'$ are top white, then the lemma holds. Otherwise a top black or top transparent term u' occurs in the innermost derivation $s \to_c^* s'$. Suppose $s \to_c^* u \to_c u' \to_c^* s'$ such that u' is the first non-top-white term in the derivation. Since u is top white, the derivation is innermost, and the collapsing reduction takes place in the outer white context, it follows that $u = C^w\{\!\{u_1,\dots,u_m\}\!\}$ where $u_1,\dots,u_m \in NF(\to_c)$, and $u' = \hat{C}^w\langle\!\langle u_{i_1},\dots,u_{i_l}\rangle\!\rangle$ for some $i_1,\dots,i_l \in \{1,\dots,m\}$.

- If u' is top black, then $u' = u_i$ for some $i \in \{i_1,\dots,i_l\}$. Since $u_i \in NF(\to_c)$, it follows that $s' = u'$. Clearly, the lemma is also valid in this case.
- In the remaining case u' is top transparent. Then any reduction step in the sequence $u' \to_c^* s'$ takes place in the respective outer white contexts because $u_{i_1},\dots,u_{i_l} \in NF(\to_c)$. Therefore, $s' = \bar{C}^w\langle\!\langle u_{j_1},\dots,u_{j_p}\rangle\!\rangle$ for some indices $j_1,\dots,j_p \in \{i_1,\dots,i_l\}$, and it follows $C^b[\dots,s,\dots] \to_c^* C^b[\dots,s',\dots]$.

□

Proposition 6.4 If $\mathcal{R}_1$ and $\mathcal{R}_2$ are semi-complete, then the relation $\to_c$ is innermost normalizing on $\mathcal{T}(\mathcal{D},\mathcal{C},\mathcal{V})$.

Proof: It is shown that every term t is innermost normalizing w.r.t. $\to_c$ using induction on $rank(t) = k$. The case $k = 0$ is trivially true and for $k = 1$ the assertion follows from Lemma 6.2 in conjunction with case (iii) below. So let $rank(t) = k > 1$. The following case analysis yields the result.

Case (i): t is top black.

Then we may write $t = C^b[\![t_1,\dots,t_n]\!]$. Since $rank(t_j) < rank(t)$, it follows from the induction hypothesis that, for every $j \in \{1,\dots,n\}$, there exists an innermost derivation $t_j \to_c^* t_j'$ such that $t_j' \in NF(\to_c)$. According to Lemma 6.3, $t = C^b[\![t_1,\dots,t_n]\!] \to_c^* C^b[t_1',\dots,t_n']$. Observe that this is also an innermost derivation. Moreover, since t_j' can be written as $t_j' = \hat{C}_j^b\langle\!\langle t_1^j,\dots,t_{m_j}^j\rangle\!\rangle$, where every top white t_i^j is an element of $NF(\to_c)$, we may write $C^b[t_1',\dots,t_n'] = \hat{C}^b\{\!\{s_1,\dots,s_m\}\!\}$ for some black context $\hat{C}^b\{\!\{,\dots,\}\!\}$ and top white terms $s_1,\dots,s_m \in NF(\to_c)$. Choose fresh variables $x_1,\dots,x_m$ such that $<s_1,\dots,s_m> \infty <x_1,\dots,x_m>$. Since $\hat{C}^b\{x_1,\dots,x_m\} \in \mathcal{T}(\mathcal{D}_1,\mathcal{C},\mathcal{V})$ and $\to_c$ is terminating on $\mathcal{T}(\mathcal{D}_1,\mathcal{C},\mathcal{V})$, it follows that each innermost $\to_c$ derivation starting from $\hat{C}^b\{x_1,\dots,x_m\}$ ends in some $\bar{C}^b\langle x_{i_1},\dots,x_{i_l}\rangle \in NF(\to_c)$. It follows from $\hat{C}^b\{x_1,\dots,x_m\} \to_c^* \bar{C}^b\langle x_{i_1},\dots,x_{i_l}\rangle$ and the special choice of the variables $x_1,\dots,x_m$ that $t \to_c^* \hat{C}^b\{\!\{s_1,\dots,s_m\}\!\} \to_c^* \bar{C}^b\langle\!\langle s_{i_1},\dots,s_{i_l}\rangle\!\rangle = t'$. It is easy to verify that $t' \in NF(\to_c)$ and that $t \to_c^* t'$ is an innermost reduction sequence.

Case (ii): t is top white. Analogous to case (i).

Case (iii): t is top transparent.
Let $t = C^t[\![t_1, \ldots, t_n]\!]$. According to cases (i) and (ii), every t_j reduces via innermost rewriting to some $t'_j \in NF(\rightarrow_c)$. Clearly, $t' = C^t[t'_1, \ldots, t'_n] \in NF(\rightarrow_c)$, $t \rightarrow_c^* t'$, and the derivation is innermost. □

Theorem 6.5 Semi-completeness is modular for constructor-sharing TRSs.
Proof: Let $\mathcal{R}_1$ and $\mathcal{R}_2$ be constructor-sharing TRSs and let $\mathcal{R} = \mathcal{R}_1 \cup \mathcal{R}_2$. We have to show that $\mathcal{R}$ is semi-complete if and only if $\mathcal{R}_1$ and $\mathcal{R}_2$ are semi-complete. The only-if direction is trivial. So let $\mathcal{R}_1$ and $\mathcal{R}_2$ be semi-complete. According to Proposition 6.4, $\rightarrow_c$ is innermost normalizing and hence normalizing. Consequently, $\mathcal{R}$ is confluent by Theorem 5.10. Finally, Proposition 3.14 states that $\mathcal{R}$ is also normalizing. □

7 Conclusions

Several sufficient conditions for the modularity of confluence in the presence of shared constructors have been stated in this paper. After all, the whole matter boils down to ensure normalization of the collapsing reduction relation $\rightarrow_c$. Perhaps this approach leads to more interesting sufficient criteria. The modularity of confluence for left-linear TRSs [RV80] and our results are complementary. It has been pointed out that semi-completeness of the constituent systems ensures normalization of $\rightarrow_c$. In fact, with the aid of Theorem 6.5, one can show that $\rightarrow_c$ is even terminating under these circumstances. It is possible that a direct proof of the termination of $\rightarrow_c$ will turn out to be simpler than the given one. This point needs further investigations.

In [KK90], Kurihara and Kaji introduced a very interesting relation $\rightsquigarrow$ called "modular reduction". Roughly speaking, if $\mathcal{R}_1, \ldots, \mathcal{R}_n$ are pairwise disjoint TRSs, then reduction steps have to be performed using the same constituent TRS $\mathcal{R}_j$ as long as possible. More precisely, $s \rightsquigarrow t$ if and only if $s \rightarrow^+_{\mathcal{R}_j} t$ and $t \in NF(\rightarrow_{\mathcal{R}_j})$ for some $j \in \{1, \ldots, n\}$. Using Toyama's Theorem they concluded that semi-completeness of $\mathcal{R}_1, \ldots, \mathcal{R}_n$ implies completeness of $\rightsquigarrow$ (see also [Mid90]). Our main result includes that this proposition remains true if the modular reduction relation is extended to constructor-sharing TRSs (the extension itself is straightforward, cf. [KO91]). This can be checked along the lines of the proof given in [Mid90] – the arguments employing Toyama's Theorem can easily be modified: just use Theorem 6.5 instead.

The results presented should be extended to conditional term rewriting systems (CTRSs). In the investigation of modular properties of CTRSs one encounters, however, complications not present in the unconditional case. For instance normalization is not modular in general (see [Mid90]).

Acknowledgements: The author is much obliged to Robert Giegerich and Aart Middeldorp for comments on a previous version of the paper and to Anke Bodzin for typesetting parts of the manuscript.

References

[DJ90] N. Dershowitz and J.P. Jouannaud. Rewrite Systems. In L. van Leeuwen, editor, *Handbook of Theoretical Computer Science, Vol. B*, chapter 6. North-Holland, 1990.

[DJK93] N. Dershowitz, J.P. Jouannaud, and J.W. Klop. More Problems in Rewriting. In *Proceedings of the 5th International Conference on Rewriting Techniques and Applications*, pages 468–487. Lecture Notes in Computer Science **690**, Springer Verlag, 1993.

[Gra93] B. Gramlich. Generalized Sufficient Conditions for Modular Termination of Rewriting. *Applicable Algebra in Engineering, Communication and Computing*, 1993. To appear.

[KK90] M. Kurihara and I. Kaji. Modular Term Rewriting Systems and the Termination. *Information Processing Letters* **34**, pages 1–4, 1990.

[Klo92] J.W. Klop. Term Rewriting Systems. In S. Abramsky, D. Gabbay, and T. Maibaum, editors, *Handbook of Logic in Computer Science, Vol. II*, pages 1–116. Oxford University Press, 1992.

[KMTV91] J.W. Klop, A. Middeldorp, Y. Toyama, and R. Vrijer. A Simplified Proof of Toyama's Theorem. Report CS-R9156, Centre for Mathematics and Computer Science, Amsterdam, 1991. Revised version to appear in Information Processing Letters.

[KO91] M. Kurihara and A. Ohuchi. Modular Term Rewriting Systems with Shared Constructors. *Journal of Information Processing* **14***(3), IPS of Japan*, pages 357–358, 1991.

[KO92] M. Kurihara and A. Ohuchi. Modularity of Simple Termination of Term Rewriting Systems with Shared Constructors. *Theoretical Computer Science* **103**, pages 273–282, 1992.

[Mid90] A. Middeldorp. *Modular Properties of Term Rewriting Systems*. PhD thesis, Vrije Universiteit te Amsterdam, 1990.

[MT93] A. Middeldorp and Y. Toyama. Completeness of Combinations of Constructor Systems. *Journal of Symbolic Computation* **15***(3)*, pages 331–348, 1993.

[Ohl93a] E. Ohlebusch. On the Modularity of Termination of Term Rewriting Systems. Report Nr. 11, Universität Bielefeld, 1993.

[Ohl93b] E. Ohlebusch. Termination is not Modular for Confluent Variable-Preserving Term Rewriting Systems. Submitted, 1993.

[RV80] J.-C. Raoult and J. Vuillemin. Operational and Semantic Equivalence between Recursive Programs. *Journal of the ACM* **27***(4)*, pages 772–796, 1980.

[TKB89] Y. Toyama, J.W. Klop, and H.P Barendregt. Termination for the Direct Sum of Left-Linear Term Rewriting Systems. In *Proceedings of the 3rd International Conference on Rewriting Techniques and Applications*, pages 477–491. Lecture Notes in Computer Science **355**, Springer Verlag, 1989.

[Toy87a] Y. Toyama. Counterexamples to Termination for the Direct Sum of Term Rewriting Systems. *Information Processing Letters* **25**, pages 141–143, 1987.

[Toy87b] Y. Toyama. On the Church-Rosser Property for the Direct Sum of Term Rewriting Systems. *Journal of the ACM* **34***(1)*, pages 128–143, 1987.

Global Program Analysis in Constraint Form

Jens Palsberg

161 Cullinane Hall, College of Computer Science, Northeastern University,
360 Huntington Avenue, Boston, MA 02115, USA, palsberg@ccs.neu.edu

Abstract. Global program analyses of untyped higher-order functional programs have in the past decade been presented by Ayers, Bondorf, Consel, Jones, Sestoft, Shivers, and others. The analyses are usually defined as abstract interpretations and are used for rather different tasks such as type recovery, globalization, and binding-time analysis. The analyses all contain a global *closure analysis* that computes information about higher-order control-flow. Sestoft proved in 1989 and 1991 that closure analysis is correct with respect to call-by-name and call-by-value semantics, but it remained open if correctness holds for arbitrary beta-reduction.

This paper answers the question; both closure analysis and others are correct with respect to arbitrary beta-reduction. We also prove a subject-reduction result: closure information is still valid after beta-reduction. The core of our proof technique is to define closure analysis using a constraint system. The constraint system is equivalent to the closure analysis of Bondorf, which in turn is based on Sestoft's.

1 Introduction

1.1 Background

Optimization of higher-order functional languages requires powerful program analyses. The traditional framework for such analyses is *abstract interpretation*, and for *typed* languages, suitable abstract domains can often be defined by induction on the structure of types. For example, function spaces can be abstracted into function spaces. For *untyped* languages such as Scheme, however, abstract domains cannot be defined in that way.

In the past decade, program analyses of untyped languages has been presented by Ayers [2], Bondorf [4], Consel [8], Jones [10], Sestoft [15, 16], Shivers [17, 18], and others. Although the analyses are used for rather different tasks such as type recovery, globalization, and binding-time analysis, they are all based on essentially the same idea:

> **Key idea.** In the absence of types, define the abstract domains in terms of *program points*.

For example, consider the following λ-term:

$(\lambda x.\lambda y.y(xI)(xK))\Delta$
where $I = \lambda a.a$, $K = \lambda b.\lambda c.b$, and $\Delta = \lambda d.dd$.

Giannini and Rocca [9] proved that this strongly normalizing term has no higher-order polymorphic type. Still, a program analysis might answer basic questions such as:

1. For every application point, which abstractions can be applied?
2. For every abstraction, to which arguments can it be applied?

Each answer to such questions should be a subset of the program points in this particular λ-term. Thus, let us label all abstractions and applications. Also variables will be labeled: if a variable is bound, then it is labeled with the label of the λ that binds it, and if it is free, then with an arbitrary label. By introducing an explicit application symbol, we get the following abstract syntax for the above λ-term.

$$(\lambda^1 x.\lambda^2 y.y^2 \ @_7\ (x^1 \ @_8\ I)\ @_9\ (x^1 \ @_{10}\ K))\ @_{11}\ \Delta$$
where $I = \lambda^3 a.a^3$, $K = \lambda^4 b.\lambda^5 c.b^4$, and $\Delta = \lambda^6 d.d^6 \ @_{12}\ d^6$.

An analysis might be able to find out that no matter how reduction proceeds:

- "I can only be applied to I", that is, an abstraction with label 3 can only be applied to abstractions with label 3;
- "At the application point dd (in Δ) both I and K can be applied", that is, at an application point labeled 12 there can only be applied abstractions with labels 3 and 4; and
- "the abstraction $\lambda c.b$ will never be applied", that is, at no application point can an abstraction with label 5 be applied.

The quoted sentences gives the intuitive understanding of the precise statements that follows. In this particular example, the labels are rather unnecessary because no name clashes happen during any reduction and because I, K, and $\lambda c.b$ are in normal form. In the presence of name clashes or reduction under a λ, however, it is crucial to use sets of program points as the abstract values.

The above questions have turned out to be of paramount importance in many analyses of untyped functional programs. Following Sestoft and Bondorf, we will call any analysis that can answer them conservatively a *closure analysis*. On top of a closure analysis, one can build for example type recovery analyses, globalization analyses, and binding-time analyses. The closure analysis answers questions about higher-order control flow and the extension answers the questions one is really interested in, for example about type recovery. The rôle of closure analysis is thus as follows:

"*Higher-order analysis = first-order analysis + closure analysis*".

Closure analysis and its extensions can be defined as abstract interpretations. They differ radically from traditional abstract interpretations, however, in that the abstract domain is defined in terms of the program to be analyzed. This means that such analyses are *global*: before the abstract domain can be defined, the complete program is required. Moreover, the program cannot take higher-order input because that would add program points. In contrast, traditional abstract interpretations can analyze pieces of a program in isolation. We will refer to all analyses based on closure analysis as *Global program analyses.*

Examples of large-scale implementations of such analyses can be found in the Similix system of Bondorf [5, 6], the Schism system of Consel [8], and the system of Agesen, Schwartzbach, and the present author [1] for analyzing Self programs [19]. The last of these implementations demonstrates that closure analysis can handle dynamic and multiple inheritance.

Sestoft proved in 1989 [15] and 1991 [16] that closure analysis is correct with respect to call-by-name and call-by-value semantics, but it remained open if correctness holds for arbitrary beta-reduction.

1.2 Our Results

We prove that closure analysis is correct with respect to arbitrary beta-reduction. We also prove a subject-reduction result: closure information is still valid after beta-reduction.

To be able to prove these results we first do the following:

- We present a novel *specification* of closure analysis that allows arbitrary beta-reduction to take place and which subsumes all previous specifications.
- We present a closure analysis that uses a *constraint system.* The constraint system characterizes the result of the analysis without specifying how it is computed. An example of such a constraint system is given in Section 1.3.
- We prove that the constraint-based analysis is equivalent to the closure analysis of Bondorf [4], which in turn is based on Sestoft's [15]. We also prove that these analyses are equivalent to a novel simplification of Bondorf's definition.

The proofs of correctness and subject-reduction then proceed by considering only the constraint-based definition of closure analysis.

In contrast to the closure analyses by abstract interpretation, the one using a constraint system does *not* depend on labels being distinct. This makes it possible to analyze a λ-term, beta-reduce it, and then analyze the result *without* relabeling first. The abstract interpretations might be modified to have this property also but it would be somewhat messy.

Our technique for proving correctness generalizes without problems to analyses based on closure analysis. The following two results are not proved in this paper:

- The *safety analysis* of Schwartzbach and the present author [13, 12] is correct with respect to arbitrary beta-reduction. This follows from the subject-reduction property: terms stay safe after beta-reduction.
- The binding-time analysis of Schwartzbach and the present author [14] that was proved correct in [11] can be proved correct more elegantly with our new technique.

These results demonstrate that *constants* and *binding-times* can be handled with our new proof technique.

1.3 Example

The constraint system that expresses closure analysis of a λ-term is a set of Horn clauses. If the λ-term contains n abstractions and m applications, then the constraint system contains $n + (2 \times m \times n)$ constraints. Thus, the size of a constraint system is in the worst-case quadratic in the size of the λ-term. Space constraints disallow us to show a full-blown example involving name clashes and reduction under a λ, so consider instead the λ-term $(\lambda x.xx)(\lambda y.y)$ which has the abstract syntax $(\lambda^1 x.x^1 \; @_3 \; x^1) \; @_4 \; (\lambda^2 y.y^2)$. The constraint system that expresses closure analysis of this λ-term looks as follows.

$$
\begin{array}{ll}
\text{From } \lambda^1 & \{1\} \subseteq [\![\lambda^1]\!] \\
\text{From } \lambda^2 & \{2\} \subseteq [\![\lambda^2]\!] \\
\text{From } @_3 \text{ and } \lambda^1 & \left\{ \begin{array}{l} \{1\} \subseteq [\![\nu^1]\!] \Rightarrow [\![\nu^1]\!] \subseteq [\![\nu^1]\!] \\ \{1\} \subseteq [\![\nu^1]\!] \Rightarrow [\![@_3]\!] \subseteq [\![@_3]\!] \end{array} \right. \\
\text{From } @_3 \text{ and } \lambda^2 & \left\{ \begin{array}{l} \{2\} \subseteq [\![\nu^1]\!] \Rightarrow [\![\nu^1]\!] \subseteq [\![\nu^2]\!] \\ \{2\} \subseteq [\![\nu^1]\!] \Rightarrow [\![\nu^2]\!] \subseteq [\![@_3]\!] \end{array} \right. \\
\text{From } @_4 \text{ and } \lambda^1 & \left\{ \begin{array}{l} \{1\} \subseteq [\![\lambda^1]\!] \Rightarrow [\![\lambda^2]\!] \subseteq [\![\nu^1]\!] \\ \{1\} \subseteq [\![\lambda^1]\!] \Rightarrow [\![@_3]\!] \subseteq [\![@_4]\!] \end{array} \right. \\
\text{From } @_4 \text{ and } \lambda^2 & \left\{ \begin{array}{l} \{2\} \subseteq [\![\lambda^1]\!] \Rightarrow [\![\lambda^2]\!] \subseteq [\![\nu^2]\!] \\ \{2\} \subseteq [\![\lambda^1]\!] \Rightarrow [\![\nu^2]\!] \subseteq [\![@_4]\!] \end{array} \right.
\end{array}
$$

Symbols of the forms $[\![\nu^l]\!]$, $[\![\lambda^l]\!]$, and $[\![@_i]\!]$ are meta-variables. They relate to variables with label l, abstractions with label l, and applications with label i, respectively. Notice that we do *not* assume that there for example is just one abstraction with label l. The reason is that we want to do closure analysis of *all* terms, also those arising after beta-reduction which may copy terms and hence labels.

To the left of the constraints, we have indicated from where they arise. The first two constraints expresses that an abstraction may evaluate to an abstraction with the same label. The rest of the constraints come in pairs. For each application point $@_i$ and each abstraction with label l there are two constraints of the form:

$$
\begin{array}{lcl}
\{l\} \subseteq \text{“meta-var. for func. part of } @_i\text{”} & \Rightarrow & \text{“meta-var. for arg. part of } @_i\text{”} \subseteq [\![\nu^l]\!] \\
\{l\} \subseteq \text{“meta-var. for func. part of } @_i\text{”} & \Rightarrow & \text{“meta-var. for body of abstr.”} \subseteq [\![@_i]\!]
\end{array}
$$

Such constraints can be read as:

- **The first constraint.** If the function part of $@_i$ evaluates to an abstraction with label l, then the bound variable of that abstraction may be substituted with everything to which the argument part of $@_i$ can evaluate.
- **The second constraint.** If the function part of $@_i$ evaluates to an abstraction with label l, then everything to which the body of the abstraction evaluates is also a possible result of evaluating the whole application $@_i$.

In a solution of the constraint system, meta-variables are assigned closure information. The minimal solution of the above constraint system is a mapping L where:

$$L[\![\lambda^1]\!] = \{1\}$$
$$L[\![\lambda^2]\!] = L[\![\nu^1]\!] = L[\![\nu^2]\!] = L[\![@_3]\!] = L[\![@_4]\!] = \{2\}$$

For example, the whole λ-term will, if normalizing, evaluate to an abstraction with label 2 ($L[\![@_4]\!] = \{2\}$); at the application point $@_3$ there can only be applied abstractions with label 2 ($L[\![\nu^1]\!] = \{2\}$); the application point $@_3$ is the only point where abstractions with label 2 can be applied ($L[\![\lambda^1]\!] = \{1\}$); and such abstractions can only be applied to λ-terms that either do not normalize or evaluate to an abstraction with label 2 ($L[\![\nu^2]\!] = \{2\}$).

One of our theorems says that the computed closure information is correct. One might also try to do closure analysis of the above λ-term using Bondorf's abstract interpretation; an other of our theorems says that we will get the same result.

Now contract the only redex in the above λ-term. The result is a λ-term with abstract syntax $(\lambda^2 y.y^2)\ @_3\ (\lambda^2 y.y^2)$. A third of our theorems says that the mapping L above gives correct closure information also for this λ-term.

In the following Section we define three closure analyses: Bondorf's, a simpler abstract interpretation, and one in constraint form. In Section 3 we prove that they are equivalent and in Section 4 we prove that they are correct.

2 Closure Analysis

Recall the λ-calculus [3].

Definition 1. The language Λ of λ-terms has an abstract syntax which is defined by the grammar:

$$\begin{array}{rlll} E & ::= & x^l & \text{(variable)} \\ & | & \lambda^l x.E & \text{(abstraction)} \\ & | & E_1\ @_i\ E_2 & \text{(application)} \end{array}$$

The labels on variables, abstraction symbols, and application symbols have no semantic impact; they mark program points. The label on a bound variable is the same as that on the λ that binds it. Labels are drawn from the infinite set Label. The labels and the application symbols are not part of the concrete syntax of Λ. We identify terms that are α-congruent. The α-conversion changes only bound variables, not labels. We assume the Variable Convention of Barendregt [3]: when a λ-term occurs in the paper, all bound variables are chosen to be different from the free variables. This can be achieved by renaming bound variables. An occurrence of $(\lambda^l x.E)\ @_i\ E'$ is called a redex. The semantics is as usual given by the rewriting rule scheme:

$$(\lambda^l x.E)\ @_i\ E' \rightarrow E[E'/x^l] \qquad \text{(beta-reduction)}$$

Here, $E[E'/x^l]$ denotes the term E with E' substituted for the free occurrences of x^l. Notice that by the Variable Convention, no renaming of bound variables is necessary when doing substitution. In particular, when we write $(\lambda^l y.E)[E'/x^{l'}]$, we have that $y^l \not\equiv x^{l'}$ and that y^l is not among the free variables of E'. Thus, $(\lambda^l y.E)[E'/x^{l'}] = \lambda^l y.(E[E'/x^{l'}])$. We write $E_S \rightarrow^* E_T$ to denote that E_T has been obtained from E_S by 0 or more beta-reductions. A term without redexes is in normal form.

The abstract domain for closure analysis of a λ-term E is called $\mathsf{CMap}(E)$ and is defined as follows.

Definition 2. A meta-variable is of one of the forms $[\![\nu^l]\!]$, $[\![\lambda^l]\!]$, and $[\![@_i]\!]$. The set of all meta-variables is denoted $\mathsf{Metavar}$. A λ-term is assigned a meta-variable by the function var, which maps x^l to $[\![\nu^l]\!]$, $\lambda^l x.E$ to $[\![\lambda^l]\!]$, and $E_1 @_i E_2$ to $[\![@_i]\!]$.

For a λ-term E, $\mathsf{Lab}(E)$ is the set of labels on abstractions (but not applications) occurring in E. Notice that $\mathsf{Lab}(E)$ is finite. The set $\mathsf{CSet}(E)$ is the powerset of $\mathsf{Lab}(E)$; $\mathsf{CSet}(E)$ with the inclusion ordering is a complete lattice. The set $\mathsf{CMap}(E)$ consists of the total functions from $\mathsf{Metavar}$ to $\mathsf{CSet}(E)$. The set $\mathsf{CEnv}(E)$ contains each function in $\mathsf{CMap}(E)$ when restricted to meta-variables of the form $[\![\nu^l]\!]$. Both $\mathsf{CMap}(E)$ and $\mathsf{CEnv}(E)$ with point-wise ordering are complete lattices where least upper bound is written $\sqcup$. The function $\langle V \mapsto S\rangle$ maps the meta-variable V to the set S and maps all other meta-variables to the empty set. Finally, we define $upd\ V\ S\ L = \langle V \mapsto S\rangle \sqcup L$.

2.1 The Specification of Closure Analysis

We can then state precisely what a closure analysis is. An intuitive argument follows the formal definition.

Definition 3. For a λ-term E and for every $L \in \mathsf{CMap}(E)$, we define a binary relation T_L on λ-terms, as follows. $T_L(E_X, E_Y)$ holds if and only if the following four conditions hold:

- If E_Y equals $\lambda^l x.E$, then $\{l\} \subseteq L(\mathsf{var}(E_X))$.
- If E_Y contains $\lambda^{l'} y.(\lambda^l x.E)$, then E_X contains $\lambda^{l'} z.E'$ so that $\{l\} \subseteq L(\mathsf{var}(E'))$.
- If E_Y contains $(\lambda^l x.E)\ @_i\ E_2$, then E_X contains $E_1\ @_i\ E_2'$ so that $\{l\} \subseteq L(\mathsf{var}(E_1))$.
- If E_Y contains $E_1\ @_i\ (\lambda^l x.E)$, then E_X contains $E_1'\ @_i\ E_2$ so that $\{l\} \subseteq L(\mathsf{var}(E_2))$.

A closure analysis of E produces $L \in \mathsf{CMap}(E)$ so that if $E \rightarrow^* E'$, then $T_L(E, E')$.

Intuitively, if $E_X \rightarrow^* E_Y$, then we can get conservative information about the abstractions in E_Y by doing closure analysis of E_X. For example, the first condition in Definition 3 can be illustrated as follows.

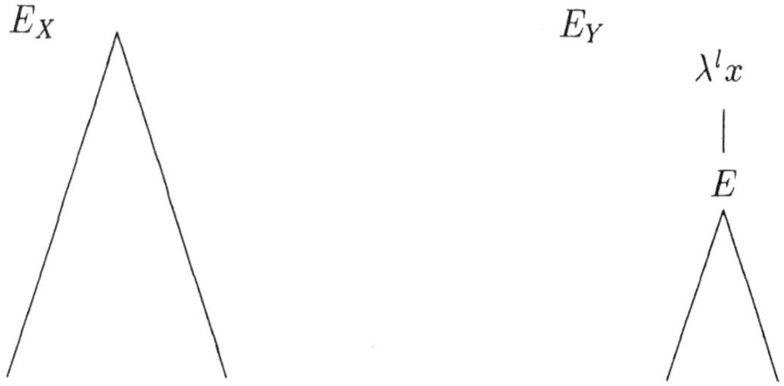

In this case, E_Y is an abstraction with label l. Thus, E_X can evaluate to an abstraction with label l. The first condition says that in this case the mapping L must satisfy $\{l\} \subseteq L(\mathsf{var}(E_X))$. In other words, the analysis must be aware that such an abstraction is a possible result of evaluating E_X.

The three other conditions in Definition 3 cover the cases where abstractions are proper subterms of E_Y. The second condition covers the case where an abstraction in E_Y is the body of yet another abstraction. The third and forth conditions cover the cases where an abstraction is the function and the argument part of an application, respectively. Here, we will illustrate just the first of these three conditions, the others are similar.

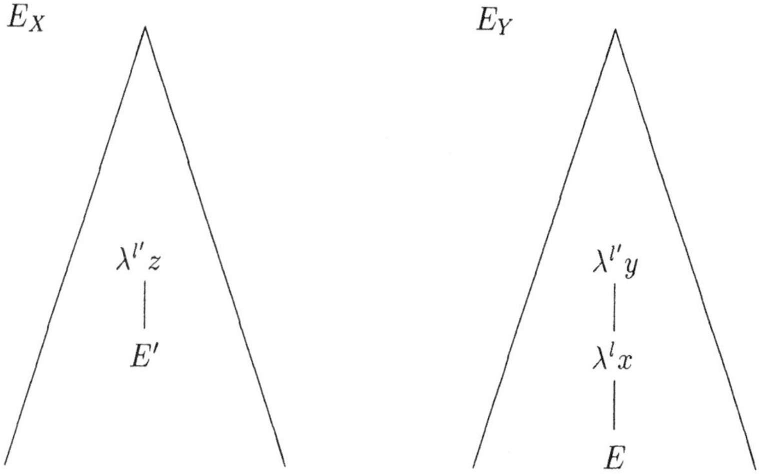

In this case, E_Y contains an abstraction with label l $(\lambda^l x.E)$. This abstraction is in turn the body of an abstraction with label l' $(\lambda^{l'} y.\lambda^l x.E)$. The second condition in Definition 3 says that in this case there must be an abstraction in E_X with label l' ($\lambda^{l'} z.E'$, the bound variable may be different) so that the mapping L satisfies $\{l\} \subseteq L(\mathsf{var}(E'))$. In other words, the analysis must be aware that some abstraction $\lambda^{l'} z.E'$ in E_X can evolve into an abstraction with a body being an abstraction with label l.

Notice the possibility that more than one abstraction in E_X has label l'. Thus, if we want closure information for "the body of the abstraction with label

l''" we must compute the *union* of information for the bodies of *all* abstractions in E_X with label l'. A similar comment applies to the third and forth condition in Definition 3. Such use of closure information is not of concern in this paper, however.

2.2 Bondorf's Definition

We now recall the closure analysis of Bondorf [4], with a few minor changes in the notation compared to his presentation. The analysis assumes that all labels are distinct. Bondorf's definition was originally given for a subset of Scheme; we have restricted it to the λ-calculus. Note that Bondorf's definition is based on Sestoft's [15].

We will use the notation that if $\lambda^l x.E$ is a subterm of the term to be analyzed, then the partial function *body* maps the label l to E.

$$\begin{aligned}
&B : (E : \Lambda) \to \mathsf{CMap}(E) \times \mathsf{CEnv}(E) \\
&B(E) = \mathit{fix}(\lambda(\mu, \rho).b(E)\mu\rho)
\end{aligned}$$

$$\begin{aligned}
&b : (E : \Lambda) \to \mathsf{CMap}(E) \to \mathsf{CEnv}(E) \to \mathsf{CMap}(E) \times \mathsf{CEnv}(E) \\
&b(x^l)\mu\rho = (\mathit{upd}\ [\![\nu^l]\!]\ \rho[\![\nu^l]\!]\ \mu, \rho) \\
&b(\lambda^l x.E)\mu\rho = \text{let } (\mu', \rho') \text{ be } b(E)\mu\rho \\
&\qquad\qquad\qquad \text{in } (\mathit{upd}\ [\![\lambda^l]\!]\ \{l\}\ \mu', \rho') \\
&b(E_1 \mathbin{@_i} E_2)\mu\rho = \text{let } (\mu', \rho') \text{ be } (b(E_1)\mu\rho) \sqcup (b(E_2)\mu\rho) \text{ in} \\
&\qquad\qquad\qquad \text{let } c \text{ be } \mu'(\mathsf{var}(E_1)) \text{ in} \\
&\qquad\qquad\qquad \text{let } \mu'' \text{ be } \mathit{upd}\ [\![@_i]\!]\ (\textstyle\bigsqcup_{l \in c} \mu'(\mathsf{var}(\mathit{body}(l))))\ \mu' \text{ in} \\
&\qquad\qquad\qquad \text{let } \rho'' \text{ be } \rho' \sqcup (\textstyle\bigsqcup_{l \in c} (\mathit{upd}\ [\![\nu^l]\!]\ \mu'(\mathsf{var}(E_2)))\ \rho')) \\
&\qquad\qquad\qquad \text{in } (\mu'', \rho'')
\end{aligned}$$

We can now do closure analysis of E by computing $\mathit{fst}(B(E))$.

2.3 A Simpler Abstract Interpretation

Bondorf's definition can be simplified considerably. To see why, consider the second component of $\mathsf{CMap}(E) \times \mathsf{CEnv}(E)$. This component is updated only in $b(E_1 \mathbin{@_i} E_2)\mu\rho$ and read only in $b(x^l)\mu\rho$. The key observation is that both these operations can be done on the first component instead. Thus, we can omit the use of $\mathsf{CEnv}(E)$. By rewriting Bondorf's definition according to this observation, we arrive at the following definition. As with Bondorf's definition, we assume that all labels are distinct.

$$\begin{aligned}
&m : (E : \Lambda) \to \mathsf{CMap}(E) \to \mathsf{CMap}(E) \\
&m(x^l)\mu = \mu \\
&m(\lambda^l x.E)\mu = (m(E)\mu) \sqcup \langle [\![\lambda^l]\!] \mapsto \{l\}\rangle \\
&m(E_1 \mathbin{@_i} E_2)\mu = (m(E_1)\mu) \sqcup (m(E_2)\mu) \sqcup \\
&\qquad\qquad \textstyle\bigsqcup_{l \in \mu(\mathsf{var}(E_1))} (\langle [\![\nu^l]\!] \mapsto \mu(\mathsf{var}(E_2))\rangle \sqcup \langle [\![@_i]\!] \mapsto \mu(\mathsf{var}(\mathit{body}(l)))\rangle)
\end{aligned}$$

We can now do closure analysis of E by computing $fix(m(E))$.

A key question is: is the simpler abstract interpretation equivalent to Bondorf's? We might attempt to prove this using fixed point induction, but we find it much easier to do using a particular constraint system as a "stepping stone".

2.4 A Constraint System

For a λ-term E, the constraint system is a finite set of Horn clauses over inclusions of the form $P \subseteq P'$, where P and P' are either meta-variables or elements of $\mathsf{CSet}(E)$. A *solution* of such a system is an element of $\mathsf{CMap}(E)$ that satisfies all Horn clauses.

The constraint system is defined in terms of the λ-term to be analyzed. We need *not* assume that all labels are distinct.

The set $R(E_1 \mathbin{@_i} E_2, \lambda^l x.E)$ consists of the two elements

$\{l\} \subseteq \mathsf{var}(E_1) \Rightarrow \mathsf{var}(E_2) \subseteq [\![\nu^l]\!]$

$\{l\} \subseteq \mathsf{var}(E_1) \Rightarrow \mathsf{var}(E) \subseteq [\![@_i]\!]$

For a λ-term E, the constraint system $C(E)$ is the union of the following sets of constraints.

- For every $\lambda^l x.E'$ in E, the singleton constraint set consisting of $\{l\} \subseteq [\![\lambda^l]\!]$.
- For every $E_1 \mathbin{@_i} E_2$ in E and for every $\lambda^l x.E'$ in E, the set $R(E_1 \mathbin{@_i} E_2, \lambda^l x.E')$.

Each $C(E)$ has a least solution namely the intersection of all solutions.

We can now do closure analysis of E by computing a solution of $C(E)$. The canonical choice of solution is of course the least one.

The closure analysis of Bondorf and Jørgensen [7] can be understood as adding two constraints to each $R(E_1 \mathbin{@_i} E_2, \lambda^l x.E')$ so that in effect the inclusions $\mathsf{var}(E_2) \subseteq [\![\nu^l]\!]$ and $\mathsf{var}(E) \subseteq [\![@_i]\!]$ are changed to equalities. Thus, their closure analysis computes more approximate information than ours. In return, their analysis can be computed in almost-linear time [7], whereas the fastest known algorithm for computing a solution of $C(E)$ uses transitive closure [12].

3 Equivalence

We now prove that the three closure analyses defined in Section 2 are equivalent (when applied to λ-terms where all labels are distinct).

Lemma 4. *If μ is a fixed point of $m(E)$, then so is it of $m(E')$ for every subterm E' of E.*

Proof. The proof is by induction on the structure of E, using that $\sqcup$ is monotone.

Lemma 5. *$C(E)$ has least solution $fix(m(E))$.*

Proof. We prove a stronger property: the solutions of $C(E)$ are exactly the fixed points of $m(E)$. There are two inclusions to be considered.

First, we prove that every solution of $C(E)$ is a fixed point of $m(E)$. We proceed by induction on the structure of E. In the base case, consider x^l. Clearly, every μ at all is a fixed point of $m(x^l)$. In the induction step, consider first $\lambda^l x.E$. Suppose μ is a solution of $C(\lambda^l x.E)$. Then μ is also a solution of $C(E)$, so by the induction hypothesis, μ is a fixed point of $m(E)$. Hence, we get $m(\lambda^l x.E)\mu = (m(E)\mu) \sqcup \langle [\![\lambda^l]\!] \mapsto \{l\}\rangle = \mu$, by using the definition of m, that μ is a fixed point of $m(E)$, and that $C(\lambda^l x.E)$ has solution μ.

Consider then $E_1 \mathbin{@_i} E_2$. Suppose μ is a solution of $C(E_1 \mathbin{@_i} E_2)$. Then μ is also a solution of $C(E_1)$ and $C(E_2)$, so by the induction hypothesis, μ is a fixed point of $m(E_1)$ and $m(E_2)$. Hence, we get $m(E_1 \mathbin{@_i} E_2)\mu = \mu$, by using the definition of m, that μ is a fixed point of $m(E_1)$ and $m(E_2)$, and that $C(E_1 \mathbin{@_i} E_2)$ has solution μ.

Second, we prove that every fixed point of $m(E)$ is a solution of $C(E)$. We proceed by induction on the structure of E. In the base case, consider x^l. Clearly, every μ at all is a solution of $C(x^l)$. In the induction step, consider first $\lambda^l x.E'$. Suppose μ is a fixed point of $m(\lambda^l x.E')$. Then, by Lemma 4, μ is also a fixed point of $m(E')$. By the induction hypothesis, μ is a solution of $C(E')$. Thus, we need to prove that μ satisfies $\{l\} \subseteq [\![\lambda^l]\!]$ and for every $E_1 \mathbin{@_i} E_2$ in E', $R(E_1 \mathbin{@_i} E_2, \lambda^l x.E')$. For the first of these, use that μ is a fixed point of both $m(E')$ and $m(\lambda^l x.E')$ to get $\mu = m(\lambda^l x.E')\mu = (m(E')\mu) \sqcup \langle [\![\lambda^l]\!] \mapsto \{l\}\rangle = \mu \sqcup \langle [\![\lambda^l]\!] \mapsto \{l\}\rangle$, from which the result follows. For the second one, consider $E_1 \mathbin{@_i} E_2$ in E'. By Lemma 4, μ is also a fixed point of both $m(E_1)$, $m(E_2)$, and $m(E_1 \mathbin{@_i} E_2)$. Using that we get $\mu = m(E_1 \mathbin{@_i} E_2)\mu = \mu \sqcup \bigsqcup_{l \in \mu(\mathsf{var}(E_1))}(\langle [\![\nu^l]\!] \mapsto \mu(\mathsf{var}(E_2))\rangle \sqcup \langle [\![@_i]\!] \mapsto \mu(\mathsf{var}(\mathit{body}(l)))\rangle)$, from which the result follows.

Consider then $E_1 \mathbin{@_i} E_2$. Suppose μ is a fixed point of $m(E_1 \mathbin{@_i} E_2)$. Then, by Lemma 4, μ is also a fixed point of both $m(E_1)$ and $m(E_2)$. By the induction hypothesis, μ is a solution of both $C(E_1)$ and $C(E_2)$. Thus, we need to prove that for every $\lambda^l x.E'$ in $E_1 \mathbin{@_i} E_2$, μ satisfies $R(E_1 \mathbin{@_i} E_2, \lambda^l x.E')$. Using that μ is a fixed point of both $m(E_1)$, $m(E_2)$, and $m(E_1 \mathbin{@_i} E_2)$ to get $\mu = m(E_1 \mathbin{@_i} E_2)\mu = \mu \sqcup \bigsqcup_{l \in \mu(\mathsf{var}(E_1))}(\langle [\![\nu^l]\!] \mapsto \mu(\mathsf{var}(E_2))\rangle \sqcup \langle [\![@_i]\!] \mapsto \mu(\mathsf{var}(\mathit{body}(l)))\rangle)$, from which the result follows.

Lemma 6. *$C(E)$ has least solution $\mathit{fst}(B(E))$.*

Proof. Similar to the proof of Lemma 5.

Theorem 7. *The three closure analyses defined in Section 2 are equivalent.*

Proof. Combine Lemmas 5 and 6.

4 Correctness

We now prove that the three closure analyses defined in Section 2 are correct. The key is to define an entailment relation $A \rightsquigarrow A'$ (Definition 8) meaning that all constraints in the constraint system A' can be logically derived from those in A. A central result (Theorem 15) is that if $E_X \rightarrow E_Y$, then $C(E_X) \rightsquigarrow C(E_Y)$.

This theorem is proved without at all considering if the involved constraint systems have solutions.

Definition 8. If A is a constraint system and H is a Horn clause, then the judgement $A \vdash H$ ("A entails H") holds if it is derivable using the following five rules:

$$\frac{}{A \vdash H} \quad \text{if } H \in A \qquad \text{(Discharge)}$$

$$\frac{}{A \vdash P \subseteq P} \qquad \text{(Reflexivity)}$$

$$\frac{A \vdash P \subseteq P' \qquad A \vdash P' \subseteq P''}{A \vdash P \subseteq P''} \qquad \text{(Transitivity)}$$

$$\frac{A \vdash X \qquad A \vdash X \Rightarrow Y}{A \vdash Y} \qquad \text{(Modus Ponens)}$$

$$\frac{A \vdash P \subseteq P'' \Rightarrow Q' \subseteq Q'' \qquad A \vdash P' \subseteq P'' \qquad A \vdash Q \subseteq Q'}{A \vdash P \subseteq P' \Rightarrow Q \subseteq Q''} \qquad \text{(Weakening)}$$

If A and A' are constraint systems, then $A \leadsto A'$ if and only if $\forall H \in A' : A \vdash H$.

Lemma 9. *$\leadsto$ is reflexive, transitive, and solution-preserving. If $A \supseteq A'$, then $A \leadsto A'$.*

Proof. The last property is immediate using Discharge. Reflexivity of $\leadsto$ is a consequence of the last property. For transitivity of $\leadsto$, suppose $A \leadsto A'$ and $A' \leadsto A''$. The statement "if $A' \vdash H$ then $A \vdash H$" can be proved by induction on the structure of the proof of $A' \vdash H$. To prove $A \leadsto A''$, suppose then that $H \in A''$. From $A' \leadsto A''$ we get $A' \vdash H$, and from the above statement we finally get $A \vdash H$. To prove that $\leadsto$ is solution-preserving, suppose $A \leadsto A'$ and that A has solution L. We need to prove that for every $H \in A'$, H has solution L. This can be proved by induction on the structure of the proof of $A \vdash H$.

The following lemmas are structured so that Modus Ponens is only used in the proof of Lemma 10 and Weakening is only used in the proof of Lemma 13.

Lemma 10. *If $A \leadsto C((\lambda^l x.E) \mathbin{@_i} E_2)$, then $A \vdash \mathsf{var}(E_2) \subseteq [\![\nu^l]\!]$ and $A \vdash \mathsf{var}(E) \subseteq [\![@_i]\!]$.*

Proof. From the assumption we get $A \vdash \{l\} \subseteq [\![\lambda^l]\!]$ and $A \leadsto R((\lambda^l x.E) \mathbin{@_i} E_2, \lambda^l x.E)$. The result then follows from $\mathsf{var}(\lambda^l x.E) = [\![\lambda^l]\!]$ and Modus Ponens.

Lemma 11. *If $A \vdash \mathsf{var}(U) \subseteq [\![\nu^l]\!]$, then $A \vdash \mathsf{var}(E[U/x^l]) \subseteq \mathsf{var}(E)$.*

Proof. By induction on the structure of E, using Reflexivity repeatedly.

Lemma 12. *If $A \rightsquigarrow C(E_X)$ and $E_X \to E_Y$, then $A \vdash \mathsf{var}(E_Y) \subseteq \mathsf{var}(E_X)$.*

Proof. We proceed by induction on the structure of E_X. In the base case, consider x^l. The conclusion is immediate since x^l is in normal form.

In the induction step, consider first $\lambda^l x.E$. Suppose $E \to E'$. Notice that $\mathsf{var}(\lambda^l x.E) = \mathsf{var}(\lambda^l x.E') = [\![\lambda^l]\!]$. Using Reflexivity we get $A \vdash [\![\lambda^l]\!] \subseteq [\![\lambda^l]\!]$.

Consider finally $E_1 \,@_i\, E_2$. There are three cases. Suppose $E_1 \to E_1'$. Notice that $\mathsf{var}(E_1 \,@_i\, E_2) = \mathsf{var}(E_1' \,@_i\, E_2) = [\![@_i]\!]$. Using Reflexivity we get $A \vdash [\![@_i]\!] \subseteq [\![@_i]\!]$.

Suppose then that $E_2 \to E_2'$. Notice that $\mathsf{var}(E_1 \,@_i\, E_2) = \mathsf{var}(E_1' \,@_i\, E_2) = [\![@_i]\!]$. Using Reflexivity we get $A \vdash [\![@_i]\!] \subseteq [\![@_i]\!]$.

Suppose then that $E_1 = \lambda^l x.E$ and that $E_1 \,@_i\, E_2 \to E[E_2/x^l]$. From Lemma 10 we get $A \vdash \mathsf{var}(E_2) \subseteq [\![\nu^l]\!]$ and $A \vdash \mathsf{var}(E) \subseteq [\![@_i]\!]$. From the former of these and Lemma 11 we get $A \vdash \mathsf{var}(E[E_2/x^l]) \subseteq \mathsf{var}(E)$. Using Transitivity we can finally conclude that $A \vdash \mathsf{var}(E[E_2/x^l]) \subseteq [\![@_i]\!]$.

Lemma 13. *Suppose $A \rightsquigarrow R(E_1 \,@_i\, E_2, \lambda^l x.E_3) \cup C(E_j)$. If $E_j = E_j'$ or $E_j \to E_j'$ or $E_j' = E_j[U_j/x_j^{l_j}]$ where $A \vdash \mathsf{var}(U_j) \subseteq \mathsf{var}(x_j^{l_j})$, then $A \rightsquigarrow R(E_1' \,@_i\, E_2', \lambda^l x.E_3')$.*

Proof. We get $A \vdash \mathsf{var}(E_j') \subseteq \mathsf{var}(E_j)$ from either Reflexivity, Lemma 12, or Lemma 11. The result then follows using Weakening.

Lemma 14. *If $A \rightsquigarrow C(E) \cup C(U)$ and $A \vdash \mathsf{var}(U) \subseteq [\![\nu^l]\!]$, then $A \rightsquigarrow C(E[U/x^l])$.*

Proof. Let ρ denote the substitution $[U/x^l]$. We proceed by induction on the structure of E. In the base case, consider $y^{l'}$. The result follows immediately from $A \rightsquigarrow C(x^l) \cup C(U)$ and Lemma 9, both if $x^l \equiv y^{l'}$ and if $x^l \not\equiv y^{l'}$.

In the induction step, consider first $\lambda^l y.E'$. Notice that $(\lambda^l y.E')\rho = \lambda^l y.(E'\rho)$. By the induction hypothesis, $A \rightsquigarrow C(E'\rho)$. Thus, we need to show $A \vdash \{l\} \subseteq [\![\lambda^l]\!]$ and for every $E_1 \,@_i\, E_2$ in $E'\rho$, $A \rightsquigarrow R(E_1 \,@_i\, E_2, \lambda^l y.(E'\rho))$. The first follows from $A \rightsquigarrow C(\lambda^l y.E')$. For the second, consider any $E_1 \,@_i\, E_2$ in $E'\rho$. Notice that either $E_1 \,@_i\, E_2$ is also a subterm of E' or $E_1 \,@_i\, E_2 = (E_1' \,@_i\, E_2')\rho = (E_1'\rho) \,@_i\, (E_2'\rho)$ where $E_1' \,@_i\, E_2'$ is a subterm of E'. In both cases the result follows from Lemma 13.

Consider finally $E_1 \,@_i\, E_2$. Notice that $(E_1 \,@_i\, E_2)\rho = (E_1\rho) \,@_i\, (E_2\rho)$. By the induction hypothesis, $A \rightsquigarrow C(E_1\rho) \cup C(E_2\rho)$. Thus, we need to show that for every $\lambda^l x.E$ in $(E_1 \,@_i\, E_2)\rho$, $A \rightsquigarrow R((E_1 \,@_i\, E_2)\rho, \lambda^l x.E)$. Consider any $\lambda^l x.E$ in $(E_1 \,@_i\, E_2)\rho$. Notice that either $\lambda^l x.E$ is also a subterm of $E_1 \,@_i\, E_2$ or $\lambda^l x.E = \lambda^l x.(E'\rho)$ where $\lambda^l x.E'$ is a subterm of $E_1 \,@_i\, E_2$. In both cases, the result follows from Lemma 13.

Theorem 15. *If $E_X \to E_Y$, then $C(E_X) \rightsquigarrow C(E_Y)$.*

Proof. We proceed by induction on the structure of E_X. In the base case of x^l, the conclusion is immediate since x^l is in normal form.

In the induction step, consider first $\lambda^l x.E$. Suppose $E \to E'$. By the induction hypothesis, $C(E) \rightsquigarrow C(E')$, so also $C(\lambda^l x.E) \rightsquigarrow C(E')$. Thus, we need to show $C(\lambda^l x.E) \vdash \{l\} \subseteq [\![\lambda^l]\!]$ and for every $E_1 \mathbin{@_i} E_2$ in $\lambda^l x.E'$, $C(\lambda^l x.E) \leadsto R(E_1 \mathbin{@_i} E_2, \lambda^l x.E')$. The first follows using Discharge. For the second, there are four cases. Notice that by Discharge we have $C(\lambda^l x.E) \leadsto R(E_1' \mathbin{@_i} E_2', \lambda^l x.E)$ for every $E_1' \mathbin{@_i} E_2'$ in $\lambda^l x.E$. In the first case, suppose $E_1 \mathbin{@_i} E_2$ is also a subterm of $\lambda^l x.E$. The result then follows from Lemma 13. In the second case, consider a subterm $E_1' \mathbin{@_i} E_2$ of $\lambda^l x.E$ so that $E_1' \rightarrow E_1$. Again, the result follows from Lemma 13. In the third case, consider a subterm $E_1 \mathbin{@_i} E_2'$ of $\lambda^l x.E$ so that $E_2' \rightarrow E_2$. Yet again, the result follows from Lemma 13. In the fourth case, consider a subterm $E_1' \mathbin{@_i} E_2'$ of $\lambda^l x.E$ so that $E_1 \mathbin{@_i} E_2 = (E_1' \mathbin{@_i} E_2')[E_S/y^{l'}]$. The substitution arises because of the contraction of a redex. From Lemma 10 we get $C(\lambda^l x.E) \vdash \mathsf{var}(E_S) \subseteq [\![\nu^{l'}]\!]$. The result then follows from Lemma 13.

Consider finally $E_1 \mathbin{@_i} E_2$. We have that for every $\lambda^l x.E$ in $E_1 \mathbin{@_i} E_2$, $C(E_1 \mathbin{@_i} E_2) \leadsto R(E_1 \mathbin{@_i} E_2, \lambda^l x.E)$. There are three cases.

Suppose $E_1 \rightarrow E_1'$. By the induction hypothesis, $C(E_1) \leadsto C(E_1')$, so also $C(E_1 \mathbin{@_i} E_2) \leadsto C(E_1')$. Thus we need to show that for every $\lambda^l x.E'$ in $E_1' \mathbin{@_i} E_2$, $C(E_1 \mathbin{@_i} E_2) \leadsto R(E_1' \mathbin{@_i} E_2, \lambda^l x.E')$. There are three cases. In the first case, suppose $\lambda^l x.E'$ is a subterm of $E_1 \mathbin{@_i} E_2$. The result then follows from Lemma 13. In the second case, consider a subterm $\lambda^l x.E$ of $E_1 \mathbin{@_i} E_2$ so that $E \rightarrow E'$. Again, the result follows from Lemma 13. In the third case, consider a subterm $\lambda^l x.E$ of $E_1 \mathbin{@_i} E_2$ so that $\lambda^l x.E' = \lambda^l x.(E[E_S/y^{l'}])$. The substitution arises because of the contraction of a redex. From Lemma 10 we get $C(E_1 \mathbin{@_i} E_2) \vdash \mathsf{var}(E_S) \subseteq [\![\nu^{l'}]\!]$. The result then follows from Lemma 13.

Suppose then that $E_2 \rightarrow E_2'$. The proof in this case is similar to the case of $E_1 \rightarrow E_1'$ so we omit the details.

Suppose then that $E_1 = \lambda^l x.E$ and that $E_1 \mathbin{@_i} E_2 \rightarrow E[E_2/x^l]$. From Lemma 10 we get $C(E_1 \mathbin{@_i} E_2) \vdash \mathsf{var}(E_2) \subseteq [\![\nu^l]\!]$. The result then follows from Lemma 14.

Theorem 16. *The three closure analyses defined in Section 2 are correct.*

Proof. From Theorem 7 we get that the three analyses are equivalent when applied to λ-terms where all labels are distinct. Thus, it is sufficient to prove that the one defined using a constraint system is correct. The proof has two steps.

In Step 1, use Lemmas 10, 11, and 12 to prove that if $A \leadsto C(E_X)$ and $E_X \rightarrow E_Y$, then both of the following properties hold:

- If E_Y contains $\lambda^l y.E$, then E_X contains $\lambda^l z.E'$ so that $A \vdash \mathsf{var}(E) \subseteq \mathsf{var}(E')$.
- If E_Y contains $E_1 \mathbin{@_i} E_2$, then E_X contains $E_1' \mathbin{@_i} E_2'$ so that $A \vdash \mathsf{var}(E_1) \subseteq \mathsf{var}(E_1')$ and $A \vdash \mathsf{var}(E_2) \subseteq \mathsf{var}(E_2')$.

In Step 2, suppose $C(E_X)$ has solution L and $E_X \rightarrow^* E_Y$. We will prove $T_L(E_X, E_Y)$ by induction on the length of $E_X \rightarrow^* E_Y$.

In the base case, $T_L(E_X, E_X)$ is immediate. In the induction step, suppose $E_X \rightarrow E_Z \rightarrow^n E_Y$. By Theorem 15, $C(E_X) \leadsto C(E_Z)$. By Lemma 9, $C(E_Z)$ has solution L. By the induction hypothesis, $T_L(E_Z, E_Y)$. To prove $T_L(E_X, E_Y)$, there are four cases to be considered.

First suppose $E_Y = \lambda^l x.E$. From $T_L(E_Z, E_Y)$ we get $\{l\} \subseteq L(\mathsf{var}(E_Z))$. From Lemma 12 we get $C(E_X) \vdash \mathsf{var}(E_Z) \subseteq \mathsf{var}(E_X)$. Finally, the result follows by using that $C(E_X)$ has solution L.

Then suppose E_Y contains $\lambda^{l'} y.(\lambda^l x.E)$. From $T_L(E_Z, E_Y)$ we get that E_Z contains $\lambda^{l'} z.E'$ so that $\{l\} \subseteq L(\mathsf{var}(E'))$. From Step 1 of this proof, we get that E_X contains $\lambda^{l'} w.E''$ so that $C(E_X) \vdash \mathsf{var}(E') \subseteq \mathsf{var}(E'')$. Finally, the result follows by using that $C(E_X)$ has solution L.

In the last two cases, suppose that E_Y contains either $(\lambda^l x.E) \ @_i \ E_2$ or $E_1 \ @_i \ (\lambda^l x.E)$, respectively. Both cases are similar to the second one, so we omit the details.

Finally, we prove our subject-reduction result.

Theorem 17. *If $C(E)$ has solution L and $E \rightarrow E'$, then $C(E')$ has solution L.*

Proof. Immediate from Theorem 15 and Lemma 9.

Acknowledgement The author thanks Nils Klarlund for helpful comments on a draft of the paper.

References

1. Ole Agesen, Jens Palsberg, and Michael I. Schwartzbach. Type inference of Self: Analysis of objects with dynamic and multiple inheritance. In *Proc. ECOOP'93, Seventh European Conference on Object-Oriented Programming*, pages 247–267, Kaiserslautern, Germany, July 1993.
2. Andrew Ayers. Efficient closure analysis with reachability. In *Proc. WSA '92, Analyse Statique*, pages 126–134, 1992.
3. Henk P. Barendregt. *The Lambda Calculus: Its Syntax and Semantics.* North-Holland, 1981.
4. Anders Bondorf. Automatic autoprojection of higher order recursive equations. *Science of Computer Programming*, 17(1–3):3–34, December 1991.
5. Anders Bondorf. *Similix 5.0 Manual.* DIKU, University of Copenhagen, Denmark, April 1993. Included in Similix 5.0 distribution.
6. Anders Bondorf and Olivier Danvy. Automatic autoprojection of recursive equations with global variables and abstract data types. *Science of Computer Programming*, 16:151–195, 1991.
7. Anders Bondorf and Jesper Jørgensen. Efficient analyses for realistic off-line partial evaluation. *Journal of Functional Programming*, 3(3):315–346, 1993.
8. Charles Consel. Binding time analysis for higher order untyped functional languages. In *Proc. ACM Conference on Lisp and Functional Programming*, pages 264–272, 1990.
9. Paola Giannini and Simona Ronchi Della Rocca. Characterization of typings in polymorphic type discipline. In *LICS'88, Third Annual Symposium on Logic in Computer Science*, pages 61–70, 1988.
10. Neil D. Jones. Flow analysis of lambda expressions. In *Proc. Eighth Colloquium on Automata, Languages, and Programming*, pages 114–128. Springer-Verlag (*LNCS* 115), 1981.

11. Jens Palsberg. Correctness of binding-time analysis. *Journal of Functional Programming*, 3(3):347–363, 1993.
12. Jens Palsberg and Michael I. Schwartzbach. Safety analysis versus type inference. *Information and Computation*. To appear.
13. Jens Palsberg and Michael I. Schwartzbach. Safety analysis versus type inference for partial types. *Information Processing Letters*, 43:175–180, 1992.
14. Jens Palsberg and Michael I. Schwartzbach. Binding-time analysis: Abstract interpretation versus type inference. In *Proc. ICCL'94, Fifth IEEE International Conference on Computer Languages*, Toulouse, France, May 1994. To appear.
15. Peter Sestoft. Replacing function parameters by global variables. Master's thesis, DIKU, University of Copenhagen, September 1989.
16. Peter Sestoft. *Analysis and Efficient Implementation of Functional Programs*. PhD thesis, DIKU, University of Copenhagen, October 1991.
17. Olin Shivers. *Control-Flow Analysis of Higher-Order Languages*. PhD thesis, CMU, May 1991. CMU-CS-91-145.
18. Olin Shivers. Data-flow analysis and type recovery in Scheme. In Peter Lee, editor, *Topics in Advanced Language Implementation*, pages 47–87. MIT Press, 1991.
19. David Ungar and Randall B. Smith. SELF: The power of simplicity. In *Proc. OOPSLA'87, Object-Oriented Programming Systems, Languages and Applications*, pages 227–241, 1987. Also published in Lisp and Symbolic Computation 4(3), Kluwer Acadamic Publishers, June 1991.

On Projective and Separable Properties

Doron Peled
AT&T Bell Laboratories
600 Mountain Avenue
Murray Hill, NJ 07974, USA
E-mail: doron@research.att.com

Abstract

A language L over the Cartesian product of component alphabets is called *projective* if it is closed under projections. That is, together with each word $\alpha \in L$, it contains all the words that have the same projections up to stuttering as α. We prove that in each of the behavior classes: ω-regular, regular and star-free ω-regular (i.e., definable by linear temporal logic) languages, the projective languages are precisely the Boolean combinations of stuttering-closed component languages from the corresponding class. Languages of these behavior classes can also be seen as properties of various temporal logics; some uses of projective properties for specification and verification of programs are studied.

1 Introduction

Consider the ω-regular languages (i.e., languages of infinite words that can be recognized by a Büchi automata) over alphabets Σ that are Cartesian products of *component* alphabets $\Sigma = \Sigma_1 \times \ldots \times \Sigma_n$. Such an alphabet arises naturally e.g., as the set of global states of a concurrent program P, where each process P_i of P has its own local component state space Σ_i. Consider a projection of the words from Σ^ω on a local alphabet Σ_i that also removes finite consecutive repetitions of letters (i.e., stuttering [15]). A language $L \subseteq \Sigma^\omega$ is called *projective* if it is closed under projection equivalence. That is, if $\alpha \in L$, and the projections of α on all the local alphabets are the same as those of β, then $\beta \in L$.

The study of classes of languages over infinite words is important for the specification of software using temporal logic: the ω-regular languages are known to correspond to the propositional temporal logic ETL (extended temporal logic) [27]. The restricted class of the ω-regular languages, recognized by counter-free Büchi automata and also known as star-free ω-regular languages, corresponds to the temporal logic LTL (linear temporal logic) [7, 17]. The translation from languages over component alphabets into temporal formulas should preserve the structure of the local component alphabets: each proposition of the formula must be related to some component alphabet, and thus the propositions of the temporal formula must be partitioned accordingly. Then, using a standard translation from languages to temporal properties, i.e., formulas in LTL, one can speak about *projective properties*.

In this paper, projective ω-regular languages (and their associated temporal logic properties) are studied. It is shown that the class of projective ω-regular languages is *exactly* the class of languages, termed *separable languages*, obtained from component properties (i.e., over the component alphabets) using the Boolean set operators *union* '$\cup$' and *parallel composition* '$||$'. That is, $L \subseteq \Sigma^\omega$ is projective if and only if $L = \bigcup_i ||_{j=1}^n L_{i,j}$ for stuttering closed ω-regular $L_{i,j} \subseteq \Sigma_j^\omega$, i.e., iff L is separable. When transferring to temporal logic, these operators correspond to the Boolean operators disjunction and conjunction, respectively.

This connection is proved first for regular languages (i.e., over finite words). The result is then lifted to ω-regular languages using Ramsey theory. Then, the proof for the ω-regular languages is adapted to the more restricted model of counter-free (i.e., star-free) ω-regular languages. Finally, these results are transferred from ω-languages to ETL and LTL properties using their correspondence with ω-regular and counter-free ω-regular languages, respectively.

It is shown that deciding projectiveness is PSPACE-hard. Thus, for the purposes where projective properties are sufficient, it is beneficial to restrict the syntax to boolean combinations of component properties. The result proved here shows this restriction results in no loss of expressiveness.

One example of a projective property is *starvation-freedom* of a program, i.e., the requirement that each process always has the opportunity to progress. This property does not constrain the order in which the various processes progress. A less trivial example is of two processes P_1 and P_2, where P_1 terminates iff P_2 terminates. Other examples include program termination and many response and fairness properties [7].

Temporal logic has established itself as one of the main tools in specifying properties of distributed and reactive programs. Algorithms for checking that a program P satisfies its temporal specification φ (e.g., [16]) suffer from problems of computational intractability, deriving from the fact that the problem is PSPACE-complete both in the size of the checked formula φ [24], and in the number n of processes of P [9].

Partial order methods for model checking [20] provide heuristics to cope with the state explosion due to the number of concurrent processes. They are based on the observation that in many cases different reorderings of concurrent events in an execution sequence (the totality of which causes the combinatorial explosion in the number of processes), do not affect the truth value of the checked formula. Thus, sequences may be grouped into equivalence classes, where the sequences in each class are equivalent up to such reordering. Partial order methods allow expanding a *reduced state graph* (a graph that represents the global states of P and the transitions between them) for P instead of the full state graph of P, with fewer states and edges. Such a reduced state graph generates only a *representative* sequence for each such equivalence class.

A reduced state graph of P can be used instead of the full state graph for model-checking properties that are not sensitive to the choice of representatives. Such properties, which are called equivalence robust [3, 20], are thus important for model checking based on partial order methods. Equivalence robustness is also important for partial order *verification* methods [11]. A property can be equivalence robust w.r.t. one program but not the other. It is shown here that the projective properties are *exactly* the properties that are equivalent robust *uniformly*, depending only on the structure of the program rather than its code.

Projective properties are also relevant with respect to concurrency control algorithms.

Such algorithms allow increased parallelism while maintaining a 'virtually-sequential' execution: each execution is equivalent to a sequential execution up to reordering the execution of atomic operations while maintaining the same internal order in each one of the processes (or transactions). These include algorithms for implementing caches [2] and maintaining serializability [19, 21]. This means that when reasoning about an implementation of a program using some concurrency control mechanism, the projective properties of the sequential programs are preserved under their concurrent implementation. Properties φ that are not projective are not guaranteed to be preserved in sequentially consistent implementations.

A practical gain lies here in the ability to model-check or verify projective properties of the sequential version of the program and to deduce that these properties hold for its concurrent implementation. The concurrent implementation can contain many more states and thus be more difficult to verify or model-check. Of course, one has to prove a correctness condition of the generic (i.e., one that can be applied to many programs) concurrency control algorithm [21]; but this is done only once for each such generic algorithm.

In the next section, projective and separable properties are formally defined. Section 3 presents the main result, connecting projective languages to Boolean combinations of component properties for ω-regular and star-free languages. Then this result is transferred to the corresponding temporal languages. It is also shown that deciding projectivity (and hence separability) of these temporal languages is PSPACE-hard. Section 4 presents applications of projective properties. Finally, Section 5 concludes the paper.

2 Projective and Separable Properties

Denote by Σ^* the set of finite words over a finite alphabet Σ. The set of infinite words will be denoted by Σ^ω. Applying the stutter-removal operator '$\natural$' to a (finite or infinite) word α, denoted $\natural\alpha$, replaces every maximal finite subsequence of identical elements by a single copy of this element. A (finite or infinite) language L over the alphabet Σ is *stuttering closed* if for each (finite or infinite, respectively) word α in L, for each word β such that $\natural\alpha = \natural\beta$, β is also in L. For example, if $aabccd \in L$, then the words $abcd$, $abccddd$ must also be in L.

Let Σ_1 and Σ_2 be two finite alphabets. We are interested in (finite and infinite) words over the combined alphabet $\Sigma = \Sigma_1 \times \Sigma_2$. Thus, each letter of Σ is a pair of two letters, one from Σ_1 and one from Σ_2. The alphabets Σ_1 and Σ_2 are referred to as component alphabets. All the definitions and results of this paper can be easily generalized to an n-component alphabet $\Sigma = \Sigma_1 \times \Sigma_2 \times \ldots \times \Sigma_n$.

Definition 2.1 *For each word $\alpha \in \Sigma^* \cup \Sigma^\omega$, denote by $\alpha|_{\Sigma_1}$ (or $\alpha|_{\Sigma_2}$) the projection of α to the letters in Σ_1 (Σ_2, respectively), where recurring letters are removed (i.e., $\alpha|_{\Sigma_1} = \natural\alpha|_{\Sigma_1}$).*

Example. Let $\alpha = \langle a_1, b_3\rangle\langle a_1, b_5\rangle\langle a_2, b_5\rangle\langle a_9, b_5\rangle$. Then $\alpha|_{\Sigma_1} = a_1\, a_2\, a_9$, and $\alpha|_{\Sigma_2} = b_3\, b_5$.

Definition 2.2 *The projections of Definition 2.1 induce an equivalence relation '$\equiv$' over finite and infinite words over Σ such that $\gamma \equiv \delta$ iff $\gamma|_{\Sigma_1} = \delta|_{\Sigma_1}$ and $\gamma|_{\Sigma_2} = \delta|_{\Sigma_2}$.*

Example. The words $\alpha = \langle a_1, b_3\rangle\langle a_1, b_5\rangle\langle a_2, b_5\rangle\langle a_9, b_5\rangle$ and $\beta = \langle a_1, b_3\rangle\langle a_2, b_3\rangle\langle a_9, b_5\rangle$ $\langle a_9, b_5\rangle$ are equivalent under '$\equiv$' since both have the same projections.

Definition 2.3 *Define $\alpha \parallel \beta$ for $\alpha \in \Sigma_1^*$ (or Σ_1^ω) and $\beta \in \Sigma_2{}^*$ (or $\beta \in \Sigma_2{}^\omega$) as the set of sequences over Σ^* (Σ^ω, respectively) such that for each $\gamma \in \alpha \parallel \beta$, $\gamma|_{\Sigma_1} = \natural\alpha$ and $\gamma|_{\Sigma_2} = \natural\beta$.*

Thus, $\alpha \parallel \beta$ is an equivalence class of the relation '$\equiv$'. Similarly, for two finite or two infinite languages over the alphabets Σ_1 and Σ_2, let $L_1 \parallel L_2$ be the union $\bigcup\{\alpha \parallel \beta \mid \alpha \in L_1 \wedge \beta \in L_2\}$. We say that $L_1 \parallel L_2$ is the *concurrent composition* of L_1 and L_2. Notice that $\alpha \parallel \beta$ and hence also $L_1 \parallel L_2$ are always stuttering closed.

For $L \subseteq \Sigma_1{}^*$ (or $\Sigma_1{}^\omega$), denote by $L\lceil_{\Sigma_2}$ the language $L \parallel \Sigma_2{}^*$ ($L \parallel \Sigma_2{}^\omega$, respectively), i.e., the subset of Σ^* (or Σ^ω, respectively) which is the same as L on its Σ_1 component and arbitrary on its Σ_2 component. Similarly define for $M \subseteq \Sigma_2{}^*$ ($\Sigma_2{}^\omega$) the language $M\rceil_{\Sigma_1}$ as $\Sigma_1{}^* \parallel M$ ($\Sigma_1{}^\omega \parallel M$, respectively).

Lemma 2.4 *For two stuttering closed languages $L_A \subseteq \Sigma_1{}^\omega$, $L_B \subseteq \Sigma_2{}^\omega$, $L_A \parallel L_B = L_A\lceil_{\Sigma_2} \cap L_B\rceil_{\Sigma_1}$.*

Proof. Immediate from the definitions. ∎

We adopt the usual notation of regular and ω-regular expressions over words, e.g., $\alpha^*, \alpha.\beta, \alpha^+, \alpha^\omega, \alpha \cup \beta$ (rather then $\alpha + \beta$), and their extensions to languages, e.g., L^*, $L_1.L_2$, $L_1 \cup L_2$.

Definition 2.5 *A regular (or ω-regular) language L over $\Sigma = \Sigma_1 \times \Sigma_2$ is called* projective *if it is closed under the projections on Σ_1 and on Σ_2. That is, if $\alpha \in L$, then for any α' such that $\alpha \equiv \alpha'$, α' is also in L.*

It is easy to see that the union, the intersection and the complement of projective languages are projective. Projective languages are also stuttering closed.

Definition 2.6 *A regular (or ω-regular) language over $\Sigma_1 \times \Sigma_2$ is* separable *if it can be written as $L = \bigcup_{i=1}^{n}(M_i \parallel N_i)$, where M_i and N_i are stuttering closed regular (ω-regular, respectively) languages over Σ_1 and Σ_2, respectively.*

An equivalence relation '$\sim$' between strings over Σ^* is a *congruence* if for each $x, y \in \Sigma^*$ such that $x \sim y$, for each $u, v \in \Sigma^*$, $u.x.v \sim u.y.v$.

Definition 2.7 *The* syntactic congruence relation *(see [6]) '$\cong_L$' of a language $L \subseteq \Sigma^*$ is the relation over Σ^* such that $u \cong_L v$ when for each $w, z \in \Sigma^*$, $w.u.z \in L$ iff $w.v.z \in L$.*

The syntactic congruence relation of a regular language has a finite number of equivalence classes [6]. Notice that a language is regular iff it is the union of, or is *saturated* by, the equivalence classes of some congruence relation with a finite index [8, 18] (i.e., a finite number of equivalence classes).

Definition 2.8 *A congruence relation '$\sim$'* saturates *an ω-regular language L if for any classes U, V of '$\sim$', if $U.V^\omega \cap L \neq \phi$, then $U.V^\omega \subseteq L$.*

Lemma 2.9 (see [25]) *Let '$\sim$' be a congruence over Σ^* of finite index. For any ω-word $\alpha \in \Sigma^\omega$ there are $\sim$-classes U, V, with $V.V \subseteq V$ (and hence $V = V^+$), such that $\alpha \in U.V^\omega$.*

Definition 2.10 *The* syntactic congruence '$\approx_L$' *for an ω-language $L \subseteq \Sigma^\omega$ is the following equivalence relation over Σ^*: $u \approx_L v$ iff for each $x, y, z \in \Sigma^*$,*

1. $x.u.y.z^\omega \in L \Leftrightarrow x.v.y.z^\omega \in L$
2. $x.(y.u.z)^\omega \in L \Leftrightarrow x.(y.v.z)^\omega \in L$.

Lemma 2.11 (see [4]) *An ω-language L is regular iff its syntactic congruence '$\approx_L$' is of finite index and saturates L. Moreover, '$\approx_L$' is the coarsest congruence saturating L.*

The temporal logic LTL allows assertions about the temporal behavior of a program using the Boolean operators, the unary modals '$\Box$' (always), '$\Diamond$' (eventually), '$\bigcirc$' (nexttime) and the binary modal '$\mathcal{U}$' (until). The stuttering closed LTL properties are exactly those that do not contain the nexttime operator [15].

The logic ETL extends LTL by allowing quantification over Boolean variables (this is not the notation used in [27], but is an equivalent notation, sometimes also called QPTL). The semantics of ETL allows a quantified variable to have different Boolean values over different states. Thus, $\exists B\,\varphi$ means that there exists a sequence (rather than a constant value) of Boolean values B for which φ is true. For example, $\forall Q\,((\neg Q \wedge \Box(Q \rightarrow \bigcirc\neg Q) \wedge \Box(\neg Q \rightarrow \bigcirc Q)) \rightarrow \Box(Q \rightarrow P))$ is an ETL formula that asserts that P holds at least in every even state. (The quantified proposition Q holds exactly in the even states, and P must hold at least whenever Q holds.) It is shown in [27] that this property cannot be formulated in LTL.

We will exploit the correspondence between ETL and Büchi automata [27], and between LTL and counter-free automata [17, 7]. Each LTL or ETL formula over the (free in ETL) propositions $\mathcal{Q}$ can be seen as a language of infinite words (ω-words). Such a language is defined over some finite alphabet Σ such that every letter of Σ corresponds to a Boolean combination of the propositions $\mathcal{Q}$. Hence $|\Sigma| = 2^{|\mathcal{Q}|}$. The handbook chapter [25] gives a comprehensive survey on ω-regular languages and temporal logics.

When the projective language L, defined over the product Σ of component alphabets, is translated to a formula φ, each component alphabet Σ_i corresponds to a disjoint set of propositions. This forms a partition $\mathcal{P}$ of the propositions that appear in the formula φ. Then the pair $\langle\varphi, \mathcal{P}\rangle$ is said to be *projective*. When clear from the context, the partition $\mathcal{P}$ is not mentioned and then the formula φ is said to be projective.

An LTL or ETL formula φ (paired with a given partition $\mathcal{P}$ of the propositions that appear in φ, which will be omitted when clear from the context) is called *separated* if it is written as a Boolean combination of stuttering closed [15] temporal formulas, each with (free, in ETL) propositions of a single subset of the partition $\mathcal{P}$. A temporal formula ψ that is logically equivalent to a separated formula is called *separable*.

Example. The LTL formula $\Box\Diamond((P \wedge Q) \vee R)$ is separable with respect to the partition $\mathcal{P} = \{\{P, Q\}, \{R\}\}$ since it is equivalent to the separated formula $\Box\Diamond(P \wedge Q) \vee \Box\Diamond R$.

Example. The LTL formula $\Box(A \rightarrow \bigcirc\Diamond(\neg B \wedge \bigcirc B)) \wedge \Box(B \rightarrow \bigcirc\Diamond(\neg A \wedge \bigcirc A))$ is separable w.r.t. the partition $\mathcal{P} = \{\{A\}, \{B\}\}$ (i.e., whenever A happens, B will change in the future from F to T, and similarly, when interchanging the A's and B's). This, somewhat surprising fact, stems from the fact that this formula is equivalent to $(\Box\neg A \wedge \Box\neg B) \vee (\Box\Diamond A \wedge \Box\Diamond\neg A \wedge \Box\Diamond B \wedge \Box\Diamond\neg B)$ (i.e., either A and B are constantly F, or they never keep changing).

Notice that the same ETL or LTL formula η (formula μ) over the predicates $\mathcal{A}$ (predicates $\mathcal{B}$, respectively) that correspond to an alphabet Σ_1 (alphabet Σ_2, respectively) expresses both a stuttering closed language L_A (L_B, respectively) and the language $L_A\lceil_{\Sigma_2}$ ($L_B\rceil_{\Sigma_1}$, respectively). Thus, using Lemma 2.4, $L_A \parallel L_B$ is expressed by the formula $\eta \wedge \mu$. Hence, we use the concurrent composition '$\parallel$' rather than intersection '$\cap$' (notice that $L_A \cap L_B = \phi$), as our language theory counterpart of the Boolean '$\wedge$' when L_A and L_B are stuttering closed with disjoint alphabets.

The main theorem in this paper will show that for both regular and ω-regular languages, the separable and the projective languages are the same. This will also be shown for the temporal logics ETL and LTL. It is quite easy to see that the separable languages (or properties, respectively) are projective. The other direction is not trivial. By choosing classes of languages (or logics) other than the above, with different expressive power, once can obtain projective language (or properties) that are not separable. For example, consider adding to LTL or ETL the modal $\mathcal{SC}(\varphi, \psi)$, which is true in a sequence if the number of changes to the truth value of φ and of ψ are the same. Let the predicates A and B be partitioned separately. Then the formula $\eta = \mathcal{SC}(A, B)$ is projective, but not separable; it is not possible to write η as a *finite* boolean combination of properties of A and of B.

Definition 2.12 *The* projective closure $L^{\succeq}$ *of a language L over an alphabet Σ is the smallest projective language over Σ that includes L.*

Notice that if L is regular (ω-regular), $L^{\succeq}$ is not necessarily regular (ω-regular, respectively). For example, if $L = (\langle a, c\rangle \cup \langle b, d\rangle)^*$, then $L^{\succeq}$ contains exactly the words over $\{a, b\} \times \{c, d\}$ in which the total number of changes between a and b in the first component is the same as the total number of changes between c and d in the second component. This is obviously not a regular language.

3 Correspondence between Projectiveness and Separability

In this section, the main results, showing correspondence between projective and separable properties for regular, ω-regular and counter-free ω-regular languages, as well as for ETL and LTL properties, are proved.

Theorem 3.1 *A language L over $\Sigma = \Sigma_1 \times \Sigma_2$ is projective iff it is separable, i.e., can be written as $L = \bigcup_{i=1}^{n}(M_i \parallel N_i)$, where M_i and N_i are stuttering closed regular languages over Σ_1 and Σ_2, respectively.*

Proof. One direction is easy: if L can be written as $\bigcup_{i=1}^{n}(M_i \parallel N_i)$, then every word of L belongs to at least one of the sets in this union, and from the definition of the concurrent composition operator '$\parallel$', it is closed under '$\equiv$' and hence each such set is projective. Finally, the union of projective languages is projective.

To show the other direction, we construct the language $L_4 = \{\alpha.\beta \mid \alpha \parallel \beta \subseteq L\}$ (after constructing some intermediate languages L_1, L_2 and L_3). The steps of the construction shows that if L is a regular projective language then so is L_4. By replacing concurrency with concatenation, we can later decompose L_4 into a finite union of languages of the form $M_i.N_i$, with $M_i \subseteq \Sigma_1^*$ and $N_i \subseteq \Sigma_2^*$. Then we can convert the concatenation back into the concurrent composition $M_i \parallel N_i$.

Let $L_1 = L \cap (\{\varepsilon\} \cup \bigcup_{a\in\Sigma_1, b\in\Sigma_2}\{\langle\Sigma_1, b\rangle^*.\langle a, b\rangle.\langle a, b\rangle.\langle a, \Sigma_2\rangle^*\}$. That is, L_1 contains the words from L in which at first only changes in Σ_1 can occur (i.e., with some fixed $b \in \Sigma_2$ as the second component) and afterwards only changes in Σ_2 can occur (i.e., with some fixed $a \in \Sigma_1$ as the first component). Then L_1 is also regular (regular languages are closed under finite union and intersection). Let $L_2 \subseteq E = (\Sigma_1 \times \Sigma_2 \times \{1, 2\})^*$ be the language obtained from L_1 by inverse homomorphism (see [8] for a proof that inverse homomorphisms preserve regularity) h^{-1} such that $h : E \mapsto \Sigma_1 \times \Sigma_2$ maps each $\langle a, b, n\rangle \in \Sigma_1 \times \Sigma_2 \times \{1, 2\}$ into $\langle a, b\rangle$ (i.e., ignores the third component).

Let L_3 be $L_2 \cap (\{\varepsilon\} \cup \bigcup_{a\in\Sigma_1, b\in\Sigma_2}\{\langle\Sigma_1, b, 1\rangle^*.\langle a, b, 1\rangle.\langle a, b, 2\rangle.\langle a, \Sigma_2, 2\rangle^*\}$. Thus, the third element is allowed to change in L_3 (only once) from 1 to 2 when changing from a fixed b to a fixed a. Let $g : E \mapsto \Sigma_1 \cup \Sigma_2$ be defined as $g(a, b, n) \triangleq$ if $n = 1$ then a else b. Finally, let $L_4 \subseteq (\Sigma_1 \cup \Sigma_2)^*$ be the language obtained from L_3 using the mapping g. Then from projectivity of L and the above construction, $\alpha.\beta \in L_4$ iff $\alpha \parallel \beta \in L$.

For example, if $\Sigma_1 = \{a, b, c\}$ and $\Sigma_2 = \{x, y, z, t\}$. Then

$$\langle a,x\rangle\,\langle b,y\rangle\,\langle c,z\rangle\,\langle c,t\rangle \in L \text{ iff } \overbrace{\langle a,x\rangle\,\langle b,x\rangle\,\langle c,x\rangle}^{\Sigma_1 \text{ chages}}\;\overbrace{\langle c,x\rangle\,\langle c,y\rangle\,\langle c,z\rangle\,\langle c,t\rangle}^{\Sigma_2 \text{ changes}} \in L,\ L_1 \text{ iff}$$

$$\langle a,x,1\rangle\,\langle b,x,1\rangle\,\langle c,x,1\rangle\,\langle c,x,2\rangle\,\langle c,y,2\rangle\,\langle c,z,2\rangle\,\langle c,t,2\rangle \in L_2,\ L_3 \text{ iff } abcxyzt \in L_4.$$

Define now the equivalence relation '$\simeq_{\Sigma_1}$' between pairs of $\Sigma_1{}^*$ as the restriction of the syntactic congruence '$\cong_{L_4}$' (see Definition 2.7) to $\Sigma_1{}^*$ words (i.e., $V \cap \Sigma_1{}^*$ is an equivalence class of '$\simeq_{\Sigma_1}$' if V is an equivalence class of '$\cong_{L_4}$'). Similarly, define '$\simeq_{\Sigma_2}$' as the restriction of '$\cong_{L_4}$' to $\Sigma_2{}^*$ words.

Now, if $\alpha \simeq_{\Sigma_1} \alpha'$ and $\beta \simeq_{\Sigma_2} \beta'$, then $\alpha.\beta \in L_4$ iff $\alpha'.\beta' \in L_4$. This follows directly from the definition of the syntactic congruences for regular languages 2.7. Thus, for each pair of equivalence classes M of '$\simeq_{\Sigma_1}$' and N of '$\simeq_{\Sigma_2}$', either $M.N \subseteq L_4$ or $M.N \cap L_4 = \phi$. Thus, every pair of a word from M and a word from N can be interleaved to form a word of L. Conversely, for each $\alpha.\beta \in L$ such that $\alpha \in \Sigma_1{}^*$ and $\beta \in \Sigma_2{}^*$ there are two equivalence classes $M \subseteq \Sigma_1{}^*$, $N \subseteq \Sigma_2{}^*$ that contain α and β, respectively. Therefore, $L_4 = \bigcup\{M.N \mid M \in\simeq_{\Sigma_1}, N \in\simeq_{\Sigma_2}, M.N \subseteq L_4\}$ (where $M \in\simeq_{\Sigma_1}$ denotes that M is an equivalence class of '$\simeq_{\Sigma_1}$'). Translating back to L, for each pair of equivalence classes M of '$\simeq_{\Sigma_1}$' and N of '$\simeq_{\Sigma_2}$', either $M \parallel N \subseteq L$ or $(M \parallel N) \cap L = \phi$. Notice that since the syntactic congruence of a regular language has a finite index, there is a finite number of such classes M and N.

Set $\overline{L} = \bigcup_{i=1}^{n}(M_i \parallel N_i)$, where for each i, M_i and N_i is a pair of equivalence classes of the syntactic congruence relation '$\simeq_{\Sigma_1}$' and '$\simeq_{\Sigma_2}$', respectively, such that $M_i.N_i \subseteq L_4$. Then, $\overline{L} = L$: it is obvious that for each sequence γ in L, $\gamma|_{\Sigma_1}$ concatenated with $\gamma|_{\Sigma_2}$ forms a word of L_4, and thus there exists a pair of equivalence classes $M_i \in\simeq_{\Sigma_1}$ and $N_i \in\simeq_{\Sigma_2}$ that contain $\gamma|_{\Sigma_1}$ and $\gamma|_{\Sigma_2}$, respectively. The concurrent composition of these classes contain γ and thus $\gamma \in \overline{L}$. Conversely, each word γ in $\overline{L}$ was obtained from the concurrent composition of two words α and β in some equivalence classes $M \subseteq \Sigma_1{}^*$ and $N \subseteq \Sigma_2{}^*$ of '$\simeq_{\Sigma_1}$' and '$\simeq_{\Sigma_2}$', respectively. According to the above construction, there is some $\gamma \in L$ such that $\gamma|_{\Sigma_1} = \alpha$ and $\gamma|_{\Sigma_2} = \beta$. Since L is projective, $\alpha \parallel \beta$ is contained in L and hence $\gamma \in L$. Finally, observe from Definition 2.7 that the equivalence classes of '$\cong_L$' are themselves projective languages. Hence, it follows that each M_i and N_i is stuttering closed as required. ∎

Lemma 3.2 *If an ω-regular language L is projective, the congruence classes of the relation '$\approx_L$' are projective.*

Proof. Directly from Definition 2.10, when setting $u \equiv v$. ∎

It follows from Lemmas 2.9 and 2.11 that a projective ω-regular language L can be written as $\bigcup_i U_i.V_i{}^\omega$, where U_i, V_i are regular *projective* languages, $V_i.V_i \subseteq V_i$ and hence also $V_i = V_i{}^+$ (i.e., V_i is closed under repetition).

Lemma 3.3 *If L is a projective ω-regular language and $L' \subseteq L$, such that $L' = Z.((X \parallel X').(Y \parallel Y')^\omega)$, with $X, Y \subseteq \Sigma_1{}^*$, $X', Y' \subseteq \Sigma_2{}^*$, $Z \subseteq (\Sigma_1 \times \Sigma_2)^*$, then $L' \subseteq Z.((X.Y^\omega) \parallel (X'.Y'^\omega)) \subseteq L$.*

Proof. Directly from the definition of projectivity. ∎

Theorem 3.4 *An ω-regular language L over $\Sigma = \Sigma_1 \times \Sigma_2$ is projective iff it is separable, i.e., can be written as $L = \bigcup_{i=1}^{n}(M_i \parallel N_i)$, where M_i and N_i are stuttering closed ω-regular languages over Σ_1 and Σ_2, respectively.*

Proof. Again, one direction is easy and similar to the proof of Theorem 3.4. We will show the other direction, namely that if L is projective it can be written in the required form. Recall that the syntactic congruence '$\approx_L$' of a projective ω-regular language L has equivalence classes which are themselves *projective regular languages* (Lemma 3.2).

We apply the construction of Theorem 3.1 to each equivalence class V_i of the syntactic congruence '$\approx_L$' of L. This construction will provide for each such regular language V_i a pair of equivalence relations '$\simeq^i_{\Sigma_1}$' and '$\simeq^i_{\Sigma_2}$'. Define a third equivalence relation '$\approx_i$' over the finite words of $\Sigma_1 \times \Sigma_2$ such that $\alpha \approx_i \beta$ iff $\alpha|_{\Sigma_1} \simeq_{\Sigma_1} \beta|_{\Sigma_1}$ *and* $\alpha|_{\Sigma_2} \simeq_{\Sigma_2} \beta|_{\Sigma_2}$. The relation '$\approx_i$' has a finite index which is the multiplication of the indexes of the equivalence classes of '$\simeq^i_{\Sigma_1}$' and '$\simeq^i_{\Sigma_2}$'. For each class V_i^j of '$\approx_i$', either $V_i^j \subseteq V_i$ or $V_i^j \cap V_i = \phi$.

Thus, the language V_i is partitioned into a finite number l_{V_i} of disjoint regular sets $V_i^1, V_i^2, \ldots, V_i^{l_{V_i}} \subseteq V_i$, which are equivalence classes of '$\approx_i$'. Furthermore, for each of the finitely many equivalence classes V_i^j of '$\approx_i$', the concurrent composition of each Σ_1-projection of a word in V_i^j with the Σ_2-projection of a word in V_i^j is contained in V_i^j (i.e., for each $\alpha \approx_i \beta$, $\alpha|_{\Sigma_1} \parallel \beta|_{\Sigma_2}$ are all equivalent under '$\approx_i$' to both α and β). Notice that since V_i is projective, each $V_i^j|_{\Sigma_1}$ and $V_i^j|_{\Sigma_2}$ are stuttering closed.

Now according to Lemma 2.9, for each word $\alpha \in L$, there exists equivalence classes U_i, V_i of '$\approx_L$' such that $\alpha \in U_i.V_i{}^\omega \subseteq L$, and $V_i = V_i{}^+$. We write α as $u.v_1.v_2.v_3\ldots$. (Notice that since $V_i = V_i{}^+$, each finite concatenation of words from the various equivalence classes of V_i also belongs to one of these classes and thus there is more than a single way to write α in the above form. However, any arbitrary choice is appropriate). Let $\Delta_\alpha(i, j)$ be the concatenation of the words $v_i.v_{i+1}\ldots v_{j-1}$. Then since $V_i = V_i{}^+$, $\Delta_\alpha(i, j)$ is itself in some partitioned class V_i^k. Thus, there is a finite partition of the pairs of integers such that $\langle m, n\rangle$ and $\langle m', n'\rangle$ are in the same class of pairs iff $\Delta_\alpha(m, n)$ and $\Delta_\alpha(m', n')$ are in the same equivalence class V_i^k. According to Ramsey theorem, there exists an infinite sequence of integers $x_1, x_2\, x_3, \ldots$ such that each pair of them are in the same set of the partition, i.e., for some k, for each $i \geq 1$, $\Delta_\alpha(x_i, x_{i+1}) \in V_i^k$.

Thus, if $u \in U_i^k$, $\Delta_\alpha(1, x_1) \in V_i^j$, and for each $i \geq 1$, $\Delta_\alpha(x_i, x_{i+1}) \in V_i^m$, then $\alpha \in U_i^k.V_i^j.(V_i^m)^\omega \subseteq L$. We can now write the language L as

$$\bigcup_{i=1}^{n}(\bigcup_{k=1}^{l_{V_k}} U_i^k).(\bigcup_{j=1}^{l_{V_i}} V_i^j).(\bigcup_{m=1}^{l_{V_i}} (V_i^m)^\omega) = \bigcup_{i=1}^{n}\bigcup_{k=1}^{l_{V_k}}\bigcup_{j=1}^{l_{V_i}}\bigcup_{m=1}^{l_{V_i}} U_i^k.V_i^j.(V_i^m)^\omega \quad (1)$$

Since L is projective, and by the construction of '$\approx_i$', every concurrent composition of an Σ_1-projection of an element of U_i^k (or V_i^j, or V_i^m, respectively) and a Σ_2-projection of an element of U_i^k (V_i^j, V_i^m, respectively) is also in U_i^k (V_i^j, V_i^m, respectively). Therefore, for each element $L_{i,k,j,m} = U_i^k.V_i^j.(V_i^m)^\omega$ in (1), it holds that

$$L_{i,k,j,m} = L'_{i,k,j,m} \triangleq (U_i^k|_{\Sigma_1} \| U_i^k|_{\Sigma_2}).(V_i^j|_{\Sigma_1} \| V_i^j|_{\Sigma_2}).(V_i^m|_{\Sigma_1} \| V_i^m|_{\Sigma_2})^\omega \subseteq L \quad (2)$$

Using Lemma 3.3 twice, the first time with $Z = U_i^k|_{\Sigma_1} \| U_i^k|_{\Sigma_2}$ and the second time with $Z = \{\varepsilon\}$, we obtain

$$L'_{i,k,j,m} \subseteq L''_{i,k,j,m} \triangleq \underbrace{(U_i^j|_{\Sigma_1}.V_i^j|_{\Sigma_1}.(V_i^m|_{\Sigma_1})^\omega)}_{L^1_{i,k,j,m}} \| \underbrace{(U_i^j|_{\Sigma_2}.V_i^k|_{\Sigma_2}.(V_i^m|_{\Sigma_2})^\omega)}_{L^2_{i,j,k,m}} \subseteq L. \quad (3)$$

Now, let $\widetilde{M}$ be the stuttering closure of a language M. It is easy to see that if M is ω-regular then $\widetilde{M}$ is also ω-regular. Then,

$$\hat{L} = \bigcup_{i=1}^{n}\bigcup_{k=1}^{l_{U_i}}\bigcup_{j=1}^{l_{V_i}}\bigcup_{m=1}^{l_{V_i}} (\widetilde{L^1_{i,k,j,m}} \| \widetilde{L^2_{i,k,j,m}}) \quad (4)$$

is of the appropriate form. Obviously, $\hat{L} \subseteq L$, since containment of each of the union elements was preserved at each step. The inclusion in the other direction holds since for every sequence $\alpha \in L$, there exists according to the above construction some $L''_{i,k,j,m}$ which contains it. ∎

Corollary 3.5 *An ETL formula φ is separable iff the property it expresses is projective (both w.r.t. the same partition $\mathcal{P} = \{\mathcal{A}, \mathcal{B}\}$ of the propositions that appear free in φ).*

Proof. The right to left direction follows directly from Theorems 3.4, Lemma 2.4, and the correspondence between the operators '$\cup$' and '$\|$' on languages with '$\vee$' and '$\wedge$', respectively, in ETL.

To prove the other direction, let φ be separable, i.e., can be written in equivalent form as a separated formula ψ. Let $\eta_1, \eta_2, \ldots \eta_n$ be ψ's stuttering closed Boolean components over the propositions $\mathcal{A}$, while $\mu_1, \mu_2, \ldots \mu_m$ are its components over $\mathcal{B}$. Then there are 2^{m+n} Boolean combinations of these components where each one can appear either negated or unnegated. From propositional logic it follows that φ can be written in an equivalent form as a disjunction of such a combination (disjunctive normal form). Each disjunct can be written as a conjunction of a (stuttering closed) formula over $\mathcal{A}$ and a formula over $\mathcal{B}$. Then, translating these subformulas to languages, it is easy to see that each such disjunct corresponds to a projective language and hence φ is projective as well. ∎

Theorem 3.4 proves that any ω-regular property can be written as a finite Boolean combination of ω-regular properties, each over a single subset of the propositions. This allows to deduce a similar connection on ETL formulas, which have the same expressive power as ω-regular languages [27]. To show that the same holds for LTL properties, it is not enough to use the fact that LTL is included in ETL; this does not guarantee that the Boolean components over either $\mathcal{A}$ or $\mathcal{B}$ of the separated formula ψ, equivalent to the projective LTL (and hence ETL) formula φ (that are guaranteed by Corollary 3.5) are themselves LTL formulas. In order to show that the above construction indeed holds for LTL, we will show first that when the language L is counter-free (i.e., star-free), one can separate it into counter-free languages on local alphabets. Then the result will follow immediately from the correspondence between counter-free ω-regular languages and LTL formulas [25].

Theorem 3.6 *A counter-free ω-regular language L over $\Sigma = \Sigma_1 \times \Sigma_2$ is projective iff it can be written as $L = \bigcup_{i=1}^{n}(M_i \parallel N_i)$, where M_i and N_i are stuttering closed* counter-free *ω-regular languages over Σ_1 and Σ_2, respectively.*

Proof. When L is counter-free, the non trivial direction in the proof of Theorems 3.1 and 3.4 needs to be repeated, showing that in each step of the construction we deal only with counter-free languages. This is based on some properties of counter-free regular and ω-regular languages.

In order to present some prerequisite results, we need to repeat some notions of monoids and their relation to regular languages. A monoid is a triple $\langle M, \cdot, 1\rangle$ containing a set M, an associative operator '$\cdot$', and a unit element (i.e., an element $1 \in M$ such that for each $m \in M$, $1 \cdot m = m \cdot 1 = m$). A monoid is *aperiodic* if there exists an integer $n \geq 0$ such that $x^n = x^{n+1}$ holds for every x in M.

Consider a congruence relation '$\sim$' over some alphabet Σ. An equivalence classes of '$\sim$' is denoted by $[v]$, where v is an arbitrary member of the class. Define $[v] \cdot [w]$ to be $[v.w]$. Then $\langle \sim /\Sigma^*, \cdot\rangle$ is a monoid with a unit element $[\varepsilon]$ (i.e., the equivalence class that contains the empty string).

1. If L is counter-free regular (ω-regular) language, then its syntactical congruence relation '$\cong_L$' ('$\approx_L$', respectively) forms an aperiodic monoid. This was proved for regular languages by Schützenberger [6, 23] and for ω-regular languages by Perrin [22].
2. Counter-free regular (and ω-regular) languages are easily shown to be closed under a finite union, intersection, complement, and stuttering closure.
3. Any equivalence class of the syntactic congruence relation '$\cong_L$' (or '$\approx_L$') for a counter-free regular (ω-regular, respectively) language L is itself counter-free. This follows from Schützenberger's theorem: for each equivalence class $\hat{L}$ of '$\cong_L$', treated itself as a regular language, it holds that $\cong_L \subseteq \cong_{\hat{L}}$, i.e., '$\cong_L$' is a refinement of '$\cong_{\hat{L}}$'. This stems from the fact that $\hat{L}$ is a union of equivalence classes (exactly one) of the congruence '$\cong_L$'. Thus, '$\cong_L$' refines $\hat{L}$'s syntactic congruence '$\cong_{\hat{L}}$' since the latter is the coarser congruence relation that saturates $\hat{L}$ [18]. Hence, there is a morphism (a mapping that preserves the operator '$\cdot$' and the unit element 1) from $\langle \cong_L /\Sigma^*, \cdot\rangle$ onto $\langle \cong_{\hat{L}} /\Sigma^*, \cdot\rangle$ such that each equivalence class $[v]$ of '$\cong_L$' is mapped into an equivalence class $[w]$ of '$\cong_{\hat{L}}$ iff $[v] \subseteq [w]$. Therefore, if $\langle \cong_L /\Sigma^*, \cdot\rangle$ is an aperiodic monoid, so is $\langle \cong_{\hat{L}} /\Sigma^*, \cdot\rangle$.

4. L is a counter-free ω-regular language iff it is a finite union of sets $U.V^\omega$, where U, V are counter-free and $V.V \subseteq V$ [25].
5. The equivalence classes of '$\simeq_{\Sigma_1}$' and '$\simeq_{\Sigma_2}$' where constructed in Theorem 3.1 (and used in Theorem 3.4) for any equivalence class V (which is counter-free regular, from 3) of the syntactic congruence relation of L using intersection with trivial counter-free regular languages. Hence, from 2, these equivalence classes are also counter-free.

Thus, it is easy to check that if the projective language L is counter-free, each one of the steps in the constructions of Theorem 3.4 produces a counter-free language. ∎

Corollary 3.7 *An LTL formula is separable iff the property it expresses is projective.*

Theorem 3.8 *Deciding projectiveness of an LTL (and ETL) formula φ w.r.t. to a given partition $\mathcal{P}$ is PSPACE-hard.*

Proof. It was shown [24] that satisfiability for LTL (and ETL) properties that contain only the modal until '$\mathcal{U}$' (and hence are stuttering closed) is PSPACE-complete. Let φ be such a formula and $\mathcal{Q} = \{Q_1, \ldots Q_n\}$ be the set of propositions that appear in φ. Denote $\neg \bigvee \mathcal{Q} = \neg(Q_1 \vee \ldots \vee Q_n)$. Without loss of generality we assume that φ is not equivalent to $\Box\neg \bigvee \mathcal{Q}$. Let Q' be a proposition that does not occur in $\mathcal{Q}$.

We present a reduction from the satisfiability of LTL to projectivity. Consider the formula $\psi = (Q' \wedge \neg \bigvee \mathcal{Q}) U (\neg Q' \wedge \varphi)$, where the modal *unless* 'U' is weaker than '$\mathcal{U}$' and satisfies $\mu U \eta = \Box\mu \vee \mu\mathcal{U}\eta$. Then, ψ is projective w.r.t. $\mathcal{P} = \{\mathcal{Q}, \{Q'\}\}$ iff φ is not satisfiable: for if φ is satisfiable, then once a proposition from $\mathcal{Q}$ becomes T (true), Q' changes from F into T and does not change thereafter. This contradicts projectivity, since if ψ was projective, it must have also allowed sequences in which Q' becomes F after the first proposition from $\mathcal{Q}$ becomes T. On the other hand, if φ is not satisfiable, ψ is equivalent to $\Box(Q' \wedge \neg \bigvee \mathcal{Q})$, which is also equivalent to $\Box Q' \wedge \Box\neg \bigvee \mathcal{Q}$. ∎

Following is a (doubly exponential) decision procedure for projectiveness of a language L, expressed as a Büchi automaton:

1. For each one of the equivalence classes W of '$\approx_L$' constructed as in [26], check that W is projective. This can be done based on the construction in Theorem 3.1: first construct the language W_4 (by constructing first W_1, W_2, W_3 from W). Then find pairs of equivalence classes M_i and N_i of '$\simeq_{\Sigma_1}$' and '$\simeq_{\Sigma_2}$', respectively, such that $M_i.N_i \subseteq W_4$. As in the proof of Theorem 3.1, set $\overline{W}$ to be $\bigcup_{i=1}^{n}(M_i \parallel N_i)$. It is easy to see that W is projective iff $\overline{W} = W$. If one of the equivalence classes W of '$\approx_L$' is not projective, then decide that L is not projective and stop.
2. Now repeat the construction of Theorem 3.4 to construct the language $\hat{L}$ in Equation (4). The language $\hat{L} \supseteq L$ contains the words β such that at least one of the words in $\beta|_{\Sigma_1} \parallel \beta|_{\Sigma_2}$ is in L. Thus, $\hat{L}$ is the minimal language that contains L and is closed under projections. (This does not contradicts the fact that not *every* projective closure of an ω-regular language is itself ω-regular, as step 1 already eliminated some languages from being projective.) Then L is projective iff $L = \hat{L}$.

The above algorithm can also be altered to return the separated formula ψ that is equivalent to φ, when φ is projective: first translate φ into a Büchi automaton. Then translate the components $\widetilde{L^1_{i,k,j,m}}$ and $\widetilde{L^2_{i,k,j,m}}$, of $\hat{L} = \bigcup_{i=1}^{n} \bigcup_{k=1}^{l_{U_i}} \bigcup_{j=1}^{l_{V_i}} \bigcup_{m=1}^{l_{V_i}} (\widetilde{L^1_{i,k,j,m}} \| \widetilde{L^2_{i,k,j,m}})$, constructed in step 2 above, to formulas. Then replacing each union by disjunction and each concurrent composition operator '||' by conjunction (from Lemma 2.4).

4 Applications of Projective Properties

4.1 Projectivity, Sequential Consistency and Serializability

Sequential consistency was formulated in [2], based on a definition of [14], as a criterion for fast memory implementations, e.g., using caches. Let M be a non-sequential implementation of a sequential (i.e., non-cached) memory M_{seq} (notice that the program may still be concurrent, while it is the memory that is considered to be sequential). The implementation must satisfy some safety consistency conditions, e.g., that the value read by a $read[x]$ operation in an execution is the same as the last value written by the most recent $write[x]$ command in that execution. We denote these conditions by $consistent(M)$. Denote the set of behaviors (executions) of a memory M by $[\![M]\!]$. Then it is required that

$$consistent(M) \wedge \forall \xi \in [\![M]\!] \, \exists \rho \in [\![M_{seq}]\!] \, \xi \equiv \rho \tag{5}$$

Now consider properties that are expressed as temporal formulas over a set of predicates, partitioned according to the different state spaces of the program's processes. It is easy to see that the requirement (5) forces any projective property φ of M_{seq}, represented as a language L (i.e., $[\![M_{seq}]\!] \subseteq L$) of the sequential memory M_{seq} to be preserved by the implementation M. This is because φ cannot distinguish between ξ and ρ when $\xi \equiv \rho$.

The consistency constraints on the implementation M makes sequential consistency a stronger requirement than just being projection equivalent to the original program. This allows preserving other properties. For example, in [14], mutual exclusion, which is *not* a projective property is shown to be preserved on such an implementation. However, in these cases, the additional non-projective properties that are preserved by the implementation depend on the combination of the consistency conditions and the actual code of the specific program. The projective properties on the other hand are preserved uniformly over all memory implementations, depending only on the structure of the program, i.e., the partition of the program into processes rather than on the actual code.

The fact that all projective properties are preserved under sequential consistent implementation can be exploited for purposes of verification: proving that a sequential consistent implementation of a program satisfies a projective property φ can be done by proving that (a) the original program satisfies φ, and (b) that the implementation indeed satisfy sequential consistency. Proving (b) is usually done once for each implementation (e.g., proving that some architecture satisfy sequential consistency). Proving (a) should be much easier than proving directly that the implementation satisfies φ.

Serializability [19, 21] is a constraint on database implementations. Instead of a set of processes, we are dealing now with a set of finite process-like *transactions*. Let M_{seq} represent the sequences of external database events (e.g., the reads and writes) of the executions in which only one transaction is allowed to execute at any time. The sequences M represent all the interleaved executions allowed by the implementation. Then (5) can be reused (with the new interpretation of M_{seq} and M) to serve as the definition of serializability. Considering properties with a set of predicates partitioned according to the various transactions, we obtain again that the projective properties are preserved.

4.2 Projectivity and Equivalence Robustness

In this section we study the connection between projective properties and partial order techniques for model checking (and verification). Partial order model checking techniques [20] use equivalence relations between executions of programs to reduce the size of the state graph used to model check that a program satisfies a property. Such an equivalence relation is induced by partial order executions, which are partially ordered sets of events [13]: two sequences are equivalent iff they are linearization of the same partial order execution.

A finite state program P over a global state space $\Sigma = \Sigma_1 \times \ldots \times \Sigma_n$ consists of a finite set of operations T and an initial state $\iota \in \Sigma$. Each operation $\tau \in T$ is a *partial* function from a subset of the components $\Sigma_{i_1} \times \Sigma_{i_2} \times \ldots \times \Sigma_{i_l}$ with indexes $in(\tau) = \{i_1, i_2, \ldots, i_l\}$ to a subset of the components $\Sigma_{j_1} \times \Sigma_{j_2} \times \ldots \times \Sigma_{j_m}$ with indexes $out(\tau) = \{j_1, j_2, \ldots, j_m\}$. (The components can correspond to local state spaces of concurrent processes of the program P.)

Denote the restriction of a state $s \in \Sigma$ to the components indexed by the set I by $s\lfloor_I$. Then an operation $\tau \in T$ can be executed from a state $s \in \Sigma$ iff $s\lfloor_{in(\tau)}$ is in the domain of τ. We also say that τ is *enabled* from s. The effect of executing τ from s is to change the state s into a state s' where $s'\lfloor_{out(\tau)} = \tau(s\lfloor_{in(\tau)})$ and the rest of the components are unchanged, i.e., $s'\lfloor_{\{1,\ldots,n\}\setminus out(\tau)} = s\lfloor_{\{1,\ldots,n\}\setminus out(\tau)}$. An execution sequence is an infinite sequence of global states $s_0\, s_1\, s_2 \ldots$, starting from the initial state, i.e., $s_0 = \iota$, by executing a sequence of operations $\alpha_0\, \alpha_1\, \alpha_2 \ldots$ from T (we assume that there always exists an enabled operation). That is, for each $i \geq 0$, (a) α_i is enabled in s_i, and (b) s_{i+1} is obtained from s_i by the execution of α_i. Denote the set of execution sequences of a program P by $[\![P]\!]$.

An execution sequence can be represented both by the sequence of operations executed, or the sequence of states generated by the execution of these operations, starting with ι. To distinguish between these the two representations, sequences of states will be denoted by $\xi, \xi', \xi_i, \ldots$, while sequences of operations will be denoted by $\vec{\xi}, \vec{\xi'}, \vec{\xi_i}, \ldots$. It will be easier to define an equivalence relation between sequences of operations rather than between sequences of global states.

We consider properties, paired with a partition $\mathcal{P}$ of their propositions which agree with the component alphabets (i.e., the local state spaces). A property φ of a program P can be seen as a language L. The program P satisfies φ iff $[\![P]\!] \subseteq L$.

A reflexive and symmetric binary *dependency* relation $\mathcal{D} \subseteq T \times T$ is used to construct an equivalent relation between execution sequences. The dependency relation $\mathcal{D}$ is defined such that $(a, b) \in \mathcal{D}$ iff

$$(out(a) \cap out(b)) \cup (out(a) \cap in(b)) \cup (in(a) \cap out(b)) \neq \phi. \tag{6}$$

That is, the operations a and b can either change the same component state space, or the execution of one of them may depend upon a component that is changeable by the other [10]. This guarantees that two independent operations that can be executed from some global state s obtaining a state s' can be executed from s in the reversed order, obtaining the same global state s'.

Two sequences of operations $\vec{\xi}$ and $\vec{\xi'}$ are *trace equivalent*, denoted by $\vec{\xi} \doteq \vec{\xi'}$, if for each pair of operations $(a, b) \in \mathcal{D}$, the restriction of $\vec{\xi}$ to the occurrences of a and b is the same as the restriction of $\vec{\xi'}$ to a and b (the restriction of a sequence to a set of letters S is obtained by erasing all the letters that are not in S). Thus, two execution sequences are considered trace equivalent if they can be obtained from each other by commuting the order of execution of adjacent independent operations. For other alternative definitions of the equivalence '$\doteq$', see [12, 5].

Each such equivalence class corresponds to a partial order execution of the program in the sense that it constitutes the set of the linearizations of the partial order [13]. Due to this connection, model checking based on reducing the state graph using the equivalence relation '$\doteq$' is traditionally called partial order model checking. The constructed state graph must generate at least one representative (i.e., a path whose sequence of edges are labeled with program operations that correspond to an execution sequence of P) for each equivalence class of '$\doteq$'. An algorithm to construct such a reduced state graph can be found in [20]. Since the generated state graph has to represent fewer sequences, it can be considerably smaller than the full state graph which generates all of them.

Lemma 4.1 *Two sequences ξ_1, ξ_2 such that $\vec{\xi_1} \doteq \vec{\xi_2}$ satisfy that $\xi_1 \equiv \xi_2$.*

Proof. Denote $op_i = \{a \mid i \in out(a)\}$, i.e., the set of operations that can change the value of the local component Σ_i. Then, $op_i \times op_i \subseteq D$. Let σ_1 and σ_2 be finite prefixes of ξ_1 and ξ_2, respectively, such that $\vec{\sigma_1} \mid_{op_i} = \vec{\sigma_2} \mid_{op_i}$. It is easy to see that according to the definitions of '$\doteq$', for each prefix σ_1 of ξ_1 there exists an appropriate prefix σ_2 of ξ_2, since from the interdependency of the operations in op_i, they must appear in the same order in both sequences. Let s_1 and s_2 be the last states of the finite sequences σ_1 and σ_2, respectively. We claim that

$$s_1 \lfloor_{\{i\}} = s_2 \lfloor_{\{i\}}. \tag{7}$$

Thus, since $\vec{\xi_1} \mid_{op_i} \doteq \vec{\xi_2} \mid_{op_i}$, the restriction of ξ_1 and ξ_2 to the ith component is the same up to stuttering.

To prove (7), construct the *occurrence graph* G of ξ_1 [5]: this directed acyclic graph contains occurrences of operations from ξ_1 as nodes, i.e., the pair $\langle a, n\rangle$ corresponds to the nth appearance of a in ξ_1. An edge from a node $\langle a, n\rangle$ to a node $\langle b, m\rangle$ exists iff $(a, b) \in D$ *and* the nth occurrence of a in ξ_1 precedes the mth occurrence of b. This is also the occurrence graph of any sequence that is trace equivalent to ξ_1, including ξ_2.

Consider now the last occurrence $\langle a, n\rangle$ of an operation from op_i in $\vec{\sigma_1}$. It is also the last occurrence of an operation from op_i $\vec{\sigma_2}$. Let G' be the subgraph of G that includes all the predecessors of $\langle a, n\rangle$ in G, i.e., the occurrences from which there is a path that ends with $\langle a, n\rangle$. It is easy to show by induction on the size of the graph G' that the values of $s_1 \lfloor_{\{i\}}$ and $s_2 \lfloor_{\{i\}}$ are uniquely determined by the transformations of the set of program operations and by the graph G', hence they are the same. ∎

The state graph generated by the partial order model checking algorithm must satisfy that it generates at least one sequence from each equivalence class rather than all the execution sequences of a program. In order to check that a program P satisfies a property

φ using the reduced state graph, φ must not distinguish between two sequences of the same equivalence class, i.e., there exists no pair of equivalent sequences $\xi \doteq \xi'$, where ξ satisfies φ and ξ' satisfies $\neg\varphi$.

Definition 4.2 *The formula φ is said to be* equivalence robust *w.r.t. a set of equivalence classes $\mathcal{R}$ if the formula φ cannot distinguish between any two sequences of the same equivalence class in $\mathcal{R}$.*

Properties that are equivalence robust w.r.t. all equivalence classes of '$\doteq$' of all finite state programs sharing some fixed component (i.e., local) alphabets will be called *uniformly equivalent robust.* Uniform equivalence robustness depends therefore only on the structure of the program, i.e., the local alphabets, rather than its code. Characterizing the equivalence robust properties is important for verification as well as for model checking methods [10, 11, 20].

Theorem 4.3 *An LTL or ETL formula φ is uniformly equivalence robust iff it is projective.*

Proof. Using Lemma 4.1, each equivalence class of '$\doteq$' is included in an equivalence class of '$\equiv$'. (we do not claim that '$\doteq$' is a refinement of '$\equiv$', since '$\doteq$' is defined only over words that are sequences of programs, while '$\equiv$' is more liberal and is defined over all the infinite words of Σ). Thus, if φ is projective, then it is uniformly equivalence robust.

To prove the other direction, we will show that if φ is not projective, there exists at least one program for which φ is not equivalence robust: let $L \subseteq \Sigma^\omega$ be the language that corresponds to φ. If the syntactic congruence '$\approx_L$' is not projective, then from its definition there exists u, v, x, y, $z \in \Sigma^*$ such that $u \equiv v$ and one of the following holds:

1. $x.u.y.z^\omega \in L$ and $x.v.y.z^\omega \notin L$, or
2. $x.(y.u.z)^\omega \in L$ and $x.(y.v.z)^\omega \notin L$.

Let α be $x.v.y.z^\omega$ if the first case holds, and $x.(y.v.z)^\omega$ in the second case.

If the syntactic congruence is projective, construct the projective closure $L^{\doteq}$ using the algorithm at the end of Section 3. In this case, the projective closure is ω-regular. Set $L' = L^{\doteq} \setminus L$. Since L is not projective, L' is not empty. Furthermore, L is ω-regular since it is the difference between two ω regular languages. From Lemma 2.9, L must contain some ultimately periodic word α, i.e., a word of the form $x.y^\omega$.

Now let $\beta_1 = \alpha|_{\Sigma_1}$ and $\beta_2 = \alpha|_{\Sigma_2}$. It follows that $\alpha \in \beta_1 \parallel \beta_2$ but is not in L. Since α is trace equivalent to some word in L, it holds that $\beta_1 \parallel \beta_2 \cap L \neq \phi$. To complete the proof, the infinite words β_1 and β_2 can be easily translated into processes P_1 and P_2 on disjoint state spaces, with alphabets Σ_1 and Σ_2, respectively. The program P is the union of operations of P_1 and P_2, with initial state that corresponds to the initial state of both processes, and with $\mathcal{D} = (\Sigma_1 \times \Sigma_1) \cup (\Sigma_2 \times \Sigma_2)$. The executions of the program P contain (among others, since no fairness requirement [7] was assumed) the sequences of $\beta_1 \parallel \beta_2$, which are all equivalent under '$\doteq$'. But $\beta_1 \parallel \beta_2$ contains both a sequence that satisfies φ (is in L) and a sequence that does not satisfy φ (e.g., the sequence α)[1]. ∎

[1]The reason for constructing programs for the words β_1 and β_2 (based on projections of the periodic word α) and not directly for the languages $L|_{\Sigma_1}$ and $L|_{\Sigma_2}$ is that not every ω-language corresponds to the set of sequences of some finite state program [1].

The practical consequence is that a reduced state graph generated by partial order methods (such as [20]) can be used for checking projective properties. For non-projective properties, the structural information about the partition of the propositions according to the components (processes) is not sufficient to determine if the reduced state graph is appropriate for checking the correctness of the property. One can still model-check non-projective properties using partial order techniques: this is done by extending the dependency relation $\mathcal{D}$, which refines the equivalence relation '$\doteq$', and hence requires more representatives. However, this comes at the expense of reducing the efficiency as it means extending the state graph [20].

Now, instead of checking for projectiveness, which was shown in Theorem 3.8 to be hard, one can use the result of Corollary 3.7, and constrain the syntax to separated formulas.

5 Conclusions

Projective languages over component alphabets where studied. The projective languages in the behavior classes of regular, ω-regular and counter-free (i.e., star-free) ω-regular languages where shown to be constructible using the operators union '$\cup$' and concurrent composition '$||$' from component languages of the corresponding class. Translating this result to temporal logics, it was shown that projective ETL (LTL) properties over a partitioned set of propositions $\mathcal{P}$ are exactly those properties that can be written as a boolean combination of stuttering closed properties over a single subset in $\mathcal{P}$.

Projective properties were shown to be important for partial order model checking methods. It was shown that they can be checked under a construction that generates at least one representative interleaving sequence for each partial order execution instead of all the sequences. Conversely, it was shown that when a property φ is not projective, there exists at least one program for which checking φ cannot rely on representatives. Other application of that projective properties include preservation of properties under hardware implementations that guarantee sequential consistency, and by distributed implementations of databases that guarantee serializability.

Deciding projectiveness was shown to be PSPACE-hard. Thus, for the cases where projective properties are important, the connection between projective properties and separable properties allows restricting the syntax to boolean combinations of component properties without loss of expressive power.

Acknowledgements. I would like to thank R. P. Kurshan for many helpful discussions on this subject. My interest in separable properties was inspired by a discussion with Amir Pnueli and Pierre Wolper.

References

[1] M. Abadi, L. Lamport, P. Wolper, Realizable and Unrealizable Concurrent Program Specifications, ICALP 1989, LNCS 372, Springer–Verlag, 1–17.

[2] Y. Afek, G. M. Brown, M. Merritt, Lazy Caching, ACM Transactions on Programming Languages and Systems 15 (1993), 182–205.

[3] K. Apt, N. Francez, S. Katz, Appraising fairness in languages for distributed programming, Distributed Computing, Vol 2 (1988), 226–241.

[4] A. Arnold, A Syntactic congruence for Rational ω-languages, Theoretical Computer Science 39 (1985), 333-335.

[5] V. Diekert, Combinatorics on Traces, LNCS 454, Springer–Verlag, 1990.

[6] S. Eilenberg, Automata, Languages and Machines, Vol. A, Academic Press, New York, 1974.

[7] D. Gabbay, A. Pnueli, S. Shelah, J. Stavi, On the Temporal Analysis of Fairness, ACM Symposium on Principles of Programming Languages, 1980, 163–173.

[8] J. E. Hopcroft, J. D. Ullman, Introduction to Automata Theory, Languages and Computation, Addison Wesley, 1979.

[9] N. D. Jones, L.H. Landweber, Y. E. Lien, Complexity of some problems in Petri Nets, Theoretical Computer Science 4, 277-299.

[10] S. Katz, D. Peled, Interleaving Set Temporal Logic, Theoretical Computer Science, Vol. 75, Number 3, 21–43.

[11] S. Katz, D. Peled, Verification of Distributed Programs using Representative Interleaving Sequences, Distributed Computing (1992) 6, 107-120.

[12] M. Z. Kwiatkowska, Fairness for Non–interleaving Concurrency, Phd. Thesis, Faculty of Science, University of Leicester, 1989.

[13] L. Lamport, Time, clocks and the ordering of events in a distributed system, Communications of the ACM 21 (1978), 558–565.

[14] L. Lamport, How to make a multiprocess computer that correctly executes multiprocess programs, IEEE Transactions on Computers, Vol. c-28, No. 9, 690-691.

[15] L. Lamport, What good is temporal logic, in R.E.A. Mason (Ed.), Information Processing 83, Elsevier Science Publishers, 1983, 657-668.

[16] O. Lichtenstein, A. Pnueli, Checking that finite-state concurrent programs satisfy their linear specification, Proceedings of the 11th ACM Annual Symposium on Principles of Programming Languages, 1984, 97–107.

[17] R. McNaughton, S. Papert, Counter-Free Automata, The MIT Press, 1971.

[18] A. Nerode, Linear Automaton Transformations, Proceedings AMS 9, 541–544.

[19] C. Papadimitiou, The Theory of Database Concurrency Control, Computer Science Press, 1986.

[20] D. Peled, All from One, One for All: on Model Checking using Representatives, Proceedings of Computer Aided Verification 93, Elounda, Greece, LNCS 697, 609–623.

[21] D. Peled, S. Katz, A. Pnueli, Specifying and Proving Serializability in Temporal Logic, 6th IEEE annual symposium on Logic in Computer Science, Amsterdam, The Netherlands, July 1991, 232–245.

[22] D. Perrin, Recent Results on Automata and Infinite Words, Mathematical Foundations of Computer Science, LNCS 176, Springer Verlag 1984, 134-148.

[23] M. P. Schützenberger, Sur les relations rationnelles functionnelles, in M. Nivat (ed.), Automata, Languages and Programming, North Holland, 103–114.

[24] A.P. Sistla, E.M. Clarke, The Complexity of Propositional Temporal Logics, Journal of the ACM 32 (1985), 733–749.

[25] W. Thomas, Automata on Infinite Objects, in J. Van Leeuwen (ed.), Handbook of Theoretical Computer Science, Vol. B, Elsvier, 133–191.

[26] T. Wilke, An algebraic theory for regular languages of finite and infinite words, Technical report 9202, 1992, Christian-Albrechts university, Kiel, Germany.

[27] P. Wolper, Temporal Logic Can be More Expressive, Information and Control 56 (1983), 72–99.

A Rank Hierarchy for Deterministic Tree-Walking Transducers*

Owen Rambow[1] and Giorgio Satta[2]

[1] Department of CIS, University of Pennsylvania,
3401 Walnut Street, Suite 400C,
Philadelphia, PA 19104
rambow@linc.cis.upenn.edu

[2] Università di Venezia, Scienze dell'Informazione
via Torino 155, 30172 Mestre – Venezia, Italy
satta@moo.dsi.unive.it

Abstract. In this paper two complexity measures are investigated for the class of deterministic tree-walking transducers. We show that, when a constant bound is imposed on the *crossing number* of these devices, the *rank* of the input tree language induces an infinite, non-collapsing hierarchy. Using this result we solve some language-theoretic questions that were left open in the literature. Our separation result can also be transferred to other classes in the family of finite copying parallel rewriting systems, since a weak equivalence relation holds between these classes and deterministic tree-walking transducers, even when the complexity measures above are bounded.

1 Introduction

Tree-to-string transducers constitute a generalization of two-ways transducers in which a sequential machine visits up and down a tree structure in checking mode, producing a translation string. If the machine is finite state and deterministic, we have the class of deterministic tree-walking transducers (DTWT) of [2] (called "tree automata" there). We can regard DTWT as generative devices controlled by some tree language. Interestingly enough, other rewriting systems have been shown equivalent to DTWT, such as the the linear generalized syntax-directed translation of [2], the finite copying top-down tree-to-string transducers of [6], the (string generating) context-free hypergraph grammars of [3] and the multiple context-free grammars of [8] (see [5] and [11] for the last two results).

Two complexity measures can be defined for the class DTWT, usually called the *crossing number* and the *rank*. The crossing number of a DTWT represents

* We are grateful to Joost Engelfriet and Ryuichi Nakanisi for helpful discussion on topics related to this paper. This research was conducted while the second author was a post-doctoral fellow at the Institute for Research in Cognitive Science at the University of Pennsylvania. The research was sponsored by the following grants: ARO DAAL 03-89-C-0031; DARPA N00014-90-J-1863; NSF IRI 90-16592; and Ben Franklin 91S.3078C-1.

the maximum number of times the automaton enters into any subtree in the input tree language; because of the determinism, this number is always finite (see [2]). The rank of a DTWT is the branching degree of the input tree language and is finite by definition.

The crossing number induces an infinite, non-collapsing hierarchy within the class of languages generated by DTWT (see [6]). Whether the rank measure induces a corresponding infinite non-collapsing hierarchy within the class of languages generated by DTWT was not known to date and the major contribution of this paper is the solution of this problem. We show that, within DTWT with crossing number bounded by $f \geq 2$, we can construct an infinite non-collapsing hierarchy by varying the rank. This result has many consequences for the theory of translation and of controlled rewriting; some of them will be discussed in this paper.

2 Definitions

In this paper, we follow standard notational conventions. For an alphabet V, we denote by V^* the set of all finite strings over V, V^+ the set of non-empty ones. Let $a \in V$, and $w \in V^*$; $\#_a(w)$ denotes the number of occurrences of a in w. Finally, for a class $\mathcal{C}$ of generative devices, $\mathcal{L}(\mathcal{C})$ denotes the class of all languages generated by $\mathcal{C}$. We start out by reviewing the definition of deterministic tree walk transducers. (We follow the definition of [2].)

A *deterministic tree walk transducer* (DTWT) is defined as a 6-tuple $M = (Q, G, \Delta, \delta, q_0, Q_F)$, where Q is a finite set of states with $q \in Q$ the initial state and $Q_F \subseteq Q$ the set of final states, $G = (V_\mathrm{N}, V_\mathrm{T}, P, S)$ is a context-free grammar, called the *underlying* context-free grammar, Δ is a set of output symbols, and δ is a mapping from $Q \times (P \cup V_\mathrm{T} \cup \{\varepsilon\})$ into $Q \times I \times \Delta^*$, where $I = \{\mathsf{up}, \mathsf{stay}, \mathsf{down}1, \ldots, \mathsf{down}n\}$ (n is the maximal branching degree of the underlying context-free grammar). Map δ determines the movements of the DTWT on a context-free derivation tree (in which the interior nodes are labeled not with nonterminals but with the production used to rewrite the nonterminal). Given the current state and the label of the current node, δ returns a new state, a move (from I), and an output string. The transition function δ is restricted in an appropriate way so that the move instruction is always interpretable with respect to the tree. The output is just the concatenation of the output from the current move with that from the previous moves. The set of output sentences of the automaton is then the set of output sentences generated when the automaton is in a final state. The class of all unordered scattered context grammars is also denoted DTWT.

We will call *crossing number* of a DTWT the maximum number of times the automaton enters into any subtree in the input tree language; as mentioned in the introduction, this number must be finite because the automaton is deterministic. Since this device can visit a subtree more than once, the output string will contain separated substrings that are derived from traversing the same structure and that are therefore in some sense related. For example, by traversing a monadic tree twice, a DTWT can generate the language $\{a^n b^n a^n b^n \mid n \geq 0\}$. By increasing the crossing number, we can increase the number of related substrings, and therefore the generative capacity of the system: if the crossing number is bounded by an integer $f \geq 1$, a transducer can count up to $2f$ but cannot produce the language $L = \{a_1^n a_2^n \cdots a_{2f+1}^n \mid n \geq 0\}$. This separation result can be proved using a pumping lemma (see for instance [6]).

The *rank* of a DTWT is the maximal branching degree of the underlying context-free grammar. In order to show that the rank also induces a non-collapsing hierarchy (for fixed crossing number) we will first define a string-rewriting system which is equivalent to DTWT and for which we will identify parameters that correspond to the crossing number and the rank of a DTWT. We choose to introduce a string-rewriting system since the class of languages that allows us to show the existence of a rank hierarchy is significantly more complex than the class of languages that shows the existence of a crossing number hierarchy; a true string rewriting systems allows us to present the proof more elegantly.

An *unordered scattered context grammar* (USCG) is defined as a quadruple $G = (V_N, V_T, P, S)$ where V_N, V_T are finite, disjoint sets of nonterminal and terminal symbols respectively, $S \in V_N$ is the start symbol and P is a finite set of productions having the form $(A_1, \ldots, A_n) \rightarrow (\alpha_1, \ldots, \alpha_n)$, where $n \geq 1$, $A_i \in V_N$, $\alpha_i \in (V_N \cup V_T)^*$, $1 \leq i \leq n$. We write $\gamma \Rightarrow_G \delta$ whenever there exist $p : (A_1, \ldots, A_n) \rightarrow (\alpha_1, \ldots, \alpha_n) \in P$ and an arbitrary permutation π of $\{1, \ldots, n\}$ such that

$$\gamma = \gamma_0 A_{\pi(1)} \gamma_1 A_{\pi(2)} \cdots \gamma_{n-1} A_{\pi(n)} \gamma_n,$$

$$\delta = \gamma_0 \alpha_{\pi(1)} \gamma_1 \alpha_{\pi(2)} \cdots \gamma_{n-1} \alpha_{\pi(n)} \gamma_n,$$

where $\gamma_i \in (V_N \cup V_T)^*$, $0 \leq i \leq n$. The class of all unordered scattered context grammars is also denoted USCG. USCGs are known to be weakly equivalent to several other regulated rewriting systems, including context-free matrix grammars, programmed grammars and state grammars. The reader is referred to [4] for details.

We now introduce a restriction on the derivation relation for USCG which we will call *locality*. Informally, locality forces each production to rewrite only symbols which were previously introduced together in a single step of the derivation. As a result, we have that in a local rewriting system the set of all derivations can be characterized by a context-free grammar, i.e., a derivation can be represented by a recognizable tree in the sense of [9]. The notion of locality was first discussed by [10]. In [7] it is shown how locality restriction characterizes a broad range of formalisms known in the literature with the name of finite copying parallel rewriting systems (see [6]).

In the following, strings $\gamma \in (V_N \cup V_T)^*$ will be viewed as sequences of symbols. An equivalence relation I_γ is said to be *associated with* γ if I_γ is defined on the set of elements of γ that are instances of symbols in V_N. A new class of rewriting systems can be obtained if we introduce associated equivalence relations in the definition of the derive relation for USCG so as to impose the locality restriction. (We overload symbol $\Rightarrow_G$.)

Definition 1. A local unordered scattered context grammar (LUSCG for short) is an unordered scattered context grammar G associated with a binary relation $\Rightarrow_G$ defined over pairs consisting of a string in $(V_N \cup V_T)^*$ and an associated equivalence relation. We write $(\gamma, I_\gamma) \Rightarrow_G (\delta, I_\delta)$ if and only if:

(i) δ is obtained from γ by using a production $p \in P$ to rewrite elements of γ that are equivalent in I_γ, and
(ii) $I_\delta = I'_\gamma \cup I$, where I'_γ makes equivalent all and only those instances of nonterminals in δ that have not been introduced by p and that correspond to instances that were equivalent in I_γ, and I makes equivalent all and only the instances of nonterminal elements of δ introduced by p.

The class of all local unordered scattered context grammars is also denoted LUSCG.

Example 1. Let $L = \{ww | w \in D_1\}$, where D_1 is the Dyck language of strings of properly balanced parentheses. Language L can be derived by the LUSCG $G_L = (V_N, V_T, P, S)$, where $V_N = \{S, A, B\}$, $V_T = \{[,]\}$ and set P consists of the following productions:

$$\begin{aligned} (S) &\rightarrow (AA), \\ (A, A) &\rightarrow ([A], [A]), \\ (A, A) &\rightarrow (AB, AB), \\ (B, B) &\rightarrow (A, A), \\ (A, A) &\rightarrow ([\,], [\,]). \end{aligned}$$

As a convention, given a string of the form $\gamma_0 A_1 \gamma_1 \cdots \gamma_{n-1} A_n \gamma_n$, $n \geq 1$, we denote with $I^{(A_1, \ldots, A_n)}$ any associated equivalence relation in which the indicated instances of nonterminals $A_1, \ldots, A_n$ are equivalent. We introduce additional notation to be used in the following. If $p : (A_1, \ldots, A_n) \rightarrow (\alpha_1, \ldots, \alpha_n)$ belongs to P, we say that $(A_1, \ldots, A_n)$ is the *left-hand tuple* of p and $(\alpha_1, \ldots, \alpha_n)$ is the *right-hand tuple* of p. Relation $\Rightarrow_G$ will sometime be written $\overset{p}{\Rightarrow}_G$ to express that production p was used in the rewriting. In order to represent derivations in G, we use the reflexive and transitive closure of $\Rightarrow_G$, written $\overset{*}{\Rightarrow}_G$.

The *reduced form* for a LUSCG G is a LUSCG derived from G by eliminating useless productions, i.e., productions that can never be used in a terminating derivation. It can easily be shown that for each LUSCG G, there is a reduced form grammar. In this paper we will always assume grammars in reduced form.

As already mentioned, the locality restriction makes it possible to represent the underlying structure of a derivation by means of a recognizable tree. The following definition specifies how this can be done. Let $G = (V_N, V_T, P, S)$ be a LUSCG. Define $P^{(0)} = \{p \mid p \in P$, there are no nonterminals in the right-hand tuple of $p\}$ and $P^{(1)} = P - P^{(0)}$. Without loss of generality, we assume that p_S is the unique production in P that rewrites S and $p_S \in P^{(1)}$.

Definition 2. The derivation grammar of G, denoted der(G), is the context-free grammar $(P^{(1)}, P^{(0)}, \Pi, p_S)$ where $P^{(1)}$ and $P^{(0)}$ are the set of nonterminal and terminal symbols respectively, p_S is the initial symbol and Π contains all and only productions of the form $p \rightarrow p_1 \cdots p_n$, where $p, p_1, \ldots, p_n \in P$ and $n \geq 1$, such that $p_1, \ldots, p_n$ together rewrite all the nonterminal symbols of G introduced by the right-hand tuple of p.

We remark that Definition 2 assumes a canonical ordering of the productions, so that two productions of $\mathrm{der}(G)$ cannot differ only in the order of the right-hand side symbols. Clearly, every derivation in G corresponds to a unique derivation in $\mathrm{der}(G)$.

We now introduce two parameters associated with grammars in the class LUSCG, that will be regarded as complexity measures in what follows.

Definition 3. Let $G = (V_\mathrm{N}, V_\mathrm{T}, P, S)$ be a LUSCG, $p \in P$, and let $\mathrm{der}(G) = (P^{(1)}, P^{(0)}, \Pi, p_S)$ be the derivation grammar of G. The fan-out of production p, written $\varphi(p)$, is the length of its tuples. The fan-out of G is defined as $\varphi(G) = \max_{p \in P} \varphi(p)$. The rank of production p, written $\rho(p)$, is defined as $\rho(p) = \max_{(p \rightarrow \alpha) \in \Pi} |\alpha|$. The rank of G is defined as $\rho(G) = \max_{p \in P} \rho(p)$.

For integers $f, r \geq 1$, r-LUSCG(f) will denote the class of all LUSCG having fan-out bounded by f and rank bounded by r. We will also write r-LUSCG for $\cup_{f \geq 1} r$-LUSCG(f) and LUSCG(f) for $\cup_{r \geq 1} r$-LUSCG(f). We remark that a grammar G must have fan-out and rank at least as great as those of its reduced form grammar. Similarly, we denote by r-DTWT(f) the class of all DTWT with crossing number bounded by f and rank bounded by r. We will write r-DTWT for $\cup_{f \geq 1} r$-DTWT(f) and DTWT(f) for $\cup_{r \geq 1} r$-DTWT(f).

The class of local unordered scattered context grammars has the same weak generative power as the class of deterministic tree-walking transducers and there is a close correspondence between fan-out and rank for the former class and the crossing number and rank parameters for the latter class. This allows us to transfer to DTWT our separation result in Section 3.

Theorem 4. *For every pair of integers $f, r \geq 1$, we have $\mathcal{L}(r$-LUSCG$(f)) = \mathcal{L}(r$-DTWT$(f))$.*

The above equivalence result is obtained by pairing devices in such a way that the underlying grammar in the DTWT corresponds to the derivation grammar of the LUSCG. In this way, the rank parameter is preserved. Furthermore, each entry by the DTWT into a subtree of a derivation tree generated by the underlying grammar corresponds to a derivation in the LUSCG starting with a separate component of the left-hand tuple of the corresponding production. Thus, all sequential visits by the DTWT to some subtree correspond to a single parallel derivation in the LUSCG of all nonterminals in the left-hand tuple of the corresponding production. Therefore, the crossing-number for that subtree corresponds to the fan-out of the starting production in the parallel derivation. In this way, the crossing number of DTWT corresponds to the fan-out of LUSCG. We refer to [7] for a formal proof, which involves showing the equivalence between LUSCG and the multiple context-free grammars of [8], and then using the equivalence between the latter and DTWT shown by [11].

3 The Rank Hierarchy

This section presents the main result of the paper. We show that the rank parameter defines an infinite (non-collapsing) hierarchy within each class LUSCG(f), $f \geq 2$. Let $G = (V_{\mathrm{N}}, V_{\mathrm{T}}, P, S)$ be a (reduced) LUSCG. We first introduce some notions that describe productions of G in terms of derivations in which they can participate.

Definition 5. A production p in P with left-hand tuple $(A_1, \ldots, A_t), t \geq 1$, covers terminal symbol $a \in V_{\mathrm{T}}$ if and only if for any integer $d \geq 1$ there exists a derivation η such that the following conditions are satisfied:

(i) η starts with p and has the form

$$(\gamma_0 A_{\pi(1)} \gamma_1 \cdots \gamma_{t-1} A_{\pi(t)} \gamma_t, I^{(A_1,\ldots,A_t)}) \stackrel{*}{\Rightarrow}_G (\gamma_0 v_1 \gamma_1 \cdots \gamma_{t-1} v_t \gamma_t, I),$$

for some equivalence relation I, where $\gamma_i \in (V_{\mathrm{N}} \cup V_{\mathrm{T}})^*$, $0 \leq i \leq t$, and $v_i \in V_{\mathrm{T}}^*$, $1 \leq i \leq t$;

(ii) string $v_1 \cdots v_t$ includes more than d instances of a.

In the following we will use symbol $\lhd$ to denote the covering relation, and we will take $p \lhd \{a_1, \ldots, a_k\}$ to mean that $p \lhd a_i$ for each i, $1 \leq i \leq k$. Furthermore, we will write $A \lhd a$ if A is a nonterminal in the left-hand tuple of some production p, which is understood from the context, and $p \lhd a$ in such a way that an unbounded number of instances of a are included in the substrings that can be derived by A.

Let $p : (A_1, \ldots, A_t) \to (\alpha_1, \ldots, \alpha_t), t \geq 1$, be a a production in P, and let $a \in V_{\mathrm{T}}$. Consider derivations in G of the form

$$\begin{aligned}(S, I^{(S)}) &\stackrel{*}{\Rightarrow}_G (u_0 A_1 u_1 \cdots u_{t-1} A_t u_t, I_1) \\ &\stackrel{p}{\Rightarrow}_G (u_0 \alpha_1 u_1 \cdots u_{t-1} \alpha_t u_t, I_2) \\ &\stackrel{*}{\Rightarrow}_G (u_0 v_1 u_1 \cdots u_{t-1} v_t u_t, I_3),\end{aligned} \tag{1}$$

where $u_i, v_j \in (V_{\mathrm{T}})^*$. If $p \not\lhd a$, it follows that there exists a constant $M_{p,a}$ such that, for any derivation of the form (1), the number of instances of a in $v_1 v_2 \cdots v_t$ is bounded by $M_{p,a}$. If $p \lhd a$, we assume $M_{p,a} = -1$. We define M_G to be the maximum among all $M_{p,a}$, $p \in P$ and $a \in V_{\mathrm{T}}$. Furthermore, let $L_M(G) = \{w \mid w \in L(G), \#_a(w) > M_G \text{ for every } a \in V_{\mathrm{T}}\}$. A production p of G is called *productive* if p is used in some derivation for some sentence in $L_M(G)$. for some sentence in L_M. This will be used to exclude productions of G that can generate only uninteresting sets of strings.

In what follows we prove a separation for classes r-LUSCG(f), $r \geq 3$. In order to do this, we define a family of languages to which we will henceforth restrict our attention.

Definition 6. Let r and f be two integers, $r, f \geq 1$. Let also $V_{\mathrm{T}}^{(r,f)} = \{a_{i,j} \mid 1 \leq i \leq r, 1 \leq j \leq f\}$ and π_r a permutation of $\{1, 2, \ldots, r\}$ defined as follows. If r is even:

$$\pi_r(i) = \begin{cases} 2i - 1, \; i \in \{1, \ldots, r/2\}; \\ 2i - r, \; i \in \{r/2 + 1, \ldots, r\}. \end{cases}$$

If r is odd:

$$\pi_r(i) = \begin{cases} i, & i \in \{1, r\}; \\ r - 1, & i = (r+1)/2; \\ r - 2(i-1), & i \in \{2, \ldots, (r+1)/2 - 1\}; \\ 2i - r - 1, & i \in \{(r+1)/2 + 1, \ldots, r - 1\}. \end{cases}$$

Language $L_{r,f}$ is specified as follows:

$$L_{r,f} = \{w_1 w_2 \cdots w_f \mid w_1 = a_{1,1}^{i_1} \cdots a_{r,1}^{i_r}, \; w_h = a_{\pi_r(1),h}^{i_{\pi_r(1)}} \cdots a_{\pi_r(r),h}^{i_{\pi_r(r)}}, \; 2 \leq h \leq f, i_j \geq 1, \; 1 \leq j \leq r\}.$$

In the following we call *segment* each substring w_h in the definition of a string in $L_{r,f}$. We will also use $\overline{a_s}$ to denote the set $\{a_{s,1}, a_{s,2} \ldots, a_{s,f}\}$, which we will refer to as a *terminal group* for $L_{r,f}$. The set of all terminal groups for $L_{r,f}$ will be denoted $\mathcal{V}^{(r,f)}$ and, for $r \geq 3$, set $\{\overline{a_i} \mid 2 \leq i \leq r-1\}$ will be denoted $\mathcal{B}^{(r,f)}$. The definition of $\lhd$ extends to a set of sets in the obvious way. We relate previous definitions by means of an example.

Example 2. Language $L_{r,f}$ can be derived by a grammar in $(r-2)$-LUSCG(f), for $f \geq 1$ and $r \geq 4$. Such a grammar is specified as follows:

$$\begin{aligned} G &= (V_{\mathrm{N}}, V_{\mathrm{T}}^{(r,f)}, S, P); \\ P &= \{p_i \mid 1 \leq i \leq 3 + 2r\}; \\ V_{\mathrm{N}} &= \{S\} \cup \{Q_j, R_j \mid 1 \leq j \leq f\} \cup \\ &\quad \{A_{i,j} \mid 1 \leq i \leq r, 1 \leq j \leq f\}; \end{aligned}$$

$$\begin{aligned} p_1 &: (S) \rightarrow (A_{1,1}Q_1 \cdots A_{1,f}Q_f); \\ p_2 &: (Q_1, \ldots, Q_f) \rightarrow (R_1 A_{r,1}, \ldots, R_f A_{r,f}); \\ p_3 &: (R_1, \ldots, R_f) \rightarrow (\alpha^{(1)}, \ldots, \alpha^{(f)}), \quad \alpha^{(1)} = A_{2,1} A_{3,1} \cdots A_{r-1,1}, \\ &\quad \alpha^{(j)} = A_{\pi_r(2),j} A_{\pi_r(3),j} \cdots A_{\pi_r(r-1),j}, \quad 2 \leq j \leq f; \\ p_{3+j} &: (A_{j,1}, \ldots, A_{j,f}) \rightarrow (a_{j,1} A_{j,1}, \ldots, a_{j,f} A_{j,f}), \quad 1 \leq j \leq r; \\ p_{3+r+j} &: (A_{j,1}, \ldots, A_{j,f}) \rightarrow (a_{j,1}, \ldots, a_{j,f}) \quad 1 \leq j \leq r; \end{aligned}$$

We have $\rho(p_1) = \rho(p_2) = 2$, $\rho(p_3) = r - 2$ and $\rho(p_{3+j}) = 1$, $\rho(p_{3+r+j}) = 0$ for $1 \leq j \leq r$; the rank of p_3 determines the rank of G. Observe that p_3 covers $\mathcal{B}^{(r,f)}$.

As a first property of the family $L_{r,f}$, we will show that any grammar in LUSCG that derives $L_{r,f}$ cannot have a production that covers more than one, but fewer than $r - 3$, terminal groups in $\mathcal{B}^{(r,f)}$, for any $r \geq 6$ and $f \geq 2$. In the following discussion, we will be referring to an implicit LUSCG for $L_{r,f}$; hence, for example, whenever we mention a symbol $a_{s,q}$, the ranges of s and q are implicitly stated.

The first lemma shows that for languages $L_{r,f}$, the properties of covering $a_{s,q}$ and of covering $\overline{a_s}$ cannot be distinguished.

Lemma 7. *If a production p covers some $a_{s,q}$, then p covers $\overline{a_s}$.*

Proof. If $f = 1$, the statement trivially holds. For $f > 1$, assume there exists $q' \neq q$ such that p does not cover $a_{s,q'}$. Consider a derivation of the form

$$\begin{aligned}(S, I^{(S)}) &\overset{*}{\Rightarrow}_G (u_0 A_1 u_1 \cdots u_{t-1} A_t u_t, I_1)\\ &\overset{p}{\Rightarrow}_G (u_0 \alpha_1 u_1 \cdots u_{t-1} \alpha_t u_t, I_2)\\ &\overset{*}{\Rightarrow}_G (u_0 v_1 u_1 \cdots u_{t-1} v_t u_t, I_3),\end{aligned} \tag{2}$$

where $u_i, v_j \in (V_{\mathrm{T}}^{(r,f)})^*$, and $t \geq 1$. (Note that such a derivation exists since we assume the grammar to be reduced.) Let m be the number of instances of $a_{s,q'}$ in $u_0 u_1 \cdots u_t$. Since p covers $a_{s,q}$, we can derive a second string in $L_{r,f}$ of the form $u_0 x_1 u_1 \cdots u_{t-1} x_t u_t$, such that the number of instances of $a_{s,q}$ in string $x_1 x_2, \cdots x_t$ exceeds $M_G + m$. Since $a_{s,q'}$ is not covered by p, the number of instances of $a_{s,q'}$ in $x_1 x_2 \cdots x_t$ is bounded by M_G. Then the number of instances of $a_{s,q}$ differs from that of $a_{s,q'}$, contradicting the definition of $L_{r,f}$.

Next we show that whenever a nonterminal A in the left-hand tuple of a productive production p covers two different symbols $a_{s,q}$ and $a_{s,q'}$, that is, two symbols belonging to the same terminal group but to different segments, then p covers the whole of $V_{\mathrm{T}}^{(r,f)}$. We prove the result in two steps.

Let a and b be two symbols in $V_{\mathrm{T}}^{(r,f)}$. Observe that, for any string w in $L_{r,f}$, the set of all terminal symbols occurring between a and b in w (including a and b) is always the same. We will call such a set the *in-between set* of a and b. From the definition of $L_{r,f}$ it follows that if a' is in the in-between set of a and b, $a' \neq a$ and $a' \neq b$, then in any string in $L_{r,f}$, all instances of a' occur between instances of a and instances of b.

Lemma 8. *Let $r \geq 2$ and let p be a productive production such that a nonterminal symbol A in the left-hand tuple of p covers (by means of p) set $\{a, b\} \subseteq V_{\mathrm{T}}^{(r,f)}$. Then p covers the in-between set of a and b.*

Proof. If the in-between set of a and b is $\{a, b\}$, the lemma holds trivially. Let a' be in the in-between set of a and b, $a' \notin \{a, b\}$, and suppose that p cannot generate more than M_G instances of a'. Since p is productive, there exists a sentential derivation using p that derives a string in $L_{r,f}$ which has more than M_G occurrences of a'. Such a derivation can be represented as

$$\begin{aligned}(S, I^{(S)}) &\overset{*}{\Rightarrow}_G (u_0 A_1 u_1 \cdots u_{k-1} A_k u_k \cdots u_{t-1} A_t u_t, I_1)\\ &\overset{p}{\Rightarrow}_G (u_0 \alpha_1 u_1 \cdots u_{k-1} \alpha_k u_k \cdots u_{t-1} \alpha_t u_t, I_2)\\ &\overset{*}{\Rightarrow}_G (u_0 v_1 u_1 \cdots u_{k-1} v_k u_k \cdots u_{t-1} v_t u_t, I_3),\end{aligned} \tag{3}$$

where $A = A_k$, $u_i, v_j \in (V_{\mathrm{T}}^{(r,f)})^*$, and $t \geq 1$. Since $p \not\triangleleft a'$ by assumption, there must be instances of a' in $u_0 u_1 \cdots u_t$. A_k generates a and b by means of p; we can therefore derive a second string in $L_{r,f}$ having the form $w =$

$u_0x_1u_1 \cdots u_{k-1}x_ku_k \cdots u_{t-1}x_tu_t$, such that x_k contains instances of a and b. But then we have instances of a' in w not occurring between a and b: this contradicts the definition of $L_{r,f}$.

We can now prove the previously mentioned result.

Lemma 9. *Let $f \geq 2$ and $r \geq 2$. If a nonterminal A from the left-hand tuple of a productive production p covers both $a_{s,q}$ and $a_{s,q'}$ in $V_{\mathrm{T}}^{(r,f)}$, for some s and $q < q'$, then p covers $\mathcal{V}^{(r,f)}$.*

Proof. Since $a_{r,q}$ and $a_{1,q+1}$ are in the in-between set of $a_{s,q}$ and $a_{s,q'}$, p must cover both $a_{r,q}$ and $a_{1,q+1}$ by Lemma 8. By Lemma 7, p must cover $\overline{a_1}$ and $\overline{a_r}$. If one nonterminal B from the left-hand tuple of p covers more than one member of $\overline{a_1}$, say $a_{1,u}$ and $a_{1,u'}$, then by Lemma 8 we have $p \lhd a_{j,u}$ for $1 \leq j \leq r$, and we are done by Lemma 7. Suppose instead that each nonterminal from the left-hand tuple of p covers exactly one member of $\overline{a_1}$. Let B be the nonterminal that covers $a_{q,1}$. If B covers any member of $\overline{a_r}$, then it must cover $a_{r,1}$. By Lemmas 8 and 7, we are done. Suppose instead that B does not cover any member of $\overline{a_r}$. Then there must be a nonterminal from the left-hand tuple of p which covers two members of $\overline{a_r}$, say $a_{r,u}$ and $a_{r,u'}$. Then by Lemma 8, p covers $a_{j,u'}$ for $1 \leq j \leq r$, and we are done by Lemma 7.

We now use previous results to derive a basic property of productive productions in G that will be used to show the major result.

Lemma 10. *Let $f \geq 2$ and $r \geq 6$. If a productive production p covers more than one terminal group in $\mathcal{B}^{(r,f)}$, then p covers $\mathcal{B}^{(r,f)}$.*

Proof. Assume that $(A_1, \ldots, A_t)$, $t \geq 1$, is the left-hand tuple of p. First we show that under the above hypotheses, if $p \lhd \{\overline{a_s}, \overline{a_{s'}}\}$ for $\overline{a_s}, \overline{a_{s'}} \in \mathcal{B}^{(r,f)}$, $s < s'$, then the only interesting case for us is $t = f$ and $A_i \lhd \{a_{s,i}, a_{s',i}\}$ for $1 \leq i \leq f$. Since p is productive, if any nonterminal A in the left-hand tuple of p covers $\{a_{s,q}, a_{s,q'}\}$, $q \neq q'$, then by Lemma 9 p covers all of the terminal groups in $\mathcal{V}^{(r,f)}$. The remaining possibility is that $t = f$ and for all i, $1 \leq i \leq f$, A_i covers exactly one terminal in $\overline{a_s}$ and exactly one terminal in $\overline{a_{s'}}$. W.l.o.g. we may assume that $A_i \lhd a_{s,i}$, $1 \leq i \leq f$. ¿From the definition of $L_{r,f}$, it follows that $A_i \lhd a_{s',i}$, $1 \leq i \leq f$. In the following, we will therefore deal only with the case $A_i \lhd \{a_{s,i}, a_{s',i}\}$ for $1 \leq i \leq f$.

Since A_1 covers both $a_{s,1}$ and $a_{s',1}$ by means of p and since p is productive, by Lemma 8 we conclude that p must also cover $a_{s+1,1}$, and hence $\overline{a_{s+1}}$ by Lemma 7. Again we restrict our attention to the only interesting case in which $A_i \lhd \{a_{s,i}, a_{s+1,i}\}$, $1 \leq i \leq f$. We now show that $p \lhd \{a_{r-1,2}, a_{2,2}\}$ by investigating the case $i = 2$. We distinguish three cases.

Case 1: r is even. It can be seen from the definition of $L_{r,f}$ that $a_{r-1,2}$ and $a_{2,2}$ are in the in-between set of $a_{s,2}$ and $a_{s+1,2}$. Since p is productive, we have that p covers $\{a_{r-1,2}, a_{2,2}\}$ by Lemma 8.

Case 2: r is odd and $s \neq r-2$. It again follows from from the definition of $L_{r,f}$

and from Lemma 8 that $p \lhd \{a_{r-1,2}, a_{2,2}\}$.
Case 3: r is odd and $s = r - 2$. Then $A_2 \lhd \{a_{r-2,2}, a_{r-1,2}\}$. By Lemma 8 and from the definition of $L_{r,f}$, p must also cover $a_{3,2}$; by Lemma 7 p covers $\overline{a_3}$. One more time we restrict our attention to the case in which $A_1 \lhd a_{3,1}$ and $A_1 \lhd a_{s,1}$. Since $s \geq 4$, we can apply the same reasoning to see that p covers $\overline{a_4}$. But since $3 \neq r - 2$, we are now in Case 2.

We may conclude that $p \lhd \{a_{r-1,2}, a_{2,2}\}$. By Lemma 7, $a_{2,1}$ and $a_{r-1,1}$ must also be covered by p. The only interesting case is if they are covered by A_1. But then by Lemma 8 $p \lhd \{a_{j,1} | 2 \leq j \leq r - 1\}$, and we are done by Lemma 7.

The following last lemma presents a property of derivations in G that will be used to "factorize" sentential derivations for sentences in L_M. We need to introduce two additional notions. Let p be a production whose left-hand tuple is $(A_1, \ldots, A_t)$, $t \leq f$. Assume the existence of a sentential derivation of the form

$$(S, I^{(S)}) \overset{*}{\Rightarrow}_G (u_0 A_1 u_1 \cdots u_{t-1} A_t u_t, I^{(A_1, \ldots, A_t)}),$$

where $u_i \in (V_{\mathrm{T}}^{(r,f)})^*$. Then $u_0 A_1 u_1 \cdots u_{t-1} A_t u_t$ is called a *p-factorized* sentential form. Let a, b, c be different symbols in $V_{\mathrm{T}}^{(r,f)}$. We say that b is *isolated* in the above sentential form whenever, for strings $x, y, v, z \in (V_{\mathrm{T}}^{(r,f)})^*$, one of the following conditions is realized: (i) $u_0 = xbycv$, (ii) $u_j = xaybvcz$ for some j, $1 \leq j \leq t - 1$, or (iii) $u_t = xaybv$. Note that whenever a terminal symbol a is isolated in a p-factorized sentential form, then p cannot generate a.

Lemma 11. *Let $f \geq 2$, $r \geq 6$. Let p be a productive production such that $p \lhd \mathcal{B}^{(r,f)}$ and let $u_0 A_1 u_1 \cdots u_{t-1} A_t u_t$, $t \leq f$, be a p-factorized sentential form. Then for every terminal group $\overline{a} \in \mathcal{B}^{(r,f)}$ there exists a terminal symbol $a \in \overline{a}$ such that a is not found in string $u_0 u_1 \cdots u_t$.*

Proof. For the sake of contradiction, assume that $u_0 u_1 \cdots u_t$ contains instances of every terminal symbol in some $\overline{a_s} \in \mathcal{B}^{(r,f)}$. First of all, we claim that no u_i, $0 \leq i \leq t$, can contain two different terminals from $\overline{a_s}$. From the definition of $L_{r,f}$ it can be seen that for any $a_{s,q}, a_{s,q'}$ in $\overline{a_s}$, $q \neq q'$, the in-between set of $a_{s,q}$ and $a_{s,q'}$ contains at least one terminal b from some $\overline{a_{s'}} \in \mathcal{B}^{(r,f)}$, $s' \neq s$. If $a_{s,q}$ and $a_{s,q'}$ are included in u_i, then b will be isolated in the p-factorized sentential form and p could not generate b, contrary to the hypotheses. This proves our claim.

Let $l = \pi^{-1}(r - 1)$, i.e., $l = r - 2$ if r is even, $l = r - 3$ if r is odd. To prove the lemma, we will distinguish three cases.
Case 1: $s \notin \{2, l\}$. If any $a_{s,q} \in \overline{a_s}$ is included in u_0, then $a_{2,1}$ to its left will be isolated and p could not generate $a_{2,1}$, contrary to the hypotheses. Similarly, if any $a_{s,q}$ is included in u_t, then $a_{l,f}$ to its right will be isolated and p could not generate $a_{l,f}$, again a contradiction. We conclude therefore that terminals in $\overline{a_s}$ are all contained within $u_1 \cdots u_{t-1}$. Since $t \leq f$, there will be some u_i, $1 \leq i \leq t - 1$, which contains two different terminals from $\overline{a_s}$, contradicting our claim.

Case 2: $s = 2$. If any $a_{2,q} \in \overline{a_2}$ is contained in u_t, then $a_{l,f}$ to its right will be isolated and p could not generate such a symbol. ¿From our claim and the definition of $L_{r,f}$, it follows that $t = f$ and each $a_{2,q}$ is contained in u_{q-1} for $1 \leq q \leq f$. Consider now A_1. Since p covers $\mathcal{B}^{(r,f)}$ and u_1 contains $a_{2,2}$, A_1 must cover at least $a_{2,1}$ and $a_{3,2}$ (which occur to the left of $a_{2,2}$ in strings of $L_{r,f}$). Since p is productive, by Lemma 8 p covers the in-between set of $a_{2,1}$ and $a_{3,2}$, which includes $a_{1,2}$; therefore p covers $\overline{a_1}$ by Lemma 7. But this is impossible, since u_0 must contain at least one instance of $a_{1,1}$ to the left of $a_{2,1}$, which is therefore isolated.
Case 3: $s = l$. If any $a_{l,q} \in \overline{a_l}$ is contained in u_0, then $a_{2,1}$ to its left will be isolated and p could not generate such a symbol. Again it follows from our claim that $t = f$ and each $a_{l,q}$ is contained in u_q, for $1 \leq q \leq f$. Consider A_2. Since p covers $\mathcal{B}^{(r,f)}$, u_1 contains $a_{l,1}$ and u_2 contains $a_{l,2}$, A_2 must cover at least $a_{r-1,1}$ and $a_{3,2}$ (which occur in between $a_{l,1}$ and $a_{l,2}$ in strings of $L_{r,f}$). Since p is productive, by Lemma 8 p covers the in-between set of $a_{r-1,1}$ and $a_{3,2}$, which includes $a_{r,1}$; therefore p covers $\overline{a_r}$ by Lemma 7. This is impossible, because u_f must contain at least one instance of $a_{r,f}$ to the right of $a_{l,f}$, which is therefore isolated.

Let p be a production satisfying the hypotheses of Lemma 11 and let p', p'' be any pair of productions that can simultaneously be used to rewrite the right-hand tuple of p. As a consequence of Lemma 11, we have that whenever p' covers $\mathcal{B}^{(r,f)}$, p'' cannot cover any terminal group in $\mathcal{B}^{(r,f)}$. This observation will be used in the proof of the following theorem, which refers to all previous results. The theorem shows that, for all sentences w in some subset of $L_{r,f}$, any derivation in G of w can be partitioned into two parts. In a sense to be made more precise below, the first part of the derivation cannot generate all of some terminal symbols in the terminal groups in $\mathcal{B}^{(r,f)}$, while the second part of the derivation uses productions that do cover $\mathcal{B}^{(r,f)}$.

Theorem 12. *Let $f \geq 2$, $r \geq 6$. Then we have $L_{r,f} \in \mathcal{L}((r-2)\text{-LUSCG}(f)) - \mathcal{L}((r-3)\text{-LUSCG}(f))$.*

Proof. A grammar in $(r-2)$-LUSCG(f) that derives $L_{r,f}$ has been presented in Example 2. To prove the statement, we show that the existence of $G \in (r-3)$-LUSCG(f) such that $L(G) = L_{r,f}$ leads to a contradiction.

Let Δ_G be the maximum number of terminal symbols in the right-hand tuple of a production of G. Let w be a sentence in $L_{r,f}$ such that $\#_a(w) > (r-3) \cdot M_G + \Delta_G$ for every $a \in V_T^{(r,f)}$, and let also ρ be a derivation in G for w. Note that every production in ρ is productive. We uniquely identify a production used in ρ in the following way. Let p_1 be the first production used in ρ, i.e., ρ has the form $(S, I^{(S)}) \overset{p_1}{\Rightarrow}_G (\alpha, I^{(\alpha)}) \overset{*}{\Rightarrow}_G (w, I')$. Observe that S is a p_1-factorized sentential form and, by the choice of w, p_1 covers $\mathcal{B}^{(r,f)}$. Let $p_{1,1}, \ldots, p_{1,k_1}$, $1 \leq k_1 \leq r-3$, be the sequence of productions used in ρ to rewrite the right-hand tuple of p_1. As already observed, Lemma 11 entails that at most one production in such a sequence can cover $\mathcal{B}^{(r,f)}$. If such a production exists, we call it p_2. We iterate the step until we arrive at some production p_l, $l \geq 1$, used in ρ such that p_l covers $\mathcal{B}^{(r,f)}$ and none of the productions that are used in ρ to rewrite the right-hand tuple of p_l covers $\mathcal{B}^{(r,f)}$.

Let $u_0A_1u_1 \cdots u_{t-1}A_tu_t$ be the p_l-factorized sentential form defined by p_l. Since p_l is productive, we invoke Lemma 11 and conclude that for every terminal group $\overline{a_s} \in \mathcal{B}^{(r,f)}$ there exists a terminal a_{s,q_s} that is not contained within string $u_0u_1 \cdots u_t$. Hence, more than $(r-3) \cdot M_G + \Delta_G$ instances of each a_{s,q_s}, $2 \leq s \leq r-1$, are generated under ρ from the non-terminals in the right-hand tuple of p_l. Now let $p_{l,1}, \ldots, p_{l,k_l}$, $1 \leq k_l \leq r-3$, be the sequence of productions used in ρ to rewrite the right-hand tuple of p_l. The right-hand tuple of p_l itself cannot contain more than Δ_G instances of each a_{s,q_s}, and therefore $p_{l,1}, \ldots, p_{l,k_l}$ must generate more than $(r-3) \cdot M_G$ instances of each a_{s,q_s}. Since $k_l \leq r-3$, by a counting argument we conclude that for each s, $2 \leq s \leq r-1$, there must be at least one $p_{l,i}$, $1 \leq i \leq k_l$, such that $p_{l,i}$ covers a_{s,q_s}. By Lemma 7, $p_{l,i}$ covers $\overline{a_s}$. Again by a counting argument, we derive that at least one production $p_{l,i}$, $1 \leq i \leq k_l$, covers two terminal groups in $\mathcal{B}^{(r,f)}$. Since $p_{l,i}$ is productive, it covers $\mathcal{B}^{(r,f)}$ by Lemma 10. This contradicts the choice of production p_l: we conclude that there can be no derivation in G for w, that is, grammar G does not exist.

We now turn to subclasses 1-LUSCG(f), 2-LUSCG(f) and 3-LUSCG(f), $f \geq 2$. Proofs of the following results are conceptually simpler than the proof of the main theorem above and are not reported here; they can be found in [7]. The next result is proved by exhibiting a construction that transforms any grammar in 3-LUSCG(2) into one in 2-LUSCG(2), without altering the derived language.

Theorem 13. $\mathcal{L}$(2-LUSCG(2)) = $\mathcal{L}$(3-LUSCG(2)).

The following theorem is proved in [7] introducing a second family of languages whose strings consist of segments with three different permutations of the same symbols (compare with $L_{r,f}$). Properties similar to the ones introduced by Lemmas 7 to 11 can then be shown in order to prove the following result.

Theorem 14. *Let f be an integer, $f \geq 3$. Then $\mathcal{L}$(2-LUSCG(f)) is properly included in $\mathcal{L}$(3-LUSCG(f)).*

Finally, separation between subclasses $\mathcal{L}$(1-LUSCG(f)) and $\mathcal{L}$(2-LUSCG(f)) can be proved by exhibiting a context-free language that is contained in $\mathcal{L}$(2-LUSCG(1)) but not in any of the subclasses $\mathcal{L}$(1-LUSCG(f)), $f \geq 1$.

Theorem 15. *Let $f \geq 1$. Then $\mathcal{L}$(1-LUSCG(f)) is properly included in $\mathcal{L}$(2-LUSCG(f)).*

4 Discussion and Remarks

By combining two independent complexity measures, we have obtained interesting separation results for subclasses of LUSCG. The technique we have adopted has been inspired by a technique used in [1] to prove the existence of an infinite non-collapsing hierarchy induced by the rank in non-simple syntax-directed translation schemata (SDTS). As already discussed in Section 2, we can view DTWT as generative devices controlled by the class of recognizable tree languages. In this way, Theorem 4 can be used to transfer our separation result to subclasses DTWT(f), for $f \geq 2$. This in turn can be combined with already known properties of the class DTWT, in order to derive interesting language-theoretic consequences that are summarized below and have been reported in a longer version of this paper ([7]).

In [7] it is shown that the languages generated by the subclass r-DTWT(f) form a substitution-closed full AFL for $r \geq 2$ and $f \geq 1$. Using the results of Section 3, it is easy to show that the class of languages generated by each DTWT(f), $f \geq 2$, is not a full principal AFL. This solves in the negative a question left open in [6].[3]

It is not difficult to show that every language generated by the class DTWT(1) can be also generated by some translator in 2-DTWT(1). This implies that a normal form can be defined for devices in DTWT(1) by imposing some bound on the rank. Our result shows that for subclasses DTWT(f), $f \geq 2$, such normal forms are not admitted. This answers a question left open in [2].

In [7] it is shown that subclasses r-DTWT, $r \geq 2$, generate all the same languages. Given our result, this means that in DTWT we can trade the rank resource with the crossing number resource. Furthermore, we have already mentioned in the introduction that there exist languages generated by 1-DTWT(f) but not by DTWT($f-1$), for any $f \geq 2$. Combining this fact with our separation result, we get a two-dimensional hierarchy for DTWT, whose elements are subclasses r-DTWT(f), $r, f \geq 1$: such hierarchy does not collapse in either of its two dimensions.

The class DTWT is closely related to the class of finite copying top-down tree-to-string transducers (yT_{fc}) of [6]. These systems take a tree as input and convert it into a string, through a series of elementary rewrite step. Each rewrite step consumes the root node of a tree in the sentential form, and rearranges the subtrees that are immediately dominated, interleaving them with terminal strings. Crucially, only a finite number of copies of each subtree can be produced during the rewriting process. Again we can restrict our attention to the input class of recognizable tree languages, and view yT_{fc} as (controlled) generative devices. It turns out that the resulting class is weakly equivalent to DTWT, as discussed in [6]. Moreover, the equivalence relation preserves the rank of the two input tree languages and matches the finite copying degree with the crossing number. Hence, the two dimensional hierarchy discussed above is also found for subclasses of yT_{fc} induced by the rank and the copying degree parameters.

Finally, the two dimensional hierarchy result can also be transferred to the string generating context-free hypergraph grammars of [3] and to the multiple context-free grammars of [8]. In particular, for context-free hypergraph gram-

[3] We are grateful to Joost Engelfriet for drawing our attention to the relevance of our result to this issue.

mars we have found a match between the crossing number and the rank parameters in DTWT, and the maximum number of tentacles in the hyperedges and the maximum number of nonterminals in productions of the hypergraph grammar; details can be found in [7].

References

1. A. V. Aho and J. D. Ullman. Properties of syntax directed translations. *Journal of Computer and System Science*, 3(3):319–334, 1969.
2. A. V. Aho and J. D. Ullman. Translations on a context-free grammar. *Information and Control*, 19:439–475, 1971.
3. M. Bauderon and B. Courcelle. Graph expressions and graph rewritings. *Mathematical Systems Theory*, 20:83–127, 1987.
4. J. Dassow and G. Păun. *Regulated Rewriting in Formal Language Theory.* Springer-Verlag, Berlin, Germany, 1989.
5. J. Engelfriet and L. Heyker. The string generating power of context-free hypergraph grammars. *Journal of Computer and System Science*, 43:328–360, 1991.
6. J. Engelfriet, G. Rozenberg, and G. Slutzki. Tree transducers, L systems, and two-way machines. *Journal of Computer and System Science*, 20:150–202, 1980.
7. O. Rambow and G. Satta. A two-dimensional hierarchy for finite copying parallel rewriting systems. Technical report, Institute for Research in Cognitive Science, University of Pennsylvania, Philadelphia, PA, 1994.
8. H. Seki, T. Matsumura, M. Fujii, and T. Kasami. On multiple context-free grammars. *Theoretical Computer Science*, 88:191–229, 1991.
9. J. W. Thatcher. Tree automata: An informal survey. In A. V. Aho, editor, *Currents in the Theory of Computing*, chapter 4, pages 143–172. Prentice-Hall, Englewood Cliffs, NJ, 1973.
10. D. J. Weir. *Characterizing Mildly Context-Sensitive Grammar Formalisms.* PhD thesis, Department of Computer and Information Science, University of Pennsylvania, 1988.
11. D. J. Weir. Linear context-free rewriting systems and deterministic tree-walk transducers. In *Proc. of the 30th Meeting of the Association for Computational Linguistics (ACL'92)*, Newark, Delaware, 1992.

Superposition in Picture Languages*

Bodonirina Ratoandromanana and Denis Robilliard

LIFL, Université de Lille I,
59655 Villeneuve d'Ascq Cedex, France.
E-mail: robillia@lifl.fr

Abstract. A word on alphabet $\pi = \{u, r, d, l\}$ can be thought of as a description of a connected picture drawn on a square grid: each letter is associated with a unit move of a pen, u coding a move up, r, d and l coding moves to the right, down and to the left. We define the notion of *superposition* of two pictures f and g as the set of pictures obtained when one draws first f and then g with the sole constraint that the resulting picture must be connected. We show that superposition does not preserve regularity of classical chain-code picture languages, as defined by Maurer and al. [12]. On the other hand, we prove, using constructive methods, that regular descriptive "branch-picture" languages, introduced by Gutbrod [8], are closed under superposition and iterated superposition.

1 Introduction

A word over $\pi = \{u, r, d, l\}$ can be understood as a program controlling a plotter or a CRT and thus describing a path on a grid-like graph. To each symbol of the alphabet $\pi = \{u, r, d, l\}$ we give the following meaning:

u : perform a drawing move up, until reaching the next vertex of the grid,
r : same as above, but moving to the right,
d : same as above, but moving down,
l : same as above, but moving to the left.

If we call picture (or also *basic* picture) a finite set of unit lines drawn on the grid, then the trace of a word in π^* corresponds to a picture, which is connected. This kind of coding is akin to the "chain-code" concept created by Freeman [7], and it enables the easy implementation of operations such as translation or up-scaling by an integer factor. The systematic study of languages over π^* was initiated by Maurer et al. [12], using methods and knowledge from formal language theory. It has inspired a trend of research, including works on geometrical properties of pictures (see [5, 6]), extensions of the encoding system ([9, 8]), complexity issues ([10, 11]), minimalization of words representing a given picture ([14, 13, 4]), and also problems related to polyominoes and tilings ([3, 2, 1, 15]).

* This research was partially supported by "GDR Mathématiques et Informatique" and ESPRIT Basic Research Action 6317 ASMICS 2

Using words to encode pictures has given birth to the notion of *drawn* picture, that is with start and end point, as opposed to basic pictures which do not include such informations dependent on the coding. There is an obvious relationship between the concatenation of chain-code picture words and the concatenation of drawn pictures (see [12]), but there is no similar concept when dealing with basic pictures, as they do not have distinguished points where to link them together. We have chosen to take the point of view of the graphic user (sketcher, artist), who rather thinks in terms of the rough, basic pictures, and then to define intuitive operations on these objects, in order to examine the adequacy of the classical encoding and of some of its refinements. Hence we propose an operator, called superposition, which realize an intuitive notion of "concatenation" of basic pictures: the superposition of two pictures f and g is the set of pictures obtained when first drawing f and then g, in such a way that the resulting picture is connected. We extend it to languages: let $\mathcal{F}$ and $\mathcal{G}$ two picture languages, then $\mathcal{F} \odot \mathcal{G} = \bigcup_{f,g} f \odot g$, with $f \in \mathcal{F}$ et $g \in \mathcal{G}$. We then show that this operator does not preserve regularity of chain code picture languages on π.

Next, we examine superposition within the frame of so-called "branch picture languages" (BPL) introduced by Roger Gutbrod [8]. Two symbols (# and \$) are added to alphabet π, with the following meaning: # means "stack the coordinates of the current vertex of the grid", and \$ means "extract the coordinates of the last vertex stored on the stack, and put the pen on this vertex" (there is no drawing while perfoming this move). A language on $\sigma = \{u, r, d, l, \#, \$\}$ is said to be *descriptive* if and only if it is well parenthesized on the pair of symbols $\{\#, \$\}$. If a regular language L over σ is descriptive then the maximum level of parenthesis of the words in L is bounded, whence L can be described with a stack of bounded depth, thus preserving implementation efficiency. In this paper, we prove that regular descriptive BPL are closed under superposition and iterated superposition.

This work intends to develop the study of operators performing on basic pictures. It confirms the adequacy and expressive power of the BPL formalism.

2 Preliminaries

2.1 Classical Chain-Code Picture Languages

Here we give a short remind of the basics of classical chain-code picture languages. For more details, the reader can refer to [12].

Let $p = (x, y)$ be a *vertex* of the discrete Cartesian plane considered as a square grid, let the alphabet $\pi = \{u, r, d, l\}$, the *up-neighbor*, respectively right, down and left, of p is $\mathrm{sh}(u, p) = (x, y + 1)$, respectively $\mathrm{sh}(r, p) = (x + 1, y)$, $\mathrm{sh}(d, p) = (x, y - 1)$ et $\mathrm{sh}(l, p) = (x - 1, y)$ (sh comes from *shift*). A *unit line* is defined by a non ordered pair of vertices $s = \{p, \mathrm{sh}(x, p)\}$, with $x \in \pi$. A *picture* is a finite set of unit lines. A picture language is a set of pictures.

A word $w \in \pi^*$ is called a *chain-code picture word*. A left to right parsing of w describes a path on the grid. If we start from vertex p, the position of the pen after drawing word wx, $w \in \pi^*$, $x \in \pi$, is recursively defined by: $\mathrm{sh}(wx, p) = \mathrm{sh}(x, \mathrm{sh}(w, p))$, with $\mathrm{sh}(\lambda, p) = p$ for the empty word λ.

The inverse of word $w \in \pi^*$, denoted $\overline{w}$, is recursively defined by: $\overline{\lambda} = \lambda$, $\overline{wu} = d\overline{w}$, $\overline{wr} = l\overline{w}$, $\overline{wd} = u\overline{w}$, $\overline{wl} = r\overline{w}$, with $w \in \pi^*$.

The *(basic) picture* represented by, or associated with, a chain-code picture word wx, starting from vertex p is recursively defined by: $\mathrm{bpic}(wx, p) = \{\{\mathrm{sh}(x, \mathrm{sh}(w, p)),\ \mathrm{sh}(w, p)\}\} \cup \mathrm{bpic}(w, p)$ and $\mathrm{bpic}(\lambda, p) = \emptyset$, with $w \in \pi^*$ and $x \in \pi$. The *drawn picture* represented by, or associated with, a chain-code picture word w, starting from vertex p is: $\mathrm{dpic}(w, p) = \{\mathrm{bpic}(w, p), p, \mathrm{sh}(w, p)\}$ (i.e. it is the triple made of the basic picture and the start and end vertices of the drawing). The *semi-drawn picture* represented by, or associated with, a chain-code picture word w, starting from vertex p is: $\mathrm{spic}(w, p) = \{\mathrm{bpic}(w, p), p\}$ (i.e. it is the basic picture and the start vertex of the drawing; this notion is slightly different from the one found in [8]).

Notice that a non empty picture can be represented by an infinity of chain code picture words, and that two chain code picture words can have same basic picture but different drawn pictures (see Fig. 1).

associated to word *urdrl* associated to infinite language $urdr(lr)^*$

○ *specifies the start vertex,* □ *specifies the end vertex.*

Fig. 1. examples of drawn pictures.

The integer translation $\mathrm{tr}_{m,n}(x, y) = (x + m, y + n)$ allows the definition of equivalence classes of basic pictures. Similarly, with a word w we associate the standard drawn (respectively semi-drawn) picture, which has its start vertex at the origin of the grid: $\mathrm{dpic}(w) = \{\mathrm{bpic}(w, (0, 0)), \mathrm{sh}(w, (0, 0))\}$ (respectively $\mathrm{spic}(w) = \mathrm{bpic}(w, (0, 0)))$; we no longer mention the start vertex. For the sake of convenience, we also write $\mathrm{sh}(w)$ instead of $\mathrm{sh}(w, (0, 0))$, and we make no distinction between equivalence classes and their standard representatives.

A picture language $\mathcal{F}$ is regular if and only if there exists a regular chain-code picture language F such that $\mathrm{bpic}(F) = \{\mathrm{bpic}(w) \mid w \in F\} = \mathcal{F}$.

Let f be a picture, we denote by $\mathrm{des}_\pi(f)$ the set $\{w \in \pi^* \mid \mathrm{bpic}(w) = f\}$; in words, it is the set of words describing picture f. This notion is extended to languages : let $\mathcal{F}$ be a picture language, then $\mathrm{des}_\pi(\mathcal{F}) = \{w \in \pi^* \mid \mathrm{bpic}(w) \in \mathcal{F}\}$. It is worth noting that for all picture f, $\mathrm{des}_\pi(f)$ is a regular set (see [12]) but if $\mathcal{F}$ is a regular picture language then $\mathrm{des}_\pi(\mathcal{F})$ is not always regular.

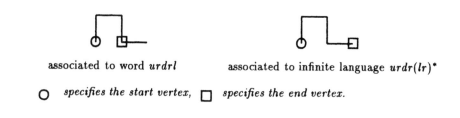

2.2 Branch Picture Languages

We give here an overview of branch picture languages (BPL). The reader is directed to [8] for a more complete survey.

Chain code picture words, within the frame of BPL, are defined over alphabet $\sigma = \{u, r, d, l, \#, \$\}$. The symbol # means "put on the stack the coordinates of the current vertex of the grid", and \$ means "extract the coordinates of the last vertex stored on the stack, and put the pen on this vertex" (there is no drawing while performing this move, so no unit lines are added to the picture). More formally:

Let $w \in \sigma^*$, the set of stack reduced words, denoted by $\mathrm{sred}(w)$, is defined by the following properties:

- $w \in \mathrm{sred}(w)$,
- If $w' = w_1\#w_2\$w_3 \in \mathrm{sred}(w)$, with $w_2 \in \pi^*$, then $w_1 w_2 \overline{w_2} w_3 \in \mathrm{sred}(w)$.

For all $w \in \sigma^*$, there exists at most only one word in $\mathrm{sred}(w) \cap \pi^*$. If this word exists, it is denoted by $\mathrm{sf}(w)$ (*stack free word*), and we have: $\mathrm{bpic}(w) = \mathrm{bpic}(\mathrm{sf}(w))$ (similarly for dpic and spic).

associated to word $rr\#u\#l\$r\$rr\#u\$rr$

• *specifies a branch point.*

Fig. 2. example of picture with branches.

A picture language $\mathcal{F}$ is said B-regular if and only if there exists a regular BPL of chain code picture words F such that $\mathrm{bpic}(F) = \mathcal{F}$.

A word is *descriptive* if it is well parenthesized on the symbols {#,\$}, i.e. if $\mathrm{sred}(w) \cap \pi^* \neq \emptyset$. A BPL L is descriptive if and only if every word in L is descriptive.

The depth of the stack needed to draw a picture is an important concept. Thus we define the following languages:

- $\mathrm{ST}_{-1} = \emptyset$,
- $\mathrm{ST}_0 = \pi^*$,
- $\mathrm{ST}_{n+1} = (\mathrm{ST}_n\#\mathrm{ST}_n\$)^*\mathrm{ST}_n$
- $\sigma_d = \bigcup_{i \geq 0} \mathrm{ST}_i$.

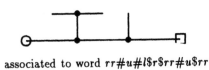

The degree of a BPL L is the smallest integer n such that $L \cap \sigma_d \subseteqq \mathrm{ST}_n$. The degree of a picture language $\mathcal{L}$ is the smallest of the degree of the BPL L such that $\mathcal{L} = \mathrm{bpic}(L)$. This notion of degree can naturally be extended to B-regular, B-Context-Free, drawn, semi-drawn picture languages, ...

The following two assertions are from [8]. They point to some relationship between degree and descriptivity.

Proposition 1. *A* BPL L *is descriptive if and only if* $L \subseteqq \sigma_d$.

Proposition 2. *Let* L *be a regular descriptive* BPL, *then* $\exists n \geq 0$ *such that* $L \subseteqq \mathrm{ST}_n$.

2.3 New Definitions about BPL

The notion of inverse must be redefined in the BPL. We can't draw the unit lines in reverse order, due to the jumps performed at every \$ symbol. We define the inverse by reversing all factors at depth 0, and leaving the rest unaffected. Thus if $w = r\#u\$r\#ur\#u\$r\$r$, then $\overline{w} = l\#ur\#u\$r\$l\#u\$l$. More formally:

Definition 3. Let L be a regular descriptive BPL of depth p, recognized by automaton $R =< \sigma, Q, F, q_0, \delta >$, then:

$$\overline{L} = n^{-1}(s(\mathrm{Mirror}(t^{-1}(\$_1 n(L)\#_1)))) \ .$$

with n, s and t being three transducers:

- n numbers parenthesis depending on the depth at which they appear, e.g.: $u\#r\$u\#l\#u\$l\$u$ gives $u\#_1 r\$_1 u\#_1 l\#_2 u\$_2 l\$_1 u$ (it is possible because the degree of regular descriptive BPL is bounded).
- $s : \begin{cases} a_{qq'} \rightarrow \overline{\mathrm{proj}_{/\pi}(R_{qq'})} \\ b_{qq'} \rightarrow E(R_{qq'}) \end{cases}$
  with E a morphism swapping $\#_1$ and $\$_1$, and $\mathrm{proj}_{/\pi}$ the projection on alphabet π.
- $t : \begin{cases} a_{qq'} \rightarrow R_{qq'} \cap (\$_1 \pi^* \#_1) \\ b_{qq'} \rightarrow R_{qq'} \cap (\#_1 \gamma^* \$_1) \end{cases}$
  with $\gamma =$ any letter or numbered parenthesis except $\#_1, \$_1$.

Proposition 4. *The inverse of a regular descriptive* BPL *is a regular descriptive* BPL.

Proof. Obvious from the definition of the inverse of a BPL. □

Definition 5. Let f be a picture, we denote by $\mathrm{des}_\sigma(f)$ the set $\{w \in \sigma^* \mid \mathrm{bpic}(w) = f\}$. Let $\mathcal{F}$ be a picture language, then $\mathrm{des}_\sigma(\mathcal{F}) = \{w \in \sigma^* \mid \mathrm{bpic}(w) \in \mathcal{F}\}$.

2.4 Superposition

Definition 6. Let f and g be two basic pictures, we define the superposition of f and g by:

$$f \odot g = \{h = f \cup \mathrm{tr}_{m,n}(g) \mid h \text{ is connected, and } m, n \in \mathbb{N}\} \ .$$

It is convenient to also have a definition in terms of picture words, so:

Definition 7. Let w_1 and w_2 be two picture words on σ, then:

$$\begin{aligned} \mathrm{bpic}(w_1) \odot \mathrm{bpic}(w_2) &= \mathrm{bpic}(\ \mathrm{des}_\pi(\mathrm{bpic}(w_1))\ \mathrm{des}_\pi(\mathrm{bpic}(w_2))) \\ &= \mathrm{bpic}(\ \mathrm{des}_\sigma(\mathrm{bpic}(w_1))\ \mathrm{des}_\sigma(\mathrm{bpic}(w_2))) \ . \end{aligned}$$

We use the following notations: $f^{\odot 0} = \emptyset$, $f^{\odot 1} = f$, $f^{\odot n} = f \odot f^{\odot(n-1)}$.

Definition 8. We call *rounded star* the closure of the superposition operator:

$$f^{\circledast} = \bigcup_{n>=0} f^{\odot n} \ .$$

We extend these definitions to languages: let $\mathcal{F}$ and $\mathcal{G}$, be two picture languages, then $\mathcal{F} \odot \mathcal{G} = \bigcup_{f,g} f \odot g$, for all $f \in \mathcal{F}$ and $g \in \mathcal{G}$, and $\mathcal{F}^{\circledast} = \bigcup_{n>=0} \mathcal{F}^{\odot n}$.

3 Results

3.1 Classical Picture Languages

Theorem 9. *Superposition does not preserve regularity of classical picture languages:*

$$\exists R_1, R_2 \in Lreg \text{ such that } \nexists R \in Lreg \text{ with } bpic(R) = bpic(R_1) \odot bpic(R_2) \ .$$

Proof. Let $R_1 = r^*ddl^*$ et $R_2 = l^*$, let us suppose that there exists an automaton $A =< \sigma, Q, F, q_0, \delta >$, with n states, recognizing language R such that $\mathrm{bpic}(R) = \mathrm{bpic}(R_1) \odot \mathrm{bpic}(R_2)$. Then there exists a word w in R associated with picture (i) in Fig. 3, where each horizontal line has the same length such that $\mathrm{dist}(ab) > n$.

Whatever way one chooses to draw this picture, the lines $[ab]$, $[cd]$ and $[ef]$ are to be drawn in a given order. Using symmetries, we can restrain our study to the following case, without loss of generality: we draw first $[ab]$, then $[cd]$, and then $[ef]$. So we pass in successive order over points b, d, c, d, f (amongst others). More formally, $w = w_1x_1x_2x_3x_4w_2$, with $\mathrm{sh}(w_1) = b$, $\mathrm{sh}(w_1x_1) = d$, $\mathrm{sh}(w_1x_1x_2) = c$, $\mathrm{sh}(w_1x_1x_2x_3) = d$, $\mathrm{sh}(w_1x_1x_2x_3x_4) = f$, with w_1, x_1, x_2, x_3, x_4, $w_2 \in \pi^*$.

We have $\mathrm{dist}(cd) > n$ and so we loop on a given state of the automaton when parsing x_3 : $\exists p \in Q$, $\exists \alpha, \beta, \gamma \in \pi^*$, such that $x_3 = \alpha\beta\gamma$ and $(q_0, w_1x_1x_2\alpha) = q = (q_0, w_1x_1x_2\alpha\beta)$ with $|\beta|_r - |\beta|_l > 0$. We deduce that automaton A recognizes words like $w_1x_1x_2\alpha\beta^*\gamma x_4w_2$, and $\mathrm{bpic}(R)$ contains pictures alike (ii) in Fig. 3. These pictures are obviously not in $\mathrm{bpic}(R_1) \odot \mathrm{bpic}(R_2)$. Contradiction. $\square$

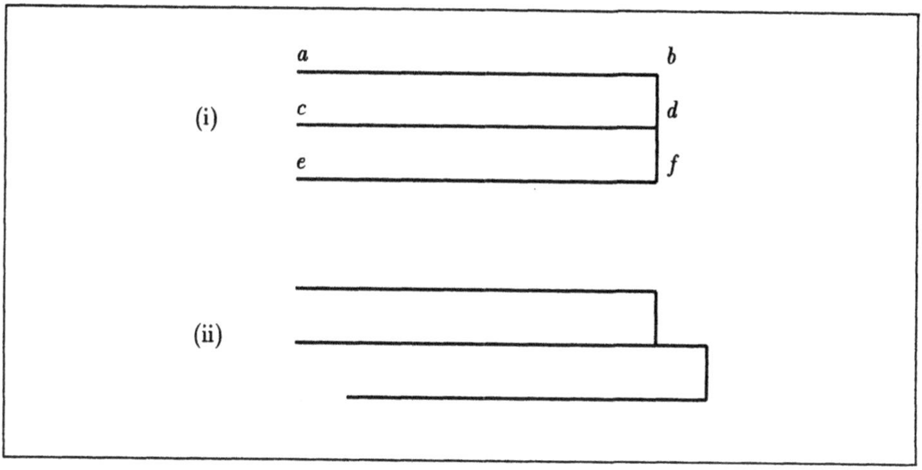

Fig. 3. pictures in bpic(R).

3.2 Branch Picture Languages

Overview. Our goal can be divided into two parts:

1. implementing the superposition operator in the BPL formalism,
2. verifying that the basic properties of regularity and descriptivity are preserved.

First we give the basic idea that enables us to achieve the first part of our goal, and then we refine it in order to obtain a constructive method and achieve the second part.

The basic idea is, given a word $w \in \sigma^*$, to take the set of words, denoted by $\mathrm{sdes}_\sigma(w)$, that have same semi-drawn picture as w: i.e. same start vertex but end vertex situated anywhere on the picture. Then, let L_1 and L_2 be two BPL, the superposition of the associated picture languages is obtained by taking the concatenation product of $\mathrm{sdes}_\sigma(L_1)$ and $\overline{\mathrm{sdes}_\sigma(L_2)}$.

Definition 10. Let $w \in \sigma^*$, $\mathrm{sdes}_\sigma(w) = \{w' \in \sigma^* \mid \mathrm{spic}(w') = \mathrm{spic}(w)\}$.

Proposition 11. *Let L_1, L_2 be two regular descriptive* BPL *then:*

$$bpic(L_1) \odot bpic(L_2) = bpic(\ sdes_\sigma(L_1)\ \overline{sdes_\sigma(L_2)})\ .$$

Sketch of proof: for every picture f in $\mathrm{bpic}(L_1)$, we have a description in $\mathrm{sdes}_\sigma(L_1)$ such that the end point is situated anywhere we want on f. For every picture g in $\mathrm{bpic}(L_2)$, we have a description in $\overline{\mathrm{sdes}_\sigma(L_2)}$ such that the start point is situated anywhere we want on g. It is obvious that the concatenation of these languages gives us a description for every possible superposition of f and g.

The operator sdes_σ just helped us in expressing what we need in a clear manner, but it does not preserve regularity (e.g.: $\mathrm{sdes}_\sigma(ur^*) \cap \{ur^*l^*d\} = \{ur^n l^n d \mid n \in \mathbb{N}\}$). The trouble comes from the fact that we try to have *every* word describing the same semi-drawn picture. In fact, for every end vertex of our semi-drawn picture, we only need one word (or a given bounded number of words) describing the associated picture. So we introduce another operator, denoted here by odes_σ, that retains those "interesting" words from sdes_σ (in fact their inverse, due to technical reasons) and keeps regularity. Here is a sketch giving some hints at the construction of odes_σ, especially the breaking in four different cases. Formal definition and proofs follow in next subsections.

Sketch of construction: given a word w in σ^* and $f = \mathrm{bpic}(w)$ its picture, we want a set L of words describing f such that for each start vertex s taken on f there is a bounded, non zero, number of words in L with s as start vertex and the start vertex of w as end vertex (remember we take the inverse of the "interesting" words from sdes_σ). To construct L we take:

1. $\{\overline{w}\}$;
2. $\{\#w''\$\overline{w'} \mid w = w'w'' \text{ and } w', w'' \in \mathrm{ST}_n\}$, i.e. we cut w at a subword of depth 0, and stick the two parts together so we start drawing where the cut occurred;
3. if $w = w'\#w''\$w'''$ with $w''' \neq 1$, $w', w''' \in \mathrm{ST}_n$, we add $\{\, \mathrm{odes}_\sigma(w'')\#w'''\$\overline{w'}\}$, i.e. we proceed as above, but the cut place is in a branch;
4. if $w = w'\#w''\$$ with $w' \in \mathrm{ST}_n$, we add $\{\, \mathrm{odes}_\sigma(w'')\overline{w'}\}$, this case could have been covered in the previous one, but it would have involved creation of superfluous empty branches.

The odes_σ Operator.

Definition 12. Let L be a regular descriptive BPL of depth p, and $R = <\sigma, Q, F, q_0, \delta>$ an automaton recognizing L. We define $\mathrm{odes}_\sigma(\mathrm{L})$ in the following way:

- if $p = 0$, $\mathrm{odes}_\sigma(L) = L_1 + L_2$
- if $p > 0$, $\mathrm{odes}_\sigma(L) = L_1 + L_2 + L_3 + L_4$

with:

- $L_1 = \overline{L}$
- $L_2 = \bigcup_{\substack{q_1 \in Q \\ q_f \in F}} \#r_{q_1 q_f}\$\overline{r_{q_0 q_1}}$
  - $r_{q_0 q_1} = R_{q_0 q_1} \cap \mathrm{ST}_p$
  - $r_{q_1 q_f} = R_{q_1 q_f} \cap \sigma^+ \cap \mathrm{ST}_p$
- $L_3 = \bigcup_{\substack{q_1, q_2 \in Q \\ q_f \in F}} \mathrm{odes}_\sigma(r_{q_1 q_2})\#r_{q_2 q_f}\$\overline{r_{q_0 q_1}}$
  - $r_{q_0 q_1} = ((R_{q_0 q_1})\#^{-1}) \cap \mathrm{ST}_p$
  - $r_{q_1 q_2} = R_{q_1 q_2} \cap \mathrm{ST}_{p-1}$

- $r_{q_2q_f} = (\$^{-1}(R_{q_2q_f})) \cap \sigma^+ \cap \mathrm{ST}_p$

- $L_4 = \bigcup_{\substack{q_1, q_2 \in Q \\ q_f \in F \\ R_{q_2q_f} = \$}} \mathrm{odes}_\sigma(r_{q_1q_2})\overline{r_{q_0q_1}}$
  - $r_{q_0q_1} = ((R_{q_0q_1})\#^{-1}) \cap \mathrm{ST}_p$
  - $r_{q_1q_2} = R_{q_1q_2} \cap \mathrm{ST}_{p-1}$

Proposition 13. *Regular* BPL *are closed under* $odes_\sigma$.

Proof. By definition of odes_σ. Notice that we call recursively odes_σ in its own definition, but with words of decreasing length and branch depth. □

Proposition 14. *Descriptivity is preserved under* $odes_\sigma$ *and:*

$$L \in \mathrm{ST}_p \Longrightarrow odes_\sigma(L) \in \mathrm{ST}_{p+1} \ .$$

Proof. By induction on depth p.

- if $p = 0$, then $\mathrm{odes}_\sigma(L) = L_1 + L_2 \in \mathrm{ST}_1$
- we suppose Prop. 14 is true for $p > 0$, let us verify it is true for $p + 1$:
  $\mathrm{odes}_\sigma(L) = L_1 + L_2 + L_3 + L_4 \in \mathrm{ST}_{p+1}$ because:
  - $L_1 \in \mathrm{ST}_p$
  - $L_2 \in \mathrm{ST}_{p+1}$
  - $L_3 \in \mathrm{ST}_{p+1}$
  - $L_4 \in \mathrm{ST}_p$

□

Proposition 15. *Let* $L \in \mathrm{ST}_p$, *then:*

$$odes_\sigma(L) \subseteqq \overline{sdes_\sigma(L)} \ .$$

Proof. By induction on depth p.

- if $p = 0$, then $\mathrm{odes}_\sigma(L) = L_1 + L_2$
  - $L \subseteqq \mathrm{sdes}_\sigma(L) \Rightarrow L_1 = \overline{L} \subseteqq \overline{\mathrm{sdes}_\sigma(L)}$
  - $r_{q_0q_1}$ and $r_{q_1q_f} \subseteqq L$
    $\Rightarrow r_{q_0q_1}\#r_{q_1q_f}\$ \subseteqq \mathrm{sdes}_\sigma(L)$
    $\Rightarrow L_2 \subseteqq \overline{\mathrm{sdes}_\sigma(L)}$
- we suppose Prop. 15 is true for $p - 1$, we verify it is true for $p > 0$:
  $\mathrm{odes}_\sigma(L) = L_1 + L_2 + L_3 + L_4$
  - same demonstration for L_1 and L_2 as for the case $p = 0$
  - $R_{q_0q_1}R_{q_1q_2}R_{q_2q_f} \subseteqq L$
    $\Rightarrow r_{q_0q_1}\#r_{q_1q_2}\$\#r_{q_2q_f}\$ \subseteqq \mathrm{sdes}_\sigma(L)$
    $\Rightarrow r_{q_0q_1}\#r_{q_2q_f}\$\#r_{q_1q_2}\$ \subseteqq \mathrm{sdes}_\sigma(L)$
    $\Rightarrow r_{q_0q_1}\#r_{q_2q_f}\$r_{q_1q_2} \subseteqq \mathrm{sdes}_\sigma(L)$
    $\Rightarrow r_{q_0q_1}\#r_{q_2q_f}\$\ \mathrm{sdes}_\sigma(r_{q_1q_2}) \subseteqq \mathrm{sdes}_\sigma(L)$
    as $r_{q_1q_2} \in \mathrm{ST}_{p-1}$, then, by induction hypothesis:
    $\Rightarrow r_{q_0q_1}\#r_{q_2q_f}\$\overline{\ \mathrm{odes}_\sigma(r_{q_1q_2})} \subseteqq \mathrm{sdes}_\sigma(L)$
    $\Rightarrow L_3 \subseteqq \overline{\mathrm{sdes}_\sigma(L)}$

- $r_{q_0q_1}\#r_{q_1q_2}\$ \subseteqq L$
  $\Rightarrow r_{q_0q_1}r_{q_1q_2} \subseteqq \text{ sdes}_\sigma(L)$
  $\Rightarrow r_{q_0q_1} \text{ sdes}_\sigma(r_{q_1q_2}) \subseteqq \text{ sdes}_\sigma(L)$
  $\Rightarrow r_{q_0q_1} \overline{\text{odes}_\sigma(r_{q_1q_2})} \subseteqq \text{ sdes}_\sigma(L)$
  $\Rightarrow L_4 \subseteqq \text{ sdes}_\sigma(L)$

□

Corollary 16. *Let $L \in \mathrm{ST}_p$, then:*

$$bpic(\ odes_\sigma(L)) = bpic(L)\ .$$

Proof. • Let us show that $\text{bpic}(\text{ odes}_\sigma(L)) \supseteqq \text{bpic}(L)$:
$\overline{L} \subseteqq \text{ odes}_\sigma(L)$
$\Rightarrow \text{bpic}(L) = \text{bpic}(\overline{L}) \subseteqq \text{bpic}(\text{ odes}_\sigma(L))$

- Let us show that $\text{bpic}(\text{ odes}_\sigma(L)) \subseteqq \text{bpic}(L)$:
  from Prop. 15 we have
  $\text{odes}_\sigma(L) \subseteqq \overline{\text{sdes}_\sigma(L)}$
  $\Rightarrow \text{bpic}(\text{ odes}_\sigma(L)) \subseteqq \text{bpic}(\overline{\text{sdes}_\sigma(L)}) = \text{bpic}(\text{ sdes}_\sigma(L)) = \text{bpic}(L)$
  □

Proposition 17. *Let $L \in \mathrm{ST}_p$ and a word $l \in L$, then:*

$$\forall w \in\ des_\pi(bpic(l)), \exists v \in \overline{\ sdes_\sigma(l)}\ \text{such that}\ spic(w) = spic(v)\ .$$

Proof. Let $w \in \text{ des}_\pi(\text{bpic}(l))$, then $\text{bpic}(l) = \text{bpic}(w)$, and there exists $v \in \overline{\text{sdes}_\sigma(l)}$ such that $\text{spic}(w) = \text{spic}(v)$, from the definition of sdes_σ. □

Proposition 18. *Let $L \in \mathrm{ST}_p$ and a word $l \in L$, then:*

$$\forall w \in \overline{\ sdes_\sigma(l)}, \exists v \in\ odes_\sigma(L)\ \text{such that}\ dpic(w) = dpic(v)\ .$$

Proof. By induction on depth p.

- if $p = 0$, then $\exists v \in \text{ odes}_\sigma(l)$ such that $\text{dpic}(w) = \text{dpic}(v)$
- we suppose Prop. 18 is true for $p-1$,let us verify it is true for $p > 0$:
  $w \in \overline{\text{sdes}_\sigma(l)} \Rightarrow \overline{w} \in \text{ sdes}_\sigma(l) \Rightarrow \text{spic}(\overline{w}) = \text{spic}(l)$
  - if $l = l_1l_2$ with $l_1, l_2 \in \mathrm{ST}_p$ and the start vertex of w is $P = \text{sh}(l_1)$, then $v = \#l_2\$\overline{l_1} \in \text{ odes}_\sigma(l)$ and $\text{dpic}(w) = \text{dpic}(v)$
  - if the start vertex of w is $P = \text{sh}(l)$, then $v = \overline{l} \in \text{ odes}_\sigma(l)$ and $\text{dpic}(w) = \text{dpic}(v)$
  - if $l = l_1\#l_2\$l_3$, with $l_1, l_3 \in \mathrm{ST}_p$, $l_3 \neq \varepsilon$ and $l_2 \in \mathrm{ST}_{p-1}$ and the start vertex of w is in l_2 (more formally: $l_2 = \alpha\beta$ and the start point of w is $\text{sh}(l_1\alpha)$), then:
    $\Rightarrow l_1\#l_3\$l_2 \in \text{ sdes}_\sigma(l)$
    $\Rightarrow \text{dpic}(\overline{w}) = \text{dpic}(l_1\#l_3\$x)$ with $x \in \text{ sdes}_\sigma(l_2)$
    as $\overline{x} \in \overline{\text{sdes}_\sigma(l_2)}$ and $l_2 \in \mathrm{ST}_{p-1}$, we have:
    $\exists t \in \text{ odes}_\sigma(l_2)$ such that $\text{dpic}(\overline{x}) = \text{dpic}(t)$
    $\Rightarrow \text{dpic}(w) = \text{dpic}(\overline{x}\#l_3\$\overline{l_1}) = \text{dpic}(t\#l_3\$\overline{l_1})$
    and $v = t\#l_3\$\overline{l_1} \in \text{ odes}_\sigma(l)$

○ if $l = l_1 \# l_2 \$$ with $l_1 \in ST_p$, $l_2 \in ST_{p-1}$, and the start vertex of w is in l_2, then:
$\Rightarrow l_1 l_2 \in \text{sdes}_\sigma(l)$
$\Rightarrow \text{dpic}(\overline{w}) = \text{dpic}(l_1 x)$ with $x \in \text{sdes}_\sigma(l_2)$
$\Rightarrow \text{dpic}(w) = \text{dpic}(\overline{x} \overline{l_1})$
by induction hypothesis:
$\exists t \in \text{odes}_\sigma(l_2)$ such that $\text{dpic}(\overline{x}) = \text{dpic}(t)$
$\Rightarrow \text{dpic}(w) = \text{dpic}(t \overline{l_1})$
and $v = t \overline{l_1} \in L_4 \subseteq \text{odes}_\sigma(L)$

$\square$

Corollary 19. *Let* $L \in ST_p$, *then:*

$$dpic(\ odes_\sigma(L)) = dpic(\ \overline{sdes_\sigma(L)}) \ .$$

Proof. Obvious from Prop. 18 $\square$

Main Results. The previous propositions enable us to derive the closure of regular descriptive BPL under superposition and iterated superposition.

Theorem 20. *Regular descriptive BPL are closed under superposition, and let* $L_1 \in ST_{p_1}$ *and* $L_2 \in ST_{p_2}$ *be two regular descriptive BPL, then*

$$bpic(L_1) \odot bpic(L_2) = bpic(\ \overline{odes_\sigma(L_1)} \ odes_\sigma(L_2)) \ .$$

Proof. • Let us show that: $\text{bpic}(L_1) \odot \text{bpic}(L_2) \supseteq \text{bpic}(\ \overline{odes_\sigma(L_1)} \ odes_\sigma(L_2))$
   Let $l_1 \in L_1, l_2 \in L_2$, and $t_1 \in \overline{odes_\sigma(l_1)}, t_2 \in odes_\sigma(l_2)$
   $\Rightarrow t_1 \in \overline{des_\sigma(\text{bpic}(l_1))}, t_2 \in des_\sigma(\text{bpic}(l_2))$
   $\Rightarrow \text{bpic}(\ \overline{odes_\sigma(l_1)} \ odes_\sigma(l_2)) \subseteq \text{bpic}(\ \overline{des_\sigma(\text{bpic}(l_1))} \ des_\sigma(\text{bpic}(l_2)))$
   $\Rightarrow \text{bpic}(\ \overline{odes_\sigma(l_1)} \ odes_\sigma(l_2)) \subseteq \text{bpic}(L_1) \odot \text{bpic}(L_2)$ (by definition of super-position)
   • Let us show that: $\text{bpic}(L_1) \odot \text{bpic}(L_2) \subseteq \text{bpic}(\ \overline{odes_\sigma(L_1)} \ odes_\sigma(L_2))$
   Let $l_1 \in L_1, l_2 \in L_2$ and $f \in \text{bpic}(l_1) \odot \text{bpic}(l_2)$
   $\Rightarrow \exists w_1 \in \overline{des_\sigma(\text{bpic}(l_1))}$ and $w_2 \in des_\sigma(\text{bpic}(l_2))$ such that $f = \text{bpic}(w_1 w_2)$
   $\Rightarrow$ (Prop. 17) $\exists x_2 \in sdes_\sigma(l_2)$ such that $\text{spic}(x_2) = \text{spic}(w_2)$
   We also have: $\overline{w_1} \in \overline{des_\sigma(\text{bpic}(l_1))}$
   $\Rightarrow$ (Prop. 17) $\exists x_1 \in \overline{sdes_\sigma(l_1)}$ such that $\text{spic}(x_1) = \text{spic}(\overline{w_1})$
   $\Rightarrow \text{bpic}(w_1 w_2) = \text{bpic}(\overline{x_1} x_2)$
   $\Rightarrow$ (Prop. 18) $\text{bpic}(w_1 w_2) = \text{bpic}(\overline{v_1} v_2)$
   with $v_1 \in odes_\sigma(l_1), v_2 \in odes_\sigma(l_2)$
   $\square$

Corollary 21. *Let* $L_1 \in ST_{p_1}$ *and* $L_2 \in ST_{p_2}$ *be two regular descriptive BPL then:*

$$degree(bpic(L_1) \odot bpic(L_2)) \leq sup(p_1, p_2) + 1 \ .$$

Proof. Obvious from 14 and 20. □

Theorem 22. *Regular descriptive* BPL *are closed under iterated superposition, and let* $L \in \mathrm{ST}_p$ *a regular descriptive* BPL, *then:*

$$(bpic(L))^{\circledast} = bpic((\ odes_\sigma(L) + \overline{odes_\sigma(L)})^*)\ .$$

Proof. • Let us show that: $(\mathrm{bpic}(L))^{\circledast} \supseteq \mathrm{bpic}((\ \mathrm{odes}_\sigma(L) + \overline{\mathrm{odes}_\sigma(L)})^*)$
$(\mathrm{bpic}(L))^{\circledast} = \mathrm{bpic}((\ \mathrm{des}_\sigma(L))^*)$
$\mathrm{odes}_\sigma(L) \subseteqq \mathrm{des}_\sigma(\mathrm{bpic}(L))$
$\overline{\mathrm{odes}_\sigma(L)} \subseteqq \overline{\mathrm{des}_\sigma(\mathrm{bpic}(L))}$
$\Rightarrow \mathrm{bpic}((\ \mathrm{odes}_\sigma(L) + \overline{\mathrm{odes}_\sigma(L)})^*) \subseteqq (\mathrm{bpic}(L))^{\circledast}$

• Let us show that: $(\mathrm{bpic}(L))^{\circledast} \subseteqq \mathrm{bpic}((\ \mathrm{odes}_\sigma(L) + \overline{\mathrm{odes}_\sigma(L)})^*)$
Let $w \in\ \mathrm{des}_\sigma(\mathrm{bpic}(L))$
$\Rightarrow \exists l \in L$ such that $w \in\ \mathrm{des}_\sigma(\mathrm{bpic}(l))$
$\Rightarrow$ (Prop. 17) $\exists x \in\ \mathrm{sdes}_\sigma(l)$ such that $\mathrm{spic}(x) = \mathrm{spic}(w)$
$\Rightarrow$ (Prop. 18) $\exists l' \in\ \mathrm{odes}_\sigma(l)$ such that $\mathrm{dpic}(x) = \mathrm{dpic}(l')$
On the other hand: $\overline{w} \in\ \overline{\mathrm{des}_\sigma(\mathrm{bpic}(l))}$
$\Rightarrow$ (Prop. 17) $\exists y \in\ \overline{\mathrm{sdes}_\sigma(l)}$ such that $\mathrm{spic}(y) = \mathrm{spic}(\overline{w})$
$\Rightarrow$ (Prop. 18) $\exists l'' \in\ \mathrm{odes}_\sigma(l)$ such that $\mathrm{dpic}(y) = \mathrm{dpic}(l'')$
$\Rightarrow \mathrm{dpic}(w) = \mathrm{dpic}(l'l'')$
$\Rightarrow (\mathrm{bpic}(L))^{\circledast} \subseteqq \mathrm{bpic}((\ \mathrm{odes}_\sigma(L) + \overline{\mathrm{odes}_\sigma(L)})^*)$
□

Corollary 23. *Let* $L \in \mathrm{ST}_p$, *then* $degree((bpic(L))^{\circledast}) \leq p+1$.

4 Conclusion

These results show that the coding with branches is more appropriate than the classical one to the description of our superposition operator. We have given special attention to the fundamental property of regularity. Are there others operators performing on basic picture, which, on the contrary, preserve that property in the classical formalism? And what can be said of the superposition in other families such as linear or context-free languages?

References

1. Danièle Beauquier. An undecidable problem about rationnal sets and contour words of polyominoes. *Information Processing Letters*, 37:257–263, 1991.
2. Danièle Beauquier, Michel Latteux, and Karine Slowinski. A decidability result about convex polyominoes. In *Lecture Notes in Computer Science*, volume 583, pages 32–45, 1992.
3. Danièle Beauquier and Maurice Nivat. Tiling pictures of the plane with two bars, a horizontal and a vertical one. Technical Report LITP 91.67, LITP, November 1991.

4. Franz J. Brandenburg and Jürgen Dassow. Efficient reductions of picture words. *Theoretical Informatics and Applications*, 27(4):49–56, 1993.
5. Jürgen Dassow. Graph-theoretical properties and chain code picture languages. *J. Inf. Process. Cybern.*, EIK 25:423–433, 1989.
6. Jürgen Dassow. On the connectedness of pictures in chain code picture languages. *Theoretical Computer Science*, 81:289–294, 1991.
7. H. Freeman. On the encoding of arbitrary geometric configuration. *Ire Transactions on Electronic Computers*, 10:260–268, 1961.
8. Roger Gutbrod. Branch picture languages. Technical report, Aachen University, 1991.
9. Friedhelm Hinz and Emo Welzl. Regular chain code picture languages with invisible lines. Technical Report 252, Graz University of Technology, 1988.
10. Changwook Kim. Complexity and decidability for restricted classes of picture languages. *Theoretical Computer Science*, 73, 1990.
11. Changwook Kim and Ivan Hal Sudborough. On reversal-bounded picture languages. *Theoretical Computer Science*, 104:185–206, 1992.
12. H. A. Maurer, G. Rozenberg, and E. Welzl. Using string languages to describe picture languages. *Information and Control*, 54:155–185, 1982.
13. Gheorge Păun, Denis Robilliard, and Karine Slowinski. Connected pictures and minimal words with blank moves. Technical Report IT-92-239, LIFL, Université des Sciences et Technologies de Lille, France, November 1992.
14. Patrice Séébold and Karine Slowinski. The shortest way to draw a connected picture. *Computer Graphics Forum*, 10:319–327, 1991.
15. Jihad Tatari and Eric Tosan. Représentation des polyominos. In *Actes de GROPLAN'92*, 1992.

A Grammar-based Data-flow Analysis to Stop Deforestation

Morten Heine Sørensen

DIKU, Department of Computer Science, University of Copenhagen, Universitetsparken 1, DK-2100 Copenhagen, Denmark. E-mail: rambo@diku.dk

Abstract. Wadler's *deforestation* algorithm removes intermediate data structures from functional programs, but is only guaranteed to terminate for *treeless* programs. Chin has shown how one can apply deforestation to all first-order programs: *annotate* non-treeless subterms and apply the *extended* deforestation algorithm which essentially leaves annotated subterms untransformed. We develop a new technique of putting annotations on programs. The basic idea is to compute a finite grammar which approximates the set of terms that the deforestation algorithm encounters. The technique extends Wadler's and Chin's in a certain sense.

1 Introduction

Modern functional programming languages like Miranda[1] [Tur90] lend themselves to a certain elegant style of programming which exploits *higher-order functions*, *lazy evaluation* and *intermediate data structures*; Hughes [Hug90] gives illuminating examples. While this programming style makes it easy to read and write programs, it also results in inefficient programs.

Early work on automatic elimination of intermediate data structures from functional programs includes Turchin's *supercompiler* [Tur80,Tur82] and Wadler's *listless transformer* [Wad84,Wad85]. The latter eliminates intermediate *lists*, but later Wadler invented *deforestation* [Wad88,Fer88], which eliminates intermediate data structures in general, and proved that the deforestation algorithm terminates when applied to *treeless* programs.

A method for applying deforestation to all first-order programs was later described by Chin [Chi90,Chi94]. Inspired by Wadler's *blazed* deforestation algorithm [Wad88] he invented an *extended* deforestation algorithm which essentially leaves *annotated* subterms untransformed. The problem remains to calculate annotations ensuring that application of the extended deforestation algorithm to the annotated program terminates; as few subterms as possible should be annotated. Chin essentially annotates non-treeless subterms.

This paper describes a new static analysis whose result can be used to ensure termination of deforestation in such a way that fewer annotations will be put on the program, compared to Chin's technique.

The remainder is organized as follows. Section 2: the language we study. Section 3: the deforestation algorithm. Section 4: the two kinds of non-termination

[1] Miranda is a trademark of Research Software Ltd.

that can arise during deforestation. Section 5: some notation for the analysis. Section 6: the idea of the analysis and how it works on the two examples from section 4. Section 7: the analysis technically. Section 8: an improvement of the basic method. Section 9: an explanation of the fact that our method extends the methods by Wadler and Chin; the improvement of Section 8 is necessary for this. Section 10: conclusion.

2 Language and notation

We study the same language as the one studied in [Fer88].

Definition 1 Object language. Let c, v, f, g range over constructor names, variable names, f-function names, and g-function names, respectively. Let t, p, d range over terms, patterns, and definitions, respectively.

$$
\begin{aligned}
t &::= v \mid c\, t_1 \ldots t_n \mid f\, t_1 \ldots t_n \mid g\, t_0 \ldots t_n \mid \text{ let } v = t \text{ in } t' \\
p &::= c\, v_1 \ldots v_n \\
d &::= f\, v_1 \ldots v_n \leftarrow t \\
&\mid \;\; g\, p_1\, v_1 \ldots v_n \leftarrow t_1 \\
&\qquad\qquad \vdots \\
&\quad\;\; g\, p_k\, v_1 \ldots v_n \leftarrow t_k
\end{aligned}
$$

g-functions have one pattern matching argument, f-functions have none. We use h to range over functions which are either f- or g-functions.

We require that no variable occur more than once in a pattern and that all variables of a right hand side of a definition be present in the corresponding left hand side. To ensure uniqueness of reduction, we require from a program that each function have at most one definition and, in the case of a g-definition, that no two patterns p_i and p_j contain the same constructor.

The semantics for reduction of a variable-free term is *lazy evaluation*, like in Miranda.

As usual we state the deforestation algorithm by rule for rewriting terms. For this, we need some notation that allows us to pick a function call in a term and replace the call by the body of the function with arguments substituted for formal parameters. Since the deforestation algorithm basically simulates call-by-name evaluation, there is always a unique function call whose unfolding is *forced*. For instance, to find out which of g's clauses to apply to $g\,(f_1\, t_1)\,(f_2\, t_2)$ we are forced to unfold the call $f_1\, t_1$. In the terminology below, the forced call $f_1\, t_1$ is the *redex* and the surrounding term $g\, []\, (f_2\, t_2)$ is the *context*. If the term is a variable or has an outermost constructor, it is an *observable*.

Definition 2 Context, redex and observable. Let e, r, o range over contexts, redexes, and observables, respectively.

$$\begin{aligned}
e &::= [] \mid g\, e\, t_1 \ldots t_n \\
r &::= f\, t_1 \ldots t_n \mid g\, (c\, t_{n+1} \ldots t_{n+m})\, t_1 \ldots t_n \mid g\, v\, t_1 \ldots t_n \mid \text{ let } v = t \text{ in } t' \\
o &::= c\, t_1 \ldots t_n \mid v
\end{aligned}$$

The expression $e[t]$ denotes the result of replacing the occurrence of $[]$ in e by t. Note that every term t is either an observable or decomposes uniquely into a context e and redex r such that $t \equiv e[r]$ (*the unique decomposition property*). This provides the desired way of "grabbing hold" of the next function call to unfold in a term.

The let-construct is not intended for the programmer; it is adopted in the language as an alternative to annotations. Instead of annotating the "dangerous" parts of a program and applying an extended deforestation algorithm which works conservatively on annotated subterms, we transform dangerous parts of the program into let-expressions and let the deforestation algorithm work conservatively on let-expressions.

3 The deforestation algorihtm

The following definition of $\mathcal{D}$ is essentially the deforestation algorithm in [Fer88]. After the algorithm we explain $\mathcal{D}$ along with the notation employed.

Definition 3 Deforestation algorithm, $\mathcal{D}$.

$$\begin{array}{lll}
(1)\ \mathcal{D}[\![\, v \,]\!] & & \Rightarrow v \\
(2)\ \mathcal{D}[\![\, c\, t_1 \ldots t_n \,]\!] & & \Rightarrow c\, (\mathcal{D}[\![\, t_1 \,]\!]) \ldots (\mathcal{D}[\![\, t_n \,]\!]) \\
(3)\ \mathcal{D}[\![\, e[f\, t_1 \ldots t_n] \,]\!] & & \Rightarrow f^{\Box}\, u_1 \ldots u_l \\
\quad \textbf{where} & f^{\Box}\, u_1 \ldots u_l & \leftarrow \mathcal{D}[\![\, e[\, t^f \{v_i^f := t_i\}_{i=1}^n \,] \,]\!] \\
(4)\ \mathcal{D}[\![\, e[g\, (c\, t_{n+1} \ldots t_{n+m})\, t_1 \ldots t_n] \,]\!] & & \Rightarrow f^{\Box}\, u_1 \ldots u_l \\
\quad \textbf{where} & f^{\Box}\, u_1 \ldots u_l & \leftarrow \mathcal{D}[\![\, e[\, t^{g,c} \{v_i^{g,c} := t_i\}_{i=1}^{n+m} \,] \,]\!] \\
(5)\ \mathcal{D}[\![\, e[g\, v\, t_1 \ldots t_n] \,]\!] & & \Rightarrow g^{\Box}\, v\, u_1 \ldots u_l \\
\quad \textbf{where} & g^{\Box}\, p_1^g\, u_1 \ldots u_l & \leftarrow \mathcal{D}[\![\, e[t^{g,c_1} \{v_i^{g,c_1} := t_i\}_{i=1}^n] \,]\!] \\
 & & \quad \vdots \\
 & g^{\Box}\, p_k^g\, u_1 \ldots u_l & \leftarrow \mathcal{D}[\![\, e[t^{g,c_k} \{v_i^{g,c_k} := t_i\}_{i=1}^n] \,]\!] \\
(6)\ \mathcal{D}[\![\, \text{let } v = t \text{ in } t' \,]\!] & & \Rightarrow \text{let } v = \mathcal{D}[\![\, t \,]\!] \text{ in } \mathcal{D}[\![\, t' \,]\!]
\end{array}$$

Notation.

The algorithm should be understood in the context of some program p. It is written in an informal meta-language; the symbol $\Rightarrow$ denotes evaluation in this language.

For f-functions, t^f denotes the right hand side of the definition for function f in p, and $v_1^f \dots v_n^f$ are the formal parameters in f's definition.

For g-functions, $t^{g,c}$ is the right hand side of g corresponding to the left hand side whose pattern contains the constructor c. Further, $v_1^{g,c} \dots v_n^{g,c}, v_{n+1}^{g,c} \dots v_{n+m}^{g,c}$ are the formal parameters of g in the clause whose pattern contains the constructor c. Here $v_1^{g,c} \dots v_n^{g,c}$ are those not occurring in the pattern (these are the same for all c) while $v_{n+1}^{g,c}, \dots v_{n+m}^{g,c}$ are the variables in the pattern (m depends on c).

The expression $t\{v_i := t_i\}_{i=1}^n$ denotes the result of simultaneously replacing all occurrences of v_i in t by t_i for all $i = 1 \dots n$.

The arguments $v, u_1 \dots u_l$ in the calls in clauses (3)-(5) are the free variables occurring in e and the t_i's. In clause (5), v is also included among $u_1 \dots u_l$ if it occurs in e or the t_i's. (In this case v occurs twice in the call[2]).

Chin's producer-consumer view of deforestation.

In clauses (3)-(5) of $\mathcal{D}$, the term t is transformed into a *residual call* to a new function.[3] This is a *fold* step. The right hand side of the new function is defined (before further transformation) to be t unfolded one step.[4] This is an *unfold* step and a *define* step. In clause (5) of $\mathcal{D}$, an *instantiation* step is performed as well.

The unfold steps propagate constructors towards the root of the term and thereby execute construction and subsequent destruction of intermediate structures. Consider, for instance, the term $g_2\,(g_1\,(f\,t_0)\,t_1)\,t_2$. Using the terminology of Chin [Chi90], the idea[5] is that the redex $f\,t_0$ through a number of unfoldings becomes a term with an outermost constructor, *produces* a constructor. This will allow the surrounding g-function g_1 to be unfolded, *consuming* exactly the outermost constructor from the term, since patterns are one constructor deep. This latter unfolding will itself through a number of subsequent unfoldings produce a constructor allowing the next surrounding g-function g_2 to be unfolded. In this way, the constructor propagates all the way to the root of the term, and transformation then proceeds to each of the arguments of the constructor in a similar fashion.

Folding to increase termination.

As is well-known, deforestation hardly ever terminates in the present formulation. The "problem" is that the same term may be encountered over and over again. Therefore we introduce a *folding scheme*. Each of the multiple recursive

---

2 This is actually a very important point; see [Sor94].

3 We assume that these new functions are collected somehow in a new program.

4 Actually the left hand side as well as the unfolding of t should be renamed; we ignore the details.

5 The following is the *desired* situation; the algorithm does not behave this well on all program, as we shall see.

calls to $\mathcal{D}$ in clauses (2),(5),(6) determine a *branch* of transformation. We assume that when a term is encountered for the second time in the same branch then transformation terminates with the generation of the residual call. No new definition is introduced, since this was done the first time the term was encountered.

When a term is encountered which differs merely in the choice of variable names from a previously encountered term in the same branch, then we assume that transformation terminates with the generation of an appropriate residual call too. This can be explicated in notation in various ways, see [Fer88,Chi94].

Effeciency of residual programs.

There are some well-known problems in ensuring that the output program of $\mathcal{D}$ is at least as efficient, and preferably more efficient, than the input.

First, there is a problem concerning duplication of computation in the case of non-linear functions. This problem is well-known in deforestation as well as in partial evaluation. Therefore we shall not be concerned with this problem here.

Second, many calls and let-expressions in the residual program may be unfolded, improving efficiency. This phenomenon is also well known in deforestation and partial evaluation, so we do not go into details here.

4 Termination problems in deforestation

Below we give two example programs which show the two kinds of problems that can occur. We show that application of $\mathcal{D}$ to each of the programs loops infinitely. We also show that with certain small changes in the programs, $\mathcal{D}$ does not loop infinitely. These changes are called *generalizations*.

The Accumulating Parameter.

Example 1. Consider the following program.

$$
\begin{array}{ll}
 & r\ l \\
r\ xs & \leftarrow rr\ xs\ Nil \\
rr\ Nil\ ys & \leftarrow ys \\
rr\ (Cons\ z\ zs)\ ys & \leftarrow rr\ zs\ (Cons\ z\ ys)
\end{array}
$$

The r function returns its argument list reversed. Applied to this program and term $\mathcal{D}$ loops infinitely. The problem is that $\mathcal{D}$ encounters the progressively larger terms $rr\ l\ Nil$, $rr\ zs\ (Cons\ z_1\ Nil)$, $rr\ zs\ (Cons\ z_2\ (Cons\ z_1\ Nil))$, *etc.* Since the formal parameter ys of rr is bound to progressively larger terms, Chin calls x an *accumulating parameter.*[6] Note that each of the problematic terms that are bound to ys is a subterm of the term which is subsequently bound to ys.

[6] The same phrase is usually used for the programming style rr is written in.

It would seem that we can solve the problem if we could, somehow, make sure that $\mathcal{D}$ could not tell the difference between the different terms that are bound to ys. This can be achieved by transforming the program into:

$$
\begin{array}{ll}
 & r\,l \\
r\,xs & \leftarrow \text{let } v = Nil \text{ in } rr\,xs\,v \\
rr\,Nil\,ys & \leftarrow ys \\
rr\,(Cons\,z\,zs)\,ys & \leftarrow \text{let } v = Cons\,z\,ys \text{ in } rr\,zs\,v
\end{array}
$$

Applying $\mathcal{D}$ to this term and program terminates with the same term and program as output. This is satisfactory.

The Obstructing Function Call.

Example 2. Consider the following term and program.

$$
\begin{array}{ll}
 & r\,l \\
r\,Nil & \leftarrow Nil \\
r\,(Cons\,z\,zs) & \leftarrow a\,(r\,zs)\,z \\
a\,Nil\,y & \leftarrow Cons\,y\,Nil \\
a\,(Cons\,x\,xs)\,y & \leftarrow Cons\,x\,(a\,xs\,y)
\end{array}
$$

The r function again reverses its argument, this time by first reversing the tail and then appending the head to this (the a function puts the element y in the end of its first argument). Now the problem is that $\mathcal{D}$ encounters the terms $r\,l$, $a(r\,zs)z_1$, $a(a(r\,zs)z_2)z_1$, *etc.* We call each of the calls to r in the redex position an ***obstructing function call***, since they prevent the surrounding term from ever being transformed.[7] Note that each of the problematic terms that $\mathcal{D}$ encounters appears in the redex position of the subsequent problematic term.

It would seem that we can solve the problem if we could, somehow, make sure that $\mathcal{D}$ could not tell the difference between the different terms that occur in the redex position. This can be achieved by transforming the program into: (the change in the *term* is actually not necessary)

$$
\begin{array}{ll}
 & \text{let } v = r\,l \text{ in } v \\
r\,Nil & \leftarrow Nil \\
r\,(Cons\,z\,zs) & \leftarrow \text{let } v = r\,zs \text{ in } a\,v\,z \\
a\,Nil\,y & \leftarrow Cons\,y\,Nil \\
a\,(Cons\,x\,xs)\,y & \leftarrow Cons\,x\,(a\,xs\,y)
\end{array}
$$

Applying $\mathcal{D}$ to this term and program terminates with the same term and program as output. This is satisfactory.

---

[7] We differ slightly from the terminology of Chin here.

Generalizations.

Let $e()$ denote a term with exactly one occurrence of () at a place where a subterm could have occurred, and let $e(t)$ denote the result of substituting t for the occurrence of ().

Turning $e(h\, t_1 \ldots t_n)$ into let $v = t_i$ in $e(h\, t_1 \ldots t_{i-1}\, v\, t_{i+1} \ldots t_n)$ is called *generalization of h's i'th argument.* In Example 1, we generalized rr's second argument.

Turning $e(h\, t_1 \ldots t_n)$ into let $v = h\, t_1 \ldots t_n$ in $e(v)$ is called *generalization of the call to h.* In example 2, we generalized the call to r.

Generalizing should be thought of as annotating. Instead of putting funny symbols on our programs we instead use a distinct language construct.

5 Tree grammars

This section introduces some notation and terminology necessary to state our analysis. We first define tree grammars which are grammars where the right hand sides of productions are terms with nonterminals. The right hand sides will be called grammar terms, and there are also notions of grammar context, grammar redex, and grammar observable. In grammar terms we do not have variables; instead we have $\bullet$ informally signifying "any variable."

Definition 4 Grammar term, redex, observable. Tree grammar. Let t, r, o range over grammar terms, grammar redexes, and grammar observables, respectively.

$$
\begin{aligned}
t &::= \bullet \mid c\, t_1 \ldots t_n \mid f\, t_1 \ldots t_n \mid g\, t_0 \ldots t_n \mid \text{let } \bullet = t \text{ in } t' \mid N \\
e &::= [] \mid g\, e\, t_1 \ldots t_n \\
r &::= f\, t_1 \ldots t_n \mid g\, (c\, t_{n+1} \ldots t_{n+m})\, t_1 \ldots t_n \mid g\, \bullet\, t_1 \ldots t_n \mid \text{let } \bullet = t \text{ in } t' \\
o &::= c\, t_1 \ldots t_n \mid \bullet
\end{aligned}
$$

$\mathcal{N}$ and $\mathcal{GT}$ denote the set of all nonterminals and grammar terms, respectively. By a *tree grammar* we mean a subset of $\mathcal{N} \times \mathcal{GT}$, which will be written $\{N_i \rightarrow t_i\}_{i \in J}$. Each $N_i \rightarrow t_i$ is called a *production.* A *finite tree grammar* is a finite subset of $\mathcal{N} \times \mathcal{GT}$. Our construction will always compute a finite tree grammar.

We shall omit the qualifier "grammar" in front of "term," "context," *etc.* when no confusion is likely to arise. Instead of tree grammars we also often use the unqualified term: grammars.

Definition 5. Define $\mathcal{F}$ to be the function which maps a term t to the grammar term which arises by replacing all variables by $\bullet$.

The unique decomposition property is preserved in a slightly modified form: given a grammar term t, exactly one of the following cases occur: 1) t is observable; 2) t can be decomposed uniquely into e, r such that $t \equiv e[r]$; 3) t can be decomposed uniquely into e, N such that $t \equiv e[N]$. So structural definitions use the extra case: $e[N]$.

Just as the notion of context is convenient for grabing hold of the redex and denoting the unfolding of the function call in the redex, we need some notation that allows us to pick an occurrence of a nonterminal and replace it with one of the right hand sides of the nonterminal in some grammar.

Definition 6 Replacement of nonterminals, $*$-derivation. Let $e()$ denote a grammar term with exactly one occurrence of () at a place where another grammar term could have occurred, and let $e(t)$ denote the result of substituting t for the occurrence of ().

Given a grammar G, G^* is the smallest grammar satisfying the closure rules:

$$\frac{N \to t \in G}{N \to t \in G^*} \qquad \frac{N \to e(N') \in G^* \quad N' \to t \in G}{N \to e(t) \in G^*}$$

A production in G^* will also be called a *derivation.*

6 Idea and examples of the analysis

This section introduces informally the analysis as well as its use; the next section introduces both rigorously. Given term t and program p, the overall method runs as follows.

1. Calculate a finite grammar G approximating the set of terms that $\mathcal{D}[\![\, t \,]\!]$ encounters.
2. Look in this grammar and calculate suitable generalizations.
3. If no new generalizations were calculated stop; otherwise perform the generalizations on the term and program and go to step 1 with the new program and term.

Grammar for the Accumulating Parameter.

Example 3. Recall the program from Section 4 showing the problem of the Accumulating Parameter. The first grammar G that will be computed for this term and program is:

$$\begin{array}{llll} F^0 & \to r \bullet \mid F^r \mid \bullet \mid V^{ys} & F^r & \to rr\ V^{xs}\ Nil \mid F^{rr}_{Nil} \mid F^{rr}_{Cons} \\ V^{xs} & \to \bullet & F^{rr}_{Nil} & \to V^{ys} \\ V^{ys} & \to Nil \mid Cons \bullet V^{ys} & F^{rr}_{Cons} & \to rr \bullet (Cons \bullet V^{ys}) \mid F^{rr}_{Nil} \mid F^{rr}_{Cons} \end{array}$$

In the grammar there are three kinds of nonterminals which we explain in turn.

1. A start nonterminal F^0. If $\mathcal{D}[\![\, t \,]\!]$ encounters t' then $F^0 \to \mathcal{F}[\![\, t' \,]\!] \in G^*$.
2. A nonterminal F^f for each f-function in the program and a nonterminal F^g_c for each clause of the definition of every g-function in the program. If a call to h occurs in the redex of some term $e[h\, t_1 \ldots t_n]$ that $\mathcal{D}$ encounters, and this term in a number of steps is transformed to $e[t']$ by performing steps in the redex, then $F^h \to \mathcal{F}[\![\, t' \,]\!] \in G^*$
3. A nonterminal V^v for every variable in the program. If t' is bound to v during the course of $\mathcal{D}[\![\, t \,]\!]$, then $V^v \to \mathcal{F}[\![\, t' \,]\!] \in G^*$.

To understand that the grammar is a safe approximation of the set of terms that the positive supercompiler encounters, the first of these three results suffice. The two latter are never actually used in the reasoning, but they motivate several ideas, for instance the technique for computing generalizations from a grammar.

Recall that the problem in Example 1 was that rr was called with the progressively larger arguments Nil, $Cons\ z_1\ Nil$, $Cons\ z_2\ (Cons\ z_1\ Nil)$, *etc.* The formal parameter of rr is ys, and in fact $V^{ys} \rightarrow \mathcal{F}[\![\, t \,]\!] \in G^*$ when t ranges over all these terms. Also recall that we noted in Example 1 that each problematic term was a subterm of the subsequent problematic term. Notice how well this is reflected by the production $V^{ys} \rightarrow Cons\ \bullet\ V^{ys}$.

The problem of the Accumulating Parameter is generally reflected by a production $V^v \rightarrow e(V^v) \in G^*$. In preventing $\mathcal{D}$ from looping the idea is to generalize all arguments corresponding to some variable v for which $V^v \rightarrow e(V^v) \in G^*$ where $e \neq ()$. So we should generalize the second argument in all calls to rr. This yields the second program in Example 1. Recalculating the grammar for the new term and program yields a grammar G with no $V^v \rightarrow e(V^v) \in G^*$ for $e \neq ()$. (This will not generally hold for the first recalculated grammar).

The grammar is computed in steps which simulate steps of $\mathcal{D}$. The overall idea in computing the grammar G_∞, approximating the set of terms that $\mathcal{D}[\![\, t \,]\!]$ encounters, is as follows.

1. $G_0 = \{F^0 \rightarrow \mathcal{F}[\![\, t \,]\!]\}$
2. $G_{i+1} = \mathcal{E}(G_i^*) \cup G_i$, where $\mathcal{E}(H)$ is a certain function which looks at each right hand side of F^0 in H and computes certain new productions representing unfolding of terms.
3. $G_\infty = \cup_{i=0}^{\infty} G_i$

Recall point 1 in the meaning of productions: that $F^0 \rightarrow \mathcal{F}[\![\, t' \,]\!] \in G_\infty^*$ for all t' that $\mathcal{D}$ encounters. The idea is that this follows from the invariant: $F^0 \rightarrow \mathcal{F}[\![\, t' \,]\!] \in G_i^*$ for all t' encountered by $\mathcal{D}$ in at most i steps.

Below we show for the example program how each step of $\mathcal{D}$ is accompanied by an addition of productions to the grammar.

Step 1. $\mathcal{D}$ starts with the term $r\ l$, whereas the initial grammar G_0 is $\{F^0 \rightarrow r\ \bullet\}$. It then clearly holds that $F^0 \rightarrow \mathcal{F}[\![\, r\ l \,]\!] \in G_0^*$.

Step 2. Then $\mathcal{D}$ moves to $rr\ l\ Nil$, whereas we add to our grammar the new productions

$$F^0 \rightarrow F^r, F^r \rightarrow rr\ V^{xs}\ Nil, V^{xs} \rightarrow \bullet$$

yielding the new grammar G_1. The first production records that we unfolded a call to r (in the empty context). The second just records the definition of r; this is the same production for all calls to r. The last production records the binding of a variable to xs. It now holds that $F^0 \rightarrow \mathcal{F}[\![\, rr\ l\ Nil \,]\!] \in G_1^*$.

This step shows the difference between nonterminals V^v and $\bullet$ in a right hand side. When we have $F^0 \rightarrow e(V^x)$ in the grammar then it means that $\mathcal{D}$ encounters the term $e(t)$ where t is some term that is bound to x at some point. When we have $F^0 \rightarrow e(\bullet)$ it means that $\mathcal{D}$ encounters the term $e(x)$ where x is some variable.

Step 3. Now $\mathcal{D}$ instantiates l to the patterns of rr and thereby encounters the terms Nil and $rr\ zs\ (Cons\ z\ Nil)$. We must add something to G_1 representing this step.

As mentioned above, the basic idea is for the grammar construction in the i'th step to compute G_i^*, where G_i is the grammar computed so far, and then unfold redexes on the right hand sides of productions for F^0. For instance, after step 1, we had $F^0 \rightarrow r \bullet \in G_0^*$, and in step 2 we computed G_0^*, and unfolded the right hand side $r\bullet$ to the new productions $F^0 \rightarrow F^r$, *etc.* The problem with this is that G_i^* may be infinite and so computation of it will loop infinitely. The solution is to compute from G_i only part of G_i^* and unfold calls on *all* right hand sides yielding at least all the right productions.

In the current step, for instance, we can derive $F^r \rightarrow rr \bullet Nil$ from the two last productions computed in step 2 and then unfold the right hand side $rr \bullet Nil$ of F^r to productions

$$F^r \rightarrow F^{rr}_{Nil}, F^r \rightarrow F^{rr}_{Cons}, F^{rr}_{Nil} \rightarrow V^{ys}, F^{rr}_{Cons} \rightarrow rr \bullet (Cons \bullet V^{ys}), V^{ys} \rightarrow Nil$$

yielding G_2. The first two productions record that we unfold the call to rr according to the different instantiations. The next two productions record the clauses of rr, and the last production records the binding caused by the unfolding. It now holds that $F^0 \rightarrow Nil, F^0 \rightarrow \mathcal{F}[\![\ rr\ zs\ (Cons\ z\ Nil)\ ]\!] \in G_2^*$.

The question arises: just how much of G_i^* should be computed in the i'th step? We must avoid looping, but compute enough to get detailed knowledge of the flow. Given $N \rightarrow e[g\ N'\ t_1 \ldots t_n]$ we must replace N' by right hand sides of form N'', $\bullet$, and $c\ t'_1 \ldots t'_k$ to see which of g's clauses will be used by $\mathcal{D}$. Given $F^0 \rightarrow N$ we must replace N by right hand side of form N' or $c\ t_1 \ldots t_n$ to recall that $\mathcal{D}$ encounters the arguments of terms with outermost constructors.

Step 4. The next terms encountered by $\mathcal{D}$ by the instantiation of zs are $Cons\ z\ Nil$ and $rr\ zs\ Cons\ z'\ (Cons\ z\ Nil)$. The grammar G_2 contains among others the productions $F^0 \rightarrow F^r$, $F^r \rightarrow F^{rr}_{Cons}$, $F^{rr}_{Cons} \rightarrow rr \bullet (Cons \bullet V^{ys})$. Here we unfold the right hand side of the last production to get

$$F^{rr}_{Cons} \rightarrow F^{rr}_{Nil}, F^{rr}_{Cons} \rightarrow F^{rr}_{Cons}, V^{ys} \rightarrow Cons \bullet V^{ys}$$

yielding G_3. Here we did not add productions for the clauses of rr, since these were already present in G_2. It now holds that $F^0 \rightarrow \mathcal{F}[\![\ Cons\ z\ Nil\ ]\!] \in G_3^*$ and $F^0 \rightarrow \mathcal{F}[\![\ rr\ zs\ Cons\ z'\ (Cons\ z\ Nil)\ ]\!] \in G_3^*$.

Note that how little of G_2^* it was necessary to compute before unfolding right hand sides, to get this.

Step 5. In the next step $\mathcal{D}$ encounters (among others) the terms Nil and z. Deriving $F^0 \rightarrow Cons \bullet V^{ys}$ from G_3 and unfolding we get the two productions $F^0 \rightarrow \bullet$ and $F^0 \rightarrow V^{ys}$.

Why did we not simply compute from $V^{ys} \rightarrow Cons \bullet V^{ys}$ the two productions $V^{ys} \rightarrow \bullet$ and $V^{ys} \rightarrow V^{ys}$? Surely this would also yield $F^0 \rightarrow \bullet, F^0 \rightarrow V^{ys} \in G_4^*$. This is true, but it would also lead the analysis to believe that ys becoms bound to *e.g.* z. In fact it *does* in this case, but in general a variable bound to a term with an outermost constructor will not necessarily be bound to the components.

We have now arrived at the final grammar.

Grammar for the Obstructing Function Call

Example 4. Recall the program from Section 4 showing the problem of the obstructing function call. The first grammar that will be computed for this program is:

$$\begin{array}{llll} F^0 & \rightarrow r \bullet \mid F^r_{Nil} & F^r_{Nil} & \rightarrow Nil \\ & \mid F^r_{Cons} \mid Nil \mid V^y & F^r_{Cons} & \rightarrow a\,(r \bullet) \bullet \mid a\, F^r_{Nil} \bullet \mid a\, F^r_{Cons} \bullet \mid F^a_{Nil} \\ V^y & \rightarrow \bullet & F^a_{Nil} & \rightarrow Cons\ V^y\ Nil \end{array}$$

Recall that the problem in Example 2 was that the progressively larger terms $r\,l$, $a\,(r\,zs)\,z_1$, $a\,(a\,(r\,zs)\,z_2\,z_1$, *etc.* were encountered, and in fact $F^0 \rightarrow \mathcal{F}[\![\, t \,]\!] \in G^*$ as t ranges over these terms. Also recall that we noted in Example 2 that each problematic term appeared in the redex position of the subsequent problematic term. Notice how well this is reflected by the production $F^r_{Cons} \rightarrow a\, F^r_{Cons} \bullet$.

The problem of the Obstructing Function call is reflected by a production $F^h \rightarrow e[F^h] \in G^*$ with $e \neq []$. In preventing $\mathcal{D}$ from looping, the idea is to generalize calls to every function h for which $F^h \rightarrow e[F^h] \in G^*$ with $e \neq []$. So we must generalize all calls to r. This yields the second program in Example 2. Recalculating the grammar for the new term and program yields a grammar G with no $F^h \rightarrow e[F^h] \in G^*$ with $e \neq []$.

7 The analysis

This section states the actual analysis. An approximation similar to the present has appeared in [Jon87], which was indeed the main inspiration for this work. Other similar grammar constructions have appeared in [And86] for approximating Term Rewriting Systems and in [Mog88] for computing binding-time annotations for a self-applicable partial evaluator with partially static structures. Turchin has also used the idea of using grammars to approximate the terms that the supercompiler will encounter, see [Tur80] (Section 5.4). He uses the grammar approximation to get better transformation in the case of nested function calls, but apparently not to ensure termination.

Recall from Example 3 that the original idea was as follows: (*i*) compute a grammar, find generalizations, perform them on the term and program, and continue this cycle until no new generalizations are found. (*ii*) compute each grammar in a number of steps. (*iii*) in each of these steps first compute the grammar G_i^* (actually something less), and then (*iv*) apply a certain unfolding function on right hand sides of F^0 in G_i^*. Below we describe these steps precisely in the order: *(iii), (iv), (ii), (i)*. The four parts of the construction are stated in each their definition; all text not appearing within the definitions is merely explanatory.

Recall from Example 3 that we should not actually compute G_i^* and apply the unfolding function to all right hand sides of F^0, since G_i^* may be infinite. Instead we compute a smaller, finite, grammar $G_i^\diamond$ in each step and then apply the unfolding function to the right hand sides of *all* nonterminals, not just those of F^0.

We now define and explain $\diamond$. The reader familiar with [And86] may read it as an implementation of the notion of *minimal incorporation*.

Definition 7. Given grammar G, $G^\diamond$ is the smallest grammar satisfying the closure rules:

$$\frac{N \rightarrow t' \in G}{N \rightarrow t' \in G^\diamond} \qquad \frac{N \rightarrow e[N'] \in G^\diamond \;\; N' \rightarrow t \in G}{N \rightarrow e[t] \in G^\diamond} \qquad \frac{F^0 \rightarrow N' \in G^\diamond \;\; N' \rightarrow t \in G}{F^0 \rightarrow t \in G^\diamond}$$

where $e \neq []$ and $t \in \{N'', \bullet, c\, t_1 \ldots t_n\}$.

The first rule says that all productions in G_i are in $G_i^\diamond$. If we have $F^0 \rightarrow t \in G_i$ where t is something giving rise to new productions, *e.g.* $e[r]$ where r is an f-function call, then, because $F^0 \rightarrow t \in G_i^\diamond$, we get these new productions by considering the productions in $G_i^\diamond$.

The second rule can be motivated as follows. Suppose that $F^0 \rightarrow g\, N \in G_i^\diamond$ and that $N \rightarrow c\, t_1 \ldots t_n$. Considering each of these two productions indepen-detly does not tell the unfolding function anything. But given the information $F^0 \rightarrow g\, (c\, t_1 \ldots t_n) \in G_i^\diamond$ the unfolding function knows that a call to g will be encountered by $\mathcal{D}$ and that the call will be unfolded to the clause for c, and the unfolding function will generate new productions to account for this.

Why must the side condition on e, t hold in this rule? Well, *a priori* the idea is to get as *many* side conditions as possible, reducing the size of $G^\diamond$. The side condition is then motivated by the fact that these replacements of nonterminals by right hand sides suffice to maintain the invariant that $F^0 \rightarrow t \in G_i^*$ for all t encountered by $\mathcal{D}$ in at most i steps, and thereby $F^0 \rightarrow t \in G_\infty$ for all t encountered by $\mathcal{D}$ at all.

For instance, if G_i contains $F^0 \rightarrow g\, N, N \rightarrow f\, t$, then $*$ would compute $F^0 \rightarrow g\, (f\, t)$ before applying the unfolding function, the latter then yielding (roughly) the new productions (1) $F^0 \rightarrow g\, F^f, F^f \rightarrow t^f, V^{v^f} \rightarrow t$. But it is enough to apply the unfolding function right away to the production $N \rightarrow f\, t$ yielding (2) $N \rightarrow F^f, N^f \rightarrow t^f, N^{v^f} \rightarrow t$. The union of the productions (2) with G_i contains all the information that the union of (1) to G_i does.

One of the unfolding rules will state that if a term with an outermost con-structer is encountered by $\mathcal{D}$, then the grammar must record that each of the constructor arguments also will be reached by $\mathcal{D}$. But it does not hold that if some function call appears in the redex and ends up being evaluated to $c\, t_1 \ldots t_n$ in the same context, then evaluation will proceed with the arguments in the re-dex; on the contrary, the redex position will change to the surrounding g-function call. Therefore, it is necessary to know for a right hand side with an outermost constructor whether it is derivable from F^0 or some other nonterminal; in the latter case $\mathcal{D}$ does not encounter the constructer term alone, it encounters it as a subterm of a bigger term. This is why the last rule is restricted to the nonterminal F^0.

Definition 8 Unfolding function.

$$
\begin{array}{ll}
\mathcal{E}[\![N \rightarrow \bullet]\!] & = \{\} \\
\mathcal{E}[\![N \rightarrow c\, t_1 \ldots t_n]\!] & = \{N \rightarrow t_1, \ldots, N \rightarrow t_n\},\ \text{if } N \equiv F^0; \\
 & = \{\},\ \text{otherwise} \\
\mathcal{E}[\![N \rightarrow e[f\, t_1 \ldots t_n]]\!] & = \{N \rightarrow e[F^f], F^f \rightarrow t^f \{v_i^f := V_i^f\}_{i=1}^n\} \\
 & \quad \cup_{i=1}^n \{V_i^f \rightarrow t_i\} \\
\mathcal{E}[\![N \rightarrow e[g\, (c\, t_{n+1} \ldots t_{n+m})\, t_1 \ldots t_n]\!] & = \{N \rightarrow e[F_c^g], \\
 & \quad F_c^g \rightarrow t^{g,c} \{v_i^{g,c} := V_i^{g,c}\}_{i=1}^n\} \\
 & \quad \cup_{i=1}^{n+m} \{V_i^{v^{g,c}} \rightarrow t_i\} \\
\mathcal{E}[\![N \rightarrow e[g\, \bullet\, t_1 \ldots t_n]]\!] & = \cup_{j=1}^k \{N \rightarrow e[F_{c_j}^g], \\
 & F_{c_j}^g \rightarrow t^{g,c_j} \{v_i^{g,c_j} := \bullet\}_{i=n+1}^m \{v_i^{g,c_j} := N_i^{v^{g,c_j}}\}_{i=1}^n \\
 & \quad \cup_{i=1}^n \{V_i^{g,c_j} \rightarrow t_i\}\} \\
\mathcal{E}[\![N \rightarrow e[N']]\!] & = \{\} \\
\mathcal{E}[\![N \rightarrow e[\ \text{let} \bullet = t \text{ in } t']]\!] & = \{F^0 \rightarrow t, N \rightarrow e[t']\}
\end{array}
$$

The same notational conventions are employed here as in the formulation of the deforestation algorithm, see Section 3.

As was explained in Example 3, $\mathcal{E}$ simulates $\mathcal{D}$'s unfolding mechanism so as to maintain the invariant $F^0 \rightarrow \mathcal{F}[\![t]\!] \in G_i^*$ for all t encountered by $\mathcal{D}$ in at most i steps. For instance from the three productions representing the unfolding of a function call, one can recover the term that $\mathcal{D}$ comes to in one step from the original right hand side.

By an abuse of notation we also apply $\mathcal{E}$ to grammars as follows.

Definition 9 Steps of the grammar construction. The grammar for term t_0 and program p is:

$$
\begin{array}{ll}
\mathcal{E}(G) & = \cup_{N \rightarrow t \in G} \mathcal{E}[\![N \rightarrow t]\!] \\
G_0 & = \{F^0 \rightarrow \mathcal{F}[\![t_0]\!]\} \\
G_{i+1} & = \mathcal{E}(G_i{}^{\diamond}) \cup G_i \\
G_\infty & = \cup_{i=0}^{\infty} G_i
\end{array}
$$

Now we can state the final algorithm, which takes as input a program and a term and returns another program and term for which $\mathcal{D}$ terminates.

Definition 10. Given term t and program p.

1. Calculate $G = G_\infty$.
2. If there exists e, e', t' such that
   (a) $F^0 \rightarrow e'(F^h), F^h \rightarrow e[F^h], F^h \rightarrow t' \in G_\infty^*$ for some F^h and with $e \not\equiv []$, then generalize all calls to h in t, p;
   (b) $F^0 \rightarrow e'(V^v), V^v \rightarrow e(V^v), V^v \rightarrow t' \in G_\infty^*$ for some V^v and with $e \not\equiv ()$, then generalize all arguments for v in t, p.
3. If no generalizations were performed stop; otherwise go to step 1 with the new term and program.

In [Sor93] we have proved:

Theorem 11. *(i) the grammar computed in step 1 of the preceding algorithm is always finite (and can be computed in a finte number of steps). (ii) the criterion in step 2 of the preceding algorithm is decidable. (iii) for every term t and program p the preceding algorithm terminates with a term t′ and program p′ such that* $\mathcal{D}[\![\, t' \,]\!]$ *in the context of p′ terminates.*

This settles the correctness issue. One might also wonder how *efficient* the analysis is. In a recent work [Sei93], Seidl reformulates the computation of the grammars of [Jon87,And86] as a normalization process of set equations, and shows that the procees can be carried out in polynomial time. We shall not be concerned with the complexity of our grammar analysis; future work may investigate whether it can be reformulated similarly to the constructions in [Jon87,And86].

8 A shortcoming and its solution

In this section we describe a shortcoming of the basic technique. A simple extension solves a certain, important class of instances of the problem, see the next section.

Example 5. Consider the following uninteresting term and program.

$$
\begin{array}{ll}
 & f\,(f'\,z) \\
f'\,w & \leftarrow f\,w \\
f\,v & \leftarrow g\,v \\
g\,(C\,u) & \rightarrow C\,u
\end{array}
$$

The first two steps in transformation are: $\mathcal{D}[\![\; f\,(f'\,z) \;]\!] \Rightarrow \mathcal{D}[\![\; g\,(f'\,z) \;]\!] \Rightarrow \mathcal{D}[\![\, g\,(f\,z) \,]\!]$. After a few more steps the transformation terminates. The grammar computed from this term and program is:

$$
\begin{array}{lll}
F^0 & \rightarrow f\,(f'\,\bullet) \mid F^f \mid V^u & \\
V^w & \rightarrow \bullet & F^{f'} \rightarrow f\,V^w \mid F^f \\
V^v & \rightarrow f'\,\bullet \mid F^{f'} \mid V^w & F^f \;\rightarrow g\,V^v \mid F^g_C \\
V^u & \rightarrow V^u & F^g_C \;\rightarrow C\,V^u \mid C\,\bullet
\end{array}
$$

Although there is no termination problem, we have $F^f \rightarrow g\;F^f \in G^*$ signifying that calls to f should be generalized. We have cheated the grammar construction by having an initial term $f\;t$ which unfolds to $e[f\;t']$ where the second call to f is not "caused" in any way by the first.

The solution to this shortcoming is to make sure that $F^f \rightarrow g\;F^f \in G^*$ only happens when the second call really is caused by the first in some way. This can be done by a theoretically simple extension as follows. Suppose that we wish to transform the term t in program p and that t contains, syntactically, n function calls. Take n copies of p. In the i'th copy, all function names and variable names are subscripted with i. In the term, subscript each function call with a unique number i between 1 and n, informally signifying that this call be evaluated in the i'th copy of p. Then compute the grammar. Now calculate generalizations from this grammar as usual. For instance, $F^{f_1} \to e[F^{f_2}] \in G^*$ does not signify infinity but $F^{f_1} \to e[F^{f_1}] \in G^*$ does. Perform generalizations on the n copies of the program accordingly, and transform the term using the n copies of the program.

Note that there is nothing new in this method, theoretically. Before transformation, we simply make n copies of the program, and change the original calls in the term into calls to the different versions. One can avoid actually making n copies of the program, see [Sor93].

Example 6. For the example, the first steps of the transformation are: $\mathcal{D}[\![f_1(f_2' z)]\!] \Rightarrow \mathcal{D}[\![g_1 (f_2' z)]\!] \Rightarrow \mathcal{D}[\![g_1 (f_2 z)]\!]$. Here we see the important point: now the two calls to f are separable—they have different numbers. Indeed, the computed grammar for this new term and program does not imply any generalizations.

9 Relation to Wadler and Chin's methods

Recall that Wadler's original formulation of the deforestation algorithm was guaranteed to terminate only when applied to a *treeless program*. In [Sor93] we prove the following proposition.

Proposition 12. *Let p be a treeless program and t an arbitrary term. Let G be the grammar computed from p and t using the extension from the preceding section. Then there is no $F^h \to e[F^h] \in G^*$ with $e \neq []$ and no $V^v \to e(V^v) \in G^*$ with $e \neq ()$.*

This implies that no treeless program will receive generalizations by our method. Hence, whenever Chin's method finds that no annotations are required, our method finds no generalizations.

On the other hand there are programs which are non-treeless and hence requires annotations by Chin's method, which do require generalizations by our method.

Example 7. Consider the (rather contrived) term and program:

$$\begin{array}{ll} & f\ v \\ f\ x & \leftarrow f'\ (C\ x) \\ f'\ y & \leftarrow g\ y \\ g\ (C\ z) & \leftarrow f\ z \end{array}$$

The reader may care to apply $\mathcal{D}$ to the term and verify that the process does not loop infinitely. The grammar is:

$$\begin{array}{llll} F^0 \to f\ \bullet \mid F^f & & F^f & \to f'\ (C\ V^x) \mid F^{f'} \\ V^y \to c\ V^x & & F^{f'} & \to g\ V^y \mid F^g_C \\ V^x \to \bullet \mid V^z & & F^g_C & \to f\ V^z \mid F^f \\ V^z \to V^x & & & \end{array}$$

The grammar does not imply any generalizations. We can see that the analysis reasons as follows. First f calls f' (*c.f.* $F^f \to F^{f'}$). In the program we can see that the argument is larger than that which f itself received. Second, f' calls g (*c.f.* $F^{f'} \to F^g$). The argument is the same as that which f' received. Finally, g calls f (*c.f.* $F^g \to F^f$). Here the argument is smaller than that which g itself received. The point is: will the argument to f get bigger and bigger in each incarnation of f, or is the decrement by g significant enough to outweigh the increment by f? Well, in the grammar we see that our analysis discovered that the argument that g binds to z when it is called from f' is the argument which f originally received (*c.f.* $V^z \to V^x$) and g then calls f with that same argument (*c.f.* $V^x \to V^z$), and this does not yield progressively larger arguments.

Note that the program is non-treeless. Chin's method would classify f' as an unsafe consumer, and annotate the argument Cx. This would in fact prevent the C in the call to f' from being eliminated by g. This shows that the grammar can detect *decrements that outweigh increments*. Our construction can also handle other violations against the treeless form.

10 Conclusion

We have presented a means of ensuring termination of deforestation which extends the amount of transformation that can be performed on programs, compared to Chin's previous method.

Acknowledgements.

I would like to thank the Wei-Ngan Chin for explaining me details of his method and for many comments to [Sor93] out of which this paper grew. Also thanks to Nils Andersen, David Sands, and Robert Glück for comments and discussions. I would like to thank Neil Jones, my supervisor, for being a great inspiration and for suggesting many improvements in [Sor93]. More formally, I also owe Neil the credit that the idea of using something similar to his grammar-based data-flow analysis in [Jon87] to ensure termination of deforestation was originally his; I merely pursued the idea. Last of all, I should express my appreciation for the patience of my (non-computer scientist) girl-friend Mette Bjørnlund, who has come to know a lot about deforestation during my writing of this paper.

References

[And86] Nils Andersen. *Approximating Term Rewriting systems With Tree Grammars.* DIKU-report 86/16, Institute of Datalogy, University of Copenhagen, 1986.

[Chi90] Wei-Ngan Chin. *Automatic Methods for Program Transformation.* Ph.D. thesis, Imperial College, University of London, July 1990.

[Chi94] Wei-Ngan Chin. Safe Fusion of Functional expressions II: Further Improvements. In *Journal of Functional programming. To appear.*

[Fer88] A. B. Ferguson & Philip Wadler. When will Deforestation Stop?. In *1988 Glasgow Workshop on Functional Programming*. August 1988.

[Hug90] John Hughes. Why Functional Programming Matters. In *Research topics in Functional Programming*. Ed. D. Turner, Addison-Wesley, 1990.

[Jon87] Neil D. Jones. Flow analysis of Lazy higher-order functional programs. In *Abstract Interpretation of Declarative Languages*. Eds. Samson Abramsky & Chris Hankin, Ellis Horwood, London, 1987.

[Mog88] Torben Mogensen. Partially Static Structures in a Self-applicable Partial Evaluator. In *Partial Evaluation and Mixed Computation*. Eds. A. P. Ershov, D. Bjrner & N. D. Jones, North-Holland, 1988.

[Sei93] Helmut Seidl. *Approximating Functional Programs in Polynomial Time*. Unpublished manuscript. 1993.

[Sor93] Morten Heine Sørensen. *A New Means of Ensuring Termination of Deforestation*. Student Project 93-8-3, DIKU, Department of Computer Science, University of Copenhagen, 1993.

[Sor94] Morten Heine Sørensen, Robert Glück, Neil D. Jones. Towards Unifying Partial Evaluation, Deforestation, Supercompilation, and GPC. In *European Symposium On Programming'94*. To appear as LNCS, 1994.

[Tur90] David Turner. An overview of Miranda. In *Research topics in Functional Programming*. Ed. D. Turner, Addison-Wesley, 1990.

[Tur80] Valentin F. Turchin. *The Language REFAL—The Theory of Compilation and Metasystem Analysis*. Courant Computer Science Report 20, 1980.

[Tur82] Valentin F. Turchin, Robert M. Nirenberg, Dimitri V. Turchin. Experiments with a Supercompiler. In *ACM Symposium on Lisp and Functional Programming*. New york, 1982.

[Tur88] Valentin F. Turchin. The Algorithm of Generalization in the Supercompiler. In *Partial Evaluation and Mixed Computation*. Eds. A. P. Ershov, D. Bjrner & N. D. Jones North-Holland, 1988.

[Wad84] Philip Wadler. Listlessness is better than lazyness: Lazy evaluation and garbage collection at compile-time. In *ACM Symposium on Lisp and Functional Programming*. Austin, Texas, 1984.

[Wad85] Philip Wadler. Listlessness is better than lazyness II: Composing Listless functions. In *Workshop on Programs as Data objects*. LNCS 217, Copenhagen, 1985.

[Wad88] Philip Wadler. Deforestation: Transforming programs to eliminate trees. In *European symposium On programming (ESOP)*. Nancy, France, 1988.

Springer-Verlag and the Environment

We at Springer-Verlag firmly believe that an international science publisher has a special obligation to the environment, and our corporate policies consistently reflect this conviction.

We also expect our business partners – paper mills, printers, packaging manufacturers, etc. – to commit themselves to using environmentally friendly materials and production processes.

The paper in this book is made from low- or no-chlorine pulp and is acid free, in conformance with international standards for paper permanency.

Lecture Notes in Computer Science

For information about Vols. 1–709
please contact your bookseller or Springer-Verlag

Vol. 710: Z. Ésik (Ed.), Fundamentals of Computation Theory. Proceedings, 1993. IX, 471 pages. 1993.

Vol. 711: A. M. Borzyszkowski, S. Sokołowski (Eds.), Mathematical Foundations of Computer Science 1993. Proceedings, 1993. XIII, 782 pages. 1993.

Vol. 712: P. V. Rangan (Ed.), Network and Operating System Support for Digital Audio and Video. Proceedings, 1992. X, 416 pages. 1993.

Vol. 713: G. Gottlob, A. Leitsch, D. Mundici (Eds.), Computational Logic and Proof Theory. Proceedings, 1993. XI, 348 pages. 1993.

Vol. 714: M. Bruynooghe, J. Penjam (Eds.), Programming Language Implementation and Logic Programming. Proceedings, 1993. XI, 421 pages. 1993.

Vol. 715: E. Best (Ed.), CONCUR'93. Proceedings, 1993. IX, 541 pages. 1993.

Vol. 716: A. U. Frank, I. Campari (Eds.), Spatial Information Theory. Proceedings, 1993. XI, 478 pages. 1993.

Vol. 717: I. Sommerville, M. Paul (Eds.), Software Engineering - ESEC '93. Proceedings, 1993. XII, 516 pages. 1993.

Vol. 718: J. Seberry, Y. Zheng (Eds.), Advances in Cryptology - AUSCRYPT '92. Proceedings, 1992. XIII, 543 pages. 1993.

Vol. 719: D. Chetverikov, W.G. Kropatsch (Eds.), Computer Analysis of Images and Patterns. Proceedings, 1993. XVI, 857 pages. 1993.

Vol. 720: V.Mařík, J. Lažanský, R.R. Wagner (Eds.), Database and Expert Systems Applications. Proceedings, 1993. XV, 768 pages. 1993.

Vol. 721: J. Fitch (Ed.), Design and Implementation of Symbolic Computation Systems. Proceedings, 1992. VIII, 215 pages. 1993.

Vol. 722: A. Miola (Ed.), Design and Implementation of Symbolic Computation Systems. Proceedings, 1993. XII, 384 pages. 1993.

Vol. 723: N. Aussenac, G. Boy, B. Gaines, M. Linster, J.-G. Ganascia, Y. Kodratoff (Eds.), Knowledge Acquisition for Knowledge-Based Systems. Proceedings, 1993. XIII, 446 pages. 1993. (Subseries LNAI).

Vol. 724: P. Cousot, M. Falaschi, G. Filè, A. Rauzy (Eds.), Static Analysis. Proceedings, 1993. IX, 283 pages. 1993.

Vol. 725: A. Schiper (Ed.), Distributed Algorithms. Proceedings, 1993. VIII, 325 pages. 1993.

Vol. 726: T. Lengauer (Ed.), Algorithms - ESA '93. Proceedings, 1993. IX, 419 pages. 1993

Vol. 727: M. Filgueiras, L. Damas (Eds.), Progress in Artificial Intelligence. Proceedings, 1993. X, 362 pages. 1993. (Subseries LNAI).

Vol. 728: P. Torasso (Ed.), Advances in Artificial Intelligence. Proceedings, 1993. XI, 336 pages. 1993. (Subseries LNAI).

Vol. 729: L. Donatiello, R. Nelson (Eds.), Performance Evaluation of Computer and Communication Systems. Proceedings, 1993. VIII, 675 pages. 1993.

Vol. 730: D. B. Lomet (Ed.), Foundations of Data Organization and Algorithms. Proceedings, 1993. XII, 412 pages. 1993.

Vol. 731: A. Schill (Ed.), DCE - The OSF Distributed Computing Environment. Proceedings, 1993. VIII, 285 pages. 1993.

Vol. 732: A. Bode, M. Dal Cin (Eds.), Parallel Computer Architectures. IX, 311 pages. 1993.

Vol. 733: Th. Grechenig, M. Tscheligi (Eds.), Human Computer Interaction. Proceedings, 1993. XIV, 450 pages. 1993.

Vol. 734: J. Volkert (Ed.), Parallel Computation. Proceedings, 1993. VIII, 248 pages. 1993.

Vol. 735: D. Bjørner, M. Broy, I. V. Pottosin (Eds.), Formal Methods in Programming and Their Applications. Proceedings, 1993. IX, 434 pages. 1993.

Vol. 736: R. L. Grossman, A. Nerode, A. P. Ravn, H. Rischel (Eds.), Hybrid Systems. VIII, 474 pages. 1993.

Vol. 737: J. Calmet, J. A. Campbell (Eds.), Artificial Intelligence and Symbolic Mathematical Computing. Proceedings, 1992. VIII, 305 pages. 1993.

Vol. 738: M. Weber, M. Simons, Ch. Lafontaine, The Generic Development Language Deva. XI, 246 pages. 1993.

Vol. 739: H. Imai, R. L. Rivest, T. Matsumoto (Eds.), Advances in Cryptology - ASIACRYPT '91. X, 499 pages. 1993.

Vol. 740: E. F. Brickell (Ed.), Advances in Cryptology - CRYPTO '92. Proceedings, 1992. X, 593 pages. 1993.

Vol. 741: B. Preneel, R. Govaerts, J. Vandewalle (Eds.), Computer Security and Industrial Cryptography. Proceedings, 1991. VIII, 275 pages. 1993.

Vol. 742: S. Nishio, A. Yonezawa (Eds.), Object Technologies for Advanced Software. Proceedings, 1993. X, 543 pages. 1993.

Vol. 743: S. Doshita, K. Furukawa, K. P. Jantke, T. Nishida (Eds.), Algorithmic Learning Theory. Proceedings, 1992. X, 260 pages. 1993. (Subseries LNAI)

Vol. 744: K. P. Jantke, T. Yokomori, S. Kobayashi, E. Tomita (Eds.), Algorithmic Learning Theory. Proceedings, 1993. XI, 423 pages. 1993. (Subseries LNAI)

Vol. 745: V. Roberto (Ed.), Intelligent Perceptual Systems. VIII, 378 pages. 1993. (Subseries LNAI)

Vol. 746: A. S. Tanguiane, Artificial Perception and Music Recognition. XV, 210 pages. 1993. (Subseries LNAI).

Vol. 747: M. Clarke, R. Kruse, S. Moral (Eds.), Symbolic and Quantitative Approaches to Reasoning and Uncertainty. Proceedings, 1993. X, 390 pages. 1993.

Vol. 748: R. H. Halstead Jr., T. Ito (Eds.), Parallel Symbolic Computing: Languages, Systems, and Applications. Proceedings, 1992. X, 419 pages. 1993.

Vol. 749: P. A. Fritzson (Ed.), Automated and Algorithmic Debugging. Proceedings, 1993. VIII, 369 pages. 1993.

Vol. 750: J. L. Díaz-Herrera (Ed.), Software Engineering Education. Proceedings, 1994. XII, 601 pages. 1994.

Vol. 751: B. Jähne, Spatio-Temporal Image Processing. XII, 208 pages. 1993.

Vol. 752: T. W. Finin, C. K. Nicholas, Y. Yesha (Eds.), Information and Knowledge Management. Proceedings, 1992. VII, 142 pages. 1993.

Vol. 753: L. J. Bass, J. Gornostaev, C. Unger (Eds.), Human-Computer Interaction. Proceedings, 1993. X, 388 pages. 1993.

Vol. 754: H. D. Pfeiffer, T. E. Nagle (Eds.), Conceptual Structures: Theory and Implementation. Proceedings, 1992. IX, 327 pages. 1993. (Subseries LNAI).

Vol. 755: B. Möller, H. Partsch, S. Schuman (Eds.), Formal Program Development. Proceedings. VII, 371 pages. 1993.

Vol. 756: J. Pieprzyk, B. Sadeghiyan, Design of Hashing Algorithms. XV, 194 pages. 1993.

Vol. 757: U. Banerjee, D. Gelernter, A. Nicolau, D. Padua (Eds.), Languages and Compilers for Parallel Computing. Proceedings, 1992. X, 576 pages. 1993.

Vol. 758: M. Teillaud, Towards Dynamic Randomized Algorithms in Computational Geometry. IX, 157 pages. 1993.

Vol. 759: N. R. Adam, B. K. Bhargava (Eds.), Advanced Database Systems. XV, 451 pages. 1993.

Vol. 760: S. Ceri, K. Tanaka, S. Tsur (Eds.), Deductive and Object-Oriented Databases. Proceedings, 1993. XII, 488 pages. 1993.

Vol. 761: R. K. Shyamasundar (Ed.), Foundations of Software Technology and Theoretical Computer Science. Proceedings, 1993. XIV, 456 pages. 1993.

Vol. 762: K. W. Ng, P. Raghavan, N. V. Balasubramanian, F. Y. L. Chin (Eds.), Algorithms and Computation. Proceedings, 1993. XIII, 542 pages. 1993.

Vol. 763: F. Pichler, R. Moreno Díaz (Eds.), Computer Aided Systems Theory - EUROCAST '93. Proceedings, 1993. IX, 451 pages. 1994.

Vol. 764: G. Wagner, Vivid Logic. XII, 148 pages. 1994. (Subseries LNAI).

Vol. 765: T. Helleseth (Ed.), Advances in Cryptology - EUROCRYPT '93. Proceedings, 1993. X, 467 pages. 1994.

Vol. 766: P. R. Van Loocke, The Dynamics of Concepts. XI, 340 pages. 1994. (Subseries LNAI).

Vol. 767: M. Gogolla, An Extended Entity-Relationship Model. X, 136 pages. 1994.

Vol. 768: U. Banerjee, D. Gelernter, A. Nicolau, D. Padua (Eds.), Languages and Compilers for Parallel Computing. Proceedings, 1993. XI, 655 pages. 1994.

Vol. 769: J. L. Nazareth, The Newton-Cauchy Framework. XII, 101 pages. 1994.

Vol. 770: P. Haddawy (Representing Plans Under Uncertainty. X, 129 pages. 1994. (Subseries LNAI).

Vol. 771: G. Tomas, C. W. Ueberhuber, Visualization of Scientific Parallel Programs. XI, 310 pages. 1994.

Vol. 772: B. C. Warboys (Ed.),Software Process Technology. Proceedings, 1994. IX, 275 pages. 1994.

Vol. 773: D. R. Stinson (Ed.), Advances in Cryptology - CRYPTO '93. Proceedings, 1993. X, 492 pages. 1994.

Vol. 774: M. Banâtre, P. A. Lee (Eds.), Hardware and Software Architectures for Fault Tolerance. XIII, 311 pages. 1994.

Vol. 775: P. Enjalbert, E. W. Mayr, K. W. Wagner (Eds.), STACS 94. Proceedings, 1994. XIV, 782 pages. 1994.

Vol. 776: H. J. Schneider, H. Ehrig (Eds.), Graph Transformations in Computer Science. Proceedings, 1993. VIII, 395 pages. 1994.

Vol. 777: K. von Luck, H. Marburger (Eds.), Management and Processing of Complex Data Structures. Proceedings, 1994. VII, 220 pages. 1994.

Vol. 778: M. Bonuccelli, P. Crescenzi, R: Petreschi (Eds.), Algorithms and Complexity. Proceedings, 1994. VIII, 222 pages. 1994.

Vol. 779: M. Jarke, J. Bubenko, K. Jeffery (Eds.), Advances in Database Technology — EDBT '94. Proceedings, 1994. XII, 406 pages. 1994.

Vol. 780: J. J. Joyce, C.-J. H. Seger (Eds.), Higher Order Logic Theorem Proving and Its Applications. Proceedings, 1993. X, 518 pages. 1994.

Vol. 781: G. Cohen, S. Litsyn, A. Lobstein, G. Zémor (Eds.), Algebraic Coding. Proceedings, 1993. XII, 326 pages. 1994.

Vol. 782: J. Gutknecht (Ed.), Programming Languages and System Architectures. Proceedings, 1994. X, 344 pages. 1994.

Vol. 783: C. G. Günther (Ed.), Mobile Communications. Proceedings, 1994. XVI, 564 pages. 1994.

Vol. 784: F. Bergadano, L. De Raedt (Eds.), Machine Learning: ECML-94. Proceedings, 1994. XI, 439 pages. 1994. (Subseries LNAI).

Vol. 785: H. Ehrig, F. Orejas (Eds.), Recent Trends in Data Type Specification. Proceedings, 1992. VIII, 350 pages. 1994.

Vol. 786: P. A. Fritzson (Ed.), Compiler Construction. Proceedings, 1994. XI, 451 pages. 1994.

Vol. 787: S. Tison (Ed.), Trees in Algebra and Programming - CAAP '94. Proceedings, 1994. X, 351 pages. 1994.

Vol. 788: D. Sannella (Ed.), Programming Languages and Systems - ESOP '94. Proceedings, 1994. VIII, 516 pages. 1994.

Vol. 789: M. Hagiya, J. C. Mitchell (Eds.), Theoretical Aspects of Computer Software. Proceedings, 1994. XI, 887 pages. 1994.